I0890026

DATE DUE

JUL 0 3 2013	

BRODART, CO.   Cat. No. 23-221

Paradise Lost?

The Florida History and Culture Series

University Press of Florida / State University System

Florida A&M University, Tallahassee
Florida Atlantic University, Boca Raton
Florida Gulf Coast University, Ft. Myers
Florida International University, Miami
Florida State University, Tallahassee
University of Central Florida, Orlando
University of Florida, Gainesville
University of North Florida, Jacksonville
University of South Florida , Tampa
University of West Florida , Pensacola

University Press of Florida

Gainesville · Tallahassee · Tampa · Boca Raton · Pensacola · Orlando · Miami · Jacksonville · Ft. Myers

Paradise Lost?

The Environmental History of Florida

Edited by Jack E. Davis and Raymond Arsenault

Copyright 2005 by Jack E. Davis and Raymond Arsenault
Printed in the United States of America on recycled, acid-free paper
All rights reserved

Chapter 9 originally appeared as Raymond Arsenault, "The Public Storm: Hurricanes
and the State in Twentieth-Century America," in *American Public Life and the Historical
Imagination*, edited by Wendy Gamber et al. (University of Notre Dame Press, 2003).
Reprinted with permission.

Chapter 13 originally appeared as Jack E. Davis, "'Conservation is Now a Dead Word':
Marjory Stoneman Douglas and the Transformation of American Environmentalism,"
Environmental History 8 (January 2003): 53–76. Reprinted with permission.

10 09 08 07 06 05   6 5 4 3 2 1

A record of cataloging-in-publication data is available from the Library of Congress.

ISBN 0-8130-2826-4

The University Press of Florida is the scholarly publishing agency for the State
University System of Florida, comprising Florida A&M University, Florida Atlantic
University, Florida Gulf Coast University, Florida International University, Florida State
University, University of Central Florida, University of Florida, University of North
Florida, University of South Florida, and University of West Florida

University Press of Florida
15 Northwest 15th Street
Gainesville, FL 32611-2079
http://www.upf.com

ACC Library Services
Austin, Texas

For
Becky Palmer Davis
Patricia Ostby Arsenault

Contents

List of Illustrations   ix

Foreword   xi

Acknowledgments   xiii

Introduction   1

Part 1. Paradise Explored and Interpreted

   1. Between Topos and the Terrain: A Brief Survey of Florida
      Environmental Writing, 1513–1821   25
      Thomas Hallock

   2. An Eighteenth-Century Flower Child: William Bartram   47
      Charlotte M. Porter

   3. A Naturalist's Place: Archie Carr and the Nature of Florida   72
      Frederick R. Davis

   4. "Improving" Paradise: The Civilian Conservation Corps and
      Environmental Change in Florida   92
      Dave Nelson

5. Water, Water Everywhere 113
   Christopher F. Meindl

Part 2. Science, Technology, and Public Policy

6. The Everglades and the Florida Dream 141
   David McCally
7. The Trials and Tribulations of *Amos Quito*: The Creation of the Florida
   Anti-Mosquito Association 160
   Gordon Patterson
8. "Nature's Navels": An Overview of the Many Environmental Histories
   of Florida Citrus 177
   Christian Warren
9. The Public Storm: Hurricanes and the State in Twentieth-Century
   America 201
   Raymond Arsenault

Part 3. Despoliation

10. Alligators and Plume Birds: The Despoliation of Florida's Living
    Aesthetic 235
    Jack E. Davis
11. Blasting through Paradise: The Construction and Consequences
    of the Tamiami Trail 260
    Gary Garrett
12. Lake Apopka: From Natural Wonder to Unnatural Disaster 280
    Nano Riley

Part 4. Conservation and Environmentalism

13. "Conservation Is Now a Dead Word": Marjory Stoneman Douglas
    and the Transformation of American Environmentalism 297
    Jack E. Davis
14. A "Monstrous Desecration": Dredge and Fill in Boca Ciega Bay 326
    Bruce Stephenson
15. "We Must Free Ourselves . . . from the Tattered Fetters of the Booster
    Mentality": Big Cypress Swamp and the Politics of Environmental
    Protection in 1970s Florida 350
    Gordon E. Harvey
16. "The Big Ditch": The Rise and Fall of the Cross-Florida Barge Canal 375
    Lee Irby

Contributors 399
Index 403

Illustrations

Figure 5.1.   Population of Florida since 1860   126
Figure 8.1.   Oranges produced by box   184
Figure 8.2.   Orange production by county   184
Figure 8.3.   Orange production versus population growth   193
Figure 14.1.   Boca Ciega Bay   341

Table 8.1.   Orange production in Florida, 1890–1992   185

Foreword

Paradise Lost? An Environmental History of Florida is the latest book in a series devoted to Florida history and culture. During the past half century, the burgeoning population and increased national and international visibility of Florida have sparked a great deal of popular interest in the state's past, present, and future. As the favorite destination of countless tourists and as the new home for millions of retirees and other migrants, modern Florida has become a demographic, political, and cultural bellwether. In an effort to explore the Sunshine State in all its complexity, past and present, the University Press of Florida has established the Florida History and Culture series.

The University Press of Florida is committed to the creation of an eclectic but carefully crafted set of books that will provide the field of Florida studies with a new focus and that will encourage Florida researchers and writers to consider the broader implications and context of their work. The series includes standard academic monographs, works of synthesis, memoirs, and anthologies. And, while the series features books of historical interest, we encourage authors researching Florida's environment, politics, literature, and popular or material culture to submit their manuscripts as well. Each book offers a distinct personality and voice, but the ultimate goal of the series is to foster a sense of community and collaboration among Florida scholars.

For centuries, explorers and soldiers, tourists and travelers have encountered Florida. In fits of rhetorical rhapsody and literary despair, writers have been bewitched and bewildered by the sheer variety of the colony, territory, and state. For every Elizabeth Bishop who waxed poetic about "the state with the prettiest name, the state that floats in brackish water," there was a Senator John Holmes of Maine who declared that Florida was so worthless that it would not be much of a "loss to the U.S. were the whole peninsula of Florida to sink into the Gulf of Mexico." Appreciating and understanding the place called Florida proved to be complicated.

Paradise Lost? represents a stunning collection of original essays aimed at understanding the environmental history of Florida. More than simply a compilation of essays, *Paradise Lost?* breaks new ground in the burgeoning field of environmental history. Edited by Jack Davis and Raymond Arsenault, the study ranges far and wide, from William Bartram's eighteenth-century wanderings to Archie and Marjorie Harris Carr's twentieth-century activism, from studies of Florida's parks, groves, and barge canals to examinations of the Everglades, Lake Apopka, and the Kissimmee River.

If ever a book could be considered homegrown, *Paradise Lost?* qualifies. Many of the essays originated in the classes of the authors or from close associations cultivated by the two scholars. The book provides a cautionary lesson in the costs of progress and the continuing struggle to preserve Florida. Tales abound of heroes and villains, of battles won and lost. In this study, nature becomes an active agent in the historical process, rarely the passive victim. Most significantly, nature occupies center stage. Readers surely will enjoy the engaged scholarship and the engaging prose.

Gary R. Mormino
Series Coeditor

Acknowledgments

As the coeditors of *Paradise Lost?* we would like to thank a number of individuals who provided us with guidance, assistance, and encouragement. In the early stages of the project, Jim Carstens, now of the University of South Alabama, was instrumental in planning and organizing the various contributions to the volume. As the book took shape, we were fortunate to work with a talented array of contributors, men and women who share our commitment to the development of environmental history as a major field of intellectual inquiry. Whatever strengths the book possesses are due in large part to their expertise and professionalism. We would also like to thank the librarians and archivists who helped us along the way, especially Jim Cusick, archivist of the P. K. Yonge Library of Florida History at the University of Florida; Kathleen Hardee Arsenault, dean of the Nelson Poynter Memorial Library at the University of South Florida, St. Petersburg; and Jim Schnur, director of Special Collections at the Poynter Library. We received expert editorial guidance from the staff of the University Press of Florida—most notably from Meredith Morris-Babb, Susan Brady, and Gillian Hillis. And we are especially grateful for the astute critical reading of the manuscript by Tim Silver of Appalachian State University and Carolyn Johnston of Eckerd College. Among the many family members, friends, and colleagues who offered us advice and encouragement during the book's long gestation, several deserve special thanks: Amelia, Anne, Kathleen, and Oscar Arsenault, John Belohlavek, Bill Belleville, Peter Belmont, Peter and Susan Betzer, Al Burt, Stephanie Cain, David Carr, Tim Clemmons, Steve Davis-Thompson, Mark Durand, Janine Farver, David Hackett Fischer, Thom Foley, John Hope Franklin, Marti Garratt, Peter Golenbook, Suzanne Hardee, Bill Heller, Jim and Lois Horton, Allen and Barbara Isaacman, Walter Jaap, Meeghan Kane, Jeff Klinkenberg, Laurie MacDonald, David Maehr, Danita Marie, Gary Mormino, Barbara Ness, Barry Reese, Monica Rowland, Sonya Rudenstine, Greta Scheid-Wells, Nevin Sitler, Rhonda Sonnenberg, John and Sheila Stewart, Suzanne St. John, Sudsy Tschiderer, Albert Vogt, David Seth Walker, and Steve and Lee Whitfield. Thanks to Kelly Buchanan, Meeghan Kane, and Edward Woodward for doing an excellent job compiling the index with skill and good humor; they went above and beyond their normal duties as Florida Studies Program graduate assistants. We would also like to acknowledge the hard work and enthusiasm of the many students who have sustained and deepened our interest in environmental history during the past fifteen years. Some of those students ended up as formal contributors to this book, but it is our hope that all of those who made their way through the mountain of readings that we inflicted upon them will take some pride in the publication of *Paradise Lost?* Finally, this book is dedicated, with love and respect, to our own personal "earth mothers": Becky Palmer Davis and Patricia Ostby Arsenault. By nurturing our sense of wonder about the natural world—and the proper place of humans within it—they deserve much of the credit for what follows.

Introduction

Beyond the sprawl that consumes so much of Florida, nature conspicuously endows the physical setting. Less evident is nature's significance to history. It was the environment's largesse that enabled the indigenous people of southern Florida to live without agriculture while retaining a sedentary existence, a rare combination of circumstances for a complex and flourishing civilization. Some among their disease-bearing Spanish conquerors believed that Florida might bestow something greater than the gold and silver that eluded them—eternal life. Four centuries later, Florida's natural charms stirred the literary imagination of Henry James, Sidney Lanier, Harriet Beecher Stowe, Stephen Crane, and others. The environment also betrayed features that fascinated minds of empirical temperament. It was primitive, diverse, accessible, and full of bountiful life. It had plants botanists had never seen, and primordial reptiles and birds that excited the emotions of even dour men of science. Few failed to speak of its splendor. In the twentieth century, pioneering ecologists gained notoriety for their studies of the Florida environment.

Humanists, by contrast, were slower to accept the environment as a scholarly resource. The state's rich cultural heritage preoccupied them instead.

But the environment was always there, an intrusive and unyielding variable, agent, or context that eventually crept into the scholars' consciousness. Archeologists studying Florida's pre-Columbian people were compelled to look to ecological science for a deeper understanding of ancient civilizations. To interpret Florida writers, literary scholars had to familiarize themselves with the canon of nature writing. Political scientists learned that water and land were at the heart of Florida politics, as did historians chronicling Florida's past.

The essays in this collection concern themselves with those two natural assets and more. Environmental historians frame questions about society, politics, and culture around the relationship between people and the natural environment. They see nature not simply as an object of human imposition but as a dynamic agent in history, one that takes an active role in shaping human choices and experiences. Beyond the imagined parameters we place upon the world around us are forces that have always affected human history. Those forces are older than humanity, and ultimately they will likely prove to be more enduring. The dean of environmental history, Donald Worster, argues that they "have long been setting the terms of our existence; they have influenced what we have done and what we have been able to do."[1]

Worster is talking about the forces of nature. Florida is an outstanding place to study nature's influence in history in large measure because so many cultures—Native American, Spanish, French, Anglo, African, southern, northern, midwestern, and others—have interacted with the indigenous environment. Comprehending those interactions is essential to expanding one's conception of Florida's past, for the natural environment embodies the values, economies, arts, literature, social relationships, and collective memory of people and their cultures. Each culture was forced to make adjustments to live with the nonhuman world, while at the same time each transformed the natural landscape in some fashion or degree. This is especially true of the twentieth century, the most dramatic period in the environmental history of Florida. During the past century—the period that receives the greatest attention in this volume—Florida has emerged from frontier conditions and ballooned into the country's fourth-largest state.

Despite nature's distinct presence in Florida's past, historians initially failed to gaze beyond human activities. The early histories of Florida, including weighty multivolume texts written by some of the state's best-recognized scholars, subordinate environmental imperatives much in the way that the texts ignore pre-European contact history. A noteworthy example of this slight to nature is the four-volume state history written by University of Florida professor Junius E. Dovell in 1952. Crafting his subject while surrounded by an impressive cohort of ecologists at his university, Dovell prefaced his study with a description of Florida as a "land of diversities," which "exist in geology, the flora and fauna, and in the people themselves." But the rest of his study strays from the direction suggested in the opening pages. Dovell and his fellow anthropocentric historians failed to consider the counterfactual. If Florida had been dry instead of wet, mountainous instead of flat, or cold instead of warm, the state's history would have been utterly different.[2]

Two monographs published in the 1940s did attempt to chart new narrative territory when they made the natural environment a centerpiece in Florida's past. Both appeared as volumes in Rinehart Books' fabled Rivers of America series. The first, *The St. Johns, a Paradise of Diversities*, by James Branch Cabell (a novelist with a naturalist bent) and Alfred Jackson Hanna, chronicled the "human drama" from the sixteenth to the nineteenth century as it revolved around the natural environment of the St. Johns River. The second, Marjory Stoneman Douglas's *The Everglades: River of Grass*, not only offered a seminal approach to the state's history; it also challenged conventional notions of wetlands as wastelands. Hanna, a Rollins College history professor, and Douglas, a south Florida writer, were alert to both nature's role in history and the goings-on in the nonhuman world of their day. Hanna served as president of the Florida Audubon Society, and Douglas later founded an influential Everglades environmental organization. She and Hanna also wrote general survey history texts that suggested a new trend in interpreting the state's past. Douglas called her 1967 *Florida: The Long Frontier* a work of environmental geography.[3]

In general, however, Florida historians were slow to heed the epistemological markers of Douglas and Hanna. Charlton Tebeau opened his 1971 *A History of Florida*, once regarded as a definitive survey text, with "Natural Endowment and First Inhabitants," a chapter that offers a detailed geographic description of his subject. But the rest of the book treats the environment as little more than a natural resource benefiting humans. In two previous books, *Florida's Last Frontier* (1957) and *Man in the Everglades* (1964), Tebeau actually came closer to following the Hanna and Douglas tradition, making considerable use of the writings of early-twentieth-century naturalists who warned that human encroachments might lead to Florida's environmental doom. Frank Chapman, Charles Torrey Simpson, John Kunkel Small, David Fairchild, and Thomas Barbour all conducted important scientific studies in the state and left behind volumes of highly accessible materials offering historically significant observations about the human-nature nexus. Still, historians before the 1980s rarely consulted the documents of the naturalists or paid heed to their alarm. Comfortable with old modes of thought and methodology, historians tended to celebrate civilization's triumphs both outside and within the context of nature. Beyond unruly floods and hurricanes, nature rarely entered their narratives. Treated as passive and inert and therefore insignificant, most of the natural world was taken for granted.[4]

Fortunately, an important catalyst for a new disciplinary direction in Florida history appeared in 1980 written by Syracuse University professor Nelson Manfred Blake. *Land into Water/Water into Land* examined the history of water management in modern Florida, an issue of considerable importance to many Floridians. According to Blake, bureaucrats and developers were the architects of a massive resculpting of the peninsula that began early in the twentieth century. The dredge-and-fill process, perfected in Florida, was their means toward the twin goals of growth and profit. As the state's population grew in hurried leaps—during the boom decades of the 1910s and 1920s, throughout the prosperous aftermath of World War II, and in the wake of residential air conditioning—humans put heavy demands on land and water. To meet the requirements of a particular venture, whether it was building a subdivision or opening agricultural acreage, one element could be easily converted into the other.[5]

Blake was writing Florida history "from the ground up," to borrow a term from environmental historian Ted Steinberg. Florida scholars took notice. Even in the absence of *Water into Land/Land into Water,* the shift to studying environmental relationships was inevitable. Living in a rapidly changing state made one acutely aware of how society organizes itself around nature. The disappearance of wild Florida was occurring in living memory, and historians only had to drive down the same streets each day to see how quickly the built environment was metastasizing. On a practical level, the archived records of explorers, settlers, soldiers, cattle barons, citrus growers, railroad magnates, and club women were flush with testimonies of the implacability of nature in human events. References to the soil, water, weather, and nonhuman life-forms were nearly as common as those to wars and elections.[6]

The essays in this collection draw on many of these records and explore Florida's past through the lens of environmental history. A principal ambition of this volume is to demonstrate the integral place of the environment in historical patterns and development. Many of Florida history's most intriguing and important questions cannot be answered or even addressed without paying attention to environmental history. Can we, for example, fully comprehend the motives behind Indian removal in Florida without knowing something about the ecological relationships of the whites who sought to control Indian land? Similar questions might be asked about the course Florida followed to the present. As a whole, this collection gives historical context to many contemporary environmental problems, and with luck it will encourage a more informed dialogue about issues such as land use and habitat preservation. We also hope to enlarge public knowledge of Florida's contributions to the American historical experience and to delineate Florida's place in the broader scope of global environmental history.

An important premise in this volume is that the indigenous flora and fauna, combined with the subtropical climate of the lower peninsula, projected qualities of a paradise, an Eden, or a dreamland. Prior to World War II, and long before tourism bureaus and travel agents used theme parks and beaches to attract visitors, the dense, wet wilderness and highly visible wildlife brought Florida to the attention of the outside world. Even before the Civil War, thousands of sightseers from Jacksonville took steamers up the St. Johns River to see such wonders as Silver Springs, described by one travel writer as, "a mysterious and beautiful freak of nature . . . [an] avenue of liquid sapphire."[7]

During the late nineteenth century, travel writers and landscape painters took the lead in crafting Florida's dreamscape image. But virtually every element of the state's popular culture contributed to the portrayal of Florida as a veritable Eden, naturally beautiful and benignly wild. Music, fiction, biographies, and architecture of the state were all "devoted to, instrumental in, or derived from Florida image making," as one student of the subject has written. Florida was a place where nature, lush and perennially colorful, constantly regenerated itself. Local chambers of commerce were quick to exploit that image. Broward County, for example, promoted itself as the "paradise of the East Coast."[8]

With great abandon, people sought such places, although not always with the same goal in mind. Some went to Florida to restore their physical health or to escape the stress and crowds of the overcivilized North. Florida was America's Riviera. Fresh and unspoiled, it symbolized a new beginning that drew not just convalescing and leisure-seeking visitors but entrepreneurs pursuing new riches. Forces of progress converged on Florida. They transformed the landscape many times over until the wilderness garden, a world of seductive natural beauty, no longer existed.

A common theme suggested in the title of this volume and running through many of the essays is that paradise in Florida seems to have been lost. Polluted water, scarred land, leaching landfill sites, acid rain, unhealthy ozone levels, beach and soil erosion, stressed reefs, depleted marine life, overpopulation, and microclimatic changes have marred Florida's dreamscape image. With only scraps of old nature left, one might argue that today's environment is an artificial one. We may think that we're seeing nature when we look out on a college campus with a pleasant pastoral setting, but what we are admiring, even when that setting includes trees older than the college, is a landscape that reveals human preferences. Environmental historians refer to places that camouflage human intervention as "second nature." Chris Warren offers a brief discussion of second nature in his essay on citrus, which has been around so long in Florida and is found in so many backyards that it feels like nature. Yet backyard fruit is like much of Florida's seemingly unspoiled green spaces and wetlands: they exist because people allow them to do so or because people have created them. Wherever possible, humans are inclined to control nature, even to the point of manipulating the way an ecosystem works. Relieve the engineers and bureaucrats of their duties in the Everglades, which is maintained by some 1,500 miles of water-control devices, and the grandest of all wetlands would likely die or degenerate into something unrecognizable.

Controlling the Florida environment has a long and mixed genealogy—French, Spanish, British, and American. Two of these groups are the focus of the opening essay in the volume's first section. Thomas Hallock is less interested in how European empires, specifically the Spanish and British, controlled nature than in how their subjects interpreted the Florida paradise. While many scholars have examined nature in nineteenth- and twentieth-century Florida literature, Hallock is the first to undertake an ecological survey of the literature—letters, journals, and books—of those Europeans who explored and settled the peninsula. Florida was not simply a paradise to these Europeans; the impressions it left with them were varied and complex. On one level, Florida was a harsh place that forced newcomers to meet the environment on its own terms. The aborigines had succeeded in doing that long before contact with Europeans, Hallock points out, while making an argument for further study of their own narrative of the landscape. In this complex real world, what emerged in the minds of Europeans and conveyed to the written word was an interesting amalgamation of truth and myth, images of the like that continued to inform perceptions for centuries to come.

The texts of European explorers abstracted the Florida environment, whether hospitable or hostile, within a particular cultural context. In *Uncommon Ground*, William Cronon argues that nature as Americans know it is an idea, existing in many forms, that represents the commingling of artifice and ecological forms.[9] Similarly, paradise was (and is) an admixture of the imagined and the actual, a dynamic concept or state of mind that varied with the sentiments and multilayered visions of a given culture and generation.

The social construction of paradise was in part the result of humans separating themselves from nature. With few exceptions, to be *of* nature was to be savage; to be apart from it was to be civilized. Western tradition has always positioned humans above the nonhuman world, with the former assuming the moral imperative to take dominion over the latter. Donald Worster observes that Western culture has a "tendency to measure everything in human terms, to reduce the world to a succession of cultural ideas, to frame everything as a confrontation between rival abstractions, or to insist on the triumph of the human imagination over the natural world." As Worster's comment suggests, environmental historians understand nature as the essential context of human existence, and the only one of the two—nature and humanity—that can survive without the other. Environmental historians regard their human subjects as one component in a larger interconnected world, and yet they recognize that those same subjects remove themselves intellectually and emotionally from nature.[10]

One of Florida's first naturalists, William Bartram, was determined to avoid such removal. Charlotte Porter's essay follows the extraordinary travels of Bartram through colonial East Florida during his four-year, 2,400-mile journey across the southern colonies. Exploring Florida when it was part of the British empire (1763–83), Bartram collected a wide range of specimens and scientific data. His journey produced the most detailed observations of Florida nature before statehood. Captured in texts as well as illustrations, Bartram's Florida is at times savage and contentious and at other times serene and inviting. But it is always exotic, an Elysium, as he calls it, and it is both real and imagined. His journal, known today as *Travels*, contains not only scientific details but equally fascinating observations of human interaction—both of Indians and British subjects—with the environment. When gazing upon a landscape, he accepted humans as part of the natural community, a perspective not taken by the ordinary naturalist or scientist of the day.

Bartram had a significant influence on Florida nature writers a century later, Porter points out, and his observations remain an invaluable tool for environmental planning—restoring paradise—in northeastern Florida.

Scores of naturalists followed Bartram to Florida over the next two centuries. One was University of Florida herpetologist Archie Carr, whom Frederick R. Davis writes about in this collection. Carr referred to natural Florida as an Eden, but for him Eden was not a pastoral landscape revealing human improvements. It was an ecological place rich in the matter of scientific study. Carr, who earned professional accolades for his pioneering work with sea turtles, carved out a distinguished five-decade career at the University of Florida, from the 1930s to the 1980s. As Davis points out, Carr's talents included a scientist's eye for observation and a writer's sense of place. Although research often took him to Central America and Africa, the place he always came back to, emotionally and intellectually, was Florida. Carr came from a long line of naturalists whose writings introduced Florida's unique biology to a national audience. But few, if any, were as eloquent and prolific as Carr. Prepared for both academic and general audiences, his writings eventually acquired a conservationist tone. Though characteristically subtle, his advocacy carried the backing of scientific knowledge and the poignancy of descriptive prose.

Most people did not see Florida from the perspective of a biologist. Whereas Carr reveled in the chaotic quality of nature, others idealized paradise as orderly, tranquil, and bountiful. Since early Western thought, paradise meant safe and easy living and a mild climate. It was reminiscent of the original garden. "The region is as quiet as in the days of Adam," the historian George Bancroft wrote from the St. Johns River in 1855 to his wife in New York; "the dense woods came down to the water's edge; the yellow jasmine in full bloom almost hung on the water. I have seen nothing like it." Paradise resonated in many of Florida's offerings; and yet Florida could also disappoint people's expectations. When and where conditions were not in harmony with perceptions of paradise, some people took it as their duty to reconstruct or improve upon the natural setting.[11]

This presumption was perhaps best illustrated in the mission of the Civilian Conservation Corps (CCC) in Florida. Dave Nelson's essay explores how the Depression-era relief agency helped to define nature for Florida residents and visitors. Provisioned with shovels, axes, and bulldozers, the young men of the corps were assigned the task of overhauling Florida's one state park and building new ones. As with national parks, the state parks were designed to conform to a wilderness ideal, meaning a place not too wild for humans and one that satisfied popular notions of natural beauty. The parks, in other words, were manufactured environments: the CCC removed unwanted indigenous vegetation and animals; planted new, sometimes exotic species; ditched and drained parts of the land; and opened up wild areas with roads, bridges, and recreational spots. In the end, the CCC reclaimed paradise from unviolated nature.

Improving paradise sometimes jeopardized Florida's ecology, the physical foundation of paradise. The natural assets of Florida do not resemble those of other states. The state is unusually flat (the desired condition for an agricultural paradise), reaching a topographical height of only 345 feet. Yet the landscape lacks uniformity. Before the days of heavy logging after the Civil War, north Florida had vast, cathedral-like longleaf pine forests, which were routinely stimulated by lightning fires. An extant and contrasting feature of terrestrial Florida—one that belies visions of paradise—is its scrublands, known among ecologists as palmetto, pine, wire-grass, and limestone flatwoods. Florida is also well known for its myriad forms of hammocks (dense hardwood and palm enclaves with an understory of organic humus): low, upland, mesophytic, and tropical. It is the only state on the continent that reaches into a subtropical climatic region, which lends diversity to its native communities of flora and fauna. With 3,000 species of temperate and tropical plants, Florida is a "botanical paradise," as John Kunkel Small once observed. Equally impressive, Florida has more bird species (475) than any continental state, ranging in size from the almost weightless ruby-throated hummingbird to the more-than-four-foot great blue heron. Their nonavian neighbors include 94 species of wild mammals, and 162 species and subspecies of reptile and amphibian fauna.[12]

None of these species could exist without water. Florida is the wettest state on the continent, with the highest rainfall and the greatest proportion of ground and surface water. Chris Meindl's essay traces the geographic history of the state's most important, most conspicuous—and most abused—natural feature. Florida's water has been polluted, moved from one place to another, and drained away. The result has been waste and miscalculations about its availability. How much surface water did Florida actually have at the time of statehood and how much it since has lost are questions foremost on Meindl's mind. He begins tackling those questions by exploring the conceptual definitions of wetlands and by illustrating their ecological importance. He also examines some of the signature water-control projects in Florida history, designed to fulfill aspirations of growth or visions of an agrarian Arcadia. If the past is indeed prelude, the future does not bode well for Florida's wetlands, Meindl speculates, for all of life's events in Florida come back to water.

Controlling water required the tools of science and technology, innovations that have usually come with the backing of either public policy or market incentives. Humanity has benefited in many ways from scientific insights and technological developments. Advances in medicine offer one case in point. At the same time, humans have acquired new powers to destroy and exploit, with people and nature suffering the impact. One need not elaborate on the development and use of the atomic bomb at the end of World War II to support this argument. For good or bad, humans can remake the world in dramatic ways. From beach renourishment to highway construction, Florida offers many examples of the power of science and technology to improve the quality of life and to alter civilization's relationship with the environment.

Air conditioning, which affects virtually every Floridian's life, puts this dynamic in perspective. Within the course of a few decades during the second half of the twentieth century, air conditioning profoundly changed the South, and Florida in particular. By making the hot and humid summer months more hospitable, air conditioning expanded tourism in Florida from a six-month to a year-round industry, stimulating phenomenal population growth and accelerating the relocation of business and industry from the Northeast and Midwest to the nation's southernmost state. The demographic change in Florida led to a regional power shift and in the process altered the politics, economy, architecture, and community life of the state. The assurance of a technologically engineered mild climate gave new life to the paradise myth, but not without a heavy price. Air conditioning has become the single greatest source of residential energy consumption in the state (Floridians spent $1.8 billion to run their air conditioners in 1997), and virtually every environmental problem associated with Florida's population growth, from urban sprawl to highway congestion, has been exacerbated by the rise of the air-conditioning culture.[13]

The second group of essays in this volume show other ways in which science and technology have complicated the human relationship with the environment. With public policy adding another layer to the mix, science and technology have not only been responsible for a host of environmental problems; they have also been employed to fix them. That has been the central paradox in the modern history of the Everglades. In 2000, Congress and the Florida legislature jointly pledged $7.8 billion to fund the Comprehensive

Everglades Restoration Project. Yet, as David McCally demonstrates in his essay, the nation's most ambitious environmental engineering rescue project is a response to a century of abuse for which science was in part responsible. Dating back to the mid-nineteenth century, Floridians used scientific studies, albeit poor ones, to reinforce their notion of the viability of converting the Everglades into dry and productive land. Advocates of Everglades drainage, McCally explains, were chasing the Florida dream, which he defines as an exotic variant of the "American desire for better life in a new world." Arguing that science and the Florida dream were mutually reinforcing, McCally examines the role of this dialectic in the destruction of Everglades ecology. He ultimately notes the irony in the shift from destruction to restoration. On one level, Floridians' relationship with the Everglades has not changed. It remains freighted with illusions about the possibilities of science to reconstruct nature to conform to the protean Florida dream. Just as Floridians believed that they could engineer an agrarian Arcadia out of a fetid swamp, they now trust that science will save them from their environmental follies.

If science for the benefit of civilization could refashion a landscape into a completely different form, it could presumably improve the quality of human life by controlling a pesky, airborne insect. For thousands of years, humans had lived with mosquitoes. But by the twentieth century, Florida residents, instilled with a progressive-era confidence that public-health initiatives could ameliorate the natural environment, decided to suffer no longer. Paradise was supposed to be a hospitable place. Gordon Patterson points out in his essay that by the 1910s scientists had come to understand the mosquito as more than a bothersome pest. Viewing the insect as a vector of diseases like malaria and as a major hazard, the State Board of Health and the U.S. Public Health Service launched what Patterson describes as a war against mosquitoes. Battles were not limited to miasmic swamps, however. In examining the comparatively crude though sometimes effective science of mosquito control in the days before pesticides, Patterson also tells the story of public health officials who struggled to free themselves from the mire of state politics.

Florida citrus, by contrast, has always been a blessed child of Florida politicians. One might think that oranges are Florida's original fruit. But the origins and history of citrus in Florida environment are complicated, as Chris Warren's contribution to this collection indicates. Warren begins with European contact and follows the journey of Florida citrus agriculture through space and time. Citrus agriculture has led a nomadic existence in Florida, prompting Warren to investigate the environmental imperatives behind its migration. He is also interested in the transformation of citrus from a crop to a product—in particular as a concentrate—and the environmental factors and technological innovations that shaped that transformation. Following citrus's journey through Florida has left Warren with many intriguing questions about the environmental history of the fruit crop. The answers to those questions beg for a larger work on this understudied subject in Florida.

If the blossoms and bright fruit of citrus evoke the color and scent of paradise, hurricanes spoil the myth. They are not simply a Florida phenomenon. They come from somewhere distant, inflict their damage, and then move on. Yet they have terrorized every culture that has established itself in Florida. Raymond Arsenault's essay tracks the historical evolution of hurricanes from private storms to public storms. Virtually everything about hurricanes was a matter of local or personal concern until the turn of the twentieth century, when hurricanes gradually became institutionalized in weather technology, the affairs of the state, and the national consciousness. Central to Arsenault's study is the argument that the advancement of forecasting technology was dependent on government activism and the growing expectation that the state take responsibility for the public's safety. The turning point in the government's role to protect U.S. citizens from wrathful storms came with the crushing hurricanes that blew through southern Florida in the 1920s and 1930s. Although the public storm had been born, it did not reach maturity until after World War II. Hurricanes, of course, continued to inflict major damage despite rising expectations of mitigation and control; and as late as 1992, Hurricane Andrew demonstrated nature's enduring power over the state.

In addition to the application of science to nature, Arsenault's essay illuminates another theme in environmental history. In popular and bureaucratic parlance, hurricanes, like earthquakes and floods, are invariably labeled natural disasters—acts of God or nature. Yet environmental historians do not see such phenomena as altogether natural. Humans lend destructive power to hurricanes and their counterparts by placing themselves in harm's way—by, for example, building and rebuilding their homes and businesses on a fault line, in a flood plain, or on a beachfront.[14] In turn, perceptions of nature's harmful tendencies harden civilization's resolve to control the nonhuman world. The unqualified belief in the human capacity to impose its will upon nature—to make it more amenable to human desires and expectations—has broadened civilization's imprint on the land. As a result, Florida has undergone a significant transformation, with old landscapes turned into something new and different. In the end, the despoliation of nature caused by human activities has been more extensive and devastating than all of Florida's hurricanes combined. As nature mends self-inflicted wounds, humans leave new scars.

Florida received its first scars some 13,000 years ago when humans migrated to the region. It is naïve to think that a culture, even one of indigenous peoples, has ever existed in perfect harmony with the natural environment. All cultures have in some way left their mark, with some more lasting than others. The environmental consequences of a sixteenth-century Calusa shell midden, for example, are insignificant when compared with those of a modern-day county landfill, and only the former has room in the paradise myth. Modern society has engineered the most important environmental damage. Leading off the collection's third organizing theme, despoliation, Jack E. Davis's essay argues that if nature embodied Florida's original image, then serious assaults on nature threatened that image. The first assaults came in the late nineteenth and early twentieth centuries, and not by developers but by hunters, when world markets awarded a monetary value to some of Florida's most distinctive flora and fauna. The "living aesthetic," which had enraptured William Bartram and his predecessors, was Florida's defining quality, what Americans wrote about and what tourists came to see and experience. The exploitation of novelties of nature, specifically alligators and plume birds, led to a level of wildlife destruction in Florida equal to that of the bison on the western plains. By the early twentieth century, lovers of wild Florida had begun grieving for a vanishing Eden.

Development is the sequel to wildlife destruction in the physical transformation of Florida in the modern period. The expansion of civilization's artifacts prevented "shot out" environments from resuming their own course of history, from returning to undisturbed, or minimally disturbed, ecological sequences. William Cronon argues that how successfully a given environment reproduces itself when people are present is the "best measure of a culture's ecological stability." In keeping with this idea, one can argue that the encroachment of the built environment on nature is a subject that deserves more attention than environmental historians have given it. In twentieth-century Florida history, the displacement of wild spaces by human-made structures is a dominant and yet clearly underexplored theme. What people built and for what reasons, why they chose a particular site, what materials they used and architectural styles they followed, what construction practices they employed, how they and their structures interacted with the natural elements, and how all these things changed over time are questions worth pursuing. One might also ask how the state and local governments influenced private decisions in residential and commercial construction. For example, the development of infrastructure—roads, bridges, and utilities—was essential to opening up wilderness spaces and advancing private development.[15]

Few public-funded construction projects in Florida raise more questions about environmental impact than does the Tamiami Trail, an asphalt ribbon built across the Everglades in the 1920s. Although the 273-mile highway connecting Miami to Tampa was completed in 1928 on the eve of the Great Depression, the idea of a roadway that, like railroads in the Great West, would benefit tourism, business, and development was conceived before Florida's first real estate boom. The Tamiami Trail did more than facilitate development, however, as Gary Garret tells us in his contribution to this collection. In addition to connecting cities once separated by wilderness, the roadway bifurcated the ecosystem of southern Florida and disrupted the lives of the Seminoles who considered the area their home. The construction of the highway was a veritable "mission of conquest" designed to subdue both nature and humans. Although the Tamiami Trail is currently regarded as a scenic highway, it inflicted "injuries to the land, water, and inhabitants that continue to be felt today and may yet prove fatal" to the Everglades.

Since European settlement, agricultural interests have been a main driving force behind infrastructure development in Florida. Similarly, in a trend that dates back to the first Spanish period, much of wild Florida (approximately 500,000 acres in the Everglades alone) has been replaced by commercial farmland. Beginning in the late nineteenth century, literature promoting land sales portrayed Florida as a farmer's paradise, a pastoral garden where the soil was rich and the climate perfect. On an aesthetic level, and certainly as illustrations in sales literature suggested, agricultural development seemed like a benign transformation of the landscape. But commercial farming gave a perverse twist to the Jeffersonian dream of the independent yeoman farmer, the intended beneficiary of land policies that facilitated corporate agriculture. Commercial farming also epitomized the commodification of the earth's bounties, mandating practices that have been particularly harmful to the environment, and generating ecological changes that reach well beyond crop fields. In American culture, nature and natural resources are virtually synonymous, and America puts great stock in resource exploitation, the fuel of the country's economic growth. The commercial development of the Everglades is one of Florida's best-known stories, with the effects of sugar growing and cattle ranching receiving considerable attention in news periodicals, scholarly studies, and the chambers of the state legislature and the U.S. Congress. The Everglades, however, account for only one of countless places in Florida where despoliation has followed agricultural development.

Lake Apopka is one such place, as Nano Riley's essay reveals. Riley examines the lake's devolution from Florida's second-largest and perhaps most beautiful body of freshwater to a virtually dead lake, reduced in size to the state's fourth-largest. Chemical pesticides and fertilizers, the essential tools of modern agriculture, turned Lake Apopka into a toxic cesspool. Just as these inorganic materials threatened indigenous wildlife, Riley informs her readers, they jeopardized the health of migrant farmworkers. Exploiting the environment went hand in hand with exploiting labor. Riley, like David McCally in his study of the Everglades, also touches on the theme of ecology restoration, a relatively new science that, as the story of Lake Apopka shows, remains at the experimental level. The state initiated efforts to clean up the lake in the 1990s, but bureaucratic mistakes led to a massive wildlife kill. Lake Apopka's devastation and rejuvenation, Riley proposes, offer lessons for the future.

The Lake Apopka cleanup initiatives were the culmination of a long history of environmental mistakes. By the late twentieth century, when the transformation of many landscapes had gone beyond the point of preservation, restoration had become the logical complement to environmental protection, the final organizing theme in this collection. The history of environmentalism in Florida and elsewhere represents a turn from progressive-era conservation to the modern environmental movement. In the former, which emerged in full force at the beginning of the twentieth century, activists were generally amateurs who performed their duties without the benefit of ecological knowledge. Their goals were often to conserve natural resources to ensure their continuous availability for commercial use. On many occasions, aesthetic qualities, spiritual benefits, or wildlife destruction—but rarely biological considerations—prompted calls for complete preservation of a wilderness area or the creation of a wildlife sanctuary. By the 1960s, however, Americans were growing increasingly wary of living in a dangerously polluted world. At the same time, ecological scientists had begun to insist that the health of nature was a barometer for human health itself. Joining forces with volunteers and concerned citizens, professional environmentalists helped to foster a powerful national environmental movement that pressed for fundamental reform.

Florida, reeling from the effects of explosive population growth and un-bridled development, supported one of the most active environmental com-munities in the country. The roots of that community go back to the dawn of the twentieth century, and women figured prominently in early conservation causes in Florida. In an essay that opens with the early years of women activ-ists, Jack E. Davis chronicles the experiences of Florida's best-known environ-mentalist, Marjory Stoneman Douglas, who in the late twentieth century led the cause to regain the ecological stability of the Everglades. Her long and socially active life spanned both progressive conservation and the modern environmental movement. Through Douglas's maturing as a full-fledged en-vironmentalist, Davis compares and contrasts those two eras, exploring the catalysts for change in American environmentalism. He ultimately debunks popular myths about Douglas's work as protector of the Everglades early in the twentieth century, noting that her environmental sensibilities evolved along with the larger movement over the course of the century.

Before Douglas emerged as a full-time Everglades activist, others in Flor-ida were working to protect the environment. One was Governor LeRoy Collins. Best known by historians for his shift on the civil rights question, Collins proved to be a stubborn environmentalist. Historians generally credit the 1962 publication of Rachel Carson's *Silent Spring* with ushering in the modern environmental movement. But, as Bruce Stephenson's essay on St. Petersburg shows, in trying to stop a major dredge-and-fill project in Boca Ciega Bay, Collins was already exhibiting a modern environmental conscious-ness in the 1950s. The development of Boca Ciega Bay reflected the growth mentality that had shaped municipal planning since the progressive era, a period when few Florida cities had zoning ordinances but when city plan-ners, including St. Petersburg's, practiced a soon-to-be-forgotten art of de-signing with nature. Stephenson's study is the story of how an environmen-tally astute governor and grassroots activists, aided by the new science of ecology, tried to demonstrate that conventional ways of thinking about the environment had desecrated the beauty and luster of Florida and the biologi-cal struts of a once-vital bay.

Twenty years later, another Florida governor found himself in a battle against developers and an entrenched growth mentality. Appalled by Flor-ida's unimpeded march toward environmental degradation, Governor Reubin Askew turned his attention to the Big Cypress Swamp, located on the north-western fringe of the Everglades. As Gordon Harvey's essay demonstrates, ecologists had educated Askew on the importance of Big Cypress as a watershed for the Everglades, which served as the habitat for numerous endangered species. Indeed, the great wetland itself was struggling to survive the onslaught of agricultural expansion around Lake Okeechobee and development in the southeast. Harvey's account of Askew's campaign to gain federal protection for the Big Cypress illuminates a new age in environmental politics, which included the unlikely environmental policies of the Richard Nixon administration, collaborative initiatives between state and federal governments, the emergence of ecological scientists as activists, and the subordination of property rights to environmental protection.

A parallel story to the Big Cypress saga, and one with similar elements, is that of the Cross-Florida Barge Canal. Located in north central Florida, the canal represented an environmental insult of significant proportion. If completed, the artificial commercial waterway would have severed the Florida peninsula, flooded wilderness areas, silted clear-running rivers and streams, and replaced one of the state's first natural attractions, the already-damaged Ocklawaha River. The undisturbed beauty of the Ocklawaha had once invited tourists and writers of the nineteenth century to speak of Florida as paradise. After many fits and starts early in the next century, Lee Irby explains in the volume's last essay, the construction of the canal began in earnest during the Cold War, though by then the canal had become a controversial project. In contrast to the Big Cypress episode, the campaign to stop the canal was led not by a governor but rather by a grassroots organization, Florida Defenders of the Environment (FDE). Founded and led by Marjorie Harris Carr, a scientist by training and the wife of Archie Carr, FDE epitomized the single-issue, citizen-based organizations that defined an important impulse in the modern movement. In the struggle over the canal, Carr and her colleagues were forced to pit scientific rationale against arguments for economic betterment, national security, and recreational benefits. The barge was stopped, but not before the restructuring of much of the river and the landscape along the canal corridor. For environmental activists, many issues were left unresolved.

Florida history is replete with ambiguous victories for environmentalists. This is not to say that developers and bureaucrats, or humans generally, have subdued nature beyond redemption or relevance. Natural forces continue to exert a powerful influence on the state, and some of the most challenging problems that Floridians face in the twenty-first century are related to their dependence on the state's natural assets. Anticipated population growth heightens the challenges. Studies project that by 2030, 23.5 million people will be living in Florida. Not only will this population put a greater demand on basic services, it will move people out to the few remaining undeveloped landscapes. Some places in Florida, such as Pinellas County, are already built out.[16]

The most dramatic problem, and central to all others, is how to sustain a balance between the water requirements of the enlarged population and an ecology that must remain healthy to yield that basic resource. Florida has a seeming overabundance of water, but as Chris Meindl tells us, Floridians have a long history of squandering it. Development continues to interfere with the region's elaborate hydrological system, and Florida, the wettest state, has already begun to mimic the challenges and dubious solutions of water supply in arid southern California. Much like Los Angeles, for example, which diverts water from lakes and rivers hundreds of miles away, communities in southern Florida are piping in freshwater from other parts of the state, altering the environment in those areas. In part to avoid "water wars" between regions, Tampa in 2003 opened the state's first and the nation's largest desalinization plant, which in theory will provide uninterrupted service to the area's two million people even in times of drought. By all appearances, technology has once again provided a panacea. For developers, businesses, utility companies, and the Southwest Florida Water Management District, desalinization is a practical solution to the demands of an expanding population—one that will allow growth to continue. Yet for activists opposed to continuing sprawl and more towering condominiums, the energy-intensive technology comes with its own set of environmental problems and gives continued reign to old destructive habits of growth.[17]

As has been argued here, loss of unspoiled places has been a central if sometimes overlooked theme in Florida history. And yet, even though engineered landscapes have come to define the state, Florida retains much of its natural bounty and beauty. By the end of the twentieth century, 530 plants and animals had made the state's list of endangered, threatened, and commercially exploited species (104 on the federal endangered and threatened list). But during this same period many more species had shown themselves to be remarkably adaptive and resilient. Some, like the alligator and white ibis, have rebounded from dangerously low population levels. These small victories for wildlife can be attributed in part to Florida's aggressive and highly organized environmental community. A reflection of that community's efforts, the state's environmental laws and regulations are the most comprehensive in the region (although they are not always aggressively enforced and are sometimes legislated around), and policymakers from both political parties have earned merit for green initiatives. Archie Carr, who regarded wildlife and wilderness losses in Florida as the "most spectacular events" in the post–World War II period, held out hope for Floridians to rise to a "new stewardship" and save what was left of predevelopment Florida. Trying to avoid falling into the "trap of nostalgia and indignation," he devoted his last book to a celebration of Florida's natural wonders. Turning his eye to the beauty that remained, he found much in which to indulge himself.[18]

The essays in this collection, too, speak about more than loss and destruction. They tell about images, cultural values, public policy making, and nature shaping cultures. They represent a wide range of topics, but altogether they constitute something less than a comprehensive examination of Florida's environmental history. As with any collection of this sort, much remains to be explored. Historians have not yet, for example, given suitable attention to the changing ecological habits of Florida Indians, the ecological stresses of commercial fishing on the marine environment, the consequences of septic tank effluence on groundwater and coastal waters, the ecological implications and politics of endangered species, and the history and impact of environmental laws and policy. The public-service career of Nathaniel Reed, environmental advisor to Republican Governor Claude Kirk and President Richard Nixon, warrants a full-scale study, as do the environmental policies of Kirk and other Florida governors. The founding of Florida Audubon in 1900, one of the earliest chapters in the country, also awaits examination. Florida tourism has received very little scholarly attention in general, and the environmental implications of thirty to fifty million annual visitors have all but been ignored.

As more students of Florida's past take an interest in environmental topics, the state's historiographical landscape will be reshaped by new sources of understanding and complexity. And as the state continues to undergo demographic and material change, public awareness of environmental issues will no doubt expand. But whether all of this will take place in the hopeful contest of a "paradise" partially regained, or in the dreaded context of a paradise lost, remains to be seen. When Europeans first came to Florida, they had grand schemes in mind. As alluring as natural Florida was, it could not satisfy their material, aesthetic, and cultural demands. Florida, for all its natural beauty and bounty, required an almost endless series of makeovers: a forest to be cleared; a river to be dammed; a wetland to be drained; a road or subdivision to be built. Today, after five centuries of European and American initiative and innovation, the result lies before us—a thriving, vital set of human communities resting on a not-so-vital base of land and water inhabited by endangered species and threatened by all manner of pollutants. The time of reckoning, if not already here, is fast approaching, and modern Floridians can ill afford to ignore the fragile foundations of the civilization that they and their ancestors have wrought. Finding and implementing solutions to Florida's environmental problems are tasks that will test the wisdom and courage of all Floridians in the twenty-first century. But it is our contention that professional historians have a special responsibility to do what they can to provide context and historical meaning for public officials and other citizens trying to address this difficult and complex set of issues. Without an informed understanding of the past—without an appreciation for the lessons of environmental history—there is little chance that today's Floridians, or tomorrow's, will be able to meet the formidable challenge of achieving a sustainable balance of natural and human interests. With this in mind, we offer the sixteen essays in this volume as the first installment of what we hope will become an increasingly important and engaged field of scholarly inquiry.

Notes

1. Donald Worster, "The Grand Canyon," *American Places: Encounters with History*, ed. William E. Leuchtenburg (New York: Oxford University Press, 2000), 361.

2. J. E. Dovell, *Florida: Historic, Dramatic, Contemporary* (New York: Lewis Historical Publishing Company, 1952).

3. Branch Cabell and A. J. Hanna, *The St. Johns, a Paradise of Diversities* (New York: Farrar and Rinehart, 1943); Marjory Stoneman Douglas, *The Everglades: River of Grass* (New York: Rinehart, 1947); Alfred Jackson Hanna and Kathryn Abbey Hanna, *Lake Okeechobee: Wellspring of the Everglades* (Indianapolis: Bobbs-Merrill, 1948); Marjory Stoneman Douglas, *Florida: The Long Frontier* (New York: Harper and Row, 1967); Alfred Jackson Hanna and Kathryn Abbey Hanna, *Florida's Golden Sands* (Indianapolis: Bobs-Merrill, 1950); Jack C. Lane, "Constructing *The St. Johns*: History as Literary Narrative," *Florida Historical Quarterly* 80 (winter 2002): 316 (quote).

4. Charlton W. Tebeau, *Florida's Last Frontier: The History of Collier County* (Coral Gables: University of Miami Press, 1957. *Man in the Everglades: 2000 Years of Human History in the Everglades National Park* was originally published under the title *They Lived in the Park: The Story of Man in the Everglade National Park* (Coral Gables: University of Miami Press, 1964).

5. Nelson Manfred Blake, *Land into Water/Water into Land: A History of Water Management in Florida* (Gainesville: University Presses of Florida, 1980).

6. Ted Steinberg, *Down to Earth: Nature's Role in American History* (New York: Oxford University Press, 2002), x.

7. Elliott James Mackle Jr., "The Eden of the South: Florida's Image in American

Travel Literature and Painting, 1865–1900" (Ph.D. dissertation, Emory University, 1977), 115 (quote); Anne E. Rowe, *The Idea of Florida in the American Literary Imagination* (Baton Rouge: Louisiana State University Press, 1986); Sidney Lanier, *Florida: Its Scenery, Climate, and History* (Philadelphia: J. B. Lippincott, 1876); Harriet Beecher Stowe, *Palmetto-Leaves* (Gainesville: University of Florida Press, 1968), 116–36, 261.

8. Mackle, "The Eden of the South," 2–3; Advertising Committee of the Fort Lauderdale Chamber of Commerce, *Broward County, Florida: The Climate Superb and You Can Prove It: The Paradise of the East Coast Between Palm Beach and Miami on the Dixie Highway and the East Coast* (St. Augustine, Fla.: The Record Company, 1918).

9. William Cronon, ed., *Uncommon Ground: Toward Inventing Nature* (New York: W. W. Norton, 1995).

10. Worster, "The Grand Canyon," 355.

11. Mircea Eliade, "The Yearning for Paradise in Primitive Traditions," *Daedalus* 88 (spring 1959): 255–67; Roderick Nash, *Wilderness and the American Mind* (New Haven: Yale University Press, 1982), 8–9; Patricia Clark, ed., "'A Tale to Tell from Paradise Itself': George Bancroft's Letters from Florida, March 1855," *Florida Historical Quarterly* 48 (January 1970): 268.

12. John Kunkel Small, *From Eden to Sahara: Florida's Tragedy* (Lancaster, Penn.: Science Press Printing Company, 1929), 112; Kathryn Ziewitz and June Wiaz, *Green Empire: The St. Joe Company and the Remaking of Florida's Panhandle* (Gainesville: University Press of Florida, 2004), 22–33; Archie Carr, *A Naturalist in Florida: A Celebration of Eden* (New Haven: Yale University Press, 1994), 97; Howard T. Odum et al., *Environment and Society in Florida* (Boca Raton, Fla.: Lewis Publishers, 1997), 3.

13. Raymond Arsenault, "The End of the Long Hot Summer: The Air Conditioner and Southern Culture," *Journal of Southern History* 6 (November 1964): 597–628; Raymond A. Mohl and Gary R. Mormino, "The Big Change in the Sunshine State: A Social History of Modern Florida," in *The New Florida History*, ed. Michael Gannon (Gainesville: University Press of Florida, 1996), 418–37.

14. For a fuller examination of this subject, see Ted Steinberg, *Acts of God: The Unnatural History of Natural Disaster in America* (New York: Oxford University Press, 2000).

15. William Cronon, *Changes in the Land: Indians, Colonists, and the Ecology of New England* (New York: Hill and Wang, 1983), 1–15.

16. Cathy Keen, "New UF Research Shows Florida to Grow More Rapidly Over Long Term," *UF [University of Florida] News*, March 13, 2002, *http://www.napa.ufl.edu/2002news/population.htm*.

17. *St. Petersburg Times*, March 18, 2003.

18. "Florida's Endangered Species, Threatened Species, and Species of Special Concern," special lists, August 1, 1991, Florida Fish and Wildlife Conservation Commission, *http://www.floridaconservation.org/pubs/endanger.html#nume*; Carr, *A Naturalist in Florida*, xv.

Part 1

Paradise Explored and Interpreted

Chapter 1

Between Topos and the Terrain

A Brief Survey of Florida Environmental Writing, 1513–1821

Thomas Hallock

An important question to emerge when assessing the early literature of Florida is, "Where do we locate the place?" Was colonial Florida the figment of European imaginations? Or should a place-oriented category ground "Florida" in the land? The question is a complicated one because of the region's uncanny ability—from the sixteenth century to the present—to provide a container for stories of the fantastic. Such was the case in 1565, when Giles de Pysière suggested to his Parisian readers that few forms of "more pleasurable entertainment" existed than reading "stories about new lands." He had in mind Florida, of course, then the distant site of controversy in an ongoing struggle with Spain. And it was the very distance that allowed him to push the limits of credibility with his story. Pysière reported of a dragon (having had the "assurance by beholding with the eye" such monstrosities or marvels "long ago seen") that pestered soldiers and settlers in Fort Caroline, the French outpost of Huguenot refugees just north of what later became St. Augustine. This monster, "with the head and neck of a serpent," flew "wherever it perceived some man, or some woman, or a child, and devoured them, and fed them to its young in the forest, so that on the trails one often found half-devoured people who were missing an arm or a leg." Some thirty men armed themselves with "arquebuses, picks, and halberds" to retaliate. They followed the dragon into the woods, massacred the lair, then shot the mother. The settlers thus "delivered" themselves from the evil beast and for this (arguably the first extinction noted in the American literary record) "thanks was given to God."[1]

The passage is remarkable, not just for the events it described, but for the unbuttoned confidence with which those remarkable events were narrated. As the unfamiliar setting (Florida) freed the author to venture into the realm of fairy tale, the status afforded by direct observation (by "beholding with the eye") lent legitimacy to an otherwise far-fetched report. Many early accounts of Florida nature worked in this way—negotiating a tension between topos and the terrain, between a more literary landscape and the physical setting. From Easter Sunday 1513 (when Juan Ponce de Leon christened the land for Spain) through the eighteenth century, Europeans ascribed names and properties to what was far-off or dimly understood. Florida came to represent, as a result, both the landmass and the place as constructed by armchair or actual travelers. Authors described a country that was claimed by several competing powers (by Spain, of course; by France briefly in the 1560s; by England after a Spanish cession in 1763; and by the United States after 1819). The scramble for possession—and the concomitant process of naming—led to a literature that was spun from a rhetorical balancing act, that defined a *place* both actual and imagined.[2] This balancing act is captured in the play between immediacy and distance in Pysière. (Florida was the far-off land, the author a firsthand observer; the combination provided a plausible setting for the fantastic.) Narratives unfolded in this way: between imagined topos and (presumably real) experiences in the physical terrain.

The role of distance in constructing a region may seem paradoxical, but it is important to consider, as critics in recent years have defined a "Florida literature" that relies upon essentialized categories of place.[3] Although the

Thomas Hallock

focus of any kind of regionalist project will probably be the land, the calls for a "real" Florida literature pose a possible dead-end—where critics will be left with a "cheerleading" function, searching for descriptions by visitors or residents (or wondering why those visitors or residents did not write more), possessing little leverage to examine artistic merit or the rhetorical sophistication in portrayals of a place. Certainly Florida merits continued analysis, particularly in our current theoretical climate. Early Americanists in recent years have turned increasingly to studies of the environment, cross-cultural encounters, the staple colonies, and to comparative approaches of Anglo and Latin American writings.[4] And while the field of colonial Florida history is well established, criticism of the literature remains fairly open. Prior work has been stunted by linguistic divides, and by the usual focus upon the Northeast or selected southern colonies like Virginia and South Carolina. The purpose of this essay is thus twofold: to survey the writings and review existing scholarship, and then to suggest a strategy for reading Florida as a literary subject. I begin with "topos"—the visionary landscape—and what happens when a vision supplants the physical terrain. The second part turns to "terrain," examining three different modes (natural history, map-based writing, and settlement narratives) in which colonizers imagined or chronicled changes in the land; in each case, the text marked a removal of some form. The concern for removals, finally, leads me to the topic of nature and Native Americans: in a literature that was about displacement, how should critics approach indigenous forms of writing? With this essay, I do not attempt to be encyclopedic but simply hope to suggest areas of possible study. For if the current interest in connections between American literature, culture, and the land should continue, then scholars will no doubt discover that some of our most valuable sources came from Florida.

Topos (Visions, Disasters, Displacements)

First, the visionary landscape—or more accurately, a seascape of God: In 1595, the eighteen-year-old Spaniard Andrés de Segura began a disastrous journey from Mexico to Spain. His fleet followed the standard route: stopping in Havana, then coasting Florida to St. Augustine, where they picked up currents that crossed the Atlantic. Off the Altamaha River in present-day South Georgia, however, the fleet met a storm. Andrés de Segura survived and later took orders as a lay Carmelite brother (along with the name Fray Andrés de San Miguel), where he had a remarkable career as an engineer (most notably designing the water system for Mexico City). Penned decades afterward, his *Relacíon* recalled in gripping detail how the shipwrecked party battled a storm to survive. The author and his mates escaped their sinking ship in a tippy makeshift box; sharks circled them, and the storms continued; the box leaked, but their depressed carpenter refused to work. Fray Andrés organized these dangers around the story of his conversion. Having promised his life to God in exchange for survival, he rhetorically weighed the "fury of the sea, winds, and fear of dying" against a divine hand. As the weather turned more severe, the crew rediscovered its courage—clearly the evidence of a "supernatural work."[5]

This recourse to the Divine was not an isolated act by a devout man but rather a motif that ran throughout the literature. Where contemporary readers might expect to find images of paradise, Florida was more often described as a hostile and/or remote wasteland. Any "paradise" was the promise of being delivered *away* from Florida; the challenges of an unpredictable environment led authors toward God. Narratives took a triangular shape as a result, meting out hardship (the heat, cold, storms, and so on) against a moral message. Florida literature in effect began with a shipwreck, with Alvar Núñez Cabeza de Vaca's *Naufragios* (1555), a mythic tale that cast the author's journey from Tampa Bay to Mexico as a pilgrimage. Cabeza de Vaca established a prototype for what might be called the "Florida survivor narrative." The basic plot: the narrator, washed ashore, would suffer through a difficult ordeal (usually involving native people), and on this landscape of duress would receive a lesson in Higher Law (figure 1.1). The theme of suffering and redemption (set upon a landscape that was both teleological and physical) provided the title to any number of works: Jonathan Dickinson's *God's Protecting Providence. Being the Narrative of a Journey from Port Royal in Jamaica between August 23, 1696 and April 1, 1697; A Narrative of the Shipwreck and Unparalleled Sufferings of Mrs. Sarah Allen, (late of Boston) on her passage in May from New York to New Orleans* (1816). With varying degrees of accuracy in topographic or ethnographic detail, these narratives roughly followed the same triangular form:

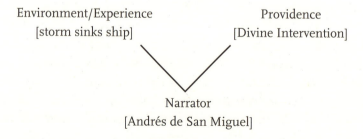

Environment/Experience   Providence
[storm sinks ship]   [Divine Intervention]

Narrator
[Andrés de San Miguel]

Thomas Hallock

The Florida of this schema was both real and imagined: Fray Andrés, Cabeza de Vaca, Dickinson, and Allen wrote from both experience and retrospect; their settings set a moral or teleological message into motion.

Intimate knowledge of place did not define colonial Florida writing—if anything, distance did. In the earliest known use of the word "Florida" in English poetry (1586), an anonymous author began with the question, "Have you not hard of Florida / A countreé by west?" As the unfamiliarity allows for promises of easy wealth (from "savage pepell" who "in the mold [soil] find glysterynge gold"), the poet would take imaginative leave for the place:

With hy!
Ye, all along the water syde
Wher yt doth eb and flowe
Are turkeyse found, and wher also
Do perles in oysteres grow;
And on the land do cedars stand
Whose bewty do excell.
With hy! Wunnot a wallet do well?[6]

The poem epitomized a Renaissance geographic view, in which the dimly understood parts were "by west"—that is, beyond known topography. In a similar example, authors described the most famous (but still distant) landmark of sixteenth-century Florida—the Fountain of Youth—almost entirely through the lens of classical learning and mythology. An early account of Ponce de León appeared in *The Decades of the New Worlde or West India* (1555), by a historian of the Spanish court, Pietro Martire d'Anghiera. In a defensive tone, Peter Martyr (as he was known in English) called the fountain a "rumour" and asked his reader "not to thynke this to bee sayde lightly or rashely." Florida was the setting of his discourse in name only: a short treatment of the water's "marvelous virtue" led him to Virgil; to Archimedes and the Cyclops; to the "current scholes of physitians and naturall philosophers"; and (thankfully for just a moment) to his own childhood bouts with constipation.[7] Such accounts invariably raise the question, "Where does one locate Florida?"

The same geography of the imagination would become still more interesting when dealing with Renaissance-era texts *from* the New World. Authors like Peter Martyr clearly performed acts of textual displacement—emptying the newly discovered realm of its own significance and (in a strategy that literary critics never tire of explicating) reconstituting that realm upon self-serving terms.[8] Two book-length works by Latin American authors, however, show how the currents of linguistic appropriation moved in multiple directions. Juan de Castellanos included a forty-eight-octet tribute to Ponce de León in his epic verse history *Elegías de Varones Ilustres de Indias*. In the seventh canto of this massive work ("Donde se cuente cómo privaron del gobierno á Joan Ponce de Leon . . . y las novedades que hubo después."), Castellanos described a journey to the northern frontier of the Caribbean: Ponce de Leon went there after facing political factions in Puerto Rico, and his travels in Florida led him to the Fountain of Youth, then to a battle with Indians, where the hero received a mortal wound. Critic Manuel Alvar classifies the *Elegías* as a "linguistic creole"—the book having "Castilian form but American content"—and the Florida episode indeed crossed borders in fascinating ways.[9] Castellanos (like others) attributed the legend of a fountain of youth to native sources: "Among the most elderly," he wrote by way of introduction, there was a place "where the oldest women unmake their wrinkles and gray hair." A comical reflection upon the healing waters, meanwhile, would locate the author in a courtly tradition:

> Estoy agora yo considerando
> Segun la vanidad de nuestros dias,
> ¡Qué de viejas vinieran arrastrando
> Por cobrar sus antiguas gallardias,
> Si fuera cierta como voy contando
> La fama de tan grandes niñerías!
> ¡Cuán rico, cuan pujante, cuan potente
> Pudiera ser el rey de la tal fuente!

> [I am now considering, / Given the vanity of our days, / that the elderly would come crawling on their knees / To exchange their traditional gallantries / If it were certain how I am telling it, / The fame of such childishness! How rich, how strong, how powerful could be the king of such a fountain!][10]

The geography of Ponce de León's fountain was nothing if not ambiguous. At one level, the poet situated Florida in a netherspace of improbability—"Si fuera cierta como voy contando." The account of Ponce de León's battle with natives (in actuality, Calusas) just a few stanzas later, however, established a primary point of reference in the Americas. The Indians attacked him with "mazas, arcos, flechas y macanas"—with maces, bow and arrow, and a type of sword made of palm wood. The latter, a *macana*, was a Taino word with possible Nahua or Quechua roots. Castellanos followed a chivalric code, in other words, in the battle against Floridians whose swords were from Meso- or South America.[11] The Florida of this *Elegía* was neither European nor American but somewhere in between.

A similar crisscrossing of the Atlantic characterized a second example, what might be called the first book by an Indian author set in the present-day United States—*La Florida* by Garcilaso de la Vega, El Inca (1605). The product of one who claimed both Incan and Spanish ancestors, the work was notable for its novelistic touches as well as for the fact that its author never set foot in the country described. More literal-minded historians of De Soto indeed can be dismissive of *La Florida* altogether, noting that "literary liberties were often taken at the expense of historical accuracy."[12] Yet Garcilaso identified with an American topic, and this identification perhaps led him to portray a more inviting landscape than his contemporaries did. As explained in the preface, his book should dispel "the bad name that that country has of being sterile and swampy." He defended the land's fertility, wrote that it "abound[ed] in everything necessary for human life," and once settled, would flourish "with the "introduction of crops and cattle."[13] But even as this author of native ancestry paused to defend indigenous people and American landscapes (seemingly to align his book more closely with physical place), Garcilaso would pen the loose equivalent of a novel—a work of fiction, indeed, whose ultimate point of reference was not Florida, but Peru.[14]

Terrain: Natural History, Surveillance, Settlement

Perhaps as often as authors imagined Florida as some vague setting, others described the land with the direct purposes of altering the physical environment. Literary scholars have given these more utilitarian writings less attention. The second part of this essay turns to three separate but interlocking genres, all of which prescribed or chronicled changes in the land: natural histories, map-based writing, and settlement accounts. Authors working in these genres sketched the outlines of new territories and boundaries; they sited future towns or forts; they anticipated the exploitation of existing natural resources; in effect, they repopulated a country. Even as these texts were often grounded in scientific knowledge of a place, by the same token, a certain amount of removal occurred; if in different ways, authors continued to negotiate between topos and terrain. These accounts came from Florida, but they cast the territory within a framework of empire—the texts were published and circulated in capital cities, removing their subject if at a rhetorical level. But what these texts had in common, to repeat a central point, was the intent of making Florida something other than what it was.

Natural History

The first, natural history, resists more than the others pat classifications of genre. A work with "natural history" in its title could focus upon any branch of knowledge (plants, insects, and so on) or a specific place; some natural histories had a more scientific basis; others used science to justify commercial pursuits; still others were tied to the most brutal episodes of European imperialism. Narratives of natural history combined taxonomy and adventure, description and meditation, religious devotion and hard-nosed practicality. But there remains a constant: taking possession in some form, at some level.[15] Panoramic surveys by Gonzalo Fernández de Oviedo y Valdés (*Historia general y natural de las Indias*) and Antonio Hererra y Tordesilla (*Historia general de los hechos de los Castellanos en las Islas y Tierrafirme del Mar Océano*) situated Florida on the northern frontier of a Spanish American empire, effectively bringing a borderland within the compass of the realm.[16] These works could include firsthand accounts of the conquistadors: Oviedo, for example, reprinted Rodrigo Rangel's narrative of the De Soto expedition. Other accounts had only secondary ties to military actions. In 1565, Francisco Lopez de Mendoza Grajales penned a detailed account of sea turtles nesting on Caribbean shores. Mendoza came to Florida as the chaplain of the Menéndez expedition; an exercise in violence, in turn, yielded one of the more vivid records of natural phenomena in the literature.[17]

Whether in the interests of science or imperial aggression, any work of natural history would have to struggle with the issue of possession at some level. In instances of hard conquest, observers collected data for tactical purposes; in seemingly benign cases (what literary critic Mary Louise Pratt calls the "anti-conquest"), observers shipped their discoveries to far-off places, conforming what they learned to European systems of knowledge.[18] During the mid-eighteenth century, this process of collection (and as I am arguing, removal) intensified in Florida for two reasons. The first was political, as the escalating rivalry between England and Spain yielded a market for descriptions of contested lands. The War of Jenkins' Ear and James Oglethorpe's unsuccessful attack on St. Augustine provide the unacknowledged background to Mark Catesby's *Natural History of Carolina, Florida, and the Bahama Islands* (1732, 1747). Although Catesby described several native species (the

Thomas Hallock

"Silver Leaf Palmetto," oaks, mangroves, the flamingo, and several other birds), his "Florida" more accurately represented the southern frontier of Carolina; his explorations of the actual peninsula were cursory at best.[19] Spain ceded Florida to the British in 1763 (in exchange for Havana), leading authors like William Roberts (*An Account of the First Discovery, and Natural History of Florida*), William Stork (*A Description of East Florida*), and Bernard Romans (*A Concise History of East and West Florida*) to often adopt the premise of a natural history for promotional ends. (As the preface of Roberts's book explained, authors should describe what was "now in our possession.")[20] The second reason was the institution of the binomial system of Carl von Linné (or Linnaeus), which led to the dispersal of his disciples around the globe. As the race to classify and name new species gathered momentum, Florida became a principal route for scientific study. The self-taught Philadelphian John Bartram parlayed a small commission that came with his appointment as "Botanist to the King" into a tour of the St. Johns River in 1765–66; ten years later, his son William crossed much of the same territory, chronicling his pilgrimage in *Travels* (1791).[21] William's famous book deserves more discussion than I can offer here (see the next chapter of this volume). I would note only that his book negotiated between conquest and science, between possession and veneration, through a pastoralism that was nonetheless a response to expansionist policies in the early United States. William couched his most cherished "native wild scenes of landscape" (the Alachua Savanna, or Paynes Prairie) alongside predictions that the same country could be "peopled and cultivated after the manner of the civilized countries of Europe."[22] Wonder for the natural world did not trump imaginative colonization, and even the most romantic vision did not blunt the acquisitional edge of republican culture.

Surveillance

Where natural histories often veered into philosophic or spiritual pursuits, the vast geographic writings about America (and therefore Florida) were tied more directly to expansion and empire. Historians of geography have argued this point at length—documenting how maps implicitly usurped the land.[23] Whether in omnibus geographic works or brief reports, early descriptions of Florida indeed took possession as their central theme. In his *Geografía y descripción de Las Indias* (1574), Juan López de Velasco observed that the Spanish, Portuguese, French, and English all gave "different names in the various maps and descriptions" to their claims; the vast expanse known as *la Florida* was called *Nueva Francia* by some, Labrador by others.[24] The authors of even the briefest dispatches described their surroundings with an eye toward tactical control. In 1558, Guido de la Bazares coasted present-day Mobile and Pensacola, issuing a reconnaissance report that included geographic coordinates, a summary of possible ports (Pensacola was the Bay of "Bas-Fonde," or deep bottom), and observations on flora, fauna, river systems, and native populations.[25] The centuries-long struggle for Florida produced a string of brief reports or chapters within book-length works, all claiming the region for one empire or another: Bazares and Velasco for Spain; John Gerar William de Brahm and Thomas Hutchins for England; Andrew Ellicott, Jedediah Morse, and John Melish for the United States.[26] A refrain that bound together map-based writing: "to convey a precise Knowledge of the Actual State and Limits of the Country," showing "where in the Course of Time, Nature and Art will introduce a Change of present Existence."[27] But even as surveys and geographies imagined changes in the land, in effect performing the very act of displacement one finds in natural histories, writings that accompanied a map were grounded in immediate knowledge of place. Maps strained to fit the contours of the land into an imperial vista, but the two seldom matched.

Two wildly different examples from mid-eighteenth-century British America illustrate this tension between topos and the terrain: De Brahm's *Report of the General Survey in the Southern District of North America* (1773) and the *Humble Petition* of Denys Rolle (1765). The former, De Brahm's *Report of the General Survey* (which accompanied a 25-foot map), charted the Atlantic coast from South Carolina to East Florida, providing coordinates to waterways, inlets, and sandbars; notes on the flora and fauna; and advice to settlers. But what makes the *Report* a surprisingly compelling read was its unflinching effort to bring scientific procedure ("the Variations of the Compass at principal places") to the "Vicissitudes of Time, Weather and Wind." The quest for accuracy pressed the geographer into a daunting calculus of time and space. De Brahm situated the inlet known as "Mukoso, alias Muskitoe," for example, "in Latitude 28°54'00 and 00°27'24" East of Saint Augustin and 00°38'24½" East of Saint Mary's," by a channel that "has near the same Water as that of Saint Augustin"; when he "surveyed it in 1765," however, water levels had fluctuated and the channel had since "shifted several times."[28] Utilitarian documents by a mathematician are rarely so fascinating, as De Brahm sought fixity to the variables of locale. And what happened to those who settled the surveyed domain? In 1764, the speculator Denys Rolle established a community on the St. Johns River (near present-day Palatka). The colony's miserable failure led Rolle to present the King's Privy Council with a *Humble Petition,* an eighty-five-page harangue (with almost fifty pages of correspondence) that catalogued the misfortunes developers could expect. (Rolle stalled in settling upon a site and feuded with the colonial government, his cattle was run off, settlers abandoned him, and a ship carrying supplies ran aground off St. Augustine.)[29] Were it not for the amusement that readers might take from a whiner's self-inflicted wounds, Rolle's *Humble Petition* would rank among the most tedious documents of early America. As a response to British calls for settling Florida in the 1760s, it testified to the difficulty of realizing the promises of a map. His *Petition* marked the gap between visionary Florida and the real one.

Settlement

A third narrative form—the settlement account—measured the gap between ambition and the actual landscape and, like Rolle's *Petition,* marked the tension between topos and terrain.[30] If Florida was paradise, these texts ask, who was to settle it? Certainly not the wealthy. A 1564 piece by John Sparke the younger in Richard Hakluyt's *Principal Navigations* reported that cultivating Florida was a task "more requisite for a prince . . . rather than for any subject." Fast forward 240 years to the Louisiana Purchase, and Juan Forbes (of the trading company Panton, Leslie and Co.) said basically the same thing: slaves in Mobile Bay could turn "useless" and "immense strips of swampland" into "useful rice plantations." Another two decades found a pamphleteer writing only as "A Gentleman of the South" inviting "commercial men" to exploit Florida's "inexhaustible quantities of natural stores"; the "thrifty population" should produce "surplus products" like cotton, sugar, rice, and indigo (not crops needed to survive).[31] The authors of such promising ventures hardly imagined working the land. It was a paradox that frontier historians have documented in case after case, from the St. Johns River to Maine: poor whites, immigrants, slaves, or Indians were to suffer the backbreaking work, while the men who wrote promotional tracts "went along for a profitable ride."[32]

The clash of expectation and reality could create narrative arc: in the meeting of Florida's topos and terrain, what happened to people who lived there? For a prime example, one need look no further than Jean Ribault's *The Whole and True Discouerye of Terra Florida* (1563), a book-length advertisement that historian of Florida literature Maurice O'Sullivan calls "one of our finest early works."[33] Ribault came to America in the spring of 1562 in search of a sanctuary for persecuted Huguenots in France. He established Charlesfort (on present-day Parris Island in South Carolina), left thirty men there, then returned to Europe having spent a matter of weeks coasting the Atlantic shoreline. Back in England, Ribault found himself in the midst of religious wars, and he landed in the Tower of London. He wrote *The Whole and True Discouerye* while the starving soldiers back in Charlesfort awaited provisions. That did not stop Ribault from describing a virtual paradise: "a good clymate, healthfull, of good temperaunce." Of the St. Johns River (which he named the River of May, having discovered it on the first of that month by the Julian calendar), he wrote that the "fairest, pleasantest and greatest medowe [there] might be seen."[34] No doubt his enthusiasm was seasonal in part. With a pen fueled by profit and having never felt the drench of a summer rain, Ribault established what is now a universally held truth: Florida is delightful in early spring.

Those who stayed after Ribault told a different story. The French experiment in religious sanctuary in America led to disaster. In 1564, René Laudonnière established a second post, Fort Caroline, south of present-day Jacksonville. The Charlesfort settlers meanwhile neglected to plant their own crops and abandoned their post when supplies ran low. According to Laudonnière, the refugees were unprepared for the open seas: they ate shoe leather, drank seawater and urine, and were eventually reduced to a lottery, where one person was to be cannibalized for food. Rival accounts (most notably by Laudonnière) depicted disaster where (according to Ribault) "nothing lackethe."[35] The demise of Fort Caroline is well known and scarcely requires my review here. (Angered by the French toehold in Florida, Philip II of Spain dispatched Pedro Menéndez de Avilés to remove the Huguenots, officially ending any French visions of paradise.) The last word came from survivors like Nicolas Le Challeux, who penned a witty "Octet" upon his return:

Who wants to go to Florida?
Let him go where I have been,
Returning gaunt and empty,
Collapsing from weakness,
The only benefit I have brought back,
Is one good white stick in my hand,
But I am safe and sound, not disheartened
Let's eat, I'm starving.[36]

Thomas Hallock

"With hi!" beckoned the poet who described a Florida of promise; "Let him go" said the poet who went.

Nature, Native Americans, and Ethnography

Such comings-and-goings, finally, leave an obvious question: What forms of environmental writing were produced by the people there before Ponce de León? The long history of natives in colonial Florida remains beyond my scope here; I would simply return to my central point—that nature writing involved a process of interpretation that was inextricably bound to colonization, that a certain amount of removal was inevitable as writers recast their subject for an audience somewhere else. This process of effacement can make it difficult to reconstruct native attitudes toward the environment. I am not suggesting a shortage of material; if one considers mediums besides paper, indeed, critics may find a rich archive. The artist Jacques LeMoyne de Morgues, for example, came to America with René Laudonnière in 1564 and left a remarkable series of sketches that captured French-Indian exchanges. An image of a tribal council depicted Saturiba, a cacique friendly to the French, in an oratorical pose: the "king" wore only a loincloth, a feather crown, and a raccoon tail; tattoos covered his chest, upper arms, wrists, thighs, calves, and ankles. Indians surrounded him (some wearing feather crowns, others draping animal pelts over their heads, none showing tattoos), drawing attention to Saturiba's ceremonial role. If we accept writing as the inscription on a surface and allow for the exchange of paper and human skin, the literary critic may ask: What did these markings on the native body mean? Can one interpret authorial intentions or cultural significance in the tattoos? How does one read the lines on his body within the context of the performance that LeMoyne depicted? Given this third-generation copy (the engraving of a drawing of a tattoo), finally, what textual history must readers consider? These questions reside at the heart of literary analysis and point to the intersection between text and interpretation that one negotiates in any act of reading.

The questions also can be daunting, posing significant challenges for readers, as sometimes valuable sources were embedded within chauvinistic ethnographic studies. Bernard Romans, for example, "subjoined" two "Indian hieroglyphic" paintings (one Choctaw, the other Creek) to *A Concise Natural History of East and West Florida*. The images possessed formal properties and a representational quality; they narrated a history that connected clans with specific animals and human events on the physical landscape. "The second is a painting in the Creek taste," Romans wrote, that displayed "ten of that nation of the Stag family" meeting enemy Choctaws at a brook called "*Oopah Ullah*." Can one untangle the "hieroglyphic" from the biases of Romans's *Natural History*? Even texts that today provide broad windows into native cultures, critics note, can be problematic sources. For example: a valuable account of the ancient Apalache ballgame, recorded by the Franciscan missionary Juan de Paiva in 1676, would suggest fascinating links between sport, society, nature, and cosmology. Paiva documented these beliefs so they could be destroyed, however, and his manuscript cobbled together the jagged pieces of a faulty translation and clerical commentary.[37] Any attempt to read native texts (and by extension the early environmental beliefs by native people), in sum, must also consider a textual history of which colonization was a part. Whether one attempts to decipher the garbled notes of a missionary or the "hieroglyphics" of a Bernard Romans, the act of interpretation was—and will always remain—an act of displacement or removal.

This leads me to a final example. Perhaps the earliest pieces of what might be called "Florida literature" survive through the Weeden Island people, a mound-building society whose pots provide a window into beliefs about the natural world in pre-Columbian Florida. Discovered in the 1920s in present-day St. Petersburg (on Weedon Island, spelled with an "o"), these artifacts have come to identify what archaeologists today call the Weeden Island I period (200–900 AD). The sacred and prestige vessels dug from the Weeden Island mounds incorporated effigies and designs of boundary crossing or anomalous species (kingfishers, spoonbills, turkey vultures, dogs); scholars today read these images figured into clay as "cultural symbols." The prestige pots in particular qualify as environmental writing, as they were "intricately incised, punctuated, and/or painted [to] depict highly stylized animals."[38] Their unearthing in burial mounds indicates a ceremonial function—a connection to rites of puberty, marriage, or dying—and cosmologies upstreamed from later sources suggest that the symbols were used to maintain a balance, or status quo. Kingfishers, for example, fly through the air, hunt in the water, and nest in the muddy banks of a river or lake. Because this species "behaved abnormally by crossing boundaries," Jerald T. Milanich explains, it was probably "awarded ritual status."[39] The pieces are in place for a literary "reading" of Weeden Island pottery: the inscribed objects possess formal properties;

they hold rich symbolic value and negotiate an allusive field; they have a rich cultural context and textual history.

But once again, these pure products of Florida cannot be read outside the dynamics of interpretation—outside the impulse to catalogue, collect, and ultimately, remove. Extracted from a grave site along Tampa Bay, these vessels are now mothballed in the permanent collections of the Smithsonian Institution. The story of their provenance, preservation, and display is fraught with irony. Today, visitors to the Weedon Island Preserve Cultural and Natural History Center may tour an education center near the mounds and, in a museum exhibit, view replicas of the pots as well as computer simulations of the vessels.[40] Through an interactive video display, visitors "handle" the artifacts for themselves; one may select an artifact, zoom in and out, turn the vessel around—all by running a finger across the touch screen. The point of the virtual tour, as Brent Weisman explains, is to "bring Weeden back to Weedon"—that is, to bring the pots back to their place, to restore (at least digitally) what archaeologists removed in the 1920s.[41]

The restoration via simulacrum (while paradoxical on the surface) is consistent with the literary history that I have sought to trace: nature writing reconstituted a place (or the products of place) through description, performing acts of removal as the territory was invented for an audience elsewhere. Ponce de Leon's fountain of youth was less the product of place than a receptacle for classical learning in the Spanish court; Pysière's tale of the dragon existed for the amusement of Parisians; William Bartram *Travels* testified to the state of learning in the early Republic. In each case, an imagined topos was defined against the actual terrain. Interpretation necessitated removal, and as example after example shows, the physical attributes of a distant colony were often separate from the prerogatives of an imperial power. Weeden Island pots have been replaced with a computer model. Where may one find the originals today? Given these dynamics between empire and place, the answer should come as no surprise: in a Smithsonian warehouse. Shelved and sorted by academics, the earliest surviving expressions of Florida's environmental imagination have been moved somewhere else.

Notes

1. Giles de Pysière, "Description of the Land and Sea Animals and Monstrous Beasts Encountered on the Island of Florida," from an essential collection of primary sources, *Laudonnière and Fort Caroline*, ed. Charles E. Bennett (Gainesville: University Presses of Florida, 1964), 74–75. A similar play between firsthand observation and

speculation informs the account of unicorns by John Sparke the younger, who wrote in 1564 that the "Floridians have pieces of Unicornes hornes, which they were about their necks." Richard Hakluyt, *Principal Navigations, Voiages and Discoveries of the English Nation* (Cambridge: Hakluyt Society, 1965), 541.

2. Convention dictated that a Spanish or Portuguese narrative of American conquest be titled a *Relacíon* (or *Relaçam Verdadeira*); these texts provided both the account of *hechos* (or deeds) and a point of *relation* between colony and empire. The term "relacíon" was usually translated to "account," which is to lose an important pun. And the definitive genre of Florida literature (if I may push this line of reasoning further) was the deposition, a genre that elevates narrative to truth. Depositions returned to Spain signed, sworn upon, sealed, and notarized by scrivener; through the elaborate apparatus of verification, at the same time, participants in the New World contest sought their advantage in court. See, for example, the report of Hernando de Manrique de Rojas, translated by Lucy L. Wenhold and reprinted by Bennett in *Laudonnière and Fort Caroline* (107–24). The "document is a series of affidavits and a description," in Bennett's words (108), and he omits the various signatures and oaths for sound editorial reasons (although this very emphasis upon veracity underscores the role that distance played in shaping the text!).

3. In their valuable anthology of Florida literature, Maurice J. O'Sullivan and Jack C. Lane break the colonial period (1530–1837) into a series of "Paradises": Spanish and French, British, the early Republic, and a grab-bag of subaltern groups (Indians and blacks). The theme is a "concern for and fascination with this 'incomparable land' and its people." *The Florida Reader: Visions of Paradise* (Sarasota, Fla.: Pineapple Press, 1991), 13. Jane Anderson Jones and O'Sullivan write that "the imaginative response to Florida was that of observer," and that "not until contemporary poets [do] we see an attempt to accept the landscape on its own terms." Introduction to *Florida in Poetry: A History of the Imagination* (Sarasota, Fla.: Pineapple Press, 1995), xiii. Annie E. Rowe makes a similar case in *The Idea of Florida in the American Literary Imagination* (Gainesville: University Presses of Florida, 1992), noting a failure to see the land on its own terms and framing the environmental literature of Florida as the story of (imaginative) colonization. Rowe's study is a valuable introduction, although her discussion of the colonial period is limited to William Bartram; for a highly condensed summary of her argument, see her entry "Literature of Florida" in *The Companion to Southern Literature,* ed. Joseph M. Flora and Lucinda Mackenthan (Baton Rouge: Louisiana State University Press, 2002), 264–68. For guides to the vast but still largely unexplored literature of Spanish Florida, see: José Fernández, "Hispanic Literature: The Colonial Period," in *Recovering the U.S. Hispanic Literary Heritage,* ed. Ramón Gutiérrez and Genaro Padilla (Houston: Arte Público, 1993), 1:253–64; William Richard Jackson, *Early Florida through Spanish Eyes,* University of Miami Hispanic-American Studies 12 (Coral Gables: University of Miami Press, 1954); E. Thomson Shields, "Beyond the Anthology: Sources for Teaching Sixteenth- and Seventeenth-Century Colonial Spanish Literature of North America," Society of Early Americanists, http://www.hnet.uci.edu/mclark/seapage.htm.

4. Philip F. Gura directed the attention of Early Americanists to the staple colonies

with his landmark article, "The Study of Colonial American Literature, 1966–1987: A Vade Mecum," *William and Mary Quarterly* 3, no. 2 (April 1998): 305–41. In turning their attention south, literary critics followed the lead of historians like Jack P. Greene. See his *Pursuits of Happiness: The Social Development of Early Modern British Colonies and the Formation of American Culture* (Chapel Hill: University of North Carolina Press, 1988). In addition to the authors cited below, the following have influenced my discussion of literary frontiers: Annette Kolodny, "Letting Go Our Grand Obsessions: Notes toward a New Literary History of the American Frontiers," *American Literature* 64, no. 1 (1992): 1–18; Peter Hulme, *Colonial Encounters: Europe and the Native Caribbean, 1492–1797* (New York: Routledge, 1992); William Spengemann, *A New World of Words: Redefining Early American Literature* (New Haven: Yale University Press, 1994); Bruce Greenfield, *Narrating Discovery: The Romantic Explorer in American Literature, 1790–1855* (New York: Columbia University Press, 1992); Terry Goldie, *Fear and Temptation: The Image of the Indigene in Canadian, Australian, and New Zealand Literatures* (Kingston: McGill-Queen's University Press, 1989). Starting points to the field of literary and ecology (or ecocriticism) include: Cheryll Glotfelty and Harold Fromm, eds., *The Ecocriticism Reader: Landmarks in Literary Ecology* (Athens: University of Georgia Press, 1996); Michael P. Branch, Rochelle Johnson, Daniel Patterson, and Scott Slovic, eds., *Reading the Earth: New Directions in the Study of Literature and Environment* (Moscow: University of Idaho Press, 1998); Ian Marshall, *Story Line: Exploring the Literature of the Appalachian Trail* (Charlottesville: University Press of Virginia, 1998); and the multiple-author contributions to "Forum on Literatures of the Environment," *PMLA* 114, no. 5 (October 1999), 1089–104, http://www.asle.umn.edu/archive/intro/pmla/pmla.html. On early American environmental aesthetics, see: Michael P. Branch, "Early Romantic Natural History Literature," in *American Nature Writers*, ed. John Elder, 1059–75 (New York: Scribner's, 1996). Book-length studies include David Mazel, *American Literary Environmentalism* (Athens: University of Georgia Press, 2000); Timothy Sweet, *American Georgics: Economy and Environment in Early American Literature* (Philadelphia: University of Pennsylvania Press, 2001); Thomas Hallock, *From the Fallen Tree: Frontier Narratives, Environmental Politics, and the Roots of a National Pastoral, 1749–1826* (Chapel Hill: University of North Carolina Press, 2003), 5.

5. Fray Andrés de San Miguel, *An Early Florida Adventure Story*, trans. John H. Hann (Gainesville: University Press of Florida, 2001), 44.

6. "The preme Rose in the grene forest" is reprinted in Jane Anderson Jones, "Florida in Renaissance Poetry," *Marjorie Kinnan Rawlings Journal of Florida Literature* 8 (1999), http://www.mccfl.edu/Faculty/Jonesj/FIP/Renaissance.html. Jones observes that the poem captures the "otherness" of the Florida landscape, and using Stephen Greenblatt's ideas of the "marvellous" to make a case for stewardship, she notes that "wonder" does not always "transform itself into understanding and an acceptance of responsibility to sustain and conserve what remains of Florida's beauty." Bartolomé de Flores has a similar play between distance and unfamiliarity in his *Obra nuevamente compuesta* (1571), a 375-line poem about the Menéndez expedition. He writes: "Y por dar mejor aviso / quiero contar las grandeza y belleza deste fértil

paruiso" [And in order to better describe it, I want to tell of the expanse, of the beauty and loveliness of this fertile paradise]. See the selection in *Florida in Poetry*, 15; for the entire poem, see the Biblioteca Virtual Miguel de Cervantes, http://www.cervantesvirtual.com/FichaObra.html?Ref=2463.

7. Pietro Martire d'Anghiera, *The Decades of the Newe Worlde or West India*, trans. Richard Eden (Ann Arbor: University Microfilms, 1966), 2d decade, 10th book, p. 87. T. Frederick Davis provides an exhaustive treatment of the Fountain of Youth in "Juan Ponce de Leon's Voyages to Florida," *Florida Historical Quarterly* 14, no. 1 (July 1935): 8–66.

8. On "wonder" as a strategy of displacement, see Stephen Greenblatt's *Marvelous Possessions: The Wonder of the New World* (Chicago: University of Chicago Press, 1991). Making a similar case, Eric Cheyfitz argues that translation is also an act of removal in *The Poetics of Imperialism: Translation and Colonization from The Tempest to Tarzan* (Philadelphia: University of Pennsylvania Press, 1997).

9. Juan de Castellanos was himself between worlds. Born in a province of Sevilla in 1522, he arrived in Puerto Rico in the early 1540s, took orders ten years later, wrote his *Elegías* in the 1560s as a priest in Tunja, Colombia [?] Isaac J. Pardo, *Juan de Castellanos: Estudio de las Elegías de Varones Ilustres de Indias* (Caracas: Universidad Central de Venezuela, n.d.), 22–37. On Castellanos as linguistic creole, see Manuel Alvar, *Juan de Castellanos: Tradicíon Española y Realidad Americana* (Bogota: Publicaciones del Instituto Caro y Cuervo 30, 1972), 56, 61.

10. Juan de Castellanos, *Elegías de Varones Ilustres de Indias. Biblioteca de Autores Españoles, desde la formacíon del lenguaje hasta nuestros dias* (Madrid: Atlas, 1944), 4:69.

11. Alvar, *Juan de Castellanos*, 243–44.

12. Edward C. Moore, foreword to *The De Soto Chronicles: The Expedition of Hernando de Soto to North America in 1539–1543*, ed. Lawrence A. Clayton, Vernon James Knight Jr., and Edward C. Moore (Tuscaloosa: University of Alabama Press, 1993), 2:ix. As the editors imply, the four major accounts that comprise *The De Soto Chronicles* offer a "feast for the taking" to the intrepid literary scholar. Those interested in literature and the environment, for example, may see how varying shades of perspective colored descriptions of the land. The harsh terrain could bring discomfort, as swamps contained mosquitoes, and "high, thick wood" provided a cover for the Indians; or authors would note native uses for the land and possible resources for settlement; finally, the terrain could interrupt an unceasing pursuit of gold, as when hostile Indians near a pond would "place water-lily leaves on their heads" to surprise the Europeans. *De Soto Chronicles*, 1:55, 70, 68.

13. On rescuing Florida's reputation, see *La Florida by the Inca* [*La Florida del Inca*], trans. Charmion Shelby, in *The De Soto Chronicles*, 2:53–54. Book 2 of *La Florida* closes with a call for settlement: "the land is very well fitted for the breeding of all kinds of cattle because it has good forests and pasture-grounds with fine water, and swamps and lakes with many reeds and rushes for hogs, which do very well on them and, by eating them, do not need grain. This suffices for an account what is in this province and of its good qualities, one of which is that it is capable of producing a great deal of silk because of the abundance of mulberries. It has also many and good fish" (253–54).

14. References to Peru in *La Florida by the Inca* are almost too numerous to cite; for an example, see the comparison of horses in Florida and llamas in South America. Garcilaso writes that the "reason horses are able to withstand the excessive labor they have undergone and now undergo in the conquests in the New World, I believe—and I have the confirmation of all the Spaniards of the Indies whom I have heard speak about this matter"—is the abundance of maize. "A proof of this is that the Indians of El Perú feed maize to the sheep [that is, llamas] that serve as beasts of burden." *La Florida by the Inca*, 220. The assurance to the reader, set off here with dashes, shows how the author freely exchanges all New World experiences, thus substituting Peru for Florida.

15. Literary studies cover several angles of natural history as a form of writing. Mary Louise Pratt situates natural history within European imperialism in her influential *Imperial Eyes: Travel Writing and Transculturation* (New York: Routledge, 1992). Pamela Regis discusses Linnaean rhetoric in *Describing Early America: Bartram, Jefferson, Crèvecoeur, and the Rhetoric of Natural History* (DeKalb: Northern Illinois University Press, 1992). Christoph Irmscher takes a thematic approach (focusing upon the narration of a self through one's collection) in *The Poetics of Natural History: From John Bartram to William James* (New Brunswick, N.J.: Rutgers University Press, 1999). For an example of the overlap between commerce and science, see Bernard Romans's dedication to John Ellis (who is cited as both a Fellow of the Royal Society and "Agent for the Province of West Florida") in *A Concise Natural History of East and West Florida*, ed. Kathryn E. Holland Braund (Tuscaloosa: University of Alabama Press, 1999), 79.

16. Antonio Hererra y Tordesilla, *Historia general de los hechos de los Castellanos en las Indias* (Madrid: 1934–35); Gonzalo Fernández de Oviedo y Valdés, *Historia general y natural de las Indias*, ed. Juan Pérez de Tudela Buesco (Madrid: Ediciones Atlas, 1959).

17. Francisco Lopez de Mendoza Grajales, "Memoire of the Happy Result and Prosperous Voyage of the Fleet Commanded by the Illustrious Captain-General Pedro Menéndez de Avilés," in *Laudonnière and Fort Caroline*, 150, 143.

18. Pratt, *Imperial Eyes*, 15.

19. Catesby tellingly conflates Spanish and British claims, writing that "the coasts of Florida, including Carolina and Virginia . . . have a muddy and soft bottom." *Catesby's Birds of Colonial America*, ed. Alan Feduccia (Chapel Hill: University of North Carolina Press, 1985), 143.

20. William Roberts, *An Account of the First Discovery, and Natural History of Florida*, ed. Robert L. Gold (Gainesville: University Presses of Florida, 1976), iii.

21. On John Bartram's journey, see Francis Harper, ed., *Diary of a Journey through the Carolinas, Georgia, and Florida: From July 1, 1765, to April 10, 1766. Transactions of the American Philosophical Society*, n.s. 33, no. 2 (1943). The best edition of William Bartram (being the only one to include detailed botanical information) is Francis Harper, ed., *The Travels of William Bartram: Naturalist's Edition* (Athens: University of Georgia Press, 1998). The starting point for any study of William Bartram is the Bartram Trail Conference website, http://www.bartramtrail.org.

22. Bartram, *Travels*, 120, 158.

23. Frontier historian Gregory H. Nobles writes that maps reflected "an attempt not

just to depict or define the land but to claim and control it" in "Straight Lines and Stability: Mapping the Political Order of the Anglo-American Frontier," *Journal of American History* 80, no. 1 (1993): 10. J. B. Harley argues that mapping provided "a medium in a wider colonial discourse for redescribing topography in the language of the dominant society" in "New England Cartography and the Native Americans," in *American Beginnings: Exploration, Culture, and Cartography in the Land of Norumbega*, ed. Emerson W. Baker et al. (Lincoln: University of Nebraska Press, 1994), 297. Literary critic William Boelhower maintains that redrawn boundaries "desemanticized" an existing place in "Stories of Foundation, Scenes of Origin," *American Literary History* 5, no. 3 (1993): 403. Benedict Anderson argues that imagined nations re*placed* existing ones through the repetition of images in print; as invented boundaries acquired the status of legitimacy through repeated publication, new "property-histories" became fixed within the colonized space; a separate "political-biographical narrative of the realm" would thus come into being. See *Imagined Communities: Reflections on the Origins and Spread of Nationalism*, rev. ed. (London: Verso, 1991), 174–75.

24. Juan López de Velasco, *Geografía y descripción de Las Indias. Biblioteca de Autores Españoles desde la formación del lenguaje hasta nuestros días*, ed. Don Marcos Jiménez de la Espadad (Madrid: Atlas, 1971), 88. His brief account of Florida, which is an overview of the empire in America, situates the Spanish claims next to the Indies and within the space and time-history of the realm—Velasco reviews the coastline, describes rivers and bays (with a focus on shipping and navigation), and notes the occupation dates of various missions and forts.

25. Guido de la Bazares, "Narrative of the voyage made by Guide de las Bazares, to discover ports and bays on the coast of Florida, for the safety of the troops to be sent thee, in the name of his Majesty, Philip II., King of Spain, under the orders of Don Luis de Velasco, Viceroy of Mexico, 1558," in *Historical Collections of Louisiana and Florida*, ed. B. F. French (New York: Albert Mason, 1875), 236–38.

26. John Gerar William de Brahm, *Report of the General Survey in the Southern District of North America*, ed. Louis DeVorsey Jr. (Columbia: University of South Carolina Press, 1971); Andrew Ellicott, *The Journal of Andrew Ellicott, late Commissioner on behalf of the United States during part of the year 1796, the years 1797, 1798, 1799, and part of the year 1800* (Chicago: Quadrangle, 1962); Thomas Hutchins, *An Historical Narrative and Topographical Description of Louisiana, and West-Florida*, ed. Joseph G. Tregle (Gainesville: University Press of Florida, 1968); Jedediah Morse, *The American Universal Geography, or a View of the Present State of all the Empires, Kingdoms, States, and Republics in the Known World, and of the United States of America in Particular* (Boston: Isaiah Thomas and Ebenezer T. Andrews, 1796); John Melish, *A Description of East and West Florida and the Bahama Islands* (Philadelphia: G. Palmer, 1813).

27. De Brahm's *Report of the General Survey in the Southern District of North America*, 63.

28. Ibid., 236. On a similar note, unfamiliarity with American nature leads to unexpected comparisons: for example, "raccoons are a kind of Foxes with Monkies Feet and Toes" (209).

29. Denys Rolle, *To the Right Honourable the Lords of His Majesty's Most Honourable*

Privy Council. The humble petition of Denys Rolle, Esq.; setting for the hardships, inconveniences, and grievances, which have attended him in his Attempts to make a settlement in east Florida, humbly praying such Relief, as in their Lordships Wisdom shall seem meet (Gainesville: University Presses of Florida 1977).

30. The classification of a "settlement narrative" may indeed be considered arbitrary, as any number of works previously cited in this article envisioned forts, farms, trade and commerce, over Indian lands. A fascinating area for further research is reports of Florida in periodicals like the *Gentleman's Magazine*. See Charles Loch Mowat, "The First Campaign of Publicity for Florida," *Mississippi Valley Historical Review* 3 (December 1943): 359–73.

31. John Sparke Jr., "The voyage made by the worshipful M. John Haukins Esquire," 543; *John Forbes' Description of the Spanish Floridas, 1804*, ed. William S. Coker (Pensacola: Perdido Bay, 1979), 21, 6; "A Gentleman of the South," *An Original Memoir, on the Floridas, with a General Description, from the Best Authorities* (Baltimore: Edward J. Coals, 1821), 8, 4. Florida as an agricultural bonanza (with others doing the work) receives a full-blown treatment from Bernard Romans's apology, who proclaims in a defense of slavery that "I cannot in good conscience forbear to give my advice to all adventurers of Florida, who desire to improve a plantation for their benefit, not to forget these useful though inferior members of society." *A Concise Natural History of East and West Florida*, 152.

32. Alan Taylor, *William Cooper's Town: Power and Persuasion on the Frontier of the Early American Republic* (New York: Knopf, 1995), 329.

33. Maurice O'Sullivan, "Florida Literature," *Forum: The Magazine of the Florida Humanities Council* (fall 2003): 22.

34. Jean Ribau[l]t, *The Whole & True Discouerye of Terra Florida*, ed. H. P. Biggar (Gainesville: University Presses of Florida 1964), 82, 87.

35. Jean Ribau[l]t is quoted from *The Whole & True Discouerye of Terra Florida*, 91; René Laudonnière reports of cannibalism in *Three Voyages*, trans. Charles E. Bennett (Tuscaloosa: University of Alabama Press, 2001), 50.

36. Le Challeux's "Octect" is reprinted in Bennett, *Laudonnière and Fort Caroline*, 164.

37. Bernard Romans, *A Concise Natural History of East and West Florida*, 151; Juan de Paiva, "Origen y Principio Del Juego De Pelota Que Los Indios Apalachinos y Yustacacanos an Estando Jugando Desde Su Infidelidad Asta El Año De 1676," in *Apalachee: The Land between the Rivers*, ed. John H. Hann, Ripley P. Bullen Monographs in Anthropology and History 7 (Gainesville: University of Florida/Florida State Museum, 1988), 331–53.

38. Jerald T. Milanich, *Archaeology of Precolumbian Florida* (Gainesville: University Presses of Florida 1994), 185.

39. Ibid., 189.

40. The Weedon Island Preserve Cultural and Natural History Center represented an attempt to connect with a history of the place. The education center's design evolved through a series of "cultural values" workshops that brought together archaeologists, anthropologists, workers for Pinellas County, and members of the Seminole tribe.

One enters the building from the east, following native custom, and the center point of the lobby embraces the four cardinal directions—east, west, north, and south. A "spirit vessel" in the center of the floor opens to the underworld; the upper world opens to a skylight. The center seeks to impart a sense of "place," leading the viewer with a deliberately constructed set of messages: "There is a complex web of connections to be explored here"; "I want to come back and see the rest"; "There is a spiritual presence in the middle of all this nature." See Gerald Hilferty and Associates, "Schematic Design Report: Weedon Island Preserve Cultural and Natural History Center," April 30, 2002.

41. Brent Weisman, "Bringing Weeden Back to Weedon," exhibit matter, Weedon Island Preserve Cultural and Natural History Center, March 2003.

Thomas Hallock

Chapter 2

An Eighteenth-Century Flower Child

William Bartram

Charlotte M. Porter

Introduction

In 1791, William Bartram (1739–1823) published a four-part narrative of a 2,400-mile journey made between 1773 and 1777. His long book had a long title, *Travels through North & South Carolina, Georgia, East & West Florida, the Cherokee Country, the Extensive Territories of the Muscogulges, or Creek Confederacy, and the Country of the Chactaws; Containing an Account of the Soil and Natural Productions of Those Regions, Together with Observations on the Manners of the Indians.*[1] Although Bartram and his contemporaries did not use the word "environment" in its present sense, the last part of his book's title acknowledged their attention to human interactions with the natural world. Published in Philadelphia, Bartram's *Travels* presented his observations about plant, animal, and human communities, old and new, for readers of a new nation, the United States.

Bartram set out on his travels to collect for a London patron, John Fothergill. Prior to the American Revolution, colonial science, particularly natural history, involved asymmetrical exchanges of specimens, drawings, and information; colonial naturalists sent to England more data than they received in return.[2] As Bartram traversed geographical, political, and social borders, he questioned the European approach to settlement.[3] Traveling with British skin traders, he observed the asymmetrical exchange of trade goods with the Lower Creeks and emerging Seminoles in East Florida.[4] Eager for European goods, their hunters were decimating animal populations. Bartram realized that the skin trade was destroying Indian cultures, the "manners" of his title, as well as needed "natural productions." The skin trade, a derivative of the English West Indian slave trade in Indian captives, also was destroying the basis of natural history. Who were the proper stewards on the frontier? In Bartram's eyes, the American Revolution brought brief reprieve to the conflict between nature's economy—an eighteenth-century idea—and human economies.

En route to trading stores, Bartram also studied the features of Florida's karst (limestone) landscape—sinkholes, springs, and wet savannas. He recognized their geometrical, if not exactly symmetrical, formations, and, in the clear spring waters, he observed equal access of predator and prey, the hunter and the hunted. In the Great Alachua Savanna, a large wet meadow in present-day Alachua County, Bartram also observed the relationship of the Indian hunter and the hunted. He predicted an additional element, future European populations.

Bartram's observations have provided tools for environmental planning in north central Florida. The present management of the Great Alachua Savanna, now Paynes Prairie Preserve State Park, uses Bartram's records (writings and drawings) for baseline reference.[5] Paynes Prairie is an important biological resource and a critical economic resource, benefiting both nature lovers and real estate developers in a dynamic, if sometimes adversarial, relationship. Restoration of biological communities that Bartram recorded is a remarkable achievement allowing public access to an expanse of the East Florida landscape as it looked at the time of the American Revolution. Missing from this vista are the Lower Creeks and Seminoles, central to Bartram's thesis of access to nature and symmetry of knowledge.

William Bartram

Besides scientific exchange and the skin trade, Bartram's *Travels* involved another asymmetry, the maturation of a late bloomer, and the author had few excuses. He and his twin sister, along with their other siblings, grew up in Kingsessing, Pennsylvania, in a comfortable home with a botanic garden.[6] His father, John Bartram, a capable self-taught botanist, corresponded on natural history topics with affluent English Quakers, and members of the prestigious Royal Society of London encouraged William's childhood interests in drawing and nature with gifts of books and paper and much advice.[7] Living outside Philadelphia, the Bartrams had access to the second-largest city in the British kingdom, and, from 1752 to 1756, William attended the Philadelphia Academy, chartered as a degree-granting college, and studied with Charles Thomson, the nation's leading classicist and, later, the second signer of the Declaration of Independence.[8] Benjamin Franklin, influential in establishing William's school, was a family friend who used his press to promote the work of William's father.[9]

As a young man, William received more advice, much tiresome, about steady ways, marriage, and tardiness, and he made one bad choice that changed his prospects. Having explored the St. Johns River with his father in 1765 for the British Land Office, William bought a tract of land near St. Augustine, and his father, against his better judgment, purchased slaves to work the property.[10] After a few months, William abandoned the place in defeat. Having expended his birthright, Bartram moved about and quit a series of occupations.[11]

In 1772, John Fothergill, a London physician and Quaker promoter of American causes, hired Bartram, by then in his thirties, to collect and draw plants.[12] The social station of his patron changed Bartram's travels from those of a ne'er-do-well to those of a welcome guest. Traveling with real estate speculators in Georgia, Bartram spent 1773 working for Fothergill, as agreed, but, camping near the Ocumulgee River, he confessed, "I was at this time rather dejected."[13] Bartram "sought comfort" in the idea of going south. Still under contract with Fothergill, he resolved to travel to the interior of East Florida.[14] He would soon find his comfort zone in the Florida interior, in Bartram's day

An Eighteenth-Century Flower Child: William Bartram

an uncharted region of the Province of East Florida poorly known to English authorities.

English East Florida

After the English gained La Florida from Spain by treaty in 1763, the Royal Ordinance created two colonies, East and West Florida, and the Ordinance Line, resented on both sides, defined the northern boundary of West Florida authorized for English settlement. West Florida extended the English colonial presence to the Mississippi River (with the exception of the French city of New Orleans). East Florida was less populous, and the British Land Office sought to repopulate lands vacated by the Spaniards and converted Indians with grants to white Protestant English householders, male and female.[15]

Seeking to promote commerce across East and West Florida through trade, the British Land Office also appealed to Creek groups to move south from other regions and relocate in the uninhabited Florida interior. Earlier in the century, the English had furnished the Creeks with guns to raid Spanish La Florida and take Indian captives for sale as slaves in the West Indies.[16] The consequences of the enslavement and relocation of Florida Indian groups resulted in depopulation, but increasingly hostile groups of Creeks, whom Bartram referred to as Lower Creeks, established themselves in a patchwork of villages across the Floridas, sometimes occupying older sites of other peoples.

Having himself succumbed to the promotion of East Florida, Bartram, a former slave owner, was cognizant of the terrible consequences of slavery. On paper, the British Land Office did not allow slavery on land grants in the Florida colonies, but the reality of the plantation system depended upon the labor of enslaved Africans. Said another way, the practice of slavery permitted English economic and aesthetic access to the East Florida landscapes removed from Indian use. A spin-off of this English access was scientific access, specifically natural history observation, and Bartram became a beneficiary.

Bartram was on hand in East Florida at the beginning and end of a decade during which the Indian skin trade replaced the Indian slave trade to accommodate British needs. With his father in 1765, Bartram had witnessed the counsel of Creek leaders called by the new English governor of East Florida to establish boundaries for land grant settlement, free passage, and trade in the province.[17] Working for Fothergill in Georgia in 1773, Bartram had had a year to observe land contests between the Cherokees and Creeks and colonists of different religious persuasions.[18] As he headed for East Florida early in 1774, he could ponder land access and community development by treaty, ordinance, and compromise, or by military, legal, and diplomatic means, as well as involuntary access (slavery) and religious access (divine right). By the time Bartram ended his travels in 1777, many of his countrymen were taking up arms against the British, to this point Bartram's only support group.

For the naturalist, the "self-evident" principle so dear and real to his former neighbors in Pennsylvania was a natural basis for settlement, access, and community identity.[19] Traveling in the Southeast, Bartram regarded the Indian nations as sovereign in their own right. Writing his book with hindsight after the American Revolution, he questioned the morality of access of former English colonists to Indian homelands. He also wondered about access of Indian peoples to benefits of the new Republic.

The Alachua Savanna

By 1791, Bartram was a well-known plant salesman and naturalist, and his book described central East Florida as a natural garden. Bartram used the most pleasing terms that English-speaking gardeners had devised. His most sophisticated readers already knew verges, meadows, borders, groves, and ponds as features derived from a long tradition of English landscape theory.[20] In his famous "Essay on Gardens" (1597), Francis Bacon, for example, had recommended dividing a garden into three parts, a "Greene wildnesse" and a "Main Garden in the midst," preferably with a "fountain." In 1660, John Evelyn, an eminent gardener, determined "to show how the aire and genious of Gardens operat vpon the humane spirits toward virtue. . . . How Caves, Grottos, Mounts, and irregular ornaments of Gardens do contribute to contemplative and philosophical Enthusiasm."[21] That is, Evelyn believed that the garden experience improved human behavior and promoted intellectual growth (if not spelling). Bartram agreed. His savannas, too, possessed "Greene wildnesse" with a "fountain" or "sparkling lake" in the center. His "fountains," of course, were not mechanical spouts, but spring-fed sinkholes, and his grottos were collapsed solution cavities, or caves. Groves encompassing the savannas offered the recommended "full Shade" to offset the airy openness of the main garden, or savanna.[22] The shade, the sparkle, the fragrance, and the greenness were purposefully contrasting qualities to benefit humankind, and, in Bartram's book, the greatest of these landscape spaces was the Great Alachua Savanna.

To meet traders bound for the Alachua Savanna, Bartram navigated his little boat upstream along the western shore of the "Indian," or St. Johns, River. Passing the time, he pondered the significance of vacated archaeological landscapes—old causeways, massive mounds, and burial sites of past Indian peoples.[23] Guessing that these structures dated to the fifteenth century, he inquired, but could not learn anything, about their past or their connections to present cultures. These sites were beyond the bounds of collective memory, and Bartram had reached the limits of his science but not his politics. These sites of vanished past peoples heightened his professed concern for the "future well-being of our Indian brethren," which was as genuine as his concern for the future well-being of European settlers.[24] In marked opposition to current French biological theory and his father's pronounced views, he did not describe native peoples as untutored savages and hateful barbarians.[25] To the contrary, "Do we want wisdom and virtue?" Bartram asked. "Let our youth then repair to the venerable council of the Muscogulges [a group of Lower Creeks]."[26] He was recommending travels to the Indian nations as an equivalent, improvement really, of the European Grand Tour, a custom whereby affluent American youths visited the grand picturesque estates of Europe to acquire taste.[27] Bartram's contemporaries valued travel as educational, and he could attest to the benefits of venerable council, but, as he also knew, the realities of travel in Indian lands made his suggestion impractical.

According to the *Travels*, Bartram arrived at the edge of the Great Alachua Savanna in April 1774. Greeting Bartram, Cowkeeper—the chief, or mico, of the resident Lower Creeks and Seminoles—gave Bartram a Creek name transliterated in the *Travels* as "Puc Puggy" and translated as "Flower Hunter."[28] This name was a Creek diminutive and derivative, perhaps equally well translated as Little Flower, Buddy, Flowery One, Flower Child, Flower Junior, Flower Scout, Fluffy Head (cottony), Whitey, or even Late Bloomer (Seedy).[29] The name, like a visa, gave Bartram safe passage in lands controlled by Cowkeeper and bore visitor responsibilities as well as benefits. Good-natured nickname or shrewd pun, the name differentiated Bartram in purpose and behavior from the skin traders with whom he traveled. In the Great Alachua Savanna, Bartram, the stalking pacifist, was about as dangerous as a butterfly, but the presence of the Flower Hunter also signaled English intent in East Florida. Finding his element in the Great Alachua Savanna, Bartram felt "placed on the borders of a new world."[30] This new world of the Alachua

Savanna—the wildflowers, the birds, the Lower Creeks, the Yamasees under Cowkeeper's protection, the allied Seminoles, the British skin traders, the fire storms, the set burns, the fish kills, and, of course, the mysterious Alachua Sink draining the savanna—provided the centerpiece of his published book. Bartram found symmetry in the parklike prairie. The prey, the bold deer, seemed to "laugh" at the young braves chasing them on their fast ponies.[31] The figure of Cowkeeper was an epitome of a Roman Caesar: "a tall well made man, very affable and cheerful, about sixty years of age, his eyes lively and full of fire, his countenance manly and placid."[32] Bartram admired his fat cattle and the natural plentitude that Cowkeeper tried to sequester for his people.[33] Cowkeeper, his English name from the herds grazing in the savanna, had to be a wise resource manager, and he kept a cool distance from other Creek groups and the English.[34]

Bartram, like many citizens of the early Republic, could not accept isolation as natural, and he suggested underground connections, "secret rocky avenues" between the "fountains" and sinkholes.[35] These horizontal solution cavities in the limestone provided passageways for species to travel to and from the surface. As for humans, Bartram noted uninhabited "desserts," or blank spaces, remaining in the landscape, in Bartram's eyes, for future European occupancy: "I make no doubt this place will at some future day be one of the most populous and delightful seats on earth."[36]

The sources of delight, the sinks, wet meadows, and spring-fed lakes of Bartram's observations were the results of ongoing solution of the surface limestone by weak organic acids.[37] Savannas, as Bartram noted, often surrounded round sinkholes, ranging in size from small dry sinks to water-filled lakes. Bartram recalled "their uniformity, being mostly circular or elliptical, and almost surrounded with expansive green meadows; and always a picturesque dark grove."[38] These sinkholes formed as solution seeps at the corners of fractures in the underlying limestone beds. With time, the solution spaces opened and the surface beds collapsed, "their superficial rims," Bartram noted, "exactly circular, as if struck with a compass, sloping gradually inwards to a point at bottom, forming an inverted cone."[39] The resulting sinkholes and surrounding drainage, or wet savannas, made circular patterns on the landscape. Because the limestone beds fractured as blocks, the fractures appeared as a grid with a surface network of circles. The *Travels* contains frequent, even repetitive, descriptions of circular insular prairies accented by jewel-like lakes. Many of these sinkhole lakes were spring-fed, because the collapse of the surface strata exposed the water table.

Bartram discussed the clarity of spring waters as a threefold medium—first, as a medium of creation; second, as a medium for equality; and third, as a medium of peace. Describing one of many spring runs near Lake George, he mused: "Although this paradise of fish may seem to exhibit a just representation of the peaceable and happy state of nature which existed before the fall, yet in reality it is a mere representation."[40] Bartram looked on as predator and prey swam amongst each other and moved aside to make room for others to pass. He wondered by what rules they achieved their state of peace: "here is no covert, no ambush; here the trout freely passes by the very nose of the alligator, and laughs in his face, and the bream by the trout."[41] In 1791, his older readers could enjoy thinking of the alligator as King George III and of the trout as the colonists. The trout, too, was a predator, and Bartram realized that, despite the medium of peace, colonial independence came at cost to nature.

Access

Natural history activities of observation and collection required fieldwork, or physical access, and Bartram needed Cowkeeper's permission, protection, and hospitality to study the natural history of the Alachua Savanna. On East Florida land grants, too, fieldwork raised the issue of trespass, circumvented by eighteenth-century European practices of hospitality. Bartram's English, Scottish, and French hosts fed him, nursed his illnesses, and provided him with credit, transportation, assistance, and servants, even though Bartram hailed from Philadelphia, a colonial hotbed of revolutionary ferment.[42]

As he traveled the sparsely settled land grants of East Florida, essentially the eastern corner of the present state between the St. Marys and St. Johns rivers, he doubted the permanence of the British land grant system as an economic and landscape model.[43] Without British military and police presence, the land grant system also could not sustain the field trips and research basic to the development of natural history. In East and West Florida, the lawlessness along byways between old and new communities made access dangerous, and without maps, scientific records lacked precision and repeatability.[44] Indeed, Bartram died in 1823 before naturalists could retrace his travels in Florida.

Bartram's *Travels*, published thirteen years after his trip, reconstructed memorable scenes of Edenic simplicity, but there had been real dangers, even for Puc Puggy the Flower Hunter. Late in July 1774, Bartram encountered a large war party of Lower Creeks camped near the trading house (near present-day Stokes Landing) on the St. Johns River.[45] The trading agent denied their leader, Long Warrior, credit, and, during the evening, a group of surly braves approached Bartram to kill a rattlesnake in their midst. Killing the snake was for them taboo.[46] Bartram killed the snake with feigned bravado in a public display and explained the taboo to his readers: he who killed rattlesnakes might become a victim of their venom.[47] His action caused him regret. Bartram confessed, "within the circle of my acquaintance, I am known to be an advocate or vindicator of the benevolent and peaceable dispositions of animal creation."[48] Outside his "circle," he recognized the trade-off of values necessary to his situation as a guest. The bullies forced him to kill the snake, but did his status as the Flower Hunter, a scientist, place him on higher ground?

The unpleasant encounter was its own retribution. The enforcement of the Lower Creek taboo frightened and disturbed Bartram because it pitted war raids for captives, or skin hunting, against flower hunting in a ludicrous context of English imperialism. Bartram felt that he had to kill the snake or be killed. That is, in a terrible moment orchestrated by the young braves, he felt powerless. In truth, he or they could have shooed away the rattler with a broom. Instead, the braves humiliated the Flower Hunter with their taboo, just as the English skin trade humiliated them with high prices, false promises, and debilitation.

Bartram later wrote that "the Animal creation are endowed with the same passions & affections We are."[49] These same passions and affections posed potential for conflicts among human communities. Bartram realized that organization of the new nation of the United States, as a compound of diverse and conflicting plant, animal, and human communities, entailed conflict with nature and therefore risked conflict with, in Jefferson's memorable phrase, nature's god. For Bartram, such conflict was the ultimate taboo, for it risked divine retribution. In a rough draft, still among his papers, he lamented that "man" would have destroyed the "whole Animal creation if his Arm were not withheld by the Supreme Creator and preserver."[50]

Asymmetry

In his drawings, Bartram often probed fateful community relationships in miniature scale, but he was unable to resolve the asymmetry of the situation. His best watercolors explored the scale of nature through the visual horizons of a cow ant, a hapless frog, a resting hummingbird, and a land snail.[51] The lives and deaths of carnivores and herbivores were mini-moments in the big picture of the world, but important to Bartram's understanding of nature. Bartram believed that species, large or small, were of equal value to the divine workmanship of created nature.[52] As he traveled, Bartram the Flower Hunter had to make difficult choices about his own workmanship, choices about what to draw, what to harvest, what to save, and what to record. Bad weather, accidents, danger, and taboo made other choices for him, but he did not confuse his incomplete science with the fullness of nature.

For Bartram, life seeped into all natural spaces like a fluid or subtle ether. His watercolors celebrated this biological continuum in a way that easily merged with the geological reality of sinkholes, solution cavities, and springs in East Florida. This continuum, however, was not tidy, and his writings and drawings, especially his exquisite pen-and-ink studies, presented nature as a chain of being with knots, kinks, and entanglements.[53] Bartram did not try to iron out these irregularities or resolve all natural communities into a precise arithmetic of "a flower for each fly."[54] There was another principle at work, the regulation of spring water communities, which filled Bartram with awe, but not understanding.

Besides the asymmetries of communities caused by human exploitation, Bartram observed natural asymmetries—range extensions of species, endemic species, and isolated populations.[55] He could not explain these phenomena but often recorded them in his drawings. Why was the spotted turtle (*Clemmys guttata*), for example, a common resident of the Atlantic colonies, found only in a small inland area of the Florida panhandle?[56] Had colonizing humans introduced these turtles from their former homelands? Fothergill, for example, had recently requested that Bartram collect North American turtles for introduction to English gardens.[57] As for ancient peoples, what had happened to the Mound Builders, Bartram wondered as he wandered about the site of Mount Royal.[58] Who had owned the discarded flint chips, literally footnotes to the presence of past observers in his drawings? Again, Bartram reached his limits as a scientist as he tried to understand the principles of species distributions and human migrations. Bartram ended his travels in January 1777 and returned to Kingsessing, where he spent the rest of his long life.[59] After the death of his father later that year, his brother, John Jr., inherited the property, including the garden.[60] The Flower Hunter, having expended his birthright, once again remained on the premises as a working houseguest and, with his brother, niece, and her husband, helped develop the garden into a nursery business.[61]

At this time, William Bartram had little choice, although he later turned down a formal offer to teach at the University of Pennsylvania. Prior to the War of Independence, there were no paid natural history professions to chose from in the colonies, because there were no profit-generating natural history collections.[62] Before the war, naturalists, including the Bartrams, sent their specimens to England for sale and exchange. This trade and the resulting prestige were asymmetrical, because the colonists, regarded as collectors without prestige in England, sent more materials and information than they received in return.

The skin trade of Bartram's experience in East Florida also was an asymmetrical exchange, because English traders demanded more and more animal products from Indian groups in exchange for limited European goods. An important concern that Bartram voiced was the Creek depletion of their hunting grounds, countered in part by Cowkeeper with the harvest of abandoned Spanish herds. The impact of the escalating slaughter of wildlife in East Florida, Bartram wrote, was "carried to an unreasonable and perhaps criminal excess, since the white people have dazzled their senses with foreign superfluities."[63] Digressing from his usually mild-mannered language, Bartram's choice of words, "criminal excess," was provocative at a time when there were no wildlife management laws regulating hunting in the United States. Again, Bartram the naturalist was the beneficiary of the skin trade on Indian lands, just as he had been the beneficiary of English courtesy on the land grants. Traveling with traders provided him with rough escort, food, translation, transport, dry storage facilities, and safety in numbers. The traders' activities and Lower Creek courtesies provided him with opportunities to learn, but he observed nothing not already known to native peoples and to many of his Spanish predecessors. He pictured natural communities organized in landscapes of scale, but, for him, all species held primary value in the economy of nature, which the skin trade perverted. Throughout his long book, Bartram reiterated the inherent worth of intact communities, not the monetary value of extracted species. Yet, back at Kingsessing, Bartram, too, made his living by catalog sales of plants, especially those given enhanced commercial value by descriptions in the *Travels*.[64] The Flower Hunter had become a Flower Trader.

Unlike the skin trade, the plant trade did not require larger and larger numbers of freshly procured specimens. Bartram, like other botanists, collected plants and propagated them in gardens for observation, exchange, and sale. The well-tended garden was like the clear spring pool, a place of moratorium. The environmental risk, of course, was the escape of unwanted introductions into the surrounding landscape. Like the skin trade, the plant trade was not sustainable, but for different reasons. Gardeners, selling their assets, seeds, bulbs, and rootstock, put themselves out of business, and, as he got older, Bartram, for one, became unwilling to travel to increasingly distant frontiers for new species.

Scientific novelty translated into economic prosperity and enhanced reputations of gardeners like the Bartrams, while the skin trade led to the depauperization and degradation of Indian participants. Bartram realized that frontier trade, in which wildlife products, guns, and alcohol were the currency, was not a sustainable economy for humans because it was not a sustainable economy for nature. Furthermore, frontier natural history, dependent on wild species and driven by novelty, was not a sustainable study of nature. The skin trade and natural history both depended upon the same frontier resources, living populations of species and people knowledgeable about their exploitation. The problem that Bartram identified was "criminal excess."

During the period of Bartram's travels, the English were not naïve about the future prospects for wildlife in the colonies. Fothergill had urged haste for natural history. "As the inhabitants increase," he wrote of colonization, animals "as well as native plants will be thinned and it is therefore of some consequence to begin their history as soon as possible."[65] Fothergill did not regard this thinning out as criminal or excessive because he did not yet have the true facts from Bartram. In this regard, the timing of the American Revolution was fortuitous. The cessation of the mails to England curtailed scientific communication between Bartram and Fothergill, and the events of war interrupted the skin trade in East Florida.

Fothergill's insight and Bartram's observations provided incentives for others.[66] The new Professor of Natural History at the University of Pennsylvania, Dr. Benjamin Smith Barton, used Bartram's records and the family garden as resources for his own publications and instruction, and Scottish poet–turned-ornithologist Alexander Wilson took drawing lessons from Bartram and his niece, Nancy Ann, at Kingsessing. Bartram lost control of his data through garden sales and friendships, and collegial contacts continued an asymmetrical trade with a different form of currency. Bartram's letters, the aspiring Wilson wrote, were "as valuable as Bank Notes to a Miser."[67] These he redeemed in his beautifully written volumes of *American Ornithology* (1808–14). This groundbreaking work introduced the possibilities of large illustrated bird books in the United States and, in a formal way, incorporated Bartram's observations as a science of birds. Throughout the elegant volumes, Wilson graciously expressed his debt to Bartram.[68]

In the United States, Wilson secured his reputation as a poet through published natural history tours, the most famous to Niagara Falls.[69] As he worked to complete the *American Ornithology,* readers met Wilson on the pages of the popular magazine *Port-Folio.* Wilson's "Rural Walk" described Bartram's. Wilson's poetry functionally refigured Cowkeeper's name of Puc Puggy as a sympathetic aura under which all naturalists could explore and hunt specimens on private lands for public good. His "The Solitary Tutor," for example, wistfully told of a melancholy soul who "Thro Georgia's groves with gentle Bartram strays."[70] Wilson mused with artistic license. In truth, these poems were displaced Florida fables, perhaps politically incorrect to situate with accuracy after Spain regained control of East Florida and West Florida. Wilson also emphasized the value of specimens for national science, and, unlike Bartram, he deposited study collections of the species that he described in Charles Wilson Peale's Philadelphia museum.[71] He began an important precedent, followed by Lewis and Clark and other nineteenth-century western explorers.[72] To complete Bartram's plant descriptions and to duplicate materials sent to England, Thomas Nuttall retraced parts of Bartram's route in the autumn of 1815, but he did not get to Florida.[73] Two years later, a party from the Academy of Natural Sciences departed Philadelphia to follow "Bartram's track" in Florida but turned back near the mouth of the St. Johns River after dangerous skirmishes with renegades.[74]

Literary Access

Writing as a naturalist fully aware of disorder, change, beauty, and decay, Bartram created a mixed idiom that makes some passages of his book confusing for modern readers. In East Florida, for example, he saw soft "porticos" among the vines, passed "pensile" banks, and pondered the "infundibuliform" cavities of sinkholes. Readers of his day enjoyed this vocabulary as the pedagogical legacy of Greek and Latin literature and found assurance in the fit of European concepts to the unsettled regions of America. Seeking neoclassical order, beautiful proportion, and classification, they were less concerned that the specifics of Bartram's itinerary were difficult for would-be travelers to reconstruct. Before Andrew Ellicott's survey of Florida published in 1803, there were few English place-names to refer to in inland East Florida.[75] The typographical errors in the published book have confounded later readers who wished to retrace his travels, but, in 1791, they were minor distractions in a major publishing event in Philadelphia.

By the time Bartram published the *Travels,* English-speaking travelers had lost easy access to Florida landscapes, now controlled by Spain. Writing about East Florida, Bartram wanted to access a meaningful human environment for his readers. The features that he sought were not land grant estates; they were features of the karst landscape—springs, sinkholes, and wet savannas. Picturesque sights were essential to the successful European Grand Tour, and Bartram's *Travels* presented the natural history of Florida as a picturesque learning experience. Having immersed himself in his sensory proximity to nature, Bartram immersed his readers, too; indeed, he drenched them in a rite of initiation to the Great Alachua Savanna. Plants saturated the air of the *Travels* with beneficial odors, and their parts, the roots of the pickerelweed (*Pontederia spp.*) and the bark of the fever-tree (*Pinckneya bracteata*), with the right touch in the right place, promised healing virtues.[76] Sounds marked the time of day. At night, Bartram recounted, Indian youths made simple music.[77] When their flutes ceased, "sylvan music" of birds and frogs chimed in to make "the shades of night more cheerful." The eyes could feast on the natural abundance, the "various grasses and flowering plants," and taste could take special delight in the wild custard fruit, or paw paw, acorns, and conte,' a jelly made of smilax root.[78]

Bartram also used examples of human behavior to engage his readers, and the most compelling examples are often his own, for Bartram's long book also is an autobiography. Bartram's travels across Indian homelands obviously occurred in real time, but his descriptions of them frequently called up "the eternal spring of virtue," that versatile time-warp of Philip Sidney's poem "Arcadia" (1590) and Thomas Lodge's novel *Rosalynde: Eupheus Golden Legacie* (1590), the main narrative source for William Shakespeare's play *As You Like It* (1599).[79] In addition to quest, the narrator of the *Travels* shares with the heroes of Shakespeare's play the elements of disguise, potion, and the opportunity for courageous acts. In the course of his book, Bartram assumed the rough dress of the English skin traders with whom he traveled. Among the Lower Creeks, he partook of the "thin drink," and, against his will, he made the right choice about a dangerous taboo. William and Shakespeare's Orlando, both unsuccessful sons, rejected the edifices of civilization and turned to nature for "friendly retreat." Both found seats on "moss-clad rocks" and discovered books in trees. In the forest, Orlando found Rosalind; Bartram found himself.

His story of coming to age placed his long book in a literary context, but Bartram's travels broke down the barriers between life and art. As Wilson also discovered, travels in the landscape were prerequisite experiences of Romanticism, and those parts of the *Travels* written about Florida found favor with the Romantic movement in Europe.[80] The 400-page *Travels* offered two of the English Lake Poets, their female companions, and their admirers ample terrain for fertile Romantic imaginations. Samuel Taylor Coleridge read the *Travels* in 1794, and William Wordsworth took the book with him to Germany in 1798.[81] The sights, scents, and sounds of the Florida landscape described reemerged in Wordsworth's "Ruth" (a love poem in the Georgia wilds) and Coleridge's "The Lime Tree Bower My Prison" (a garden poem about solitude).[82] Wordsworth's heroine Ruth owed much to Shakespeare's Rosalind, and her lover clearly was the naturalist Bartram dressed up in Creek attire. Scholars have identified Bartram's description of Salt Springs run with Alph, the sacred river in the magical place of "Xanadu" in Coleridge's poem "Kubla Khan."[83] Again, Xanadu was a chain of parklike savannas in a karst landscape.

And there were gardens bright with sinuous rills
Where blossomed many an incense-bearing tree;
And here were forests ancient as the hills.[84]

Prose writers, too, discovered the romance of Bartram's *Travels*. In France, François-René de Chateaubriand situated *Atala,* his novella of 1801, in the botanical landscape of Bartram's Alachua Savanna.[85] Chateaubriand was no naturalist, but he detailed the floating islands of water lettuce (*Pistia stratiotes*) and erect yellow flowers of spatterdock (*Nuphar spp.*), described in the *Travels*, "two or three feet above the surface of the water, each upon a green starol, representing the cap of liberty."[86]

Chateaubriand had spent five months of 1791 traveling between Baltimore and Niagara Falls. He was making his own Grand Tour, despite momentous political events occurring in his native France. Chateaubriand did not visit Florida, at this time under Spain's control. After reading Bartram's *Travels*, Chateaubriand did not need to risk a dangerous trip to invoke the moist green world of the Alachua Savanna. As French citizens invented a new calendar, Bartram's book suggested a better "calendar," the migrations of birds.[87]

These annual events of long standing, of course, were time markers for Indian peoples living, Bartram believed, in a deeper history than their new neighbors. This deeper history provided the love story of *Atala*, too, with a compelling dimension.

In East Florida, Bartram found his muse, the source for signs of springtime in the Northeast. "Most of those beautiful creatures, which annually people and harmonize our forests and groves, in the spring and summer seasons," he claimed, "are birds of passage from the southward."[88] These birds celebrated "their nuptials" with song. These are tender words, and the naturalist has framed his journey in terms attractive to the delicate feelings and sensibilities attributed to a growing audience for natural history, women of the early Republic. Many portraits of ordinary women show their interests in nature through their companions—flowers, books, and pets, songbirds, squirrels, and chipmunks. By the 1790s, Peale was targeting women in advertisements and promotional literature for his museum programs.[89] In addition to the assistance of Peale's talented children and nieces at the museum, Wilson's contributions and his poetry cultivated a female audience for natural history in general and Bartram's *Travels* in particular.[90]

Bartram's literary access became important again after the United States acquired Florida as a territory in 1821. Magazines such as the *Cabinet of Natural History* and *Rural American Sports* and popular bird manuals reprinted long sections of Bartram's *Travels* describing Florida.[91] The visual elements organizing Bartram's word-pictures of the wet savannas worked so well that they shaped the artistic and moral visions of others. For example, a lawyer turned Native American advocate, George Catlin traveled in the Florida panhandle during the winter of 1834–35, and, after a short visit in Pensacola, painted a small Florida landscape. The subject is a circular flower-filled prairie with a central "fountain" of water.[92] Bartram's book, not the season of Catlin's visit, provided this image of springtime.

Catlin may have learned other lessons, too, from Bartram's *Travels*. After the Indian Removal Act of 1828, there were fewer people in Florida than at any other time since the arrival of Ponce de León in 1513.[93] The resident Amerindian genus loci that had given Bartram's wet meadows significance became a casualty of United States policies. In 1837, to picture the Florida Seminoles, Catlin had to go to Fort Moultrie, North Carolina, where they were imprisoned. These individuals were victims of hostile military actions that Bartram predicted almost forty years earlier in the introduction to his book.

Charlotte M. Porter

Catlin's route crossed that part of Florida avoided by the great bird painter John James Audubon. In 1832, a late winter search for waterbirds on the St. Johns River disappointed Audubon, and, surrounded by alligators, he feared for the safety of his Newfoundland dog, Plato. Audubon, feeling misled, attributed a premature land boom in northeastern Florida to Bartram's "flowery sayings," and he soon departed the region for the Florida Keys.[94] Communication was key, and, in the *Travels*, Bartram tried to find suitable address to engage the reader and to access natural history communities poorly known to science. Bartram also was trying to negotiate a treaty with his readers, the peaceable disposition of wildlife and Indian well-being in exchange for scientific information.

Adam's Rib

Bartram's *Travels* had product tie-ins that facilitated reader engagement with the issues raised in his book. After 1803, readers could see Peale's portrait of Bartram hanging in the museum's gallery.[95] They could view and purchase Florida plants from Bartram's garden in Kingsessing, and they could enjoy growing these plants in their own gardens, if for no other reason than to heighten the literary effects of *Atala* and poetry by Wordsworth and Coleridge. Reciting verses of "Kubla Khan," they could actually breathe the fragrance of "incense-bearing" trees. These gardens, indebted to Bartram's travels, were intimate theme parks, later developed with redundancy on a grander scale in Florida by Walt Disney and his imitators. Sidney Lanier and Harriet Beecher Stowe, early promoters of ecotourism in Florida after the Civil War, also exploited Bartram's legacy. Mrs. Stowe, famous author of *Uncle Tom's Cabin*, moved to Mandarin, along the banks of the St. Johns River. From her modest home, a popular whistle-stop for steamboat tourists, she wrote a travel guide, *Palmetto-Leaves*, in the form of letters to other women. Many of the destination points that she featured were places described by Bartram, for Stowe shared his enthusiasm for freshwater environments. In her book, Stowe also acknowledged the difficult issue of labor in eastern Florida, still a place with no white workforce. Stowe apologized, "we never pretended that Florida was the Kingdom of Heaven," but "it is a child's Eden."[96]

The illusion of Florida as paradise has a firm hold on the popular imagination, and a 2001 issue of *National Geographic*, perhaps with unthinking reference to Stowe's remark, illustrated an article about Bartram's travels with sepia photographs of a young child frolicking about in his birthday suit.[97] The East Florida of Bartram's travels was not a place for unattended youngsters, and Bartram did not talk about nude children in his book of *Travels*. He did spy on some chaperoned Cherokee maidens bathing in a river, and he did use the terms "natural garden" and "paradise" as allusions to Eden.[98]

Returning to the larger theme of this volume, Paradise Lost, students of literature can enjoy a real connection between John Milton's poem of that name and the second edition of Bartram's *Travels* published in England in 1792 by Joseph Johnson. With a good instinct for selling books, Johnson, a liberal publisher, hired the artist William Blake to engrave plates for *Loves of the Plants*, a dicey scientific poem by Erasmus Darwin about the sex lives of plants. Darwin, the grandfather of evolutionist Charles Darwin, had published an earlier edition of the poem, but in 1792, Johnson reprinted Darwin's eclectic verses and Blake's plates in a two-part volume with a less flamboyant title, *The Botanic Garden*.[99] Johnson's London bookshop, a meeting place for American intellectuals, cultivated readers for Darwin and Bartram on both sides of the Atlantic.[100] Johnson's edition of Bartram's book also resulted in a more unified whole, and both authors became famous (if not rich) through Johnson's second editions of their work. Darwin's poem became a best seller, and within a few years, Bartram's book was translated into several European languages.

Blake's skills were key to the meteoric success of Darwin's book and, indirectly, the welcome reception of Bartram's book first in England and then on the Continent. An advocate of revolution, the mystical artist Blake also a claimed to be Milton's spiritual reincarnation.[101] In 1793, much of Blake's album, *America: A Prophecy*, would have made many readers of Bartram's *Travels* blush. The luminous beauties that he illustrated in picture and in verse were not the modest chaperoned maidens of Bartram's account. To the contrary, like the flowers of Darwin's poetry, the young women of Blake's prophecy, exposed by the light of rebellion, glowed "with the lusts of youth."[102] Milton, too, might have rolled over in his grave or, at least, covered his ears, as Blake exhorted the spirits of their sisters, "pining in the bonds of religion to find renewed life."[103] Not "asham'd of his own song," Blake continued on his vision quest with *Europe: A Prophecy* and illustrations for Dante's *Purgatorio* and *Inferno*.[104] Women and their body parts are everywhere evident in these works—as comparisons to men, objects of desire, and bundles of nerves. In Blake's *America*, human figures swim through the medium of desire, like Bartram's fish seeking the light in the karst underground of East

Florida. Blake's daring neo-mythology sexualized the cosmos of Bartram's East Florida with the license of Erasmus Darwin's science.

The deeper message of Bartram's *Travels* needed more illustrations, and, in London, Blake would have been an exciting choice for the task. Johnson apparently did not have access to collections of Bartram's drawings already in England or lacked the funds to pay Blake to engrave them or to make original illustrations. Blake was restless, and his cataclysmic revolutions paralleled Bartram's outcry against human abuse of nature. Both Bartram and Blake regarded nature as the divine creation, but with an important difference, which, despite the centuries, is a modern difference. Channeling Milton, Blake exploited vocabulary and grammatical constructs, now obsolete, to address spiritual redemption. Bartram, whose language, too, can be trying, spoke in the present voice, not apocalyptic visions, to address the stewardship of biological and human communities. "Criminal excess," Bartram's label for overexploitation of wildlife resources, was an emphatic pronouncement in a book that stands as an anthem of nature and national prayer.[105]

Conclusion

In 1774, William Bartram's travels in East Florida presumed two levels of access, physical and scientific, dependent upon passageway and permission. First, the routes of British skin traders permitted physical access tightly bound to the season and locale of natural resources. Second, a contract with a wealthy English patron and a network of courtesy permitted scientific access loosely bound with an itinerary of time and place. In the Alachua Savanna, Bartram realized that he needed a third access, the invitation of the Creek residents, supported by their protection and cooperation. By 1791, Bartram's book required a fourth access, literary access, to integrate his colonial nature studies with the agenda of the early Republic. Literary access used the vocabulary of natural history and the arts, and Bartram's language mediated his scientific interests with the esthetics of liberty. In the interior of East Florida, exuberant spatterdocks lifted their caps of liberty in example to passers-by, and spring runs and spring-fed sinkholes provided transparent pools for reflection. The beauty of the Great Alachua Savanna substantiated the Declaration of Independence, the self-evident in nature, and the Flower Hunter responded as a scientific observer happy in nature's bounty.

The asymmetries of colonial natural history and the skin trade, however, were disastrous for Bartram's Creek hosts. After his travels, these asymmetries also compromised Bartram's formal contributions as a scientist, despite his positive influence upon other naturalists, artists, and writers. Today's media shrinks might view the *Travels* as the product of a mid-life crisis. It is a large and complex book in which a prodigal son paid tribute to his father's scientific achievements and a Creek mico empowered a Flower Child. The Florida experience was essential to Bartram's book, reputation, and personal growth. For more than two centuries, Bartram's idiom of science and sentiment has promoted responsible nature study, travel, and stewardship in Florida.

Notes

1. The inexpensive and widely available edition cited as *Travels* in this paper is Mark van Doren, ed., *Travels of William Bartram* (1928; New York: Dover Publications, 1955); see an insightful review by N. Bryllion Fagin, "Bartram's *Travels*," *Modern Language Notes* 46 (May 1931): 288–89. Francis Harper, ed., *The Travels of William Bartram: The Naturalist's Edition* (New Haven: Yale University Press, 1958), now available in paperback, provides invaluable annotations.

2. See Charlotte M. Porter, "Mark Catesby's Audience and Patrons," in Mark Catesby, *Opening the Door to a New World* (Boca Raton: Florida Atlantic University, 2001), exhibition catalog.

3. *Travels*, 73, 102.

4. Ibid., 182–83; see also Robin F. A. Fabel, "British Rule in the Floridas," in *The New History of Florida*, ed. Michael Gannon (Gainesville: University Press of Florida, 1996), 142.

5. Personal communication with Howard Adams, District 3 park ranger, Paynes Prairie Preserve State Park, in an effort assisted by the Florida Federation of Garden Clubs, notably Helen G. Cruickshank, ed., *William Bartram in Florida, 1774* (n.p.: Florida Federation of Garden Clubs, 1986), 87–113, and the Bartram Trail Conference; see their *Bartram Heritage* (Montgomery: Bartram Trail Conference, 1979). Trail enthusiasts can consult Charles D. Spornick, Alan R. Cattier, and Robert J. Greene, *An Outdoor Guide to Bartram's Travels* (Athens: University of Georgia Press, 2003), 125–76; and Brad Sanders, *Guide to William Bartram's Travels* (Athens, Ga.: Fevertree Press, 2002), 96–134.

6. Joseph Kastner, *A Species of Eternity* (New York: Alfred A. Knopf, 1977), 79–81; Clark A. Elliott, *Biographical Dictionary of American Science: The Seventeenth through the Nineteenth Centuries* (Westport, Conn.: Greenwood Press, 1979), 26.

7. Concern for William fills letters of 1756–68 in Edmund Berkeley and Dorothy Smith Berkeley, eds., *The Correspondence of John Bartram, 1734 to 1777* (Gainesville: University Press of Florida, 1992), 393, 394, 404, 418, 655, 665–66, 667, 680, 683, 685, 697, 704.

8. Ernest Earnest, *John and William Bartram, Botanists and Explorers* (Philadel-

phia: University of Pennsylvania Press, 1940), 87, 89–90; J. Edwin Hendricks, *Charles Thomson and the Making of a New Nation, 1729–1824* (Canbury, N.J.: Associated University Presses, 1979), 7–8.

9. John Bartram and Franklin founded the Philosophical Society in 1743; see Edmund Berkeley and Dorothy Smith Berkeley, *The Life and Travels of John Bartram: From Lake Ontario to the River St. John* (Gainesville: University Presses of Florida, 1982), 113–14.

10. See Henry Laurens to John Bartram, August 9, 1776, *Correspondence*, 670–73.

11. Thomas P. Slaughter, *The Natures of John and William Bartram* (New York: Vintage Books, 1997), 107–31.

12. Kastner, *Species of Eternity*, 85.

13. For William's side of the story and trip summary, see his letter to John Bartram, March 27, 1775, *Correspondence*, 768–70.

14. *Travels*, 69.

15. Charles Lowe Mowat, *East Florida as a British Province: 1763–1784*, ed. Rembert W. Patrick (1943; facsimile edition, Gainesville: University of Florida Press, 1964), 53–62.

16. For an introduction to a large literature, see Jerald T. Milanich, *Florida Indians and the Invasion from Europe* (Gainesville: University Press of Florida, 1995), 222–31. For the market value and economic impact of the West Indian slave trade, see Eric Williams, *From Columbus to Castro: The History of the Caribbean, 1492–1969* (New York: Harper and Row, 1970), 150–51.

17. See note in *Correspondence*, 663; and Mowat, *East Florida*, 21.

18. For a detailed discussion, see Edward J. Cashin, *William Bartram and the American Revolution on the Southern Frontier* (Columbia: University of South Carolina Press, 2000), 7–67.

19. Charles A. Miller discusses Jefferson's confusing use of the word "nature" in *Jefferson and Nature: An Interpretation* (Baltimore: John Hopkins University Press, 1988), 91–94. Bartram used the term "self evident" to construct an argument in a document about human dignity; see note 51.

20. For an overview, see John Dixon Hunt, *Garden and Grove: The Italian Renaissance Garden in the English Imagination: 1600–1750* (Princeton, N.J.: Princeton University Press, 1986), 42–58.

21. Quoted and discussed in David Crown, *The English Garden: Meditation and Memorial* (Princeton, N.J.: Princeton University Press, 1994), 63.

22. Examples of Bartram's uses of these landscape terms are in *Travels*, 42, 178, 186,196, 202, 203.

23. Ibid., 406–8.

24. Ibid., 27.

25. For French ideas, see Charlotte M. Porter, *The Eagle's Nest: Natural History and American Ideas, 1812–1842* (Tuscaloosa: University of Alabama Press, 1986), 9, 15–16, 17, 49–50; for John Bartram's views, see his letters of July 6, 1761, and September 30, 1763, in *Correspondence*, 525, 609.

26. *Travels*, 387.

27. Carl and Jessica Bridenbaugh emphasize the custom of the Grand Tour after 1748; see *Rebels and Gentlemen in Philadelphia in the Age of Franklin* (New York: Oxford University Press, 1962), 194–216. For discussion of the picturesque, see Mavis Batey, "The High Phase of English Landscape Gardening," in *British and American Gardens in the Eighteenth Century*, ed. Robert P. Maccubbin and Peter Martin (Williamsburg: Colonial Williamsburg Foundation, 1984), 45.

28. Personal communication with Jason Jackson, assistant curator of ethnology, Sam Noble Oklahoma Museum of Natural History; this list, a work in progress, needs more input from native Creek speakers.

29. *Travels*, 163.

30. Ibid., 166.

31. Ibid.

32. Ibid., 164.

33. Ibid., 165–70.

34. John K. Mahon and Brent R. Weisman, "Florida's Seminole and Miccosukee Peoples," in *New History*, ed. Michael Gannon, 188–89; Gregory A. Waselkov and Kathryn E. Holland Braund, eds., *William Bartram on the Southeastern Indians* (Lincoln: University of Nebraska Press, 1995), 50–51, 234, 243.

35. *Travels*, 178.

36. Ibid., 211

37. For an excellent explanation, see Sam B. Upchurch and Anthony F. Randazzo, "Environmental Geology of Florida," in *The Geology of Florida*, ed. Antholy F. Randazzo and Douglas S. Jones (Gainesville: University of Press of Florida, 1997), 221–31.

38. *Travels*, 156.

39. Ibid., 177.

40. Ibid., 151, 196.

41. Ibid., 151.

42. See *Travels*, 72, 77, 258, 328–29, 340.

43. Ibid., 97, 213.

44. See letter of John Bartram, August 26, 1766, *Correspondence*, 676, and *Travels*, 75.

45. *Travels*, 214.

46. Ibid., 218.

47. Ibid., 220.

48. Ibid., 222.

49. See sentiments scribbled on the back of a letter from Benjamin Smith Barton dated September 14, 1795 in the Bartram Papers, Historical Society of Pennsylvania, Philadelphia.

50. See undated manuscript on human dignity, in my view a suppressed 1789–90 draft for introduction to the *Travels*, in the Bartram Papers.

51. See Charlotte M. Porter, "The Drawings of William Bartram (1739–1823), American Naturalist," *Archives of Natural History* 16 (1989): 294–95, and James Rosen, "William Bartram's Sketches: The Field and the Image," *Tipularia* 7 (1992): 8–11, 59.

52. *Travels*, 15, 21.

53. See reproductions of Bartram's ink drawings in the Fothergill album at the British Museum (Natural History), London, in Joseph Ewan, ed., *William Bartram: Botanical and Zoological Drawings, 1756–1788* (Philadelphia: American Philosophical Society, 1968), plates 4–36; the entire album was reproduced digitally in 2003 by Alecto Historical Editions, London.

54. *Travels*, 23.

55. See Porter, "Drawings," 293–94.

56. Hobart M. Smith and Edmund D. Brodie Jr., *Reptiles of North America: A Guide to Field Identification* (New York: Golden Press, 1982), 42.

57. For example, see letter dated 1755, *Correspondence*, 391–92.

58. *Travels*, 101–2, 104. See John Howard Payne's copy of Bartram sketch of Mount Royal in Waselkov and Braund, eds., *William Bartram on the Southeastern Indians*, 179; see also Milanich, *Florida Indians*, 21, 83, 89, 179.

59. Charlotte M. Porter, "Philadelphia Story: Florida Gives William Bartram a Second Chance," *Florida Historical Quarterly* 51 (January 1993): 319.

60. Berkeley and Berkeley, *Life and Travels*, 291.

61. D. Roger Mower Jr., "Bartram's Garden in Philadelphia," *Antiques* (March 1984), 634. See also Slaughter, *Natures*, 224–57.

62. Brooke Hindle, *The Pursuit of Science in Revolutionary America* (New York: W. W. Norton, 1974), 302–11.

63. *Travels*, 184.

64. See garden catalogs with price lists in the Bartram Papers.

65. Fothergill to John Bartram, May 1, 1769, in *Chain of Friendship: John Fothergill of London, 1735–1780*, ed. Betsy C. Corner and Christopher C. Booth (Cambridge: Harvard University Press, 1971), 303.

66. Francis Harper, "Proposals for Publishing Bartram's Travels," *Yearbook for 1945* (Philadelphia: American Philosophical Society, 1946), 78; Benjamin Smith Barton to William Bartram, August 26, 1787, and February 19, 1788, Bartram Papers.

67. Letter of March 4, 1803, in Clark Hunter, *The Life and Letters of Alexander Wilson* (Philadelphia: American Philosophical Society, 1983), 202.

68. See Alexander Wilson's nine-volume *American Ornithology, or the Natural History of the Birds of the United States* (Philadelphia: Bradford and Inskeep, 1808–14), the last volume published posthumously.

69. See Alexander B. Grosart, ed., *The Poems and Literary Prose of Alexander Wilson*, 2 vols. (Paisley, Scotland: Alexander Gardner, 1876), which includes his life and letters.

70. Alexander Wilson, "The Foresters, Description of a Pedestrian Tour to the Fall of Niagara in the Autumn of 1804," *Port-Folio* 2, July 1809, 70–77, and "A Pilgrim," *Port-Folio* 3, June 1810, 499–511.

71. Many of these specimens, which the author exhibited for the Bicentenary, still exist in excellent condition at the Museum of Comparative Zoology, Harvard University.

72. Charles Coleman Sellers, *Mr. Peale's Museum: Charles Willson Peale and the First Popular Museum of Natural Science and Art* (New York: W. W. Norton, 1980), 172–87. For Bartram's mention of music, see *Travels*, 141, 206–7.

73. Jeannette E. Graustein, *Thomas Nuttall, Naturalist: Explorations in America, 1808–1841* (Cambridge: Harvard University Press, 1967), 98–113.

74. Porter, *Eagle's Nest,* 91–93.

75. See, for example the "New and Accurate Map of East and West Florida" (1763), reproduced in *New History,* ed. Michael Gannon, 135.

76. *Travels,* 71.

77. Ibid., 141, 206.

78. Ibid., 186. Page 201 describes the preparation of conté.

79. J. C. Maxwell, "Shakespeare: The Middle Play," in *The Age of Shakespeare,* ed. Boris Ford (Baltimore: Penguin Books, 1955), 203.

80. For an interesting introduction, see Charles Rosen and Henri Zerner, *Romanticism and Realism: The Mythology of Nineteenth-Century Art* (New York: W. W. Norton, 1984), 9–48; L. Hugh Moore, "The Aesthetic Theory of William Bartram," *Essays in Arts and Sciences* 12, no. 1 (March 1983): 17–35; and Berra Grattan Lee, "William Bartram: Naturalist or 'Poet'?" *Early American Literature* 7 (fall 1972): 24–29.

81. See Fagin's note, "Bartram's Travels," 288.

82. Discussed at length in N. Bryllion Fagin, *William Bartram: Interpreter of the American Landscape* (Baltimore: John Hopkins University Press, 1933), 128–49.

83. Harper, *Naturalist's Edition,* 363.

84. I. A. Richards, ed., *The Portable Coleridge* (New York: Viking Press, 1971), 157.

85. François-René de Chateaubriand, *Atala* (1802; Paris: Les Editions Bordas, 1968), 72; see also Irving Putter, trans., *Atala/René* (Berkeley and Los Angeles: University of California Press, 1967), 18.

86. *Travels,* 107.

87. Ibid., 234.

88. Ibid., 235.

89. See works by Denison Limner (possibly Joseph Steward), Joshua Johnson (a black freedman who may have learned his craft with a Peale family member), and Susan C. Waters (an itinerant Quaker painter, although married, who retired to painting animals and still lifes), in the Edgar William and Bernice Chrysler Garbisch Collection, National Museum of Art, Washington, D.C.

90. Peale showed women participating in museum activities in two of his greatest oil paintings: *Exhumation of the Mastodon,* 1806–8, Peale Museum, Baltimore City Life Museums; and *The Artist in his Museum,* 1822, Philadelphia Academy of Fine Arts. Frances Wright was outspoken in her reaction; see David R. Brigham, *Public Culture in the Early Republic: Peale's Museum and Its Audiences* (Washington, D.C.: Smithsonian Institution Press, 1995), 53.

91. See Thomas Nuttall, *A Popular Handbook of the Ornithology of Eastern North America,* ed. Montague Chamberlain, 2d rev. ed. (Boston: Little, Brown, 1896), 1:xxxvi–vli.

92. George Catlin, *Beautiful Savannah in the Piney Woods of Florida,* oil on canvas, National Museum of American Art, Smithsonian Institution, Washington D.C., discussed by Dorothy White, *Florida Painters* (St. Petersburg: St. Petersburg Historical Society, 1984), unpaginated exhibition catalog.

93. Charles W. Tebeau, *A History of Florida* (Coral Gables: University of Miami Press, 1971), 133.

94. Quoted by Kathryn Proby, *Audubon in Florida* (Coral Gables: University of Miami Press, 1974), 31.

95. Peale also made a published engraving of this portrait, now part of the Independence National Historical Park Collection, Philadelphia.

96. Harriet Beecher Stowe, *Palmetto-Leaves,* ed. Mary B. Graff and Edith Cowles (1873; facsimile edition, Gainesville: University of Florida Press, 1968), 129.

97. Note photographs by Annie Griffiths Belt for Glen Oeland, "A Naturalist's Vision of Frontier America: William Bartram," *National Geographic* 199, no. 3 (March 2001): 112, 114–15.

98. *Travels,* 289.

99. Gerald P. Tyson, *Joseph Johnson: A Liberal Publisher* (Iowa City: University of Iowa Press, 1979), 120–23, makes no mention of Bartram, however, even though, as Fagin has noted, Johnson made minor changes throughout Bartram's book.

100. Erasmus Darwin, *Loves of the Plants, a Poem with Philosophical Notes,* is part 2 of *The Botanic Garden* (London: J. Johnson, 1792).

101. A handy full-color introduction to a voluminous and esoteric literature is William Blake, *America: A Prophecy* and *Europe: A Prophecy* (Mineola, N.Y.: Dover, 1983).

102. Blake, *America,* text to plate 15, also 21, 44.

103. Ibid.

104. Blake, *Europe,* 23–41, 45–47.

105. See also Pamela Regis, *Describing Early America: Bartram, Jefferson, Crevecoeur and the Influence of Natural History* (Philadelphia: University of Pennsylvania Press, 1992), 40–78.

Chapter 3

A Naturalist's Place

Archie Carr and the Nature of Florida

Frederick R. Davis

Over the course of a career that lasted five decades, Archie Fairly Carr Jr. (1909–87) became one of Florida's most distinguished naturalists and conservation biologists. While many of Carr's achievements in science and conservation actually took place outside the United States in Central America, his first passion remained the landscapes and wildlife of Florida. Throughout his writing for scientific and popular audiences, Carr incorporated a strong appreciation of place. Most of his early publications dealt with the fish and reptiles of Florida. When he later visited and lived in other countries, including Honduras, Costa Rica, and Nyasaland (now Malawi), the ecosystems of

Florida provided his basis of comparison. Carr's research on sea turtles (for which he is best known) began in Florida. Later in life, he became a vocal advocate for the protection of Florida's wild lands and wildlife, and he incorporated the history of Florida to bolster his arguments.

Archie Fairly Carr Jr. was born in Mobile, Alabama, on June 16, 1909, to Archibald Fairly Carr Sr. and Louise Deaderick Carr.[1] Carr's father was a Presbyterian preacher who enjoyed hunting in his spare time. Louise Carr had planned to be a concert pianist until an injury forced her to change course and become a piano teacher. After a few years in Mobile, the Carr family moved to Fort Worth, Texas, where Archie's brother, Thomas Carr, was born in 1917. In Fort Worth, the young Archie kept a menagerie of resident animals: horned toads, turtles, snakes, frogs, and an armadillo. In 1920, the Carr family moved to Savannah, Georgia, where Carr's father became the preacher at the First Presbyterian Church of Savannah. With each of their moves, Archibald senior, known to his family as "Parson," found a church in which to preach as well as places to hunt and fish. Each summer he took his two sons on an extended fishing trip. Unfortunately, one summer (ca. 1927), young Archie contracted osteomyelitis in his left arm and became extremely ill. After seven operations over the next two years, Carr's elbow joint had to be immobilized. Unable to extend his left arm, Archie always had a characteristic stance. It was also in Savannah that Archie's love of languages began to emerge as he learned to speak Gullah from stevedores who had learned the language from former slaves. Later in life, he would recall interpreting for Gullahs and 'Geechees on the Savannah docks.[2]

In addition to fishing, Archie and his brother also hunted ducks, quail, and turkeys with their father. It was probably through hunting that Archie developed his deep appreciation of natural history. After high school, Archie started at Davidson College in North Carolina (an aunt lived nearby). He fed his interest in languages by learning Spanish from his Cuban roommate. In 1930, his parents and brother moved to Umatilla, Florida (located between Ocala and Orlando). Archie transferred to Rollins College while he waited to be admitted to the University of Florida. Although he spent only one month at Rollins, he was fortunate to encounter an English professor who recognized Archie had a talent for writing and encouraged him to develop it. After that, Archie was accepted at the University of Florida, where he received three degrees and spent most of his career.

Archie Carr pursued his interest in writing at Florida and received his B.A. in English (1932), and his first degree played a critical role in his development as a writer. He immediately went on for an M.S. in zoology (1934). While the Department of Zoology was still developing, it attracted several professors from the University of Michigan to build the program. Two of the original faculty members—J. Speed Rogers and Theodore Hubbell—were entomologists, but they encouraged their graduate students to examine the natural history of a taxa (biological group) in Florida. Thus, Carr focused on reptiles and amphibians, while other graduate students received their degrees by studying the spiders of Florida and the mayflies of Florida. Hubbell and Rogers also professed an approach to the study of biology that incorporated a broader societal concern, a view that appeared prominently in the text they wrote for biology classes: *Man and the Biological World*.[3] Carr was the first person to receive a doctorate in zoology at the University of Florida (1937). For his dissertation, he wrote "A Contribution to the Herpetology of Florida," which was later published as a book in the Biological Sciences series of the University of Florida.[4]

In 1934, while he was still a master's student, Archie Carr published his first paper, "A Key to the Breeding-Songs of the Florida Frogs," in the second issue of a relatively new journal called the *Florida Naturalist*. The simplicity of his directions and the twenty-four steps that followed belied the considerable effort behind producing such a key. In the first place, Carr did not have recording material at his disposal to compare frogs' breeding calls. Most frogs (even males lost in the throes of breeding season) cease and desist their calls upon the approach of large mammals like humans. To make matters even more difficult, frogs have a tendency to give their calls from the safety of extremely wet areas. In creating his key, Carr had to isolate a given call, track it to a specific frog without disturbing the caller, and identify it to species. Carr warned of particular difficulties with tree frogs (genus: *Hyla*): "Be certain that you have limited your attention to the call of one frog and are not listening to the sounds made by several. It is sometimes difficult to isolate an individual call, especially in large choruses of *Hylas*."[5]

Carr sent his "Key to the Breeding-Songs of the Florida Frogs" to several of the established herpetologists in the United States: Thomas Barbour (Museum of Comparative Zoology, Harvard University), Leonhard Stejneger (U.S. Museum), Helen Gaige (Museum of Zoology, University of Michigan), Edward H. Taylor (University of Kansas), Albert Hazen Wright (Cornell University), and M. Graham Netting (Carnegie Museum, Pittsburgh). One of the most enthusiastic responses to the "Frog Key" came from Thomas Barbour: "Thank you ever so much for the copy of 'The Florida Naturalist' containing your article, 'A Key to the Breeding-Songs of the Florida Frogs.' This is very interesting and I am glad to have it."[6] Barbour (1884–1946) served as director of the Museum of Comparative Zoology at Harvard University (MCZ) from 1927 until his death in 1946.[7] Like Archie Carr, he became interested in reptiles and the natural history of Florida at an early age—in Barbour's case, while recovering from typhoid fever in Florida in 1898. All his degrees came from Harvard University (A.B. 1906, A.M. 1908, and Ph.D. 1911), where he remained for his entire career. Barbour's father was a wealthy businessman who left him a large inheritance that funded his pursuits as a naturalist and herpetologist, which included contributing to the development of Barro Colorado Island in Panama as a research station (now part of the Smithsonian Tropical Research Institute). He also used his own funds to support promising herpetologists like Carr and the herpetological journal *Copeia*. In the final years of his life, Barbour wrote several lengthy travel narratives on his experiences as a naturalist, including *That Vanishing Eden*, which was devoted to environmental decline in Florida.[8] Few people had greater influence on Archie Carr than did Thomas Barbour.

Carr's correspondence with other herpetologists reveals insights into the practice of natural history during the first half of the twentieth century. Many universities in the United States were in the process of expanding their research collections. Some of the herpetologists recognized in Carr the opportunity to obtain specimens (the stuff of material practice in natural history) from northern Florida, which was generally poorly represented in collections.[9] M. Graham Netting, curator of herpetology at the Carnegie Museum in Pittsburgh, expressed his gratitude for the "Frog Key" and asked to subscribe to the new journal. Later, Netting requested that Carr collect specimens for the Carnegie Museum. Apparently, Carr viewed this as an opportunity and almost immediately sent several examples. Further correspondence is filled with references to species sent and received and collecting trips in Florida. Other prominent herpetologists such as Albert Hazen Wright of Cornell University fondly recalled collecting trips with Archie Carr: "Mrs. Wright and I will never forget the collecting trip we took with you boys, and the kindly favors which you extended to us."[10] In many respects, Florida represented a biological terra incognita and was an ideal location for biological exploration. The problems that Carr discussed with his network of herpetologists related to the continuation of the naturalist tradition of the nineteenth century, while the concerns of his mentors at the University of Florida introduced him to the still relatively new study of ecology.[11]

Archie Carr's early publications all share three features: a subject in herpetology or ichthyology, a local orientation, and lively writing. Frogs, snakes, fish, and of course turtles served as subjects for Carr's early papers. Given the scientific community's limited knowledge of Florida herpetology and the location of the University of Florida in north central Florida, it made sense that he covered local species (thus adding a geographical component to the practice of natural history). But what makes Archie Carr's early publications unique is their engaging style. One hardly expects interesting reading from a paper entitled "The Gulf-Island Cottonmouths" in the journal *Proceedings of the Florida Academy of Sciences,* but after relaying folk tales about large aggregations of snakes on Gulf islands, Carr provided an entertaining account of his expedition to check the veracity of this claim. Having found and collected one cottonmouth, Carr saved a companion by impaling him with his collecting tool: "To my alarm I perceived a broad, black head, belonging to a body hidden under the leaves directly in Bellamy's path, where he could not fail to step on it. Since his feet were clad only in low quarter tennis shoes, and since the two steps that would place him squarely over the snake were being executed with energy, I made recourse to the only means of stopping him that I could conceive at the instant—I jabbed him viciously with the gig, adorned though it was with the still-living cottonmouth."[12] In reading a description like this, one could forget that Carr was writing in a scientific journal. The levity of this particular description failed to mask Carr's sincerity as a scientist. Musing on reasons why with little effort he had collected thirteen cottonmouths on a small island, Carr noted the prevalence of chicks and eggs in a rookery and their potential as food for snakes (seven of which had empty stomachs). Moreover, Carr defended his interest in the claims of local nonscientists in determining the species of snakes on the island: "In defense I can only remind you of the attitude of slightly pained, though conciliatory, unresponsiveness with which the professional zoologist always receives the reports of the amateur. He expects to learn nothing of importance and, consequently, rarely does."[13] This willingness to endure and explore the stories of locals would serve Archie Carr's story telling and scientific research throughout his life.

After receiving his doctorate in 1937, Carr became a member of the faculty in the Department of Zoology, and he married another young naturalist, Marjorie Harris. Marjorie had received her B.S. in biology at Florida State College for Women (now Florida State University). She worked as a wildlife technician for the U.S. Fish and Wildlife Service right out of college (the first woman to hold this position in the United States). By all accounts, it was love at first sight when Marjorie took a box of sick quail to Flint Hall at the University of Florida, where Carr's office was located. Archie and Marjorie were married in January 1937, within a few months of meeting, but they kept their marriage secret until Carr completed his doctoral dissertation in May 1937.

As Archie Carr was completing his doctorate, he wrote to Thomas Barbour about the possibility of visiting the collection at the Museum of Comparative Zoology in Cambridge, Massachusetts. Barbour responded enthusiastically. In a later letter about a technical problem, he again extended his invitation: "If I can give you any more information let me know and also let me know whether you would like to come up here for a month this summer and look at turtles here?"[14] The independently wealthy Barbour devoted some of his resources to facilitating the work of promising herpetologists, and from this point on, Archie Carr was a chief beneficiary of Barbour's intellectual and financial patronage. Although the actual dollar value of Barbour's financial support was fairly minimal, it was the marginal amount that made it possible for the Carrs to spend seven summers (1937–43) at Harvard. During this time, Archie Carr matured as a herpetologist, naturalist, and writer. In addition to travel plans, herpetological notes, and gossip, the correspondence between the Carrs and Barbour, or "TB," as he was affectionately called, is filled with references to gifts of books on Floridiana, paintings, maps, specimens, and even Florida oranges and limes. So profound was Barbour's affection for the Carrs that in his autobiographical narrative, *Naturalist at Large,* he acknowledged: "Others who have contributed greatly to my happiness on numberless occasions have been Margaret Porter Bigelow, to whom, with Archie and Margie Carr of the University of Florida, I presume to feel in *loco parentis.*"[15] Carr's early research suggests significant intellectual indebtedness to Barbour.

In the course of work on his doctoral dissertation, Carr observed that two species of turtles in the genus *Pseudemys* intergraded (that is, they shared taxonomic characteristics) in north Florida (recall the early correspondence between Carr and Stejneger). It was this genus that provided Carr's first major intellectual challenge, and he published several papers on its taxonomy. In his taxonomic work, Carr fell in between the two categories of taxonomists. Most taxonomists function as either "lumpers" or "splitters." Lumpers tend to "lump" separate races under a single species, whereas splitters "split" distinct races into species. In his revision of the *Pseudemys* genus, Carr functioned in both roles. In his first paper on the subject (1935), Carr lumped

Pseudemys floridana and *P. concinna* into the single species *P. floridana* with two subspecies.[16] His second paper (1937) split *P. floridana suwanniensis* (a new subspecies) from *P. mobiliensis*.[17] Carr returned to lumping in his next paper (1937) by combining *P. scripta* and *P. troostii*, but he declined to suggest a change in nomenclature.[18] As Barbour noted, this is the sort of work that some scientists dismissed as pedantry, but among naturalists and herpetologists like Leonhard Stejneger, taxonomy was a serious matter.

With the completion of his dissertation and later work at the MCZ, Carr became an acknowledged authority on *Pseudemys* and turtles in general. It was in this capacity that he suggested a change to Thomas Barbour, who was preparing the fifth revision of *A Check List of North American Amphibians and Reptiles* (1943). When he published his dissertation as a book titled *A Contribution to the Herpetology of Florida* (1940), Carr lumped two snapping turtles —*Chelydra serpentina* (Linnaeus) and *Chelydra osceola* (Stejneger)—into a single species (*C. serpentina*) with two subspecies.[19] In reclassifying *C. osceola*, Carr incurred the ire of his old contact Leonhard Stejneger, who had written the original description of the species. Taxonomy is an inherently historical practice, and the author of an original description (Stejneger, in this case) achieves a certain distinction in attaching his name to the species as describer. Stung by Stejneger's vehemence but convinced of his clear understanding of the problem, Carr responded at length to Barbour. In a six-page letter, Carr answered each of Stejneger's criticisms meticulously. Carr aligned himself with the work of naturalists while recognizing a transition to statistical and genetic approaches within university biology departments. That he directed his response to Barbour, and not to Stejneger, indicates the strong aversion to confrontation that Carr maintained throughout his life. Barbour recognized the validity of Carr's argument but diplomatically deferred to his senior collaborator: Stejneger's death on January 31, 1943—reported to Carr by Barbour via telegram—ended the debate. This episode indicates the development of Carr's intellectual commitments and confidence as an independent scientist.

One of the greatest honors that a taxonomist can bestow upon a friend or colleague is to name a species in his honor. In a tribute to his mentor, Thomas Barbour, Archie Carr named a newly discovered turtle species for him: *Graptemys barbouri*, which Carr and Lewis J. Marchand found in the Chipola River near Marianna, Florida. In the paper that described the turtle, the authors suggested that the species had escaped previous detection by descending to the bottom of deep, fast-flowing, rock-bottomed rivers. To circumvent the turtle's guile, Carr and Marchand had utilized water goggles. In the conclusion of the paper, they paid tribute to Barbour: "It seems altogether proper and pleasant to associate with this new species the name of Doctor Thomas Barbour, who has contributed extensively to our knowledge of Florida reptiles and amphibians."[20]

About the same time that Carr was honoring Barbour, he created a witty parody of a taxonomist's raison d'être: the taxonomic key. While he was still in graduate school, Carr had published two taxonomic keys; one described the breeding calls of frogs and the other facilitated the identification of the fishes of Alachua County (Gainesville lies in Alachua County). Like all keys, these publications were tools for biologists and naturalists attempting to sort out the identifications and relationships of resident species. Having used a key to identify local species, a biologist could focus on aspects of behavior and interrelations among the animals, that is, life histories. Of course, Archie Carr knew the form well, and he was able to construct a parody of his key to fishes for the annual meeting of the American Society of Ichthyologists and Herpetologists on April 3, 1941. From the title of the mythical journal of publication *Dopeia* (after *Copeia*) to the least significant footnote, the parody is filled with inside jokes and mockeries of the practice of natural history. In the "Forward!" (*sic*), Carr deflated the pretensions of taxonomic keys: "The zoological key of today is perhaps the most unstimulating and oppressive of all literary forms. Stripped of all the more succulent verbiage, its style desiccated and uninspired, and its technical arrangement often so cryptic as to render it well-nigh incomprehensible, the key may not, in any sense, be called good reading."[21] As Carr's key progresses, it becomes increasingly complicated, with long series of reference letters, gratuitous quotations in foreign languages, cross-references, unintelligible contractions, and bad advice, such as the following: "To aid in separating the forms to follow it is almost mandatory that the reader carefully jab either of the side spines of the specimen into the fleshy part of his thumb, recording his sensations in detail."[22] Most ichthyologists would be able to relate to the experience recalled by such "advice." The key also called on the user's common sense in several references to the identification of the catfish: "Any damn fool knows a catfish."[23] Like the debate with Stejneger, the key suggests Carr's growing confidence in his expertise. In addition, Carr became renowned for his wit among ichthyologists and herpetologists. But having a sense of humor did not obscure Carr's abilities as a scientist, and Albert Hazen Wright of Cornell soon invited him to write a handbook on the turtles of North America. When it was published in 1952,

The *Handbook of Turtles* received the Daniel Eliot Giraud Medal of the National Academy of Sciences.

During his seven summers at the MCZ, Carr published his first paper on sea turtles (with the exception of references in his dissertation and *Contributions to Florida Herpetology*). "Notes on Sea Turtles" included, like many of his early publications, a taxonomic key that made it possible to distinguish the species of sea turtles (due to the infrequency of encounters, even herpetologists confused the species). Carr also raised the point that the common name of the so-called bastard turtle should be switched from the bastard turtle to the ridley turtle as fisherman and turtle hunters along the Gulf coast commonly referred to it. Like Carr's investigation of water moccasins on Seahorse Key, this paper reflected his respect for local, anecdotal, nonscientific evidence and moreover his belief that scientists should defer to or at least recognize that knowledge: "Thus, although the term 'bastard turtle' is admittedly a venerable one . . . I nevertheless propose that it be relegated to synonymy. It is my conviction that in such cases priority should bow to prevalence, that a common name which is not common is a mockery; and henceforth I shall use ridley."[24] That is, in developing common names for species, scientists should recognize vernacular usage and local knowledge. During his life in science, Archie Carr returned repeatedly to the anecdotal claims of locals for both evidence and working hypotheses. Thus, this paper reveals Archie Carr's commitment to the wisdom of nonscientists and his interest in sea turtles, which would become the focus of his life's work.

For a naturalist like Archie Carr, place mattered. In his early development, Carr's studies were local: his backyard and the southern pine and mixed hardwood forests he came to know on hunting trips with his father. College and graduate school (and an automobile) meant greater independent mobility and extended trips throughout Florida. Finishing school and obtaining a full-time job meant still greater mobility: summers in Cambridge with his mentor, Thomas Barbour, and trips to Mexico, the Caribbean, and Honduras, where Carr would spend more than four years with his young family exploring the tropical highlands and lowlands. Based on these explorations, he wrote the book *High Jungles and Low* (1953). Further wanderings gave Carr critical data on the status of sea turtles in the Caribbean and Costa Rica. Such travels convinced Carr that the breeding grounds of sea turtles had been severely reduced and that Tortuguero in Costa Rica sustained the largest colony of green sea turtles in the Caribbean. Carr's extensive Caribbean wanderings and numerous encounters in search of nesting sea turtles became the subject of his second popular work, *The Windward Road* (1956). In 1952, Lewis Berner, one of Carr's colleagues, received an invitation to conduct entomological surveys in Nyasaland (now Malawi), Africa, for an English engineering firm, Sir William Halcrow and Partners, which was conducting feasibility studies for various major engineering projects in the English colonies around the world. Berner in turn asked Archie Carr to join him, and the two spent several months traveling around Africa. This experience (and three additional trips to survey sea turtles) inspired Carr to write *Ulendo* (1964), his third popular travel narrative. While each of these books has as its subject a place distant from Florida, Carr regularly draws comparisons with his beloved Florida.

During his early career, Carr's research was largely confined to Florida and the Caribbean, but two factors motivated his desire to extend his explorations to other lands. First and foremost, it had become very clear to Carr that sea turtles had a nearly global range and that a biologist could study these species only by following them to the distant oceans and beaches of the world. Carr's other reason had less to do with his particular expertise than with the passions of any naturalist. To explore life, to compare life-forms, to understand the relationship between life and geography, which is to say biology and place, naturalists travel.

While he was researching and writing the *Handbook of Turtles* (1952), it occurred to Carr that he needed field experience with the species of sea turtles that did not occur in Florida.[25] So he wrote to Thomas Barbour for advice on where he might obtain grants that would support several weeks of research at the Pacific coast turtle fisheries. Barbour responded with typical aplomb pledging MCZ funds in the amount of $100 for a collecting trip to Key West and $500 for an expedition to the west coast of Central America. In a postscript, Barbour noted that Costa Rica might be the best site for research and suggested a contact: "Wilson Popenoe can easily put you up at the Agriculture School in Honduras, and you can discuss with him there (as he is very familiar with the situation) where will be the best point on the Pacific Coast to find a turtle fishery established and then to proceed accordingly. He knows all the local ropes! Let me know if you want any detailed introductions and so forth."[26] As a result of Barbour's casual afterthought, Archie Carr and his growing family spent nearly five years on leave from University of Florida teaching at the Escuela Agricola Panamerica.

Between 1944 and 1960, Carr devoted much of his time to the study of sea turtles and tropical ecosystems, but Florida continued to serve as his touchstone of natural history. In *High Jungles and Low,* his first popular travel narrative, Carr confined his observations to the highland and lowland tropical rainforests of Honduras. He did include occasional comparisons to the ecosystems of Florida. For example, a wet savanna reminded him of the Everglades: "a wet savanna set with scattered little islands (we call them hammocks back in Florida) of Caribbean pine and skinny, broad-leaved palms, producing a landscape strongly reminiscent of the Florida Everglades."[27] The realization that a jaguar had been following a companion in Honduras reminded Carr of an analogous situation when, from the vantage of a deer stand, he watched a bobcat trail behind another hunter in the Florida scrub.

By the time Carr published *The Windward Road* in 1956, he had completed extensive surveys of the islands and coastal shores of the Caribbean in search of nesting and feeding grounds of sea turtles with the support of the American Philosophical Society and the National Science Foundation. One of the most efficient (and for Carr most enjoyable) strategies for locating sea turtles was to interview the older sea captains and residents who depended upon turtles for their livelihood and sustenance. Carr's gift for blending observations of nature and culture appears in full form in *The Windward Road,* but the significance he attached to Florida underwent a subtle but significant shift as well. Florida played a central role in Carr's argument for the conservation of sea turtles. Adopting the historian's perspective, Carr castigated the turtle industry for its lack of awareness of the plight of sea turtles. He noted that as much as any other organism, sea turtles fed European exploration and colonization of the Caribbean. Yet those who continued to hunt for sea turtles had no sense of history and assumed that relatively constant populations reflected past concentrations, but Carr as a proto-environmental historian knew better. The turtle fishery of the twentieth century represented a shadow of its former greatness. Carr explained: "One by one the famous old rookeries were destroyed. The first to go was Bermuda and next the shores of the Greater Antilles. The Bahamas were blanked out not long after, and boats from there began to cross the Gulf Stream to abet the decimation in Florida, where the crawl was once more common than the hen coop—where Charles Peake caught 2,500 greens about Sebastian in 1886 and in 1895 could take only 60; where vast herds foraged in the east-coast estuaries and on the Gulf flats of the upper peninsula and a great breeding school came each year to Dry Tortugas."[28]

In this statement, Florida served as a prime example of environmental degradation. While Carr worried about the status of sea turtles around the

Caribbean, the state of turtle rookeries in Florida seemed hopeless, especially when placed in historical perspective. Nevertheless, Carr's eloquence captured the interest and philanthropy of a publisher's representative named Joshua Powers, who launched the Caribbean Conservation Corporation by sending copies of *The Windward Road* to two dozen of his friends. Ultimately, the CCC garnered goodwill for sea turtle research and conservation throughout the United States and Latin America by supporting the research efforts of Archie Carr, who served as its technical director. Carr won two major writing awards for *The Windward Road*. *Mademoiselle* published "The Black Beach," a chapter from the book, as a short story, and it won the O. Henry Prize for short-story writing in 1956. Also, Carr received the John Burroughs Medal of the American Museum of Natural History for nature writing in 1957.

The farther Carr traveled from Florida, the more the landscapes and wildlife reminded him of those back home. Throughout his longest trip to Africa, and the resulting book *Ulendo,* Carr drew comparisons with Florida. But when he returned home, Africa came with him. In a tour de force of nature writing, "The Bird and the Behemoth," Carr recounted spotting an egret near a dragline dredge on his morning commute across Paynes Prairie just south of Gainesville. The image of the machine and the bird produced in Carr's lively mind a moment of gestalt that aligned prehistoric, early, and modern Florida with present-day Africa. Carr called the bird a "buff-back" (though he acknowledged the accepted common name for the species: cattle egret). The presence of the cattle egrets on Paynes Prairie struck a nerve because Carr remembered that when he first arrived in Florida some three decades prior, snowy egrets dominated the wet prairies, and scrawny cattle, descendants of old Spanish livestock, wandered unfenced woods and prairies. Modern ranching subsequently replaced much of that with fenced, cultivated pastures, and purebred cattle. Grasshoppers flourished in the new pastures, Carr noted, and snowy egrets left the marshes to exploit this new resource.

But without stretching the imagination too much, Carr imagined the dredge as a great beast: a mechanized version of the megafauna of Africa and the large animals that roamed Florida during the Pleistocene:

Continuously since Africa became a refuge for the Ice Age megafauna, the buff-back heron has lived as a working part of the savanna community, the companion of elephants, rhinos, zebras, giraffes, wild asses, and a whole world of antelope. For the snowy egret, there have, for a few hundreds or thousands of years, been only frogs and fishes. But for him too, not so very long ago there was ponderous company to keep. Through millions of years Florida was spread with veld or tree savanna much like the Zambezi delta land today. Right there in the middle of Paynes Prairie itself, there used to be creatures that would stand your hair on end. Pachyderms vaster than any now alive grazed the tall brakes or pruned the thin-spread trees. There were llamas and camels of half a dozen kinds, and bison and sloths and glyptodonts, bands of ancestral horses, and grazing tortoises as big as the bulls.[29]

Pleistocene Florida and its spectacular wildlife had disappeared so many millennia past. Remnants of such landscapes were giving way to ranchers and their cattle, while cattle and their herders were gradually destroying the remaining Ice Age refugia left in Africa. Carr's narrative of environmental declension was heading for a disastrous conclusion: "There is a growing emptiness around us, and we fill it with noise, and never know anything is gone. But the buff-back remembers other times, with great game thundering through all the High Masai. And back home you come upon a raging dragline with a wisp of a snowy heron there, dodging the cast and drop of the bucket as if only mammoth tusks were swinging—and what can it be but a sign of lost days and lost hosts that the genes of the bird remember?"[30]

By the 1960s, the center of Carr's sea turtle research had shifted to Tortuguero in Costa Rica, but Carr reported on several preliminary studies he conducted in Florida at Cedar Key in *So Excellent a Fishe,* Carr's only book devoted exclusively to sea turtles. Cedar Key, located about 45 miles from Gainesville, was the site of a turtle fishery. As at other sites, Carr gleaned considerable information from the local fishermen. In fact, it was in Cedar Key that Carr became convinced that sea turtles engaged in impressive feats of homing. Though Carr expressed amazement at the feats, the fishermen took for granted homing ability in sea turtles. Once the turtle-tagging program was running smoothly at Tortuguero, Carr drew comparisons between the results there and those at Cedar Key. The turtles that appeared at Tortuguero were for the most part adults, while those at Cedar Key tended to be younger subadults: "Although there is not a scrap of solid evidence to prove it, logic suggests that the Cedar Key turtles come from Tortuguero. In a roundabout but quite real way, the west coast of peninsular Florida is downstream from Tortuguero."[31]

In 1973, Archie Carr wrote *The Everglades* for Time-Life Books. As it happened, this would be the only book devoted solely to Florida published by

Carr during his lifetime (*A Naturalist in Florida* was published posthumously). Like every book in the Time-Life American Wilderness series, Carr's *The Everglades* is a lavishly illustrated book. For the most part, Carr restricted his descriptions to the state of the Everglades in the 1970s rather than allowing himself to wax nostalgic about what the unique wet prairie had been in times past. Inevitably, environmental degradation became Carr's subject. Rather than focusing on the obvious and direct effects of smog or pollution, Carr emphasized the subtle yet equally pernicious changes brought about by the introduction of exotic species of plants and animals: "There are more ways to pollute a landscape than by loading it with sewage, smog and beer cans. You can load it with exotic plants and animals. Whether brought in intentionally or accidentally, these are likely to change the landscape. The changes they make are rarely good, and often are atrocious."[32] Carr then cited several examples: armadillos, walking catfish, cajeput, Brazilian pepper, and Australian pines, each of which initiated significant changes in the landscapes of Florida.

Development posed less of a problem in the Everglades for a simple reason in Carr's opinion: mosquitoes. He wrote: "Thank the Lord for the mosquitoes. The world owes them a lot for their part in preserving Cape Sable. A heroic statue of a mosquito in bronze ought to be set up on a hurricane-proof pedestal, a huge plinth of Key Largo limestone perhaps, at some commanding point on the cape." The mosquito swarms in the Everglades were as bad as anywhere in the world, and according to Carr much worse at certain times of the year in places like Madeira Bay. Mosquitoes posed a serious deterrent to colonization and development. Nevertheless, mosquitoes failed to halt development of other places such as Marco Island, the largest of the Ten Thousand Islands and the site of a recent (1973) development project that cost half a billion dollars. Ultimately, Carr reduced the crisis of environmental degradation in Florida to a basic choice: "I went away confident that the choice that southern Florida faces is not between water for birds and water for people, as short-sighted boosters were proclaiming a little while ago. The question is, rather, whether both shall survive on a shared water ration in a magic but pitifully fragile land."[33]

During the 1960s and 1970s, Carr devoted considerable time and energy to international conservation efforts, but such activities did not preclude advocacy on behalf of the landscapes and species of Florida. In 1969, Carr fought against the construction of a major road across the University of Florida that would pass near the north shore of Lake Alice (formerly called

Jonah's Pond). In a letter to the president of the university, Stephen C. O'Connell, Carr enclosed excerpts from two of his books, *The Reptiles* and *Ulendo*. In *The Reptiles*, he wrote: "Jonah's Pond is one of the solid assets of the University of Florida. It is a sinkhole lake with tree-swamp at one end and open water at the other, and all through it a grand confusion of marsh creatures and of floating and emergent plants. The place is a little relic of a vanishing past, and incredibly, it lies on the campus of a university with 13,000 students, less than half a mile from where I'm writing now."[34] This passage went on to reveal the destruction of thousands of reptiles killed by speeding cars on highways (like the one planned for the border of Lake Alice). In *Ulendo*, Carr offered a comparable description of Lake Alice as a remnant of old Florida.

Carr acknowledged the practical arguments for the roadway, but he countered such claims with several practical reasons for the preservation of Lake Alice, such as the lake's contribution to the material resources of the university, its value as a teaching resource, its ameliorative effect on faculty and staff, and its status as a Florida showcase for visitors to the university. But the single most practical justification for the preservation of Lake Alice was as a model for students: "Perhaps the most important practical by-product of this exchange of a priceless suburban wildlife preserve for a high-speed road through the campus is the damage it will do to the sense of values of our students. At a time when the dismal signs of hand-to-mouth urbanization are everywhere so clear, it would appear an inescapable responsibility of any university to show, by every possible example, that there are better ways to live."[35] In each of these passages, Carr advocated for the preservation of two remnants of Florida: natural and historical, both of which held inherent value. As a result of Carr's writings and contributions from additional faculty, Lake Alice continues to provide an oasis of natural tranquility on an increasingly developed campus.

Carr also participated in a less direct way in several other major campaigns on behalf of Florida wildlands and not just Gainesville's landscapes. In 1970, E. O. Wilson, the Harvard biologist, solicited Carr's support for a successful Nature Conservancy initiative to purchase and preserve Lignumvitae Key in south Florida. That same year, Carr advocated for the transfer of Paynes Prairie (the site of "The Bird and the Behemoth" in *Ulendo*) into public ownership by writing letters to the Governor's Assistant for Conservation. All these efforts were minor when compared with Marjorie Carr's ongoing campaign to save the Ocklawaha River and to stop the Army Corps of Engineers from completing the Cross-Florida Barge Canal.[36] There is no doubt that Archie Carr contributed to this effort directly by writing letters of support for the campaign and securing the contributions of colleagues at the University of Florida and other universities. Their expert testimony and analysis resulted in one of the first comprehensive environmental impact statements completed of a federally mandated project.[37]

While *The Everglades* was the last book that Carr published during his lifetime (save for second editions), he continued to write about Florida. In the late 1960s, he began to write a book about Florida, but he was mindful of the risks that attended writing about a narrative so fraught with declension: "When I set out to write this book I immediately sensed a danger looming. It was that I was almost bound to fall into the trap of nostalgia and indignation, of turning this book into a diatribe against the passing of original Florida. Because to anyone who has known Florida as long as I have, and whose main interest in the place has been its wild landscapes and wild creatures, the losses have been the most spectacular events of the past three decades."[38] With his extensive knowledge of Floridiana, Carr could cite several prior lamentations: John K. Small's *From Eden to Sahara* and Thomas Barbour's *That Vanishing Eden*.[39] Carr knew the latter work particularly well since he discussed the destruction of Florida's wildlands at length with his old friend and mentor. In reflecting on these works, Carr had an epiphany: "So being a naturalist, living in the woods, and having the peculiar background I have, I am especially susceptible to the disease of bitterness over the ruin of Florida— over the partly aimless, partly avaricious ruin of unequaled natural riches of the most nearly tropical state. But in my case I decided simply, 'What the hell, you cry the blues and soon nobody listens.' And that made me see that there was really no sense writing another vanishing Eden book at all."[40]

So rather than lamenting what had been, Carr celebrated what was left. His essays on Florida appeared in *Audubon* (the magazine for the National Audubon Society) and *Animal Kingdom* (the magazine for the New York Zoological Society). Marjorie Carr collected and published an edited volume of these and other Florida essays under the title *A Naturalist in Florida: A Celebration of Eden*.[41] In these essays, most of which he wrote during his final years, Carr returned to the place he knew best. "All the Way down upon the Suwannee River" skips lightly from past to present to prehistoric and back as Carr cites William Bartram's description of the river and its Indian inhabitants; recounts battles of the War of 1812 and the Civil War; revels in the pleasure of floating down the cool, spring-fed river; exults in the discovery of teeth of mammoths and mastodons; and warns of the perils of overuse for recreation.[42] Carr's narrative of the Suwannee flows smoothly between nature and culture like the best environmental history. Similarly, in telling the tale of Florida jubilees (aquatic animal congregations), Carr weaves together strands of biology, paleogeography, Cracker culture, Bartram's *Travels,* and, inevitably, declension. As promised, Carr kept his sense of regret in check, only occasionally lapsing into despair over the loss of this landscape or that animal. Here he ponders the demise of the Wacahoota jubilees: "And sadly, it may have to stand for quite a while, because the Wacahoota jubilees are finished. As they became more widely known in town people started coming out in greater numbers. Their trespassing annoyed the owner and moved him to modify the landscape in ways that changed the character of the flow in the jubilee stream out of Moore's Prairie. I don't know what he did back there, but since then there has been no Wacahoota jubilee, and apparently there will never be another."[43]

If Carr saw in culture the roots of the destruction and degradation of nature, he ultimately considered culture to hold the seeds of hope for natural Florida as well. In an essay for *Born of the Sun* (the official Florida Bicentennial commemorative book), he took heart from the partial recovery of several species: manatees, alligators, otters, beavers, and wading birds (herons and egrets). All of these animals had been hunted to the brink of extinction in Florida during Carr's lifetime. Offsetting such optimism was the realization that unique ecosystems like the large Florida springs were in a state of decline. Carr attributed such declension to a variety of factors, but chiefly the efforts of subsistence fishermen who used dynamite to catch fish, euphemistically termed "cut-bait fishermen." Cut-bait fishing had left the majority of springs denuded of life with little hope of recovery. And yet, Archie Carr gazed into the hearts of Floridians and found good reasons for hope: "In listing some reasons for optimism over the state of nature and man in Florida, one favorable development outweighs all the rest. It is not another species on the mend or a new park or preserve or sanctuary established. It is rather a change in the hearts of the people. Although original Florida is still undergoing degradation, an assessment of the trends would show the rate of loss being overtaken by growth of a system of ecologic ethics, by a new public consciousness and conscience. . . . The rise of this new stewardship gives heart to opponents of ecologic ruin everywhere and brings promise of better times for man and nature in Florida."[44]

Such a statement reflected a considerable shift in Carr's thoughts on Florida, nature, and history. In several examples noted above, Carr equated historical Florida with natural Florida. This new configuration suggests that the rise of American environmentalism transformed the relationship between nature and culture, causing Carr to ponder the role of human agency in the past, present, and future of natural Florida.[45] A profound sense of place resonates throughout Carr's writings. Just as he constructed lasting images of Florida, that sense of Florida shaped Archie Carr.

Notes

1. Biographical details courtesy of Thomas Carr, interview by author, January 7, 1998.

2. See Archie Fairly Carr, *High Jungles and Low* (Gainesville: University Press of Florida), 193.

3. James Speed Rogers and Theodore Huntington Hubbell, *Man and the Biological World* (Gainesville, Fla.: Kallman Publishing Co., 1940).

4. See Archie Fairly Carr, *A Contribution to the Herpetology of Florida* (Gainesville: University of Florida, 1940).

5. A. F. Carr, "A Key to the Breeding-Songs of the Florida Frogs," *Florida Naturalist* 1, no. 2 (1934): 22.

6. Thomas Barbour, "Letter to Archie Carr (24 January 1934)," in Archie F. Carr Jr. Papers, Department of Special Collections, George A. Smathers Library, University of Florida.

7. Biographical material on Thomas Barbour may be found in his autobiographical travel narrative, Thomas Barbour, *Naturalist at Large* (Boston: Little, Brown and Company, 1943); "Barbour, Thomas (1884–1946)," in *Contributions to the History of Herpetology*, ed. Kraig Adler (Oxford, Ohio: Society for the Study of Amphibians and Reptiles, 1989); Arthur Loveridge, "Thomas Barbour—Herpetologist," *Herpetologica* 3 (1946); and Emmet R. Dunn, "Thomas Barbour 1884–1946," *Copeia* (1946).

8. Thomas Barbour, *That Vanishing Eden: A Naturalist's Florida* (Boston: Little, Brown and Company, 1944).

9. For perspectives on the material culture of natural history, see Nicholas Jardine, James A. Secord, and E. C. Spary, eds., *Cultures of Natural History* (Cambridge: Cambridge University Press, 1996).

10. Albert Hazen Wright to Archie Carr, April 20, 1936, Carr Papers.

11. See Paul Lawrence Farfer, *Finding Order in Nature: The Naturalist Tradition from Linnaeus to E. O. Wilson*, Johns Hopkins Introductory Studies in the History of Science (Baltimore: Johns Hopkins University Press, 2000).

12. A. F. Carr Jr., "The Gulf-Island Cottonmouths," *Proceedings of the Florida Academy of Sciences* 1 (1935): 88.

13. Ibid., 87.

14. Thomas Barbour, "Letter to Archie Carr, Jr. (April 30, 1937)," Carr Papers.

15. Barbour, *Naturalist at Large*, 311.

16. A. F. Carr, "The Identity and Status of Two Turtles of the Genus Pseudemys," *Copeia* 3 (1935): 147–48.

17. A. F. Carr, "A New Turtle from Florida, with Notes on *Pseudemys floridana mobiliensis* (Holbrook)," Occasional Papers for the Museum of Zoology, University of Michigan 348 (1937): 1–7.

18. A. F. Carr, "The Status of *Pseudemys scripta* and Pseudemys troostii," *Herpetologica* 1 (1937): 75–77.

19. Carr, *A Contribution to the Herpetology of Florida*, 99.

20. A. F. Carr and Lewis J. Marchand, "A New Turtle from the Chipola River, Florida," *Proceedings of the New England Zoological Club* 20 (1942): 97.

21. A. F. Carr Jr. "The Fishes of Alachua County, Florida: A Subjective Key," *Dopeia*, ser. B., vol. 3, part Q, no. X (April 3, 1941): vi. The key was later reprinted in Archie Fairly Carr and Marjorie Harris Carr, *A Naturalist in Florida: A Celebration of Eden* (New Haven: Yale University Press, 1994), 125–38.

22. Ibid.

23. Ibid.

24. Archie Carr, "Notes on Sea Turtles," *Proceedings of the New England Zoological Club* 21 (1942): 1–16.

25. See Archie Fairly Carr, *Handbook of Turtles: The Turtles of the United States, Canada, and Baja California* (Ithaca, N.Y.: Comstock, 1952).

26. Thomas Barbour, "Letter to Archie Carr (8 November 1944)," Carr Papers.

27. Carr, *High Jungles and Low*, 141.

28. Archie Fairly Carr, *The Windward Road: Adventures of a Naturalist on Remote Caribbean Shores* (New York: Knopf, 1956), 242.

29. Archie Fairly Carr, *Ulendo: Travels of a Naturalist in and out of Africa* (New York: Knopf, 1964), 205–6.

30. Ibid., 225.

31. Archie Fairly Carr, *So Excellent a Fishe: A Natural History of Sea Turtles* (Garden City, N.Y.: Natural History Press [for the American Museum of Natural History], 1967), 103.

32. Archie Fairly Carr, *The Everglades* (New York: Time-Life Books, 1973), 157.

33. Ibid., 169.

34. Archie Fairly Carr, *The Reptiles* (New York: Time-Life Books, 1963), 170.

35. Archie Carr, "Letter to Stephen C. O'Connell (17 October 1969)," Carr Papers.

36. Space limitations preclude thorough analysis of Marjorie Carr's efforts to save the Ocklawaha River. See Lee Irby, "A Passion for Wild Things: Marjorie Harris Carr and the Fight to Free a River," in *Making Waves: Female Activists in Twentieth-Century Florida*, ed. Jack E. Davis and Kari A. Frederickson, 177–98 (Gainesville: University Press of Florida, 2003); and Sallie R. Middleton, "Cutting through Paradise: A Political History of the Cross-Florida Barge Canal" (Ph.D. diss., Florida International University, 2001).

37. See Florida Defenders of the Environment, Environmental Impact of the Cross-Florida Barge Canal with Special Emphasis on the Ocklawaha Regional Ecosystem (Gainesville, 1970).

38. Archie Carr, *A Naturalist in Florida: A Celebration of Eden,* ed. Marjorie Harris Carr (New Haven: Yale University Press, 1994), xv.

39. John Kunkel Small, *From Eden to Sahara: Florida's Tragedy* (Lancaster, Pa.: Science Press Printing Company, 1929); Barbour, *That Vanishing Eden.*

40. Carr, *A Naturalist in Florida,* xv.

41. Ibid.

42. Ibid., 51–72.

43. Ibid., 30.

44. Ibid., 244. See also Beth R. Read and Joan E. Gill, *Born of the Sun: The Official Florida Bicentennial Commemorative Book* (Hollywood, Fla.: Florida Bicentennial Commemorative Journal, 1975).

45. For an overview of human agency and nature, see Ted Steinberg, *Down to Earth: Nature's Role in American history* (Oxford: Oxford University Press, 2002).

Chapter 4

"Improving" Paradise

The Civilian Conservation Corps
and Environmental Change in Florida

Dave Nelson

In 1941, Highlands Hammock State Park's Civilian Conservation Corps (CCC) camp published a brochure that directed visitors to "see the beauty of Florida's unspoiled nature." Across the state between 1933 and 1941, the CCC—a New Deal work-relief program to employ single, young males—worked to enlarge and improve Florida's natural areas. The program was considered a success by most observers and remained popular for more than seventy years. But in the parks, recreation areas, and forests that the CCC created, the result was anything but unspoiled. Vistas were created, trees planted, native species removed, natural processes such as fires and water flow were halted, and exotics introduced. Therefore, the program's results for the modern observer remain ambivalent. Although a successful welfare program, as well as a prime agent in spurring governmental preservation efforts and fostering popular environmental awareness, the CCC also altered many of Florida's ecosystems and brought long-lasting environmental change to Florida.

Unlike most of the New Deal programs, the Civilian Conservation Corps was a personal project of newly elected President Franklin Roosevelt. A devout conservationist, Roosevelt cultivated one of the nation's healthiest private forests at his home in Hyde Park, New York, planting ten to fifteen thousand trees a year.[1] As Labor Secretary Frances Perkins once observed, Roosevelt hated seeing trees cut and not replaced.[2] As early as 1910, Roosevelt fought for reforestation programs for New York State's Fish and Game Commission.[3]

Within eight days of taking office as president, Roosevelt personally drew up plans for a national conservation army. As he would soon explain in a "fireside chat" radio broadcast, Roosevelt proposed a civilian corps "to be used in simple work" that would "confine itself to forestry, the prevention of soil erosion, flood control and similar projects."[4] To make the corps a reality, Roosevelt had to first organize it and get it passed through Congress. His hand-drawn organizational chart listed a director who oversaw all operations, and who was to be appointed by the president. Representatives from the departments of Labor, War, Interior, and Agriculture would oversee various logistics of the program. Labor would be in charge of selection. The transportation, conditioning, policing, and housing of the enrollees (as the corps volunteers were called) would be handled by the U.S. Army. As for the choosing, prioritizing, and supervision of the various work projects, Roosevelt selected two government-service organizations. The U.S. Forestry Service would oversee all forestry projects, whether on federal, state, or private property, constituting the majority of CCC work projects. The Interior Department's National Park Service would supervise any park projects, including those in state parks. To handle the various agencies, an advisory council was set up, with representatives from all participating agencies as members.[5]

The same executive order (No. 6101) that set up the Council also named a director—labor leader Robert Fechner, former president of the International Association of Machinists, and one-time vice president of the American Federation of Labor (AFL). Withdrawn, homely, and a self-labeled nonintellectual (he once described himself as a "potato bug among dragonflies"), Fechner was appealing to Roosevelt not for his conservation experience—which was nil—but rather for his acceptance among the CCC's only major critics, the labor interests.[6] Fearing its military aspects and possible job competition, labor leaders were assuaged with Fechner's appointment. While not a conservationist, Fechner nevertheless remained devoted to FDR's conservationist goals. His assistant, James McEntee, took over upon Fechner's death in 1939 but differed little in his administration.

On March 21, 1933, Roosevelt sent a message to Congress asking for an Emergency Civilian Works (ECW), the official name for the CCC until 1937.[7] Ten days later, the bill passed both houses. As set up, the corps would accept all single, unemployed men between the ages of eighteen and twenty-five. On April 14, Native Americans were allowed into the corps. And because of the well-publicized Bonus Marches of 1932 and 1933, provision was also made to include World War I veterans, despite the age restrictions.[8] (The Bonus Marches were held by World War I veterans, who were demanding that their military bonuses be paid immediately to soften economic hardship during the Depression.) Enrollees would be paid thirty dollars a month, with twenty-five dollars sent home to their dependents. They would be organized into camps of two hundred men serving six-month terms with the option of renewing their stints for up to two years. Roosevelt wanted the men recruited quickly, with a goal of 250,000 enrollees by July 1, 1933.[9] The first camp was in Luray, Virginia, and was set up on April 17, 1933.[10] When the July deadline rolled around, director Fechner reported there were 274,375 enrollees, with camps planned in every state.[11] The Association of American Forestry reported that by July 1933, 16,000 civilians also were employed as auxiliary help.[12] The CCC was finally under way.

The CCC in Florida was up and running in less than six months. The first camp opened in the Osceola National Forest in August 1933.[13] By October, there were 3,500 Florida enrollees in twenty-two camps.[14] The State Board of Public Welfare selected and approved the enrollees, while the State Board of Forestry chose and supervised the projects (in consultation with and under the overall jurisdiction of the U.S. Forest Service and National Park Service).[15] The State Board of Forestry was, by any measure, the major driving force behind the Florida CCC program. Originally created in 1927 to conserve and develop Florida's forest resources through tree planting, nurseries, fire prevention, and public education, the Board of Forestry consisted of five board members appointed by the governor. In its first year of existence, the board chose Harry Lee Baker as state forester.[16] Originally the state inspector for the

U.S. Forest Service, the Michigan native gained prominence in Florida forestry circles in 1927 when he authored the Florida Forestry Association's *Forest Fires in Florida*.[17] That publication—an illustrated booklet about the ill effects of fire on the state published in cooperation with the U.S. Forestry Service—effectively legitimized fire suppression in Florida. By 1933, Baker was the de facto head of Florida's CCC work projects. Therefore, as on the national level, the Florida CCC program was controlled and influenced by someone who believed in "scientifically" managed consumptive use of forests—otherwise known as conservation.

In Florida, as in much of the nation, many people by the early 1900s began to formulate and follow the ideals of conservation. Unlike preservation, which involved removing presumably pristine natural areas from human development, conservation embraced the concept of "wise use"—to use former U.S. Forester Gifford Pinchot's much-used phrase.[18] For conservationists, nature was valuable only when humans were able to use it. And anything that was considered unusable or unproductive—such as wetlands and dry prairies—was seen as wasteful. The greatest good for the greatest number of people was the driving motto of Florida progressives.[19] These were not supporters of John Muir's deferential view of natural preservation. Nature required action, not passivity. Ecosystems, wildlife, and natural resources represented potential, one that humans needed to realize. But conservationists also believed that natural resources, such as water, woods, minerals, and soil, were vulnerable to careless choices including overproduction, uncontrolled fires, and poor planning. Therefore, "wise" planning and use was needed to ensure resource availability for future generations.

No one in Florida better represented this ideal than May Mann Jennings, often referred to as the "Mother of Florida Forestry." The wife of Florida governor William S. Jennings, who served from 1901 to 1905, May Mann Jennings was a powerful political activist in her own right.[20] One historian has described Jennings as the most powerful woman in Florida during the 1910s and 1920s. And by the 1930s, no one in the state would exert more influence over the Florida CCC in its early days than Jennings.

Commonly regarded as her governor-husband's "right-hand man," Jennings cemented her influential standing in the state through her role as the long-serving president of the Florida Federation of Women's Clubs (FFWC), an umbrella group organized in Green Cove Springs in 1895 to orchestrate activities and causes of Florida's women's clubs.[21] When her husband was still governor, Jennings used her position to push for drainage of the Everglades, which she and others felt was a "moral imperative."[22] They felt that under the miles of swampland lay Florida's richest soils, a resource that would benefit thousands of people. Though the project ultimately failed, and in the process wreaked environmental havoc on the fragile ecosystem, it vividly demonstrated how Jennings and many of her fellow conservationists looked toward the natural world as an answer to solving society's ills, material and otherwise. Also imbedded within the drainage project was the belief that humans needed to improve upon nature through direct intervention.

Armed with those beliefs on conservation, Jennings led the creation of the two agencies that would supervise Florida's CCC projects: the Florida Forest Service and the Florida Park Service. In collaboration with her son, S. Bryan Jennings, May Mann Jennings wrote the legislation for the creation of the Forestry Board, and for the state's first attempt at a park service.[23] The board survived; the park service did not. Then in 1933, Jennings sought and received Florida's first state park CCC camp in Florida for the privately owned Royal Palm State Park, originally created in 1915 by the FFWC to save Paradise Key from development.[24] (All park-related CCC camps were referred to as state park camps.) Earlier that year, CCC director Robert Fechner, at Secretary of the Interior Harold Ickes's urging, approved the use of CCC labor for park creation.[25] The following year, Jennings urged the Florida Forestry Board and Governor Dave Sholtz to create a park service for Florida, and use CCC labor to construct its parks.[26] Anxious for federal funds, the board drafted the bill—codified as Chapter 17025—that established the Florida Park Service within the Florida Forest Service and to be built by the National Park Service and the Civilian Conservation Corps.[27]

For a discussion of environmental change and the CCC in Florida, the creation of Florida's state parks is key. As in other areas of the nation, there were two major types of CCC projects in Florida: forestry projects and state park projects. (Others existed, such as soil conservation, and by the early 1940s, military camps, but their overall impact was negligible.) Forestry projects consisted primarily of fighting fires, and planting trees. But while comprising only a small percentage of CCC projects, state park projects are the most informative, for they required a higher intensity of environmental activities, involving several ecosystems within the park bounds. Taking into consideration that conservation-minded foresters created parks for the enjoyment of the general public, Florida's state parks were a melding of popular ideals of the natural world with the utilitarianism of professional land managers—the USFS and the NPS, as well as their two Florida counterparts. State parks were more than fenced-off wilderness areas—they were created entities, carved out of the native environment, to serve as showcases for the CCC as well as public parks. And that creation process best demonstrates the types of environmental change the CCC brought to Florida.

All total, the CCC constructed the first seven Florida state parks, forming the core of today's 158-unit-strong park system.[28] The first was Highlands Hammock State Park, in Sebring, in central south Florida. This park boasted one of the last virgin hammocks in state, with trees soaring over 100 feet into the air. Nearby was Myakka River State Park, just outside of Sarasota. Along with the Myakka River, and its adjacent two large lakes, the 20,000-acre park housed a large, dry prairie, typical of the type found across south Florida. Approximately an hour north in Hillsborough County was Hillsborough River State Park, consisting of the eponymous river, longleaf pine forests, and acres of wetlands. In north Florida, four state parks were built: Fort Clinch, Goldhead Branch, Florida Caverns, and Torreya state parks. Aside from historic Fort Clinch, located on the northern tip of Amelia Island among the barrier island's hammock and sand dunes, the parks were natural in character. Goldhead Branch State Park encompassed several freshwater lakes, extensive sandhill pine forests, a spring-fed creek, and a deep, lush ravine. The Florida Caverns were limestone caves indigenous to north Florida with its karst topography. Also within the park was a natural land bridge formed by the disappearing Chipola River. Finally, there was Torreya State Park on the banks of the Apalachicola River, home to 100-foot bluffs and the extremely rare torreya tree.[29] In addition to the state parks were several city and private parks, including Greynolds Park, Royal Palm State Park, Fairchild Tropical Gardens, and Matheson Hammock—all located in south Florida.

Although relations between the two were often strained, the FPS and the CCC rarely conflicted on the issue of altering Florida's natural environment to achieve their goals. Both agencies believed that parks were built environments—not preserved wilderness areas made accessible. As CCC superintendent for Myakka River State Park, A. D. Lawson, wrote in a narrative report from 1935: "It seems to have always been the rule for men to pick up where nature left off, and complete a beautification project."[30] One enrollee at Goldhead Branch State Park wrote in his camp newspaper that the park was "carved out of the wilderness," suggesting the natural features were unfinished, and required human intervention.[31] In another report, this time at Highlands Hammock State Park, the project superintendent described his men's efforts as the "work of a creative artisan."[32] The root concept informing these statements was the idea that nature was a wild entity that needed to be tamed, sanitized, and improved upon. This was park creation in its most literal sense.

With the possible exception of landscape architect Frederick Law Olmsted, no one influenced park creation more than the National Park Service. Created as a government agency in 1916 under President Woodrow Wilson, its roots date back to 1872 with the federal acquisition of Yellowstone.[33] Under conservation advocate President Theodore Roosevelt, the national park properties increased dramatically. These early parks, patrolled by army rangers on horseback, were devised to protect an image held by many of the time: that of a romantic wilderness devoid of human presence. For instance, in the West scores of Native Americans were dispossessed of their lands during this process.[34] (In the 1930s, mountain families were similarly displaced during the construction of the Blue Ridge Parkway and Smoky Mountain National Parks.) When ex-Borax manufacturer Stephen Mather nudged friend Secretary of the Interior Franklin Lane to offer better protection of these roped-off wild areas, he soon found himself in charge of a newly created government agency in 1916.[35] By the 1920s, under Mather's direction, new methods of park building were developed that combined the idealism of a romantic natural world with the active, hands-on approach of landscape architects. Master planning, planting schedules, fire suppression, and woods improvement all became standard operating procedure for the NPS. By the time the NPS took charge of state park work for the CCC in 1933, they had developed park creation into a well-honed skill.[36]

One of the best examples of park creation in Florida was at Greynolds Park, a city park located near the Oleta River in Dade County. Built out of an abandoned rock quarry, the CCC planted hundreds of trees and created waterways and an artificial "lookout mound."[37] The end result was a visually perfect yet completely fabricated forest. At Fort Clinch State Park in Fernandina, the CCC leveled several sand dunes to provide a clear vista of the ocean for the beach casino being built on-site.[38] Several other of the park's massive sand dunes were bisected by the park drive, with futile efforts made to stabilize the ever-shifting sand mounds with grass plantings and sand fences.[39] As historian Phoebe Cutler once described it, the NPS used the CCC to create natural areas that conformed to an idealized version of the "eastern woodlands," creating "an elaborate artifice."[40]

That artifice began with a master plan, a practice developed in the NPS.

Dave Nelson

Each park had a master plan, a blueprint for the building and the layout of the park. The master plans for Myakka, Torreya, and Hillsborough state parks housed today at the Florida State Archives reveal that most of the vistas and other natural areas visitors encountered were created whole cloth from scratch. Trees were planted in layers, foreground and background, with integrated species so that no area would be bare at any one time throughout the year. As the pictorial review for CCC Company 2444 at Goldhead Branch State Park described that camp's achievements, the men changed "what was once a wilderness into a beautiful scenic recreational area."[41] The finished product in Florida's parks and forest recreation areas was closer to a large garden than a preserved wild area.

One of the first steps taken at the state parks was a "general clean-up." While the name may conjure images of removing trash and litter from the park grounds, this was not the case. As described by one superintendent in a 1934 narrative report, general cleanups consisted of work crews roaming through the forests, removing all dead trees, snags, and stumps.[42] Another superintendent explained that cleanups were undertaken so that "the scars of past fires and timber cutting are obliterated." Often dynamite was used to remove the larger stumps. The idea was to allow the woods to "breathe." (The other name used in a few reports for these activities is even more revealing: woods improvement.) According to CCC monthly narrative and inspection reports, all state park camps, along with several forest-based camps, devoted a large portion of their workload (tabulated in reports as "man days") to general cleanups.

Because the sought ideal minimized the environment to healthy trees surrounded by safe, friendly animals, several plant and animal species were targeted for removal. For the cleanup crews, palmettos—Florida's predominant ground-covering plant—were considered especially undesirable. In another narrative report, progress on a cleanup project was described as slow going "as there is a heavy growth of palmetto on the greater portion of the area."[43] Also considered unacceptable at state parks were gar, catfish, and turtles, which the NPS and FPS believed interfered with sport fishing. Reports from Myakka River State Park are filled with photos of enrollees netting and spearing turtles and gar from Myakka Lake.[44] Myakka's project supervisor boasted in a monthly report, "We have been destroying quantities of killer gar, savage catfish, and ferocious turtles. The men have been very interested in this activity."[45] Plant life was also raked out of most freshwater areas. "There would be nothing floating there in all the water," remembered one former enrollee.[46]

As he explained further, it was not a problem for the CCC crews to keep out the flora once removed, "'cause we kept it down. The moment [the plants] would start to grow, we'd get it out of there."[47]

In a few cases, the CCC would replace what it removed with more desirable species. A June 1935 report from Myakka mentioned that into Myakka Lake "have been transferred thousands of game fish."[48] Deer, another acceptable species, was re-introduced into several parks. After a disastrous deer-tick infestation in the mid-1930s, the Florida State Livestock Sanitary Board—partly funded through the Works Progress Administration—paid citizens to kill thousands of deer.[49] Deer populations in several areas, including Myakka River State Park, were wiped out.[50] The CCC camp at Vilas, in the Apalachicola National Forest, raised deer for re-introduction across the state.[51] According to one former enrollee from Goldhead Branch State Park, deer were so desirable that bobcats ("wildcats") were trapped and removed from park grounds because they sometimes were known to kill deer.[52] At Goldhead Branch as well as Highlands Hammock state parks, feeding deer was a daily activity for enrollees. Enrollees' deer feed included table scraps, candy, and cigarettes. One deer at Goldhead Branch State Park became so accustomed to its daily feedings that the camp superintendent was treed for several hours when he found himself out of cigarettes.[53]

But the animals that received the most attention were snakes—universally despised by all involved. During off-times, it was common practice for enrollees to go on snake hunts. Camp newspapers regularly reported the number of snake kills at their camps. One example is found in Highland Hammock State Park's CCC camp's newsletter, *C-bring C-amp C-ourier*, which reported in 1934 that "courageous members of this company" killed three snakes in the past week.[54] The article encouraged more such activity. The *Myakka Rattler* reported that one crew at the park's CCC camp killed over thirty diamondback rattlesnakes during January 1935.[55] "It seems that the survey crew has all the luck with the rattlers," the article opined. "By the time they leave the camp, the palmettos will be hiding nothing but rabbits. Let's hope."[56] The CCC camp at Goldhead Branch State Park held a snake-killing contest, which netted seventeen rattlers.[57] As reported in that camp's newsletter, "taming the woods has become the hobby of many."[58] Highland Hammock's CCC camp newspaper proposed a more moderate approach: "Never disturb a snake—unless poisonous. Most snakes are useful to humanity. They destroy other snakes."[59]

Although the CCC perceived wetlands as unproductive wasteland, the corps "improved" wetlands to rid forests and parks of yet another unwanted pest—mosquitoes. At all seven state parks, and most forests, wetlands were drained with ditches and culverts to keep down the mosquito populations. Such drainage altered the surrounding ecosystems, changed the soil composition, and resulted in loss of habitat and species migration. These efforts were not always successful. According to one United States Forest Service inspection of Florida's CCC camps, "drainage is quite a problem in some sections of the state."[60] Nevertheless, truck trails were built up high to facilitate water drainage into the deep ditches dug out on either side of the road.[61] The near-universal opinion held by CCC crews and park staff was that Fort Clinch had the most severe mosquito problem. Along with drainage ditches and culverts, pyrethrum spray was used extensively.[62] One former Fort Clinch CCC enrollee remembered their meager defenses against the biting insects. Each man would "take a gallon of citronella and hand pumps" to the work site each day.[63] "We made sure to keep our clothes on."[64]

Although considered routine at the time, general cleanups best reveal the attitude that CCC administrators held about how the wilderness should appear in a perfect world: clean, safe, uncluttered, and picturesque. But these efforts paled in comparison with the time and worrying put into protection of the woods from fire.

It was a common belief across the nation that fire was a destructive force to forests and parks. As famed CCC-promoter Roy Hoyt wrote in the 1930s: "Fire is the great enemy of men in the forest. Protection against fire, and the suppression of fire, are necessary if man is to gain or maintain his control over the natural resources."[65] Fire suppression and prevention was one of the main reasons for the creation of the CCC back in 1933. A 1937 memorandum from Florida forester Harry Lee Baker to all CCC camp superintendents contained the reminder that firefighting has "priority over all other camp work."[66] That year's instructions on fire control sent out to all Florida camps from the U.S. Forest Service likewise said that fire suppression had priority "over all other jobs, regardless of the day or hour."[67] Similarly, the 1938–39 Florida CCC fire plan stressed that "work in firefighting takes precedence over all other work."[68] CCC veteran George Lecouris remembered that his Apalachicola National Forest camp's purpose was to simply "fight fires and build roads."[69] At the camp level, such priority was even stressed in the camp-printed newspapers. One example was from Goldhead Branch State Park's newspaper *Tent Town Topics*, which mentioned, "It is the work of the camp to fight fires as well as prevent fires."[70]

But for Florida, fire played a much different role than it did in other areas of the nation. For thousands of years, fires annually swept across the Florida landscape, shaping ecosystems and providing niches for many species. Native Americans and early settlers were aware of this cycle and adjusted their lives accordingly, often conducting burns to create desirable habitats that affected game animals. But by the 1930s, as development increased and natural areas dwindled, Floridians were generally unaware of fire's role in the state and followed a strict no-fire policy. Antifire prejudices were fueled further by the U.S. Forestry Service's expansive campaign to educate the nation on the benefits of fire suppression.[71] As May Mann Jennings said in a 1934 speech to the State Chamber of Commerce, "Fires in no instance should be allowed."[72] Both the CCC and the Florida Forestry and Park Service held the erroneous belief that 99 percent of all fires in Florida were human-created.[73] In fact, Florida is considered by many biologists and ecologists to have more lightning strikes than anywhere else in North America, resulting in hundreds of fires every year. Nevertheless, many observations of Florida's state park and forest properties by CCC personnel remarked upon the effects of "intentional" fires. CCC state inspector C. R. Vinten described Goldhead as "a scene of desolation which resulted from years of continuous burning."[74] A CCC narrative report from Myakka River State Park remarked that it was "common practice to burn the surrounding country," and therefore "fire breaks around the property . . . were most necessary."[75] CCC fire reports invariably blamed fires upon the local residents. One report mentioned that "the cowboys could not resist the temptation to set the world on fire."[76] The fear of the FPS and the CCC/NPS was that a fire would destroy one of the newly created state parks.

The widespread fear of fires at the time is understandable when viewed from the CCC's perspective. It was not until the 1960s that biologists and ecologists began to understand the role fire played in Florida's ecosystems.[77] Few areas are more desolate than a recently burned forest, with its smoldering black ground and charred trees. As May Mann Jennings once described such an area: "Charred wood and smoked choked atmosphere is not inviting to either visitors, nor home folks who travel our splendid highways. We certainly must stop this vandalism."[78] Yet within weeks—even days—green shoots spring up, flowers blossom, and trees germinate, creating a springlike atmosphere. As ecologist Ronald Myers wrote in *Ecosystems of Florida*, many areas "have evolved in response to frequent, low intensity fires."[79] Plants such as turkey oaks, longleaf pines, and wiregrass depend on fire for seed germination and flowering, while animals such as gopher tortoises, red-cockaded woodpeckers, Sherman's fox squirrels, and indigo snakes require it for foraging and habitat maintenance.[80] Without fire, such species would migrate or perish, and leave many areas vulnerable to larger, more damaging fires, as well as exotic invasion. But in the 1930s, little of this was known, and fear of fire as a destructive agent ran unchecked by empirical evidence proving otherwise.

The CCC responded to this fear with extensive fire-prevention efforts. Enrollees cut fire lanes 14 feet wide throughout the parks and forests. Camps made cooperative agreements with local fire agencies, and each enrollee was trained in fire-fighting techniques.[81] Enrollees worked rotating fire shifts, staying in camp every other weekend in case of a fire breakout. At Highlands Hammock, project superintendent A. C. Altvater required a minimum of seventy-five enrollees present in camp at all times.[82] Other camps had similar policies. Every camp was required to maintain two fire tool boxes, equipped with rakes, flaps, shovels, machetes, and backpack water pumps.[83] Also required at the door of every building were two sand-filled barrels, the CCC equivalent of the modern fire extinguisher.[84]

Fire prevention was also extended to the general public. Brochures, radio announcements, and newsreels at movie theaters warned of the ill effects of forest fires. These efforts reached a climax in 1934 when Governor Dave Sholtz designated December 2–8 as Forest Fire Prevention Week.[85] "It is a source of much concern to the state that thousands of wood fires are permitted to burn vast acres in Florida . . . to the disgust and disappointment of our winter residents and visitors," explained Governor Sholtz's proclamation.[86] CCC camps held parades in several cities that week, including Sarasota, Jacksonville, Ocala, Pensacola, Marianna, Tallahassee, and Lake City.[87] As promoted in these efforts, CCC enrollees were considered the "first line of defense" and followed the motto: "Fight a fire when found, and talk about it afterwards."[88]

Once the fire was found, the nearest CCC camp was called into action. Fires on state and federal lands, especially within the expensive state parks, took first priority. Below that fell any land owned by a person or group armed with a cooperative agreement with the state. Such agreements required the owner to aid in fire fighting and to follow state standards on forest maintenance. Finally, fires within a 50-mile radius of the camp that could threaten state or federal lands might be considered for CCC extinguishing. Most of the fires fought were small affairs, few more than a dozen or two acres. However, a few were quite large. CCC veteran George LeCouris recalled working on one fire in the panhandle for two weeks.[89]

Enrollees knew from their training that "in fire control work, speed counts. Travel to a fire is not a pleasure trip. Every single minute counts."[90] Fires were usually fought by hand. "We had shovels, we had flaps, and you'd go beat the fire down," remembered LeCouris. Many carried a knapsack water pump on their backs.[91] "When we'd run out of water, we'd wade out into a pond or a lake, and we'd just sink down, and fill our water up."[92]

On March 3, 1941, everyone's worst fear was realized. That morning, newly appointed FPS director Lewis Scoggin received the following telegram from Goldhead Branch's park superintendent L. R. Brodie: "Fire swept through park yesterday, and last night. Buildings all saved. Half of acreage burned. Under control now."[93] It was the beginning of Florida's fire season that year, and the longleaf pine sandhill community was a prime area for forest fires. A fire had begun off park grounds to the south.[94] But as winds blew north, burning leaves were blown into the park. Within minutes, dozens of small fires ignited throughout the park. After Brodie shot off the telegram to Scoggin, the fire erupted again. By the time the fire burned itself out, three-fourths of the park was burned, including the picnic area, the ravine, and the land surrounding the spring-fed Sheeler Lake. "There is no doubt but that these fires were deliberately set," concluded Brodie.[95] That June, an emergency conference was held between the NPS and the state parks to discuss how to improve fire protection.[96] Too much federal money had been invested to neglect fire protection. The worries were misplaced, however. Goldhead Branch's forests rebounded within months.

One activity for which the CCC was most well known—tree planting—was also one of its most ambivalent. In one sense, the CCC replaced thousands of trees in Florida lost to decades of rampant clear-cutting by residents and timber companies. Some scholars calculate that as many as 16 million acres of virgin forestland were lost in the years before 1933.[97] Using two-man crews, with one man digging with a grub hoe, the other planting the tree seedling— the CCC planted well over 3 million trees in the Sunshine State from 1933 through 1941.[98] The results were immediate and long lasting. Included was the expansion of two national forests (the Ocala and Choctawahatchee national forests)[99] and the creation of two new ones (the Osceola and Apalachicola national forests), as well as several wildlife preserves and state forests.[100] Signs posted across the state, as well as promotional brochures, articles, and radio broadcasts created by the CCC, heralded the restoration of Florida's forests.

What the PR did not mention was what types of forests were being restored. Slash pines, oaks, and even invasive exotics such as Australian pines were planted indiscriminately in the forests and parks. CCC enrollees planted over one hundred Australian pines each at Myakka and Highlands Hammock state parks.[101] Natural ecosystems such as wetlands, prairies, and longleaf pine communities were transformed into what the Florida Forestry Service believed was the ideal environment: slash pine forests with a clean understory. As CCC director Fechner once wrote, the CCC planted "quick growing trees" for maximum effect.[102] The goal, even at the state parks, was to increase Florida's timber supply. Replacing an area's native flora with slash pine altered not only the soil composition but also the water flow and the type of wildlife the land now supported. In many forests, the slash pines usually were planted in close rows that stressed the trees, while the resultant pine needle litter killed the wire and other native grasses. At Myakka, enrollees attempted to turn the natural prairie—seen as a wasteland "where there was just palmettos and nothing else"—into a pine forest.[103] Over 100,000 slash pine trees were planted in the prairie, the native habitat to the indigenous crested caracara, the Florida sand crane, the gopher tortoise, and acres of wire grass and palmettos.[104]

Ironically, despite the intense planting of pine trees, many conservationists, as well as some botanists and the general public, often considered the pine tree as aesthetically unappealing. For state parks and other recreation areas, the CCC often turned to exotic species. One example can be found in a May 1937 exchange between the University of Florida's College of Agriculture and the Florida Forest Service. The college sent 200 African Mahogany trees and 1,000 Australian pines to Highlands Hammock State Park.[105] Three hundred of the Australian pines were sent to the CCC nursery in the Olustee-based camp, and the rest were spread throughout the state's various parks and forests.[106] Melaleuca were planted to dry out unwanted wetlands.[107] In a similar vein, at Goldhead Branch State Park, the deep ravine at the park's headspring was stripped of much of its native plant life to "improve its attractiveness."[108] If Florida's natural environment did not match the idealized image held by the CCC, then it would be altered until it did. And in late 1941, the CCC itself would be forever altered.

The sudden Japanese attack at Pearl Harbor on December 7, 1941, signaled the end for the CCC, along with the other New Deal work-relief programs as "Dr. Win-the-War" replaced "Dr. New Deal." Already, many CCC camps in Florida and elsewhere were closing, while the remaining camps worked almost entirely on defense projects. By the end of 1942, all CCC camps had been shut down, and their equipment transferred to the War Department. The New Deal was over.

For Florida, times were changing in others ways as well. Several state park properties (for example, future Tomoka, Suwannee River, and Hugh Taylor Birch state parks) remained undeveloped until well after 1945. Existing state parks were either closing or catering to the military. At the same time, both the U.S. and Florida forest services began flirting with—albeit in a very limited sense—controlled burns. However, the focus was solely on fuel reduction as a fire prevention tool, not on ecological rehabilitation. Still, the political and social climate the CCC thrived within for nine years was fast disappearing. But the effects of their labors would last for decades.

At a CCC reunion at Highlands Hammock State Park in 2002, one CCC veteran approved of the park's "beautiful" appearance. Before sitting down for an interview, the veteran remarked that keeping fires out must have done the trick.[109] The following year, former CCC enrollee Buck Heath, a veteran of camps at Florida Caverns State Park and the Apalachicola National Forest, hesitated during an oral history recording when asked why the palmettos were removed at the park. After a moment, incredulous at the question, he answered, "Why? Because we were building a park."[110] For him, and most of the others involved in Florida's CCC program, parks and managed forests were considered glimpses into paradise, but only after humans had completed the job of nature and improved on it for human consumption.

Notes

1. Arthur M. Schlesinger Jr., *The Age of Roosevelt: Crisis of the Old Order, 1919–1933* (Boston: Houghton Mifflin, 1958), 336; T. H. Watkins, *The Hungry Years: A Narrative History of the Great Depression in America* (New York: Henry Holt and Company, 1999), 160.

2. Frances Perkins, *The Roosevelt I Knew* (New York: Viking Press, 1946), 177.

3. John Salmond, *The Civilian Conservation Corps, 1933–1942: A New Deal Case Study* (Durham, N.C.: Duke University Press, 1967), 6.

4. Quoted in Watkins, *Hungry Years*, 158.

5. John Paige, *The Civilian Conservation Corps and the National Park Service, 1933–1942: An Administrative History* (Washington, D.C.: National Park Service, U.S. Dept. of the Interior, 1985), 12; Salmond, *Civilian Conservation Corps*, 27.

6. Salmond, *Civilian Conservation Corps*, 28.

7. For clarity's sake, the term "Civilian Conservation Corps" (and its abbreviation, CCC) will be used throughout this paper. Watkins, *Hungry Years*, 158; David Kennedy, *Freedom from Fear: The American People in Depression and War, 1929–1945* (New York: Oxford University Press, 1999), 144.

8. Paige, *CCC and the NPS*, 15; Salmond, *Civilian Conservation Corps*, 36. For more on World War I veterans' bonus marches, and their entrance into the CCC, see Jennifer D. Keene, *Doughboys, the Great War, and the Remaking of America* (Baltimore: Johns Hopkins University Press, 2001).

9. Paige, *CCC and the NPS*, 13; Salmond, *Civilian Conservation Corps*, 45.

10. Watkins, *Hungry Years*, 162; Leslie Alexander Lacy, *The Soil Soldiers: The Civilian Conservation Corps in the Great Depression* (Radnor, Pa.: Chilton Press, 1976), 20.

11. Salmond, *Civilian Conservation Corps*, 45.

12. "With the Civilian Conservation Corps," *American Forests* 39 (July 1933): 302.

13. Charlton Tebeau, *A History of Florida* (Coral Gables: University of Miami Press, 1971), 402. Historian John F. Sweets identifies the Eastport camp (P-54) in Duval County as the first CCC camp in Florida in his "CCC in Florida," *Apalachee* 6 (1967): 79.

14. This included camps in one state forest, fourteen private forests, six national forests, and one biological survey. Camp Directories, 1933–1942, RG 35, box 10, folder 5, National Archives (NARA).

15. Records of the State Welfare Board, box 1, folder "Minutes, 1935," Florida State Archives (FSA).

16. State Planning Board, *Summaries of the Park, Parkway, and Recreational Area Study and Forest Resources Survey for Florida* (Tallahassee: State of Florida, 1939), 46. Baker was appointed April 1, 1928.

17. Harry Lee Baker, *Forest Fires in Florida* (Jacksonville: Florida Forestry Association, 1926). A copy of this publication can be found in the Florida State Library.

18. Gifford Pinchot was Theodore Roosevelt's chief forester as well as a leading member of the progressive movement. He is also the most closely linked American to the concept of conservation. For more on Pinchot, see Martin Fausold's *Gifford Pinchot, Bull Moose Progressive* (Syracuse, N.Y.: Syracuse University Press, 1961).

19. David McCally, *The Everglades: An Environmental History* (Gainesville: University Press of Florida, 1999), 86.

20. Historian and Jennings biographer Linda Vance called her the most powerful woman in Florida during the early 1900s. Linda D. Vance, *May Mann Jennings, Florida's Genteel Activist* (Gainesville: University Press of Florida, 1985), 79.

21. Vance, *May Mann Jennings*, 37.

22. McCally, *Everglades*, 86.

23. Ney Landrum, ed., *A History of the Southeastern State Park Systems* (Association of Southeastern State Parks, 1992), 26; Chapter 12283, *Laws of Florida* (Tallahassee: State of Florida, 1927), 1178–82.

24. Jennings to Governor Dave Sholtz, October 20, 1933, May Mann Jennings Papers, box 19, folder: "Correspondence 1934–June–December," P. K. Yonge Library of

Florida History, University of Florida, Gainesville (hereafter cited as PKY). For more on Jennings and Royal Palm State Park, see Linda D. Vance's article "May Mann Jennings and Royal Palm State Park" in *Florida Historical Quarterly* 55 (summer 1976): 1–17. The park was created by the Florida Federation of Women's Clubs (hereafter cited as FFWC) in 1915 to save Paradise Key from development. Today, it is encompassed within the Everglades National Park.

25. Conrad L. Wirth, *Parks, Politics, and the People* (Norman: University of Oklahoma Press, 1980), 88.

26. February 8, 1934, page 338, vol. 15, Minutes of the Trustees of the Internal Improvement Fund, FSA.

27. The bill was Senate Bill 558, vol. 91 (1935 Acts), Acts of the Legislature, FSA; *Laws of Florida*, 1935.

28. Oleno State Park in Columbia County was originally a forest ranger training facility. It did not join the Florida Park Service until 1941. Malsberger to Carlos Maxwell, June 4, 1941; W. F. Jacobs to Malsberger, October 19, 1940, Florida State Park project files, 1933–42, 1988–89, box 1, folder: "Oleno—General files," FSA.

29. Also located within the park was the less publicized, but equally rare Florida yew. Both trees are found only within a 20-mile stretch along the Apalachicola River. In the 1940s and 1950s, a few local promoters circulated the notion that the area was the site of the Garden of Eden, inexplicably using the torreya tree as their proof.

30. February 4, 1935, Narrative Report, FL SP-4, Myakka State Park files.

31. *Pick and Spade* 3, no. 2 (March 1939).

32. Narrative Report, July 1934, Highlands Hammock State Park files.

33. For more on the National Park Service's origins, see William C. Everhart, *The National Park Service* (Boulder, Colo.: Westview Press, 1983); Linda Flint McClelland, *Building the National Parks: Historic Landscape Design and Construction* (Baltimore: John Hopkins University Press, 1998); John Paige, *The Civilian Conservation Corps and the National Park Service, 1933–1942 : An Administrative History* (Washington, D.C.: National Park Service, U.S. Dept. of the Interior, 1985); Mark David Spence, *Dispossessing the Wilderness: Indian Removal and the Making of the National Parks* (New York: Oxford University Press, 1999); Conrad Wirth, *Parks, Politics, and the People* (Norman: University of Oklahoma Press, 1980).

34. For more on Native American removal from national parklands, see Spence's *Dispossessing the Wilderness*.

35. Everhart, *The National Park Service*, 13–16.

36. For information on the National Park Service's involvement with the CCC outside of Florida, see Paige's *CCC and the NPS*.

37. Ibid.

38. O. B. Taylor, National Park Service regional biologist to M. Perkins, April 16, 1940, Folder: "Florida-Fort Clinch," Records of the Wildlife Technician, RG 79, NARA.

39. Ibid.

40. Phoebe Cutler, *Public Landscape of the New Deal* (New Haven and London: Yale University Press, 1985), 66.

41. *Pictorial Review* , Co 2444, (Starke, Fla.: CCC Co. 2444, 1939), 25, found in

Florida State Parks project files, 1933–42, 1988–89, box 1, folder: "Goldhead Misc. Collection," FSA.

42. Narrative report by C. R. Vinten, SP-3, November 19, 1934, Highlands Hammock State Park files.

43. November 26, 1934, Narrative Report, FL SP-4, Myakka State Park files.

44. Copies of these photos can be found in the Myakka State Park files.

45. Narrative report by A. D. Larson, June 1935, SP-4, Myakka State Park files.

46. Oscar Manigo Oral History (OH hereafter), 5, Myakka State Park files.

47. Ibid.

48. Narrative report by A. D. Lawson, June 1935, Myakka State Park files.

49. For more information on the State of Florida's tick-eradication program, see record group 293, Records of the State Sanitary Livestock Board, Tick Eradication files 1933–51, FSA.

50. Interviews with local longtime residents by park staff in the 1980s mention the lack of deer in the 1930s and 1940s. A few attributed their absence to overhunting. See Myakka River State Park files.

51. Ansley Hall OH, interview by the author, November 2, 2002, New Deal Initiative (NDI), Reichelt Oral History Program, Florida State University, p. 7.

52. Tracy Baker, interview by Capt. Alogna and Ranger Worthington of the Florida Park Service (hereafter FPS), November 26, 1977, 3, Florida State Parks project files, 1933–42, 1988–89, box 1, folder: "Goldhead Misc. Collection," FSA.

53. Mr. A. B. Weissinger was the camp superintendent. Tracy Baker, interview by FPS Capt. Alogna and Ranger Worthington, November 26, 1977, 3–4, Florida State Parks project files, 1933–42, 1988–89, box 1, folder: "Goldhead Misc. Collection," FSA.

54. August 15, 1934, *C-bring C-amp C-ourier* 1:2.

55. February 1935, *Myakka Rattler* 2:18.

56. Ibid.

57. December 7, 1934, *Tent Town Topics* 1:10.

58. Ibid.

59. August 15, 1934, *C-bring C-amp C-ourier* 1:2.

60. Inspection Report, State of Florida, by S. M. Shanklin, February 17, 1937, General Correspondence, box 40, folder: "Supervision Policy—firebreaks and truck trails," RG 95, NARA.

61. C. F. Evans to Harry Lee Baker, March 8, 1934, General Correspondence, box 40, folder: "Supervision Policy—firebreaks and truck trails," RG 95, NARA.

62. Carl P. Russell to C. R. Vinten, March 11, 1938, Records of the Regional Wildlife Technician, 1936–42, folder: "Florida-Fort Clinch," RG 79, NARA.

63. Fred White OH, Samuel Proctor Oral History Program (SPOHP), University of Florida, 35.

64. Ibid.

65. Roy Hoyt, *We Can Take It: A Short Story of the C.C.C.* (New York: American Book Company, 1935), 66. This was a publication sanctioned by the federal government to promote the CCC. Hoyt was also the editor of the national CCC newspaper, *Happy Days*.

66. Baker to All Camp Superintendents, November 12, 1937, State Park Projects files 1936–1945, box 3, folder: "Gold Head Protection—Fire Control," FSA.

67. "Fire Control Instructions to District Rangers and Project Superintendents," n.d. (1937), General Correspondence—ECW Inspections, AL-TX, box 30, folder: "ECW Inspections—Florida National Forests, 1937," RG 95, NARA.

68. "Firefighting Plan for 1938–9," by C. H. Vinten, 1938, State Park Projects files 1936–1945, box 3, folder: "Gold Head Protection—Fire Control," FSA.

69. George LeCouris OH, interview by the author, November 2, 2002, NDI, 9.

70. December 7, 1934, *Tent Town Topics*, Co. 1421, SP-4.

71. For an examination of the evolution of federal policy on forest fires, see Stephen J. Pyne's *Fire in America: A Cultural History of Wildland and Rural Fire* (Princeton, N.J.: Princeton University Press, 1982).

72. Florida State Chamber of Commerce Speech (1934), May Mann Jennings Papers, box 19, folder: "Correspondence 1934–June–December," PKY.

73. *Fifth Biennial Report of the Florida Forest and Park Service, July 1, 1936–June 30, 1938* (Tallahassee: State of Florida, 1938), 11.

74. Vinten to National Park Service Regional Office, August 28, 1940, Florida state park project files, 1936–45, box 3, folder: "Goldhead reports," FSA.

75. Narrative Report by Earl Porter, November 26, 1934, Myakka State Park files.

76. Ibid.

77. In 1962, the Tall Timbers Research Station in north Leon County held the first annual Fire Ecology Conference, which presented the latest research on the benefits of fire to maintaining many of Florida's native ecosystems, such as dry prairies and longleaf pine forests. By the late 1960s, due in large part to Tall Timbers–sponsored research, many government agencies and private land managers were using controlled burns.

78. Florida State Chamber of Commerce Speech (1934), May Mann Jennings Papers, box 19, folder: "Correspondence 1934–June–December," PKY.

79. Ronald L. Myers, "Scrub and High Pine," in *Ecosystems of Florida*, ed. Ronald L. Myers and John J. Ewel (Gainesville: University Presses of Florida, 1990), 189.

80. Myers, 189–90.

81. Highlands Hammock hosted one fire-fighting school in 1938. Every state park project superintendent attended, along with several foremen, FPS employees, and a few enrollees. "Report of the Fire Suppression and Prevention School, 18 November 1938," State park project files, 1936–45, box 4, folder: "Highlands Hammock protection—fire control," FSA.

82. Altvater to Highlands Hammock foremen, December 6, 1938, State park project files, 1936–45, box 4, folder: "Highlands Hammock protection—fire control," FSA.

83. Ibid.

84. Associate Civil Engineer J. H. Stone to Regional ECW Officers, December 8, 1938, General Correspondence—ECW Inspection, box 28, folder: "Inspection Reports—Florida, FY1937," RG 95, NARA.

85. *Tent Town Topics*, December 7, 1934; *Jacksonville Journal*, December 8, 1934.

86. Proclamation, November 15, 1934, Governor Dave Sholtz papers, 1933–37, box 45, folder: "Forestry, 1934," FSA.

87. *Jacksonville Journal*, December 8, 1934.

88. Baker to All CCC camp superintendents, November 12, 1937, State park project files, 1936–45, box 3, folder: "Goldhead—fire control," FSA.

89. George LeCouris OH, NDI, 22.

90. Fire Control Instructions to Project Superintendents, 1937, p. 3–4, General Correspondence, ECW Inspections, folder: "ECW Inspections, Florida National Forests, 1937," RG 95, NARA.

91. Harry Bush OH, SPOHP, 22; LeCouris OH, NDI, 11.

92. George LeCouris OH, NDI, 11.

93. L. R. Brodie to Scoggin, June 21, 1941, State park project files, 1936–1945, box 3, folder: "Goldhead—fire control," FSA.

94. On March 6, 1941, Brodie wrote a three-page memo to Scoggin describing the fire. State park project files, 1936–45, box 3, folder: "Goldhead—fire control," FSA.

95. Ibid.

96. "Notes of Fire Protection Conference, Florida State Parks," June 20, 1941, State park project files, 1936–45, box 1, folder: "Florida Caverns—fire control," FSA.

97. Jerrell H. Shofner, "Roosevelt's 'Tree Army': The Civilian Conservation Corps in Florida," *Florida Historical Quarterly* 65 (April 1987): 434.

98. Char Mills, *Gifford Pinchot and the Making of Modern Environmentalism* (Washington, D.C.: Island Press, 2000), 134.

99. The Ocala and Choctawahatchee National Forests were both created in 1908 by President Theodore Roosevelt. In 1940, the majority of the Choctawahatchee property was transferred to the War Department to form the nucleus of Eglin Air Force Base. The staff of the Apalachicola National Forest today administers the remaining property.

100. "Report of Inspection, Florida National Forests," October 18, 1937, RG 95, General Correspondence, box 12, folder: "CCC-Inspection-Florida," NARA.

101. C. H. Coulter to Schaffer, May 10, 1937, State park project files, 1936–45, box 4, folder: "Plants and Plantings," FSA.

102. Robert Fechner, "My Hopes for the CCC," *American Forests* 45 (January 1939): 10.

103. Oscar Manigo OH, Myakka State Park files, 3.

104. Much modern debate has gone into the origins of dry prairies. Many contend that they were human-created, perhaps through repeated burning by indigenous peoples. Therefore, the CCC's assessment may have been partially correct, with the exception of a few centuries. *Myakka River State Park Unit Plan* (Tallahassee: Florida Department of Environmental Protection, State of Florida, 1999), 33; *Ecosystems of Florida*, 117–18.

105. H.S. Wolfe to Assistant Forester C. H. Coulter, May 5, 1937, State park project files, 1936–1945, box 4, folder: Plants and Plantings," FSA.

106. Coulter to FPS director C. H. Schaffer, May 10, 1937, State park project files, 1936–45, box 4, folder: "Plants and Plantings," FSA.

107. FPS Ranger Paula Benshoff, personal communication, March 10, 2002.

108. Malsberger to SP-5 Landscape Architect, October 11, 1939, State park project files, 1936–42, box 3, folder: "Goldhead reports—General," FSA.

109. Paul Digiralomo, interview by the author, November 2, 2002. Notes in author's possession. Interview stored with the New Deal Initiative, Florida State University.

110. Buck Heath, interview by the author, July 2003, notes in author's possession.

Chapter 5

Water, Water Everywhere

Christopher F. Meindl

It is hard to think about Florida's environmental history without also think-ing about water. Its presence is apparent in so many contexts: along more than a thousand miles of coastline (and many more miles if one includes the shorelines of Florida's thousands of islands); in rivers, creeks, and thousands of lakes that dot the landscape (not to mention hundreds of thousands of backyard swimming pools); in enormous groundwater aquifers that store bil-lions of gallons, some of which squirts to the surface in the form of fabled springs; in driving rains from frequent thunderstorms and occasional hurri-canes; and even in the air around us (in the form of water vapor) eliciting complaints that it feels "muggy." Indeed, all of this water has combined with Florida's mostly flat terrain to create millions of acres of swamps, sloughs, mangroves, and marshes, collectively called wetlands. Florida's wetlands were once considered a ubiquitous nuisance, but in recent decades wetlands have emerged near the top of the environmental agenda—witness the $7.8 billion attempt to restore parts of the Everglades to some semblance of its pre-drainage condition, or try converting a swamp into a strip mall and watch how fast environmental activists and government regulators attempt to block such plans.[1]

Although most people would recognize a wetland if dropped off in the midst of a cypress dome or led on a hike through the Everglades, wetlands are difficult to define precisely. As late as the early twentieth century, wetlands were defined in terms of agriculture—they were places where moisture was sufficient to render land unfit for cultivation. Not until the 1950s did the scientific community begin to use the term "wetlands" (as opposed to wet land), and only then did government scientists begin to develop conceptual definitions of wetlands. For example, according to the U.S. Army Corps of Engineers, the term "wetlands" refers to "those areas that are inundated or saturated by surface or ground water at a frequency and duration sufficient to support, and that under normal circumstances do support, a prevalence of vegetation typically adapted for life in saturated soil conditions." Another way of defining wetlands is as follows: wetlands are transition zones between deepwater environments that are always submerged, and upland environments that are practically never flooded. Within this transition zone are environments that are inundated or soggy a large percentage of any given year, but there are also "dry end" wetlands that have water at or near the surface for only a few weeks during an average year. In fact, most wetlands are dry for at least part of any given year, and this is an enormous source of confusion to many people who wonder why such a place can be protected as a wetland. But my grandfather always used to say, "Only a fool would buy land in Florida *before* checking the property immediately after a good rain." The truth is that a given wetland can look different throughout any given year, and it can display different hydrologic conditions from one year to the next; at the same time, there is much geographic diversity within this group of environments known as wetlands.[2]

Governments may pass laws calling for wetland protection, but this does not end the matter. Conceptual definitions of wetlands might be sufficient for the scientific community, but such characterizations are of little comfort to government regulators charged with the responsibility of protecting wetlands. Since wetlands are frequently fluctuating transition zones, wetland delineation has become mired in controversy because developing rules to determine the precise boundaries of wetlands is more a matter of public policy—and, ultimately, politics—than of science. Property-rights advocates prefer a narrow definition of wetlands so that less property will be subject to wetland protection legislation. Yet environmentalists prefer a more broadly construed definition of wetlands so that more land is protected.[3]

Why protect swamps in the first place? It turns out that many wetlands provide a host of ecological functions of social value, such as floodwater storage and flood-peak reduction, water purification, groundwater recharge, aesthetic and recreational values, plant and animal habitat, breeding grounds for many commercially valuable fish and shellfish, and storm abatement along the coast. It is important to note that not all wetlands provide all the above benefits; nor do they necessarily provide them all of the time. Indeed, some wetlands provide few if any of these ecological functions and related social values. Still, many Americans have decided that wetlands are worth protecting, so the federal government and many state and local agencies (including many in Florida) have taken steps to acquire wetlands and otherwise prevent their destruction.[4]

Wetlands have always been a large (if declining) part of the Florida landscape. Accordingly, this chapter—devoted to the environmental history of wetlands in Florida—will address three significant wetland-related issues. First, one must have some sense of the geographic diversity of Florida's wetlands in order to appreciate the difficulty policy makers and regulators have in defining and protecting wetland landscapes. Second, since recent wetland public policy has been based on the idea that many wetlands have been converted to other uses at an alarming rate, it is important to examine attempts to determine wetland acreage in Florida over time. This dovetails with a third issue, an analysis of wetland public policy development in Florida and the rest of the United States. In short: what is the nature of Florida wetlands? How many wetlands did Florida used to have, and how many remain? What has been the experience of wetland loss and subsequent attempts to protect wetlands here in Florida? This essay answers these questions and others about the changing nature of wetlands in Florida.

Florida wetlands are a diverse lot including many types that are not present in other states. Indeed, according to Katherine Ewel—a leading authority on Florida wetlands—"the unique combination in Florida of high fire frequency, low topography, high surficial groundwater tables, and seepage from deep groundwater aquifers has produced a collage of wetlands that is unmatched in diversity." This diversity has complicated the process of wetland inventory because many of these environments are easily confused with similar terrestrial (especially forested) environments. Moreover, Florida's many different wetlands create complications for the regulatory community because any set of wetland protection rules must be applied to a wide variety of environments. In order to facilitate discussion of these environments, Florida wetlands can be divided into five categories: river swamps, still-water swamps, freshwater marshes, saltwater marshes, and mangroves. Such a framework may not survive technical scrutiny, but it serves as an effective gateway to understanding Florida's many wetland systems.[5]

The word "swamp" usually refers to many different kinds of forested wetlands. Although most of Florida's swamps were logged between the late 1800s and the 1950s, nature has replaced most of the extracted trees, so these forested wetlands are still widely distributed throughout the state. Differences in hydroperiod (the length of time that soils are saturated during the year), fire frequency, organic matter ("peat") accumulation, and water source create at least thirteen different Florida swamp types, which can be grouped in two major divisions: river swamps and still-water swamps.[6]

As their name suggests, *river swamps* lie adjacent to rivers, creeks, and spring runs, and most of these are located in north and central Florida. As a group, these swamps share several characteristics. For one thing, river swamps are Florida's most diverse and productive wetlands because of the periodic movement of water (and nutrients) through them. In spite of substantial logging activity in north Florida since the 1870s, the relative lack of development in this region combined with the state's efforts to purchase property here have resulted in the preservation of extraordinarily diverse river swamps. In any event, river-based wetlands also generally have shorter hydroperiods (compared with other swamps) because they are flooded only when the neighboring river receives more water than its channel can accommodate. Standing water usually lasts for less than six months per year—and in many cases this water lasts only a month or so. Furthermore, virtually all swamps burn periodically (usually during a drought or dry time of year), and dead organic matter in the form of leaf litter or peat deposits serves as fuel. Such fires help maintain the character of the swamp by eliminating competitive (and less fire-tolerant) plants and by ensuring a lower surface elevation by sending much organic matter up in smoke. Maintaining a swamp's lower surface elevation allows water to accumulate, preventing less flood-tolerant plants from invading. Having said this, fire is a relatively infrequent occur-

Christopher F. Meindl

rence in these less frequently flooded swamps—perhaps once per century. "Drier-end" swamps (especially those river swamps that are flooded for just a handful of weeks per year) encourage rapid decomposition of dead organic material because less frequent flooding provides more opportunities for efficient aerobic (oxygen-consuming) decomposer organisms to consume dead plant tissue that might otherwise serve as fuel. Leading examples of Florida's river swamps include those along the massive Apalachicola River (between Pensacola and Tallahassee); those along low-lying portions of the Suwannee River, which begins in south Georgia's Okefenokee Swamp and winds its way to the Gulf of Mexico north of Cedar Key; and those along the Silver River, which carries water emanating from Silver Springs toward the swamp-bounded Ocklawaha River just east of Ocala.[7]

If river swamps share many characteristics, the same cannot be said of *still-water swamps*. Cypress swamps, lake-fringe swamps, mixed hardwood, and melaleuca swamps all have what might be described as "intermediate" hydroperiods: they are typically flooded between six and nine months each year. Many of these receive water oozing up from shallow groundwater sources, but some cypress swamps receive most of their water from rain, which means they are more nutrient-deficient than other swamps. Indeed, the Big Cypress Swamp (adjacent to Everglades National Park) is a predominantly rain-fed, and thus nutrient-deficient, swamp. Meanwhile, although hydric hammocks have relatively short hydroperiods (flooded less than six months per year), bay swamps, gum ponds, and shrub bogs have longer hydroperiods—they usually remain flooded more than nine months per year. At the same time, it must be kept in mind that practically all wetlands dry out for at least some time during the year, and this is an important time for plant seedlings to become established before standing water returns.[8]

The moderate-to-long hydroperiod of many still-water swamps dramatically reduces the rate of organic matter decomposition, which results in many of these wetlands having thick accumulations of peat. Large quantities of peat can serve as a source of fuel during the modest dry season. Although some still-water swamps burn every twenty years (on average), south Florida's Big Cypress Swamp (so named for its tremendous extent—570,000 acres—rather than for the size of its mostly dwarfed cypress trees) is an example of a swamp that burns more frequently—usually once per decade. Finally, although many wetlands are wet because they are places where groundwater discharges at the surface, central Florida's Green Swamp is an example of an important groundwater recharge wetland. Real estate developers historically have not been very concerned with this—but water managers have been because groundwater is the source of water for millions of Floridians, thousands of Florida farms, and hundreds of its springs.[9]

At the opposite end of the wetland spectrum are *freshwater marshes,* which are dominated by herbaceous (rather than woody) plants rooted in, and generally emergent from, shallow water that stands at or near the surface for much of the year. Like their swampy cousins, freshwater marshes are a diverse lot; James Kushlan describes six different marsh types (based upon vegetation), and the Florida Natural Areas Inventory lists nine different types of marshes in Florida. Unlike swamps, which can be found throughout Florida's panhandle and up and down the peninsula, Florida's freshwater marshes are far more numerous and extensive in the central and especially southern portions of the state. This is due in large measure to the fact that northern Florida is more elevated, has more rolling topography, and is therefore a bit better drained than much of the rest of the state.[10]

Most marshes are flooded at least once each year, although some may flood only during wet years (which can make their identification and boundary delineation difficult). Confusing matters even further is the fact that annual variation in precipitation can cause significant differences in water depth and extent of flooding at a single marsh site. In any event, deep-water marshes (dominated by floating leaf plants) have the longest hydroperiods, generally greater than nine months each year. Meanwhile, submersed marshes are only somewhat less frequently flooded, with water levels typically a bit lower than in deepwater marshes; as a consequence, submersed marshes may contain a thin distribution of emergent plants species that normally cannot tolerate deeper water. As a result of the relatively long hydroperiod, organic matter is normally produced at faster rates than it can be decomposed, so deepwater and submersed marshes usually have significant accumulations (more than 3 feet deep) of peat. In addition, the dominating presence of water for much of the year reduces fire frequency to about once every three to five years (which is infrequent compared with other Florida marshes). It is important to note, however, that fire can occasionally sweep through even flooded marshes, burning the exposed portions of plants.[11]

Other marshes are usually flooded only six to nine months per year, and they can have layers of organic matter at least 3 feet deep. Indeed, around 1900, the dense saw-grass marshes of the Everglades near Lake Okeechobee rested upon peat deposits that were more than 10 feet deep, while the southerly portions of the Glades featured sparse saw-grass stands resting on peat accumulations barely inches deep. In terms of fire, Florida marshes are adapted to recurring fires, many burning every two to three years. According to James Kushlan, "Fire plays a crucial role in the ecology of Florida's marshes by limiting the invasion of woody vegetation, affecting the composition of the herbaceous community, and retarding, or occasionally reversing, peat accumulation."[12]

Inland swamps and marshes account for roughly 90 percent of Florida's wetlands today, and since much of the state's population growth over the past century has accumulated in coastal areas, coastal zone wetlands have been under intense development pressure. Like inland wetlands that can be divided between those dominated by trees and those featuring mostly grasses and sedges (saw grass, for example, is a sedge), Florida's coastal zone wetlands may be similarly divided. Salt marshes are coastal ecosystems with communities of herbaceous, salt-tolerant plants occupying intertidal zones that are at least occasionally flooded with salt water. Alternatively, mangrove swamps are coastal wetlands dominated by trees or shrubs that share certain characteristics that allow them to survive in this harsh environment. Both salt marshes and mangrove forests develop in areas with little or no wave energy, so they are not found in conjunction with sandy beaches and roaring surf. Moreover, plants (and animals) in both environments must be able to cope with periodic inundation as well as salt, and there are relatively few species that can do this successfully.

Florida's salt marshes are frequently dominated by a small number of species of plants, and according to Clay Montague and Richard Wiegert, the different zones of a salt marsh "correspond to subtle changes in elevation, which result in changes in depth, duration, and frequency of inundation by saline water to which coastal marsh plants are especially sensitive." For example, plants that are a bit more flood-tolerant are more likely to occupy lower-lying (usually seaward) portions of salt marshes. By contrast, less flood-tolerant salt-marsh plants (which are usually a bit more salt-tolerant) occupy the slightly higher, less frequently flushed portions of marshes that can accumulate higher concentrations of salt over time as occasional floodwaters evaporate and leave salt behind.[13]

Salt marshes are typically crisscrossed by a series of zigzagging tidal creeks that allow seawater to enter portions of the marsh during high tide. These same creeks serve as conduits for exiting water during low tide. Tidal creeks (especially the edges) provide hiding places for many juvenile species of fish and shellfish, but they also facilitate the flow of energy and valued predatory animals such as snook, red drum, herons, and ibises. Periodic inundation and the presence of salt impose formidable obstacles for both plants and animals, and relatively few species can tolerate these stresses. Yet those that can are usually very abundant. Fiddler crabs are a leading example of one of the few but permanent animal residents of salt marshes. These tiny crabs (and their burrows) are a ubiquitous and voluminous feature of Florida salt marshes, and they play an important role in aerating the soil, consuming detritus (decaying plant material), and serving as a source of food for other animals.[14]

Most of Florida's salt marshes appear in one of four portions of the state's coast: northeast, northwest, southern, and central Florida's Indian River Lagoon. According to Montague and Wiegert, "the types of plants as well as the extent of salt marshes vary considerably around the state owing to a combination of large latitudinal change and geographic differences in tidal range, local relief, and wave energy." Roughly half of Florida's remaining salt marshes can be found along Florida's northwest coast, or "Big Bend," from north of Tampa Bay to Pensacola. The relative lack of economic development in this region has combined with a gently sloping continental shelf offshore to maintain extensive, low (wave) energy, and irregularly flooded salt marshes. Another 20 percent of the state's salt marshes lie along Florida's northeast coast, from just south of St. Augustine up to the Georgia border. East central Florida's Indian River Lagoon (especially near Cape Canaveral) hosts 10 percent of the state's salt marshes, although as Gordon Patterson relates in another essay in this volume, many of these have been altered in order to control the hoards of mosquitoes that plagued people in the area. My father, who helped set up camera sites for filming early missile launches at Cape Canaveral in the 1950s, observed that he and his co-workers would come in from the field looking like bears—they were completely covered by mosquitoes. Finally, an additional 20 percent of Florida's salt marshes struggle to compete with mangrove forests along coastal portions of the southern half of the peninsula.[15]

Part of the reason that salt marshes are not particularly prevalent in south Florida is due to the presence of mangroves. Globally, there are a few dozen species of mangrove trees, but Florida is home to red, black, and white mangroves. These trees (and other members of the surrounding ecosystem) are often collectively referred to as mangrove swamps or mangrove forests. It is thought that mangroves, by virtue of their taller stature, are able to out-com-

Christopher F. Meindl

pete (by shading out) typical salt-marsh grasses and sedges. Freezing air temperatures for more than a few hours are the enemy of most mangrove trees. Although a shrubby form of black mangrove can be found scattered along portions of the northern Gulf of Mexico coast, red and white mangroves are almost never found north of a line across Florida extending roughly from Cedar Key on the Gulf coast to just north of Daytona Beach on the Atlantic coast. Indeed, Florida's southernmost counties of Lee, Collier, Monroe, and Miami-Dade are home to about 90 percent of Florida's mangrove swamps, but during severe winters, many mangrove trees are killed, and surviving trees may be limited almost entirely to portions of these four counties.[16]

Mangrove trees not only display morphological adaptations (such as specialized root systems) to cope with flooding, they have physiological mechanisms that allow them to exclude or excrete salt. Red mangroves, for example, have exposed prop roots that look almost like long fingers, literally propping the rest of the tree above water. The above-ground portions of these roots are believed to allow oxygen to make its way through frequently submerged portions of root systems. Alternatively, black mangroves can survive flooding because they have a radial pattern of below-ground roots extending from the base of the tree—and an associated field of pneumatophores (asparaguslike appendages of the roots) that extend up and frequently out of water. Although red mangroves have become well adapted to excluding much salt as its roots take in water, and black mangrove leaves are frequently salt-encrusted because they excrete salt—most mangroves are thought to engage in at least some salt exclusion and salt excretion.[17]

As we have seen, Florida wetlands are a diverse lot. What is nearly universal, however, is that fact that for much of American history, most people considered wetlands a nuisance.[18] The state's ubiquitous water, oppressive heat, and countless bugs and reptiles prompted early-nineteenth-century Virginia congressman John Randolph to exclaim that he "would not give up an eligible position in hell for all Florida."[19] Indeed, wetlands in Florida and the rest of the United States have long been despised environments. This is not hard to understand. Historically, wetlands prevented or severely hampered traditional agriculture, and they served as a refuge for birds and other animals that ate nearby crops and livestock—no small concerns to earlier generations, most of whom made their living farming. Waterlogged landscapes also impeded travel by people lucky enough to own an automobile, let alone those still moving by horse and buggy. And even if one could overcome the unpleasantness of hordes of insects, worse still were the smelly swamps, marshes, and bogs that were thought to be the source of miasmatic gases that caused debilitating diseases such as malaria. Perceptions of wetlands changed little (if at all) when scientists discovered at the end of the nineteenth century that malaria is spread by certain species of mosquitoes that inhabit wet places.[20]

Florida has always been a wetland-dominated landscape. The state's total land area is roughly 35 million acres, and most observers agree that well over half of Florida once consisted of wetlands; exactly how much may never be known with certainty. By contrast, it is estimated that the lower forty-eight United States were once just 11 percent wetlands. When Florida took its place alongside other states in the Union in 1845, state officials almost immediately asked the federal government to study south Florida (dominated by the Everglades) to determine its potential value. Two years later, Congress authorized Buckingham Smith to prepare such a report, which he submitted in 1848. Smith opined that for anybody "of practical, utilitarian thought, the first and abiding impression is the utter worthlessness to civilized man, in its present condition, for any useful or practical object, of the entire region." He could not think of a solitary inducement to offer the prospective south Florida settler. Much the same might have been said about most of the rest of the state at that time. Still, Smith did conclude that draining the Everglades would be well worth the cost, though it would be more than a half century before any such work would be attempted.[21]

The U.S. Congress granted control of wet and overflowed land to Florida and more than a dozen other states in the Swamp Land Acts of 1849, 1850, and 1860. Since wetlands (especially in the relatively poor South) appeared to stand in the way of economic development, Congress gave wetlands to states to sell—and then use the proceeds to fund their "reclamation." Ironically, in the early twentieth century, when people spoke of reclaiming wetlands (or deserts), they thought in terms of modifying the landscape to enhance agricultural and urban development. Today, however, wetland reclamation involves restoring previously drained wetlands.[22] As a result of the Swamp Land Act of 1850, Florida laid claim to 22,273,208 acres it called wet and overflowed lands; the state ultimately gained title to 20,325,013 acres of wetlands (which accounted for almost 59 percent of Florida's land area). Although large wetland areas (such as the Everglades or the marshes that served as the headwaters of the St. Johns River) were not surveyed in detail, Florida's claims were based mostly on field notes of federal government surveyors.[23]

Only land that had not already been sold (and was still technically property of the federal government) could be claimed under the terms of the Swamp Land Acts. States like Ohio ultimately received very few wetlands from this legislation because most of their wet land had already been sold to pioneers and speculators. Yet Florida's liquid landscape, complete with alligators, snakes, and mosquitoes, proved unattractive to most of the nation's restless and footloose population through the late 1800s and early 1900s—and it attracted precious few of the millions of foreign immigrants who fled Europe and other places during this time period. Since it seems unlikely that Florida's scrappy nineteenth-century "Cracker" pioneers bought more than a few acres of wetlands from the U.S. government (prior to the Swamp Land Acts), it has been assumed that Florida's endowment of wetlands as of the 1780s consisted of the 20,325,013 acres granted to Florida under the terms of the Swamp Land Act of 1850. At the same time, it is also reasonable to assume that several of the large land grants made to individuals during the early Spanish and English periods in Florida's history consisted of at least some wetlands (land privatized before the state received title to over 20 million acres of presumably wet land); so Florida may have at one time been covered by more than 20.3 million acres of wetlands (perhaps more than 60 percent of the state).[24]

Throughout the latter half of the nineteenth century, wetlands were routinely drained across the midwestern states, but not in Florida. Of course, that did not mean Florida's wetlands remained under state control. Florida officials granted enormous quantities of land (much of it wet) to corporations in return for railroad construction, even though fewer than half of the 564 railroads chartered ever laid track. According to Luther Carter, "half the nation was a newly opened frontier made up of states vying to attract people and money; in bidding for Florida's share, state officials knew that the only major negotiable assets at their command were the public lands, and these they gave away recklessly." Then came Philadelphia businessman Hamilton Disston, who purchased 4 million acres of central and southern Florida swampland for $1 million in 1881. Although there was much controversy over how much land Disston actually reclaimed, his engineers dug miles of canals and achieved modest agricultural success near St. Cloud (southeast of Orlando). The nationwide Panic of 1893 then dealt a crippling blow to these efforts, and, swamped with financial problems, Disston killed himself in 1896, effectively ending his company's operations in Florida.[25]

Floridians did not engage in significant wetland drainage until closer to the middle of the twentieth century, but that did not stop them from trying. In

1912, promoters attempted to give birth to Fellsmere, an agricultural community between Melbourne and Vero Beach situated on the edge of expansive marshes that formed the headwaters of the St. Johns River. Excessive rainfall in 1916 left the town underwater and settlers scurrying for higher ground. Further development in the region occurred years later.[26]

Early attempts to develop Fellsmere were almost as much ballyhooed as the spectacular wetland reclamation project in the Everglades. Initiated by Governor Napoleon B. Broward in 1906, this project—surrounded by controversy then and now—took several decades to complete. No less a figure than Frank Stoneman—father of the famous Everglades defender Marjory Stoneman Douglas—spoke out early and often against Broward's plan to drain the Everglades. Yet Stoneman's efforts to derail early-twentieth-century Everglades reclamation were overshadowed by daunting hydrological engineering problems, a congressional investigation in 1912 prompted by charges of real estate fraud, a lack of money, and killer hurricanes in 1926 and 1928 (which collectively claimed over 2,200 lives near Lake Okeechobee). Not until the late 1940s, when the federal government began to devote its substantial resources to the work (through the U.S. Army Corps of Engineers), would wetland reclamation continue in the Everglades. Not only were roughly 700,000 acres of farmland eventually carved out of what used to be the Everglades just south of Lake Okeechobee (today's Everglades Agricultural Area), urban development along the southeast Florida coast from West Palm Beach to Miami pushed several miles inland into the Glades.

The fact that it took so long to make parts of the Glades agriculturally productive was not the fault of Thomas Elmer Will, a tireless advocate of early-twentieth-century reclamation in the Everglades. Although Will became involved with some infamous real estate hucksters in the region, he had no interest in selling land by the gallon. Indeed, he was deeply committed to establishing rural settlement in the Glades, working as hard as anyone in attempting to hack a settlement out of the saw grass. Like so many others, however, Will was eventually flooded out of his home in the Glades, but he continued to support efforts to reclaim the region's wetlands from his house in Ft. Lauderdale until his death in 1937. Nowadays, state and federal government authorities are engaged in a much debated multidecade $7.8 billion plan to restore parts of the Everglades.[27]

Meanwhile, in 1907, the U.S. Department of Agriculture (USDA) published the first comprehensive survey of wetlands in the eastern United States. (The report ignores Montana, Wyoming, Colorado, New Mexico, and all other western states probably because these states accounted for less than 8 percent of all wetlands in the lower forty-eight states The USDA derived its estimate by sending out questionnaires to one or more officials in each county in each state, including Florida. Respondents were instructed: "if you have not a record of the exact amount of swamp land, give us the best estimate you can form after consulting the county surveyor and others familiar with the lands in the county."[28] The report concludes that in the eastern portion of the U.S. there were some 77 million acres of wetlands "that can be reclaimed and made fit for cultivation by the building of simple engineering structures."[29] The report's map reveals that almost 19.8 million of those wetland acres were in Florida. It is instructive that respondents were asked to list wetlands in one of three categories: (coastal) salt marsh, swamp, or overflowed (by rivers) land. Moreover, the report's author (James O. Wright, who became involved in early efforts to drain the Everglades) acknowledged that not all wetlands are suited for agriculture. In light of Wright's admission, it is likely that his estimate did not include thousands of acres of mangrove swamps and possibly other wetlands unsuited to agriculture even if drained. Inasmuch as a mid-1950s wetland inventory found more than 500,000 acres of mangroves in Florida, if we add this to the 19.8 million acres in Wright's report, it is possible that there may have been on the order of 20.3 million acres of wetlands in Florida during the early 1900s—and that very few of the state's wetlands had been drained up to 1907.[30]

In the early 1920s, the USDA tallied 16,846,000 acres of Florida land unfit for crops without drainage. Although this estimate may have once again ignored those wetlands deemed unfit for cultivation even after drainage (such as mangroves), this USDA estimate would appear to suggest that Florida lost as many as 3.5 million acres of wetlands between statehood and 1920—with virtually all of that loss occurring since 1907. Florida had finally begun to attract a few settlers (figure 5.1), and there was undoubtedly some wetland drainage in the state during this time, but it seems unlikely that so few people were responsible for draining 3.5 million acres of wetlands from 1907 to 1920. Meanwhile, the Florida Department of Agriculture's Ralph Stoutamire claims that Florida had a grand total of 17.9 million acres of unreclaimed swamp and overflow lands in 1920. Stoutamire appeared to be working from the USDA data, and he may have included all wetlands—even those that could never be used for agriculture.[31]

In any event, by the 1950s the scientific community realized that wetland loss was taking its toll on the nation's wildlife. As a result, the U.S. Depart-

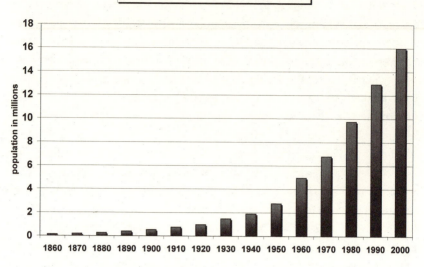

Population of Florida since 1860

Figure 5.1. Population of Florida since 1860.

ment of the Interior's Fish and Wildlife Service (FWS) undertook a project to identify the extent, distribution, and quality of the nation's remaining wetlands in terms of their value as wildlife habitat. FWS staff used a variety of published maps and a new tool—photographs taken from aircraft—to develop their inventory of the nation's wetlands. The report's authors readily admit that their concern lay with wetlands that served as home to waterfowl and other wildlife. This inventory, completed in 1954, suggests that Florida had almost 17.2 million acres of wetlands. Although urban development undoubtedly accounted for the conversion of some wetlands to homes and businesses, agriculture was probably the most significant source of wetland loss up to this point, especially in the Everglades and in the marshes forming the headwaters of the St. Johns River near Fellsmere.[32]

Meanwhile, wetland conversion to other land uses continued practically unabated until the 1970s, both in Florida and the rest of the United States; but people outside the scientific community were finally beginning to understand the many ecological functions and values provided by these environments. Accordingly, in 1974, the FWS directed its Office of Biological Services to conduct yet another inventory of the nation's wetlands. This marks the birth of an institution eventually known as the National Wetlands Inventory (NWI, now with offices in St. Petersburg, Florida). The goals of the NWI

Christopher F. Meindl

include producing and disseminating information on the characteristics and extent of wetlands in the United States and providing data to decision makers who manage the nation's resources. Moreover, the 1986 Emergency Wetlands Resources Act directs the U.S. Department of the Interior (through the FWS) to produce status and trends reports for U.S. wetlands every ten years and to produce wetland maps for all fifty states. Congress amended this act three years later by asking the FWS to produce an estimate of the nation's wetlands as of the late eighteenth century.[33]

During the late 1970s, FWS scientists laid important groundwork that helps guide wetland inventory activity to this day. One of the first problems they confronted was that of classifying and organizing different wetland types. Florida's wetland diversity is surpassed by a bewildering variety of wetland types across the United States. Prior to the late 1970s, there existed a rich vocabulary of regional wetland terminology and a host of wetland classification schemata—none of which proved satisfactory to the team of scientists preparing to inventory the nation's wetlands. To correct this problem, the team produced a new wetland classification scheme that could be used anywhere in the United States. Indeed, the elaborate *Classification of Wetlands and Deepwater Habitats of the United States* is not only the most frequently cited wetland classification scheme in this country, it also has been adopted for use in many foreign countries as well.[34]

In addition, FWS personnel had to settle upon a methodology for inventorying wetlands. Since relatively inexpensive satellite imagery is not accurate enough to identify myriad small wetlands, and deploying biologists into the field to engage in exhaustive ground-level surveys of all of the nation's wetlands would be prohibitively expensive, the FWS decided to analyze aerial photography. Even the examination of air photos for the entire United States would be prohibitively expensive and would take many years to complete, so a group of statisticians and other scientists from Colorado State University led by W. E. Frayer created a sampling design of 3,635 sample plots (each of which is 2 square miles) from all over the lower forty-eight states. Results could then be extrapolated from this sample to provide valid estimates of wetland acreage for the entire country (minus Alaska and Hawaii). Some states, such as Florida, had a sufficient number of sample plots to develop estimates of wetlands in these states.[35]

Confounding any analysis of twentieth-century wetland inventories are wildly different results produced by authors covering the same time period.[36] For example, John Hefner used Florida's 656 sample plots from the NWI's first nationwide study to estimate changes in the acreage of Florida wetlands from the 1950s to the 1970s. His analysis suggests that in the middle 1950s, Florida had approximately 12,779,000 acres of wetlands—about 4.4 million acres *fewer* than the aforementioned Shaw and Fredine's middle-1950s estimate for Florida. This is a problem in and of itself, but the implications of this estimate extend back to the early 1900s. Hefner claims that Florida had just 11,334,000 acres remaining as of the middle 1970s—translating into what he claims is a twenty-year loss between the mid-1950s and mid-1970s of 1,455,000 acres (or 727,500 acres every ten years)—during an era that W. E. Frayer and John Hefner claim is the peak of wetland loss in Florida. If Hefner's estimate for the 1950s is correct, and if the original estimate of 20.3 million acres is even close to correct, Florida may have lost over 7.5 million acres of wetlands in the first five decades of the twentieth century. Therefore, Florida would have to have lost more than twice as many wetlands (1.5 million acres) per decade for five consecutive decades in the early twentieth century before the "peak loss" period beginning in the middle 1950s (in which less than 750,000 acres of wetlands were lost each decade).[37]

As figure 5.1 reveals, Florida's population grew by just over 2.2 million in the half century between 1900 and 1950; but it grew by more than 4 million in the twenty years between 1950 and 1970. One might be tempted to agree with Frayer and Hefner that wetland loss in Florida peaked during the decades following World War II. Yet any attempt to correlate population growth with wetland loss is fraught with difficulty, in large measure because wetland loss across the nation in this era is more closely related to changes in agricultural land use. Unfortunately, much of the available agricultural land-use data obtained since 1900 is not directly comparable.[38]

Adding to the confusion are investigators who have used satellite imagery in an effort to inventory wetlands. For example, Paul Hampson prepared a map of Florida wetlands based on satellite imagery taken between 1972 and 1974. His analysis of satellite imagery suggests that Florida had just over 8.3 million acres of wetlands in the middle 1970s. In addition, Randy Kautz made use of late 1980s satellite data in an effort to create a wildlife habitat map of Florida. He estimates that Florida had approximately 8.2 million acres of wetlands during the late 1980s. (Recall that Hefner used a sample of air photos to develop an estimate of over 11.3 million acres of wetlands in Florida during the middle 1970s.) Satellite data have the advantage of being very comprehensive; we can obtain imagery for the entire state at a reasonable cost. Unfortunately, such images suffer from less than ideal resolution.

Christopher F. Meindl

In other words, we cannot accurately determine as much from these satellite images as we can from readily available (but more expensive and less comprehensive) air photos. During the early 1990s, the Federal Geographic Data Committee confirmed that conventional aerial photo interpretation techniques lead to more accurate determination of wetlands than relying upon satellite data.[39]

In any event, by the early 1970s, the nation's deteriorating environment led an increasingly impatient public to demand environmental protection—even for wetlands. In 1972, Congress responded by amending what has become known as the Clean Water Act by creating (among other items) section 404, a provision that gives the U.S. Army Corps of Engineers authority to issue (or deny) permits for disposing of dredged or fill material into waters of the United States, including wetlands. After nearly two centuries of encouraging economic development through structural modifications of the landscape (including wetland drainage), the corps initially resisted its new mission, but it has finally become somewhat more of an obstacle to wetland loss. Indeed, the corps is now caught in the cross fire between developers who see no reason why they should be prevented from using their property as they see fit (including draining and filling wetlands) and environmental advocates who fear the loss of wetland functions and values with the approval of each new ditch. Environmentalists have attacked the corps' wetland-permitting record in Florida, citing the corps' own data that the COE approved over 25,000 permits to develop wetlands (most of them very small) in Florida between January 1993 and June 2001 while denying only 34 such permit applications. Corps staffers admit they are overrun with permit applications and that they are under pressure to "speed up" the permitting process—but it is also true that the wetland permitting process leads many applicants and potential applicants to either cancel their development plans or modify them in order to protect wetlands.[40]

The impact of section 404 and other wetland protection legislation can be seen in the NWI's wetland status and trends report covering the middle 1970s to the middle 1980s. Frayer and Hefner found that Florida had 11,298,600 acres of wetlands in the mid-1970s and 11,038,300 acres in the mid-1980s. This translates into a gross loss of 260,030 acres of wetlands during the ten-year period—substantially less than the losses Hefner claims for the 1950s to 1970s. Today, the Clean Water Act's section 404 is among a couple dozen federal statutes that help protect (usually indirectly) the nation's wetlands. One of the more important and direct methods of wetland protection came near the end of 1985 with the passage of the so-called "swamp-buster" provision of that year's Farm Bill. Before the swampbuster law, many farmers not only received federal government subsidies for crops produced on wetlands that had been recently converted to cropland, they even received technical and financial assistance from the USDA to help them drain wetlands to begin with. Congress put an end to this practice by eliminating all subsidies to farmers who drained wetlands to produce crops. While this does not prohibit farmers from draining wetlands to raise crops for which no subsidy is received, it substantially reduces wetland drainage incentives for many farmers. Finally, in early 1989, President George Bush announced his support for a policy of "no net loss" of wetlands. The idea behind this catchy phrase is that for each acre of destroyed wetlands, at least one acre of wetlands must be created elsewhere. Such a policy, however, hinges on the shaky assumption that created wetlands will provide the same functions and values as natural wetlands. Not only has wetland creation thus far failed more often than not, there is also the problem of "new" wetlands being so far from a developed site that for all practical purposes, the developed site effectively loses functions and values formerly provided by wetlands.[41]

Meanwhile, in Florida prior to the 1980s, state law provided only indirect protection for wetlands. For example, in Florida Statute 403.021, the legislature declared that it was public policy to conserve water and maintain its quality. Such a statute provides only implicit recognition of wetlands' role in enhancing water quality. In 1984, however, the Florida legislature remedied this shortcoming by passing the Warren S. Henderson Wetlands Protection Act, explicitly recognizing the role of wetlands in maintaining water resources. The Henderson Act authorized the state's Department of Environmental Regulation (now the Department of Environmental Protection, or DEP) to adopt rules and regulatory programs to help protect wetlands. According to Florida's DEP, Florida does not have a goal of no net loss in terms of wetland *acreage*; but its regulatory rules are written and implemented in such a manner that attempts to achieve no net loss of wetland *function*. This has become an important issue in recent years as it has become clear that different wetlands (natural and created) provide different functions and benefits.[42]

The value of additional wetland protection legislation can be seen in a recent wetland inventory. In a report published in 2003, the NWI examined wetland changes from 1985 to 1996. Although Frayer and Hefner estimated that Florida had just over 11 million acres of wetlands in the middle 1980s, Thomas Dahl reports that Florida really had about 11,455,000 acres of wetlands in 1985. Dahl explained that his 1985 estimate is higher than Frayer and Hefner's mid-1980s figure because he had access to more detailed aerial photographs that allowed a more precise accounting of traditionally hard to determine forested wetlands (Dahl, personal communication). In any event, Dahl contends that Florida had approximately 11.4 million acres of wetlands in 1996, representing a total loss of some 55,000 acres during the eleven-year period. Clearly, Florida's rate of wetland loss has declined dramatically since the 1950s, probably the result of both federal and state wetland protection policies enacted since 1972.[43]

Wetland losses in the Sunshine State have been mirrored by similar losses across the nation. Florida probably had at least 20.3 million acres of the lower forty-eight states' total of 221 million acres wetlands as of the 1780s. Accordingly, Florida's wetlands probably covered at least 59 percent of the state while covering just 11 percent of the lower forty-eight states. By the 1990s, however, Florida probably had about 11.4 million acres of wetlands, representing a loss of almost 44 percent (therefore, the state is now roughly 30 percent wetland). Meanwhile, the lower forty-eight states probably had around 105 million acres of wetlands in the 1990s, representing a loss of approximately 52 percent since the 1780s (meaning the conterminous United States is now about 5 percent wetland). Florida may have lost a smaller percentage of its original wetland base than the national average, but because it began with far more wetlands than any other state, it lost more acres than any other state. Finally, although Florida's percentage of wetlands lost since the 1780s is a bit below the national average, some states have lost an even smaller percentage of their wetlands (Montana, 27 percent; Georgia, 23 percent; and New Hampshire, only 9 percent), while others lost a much larger percentage of their original wetland base (Indiana, Missouri, Iowa and Ohio, between 87 and 90 percent; California 91 percent).[44]

Florida has always been practically synonymous with water, and indeed, the state was born from water. Much of Florida's dirt and underlying geology reveals that virtually all of the state used to form part of the ocean floor. Yet even after modern Florida's most recent emergence from the sea (it appears to have been repeatedly submerged and exposed over the past several million years), Florida's soggy landscape helped retard its growth and development. In 1880, for example, while Florida (almost 60 percent wetland) had just 269,493 people—nearby South Carolina (originally about one-third wetland) counted just under 1 million residents; Alabama (not even one-quarter wetland) had over 1.2 million; and Georgia (originally just over 18 percent wet-land) had over 1.5 million people. Toward the end of the nineteenth century, people began to modify this watery wilderness sticking off the southeast corner of the United States. As Nelson Blake's aptly titled book makes clear, Floridians busied themselves turning *Land into Water* (especially along the coast where wetlands were converted into beaches or a series of finger-shaped strips of residential property surrounded by canals)—and turning *Water into Land* (draining wetlands for urban and agricultural develop-ment).[45]

What is not entirely clear is how much of Florida was wetland when Con-gress granted the state ownership of all its unsold swamps in the middle nineteenth century. Florida officials claimed to have had more than 22 mil-lion acres of wetlands but ultimately received title to 20.3 million acres from the federal government. We may be correct in accepting that Florida had over 20 million acres of wetlands in 1850, but problems remain. No one doubts that millions of acres of Florida wetlands have been converted to farms and urban areas, but how do we rectify Shaw's and Fredine's 1954 estimate of 17.2 million acres of wetlands with Hefner's mid-1950s estimate of just under 12.8 million? Alternatively, if we accept Hefner's 1955 estimate of nearly 12.8 million acres of swamps, marshes, and mangroves—how could such a thinly populated state have drained some 7.5 million acres of wetlands between 1907 and 1955, when Frayer and Hefner argue that much of the drainage was accomplished in the post–World War II era up to the 1970s?

What *is* clear is that the rate of wetland loss in Florida has slowed dramati-cally since the middle twentieth century. Although there is much uncertainty regarding how many wetlands Florida may have lost during the first half of the twentieth century, two separate studies suggest that Florida had about 11.3 million acres in the 1970s. Dahl's 1996 estimate of 11.4 million wetland acres for Florida indicates that earlier estimates probably missed some hard-to-detect wetlands (especially forested swamps). Increased public awareness of wetland functions and values—and public policies intended to protect Flor-ida's remaining wetlands—appear to have greatly reduced the rate of wetland loss in the Sunshine State.[46]

Defenders of Florida's wetlands would do well to resist the urge to rest in light of recent success. Massive migration into Florida continues to fuel ever-increasing demand for additional land and water resources. Researchers at the University of Florida forecast the state's population will swell to over 24 million by 2030. Although many Florida wetlands are protected, many others

Christopher F. Meindl

are not—and natural wetlands are increasingly "sacrificed" to development while at least nominally being replaced by "created" or restored wetlands. The scientific literature cautions against assuming that created wetlands will function the same way as natural wetlands. So far, it appears that *restored* swamps and marshes are more likely to function like "natural" wetlands than are upland landscapes that have been reshaped into "created" wetlands. Yet many ecologists insist that we can eventually learn how to restore and create wetlands that provide substantial functions and values to people. More insidious, however, is the threat from below the surface. Many wetlands are wet because they receive seepage from groundwater or nearby springs. Florida's phenomenal population growth continues to significantly increase demand for water, much of it pumped from the ground. Withdrawals of groundwater for public consumption could reduce water tables to the point that some wetlands and springs dry up. Some might call such talk needlessly alarmist, but who would have thought in 1950 that Florida's population of less than 3 million would have ballooned to nearly 16 million in just a half century?[47]

Notes

1. Edward A. Fernald and Elizabeth D. Purdum, eds., *Atlas of Florida* (Gainesville: University Press of Florida, 1992), 2; Steven Davis and John Ogden, eds., *Everglades: The Ecosystem and Its Restoration* (Delray Beach, Fla.: St. Lucie Press, 1994); K. A. Tzoumis, "Wetland Policy Making in the U.S. Congress from 1789 to 1995," *Wetlands* 18 (December 1998): 447–59.

2. David Moss, "Historic Changes in Terminology for Wetlands," *Coastal Zone Management Journal* 8 (1980): 215–25; U.S. Army Corps of Engineers (USACOE), *USACOE Wetlands Delineation Manual*, U.S. Army Engineers Waterway Experiment Station Technical Report Y-87-1 (1987): 12; National Research Council, *Wetlands: Characteristics and Boundaries* (Washington, D.C.: National Academy Press, 1995); William J. Mitsch and James G. Gosselink, *Wetlands*, 3rd ed. (New York: John Wiley, 2000).

3. David Policansky, "Science and Decision Making for Water Resources," *Ecological Applications* 8 (August 1998): 610–18; Jon Kusler, "Wetlands Delineations: An Issue of Science or Politics?" *Environment* 34 (March 1992): 7–11, 29–37.

4. Mitsch and Gosselink, *Wetlands*, 571–91.

5. Katherine C. Ewel, "Swamps," in *Ecosystems of Florida*, ed. Ronald L. Myers and John J. Ewel (Gainesville: University Presses of Florida, 1990), 285.

6. Ibid., 281–323.

7. Ibid.; Kathryn Ziewitz and June Wiaz, *Green Empire: The St. Joe Company and the Remaking of Florida's Panhandle* (Gainesville: University Press of Florida, 2004).

8. Ewel, "Swamps," 281–323.

9. Ibid.; Edward A. Fernald and Donald J. Patton, eds., *Water Resources Atlas of*

Florida (Tallahassee: Florida State University, Institute of Science and Public Affairs, 1984).

10. James A. Kushlan, "Freshwater Marshes," in *Ecosystems of Florida,* ed. Ronald L. Myers and John J. Ewel (Gainesville: University Presses of Florida, 1990), 324–63.

11. Ibid., 324–63.

12. Ibid., 334.

13. Clay L. Montague and Richard G. Wiegert, "Salt Marshes," in *Ecosystems of Florida,* ed. Ronald L. Myers and John J. Ewel (Gainesville: University Presses of Florida, 1990), 490.

14. Ibid., 481–516.

15. Ibid., 487.

16. William E. Odum and Carole C. McIvor, "Mangroves," in *Ecosystems of Florida,* edited by Ronald L. Myers and John J. Ewel (Gainesville: University Presses of Florida, 1990), 517–48.

17. Ibid.

18. New England salt marshes are a partial exception to this generalization because people have used the salt hay from these marshes to feed livestock for centuries. See Robert LeBlanc, "The Differential Perception of Salt Marshes by the Folk and Elite in the 19th Century," *Proceedings of the Association of American Geographers* 5 (1973) 138–43. Likewise, the wetland-dominated landscape of southern Louisiana has been home to Cajuns and others for several centuries. See Gay Gomez, *A Wetland Biography: Seasons on Louisiana's Chenier Plain* (Austin: University of Texas Press, 1998).

19. As quoted in Nelson M. Blake, *Land into Water/Water into Land: A History of Water Management in Florida* (Gainesville: University Presses of Florida, 1980), 13.

20. Christopher F. Meindl, "Past Perceptions of the Great American Wetland: Florida's Everglades during the Early Twentieth Century," *Environmental History* 5 (July 2000): 378–95; Ann Vileisis, *Discovering the Unknown Landscape: A History of America's Wetlands* (Washington, D.C.: Island Press, 1997); Roger A. Winsor, "Environmental Imagery of the Wet Prairie of East Central Illinois, 1820–1920," *Journal of Historical Geography* 13 (1987): 375–97; Kenneth Thompson, "Insalubrious California: Perception and Reality," *Annals of the Association of American Geographers* 59 (March 1969): 50–64.

21. The quotation from Buckingham Smith's report can be found in the following: U.S. Senate, 62nd Cong., 1st sess., 1911, Document 89, *Everglades of Florida, Acts, Reports, and other Papers, State and National, Relating to the Everglades of the State of Florida and their Reclamation* (Washington, D.C.: Government Printing Office), 52; Thomas E. Dahl, *Wetlands: Losses in the United States 1780s to 1980s* (Washington, D.C.: U.S. Department of the Interior, Fish and Wildlife Service, 1990).

22. In this regard, see the first two chapters of Bill Belleville's *River of Lakes: A Journey on Florida's St. Johns River* (Athens: University of Georgia Press, 200). Belleville makes frequent use of the term "reclamation" as he discusses efforts by the St. Johns River Management District to restore marshes that had been drained for agriculture.

23. Samuel P. Shaw and C. Gordon Fredine, *Wetlands of the United States: Their*

Extent and Their Value to Waterfowl and other Wildlife, Fish and Wildlife Service Circular 39 (Washington, D.C.: U.S. Department of the Interior, 1956); James O. Wright, *Swamp and Overflowed Lands in the United States: Ownership and Reclamation,* Office of Experiment Stations Circular 76 (Washington, D.C.: U.S. Department of Agriculture, 1907).

24. Dahl, *Wetlands 1780s to 1980s*; Ary J. Lamme and Christopher F. Meindl, "A Vibrant Cultural Boundary in Florida," *Southeastern Geographer* 42 (November 2002): 274–95.

25. Linda D. Vance, *May Mann Jennings: Florida's Genteel Activist* (Gainesville: University Press of Florida, 1985); Luther J. Carter, *The Florida Experience: Land and Water Policy in a Growth State* (Baltimore: Johns Hopkins University Press, 1974); J. Dovell, "A History of the Everglades of Florida" (Ph.D. diss., University of North Carolina, 1947); Alfred J. Hanna and Kathryn A. Hanna, *Lake Okeechobee: Wellspring of the Everglades* (Indianapolis: Bobbs-Merrill, 1948); Hugh Prince, *Wetlands of the American Midwest* (Chicago: University of Chicago Press, 1997); Christopher F. Meindl, "On the Eve of Destruction: People and Florida's Everglades from the Late 1800s to 1908," *Tequesta* 63 (2003): 5–36.

26. Belleville, *River of Lakes,* 15–16.

27. David McCally, *The Everglades: An Environmental History* (Gainesville: University Press of Florida, 1999); A. B. Bottcher and F. T. Izuno, eds., *Everglades Agricultural Area* (Gainesville: University Press of Florida, 1994); J. E. Dovell, "Thomas Elmer Will, Twentieth-Century Pioneer," *Tequesta* 8 (1948): 21–55; Christopher F. Meindl, "Frank Stoneman and the Florida Everglades during the Early Twentieth Century," *Florida Geographer* 29 (1998): 44–54.

28. Wright, *Swamp and Overflowed Lands in the United States,* 7.

29. Ibid., 8.

30. Ibid.; Shaw and Fredine, *Wetlands of the United States*; Christopher F. Meindl, Derek H. Alderman, and Peter Waylen, "On the Importance of Environmental Claims-Making: The Role of James O. Wright in Promoting the Drainage of Florida's Everglades in the Early Twentieth Century," *Annals of the Association of American Geographers* 92 (December 2002): 682–701; Aaron Purcell, "Plumb Lines, Politics and Projections: The Florida Everglades and the Wright Report Controversy," *Florida Historical Quarterly* 80 (fall 2001): 161–97.

31. Ralph Stoutamire, *Drainage and Water Control in Florida,* Department of Agriculture Bulletin 51 (Tallahassee: State of Florida, 1931); L. C. Gray, O. E. Baker, F. J. Marschner, and B. O. Weitz, "The Utilization of Our Lands for Crops, Pasture and Forests," in U.S. Department of Agriculture, *Agriculture Yearbook 1923* (Washington, D.C.: U.S. Government Printing Office, 1923), 425.

32. Shaw and Fredine, *Wetlands in the United States,* 17.

33. B. O. Wilen and M. K. Bates, "The U.S. Fish and Wildlife Service's National Wetlands Inventory Project," *Vegetatio* 118 (1995): 153–69; Dahl, *Wetlands 1780s to 1980s.*

34. Moss, "Historic Wetland Terminology"; L. M. Cowardin, V. Carter, F. C. Golet, and E. T. LaRoe, *Classification of Wetlands and Deepwater Habitats of the United States* (Washington, D.C.: U.S. Fish and Wildlife Service, 1979).

35. Wilen and Bates, "National Wetlands Inventory Project, 1995"; W. E. Frayer, T. J. Monahan, D. C. Bowden, and F. A. Graybill, *Status and Trends of Wetlands and Deepwater Habitats in the Conterminous Unites States, 1950s to 1970s* (Fort Collins: Colorado State University, 1983).

36. Variation of wetland estimates between authors is not unique to Florida. See R. Harold Brown, *The Greening of Georgia: The Improvement of the Environment in the Twentieth Century* (Macon, Ga.: Mercer University Press, 2002), 45.

37. John M. Hefner, "Wetlands in Florida: 1950s to 1970s," *Proceedings of the Conference: Managing Cumulative Effects in Florida Wetlands,* ed. E. D. Estevez, J. Miller, J. Morris, and R. Hamman (Madison, Wisc.: Omnipress, 1986), 23–31; W. E. Frayer and John M. Hefner, *Florida Wetlands: Status and Trends, 1970s to 1980s* (Atlanta: U.S. Fish and Wildlife Service, 1991).

38. Thomas E. Dahl, *Status and Trends of Wetlands in the Conterminous United States, 1986 to 1997* (Washington, D.C.: U.S. Department of the Interior, Fish and Wildlife Service, 2000); Thomas E. Dahl, Craig E. Johnson, and W. E. Frayer, *Status and Trends of Wetlands in the Conterminous United States, Mid-1970s to Mid-1980s* (Washington, D.C.: U.S. Department of the Interior, Fish and Wildlife Service, 1991).

39. Randy S. Kautz, "Space Age Habitat Mapping," *Florida Wildlife* 45 (May/June 1991): 30–33; Paul S. Hampson, *Wetlands in Florida,* Florida Bureau of Geology Map Series 109, (Tallahassee: Florida Bureau of Geology, 1984); Federal Geographic Data Committee (FGDC), *Application of Satellite Data for Mapping and Monitoring Wetlands,* FGDC Wetlands Subcommittee Technical Report 1 (Reston, Va.: U.S. Geological Survey, 1992).

40. Roy R. Carriker, "Wetlands and Environmental Legislation Issues," *Journal of Agricultural and Applied Economics* 26 (July 1994): 80–89; Derek Catron, "Wetlands under Siege," *Daytona Beach News-Journal,* January 27, 2002; David Sunding and David Zilberman, "The Economics of Environmental Regulation by Licensing: An Assessment of Recent Changes to the Wetland Permitting Process," *Natural Resources Journal* 42 (winter 2002): 59–90.

41. Frayer and Hefner, "Florida Wetlands 1970s to 1980s"; Ralph E. Heimlich, Keith D. Wiebe, Roger Claassen, Dwight Gadsby, and Robert M. House, *Wetlands and Agriculture: Private Interests and Public Benefits* (Washington, D.C.: U.S. Department of Agriculture, Economic Research Service, 1998); P. H. Brown and C. L. Lant, "The Effect of Wetland Mitigation Banking on the Achievement of No-Net-Loss," *Environmental Management* 23 (April 1999): 333–45; U.S. General Accounting Office, *Wetlands Overview: Problems with Acreage Data Persist,* GAO/RCED-98-150 (1998) July.

42. David Gluckman, "The History behind the Legislative History of the Cumulative Effects of Wetland Destruction," *Proceedings of the Conference,* 229–34; *Summary of the Wetland and Other Surface Water Regulatory and Proprietary Programs in Florida,* May 22, 2002, accessed on September 22, 2003, at www.dep.state.fl.us/water/wetlands/docs/erp/overview.pdf; Christopher F. Meindl, "Wetland Diversity: The Limits of Generalization," *Journal of Geography* (forthcoming).

43. Thomas Dahl, *Florida's Wetlands: An Update on Status and Trends, 1985 to 1996* (Washington, D.C.: U.S. Department of the Interior, Fish and Wildlife Service, 2003).

Christopher F. Meindl

44. Dahl, *Wetlands 1780s to 1980s*, 6; Dahl, *Status and Trends of Wetlands*, 9.

45. Anthony F. Randazzo and Douglas S. Jones, eds., *The Geology of Florida* (Gainesville: University Press of Florida, 1997); Blake, *Land into Water/Water into Land*.

46. Tzuomis, "Wetland Policy Making," 447–59.

47. The University of Florida's Bureau of Economic and Business Research is constantly engaged in forecasting Florida's population, and the figures cited in this section are found at www.napa.ufl.edu/2003news/population.htm; William J. Mitsch, Xinyuan Wu, Robert W. Narin, Paul E. Weihe, Maiming Wang, Robert Deal, and Charles E. Boucher, "Creating and Restoring Wetlands," *BioScience* 48 (December 1998): 1019–30; Dennis F. Whigham, "Ecological Issues Related to Wetland Preservation, Restoration, Creation, and Assessment," *Science of the Total Environment* 240 (1999): 31–40.

Part 2

Science, Technology, and Public Policy

Chapter 6

The Everglades and the Florida Dream

David McCally

There is an old joke about the Florida East Coast Railway. Infamous for its leisurely pace and frequent stops, the line's trains often tried the patience of their passengers. On one particularly slow run, the story goes, a woman became so exasperated that she approached the conductor, seeking an explanation for the train's failure to meet its schedule. "Conductor," the lady demanded, "can't you run any faster than this?" to which the quick-witted conductor supposedly replied, "Yes, ma'am, I can, but I've gotta' stay with the train."

The engineers and scientists who have only recently completed a massive restudy of south Florida's water-control system, like the bemused conductor, found themselves hampered with the necessity of staying with an unsatisfactory vehicle: namely, the legacy of the Florida dream. The definition of the Florida dream, like that of pornography, remains elusive, even while observers readily recognize its physical manifestations. In the case of the Florida dream, these physical manifestations assume three major forms: the idyllic days of beachside ease, the promise of subtropical agriculture, and the vision of a verdant suburbia. If these expressions of the Florida dream seem too eclectic to characterize any single idea, then the extreme environmental restructuring that so many of these beaches, farms, and suburbs underwent will provide the analytic insight required to understand at least the nature of the dream.

The Florida dream represents a variant of the American desire for a better life in a new world, except that Florida offered Americans a world not only new but also exotic. Like the lover who embraces his\her beloved in spite of the other's flaws, Americans have drawn Florida into their hearts, secure in the knowledge that the state's shortcomings could be corrected over time. But, as so many lovers have discovered, correcting shortcomings too often destroys the very qualities that excited passions in the first place. Similarly, in Florida, the attraction of an exotic world excited dreams that led to the destruction of the very stuff upon which the dream rested, and the Everglades, the most exotic feature of south Florida, endured the most thoroughgoing restructuring of all.

Beginning in 1983, the State of Florida and the federal government devised a new plan for south Florida and its surface water. It took until October 1998 for this process to come to fruition, when the United States Army Corps of Engineers issued the *Central and Southern Florida Project Comprehensive Review Study,* a complex blueprint that promised not only to ensure the adequacy of south Florida's freshwater supply but also to restore the environmental health of the beleaguered Everglades.[1] As a piece of environmental engineering, the *Comprehensive Review Study* (which served as the blueprint for the Comprehensive Everglades Restoration Project passed by Congress in 2000) has been heavily influenced by the Florida dream, and it is herein that the problems with the study lie.

Formulated only after receiving contributions from dozens of diverse groups, the *Comprehensive Review Study* represents a social document that expresses what I call the social epistemology of the Florida dream. That is, the study expresses the *way* in which a broad range of Floridians *know* how to solve their society's problems. These solutions involve three elements, and science represents the most important component of Florida's social episte-

David McCally

mology. Science will save us, Floridians tend to agree, but few stop to consider the social context that guides scientific inquiry. The political process represents the next element in the state's social epistemology. The politics of the negotiated consensus and the rule of law, most residents fervently believe, will result in the greatest good to the greatest number. A simplistic economic principle represents the final element of Florida's social epistemology. An economy based on ever-increasing consumption and continuous growth, Floridians argue, will solve all the problems that have plagued human beings since at least the dawn of history. Taken together, these three elements constitute the underpinnings upon which any attempt to restore the Everglades rests, and this social epistemology will ultimately determine the success or failure of any effort to restore the environmental health of south Florida.

The *Comprehensive Review Study* represents the latest in a long line of scientific studies of the Everglades. Granted, its predecessors can in no way compare with this most recent effort for sheer size, but each, in its own way, represents the flowering of its own era's scientific knowledge. Each also contains flaws that would only become apparent after its implementation, and each represents what Cathleen C. Vogel has so aptly characterized as a "volatile mix of science and politics."[2] Examining the *Comprehensive Review Study* as a step in a historical process will provide Floridians with a more realistic appraisal of what to expect from this, only the latest, plan to exert human control over the Everglades.

The history of the scientific study of the Everglades begins in 1847, when Buckingham Smith, a Harvard-educated attorney who resided at St. Augustine, made what he called a "reconnoissance" of the region at the behest of the United States Treasury. Smith spent some three months on his reconnaissance, sailing along the coast and exploring the various streams that flowed from the 6,200-square-mile interior wetlands, before he concluded that the entire region could be effectively drained at a cost of from $300,000 to $500,000, while creating hundreds of thousands of fertile acres suitable for farming. Although his efforts appear cursory to the modern observer, Smith assured his approving employers that he had "obtained all the information within my power, as to that portion of the peninsula below 28 degrees north latitude," and his opinions did, indeed, reflect state-of-the-art scientific knowledge of his day.[3]

The studies that followed the Smith Report had three characteristics in common. All of these studies—the Wright Report of 1911; the Mead, Metcalf, and Hazen Report of 1912; the Randolph Report of 1913; the Everglades Engineering Board of Review Report in 1927; and the *Comprehensive Report on Central and Southern Florida for Flood Control and Other Purposes* of 1949, which formed the basis for the system now in place—rested on the finest scientific data that were available when they were written. In addition, each of these reports came in the wake of challenges to the vision of unlimited growth, and each reiterated the idea that a properly managed environment would provide the foundation for the fruition of the Florida dream.

Beginning in 1906, the drainage of the Everglades started without any study at all. Florida's governor, Napoleon Bonaparte Broward, believed that drainage of the state's interior wetlands depended on nothing more than gravity. Indeed, he ran for governor on the campaign slogan "water will run downhill." That is, he believed that the elevation of the surface of Lake Okee-chobee divided by the distance between the lake and the coast guaranteed sufficient fall for canals, without pumps, to accomplish drainage, and he remained untroubled by any thoughts of complications. After only a hurried survey, the governor chose the Fourth of July 1906 to set the dredge *Everglades* to work in the New River at Fort Lauderdale, and the era of Everglades drainage came to life.[4]

In order to get the state legislature to approve his drainage scheme, Broward had to create a political consensus in favor of the enterprise. In 1906, by far the majority of the state's citizens lived in the northern tier of counties, and they did not want their tax dollars to pay for what they viewed as the foolishness going on down south. Because of this political reality, Broward established the Everglades Drainage District in 1905, with the mandate that all drainage operations would be paid for by the sale of reclaimed land or by a drainage tax levied on real estate within the district. Growth, the governor believed, would pay for the expenses of draining the wetlands.

But events proved Broward wrong. The railroads, which owned most of the land within the drainage district, challenged the drainage tax in court, and the sale of undrained land proved difficult. At this juncture, Richard J. Bolles, a land developer from Colorado, expressed an interest in Everglades real estate, and Broward agreed to sell him 500,000 acres of land for $1 million. The state agreed that the purchase price would be applied to the excavation of the proposed system of five drainage canals, and Bolles hoped to realize a huge profit from the sale of the land these ditches would reclaim—seemingly a good deal for both parties.[5]

Bolles proved himself a most adept salesman. Even though the land he owned had been neither surveyed nor drained, the promoter set about arousing interest in his tract. Bolles enticed prospective buyers with the promise that a ten-acre plot of Everglades land could provide the basis for a successful truck farm, and he assured his prospects that Florida's mild winters meant that their produce would arrive at the market during a time of scarcity. To further stimulate interest, Bolles devised a lottery scheme. Under this plan, the size of the farms varied—8,000 were of ten acres, 3,620 were twenty acres, 250 were forty acres, 100 were eighty acres, twenty were 160 acres, eight were 320 acres, and two were 640 acres. Even though all buyers would pay $240 for a ten-acre plot, the exact location and size of the individual parcels would be determined by a drawing after all of the land had been sold. Bolles's lottery proved so successful that by March 1911 more than 10,000 farms had been sold, and Bolles offered reduced train fares so that the new owners could come to Fort Lauderdale for the drawing.[6]

The drawing caused Bolles's bold scheme to flounder. When the excited new landowners arrived in Fort Lauderdale, they found a carnival atmosphere where optimism knew no bounds, but everything changed after Bolles held his lottery. It was then that gullible northerners—most of whom had bought their real estate sight unseen—discovered that water still covered their land, and to make matters worse, few could be sure of the exact location of their plots since surveying remained sketchy. Outraged, many of Bolles's customers demanded their money back, but the promoter responded by blaming the state for not following through on its promise to provide drainage and refused to accommodate them. With few options, most of the Everglades landowners gave vent to their anger by stopping payment of their installments, an action that not only affected the promoter's profits but also imperiled the state's drainage scheme, since defaulting landowners could hardly be expected to pay drainage taxes.

In response to this threat to their version of the Florida dream, boosters turned to science. The newly formed U.S. Department of Agriculture's Bureau of Irrigation and Drainage Investigations had been created to offer scientific assessments of the many drainage and irrigation projects that had sprung up around the country during the early years of the twentieth century. Speculative in nature, these projects offered Americans the promise of economic growth associated with new agricultural frontiers, but potential investors preferred to place their trust in scientific assessments rather than in the claims of the land salesmen, whom they feared could not be completely trusted. For their part, Florida's land salesmen hoped that the bureau's upcoming report would resuscitate their venture.

The Wright Report on the feasibility of Everglades drainage provides the best historical example of the volatile mix that science and politics can create. Wright, the drainage engineer who wrote the report, allowed his professional judgment to be swayed by the politics of land development that dominated the Florida political scene during the early years of the twentieth century. While writing the report, Wright formed a close alliance with Florida's Governor Napoleon Bonaparte Broward and U.S. Senator Duncan U. Fletcher. Both men ardently supported drainage of the Everglades, and both freely engaged in land speculation. For his part, Wright allowed their enthusiasms, and his ambitions, to color the paper that he wrote for the Bureau of Irrigation and Drainage Investigations.

Wright was a man on the make. Earlier in his career, while working for the bureau in North Carolina, the drainage engineer demonstrated little concern about conflicts of interest between his role as a federal official and that of private investor. While working in his official capacity on the Mattamuskeet Lake reclamation project, Wright became financially involved with companies interested in that project, and he even lobbied the North Carolina legislature on their behalf. Circumstantial evidence supports the conclusion that Wright hoped to use his official position to help himself, and others, profit from Everglades land as well.[7]

Wright's draft of the Everglades report contained egregious errors, all of which added to the optimism of drainage boosters. These errors were especially glaring with regard to the relationships among rainfall, evaporation, and runoff. Wright calculated evaporation at nine inches per month, even though there were only two months during the year when, on average, that amount of rain fell in the Everglades. This meant, according to a colleague's testimony before a congressional committee, that "there would be no runoff whatever." Indeed, extrapolating from Wright's calculations led his fellow drainage engineer to the conclusion that Lake Okeechobee "would finally dry up," because rainfall could not be expected to maintain its water level.[8]

The controversy over Wright's report began in May 1909, when he submitted a draft of it to his superiors at the bureau, and came to a head in February 1912, when the Moss Committee in the U.S. House of Representatives conducted hearings to investigate the bureau's role in the hotly controversial sale of land in the Everglades. Committee members discovered that during the sales campaign, Bolles's land agents freely quoted Wright's optimistic appraisal of drainage prospects and provided excerpts from his as yet unpublished report to their prospective buyers. In addition, the State of

Florida gave wide circulation to these excerpts following the disastrous lottery drawing, despite the debate within the bureau over their accuracy, after Broward, Wright, and Fletcher colluded to make the information public. Intended to head off a crisis, the state's release of these portions of the Wright report had the opposite effect. As testimony before the Moss Committee grew more damning, the public came to accept the notion that both the federal government and Florida's state government conspired with land developers to dupe the general public into buying land by the gallon in the Everglades.

Wright's actions during the controversy over his report leave little doubt that he committed fraud, but no one has accused anyone connected with today's *Comprehensive Review Study* of any form of dishonesty. Indeed, the number of professionals engaged in the study would require a conspiracy worthy of an *X Files* plot to perpetrate such chicanery in the new restudy. But historians of science have long argued that science, like any other human activity, is socially embedded. By this they mean that scientists can no more escape the values and norms of their society than can any other citizen. This does not mean that scientists knowingly kowtow to the interests of the politically powerful or accommodate the views of the economically well heeled; rather, it implies that the process of scientific investigation conforms to the decision-making process of the larger society as expressed in its social epistemology. In Florida, adherence to the social epistemology means embracing the Florida dream, and in this respect, the *Comprehensive Review Study* closely resembles its predecessors.

Rather than easing the crisis, the Wright Report created an atmosphere poisonous to a speculative venture such as the sale of Everglades land. Indeed, as the Moss Committee hearings would reveal, prospective investors could not trust even the opinions of federal agencies to give them an unbiased appraisal of the prospect of financial success in a newly reclaimed district. Amid this atmosphere of mistrust, land sales virtually ceased. Indeed, one developer ruefully admitted that, by May 1912, "even a ten-acre sale is as rare as a cold day in June."[9]

The desire for profit motivated the people who wanted to develop the Everglades, and they needed a clear-headed business assessment of the practicality of their ventures. Accordingly, on July 23, 1912, the Everglades Land Sales Company hired three nationally known drainage engineers, Leonard Metcalf, Daniel W. Mead, and Allen Hazen, and instructed them to restudy the drainage efforts already in place and to make recommendations for improvements. This group, which became known as the Board of Consulting Engineers, relied on the scientific data they obtained from the state's Internal Improvement Fund, the Army Corps of Engineers, and the United States Weather Service. Additionally, the members of the board traveled extensively within the Everglades, traversing all the canals constructed by the state.

Their report, issued on November 12, 1912, argued that the state's canal system could not drain the entire region, and further, went on to question the economic desirability of such widespread reclamation. The consulting engineers found particular fault with the Miami canal. Running from the shore of Lake Okeechobee to the mouth of the Miami River, the canal provided little drainage; indeed it often ran backward (toward Lake Okeechobee). The canal had, in fact, been constructed at the urging of Miami's boosters, who wanted the city to have access to the new system of canals, touted by former governor Broward as having the dual purpose of drainage and transportation. The drainage engineers pointed out that this canal could not perform either function, since it was too shallow for large boats and lacked the lateral canals necessary for effective drainage. Indeed, the Miami canal often reversed its flow, pushing water back into Lake Okeechobee, after periods of locally heavy rainfall.

But the prescience of the environmental judgments contained in the Mead, Metcalf, and Hazen Report most impress modern readers. The consulting engineers understood that drainage from the upper Everglades threatened the previously high and dry land of the Miami rocklands of the Atlantic Coastal Ridge with flooding, and they also knew that dried organic soils would easily catch fire, destroying the very fertile resource reclamation promised to create. Additionally, the report correctly evaluated the threat of subsidence, which refers to the loss of organic soil elevation due to compaction and the biochemical action of aerobic bacteria (these bacteria literally eat the organic components of the soil), once water has been removed from the surface of the Everglades. Finally, the report demonstrated an understanding of plant succession, arguing that drainage would quickly change marshlands into jungle unless quickly followed by farmers. In light of these environmental realities, the engineers advised their employers that diking and draining limited areas of the wetlands that could be quickly sold and developed made the most economic sense, concluding that "slow, substantial, progressive development" was "ultimately the best for all concerned."[10]

But this news did not meet an enthusiastic reception among those who had staked their political reputations or economic futures on Everglades drainage. In order to breathe new life into the Florida dream of an agricultural cornucopia in the Everglades, the state's politicians initiated their own study. A new scientific survey, these boosters agreed, had the potential to revive Everglades land sales, but only if the new study bore the imprint of engineers of unquestioned ability and rectitude. They found such men in Marshall O. Leighton, Edmund T. Perkins, and Ishom Randolph. No more distinguished panel could be assembled, and its chairman, Ishom Randolph, occupied a position at the very pinnacle of his profession. Randolph had served as the supervising engineer of the Chicago Sanitary District, where he supervised construction of the Chicago Drainage Canal in 1900. This canal reversed the flow of the Chicago River, directing the city's sewage away from Lake Michigan, and the successful completion of the project earned Randolph appointment to the Panama Canal Commission, where he served as the personal technical advisor to President William Howard Taft when he toured the canal in 1908. In 1913, when he accepted the chairmanship of the Everglades Engineering Commission, he was the most respected and trusted civil engineer in the United States.[11]

The commission's findings, known as the Randolph Report, could not have been more in tune with drainage boosters' hopes. The report announced that drainage was not only feasible but also economically viable. The Randolph Report did find fault with the execution of the state's plan, but it reaffirmed the twin ideas that drainage could be accomplished at a reasonable cost and that the reclaimed land would be among the nation's richest. To correct existing shortcomings, the commission proposed widening and deepening the existing drainage canals and constructing a new canal linking Lake Okeechobee with the St. Lucie River. Randolph believed this new canal, with the aid of the Caloosahatchee canal on the western shore, would control the level of the lake, by providing an outlet for water that entered it from the north, and then the expanded drainage canals would have no problem conveying the rainfall that fell in the Everglades proper to the Atlantic Ocean. The total cost of the works, the report maintained, would be around $6.7 million, only $700,000 more than the $6 million bond issue authorized earlier that year by the Florida legislature.[12]

Viewed with the benefit of hindsight, this happy intersection of acceptable cost and desired results seems too good to be true, but no such thoughts troubled the minds of those who believed in Everglades reclamation. From 1913 until 1928, the Randolph Report served as the template for Everglades drainage, but the plan had flaws that became more apparent as drainage proceeded.

Subsidence represented the most glaring flaw. As drainage became more effective, the newly reclaimed soil seemed literally to disappear. Drops in elevation could be quite dramatic in the first years following drainage, nearly 5 feet along the lake's southern shore, and the process continued, slowing but not stopping, as long as the land remained drained. As a result of this subsidence, the relationship between the lowered level of Lake Okeechobee and adjacent land remained roughly the same, forcing farmers to build a dike to keep the lake from inundating their fields during times of heavy rain. Poorly constructed, the dike burst when hurricanes passed over the peninsula during 1926, when more the 600 people died, and in 1928, when at least 2,000 —and likely many more—perished.[13] To make matters worse, the flood of 1928 proved that the St. Lucie control canal could not prevent the lake's overflow during bouts of heavy rain. Completed in 1927, economy measures had reduced its size from that proposed in the Randolph Report, but the 1928 storm would likely have burst the dike even with the increased flow.

The hurricanes of 1926 and of 1928 dealt the Florida dream a one-two punch. The first storm had devastated much of the booming city of Miami and surrounding towns, bringing the prosperity tied to rapidly rising real estate prices to an end. The hurricane that followed destroyed much of the taxable property in the Everglades Drainage District, and this destruction made recovery all the more difficult because funding to build effective public works still had to come from within the district. But this was about to change.

The Great Depression came early to Florida, beginning with the collapse of the land boom after the 1926 hurricane, but the rest of the nation, too, fell into dire economic straits after the stock market crash of October 1929. As the nation struggled to regain its economic footing, its leaders blundered toward a new political consensus. The Great Depression spawned a politics that stressed a more activist role for the federal government in the nation's economy, and an important element of that role would involve public works. Beginning during Herbert Hoover's administration, the nation's political leaders began to see public works spending as a way to prime the nation's failing economic pump. The new political climate greatly benefited those who wanted to further the Florida dream by bringing the federal government's immense spending power to bear in the Everglades.

Meanwhile, in the Everglades, a new crisis set in motion yet another study. Following the 1926 storm, the State of Florida created the Everglades Engineering Board of Review and charged it with assessing the entire Everglades reclamation project. In its report of 1927, to the amazement and disgust of flood survivors, the board found fault with neither the Randolph Report nor Fred C. Elliott, the state's chief drainage engineer. The board did, however, offer modifications of the existing plan based on "study of more accurate and extensive data, not available to the Randolph Commission," consisting of an extensive system of new canals. But the combination of dire economic times and extensive physical destruction had so damaged the economic status of the reclamation project that drainage operations were suspended in June 1927, and by July 1928 even the district's clerical staff was cut to a minimum.[14]

The state board, however, did not investigate the Everglades' problems alone. The United States Army Corps of Engineers, too, had launched a study of the drainage project at the behest of Florida congressman Herbert Draine, and this investigation, coupled with the newly emerging political consensus, led to the first extensive involvement of the corps in the Everglades. But the new political consensus had not quite carried the day during the late 1920s, and Major General Edgar Jadwin came from the old school. He believed that the corps should step in only after the state had expended all its resources, and even then, the general thought the corps should limit its role to public works having a "direct connection with navigation."[15] And there the matter may have stayed, except that the widespread physical destruction and heavy loss of life caused by the hurricane of 1928 forced the general to change his mind. When Jadwin presented his findings to Congress on January 31, 1929, he proposed that the corps not only build a new dike but also expand the Caloosahatchee and St. Lucie canals. The corps proposed that the combination of a larger and stronger dike, coupled with control canals large enough to accommodate the rain that even a hurricane could bring, would finally create effective drainage within the Everglades.[16]

Jadwin was right. After their completion in 1938, the new structures ensured that the waters of Lake Okeechobee no longer inundated the Everglades, and for the first time, drainage became effective over large areas of the wetlands. But neither Jadwin nor drainage boosters had any idea of the environmental complications that effective drainage would create.

As the land dried, three major environmental problems became apparent. First, effective drainage meant that soil subsidence greatly increased, to the alarm of agriculturalists, who saw the very resource they hoped to create vanish before their eyes. Even more alarming, growers witnessed the destruction of thousands of acres of rich soils as both naturally occurring and man-made fires consumed the dried organic matter at an alarming rate. Finally, residents of Miami found that removing surface water meant that their underground freshwater supply became the victim of saltwater intrusion, as ocean water filled the void left by too little surface water percolating into the Biscayne Aquifer, urban south Florida's sole source of freshwater.

The solution to these problems came in the wake of World War II. The Allied victory had given birth to two contradictory ideas in American politics. First, America and its political leaders took great pride from their triumph, and the victory did much to convince Americans of the ability of the federal government to achieve great ends. But amidst this postwar pride and optimism lingered a second idea; that is, a great fear that the end of wartime production meant a return of economic hard times. Taken together, these ideas combined to bring unprecedented federal involvement in south Florida water management as the corps conceived of the final solution to the district's perennial water-control problem.

No longer uneasy about involvement in large-scale public works projects, the federal government once again turned to the Corps of Engineers for a plan that would accommodate both agriculture and urban growth in south Florida. The corps, joined by such scientific organizations as the Soil Science Society of Florida, obligingly set about studying ways to implement comprehensive water control in south Florida. The new plan, the *Comprehensive Report on Central and Southern Florida for Flood Control and Other Purposes*, provided the foundation for finally making the Florida dream a reality.

The Soils Science Society had patiently studied the Everglades' soils throughout the late 1930s and 1940s and had concluded that much of the Everglades was not suited to agriculture. Accordingly, the 1947 plan divided the entire Everglades into a system of self-contained zones consisting of the Everglades Agricultural Area, south of Lake Okeechobee, where the soil was deep; three Water Conservation Areas, along the border of the Miami rocklands, where the soils were too shallow for agriculture; and Everglades National Park, at the southern tip of the peninsula, where wild lands would support native plants and animals. Dikes would keep these zones separate, but pumps and gated spillways would ensure that water could be transferred between the zones at human discretion. These water-control structures would ensure that the Agricultural Area could maintain its optimum water level in times of either drought or flood, and they would also maintain enough water in the Conservation Areas to recharge the Biscayne Aquifer,

David McCally

with enough left over, the corps assured naturalists, to supply the needs of the national park. Advocates of the plan insisted that the new water-control works would eliminate the ills associated with both flooding and too much aridity that had plagued the Everglades since the inception of drainage in 1906.

Although the scientists and engineers agreed on the new plan, creating a political consensus to support the *Comprehensive Report* proved more difficult. South Florida's largest land holders, led by Ernest Graham (father of U.S. senator Bob Graham), Sam Collier, and John Lykes, objected to many of its provisions, especially the proposal to raise the water table along the border of the Miami rocklands. Fearful that the raised water table would have adverse effects on their holdings, this group exerted its influence in the state legislature and nearly succeeded in having the Everglades Drainage District abolished during the 1947 session.[17] But nature intervened, in the form of a September hurricane. The storm dumped heavy rains on south Florida that continued through the fall, but the drainage canals transported the water to the coast, where the urban centers on the Miami rocklands experienced widespread flooding.

Residents of the Coastal Ridge believed that the proposed water conservation areas would have prevented the flooding, and they demanded construction of the works proposed in the *Comprehensive Plan*. Faced with overwhelming support for the new plan, Graham and his allies made the best deal they could. Since the inception of reclamation, drainage taxes had been accessed on acreage, based on the estimated benefits that various tracts could expect, but modern conditions, the large landowners argued, made this mode of taxation obsolete. Because the rapidly growing urban areas would derive the most benefit from the *Comprehensive Plan*, Graham and his allies believed that the residents of these cities should pay the lion's share of the costs. On May 14, 1949, the affected parties sent representatives to the Okeechobee County courthouse, where they came to an agreement on taxes that placated all parties. The new water-control works would be paid for by an ad valorem tax, shifting much of the cost from rural landholders to city dwellers, and a new political consensus had been reached.[18]

The water-control system proposed by the *Comprehensive Plan* took more than two decades to complete. During these years, the population of the urban centers along the Atlantic Coastal Ridge experienced growth that not even the district's most ardent boosters could have foreseen in 1949. By the mid 1970s, this rapid growth had posed yet another challenge to the Florida dream, and once again, this challenge centered around water.

In the eyes of those who wanted to maintain the momentum of the Florida dream, south Florida's water conservation areas conserved too little water. The conservation areas had, as planned, provided enough freshwater to the Biscayne Aquifer to inhibit saltwater intrusion, but this shallow aquifer could no longer meet the water demands of south Florida's greatly expanded population. Advocates of the Florida dream began to envision a water-control system that would not only allow recharge of the Biscayne Aquifer but also expand the freshwater carrying capacity of south Florida's aquifers.

Lying below the Biscayne Aquifer, separated from it by a layer of impervious clay known as the Hawthorne Formation, is the Floridan Aquifer. Originating in northern Georgia, this large aquifer underlies most of peninsular Florida, but south of Lake Okeechobee its water is too mineralized for either human consumption or agricultural use. In spite of this problem, local boosters began to view this aquifer as the savior of the Florida dream. If the water that left the conservation areas as runoff could be intercepted and injected into this deep aquifer, scientists believed, it could well form a freshwater bubble amid the nonpotable water. Then water from this bubble could be drawn out, when needed, for human use. Once again, science came to the rescue of the Florida dream, in the form of the recent *Comprehensive Study Review.*

Along with science, the rule of law and consensus politics that so dominate the American decision-making process have also contributed mightily to the *Comprehensive Study Review.* Indeed, the study itself grew from a 1988 lawsuit filed by Acting U.S. Attorney Dexter Lehtinen, who argued that the state government had failed to abide by federal laws mandating the restoration of the damaged Everglades ecosystem. After state officials settled the lawsuit, Everglades restoration passed from the hands of attorneys to the province of scientists, but this change of venue did not mean that the plan escaped the realm of consensus politics. No single issue better illustrates the power of this political process than does the fate of the flow-way.

The Science Sub-Group met in October 1993 and determined to "prepare an overview summary addressing Ecosystem Restoration" for south Florida. The report it issued on November 15, 1993, represented the considered opinion of a distinguished panel of scientists. On page one of that document, the authors stated that "an important lesson from history is that, in this ecosystem, any successful restoration plan developed must encompass the whole regional ecosystem, not geographic areas in isolation." The Science Sub-Group proposed a natural systems model based on a rain-driven formula as a way to reconstruct the region's hydrologic past, and experts insisted that no real environmental restoration could occur unless the predrainage Everglades' dynamic storage, sheet flow, and large spatial extent were restored. To accomplish these ends, the scientists of the Sub-Group insisted that the Everglades should be reconnected with its headwaters, Lake Okeechobee. In order to bring about this result, the Sub-Group proposed a flowway through the Everglades Agricultural Area that would mimic the predrainage system.[19]

Abundant historical data support the Sub-Group's contention that Lake Okeechobee served as the headwaters of the predrainage Everglades, most notably reports by the New Orleans *Times-Democrat* expedition that transversed the Everglades north to south in 1883, and the integrity of the twenty scientists listed as preparers of the report has not been questioned. The flowway, however, has been discarded in the plan recommended by the *Comprehensive Review Study*, as has the Sub-Group's contention that environmental restoration cannot occur unless dynamic storage, sheet flow, and large spatial extent are restored.

In the place of the rain-driven natural systems model, the *Comprehensive Review Study* offers a computer model of sheet flow that leaves Lake Okeechobee and the Everglades Agricultural Area—more than 400,000 of cultivated acres adjacent to the lake's southern shore—outside consideration. Rather than dynamic storage, which refers to the ability of the Everglades' organic soils to trap enough water to carry the wetlands through the winter dry season, the *Comprehensive Review Study* proposes storing water in three hundred injection wells as well as in two abandoned limestone quarries. Instead of large spatial extent, the *Comprehensive Review Study* proposes the creation of a system that "will be different from any former version of the Everglades. . . . [S]maller and somewhat differently arraigned than it was in the past . . . it will be a new Everglades.[20]

The reasons for these changes stem from the nature of science as a socially embedded activity: that is, science as reformulated by the demands of consensus politics and the desire for unrestricted growth. The *Comprehensive Review Study* very straightforwardly acknowledges that "Stakeholders and other interested parties helped shape the recommended plan from late 1997 through most of 1998," but it leaves unaddressed the question of how much the activities of these stakeholders and other interested parties contributed to the environmental crisis in the Everglades.

Rather than tackling these difficult questions, the *Comprehensive Review Study* treats the environmental ills of the region as little more than a problem

of engineering, asserting that "When the Central and Southern Florida Project was designed in the late 1950s only about 500,000 people lived in the
region, and it was estimated there might be as many as two million by the
year 2000. Today's population of approximately six million is three times as
many people as the system was designed to serve." The new system, the *Comprehensive Review Study* blandly asserts, will serve "eight million by the year
2010, and from twelve to fifteen million by 2050," but it leaves unaddressed
how the population of south Florida can double while living cheek by jowl
with a healthy Everglades.[21]

Indeed, the *Comprehensive Review Study* gives short shrift to environmental restoration. The study offers three proposals aimed at restoring the environmental health of the Everglades, the first two of which affect the movement of water, while the third concerns itself directly with environmental
restoration. The new plan calls for the removal of about 500 miles of dikes
and levees, just over one-third of the total of such structures in the Everglades, and elevating 20 miles of the Tamiami Trail (U.S. 41), which crosses
the Everglades east to west. These changes, no doubt, have the potential to
improve sheet flow within the Everglades; that is, if the 12 to 15 million people
who live in south Florida by 2050 have not consumed it all. Finally, the *Comprehensive Review Study* calls for the creation of 30,000 acres of saw-grass
marsh along the border of the Atlantic Coastal Ridge. This human-made
marsh, combined with a similar 40,000-acre marsh already being built at the
southern edge of the Everglades Agricultural Area, has been designed to filter
out the contaminates contained in urban and agricultural runoff.[22]

From the perspective of the naturalist, these filtration marshes offer the
most telling criticism of the *Comprehensive Review Study*. Although touted as
part of a plan for a sustainable Everglades, marsh building does not constitute environmental restoration, at least not in the sense of creating habitat for
wildlife. Major Archie Williams, who chronicled the 1883 trip of the New
Orleans *Times-Democrat* through the predrainage Everglades, expressed this
idea best when he called the saw-grass portions of the Everglades "sawgrass
deserts" and told his readers that within the dense stands of saw grass, "a
deathlike oppressive stillness prevailed," in an area "utterly devoid of game of
any kind" where, indeed "there was no fish in the water, no birds in the air."[23]
If, as the authors of the *Comprehensive Review Study* suggest, their goal is
sustainability, that sustainability is seemingly directed more at the life of the
Florida dream than at the fauna of the Everglades.

To re-create a viable ecosystem in the Everglades will require dramatic

David McCally

changes in our state's social epistemology, dramatic changes that have not found expression in the *Comprehensive Review Study*. Epistemological change implies not so much a change in *what* we know, as it does a change in *how* we use that knowledge. The wisdom of the past can provide some guidance here. The Taoist adept Lao Tsu, writing in the sixth century B.C.E., suggests a guide for Florida's environmental future when he writes:

> A small country has fewer people.
> Though there are machines that can work ten to a hundred times
>   faster than man, they are not needed.
> The people take death seriously and do not travel far.
> Though they have boats and carriages, no one uses them.
> Though they have armor and weapons, no one displays them.
> Men return to the knotting of rope in place of writing.
> Their food is plain and good, their clothing fine but simple, their
>   homes secure;
> They are happy in their ways.
> Though they live within sight of their neighbors,
> And crowing cocks and barking dogs are heard across the way,
> Yet they leave each other in peace while they grow old and die.[24]

Such wisdom and the limited consumption and simplicity of life that it advises will be required if Americans expect to live in a healthy environment, even as that environment comes more and more under human control, and the Everglades will offer a test case. Ultimately, the need to be wise enough to recognize that environmental sustainability will require them to adapt their social epistemology to the realities of the natural world must replace the current drive to convert all of the natural world to human needs.

Notes

1. The corps issued one report in October 1998 and a rewrite in April 1999.

2. Cathleen C. Vogel, "The Everglades: A Volatile Mix of Science and Politics," July 1997, report in possession of author.

3. *Report of Buckingham Smith, Esq.*, Senate Document 242, 30th Cong., 1st sess., 1848, 10, 17.

4. See State of Florida, *Minutes of the Trustees of the Internal Improvement Fund* 6 (1906): 96–97; and Nelson Manfred Blake, *Land into Water/Water into Land: A History of Water Management in Florida* (Gainesville: University Presses of Florida, 1980), 97–98.

5. See House Committee on Expenditures in the Department of Agriculture, *Everglades of Florida Hearings*, 62nd Cong., 1st sess., 1912, 143–44; and *Minutes of the Trustees* 7 (1909): 502–53.

6. See "Florida Fruit Lands Review" (Kansas City: Florida Fruit Lands Company, n.d.), P. K. Yonge Library of Florida History, University of Florida, Gainesville; and Philip J. Weilding and August Burghard, *Checkered Sunshine: The Story of Fort Lauderdale, 1793–1955* (Gainesville: University of Florida Press, 1966), 38–40.

7. *Majority Report*, Senate Report 1207, 62nd Cong., 2d sess., 1912, 2–3.

8. *Everglades of Florida Hearings*, 343–44, 352.

9. Thomas E. Will to Mr. Knott, May 8, 1912, Thomas Elmer Will Papers, box 1, P. K. Yonge Library of Florida History.

10. Daniel W. Mead, Allen Hazen, and Leonard Metcalf, *Report on the Drainage of the Everglades with Special Reference to the Lands of the Everglades Land Sales Company, Everglades Land Company, Everglades Sugar and Land Company in the Vicinity of Miami, Florida* (Chicago: Board of Consulting Engineers, 1912), 33.

11. Dumas Malone, ed., *Dictionary of American Biography* (New York: Charles Scribner's Sons, 1935), 359–60.

12. *Florida Everglades: Report of the Florida Everglades Engineering Commission to the Everglades the Board of Commissioners of the Everglades Drainage District and the Trustees of the Internal Improvement Fund, State of Florida, 1913*, Senate Document 379, 63rd Cong., 2nd sess., 1914, 5.

13. Anson Marston, S. H. McCory, and George B. Hills, *Report of the Everglades Engineering Board of Review to Commissioners of Everglades Drainage District* (Tallahassee, Fla.: T. J. Appleyard, 1927), 48, 71; and Kelly H. Brooks, "Lake Okeechobee," *Environments of South Florida, Present and Past*, ed. Patrick J, Gleason (Coral Gables: Miami Geological Society, 1984), 2:257.

14. *Report of the Everglades Engineering Board of Review*, 1–3; and *Minutes of the Trustees of the Internal Improvement Fund* 17 (1929): 275–76.

15. *Caloosahatchee River and Lake Okeechobee Drainage Areas, Florida. Letter from the Secretary of War, Transmitting Report from the Chief of Engineers on Survey of Caloosahatchee River and Lake Okeechobee Drainage Areas, Florida, with View of Improvement for Navigation and the Control of Floods*, House Document 215, 70th Cong., 1st sess., 1928, 50.

16. *Letter from the Chief of Engineers, United States Army, Transmitting to the Chairman of the Committee of Commerce, United States Senate, in Response to a Letter Dated December 6, 1928, a Report on the Caloosahatchee River and Lake Okeechobee Drainage Areas, Florida, with a View to Improvement for Navigation and the Control of Floods, April 9, 1928*, House Document 215, 70th Cong., 1st sess., 1928, 23.

17. Blake, *Land into Water/Water into Land*, 176; Mr. Franklin to Sam Collier, August 19, 1947, box 32, Ernest Graham Collection, P. K. Yonge Library of Florida History.

18. "House Group OKs Flood Control," *Miami Herald*, May 17, 1949.

19. Science Sub-Group, "Federal Objectives for the South Florida Restoration by the Science Sub-Group of the South Florida Management and Coordination Working Group," November 15, 1993, i, 1, 17, 23, 26, 28.

David McCally

20. Cathleen C. Vogel, "Central and Southern Florida Project Comprehensive Review Study: Road Map or Roadblock for the Future? A Case Study in Water Resource Planning in the Age of Ecosystem Management," October 1998, 16–18, University Council on Water Resources website, http://www.ucowr.siu.edu/updates/pdf/VIII_A12.pdf.

21. Ibid., 9, 12, 15.

22. Ibid., 16.

23. A. P. Williams, "North to South through the Everglades in 1883," pt. 2, ed. Mary K. Wintringham, *Tequesta* 24 (1964): 62, 81.

24. Lao Tsu, *Tao Te Ching*, trans. Gia-Fu Feng and Jane English (New York: Vintage Books), 80.

Chapter 7

The Trials and Tribulations of Amos Quito

The Creation of the Florida Anti-Mosquito Association

Gordon Patterson

"It is the plain and sober truth," Colonel Raymond Turck, Florida's chief medical officer, declared to the 150 would-be mosquito warriors, "that we humans are engaged in a battle for self-preservation."[1] Turck's stirring words came on December 6, 1922, at the Palmetto Club in Daytona at a gathering of the state's antimosquito forces. Turck, a former member of the Royal Canadian Mounted Police who later pursued Pancho Villa and had been awarded the Distinguished Service Medal in World War I for his valor in the 1918 Meuse-Argonne offensive, told his audience this was a battle that would determine the fate of the human race. No less authority than Leland Osian

Howard, the nation's principal entomologist, had put it in the starkest of terms: "The insect world is a menace to the dominance of man on this planet."[2] Turck was even more explicit. The struggle between humans and insects in general and between man and mosquitoes in particular was a war "which will in all probability end in the extermination of one side or the other."[3]

Florida's war against mosquitoes grew into a powerful statewide movement during World War I and the early 1920s. Few Floridians in 1916 would have anticipated the emergence of an organized antimosquito crusade. Until 1917, the State Board of Health (FSBH) had led the campaign against mosquitoes. Adversity often sparks growth and development. This was the case for the antimosquito movement. Sidney J. Catts's victory in the 1916 gubernatorial race signaled the beginning of a series of budget cuts and hostility to the Health Board's antimosquito initiatives in Tallahassee. Catts, a reactionary who campaigned on a platform that combined anti-Catholicism (make priests turn down their collars and open all convents), Prohibition, and a call for the repeal of conservation laws, opposed the State Board of Health's antimosquito initiatives. Shortly after his inauguration, Catts forced Joseph Porter, a passionate advocate of mosquito control, to resign his position as state health officer and installed a panel of directors at the Board of Health sympathetic to his antediluvian agenda. The new directors named W. H. Cox to lead Florida's public health program. Cox asked the veteran mosquito researcher Hiram Byrd to serve as the board's new scientific secretary.[4]

Porter and his antimosquito confederates did not despair. There was evidence of a growing interest in mosquitoes and mosquito control throughout the state. In 1913, U. C. Loftin devoted his master's thesis at the University of Florida to exploring Florida's mosquitoes.[5] Three years later, eleven men met in Gainesville and organized the Florida Entomological Society, marking Florida as the first southern state to form an entomological body. In 1917, the society boasted one hundred active members. Just as the governor forced the Board of Health to curtail its antimosquito campaign, the Florida Entomological Society launched the *Florida Buggist*.[6]

Porter's dismissal was the opening salvo in Catts's effort to shrink the Board of Health. Evidence of change in the Board of Health's policies was soon apparent. In May 1917, Catts's political appointees announced their intentions in an editorial in *Florida Health Notes*. "The new State Board of Health," the directors wrote, "has assumed its responsibilities and it is pertinent at this juncture to set forth its position. The Board is fully aware that it takes up duties under unusual circumstances; under circumstances in which it expects every official act to be the subject of contention."[7] The expansion and reorganization of the board during Porter's reign fell under withering criticism. The new directors alleged that Porter had allowed his passion for improving public health in general and antimosquito measures in particular to get out of hand. Worse still, they claimed Porter had ineptly managed the budget of the FSBH. "Finances were in a bad condition," the directors wrote, "and bills had accumulated."[8] They ordered Cox to cut expenditures. Health officials curtailed public health education programs. The Health Train was permanently derailed. Perhaps most significant of all, the directors slashed the Health Board's budget by 25 percent.[9]

If Governor Catts and his cronies hoped that Porter would quietly pass into retirement, they were disappointed. "Big Joe" Porter refused to abandon his life's work. He fired off a letter to his old friend Dr. William Gorgas, Woodrow Wilson's surgeon general of the U.S. Army, requesting Gorgas to reactivate his army commission. Gorgas, famed for his work in suppressing yellow fever in the Panama Zone, restored Porter's rank as lieutenant colonel and assigned him to serve as the surgeon for Camp Johnson outside Jacksonville.[10] This allowed Porter to maintain contact with his antimosquito confederates at the state health office.

George Simons was Porter's paladin in Jacksonville. In 1916, Porter recruited Simons, a recent graduate of Massachusetts Institute of Technology, to lead the Board of Health's Bureau of Engineering and develop an antimosquito program. Porter's forced departure and the budget cuts failed to dampen Simons's ardor. If anything, they sharpened his resolve. "We are in a state of war," an anonymous contributor to *Florida Health Notes* declared six months after Porter's firing. Less than twenty years had elapsed since the discovery that mosquitoes transmitted malaria. Some states such as New Jersey had made great strides in reducing mosquito-borne diseases. Florida, the writer opined, "has as much cause to enter whole-heartedly into this mosquito warfare as any people on earth." The "Entente Mosquitoes" have brought a "reign of terror" to Florida. The time has come to make the "chronic malaria carrier . . . a thing of the past."[11]

The United States' entry into World War I catalyzed new antimosquito initiatives. In the spring of 1918, the U.S. Public Health Service (USPHS) dispatched C. N. Harrub, Porter's friend and a federal sanitary engineer, to Florida to organize mosquito-control efforts at the U.S. Government Military Reservation in Jacksonville. Harrub asked Porter's advice on who was best qualified to organize an antimosquito campaign. At Porter's suggestion, Harrub requested that George Simons make a sanitary survey in order to "remedy and eliminate nuisances of potentially dangerous character."[12]

Army officials feared that recruits would contract malaria from the local population. Harrub and Simons developed a detailed plan to protect the military installation from mosquito-borne diseases and proposed a twofold strategy. On base, the military would enforce a stringent sanitation regimen. Barracks would be screened, trash and rubbish cleared, and any pools of standing water drained or treated with oil or kerosene. The greater threat came from outside the base from *Anopheles quadrimaculatus* mosquitoes that abound in the flat piney woods of north Florida.

Worldwide there are more than four hundred species of *Anopheles* mosquitoes, and roughly seventy of these are competent vectors of the malaria plasmodia. In Africa, the *Anopheles gambiae* and *An. funestus* pose the most significant threat.[13] In Florida, at least thirteen species of *Anopheles* mosquitoes are potentially vectors for malaria.[14] Three of these species are particularly troublesome. *An. atropos,* a brownish-black mosquito that breeds in brackish water, is a fierce biter, but not known as a vector for malaria. *An. crucians,* distinguished by pale scales on its wings, is a competent vector for malaria that prefers to feed on livestock and other large mammals. *An. quadrimaculatus* is the principal vector of malaria to humans in Florida. Taxonomists now consider this mosquito a species complex composed of five different but similar mosquitoes. *An. quadrimaculatus* breeds in freshwater, feeds during the night, and distinguishes itself by "having four, more or less distinctive spots on the wings."[15]

The key lay in preventing *An. quadrimaculatus* from reaching the military encampment at Jacksonville. Harrub and Simons knew that the flight range of *An. quadrimaculatus* was seldom more than 2 miles. They concluded that Camp Johnson could be protected if mosquito breeding could be eliminated in an area 1 to 3 miles around the camp's perimeter. They prepared a detailed plan of drainage ditches that would allow the runoff of water and prevent mosquito breeding.

Porter approved Harrub and Simons's program of ditching and drainage. Until World War I, antimosquito measures aimed at preventing insect bites, but at Camp Johnson public health officers sought to eliminate the problem's source. "No where in Florida," *Florida Health Notes* reported, "has the importance of Malaria Control Work been realized as much as in the territory surrounding the U.S. Government Reservation at Jacksonville."[16]

After Porter's forced resignation, George Simons became the single most important advocate for mosquito control at the Health Board. Simons believed that the antimosquito campaign's success at Camp Johnson was only a beginning. An editorial in *Florida Health Notes* supported Simons's position. The time had come to organize a campaign against mosquitoes. "*Every mosquito breeding place in this state,*" an unnamed writer in *Florida Health Notes* declared in italics, "*can be either eliminated or else treated to such an extent that the mosquito nuisance will be greatly decreased.*"[17] Simons announced that the Health Board's Bureau of Engineering was willing to prepare plans for "the eradication of mosquito breeding places" anywhere in the state.[18]

Relations between Governor Catts and the Health Board worsened after World War I. In 1919, W. H. Cox resigned as the state's medical officer. Dr. Ralph Greene agreed to complete Cox's term. Greene, a respected physician and advocate of an expanded role for the Health Board, sympathized with Simons's desire to broaden the antimosquito effort. Budgetary restrictions, however, obliged Greene to make further cuts in health programs, including suspending publication of *Florida Health Notes*. Despite these cutbacks, Simons continued to look for ways to create a statewide mosquito-control program.[19]

Late in 1919, the Burton-Swartz Cypress Company and the Perry City Council asked Simons to prepare a malaria survey for Taylor County. The two thousand citizens of Perry were at an epidemiological crossroads. Located roughly 20 miles from the Gulf in the heart of Florida's timber country, Perry served as the hub for north central Florida's logging industry. The county's flat piney woods and cypress swamps were both a blessing and a curse. The region's economy was based on the sawmills and lumber companies. The same low, wet, piney woods and cypress swamps were an ideal habitat for *An. quadrimaculatus*. Malaria was endemic. Local pharmacists and drugstore owners maintained that Perry's residents collectively spent at least $3,000 annually for quinine. Physicians estimated that 50 percent of the people suffered from malaria.[20] The county had the highest death rate from malaria in Florida.[21]

Perry presented an opportunity to prove to skeptics that mosquito control could eliminate malaria. The first step was to identify the intensity of the malaria problem and to determine the disease's focal points. Simons's health inspectors fanned out across the county in early January. The house-to-house canvass produced shocking results. Simons estimated that fully 65 percent of the population of Taylor County's residents tested positive for malaria.[22] "The entire populace," he concluded, "was more or less discouraged over the town's future."[23] Immediate action was necessary if Perry were to be delivered from the scourge of malaria.

On January 16, 1920, the *Taylor County Herald* reported that the State Board of Health and the USPHS had teamed up to organize an antimalaria campaign in Perry.[24] Simons intended the Perry Project to serve as a model for future antimosquito initiatives. Earlier antimalaria campaigns had failed because of insufficient study and lack of coordination. In Perry, Simons promised to employ every available means of suppressing *An. quadrimaculatus* mosquitoes.

In 1920, a sanitary engineer like George Simons had recourse to a handful of tried-and-true mosquito-control strategies. Long-term success meant preventing mosquitoes from breeding. Two mechanical options were available; both involved shoveling dirt. Mosquitoes need water for their eggs to hatch into larvae. The most effective way of stopping mosquitoes from breeding is to fill in low areas so water cannot collect, but the problem with this approach is that it is an expensive, time-consuming process. The other approach is to dig runoff ditches that prevent water from collecting. At Camp Johnson, Simons had based the control program on ditches stocked with a species of minnows known as *Gambusia affinis* that thrive on a diet of mosquito larvae. In the 1920s, advocates of mosquito control believed *Gambusia affinis* presented an effective biological means of control so long as the minnows had access to mosquito larvae.

What made the Perry Project unique was that Simons planned to develop a comprehensive strategy based on biological and simple mechanical means in Perry. Eliminating breeding areas and giving minnows access to mosquito larvae were essential for long-term success. The people of Perry, however, needed immediate protection. Simons recommended that health workers spray oil and kerosene on standing bodies of water. Since mosquito larvae must breathe in order to survive, a thin oil sheen on top of a pond or on the surface of a rain barrel causes them to suffocate. This is a chemical means of control. Finally, in pursuing a cultural approach to mosquito control, Simons called for a countywide education program to alert the citizenry of the measures to take to protect themselves from the *Anopheles* threat. Simons's plan offers a sharp contrast with pesticide-based mosquito control, which developed in the 1940s after the discovery of the toxicant power of DDT. Had DDT been available, Simons would undoubtedly have employed it. In 1920, he used the tools that were available.

Simons prepared a topographical map of Taylor County. The USPHS sent J. G. Foster, a sanitary engineer, to assist Simons in drafting the plan. Simultaneously, Simons reviewed the available meteorological records. He believed that improving the flow of two creeks and lowering the water level in the adjacent pine woods held the key to solving the *An. quadrimaculatus* problem. Dredging the creeks was a start. Later, county workers would need to add additional canals to facilitate the runoff of storm water. While the ditching was underway, Simons recommended a series of immediate measures. Ponds and streams should be treated with oil while local workers stocked the county's creeks, ditches, and any standing water with minnows. Finally, Simons told county officials that all houses were to be tightly screened and 170,000 doses of quinine distributed in Perry.[25]

Financing the project presented a formidable challenge. Ralph Greene agreed to donate Simons's engineering expertise. Digging an estimated 4.1 miles of drainage ditches would cost a substantial amount of money. Late in January, the city council and representatives of the Burton-Swartz Cypress Company met and listened to the Simons's proposal. Perry's city council promised to make every effort "toward the carrying into effect" of the mosquito-control project. In March, the council passed ordinances requiring the installation of screening throughout the city.[26]

Between January and May, the Perry City Council, Taylor County officials, and the Burton-Swartz Cypress Company wrestled with the funding issue. Eventually, a compromise emerged. In May, the council brought forward a bond issue that allocated $15,000 for the drainage project. The Burton-Swartz Cypress Company agreed to contribute $10,000 to the project, while Taylor County officials added $3,000. Work on digging the main ditch and lateral lines was completed in November, with more than 46,000 cubic yards of earth excavated. When work was completed, Simons's team had opened an additional 3 miles of creek beds, cleared fifteen acres of land, dynamited an old dam, and constructed 3 new bridges.[27]

The Perry campaign transformed mosquito control in Florida. The project dwarfed earlier undertakings. George Simons described the Perry Project as "one of the largest of its kind in this country."[28] Even the proponents of mosquito control were surprised at the project's success. One year after the work's completion, Simons's inspectors canvassed the community. They were astonished. There had been a 90 percent reduction in the malaria infection rate.[29]

Mosquito control revitalized Perry. The owner of the Burton-Swartz Cypress Company wrote Simons and described the positive consequences of mosquito control. "Before your work here," E. G. Swartz wrote, "there were times in the late summer and autumn months that our business was seriously handicapped by being forced to operate our plant shorthanded, due entirely to malaria among our employees." The company, Swartz added, would rather "spend $100,000 than return to the old conditions. We could do that, I am sure, and then be ahead of the deal."[30] J. H. Scales, a local banker and member of the Florida Senate, echoed Swartz's enthusiastic appraisal. "The anti-mosquito campaign in Perry," Scales wrote to Simons, "by the State Board of Health was the greatest undertaking and success ever achieved. . . . Doctors tell me that they have less than one-tenth the malaria and chill patients than three years ago. The mosquito has been 90 percent eliminated from Perry since you put over the anti-mosquito campaign."[31]

Simons's crusade for mosquito control was not restricted to Perry. He found an unexpected ally 100 miles to the south in the phosphate mining lands of Polk County in Brewster, Florida. Brewster was a company town. Most of the 1,500 residents worked in one of the American Cyanamid Company's nearby mines. The phosphate country was an ideal breeding place for insect pests and infectious diseases. Hookworm was endemic among the town's children. Open privies and poor garbage disposal combined to make typhus and typhoid constant threats. Between 40 and 80 percent of the population suffered from malaria. At any given time, sickness kept between eighty and one hundred American Cyanamid workers from the mines.[32]

William J. Buck, the town's physician, persuaded the American Cyanamid Company to support a citywide public health initiative. Buck modeled his program on Simons's initiatives, recommending that the company tightly screen homes and buildings. Regular garbage service was instituted. A team of five health inspectors enforced strict compliance with the sanitation code.

The mosquito problem proved the most vexing challenge. Ditching was ineffectual. "The first few weeks of our work demonstrated," Buck wrote in a 1920 report, "the impossibility of eliminating the mosquito by drainage and oiling alone; however, close and repeated inspection failed to reveal mosquito larvae in several of the larger ponds and several of the slow moving weed-filled streams, the natural habitat of the *Anopheles*."[33] Buck discovered that the ponds and streams that were free of mosquitoes were populated with *Gambusia affinis*.

Buck hit on the idea of basing the campaign around minnows. His first step was to establish a minnow-breeding pond. Once assured that he had a sufficient supply of minnows, he outfitted what was probably the first mosquito-control vehicle in Florida history. In the 1950s, a generation of Floridians became accustomed to trucks spraying toxic chemicals. In 1920, Buck's "mosquito wagon" consisted of several water barrels filled with *Gambusia affinis* and was pulled by a team of horses. Buck's sanitary inspectors monitored an area within a mile-and-a-half radius of Brewster. When they found *An. quadrimaculatus* hot spots, they dispatched the "mosquito wagon" to seed the problem area with minnows.

The amazing thing was that it worked. In 1921, Raymond Turck visited Brewster shortly after succeeding Ralph Greene as the state's medical officer. The tiny fish had rejuvenated the town. The antimosquito program had miraculous effects. "I tried hard to find a mosquito," Turck declared. "I even sat out on an unscreened veranda step and wandered about in the bushes and on the edge of a pond at dusk trying to locate at least one mosquito. Not one. Not a bite."[34] A year earlier, Brewster had been a "pest hole." Turck maintained that Buck's sanitation initiative had succeeded in making Brewster one of the healthiest places to live in Florida.[35] In December 1923, William Buck reported that Brewster's malaria infection rate "had been reduced to a fraction of one per cent."[36]

Ironically, Florida's proponents of mosquito control suffered a decisive setback just when evidence of the successful antimosquito work in Perry and Brewster was coming to light. In 1921, the legislature slashed the Board of Health's budget by 50 percent.[37] The Board of Health had lost three-quarters of its funding in four years. Dr. Raymond Turck replaced Ralph Greene as state health officer. The newly created bureaus of Child Welfare and Venereal Disease were abolished. Turck ordered his directors to slash their expenditures.[38]

George Simons refused to moderate his efforts. If politicians failed to recognize the importance of the war against mosquitoes, Simons vowed he would show them. He was convinced that the state's growth depended on winning the battle against mosquito-borne diseases. An outbreak of dengue fever along the southeast Florida coast in the fall presented Simons with the opportunity he needed. Miami was particularly hard hit. By December, the Miami City Commission resolved to launch an antimosquito program. Real estate sales had been booming. The commissioners believed that Miami's future hinged on the winter visitors' belief that Miami was a healthy place. Perry and Brewster gave Miami city officials cause for hope. They asked Simons to help them devise a mosquito-control program.

Miami's city commission adopted Simon's model mosquito ordinance on March 1922. They allocated $10,000 for the "mosquito campaign."[39] By midsummer, five newly hired mosquito inspectors and nine "oilers" were at work. The mosquito inspectors surveyed the city every ten days.[40] They identified areas where *Ae. aegypti* mosquitoes were breeding, monitored problem spots, enforced compliance with antimosquito ordinances, and provided the oilers with their larviciding assignments. In April, the oilers sprayed 1,200 gallons of oil that local garages had donated to the control program.[41]

Success in the "Miami Mosquito Campaign" was predicated on the public's understanding of the campaign's objectives and active support for the control initiatives. Five mosquito inspectors and nine oilers could not eliminate every *Ae. aegypti* breeding place. A substantial portion of the commission's $10,000 allocation was devoted to educating the public on the nature of the mosquito threat and the available control measures. On April 15, the *Miami Daily Metropolis* published the first in a series of "Bulletins on the Mosquito Campaign."[42] Sanitation officials mailed form letters to businesses and civic organizations describing the benefits of mosquito control. Simons, who spent much of March through May commuting between Jacksonville and Miami, followed up the letters with a public campaign based on slogans, speeches, and newspaper articles.[43] The centerpiece of the public education program was a thirty-six-page booklet titled *Mosquitoes and Mosquito Control* that George Simons and George Moznette, a United States Department of Agriculture entomologist based in Miami, had prepared. Local health officials distributed 5,500 copies throughout the city.

Simons's and Moznette's thirty-six-page booklet was noteworthy. First, this was the first practical guide to mosquito control published in Florida. Second, the booklet offered an outline of the essentials of mosquito control for the general public. "The purpose of this bulletin," the authors explained, "is to present to the layman a plain and reasonably accurate account of the importance and the breeding habits of the more important health and economic species of mosquitoes in Florida, to discuss fully the underlying principles of control, and, finally, to impress upon everyone the urgent need for co-operation in eliminating mosquito breeding places."[44] Each section of the booklet contributed to the goal of devising and implementing an effective mosquito-control program.

"Mosquito control," Simons and Moznette maintained, "is more than a dream or idle fancy."[45] They argued that the state's prosperity was tied to success in controlling mosquitoes. Currently, "hundreds of thousands of dollars,—yes millions—in damages in Florida can be charged directly to mosquito prevalence."[46] As new residents streamed into Florida, these costs would grow.

Effective mosquito control began with "understanding the life stages and habits of the several species of mosquitoes."[47] Simons and Moznette divided the possible control measures into two groups. Primary measures included efforts to prevent mosquitoes from breeding. Secondary measures consisted of the steps that individuals could take to prevent being bitten by mosquitoes. Since mosquitoes need water to breed, drainage and filling low areas were the two most effective primary measures. Other primary methods included use of oil as a larvicide and the introduction of minnows into mosquito-breeding areas. Screening and mosquito netting for beds served as a secondary or final line of defense against adult mosquitoes.

Simons and Moznette's message was positive. Individuals should not feel overwhelmed. Mosquitoes can be controlled. Success in the war against mosquitoes depended on an informed and educated citizenry. "The public," Simons and Moznette concluded, "can do everything through its collective citizenry; upon its enthusiasm and interest rests the final success of the program."[48]

The summer of 1922 provided the crucial test for Miami's Mosquito Control Campaign. Simons watched as the number of cases of dengue fever soared in the spring and summer of 1922. The disease accompanied travelers on the state's highways and rails. A dengue epidemic broke out in Tallahassee in mid-July following the annual state teachers' education program. A few weeks later, the state's annual militia encampment brought the disease to Jacksonville. No city, however, was as hard hit by the dengue outbreak as Tampa.

City officials in Tampa ignored the mosquito threat throughout the spring. Early in July, Tampa's health officer, Dr. J. R. Harris, announced that cases of dengue fever had risen to epidemic proportions. The situation reached a crisis point in August. "Our equipment," Harris declared, "is totally inadequate to wage a general campaign against mosquitoes."[49] Some officials estimated that there were 2,500 cases of dengue in the city. Others thought that the number might be as high as four thousand.[50] Tampa's city manager tried to calm the public's fear. "If the people of Tampa will cooperate," A. W. Hall observed, "by emptying all the old barrels and tin cans and cutting the weeds on their own premises, I believe the situation can be controlled."[51] Despite Hall's optimistic forecast, the dengue epidemic intensified in July. The commissioners fired Hall. The new city manager, Lesley Brown, sent an urgent request to the State Board of Health asking that George Simons organize Tampa's war against mosquitoes.

Simons presented his recommendations to a special meeting of the city commission in August. The city had done next to "nothing at all, comparatively speaking" to eradicate mosquitoes.[52] As a first step, commissioners must allocate sufficient funds for mosquito control. "Miami," Simons explained, "taking steps early in the season to prevent the recurrence there of an epidemic of dengue such as raged last season, has expended $15,000 on mosquito eradication. At this rate the city of Tampa should immediately expend $50,000 on mosquito eradication."[53]

Without decisive action, Simons warned the disease would spread. "Conditions at the city dump," he declared, "were an abomination."[54] Cleaning the dump was a beginning. "You have cut a few weeds," Simons acknowledged, "but weeds are not mosquito breeding places. You should not spend emergency money for cutting weeds when you can use the money to much better advantage . . . to eradicate the dengue fever carrying mosquito."[55] Simons recommended that city commissioners pass a "model ordinance" that would divide the city into sanitation districts. Health and sanitary inspectors were needed to monitor neighborhoods for mosquito-breeding places. Finally, health officers needed to rigorously enforce screening laws.

The dengue epidemic threatened Tampa's future. Real estate developers and businesses dependent on tourists feared that newspaper reports of the epidemic would harm the city. Simons ridiculed this position. Tampa's development depended on the commission's success in devising an effective mosquito-control program. "There has been some criticism," Simons acknowledged, "of your newspapers because they have carried facts about the dengue fever, but I tell you, gentlemen, that the best advertisement you can get for your city is to spread abroad the knowledge that you have an active health department which is making definite efforts to control and stomp out the fever."[56] The decision lay with the commissioners. If they adopted the proposed "vigorous measures," Simons was optimistic. He estimated that "the work can be completed by late fall, in ample time to have a mosquito-less and dengue-less city before the annual influx of tourists and winter visitors."[57]

The city commission embraced Simons's recommendations. Eight new health inspectors were hired. City officials enlisted Boy Scouts to serve as auxiliary sanitary inspectors. Convicts were assigned to clean the city dump.[58]

The commissioners approved the model antimosquito ordinance. Most important of all, City Manager Brown announced that "funds for waging the anti-mosquito warfare" would be taken from "special funds of the city not designated for use for other purposes."[59] Tampa's leaders promised that the "work now underway by the city in its campaign will be continued until health officials are satisfied that all menaces to the city's health have been eradicated."[60]

The 1922 dengue epidemic proved a blessing. There had been more than 200,000 cases in Florida during the summer epidemic.[61] Miami was spared. Later, Simons told Raymond Turck that "the dengue situation throughout the state [had] put the people in a mood to be receptive to constructive plans that would control mosquito-borne infections."[62] Simons concluded that victory in the war against mosquitoes hinged on rallying public support for the campaign. Perry and Brewster had demonstrated that mosquito control could eliminate malaria. The Miami Mosquito Campaign succeeded in preventing a dengue outbreak within the city. The recent statewide dengue outbreak had made the public mindful of the human and economic costs of mosquito-borne diseases.

The legislature's cutbacks in the Board of Health's budget convinced Simons and Turck that the campaign for mosquito control must cultivate its own political base. In August, Simons mapped out a strategy for rallying the public behind the "Suppress the Mosquito" banner. Simons organized a speaking tour that took him across the state. During the fall, Simons visited Daytona Beach, New Smyrna, Titusville, West Palm Beach, and Gainesville. Later, Simons carried his antimosquito message into the panhandle, speaking in Monticello and Tallahassee.

Simons did not vary his speech. First, he described the magnitude of the mosquito problem. In the past, yellow fever had ravaged Florida. Malaria and dengue continued to inflict tremendous economic costs. Then, Simons pointed to the success of the Perry Project and Miami's antimosquito measures. A mosquito-less Florida was not a utopian idea. It was, Simons concluded, every "community's obligation" to bring the "great benefit of mosquito control" to Florida.[63]

"The call has gone forth," Simons declared, "the gong has sounded its knell, and all is in readiness to try *Amos Quito*. The judges, witnesses, and numerous court attendants have been duly summoned to appear in Daytona ... for the trial and execution proceedings."[64] Simons promised that the Day-

Gordon Patterson

tona Conference would inaugurate a new stage in the war against mosquitoes. Florida's war against mosquitoes, Simons warned, *"is not work to be accomplished over night or even over a brief period of time.* Mosquito eradication measures take time and after the start has once been made the citizens must be reasonably patient and considerate and not judge hastily the ultimate results after only a short period of work."[65]

One hundred and fifty mosquito warriors traveled to Daytona in December 1922. Their objective was to launch a statewide crusade for mosquito control. The "intensive educational publicity campaign" generated tremendous press coverage.[66] "Seldom a day passed," George Simons recalled, "without the insertion of some little news item recalling to mind the Daytona Conference."[67] Representatives from city governments, county authorities, citizens groups, the federal government, as well as industry and commerce gathered to formulate a strategy for waging war against the state's number-one pest.

The meeting's tone was militant. "The next war," State Health Officer Lt. Colonel Raymond Turck told the delegates, "will be that waged with insects destructive of human life."[68] Physicians, entomologists, and engineers had proved it was possible to control mosquitoes. The delegates confronted the question of whether Florida had the resolve necessary for the task. Turck told them that the battle would be lost if the nation "continues its apathetic policy." A vigorous mosquito control would transform the state. "Florida," Turck continued, "can be made a health paradise if a goal is established and all work toward it."[69]

The participants at the Daytona Meeting answered Turck's call for action affirmatively. On December 7, they voted to organize the Florida Anti-Mosquito Association (FAMA). They chose Joseph Porter to be the association's first president. Porter's election ensured the organization's credibility. His career was synonymous with the fight to eliminate mosquito-borne diseases. Raymond Turck introduced Porter's presidential address. "Twenty-five years hence," Turck observed, "we will look back to this momentous date in Florida's history. It will be remembered as the natal day of an organization which I am confident, will bring about the realization of the titanic work of controlling, if not eradicating the mosquito from the state."[70] Taking the gavel, the seventy-five-year-old Porter echoed Turck's enthusiasm. The goal was clear. Victory over the mosquito was assured, Porter declared, if the people of Florida "keep everlastingly at it."[71]

Notes

1. "State-Wide Mosquito Campaign Is Launched," *Daytona News,* December 10, 1922, newspaper clipping, Florida State Board of Health Scrapbook, Lee County Mosquito Control, 22.

2. Ibid.

3. Ibid.

4. Albert V. Hardy and May Pynchon, *Millstones and Milestones: Florida's Public Health from 1889,* Florida State Board of Health Monograph Series No. 7 (Jacksonville, 1964), 30.

5. U. C. Loftin, "Mosquitoes Found about Gainesville," *Florida Buggist* 3 (September 1919): 1.

6. A. N. Tissot, "A Brief History of the Florida Entomological Society," *Florida Entomologist* 22 (February 1939): 8–9.

7. Hardy and Pynchon, *Millstones and Milestones,* 30.

8. Ibid.

9. Ibid.

10. Ibid., 28.

11. "The Entente Mosquitoes," *Florida Health Notes* 12 (September 1917): 1.

12. George Simons, in *Thirtieth Annual Report of the State Board of Health, 1918* (Jacksonville, 1919), 152.

13. Awash Teklehaimanot and Pushpa R. J. Herath, "The Mosquito: Public Enemy Number 1," *World Health* (September-October 1991): 21.

14. "Man's Great Enemy . . . the Mosquito," *Florida Health Notes* 48 (March 1953): 56.

15. Elisabeth Beck, *Public Health Pest Control Manual: Applicator Training Manual,* revised by Thomas Loyless (Tallahassee: Florida Department of Agriculture and Consumer Services, 1999), 18. See Jai K. Nayar, C. D. Morris, and R. H. Baker, "Human Malaria," Florida Medical Entomology On-Line Publications PH1002, http://www.ifas.ufl.edu/~veroweb/olpub/malaria.htm (accessed June 15, 2002), 3.

16. "Malaria Control Work," *Florida Health Notes* 13 (November 1918): 80.

17. "Malaria Control Work," *Florida Health Notes.*

18. Ibid.

19. George Simons in *Thirty-First Annual Report of the State Board of Health of Florida* (Jacksonville, 1921), 35.

20. "Most Extensive Malarial Eradication Work in the United States Being Conducted by State Board Health Board in Perry, Fla.," *Jacksonville Times-Union,* September 12, 1920, newspaper clipping, Florida State Board of Health Scrapbook, Lee County Mosquito Control, 1.

21. In 1919, the malaria mortality rate per 100,000 in Perry and Taylor County was 405 and 147, respectively. See "State-Wide Mosquito Campaign Is Launched," *Daytona News,* December 10, 1922; and Hardy and Pynchon, *Millstones and Milestones,* 32.

22. "Most Extensive Malarial Eradication Work."

23. George Simons, "Biennial Report for 1921–1922 Bureau of Engineering,"

Thirty-Second Biennial Report of the State Board of Health of Florida (Jacksonville, 1923), 197.

24. "Malarial Fight to Begin Soon," *Taylor County Herald,* January 16, 1920.

25. "Most Extensive Malarial Eradication Work."

26. "Council Passes Screening Law: All Homes and Places of Abode Must be Properly Screened against Mosquitoes," *Taylor County Herald,* March 5, 1920, 1.

27. George Simons, "Biennial Report for 1921–1922 Bureau of Engineering," *Thirty-Second Biennial Report of the State Board of Health of Florida* (Jacksonville, 1923), 197.

28. Simons, "Biennial Report for 1921–1922 Bureau of Engineering," 196.

29. Hardy and Pynchon, *Millstones and Milestones,* 33.

30. Simons, "Biennial Report for 1921–1922 Bureau of Engineering," 197.

31. Ibid., 199.

32. Raymond Turck, "Address to Anti-Mosquito Conference," Daytona Beach, December 6, 1922, unidentified newspaper clipping, Florida State Board of Health Scrapbook, Lee County Mosquito Control, 31.

33. Turck, "Address to Anti-Mosquito Conference."

34. Ibid.

35. Ibid.

36. "Anti-Mosquito Association to Fight for Entire Elimination of Malaria Mosquito," unidentified newspaper clipping, December 6, 1923, Florida State Board of Health Scrapbook, Lee County Mosquito Control, 62.

37. Hardy and Pynchon, *Millstones and Milestones,* 31.

38. Ibid.

39. "East Coast Waging War on Mosquito, unidentified newspaper clipping, June 28, 1922, Florida State Board of Health Scrapbook, Lee County Mosquito Control, 2.

40. "During May there were 3,125 mosquito inspections and mosquito breeding places were found as follows: 7340 tubs, 1,469 buckets, 1,371 water barrels, 1,440 catch basins, 476 cisterns and tanks, 57 fountains, 85 flower urns, 21 ditches, 148 ground depressions, 28 derelict craft, 3,186 miscellaneous containers such as tin cans broken and useless crockery, dishes and kitchen utensils." See "East Coast Waging War on Mosquito," unidentified newspaper clipping, June 28, 1922, Florida State Board of Health Scrapbook, Lee County Mosquito Control, 2

41. Ibid.

42. "Bulletin No. 1: The Mosquito Campaign," *Miami Daily Metropolis,* April 15, 1922, 2.

43. Simons, "Biennial Report for 1921–1922 Bureau of Engineering," 195–96.

44. George W. Simons and George F. Moznette, *Mosquitoes and Mosquito Control,* 4th ed. (Florida State Board of Health, Jacksonville, 1924), 3.

45. Ibid., 19.

46. Ibid., 4.

47. Ibid., 19.

48. Ibid., 34.

49. "Dengue Near an Epidemic in City Now," *Tampa Daily Times,* July 10, 1922.

50. "Claim 2,500 Victims of Dengue Here: Alarming Spread of Disease Shown in Survey," *Tampa Daily Times*, July 11, 1922.

51. Ibid.

52. "Outlines Plan for Mosquito Campaign," *Tampa Morning Tribune*, August 23, 1922.

53. "Campaign to Cover Tampa Like a Blanket: Quick Action Follows Simons Report to Commission," *Tampa Daily Times*, August 23, 1922.

54. Ibid.

55. Ibid.

56. Ibid.

57. Ibid.

58. "City Launches Campaign to Drive out Mosquitoes," *Tampa Morning Tribune*, August 24, 1922.

59. Ibid.

60. "Inspectors Make Rounds of Premises: City Adds Eight Men to Force in War on Mosquitoes," *Tampa Daily Times*, August 24, 1922.

61. "State Health Board to Combat Mosquito Menace: Asks Funds," unidentified newspaper clipping, February 22, 1923, Florida State Board of Health Scrapbook, Lee County Mosquito Control, 29.

62. George Simons, "Biennial Report for 1921–1922 Bureau of Engineering," *Thirty-Second Biennial Report of the State Board of Health of Florida* (Jacksonville, 1923), 200.

63. Ibid.

64. George Simons, "Bureau of Sanitary Engineering," *Florida Health Notes* 14 (December 1922): 8.

65. Ibid., 8.

66. George Simons, "Report of the Bureau of Engineering," *Thirty-Second Biennial Report of the State Board of Health of Florida* (Jacksonville, 1923), 200.

67. Ibid.

68. Raymond Turck quoted in "Declare War on Mosquito," *St. Petersburg Times*, December 7, 1922.

69. Ibid.

70. Ibid.

71. Vida Lester MacDonell, "History of the Florida Anti-Mosquito Association," *Proceedings of the Tenth Annual Meeting of the Florida Anti-Mosquito Association*, Clearwater, Fla., March 14–15, 1932.

Chapter 8

"Nature's Navels"

An Overview of the Many Environmental Histories of Florida Citrus

Christian Warren

In the winter of 1912, a major land boom was just warming up in the Tampa Bay area, on Florida's Gulf coast. In St. Petersburg, Midgley Realty offered prospective home builders more than a stake in the speculation, more than a title to an empty lot. In addition to such expected amenities as easy access to the trolley line and cement sidewalks, each of Midgley's lots featured "14 fine grapefruit trees." An attractive landscaping feature on a two-acre tract, perhaps, but on the 50 x 135-foot lots Midgley was peddling, fourteen grapefruit trees would have left very little room for houses.[1] Just what was being sold here? Clearly, Midgley was parceling out what had been a working citrus grove (in fact, his Floriana Park subdivision was located on Tangerine Avenue). But he was also marketing a relationship to nature's bounty, to healthful natural foods, and to the salubrious climate that fueled the growing real estate frenzy.

This incident raises several questions about the specifics of an environmental history of citrus in Florida; but these questions suggest how, in turn, a comprehensive environmental history of citrus (the mere outline of which is presented here) might explore many of environmental history's central themes. First, citrus agriculture addresses environmental history's most traditional subject: land, water, climate, and the impact of humans' economic activities, including the impact of local and distant markets, and the erasure of the frontier. Florida offers a unique laboratory for testing frontier theses. The peninsula's very shape (Marjory Stoneman Douglas called it the "Long Frontier") and that frontier's belated "closing" make Florida a very different stage upon which to test the Turnerian script.[2] The particular role for citrus in this story includes not only where and why citrus regions arose but also the history of competing land uses and visions for Florida's future.

The vast scale of citrus production raises a second theme in environmental history: "second nature." How did this commercial, agricultural product come to be seen as a "natural" part of Florida's landscape? To what extent did distant economic decisions and new technologies further remove citrus from the natural world? And how has this product, so closely associated with a pure and healthy nature, been used to market other commodities, including the commodified concept of a naturally healthy Florida?

A complete history of Florida citrus would also consider the themes of environmental health and the irony-laden theme of built environments. Chemical fertilizers and pesticides have had important health implications for the workers who tend groves and harvest fruit (making citrus agriculture an environmental justice issue) as well as for the health of all who play in or drink from Florida's waters. And as a visit to almost any Florida suburb will make clear, backyard citrus trees, far removed from any explicitly commercial setting, play an important role as markers of the natural in the "built environment," a place of increasing interest to environmental historians. This essay focuses on land and climate as they shaped Florida's developing citrus industry, and the technological and economic developments that transformed citrus from plant to crop to product. And while it cannot adequately address environmental health and the built environment, these themes are never completely out of mind, and reappear now and again as a call for a thorough investigation of each.

Few features of the Florida landscape seem more "natural" than citrus trees. In 1992, Florida citrus groves covered almost a million acres with their parti-colored geometry.[3] In addition, all manner of citrus trees adorn suburban backyards throughout most of the state. And wild citrus—rough lemons, sour oranges—grow wherever soil, climate, and water allow. The ubiquity and variety of Florida citrus suggest a natural affinity and an ancient Florida heritage. In reality, citrus is no more a Florida native than wild boars or sugarcane, both of which were early elements of the "Columbian Exchange." It remains unclear which early Spanish settler first planted citrus in Florida, but like the swine that escaped Spanish settlements, oranges quickly dispersed over the landscape.[4] In 1562, French explorer Jean Ribault noted Timucuan Indians along the St. Johns River growing "citrons" along with native and other Old World crops. By 1579, Spanish correspondents described successful orange cultivation in St. Augustine, though citrus never became an important agricultural product for the Spanish Floridians.[5]

People brought citrus to Florida not for its natural beauty but for the wealth it promised. Pursuing that goal pitted the citrus farmer against the land, the climate, biological pests and other natural obstacles, as well as economic factors such as geographic and temporal distances to markets. The rise of commercial citriculture in Florida raises the oldest and most persistent subject of environmental history: in Donald Worster's words, "productive technology as it interacts with the environment" in order to understand "the various ways people have tried to make nature over into a system that produces resources for their consumption."[6] Florida's early citrus growers struck a balance between the risk of freezes and access to markets. Climate and natural geography—high land near navigable rivers or deep ports—initially confined Florida's citrus region to the St. Johns area and northeast Atlantic coast. Eventually, devastating freezes and a long-term trend toward cooler winters pushed citrus production southward, toward a climate for which the trees were better suited.

Intense citriculture in Florida began with the English occupation (1764–83). By the late 1600s, English planters had expanded their operations in Barbados to South Carolina. They fully expected citrus to thrive; after all, the Carolina sea islands lay at around 32 degrees north latitude, the same latitude as Morocco; more reassuring, Valencia, Spain, lay at 38 degrees. Eager colonists did not take full account of the climatic differences between western and eastern continental shores, or of the Gulf Stream's mediating effects on Western Europe's climate. This so-called latitude fallacy provoked numerous misjudgments that plagued settlers in North America from Florida to Nova Scotia.[7]

Ironically, the climate in the Southeast during the hundred years preceding the major freeze of 1835 fully accorded with English planter's expectations, and citrus production flourished in English groves in Charleston and Georgia—and northern Florida after 1763. British surveyors had noted wild oranges growing in the woods south of St. Augustine, and British growers quickly added citrus to the list of products exported from Florida. In addition to the indigo and naval stores that filled their holds, British ships carried dried orange peels, and casks of orange "juice," usually watered, and preserved with sugars, spices, and spirits.[8] Most of these products were derived from wild orange trees, but a number of planters cultivated sweet oranges. New York exporter Jesse Fish acquired a large estate on St. Anastasia Island from departing Spaniards in 1763 and held it after Florida was returned to Spanish rule in 1784. From the early English occupation, fruit and juice from Jesse Fish's groves gained international renown.[9]

After 1821, when Spain ceded Florida to the United States, citriculture expanded rapidly along the St. Johns, the Indian, and the Halifax rivers on the Atlantic coast, and along the Hillsborough River on the Gulf coast. Demand for young trees outstripped what nurseries and wild groves could supply. On Merritt Island, on the eastern shore of the Indian River, Douglas Dummett, a captain in the Florida militia and son of a Barbadian planter, developed a commercial technique for budding sweet China oranges onto the stump of the hardy wild (but sour) Spanish oranges. "Topworking" produced bearing trees in only three years. Demand for Dummett's "Indian River oranges" helped spur Florida's first citrus boom. By the early 1830s, citrus was the chief agricultural product of Florida's eastern coast, with annual citrus exports exceeding 2 million oranges from St. Augustine alone.[10]

Then, in February 1835, a crushing freeze ended the nearly century-long warm spell. Popular opinion blamed a wayward iceberg off the Florida coast for the chill; but whatever the cause, Sunday, February 8, brought four days of chilling winds, record low temperatures, and death to thousands of citrus trees. At St. Augustine, temperatures fell to as low as 7 degrees Fahrenheit, and for twenty-four hours remained below 21 degrees. The shores of the St. Johns froze, and orange trees as far south as 28 degrees north latitude died back to the roots. Many growers, according to one contemporary observer, "were hurled in a night from the seat of affluence into the lap of poverty and distress."[11]

Although "Cold Sunday" prompted most Georgia growers to abandon citrus production, groves in the St. Augustine area slowly recovered, and the center of Florida citrus production shifted only slightly southward. The freeze drastically changed the nature of those groves, however. Most of the wild orange trees died back in 1835, and new groves were nearly always top-worked on the surviving wild roots or on new sour orange rootstock, frequently with buds of hardy sweet oranges from Douglas Dummett's Merritt Island groves.[12]

Freezes continued to cull northern groves periodically, and a serious infestation of purple scale, a parasitic insect, plagued growers across the state from 1838 through the 1850s.[13] Despite freezes and bugs, production continued to expand; and while the center of production inched ever southward, undeveloped lines of transportation more than the impact of climate limited the geography of that expansion. Fresh citrus is a bulky and perishable commodity, requiring ready access to markets. With no railroads serving central Florida, growers were confined to the coasts and navigable rivers. Between 1835 and the end of the Civil War, growers set in many new groves farther up the St. Johns. In 1865, East Florida growers were harvesting citrus from ten thousand trees. Every winter they loaded their fresh fruit onto paddleboats for transportation down the Ocklawaha and St. Johns to Jacksonville and points north.[14]

The end of the Civil War marks the beginning of the modern Florida citrus industry. Between 1865 and the great freeze of 1895, northern money, transportation technology, and human capital defined the geography of Florida's orange belt. For nearly a century, three areas would dominate Florida citrus production: the Ridge, a high (by Floridian standards) region running along the center of the peninsula from Lake County south to Highlands County; the Indian River region on the Atlantic coast; and the Tampa Bay area on the Gulf coast. But the postbellum years also saw citriculture expand along the northern rivers and adjacent to new rail lines. Whether they chose those areas destined to define the orange belt or worked groves fated for frosty extinction, Florida's Gilded Age growers were driven by land speculation and citrus's reputation for good returns. The relative absence of hard freezes fueled "orange fever."

Perhaps as important as the mild climate was the proselytizing of northern speculators, consumptive health seekers, and do-gooders who spread the gospel of easy money, clear lungs, and clean consciences awaiting those who would stake a claim in Florida. Marion County grower F. G. Sampson recalled some of the promoters' boasts: "We were told that an orange tree planted on good land would never need fertilizing, that they had no insect enemies . . . and that oranges could never sell for less than two cents each at the grove."[15] Harriet Beecher Stowe's claims for quick riches through citriculture were considerably more realistic than those of railroad promoters and land speculators. But the steady stream of dispatches she sent to the *Christian Union* from her winter home in Mandarin, on the eastern shore of the St. Johns, made her one of the most famous of these promoters. Stowe enthusiastically reported on subjects ranging from the state's flora and fauna to its citrus business, as well as on her efforts in the betterment of the former slaves, and the moral improvements her brand of reform might bestow on the South.[16]

But Stowe was not a typical grower. Her Mandarin grove contained a little over one hundred trees and was already established when she and Calvin Stowe bought their winter home. More typical is John Tenney, a northern lumberman who bought timberland in Palatka in 1865. After harvesting his pine trees, he decided to clear the land and "set out orange trees." Tenney was not the only one in Palatka with this idea. "We were not left alone but a few months, as people began to come in, all infected with orange fever that had become chronic all over the state."[17]

Orange fever transformed much of central Florida's landscape. Gainesville in the 1880s was not merely surrounded by groves—they appeared to be swallowing the municipality. An advertisement for a two-acre lot in town boasted "158 orange trees planted out, from five to eight years old," while at the Alachua County courthouse, crews razed ancient oaks to make room for orange trees. Groves appeared along the shores of hundreds of small lakes perforating the Ridge. First developed were those with access to navigable rivers, but as the railway's tendrils spread out from the main trunks, almost the entire Ridge gained quick access to northern markets.[18]

Florida orange growers produced around 100,000 90-pound boxes during the 1874–75 season; by 1884, annual citrus production reached 625,000 boxes, and by the 1890 census, that number had shot to over 3 million. Another measure of the pace of growth near the end of the nineteenth century is the ratio of bearing to nonbearing trees. In 1890, growers harvested oranges from 2.7 million trees and eagerly tended another 7.4 million immature trees. Production peaked with the 1893–94 harvest of just over 5 million boxes, a number that would not be exceeded until 1909, fifteen years after the devastating freeze of 1894–95.[19]

The "big one" was actually two freezes: one in late December, the other in February. Either could have destroyed the remaining crop and killed many young trees, but their combined effect wiped out entire orchards, including grand, hardy veterans of many a cold snap. The December freeze arrived on the 29th, bringing temperatures as low as 12 degrees Fahrenheit in Tallahassee, and 19 degrees in Tampa, where the Weather Bureau recorded a high of only 39 degrees. Only half the crop had been harvested; the rest froze on the tree. January brought warmer weather and rain, and damaged trees began to recover. At this most vulnerable time, the February freeze hit. Lottie Conrad of DeLand recalled that the February freeze "came so quickly and finally, with terrible strong winds and torrents of freezing rain, causing the now running sap in the trees to freeze. All night long one could hear the cracking open of the bark of the trees, as if one were cracking walnuts."[20]

Unlike the 1835 freeze, or a bruising four-day cold snap in 1886, the freeze of 1894–95 prompted a significant permanent southward shift in citrus growing. Years later, longtime Florida residents told of disillusioned growers abandoning their groves before their frozen oranges thawed, locking their houses and heading back north.[21] Agricultural statistics for the next twenty years suggest that more frequently they bought land farther south and set out new groves (see figure 8.1). Among counties centered above 29 degrees north latitude that reported citrus production in the census of 1890, almost 82 percent recorded no production at all for four years after the big freeze, while only 20 percent of those counties at or below 29 degrees were completely knocked out; production in another 20 percent of southern counties actually increased.[22] By 1909, over two-thirds of the northern counties were still growing fewer oranges than twenty years before, while nearly three-fourths of the southern counties had increased production, dramatically in many cases.[23]

Those areas that escaped the cold's icy fingers gained both value and reputation. Set on high land below the 28th parallel, with plenty of lakes to moderate the cold winds, Keystone City's groves escaped the freeze, prompting its jubilant citizens to rename their town Frostproof.[24] The Tampa Bay area, and especially the Pinellas peninsula, saw a dramatic influx of both citrus trees and people. Between 1890 and 1910, Hillsborough County's population and orange production increased fivefold. The move south was encouraged by land promoters and railroad men who took advantage of the increased desirability of southern land. Railroad magnate Henry Flagler, reassured by Julia

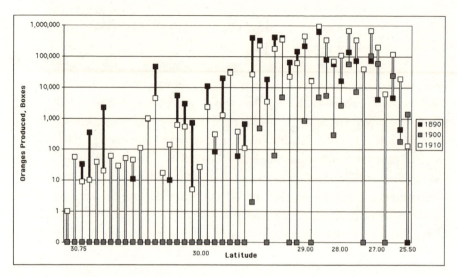

Figure 8.1. Oranges produced by box.

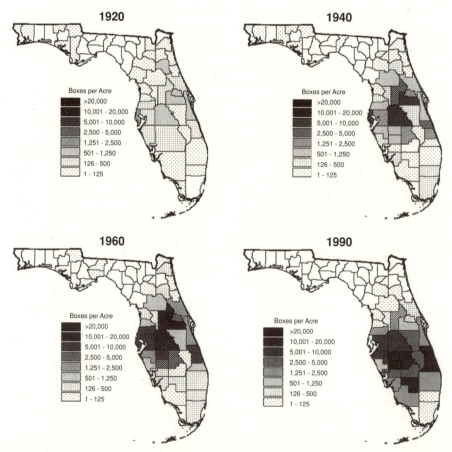

Figure 8.2. Orange production by county.

Tuttle—who had just purchased large tracts of citrus land in what would soon become Miami—that the region was well below the frost line, rushed ahead with a proposed rail line to Florida's southeast shores and made low-interest loans to help farmers of freeze-damaged groves along existing rail lines.[25]

The decade after 1894 was punctuated by severe freezes, pushing groves farther south as most Florida growers developed a healthy respect for winter's chills. With only die-hards growing citrus in the northern third of the state, it would appear that by the beginning of the twentieth century, climate had fully exerted its influence on the distribution of Florida's citrus groves. Occasional severe freezes, such as those that devastated citrus groves in the 1980s, hit northern counties hardest, continuing the citrus belt's southward retreat.[26]

The geographic and climatic history of citrus may be interpreted as growers' lessons from nature's catechism, a rigorous tutorial in respecting the limits of climate, season, and geography. But there were other lessons as well. Florida's citrus growers devised technologies to maximize production of the most marketable fruits. In addition, they employed every new technology to expand the citrus region, reach more distant markets, and control the economic consequences of their season-bound and climate-prone supply. Orange production and productivity statistics for the last century reveal how successful this venture was. The number of acres in Florida producing oranges increased nearly five times from 1890 to 1992, but enhanced productivity produced increased yields to over forty-three times. Growers in the last quarter of the twentieth century harvested from ten to fifteen times as many oranges per acre as their counterparts a century earlier, with each bearing tree producing between two and three times as many oranges (see table 8.1). This change suggests that the "nature" of the citrus tree itself was malleable,

Table 8.1. Orange Production in Florida, Selected Statistics

	Boxes Harvested	Acres Producing	Trees (bearing)	Boxes/Acre	Boxes/Tree
1890	3,146,740	144,769	2,725,272	21.74	1.15
1919	5,930,422	3,645,811			1.63
1929	9,720,998	198,614	9,002,362	48.94	1.08
1939	24,047,105				
1949	49,966,938				
1959	79,525,907		24,005,043	3.31	
1969	132,732,960	399,474	44,443,425	332.27	2.99
1978	164,993,294	692,193	47,741,466	238.36	3.46
1992	136,368,008	691,988	53,592,022	197.07	2.54

An Overview of the Many Environmental Histories of Florida Citrus

and that we should consider it not only in its climatic and geographic settings but as a manufactured product in isolation, from the roots up.

Most people reflexively see a healthy and productive citrus tree as an object of natural beauty. Harriet Beecher Stowe expressed this sentiment eloquently: "The orange-tree is, in our view, the best worthy to represent the tree of life of any that grows on our earth. It is the fairest, the noblest, the most generous, it is the most upspringing and abundant, of all trees which the Lord God caused to grow eastward in Eden." Stowe granted her subject human moral attributes, and rated its "natural" attributes according to human economic needs ("most generous," "abundant"). Perhaps it *is* natural that the orange is so attractive, but much of what Stowe admired so in her beloved orange tree, "thirty feet high, with spreading graceful top, and varnished green leaves, full of golden fruit," are characteristics derived as much from human intervention as from the "Lord God."[27] The wild citrus that evolved millions of years ago in Southeast Asia produced a bitter fruit. It seems likely that people from many areas domesticated the wild species simultaneously, although literary and biological evidence suggests southern China was the heart of early domestication. By 4000 BCE, early citriculture had produced lemons, limes, and oranges. The domesticated species—bred and tended for human needs—thrived; wild citrus on the other hand, perhaps reviled by then for its weedlike "upspringing" nature and abundance, gradually slipped into extinction.[28]

The technology of modern citrus production removes the typical tree even further from its natural ancestry. Almost every fruit-producing citrus tree is held to the earth and nurtured by roots of an altogether different variety. As mentioned in the swift survey above, growers since the early nineteenth century have relied on joining buds of bearing stock to rootstock of hardy but unpalatable citrus varieties. Prior to the twentieth century, sour oranges—the ancestors of trees propagated by the earliest Spanish visitors—provided the most popular rootstock; they continue to be used in heavy or moist soils. Most of the citrus planted in the higher, sandy soils of the Ridge was grown on rough lemon rootstock until the 1960s, when a long run of problems in sweet oranges grown on rough lemon rootstock prompted growers to shift to a range of other rootstocks, such as hybrids developed early in the century by Florida grower W. T. Swingle.[29]

Careful breeding and selection of root and scion stock operate on the tree itself. Other technologies act to alter the citrus tree's relation to its environment. From the beginning of the industry, citrus growers employed all the conventional agricultural tools of irrigation, fertilizers, and pesticides. A complete environmental history of Florida citrus must address each of these technologies in detail, analyzing how their use was shaped by economics, government, and especially as they affected the environment.[30] For the purposes of this brief survey, however, I will focus on technologies that seek to mitigate the effects of climate.

Florida's frequent chilly lapses from the semitropical ideal prompted growers to harness wind, water, and fire to soften winter's occasional chills. The typical Florida cold front rushes south from the Arctic, announced by wind and rain, but arriving as a heavy, dry blanket of cold, clear air. With no insulating clouds, the ground quickly gives up its heat at night, producing an inversion layer where the air at ground level is much cooler than a couple dozen feet above.

Citrus growers found that when the air is still, a series of evenly spaced fires—seventy per acre is typical—can raise the temperature of this thin blanket of air by several degrees. Where lumber was plentiful and close at hand, growers kept small piles of "lighter wood," or rosin-rich heart of pine, throughout the groves; junk tires were another popular source of fuel. As pine became scarce, most growers came to rely on oil heaters (sometimes called "smudge pots"), which might be easily lit or extinguished. Grower Buddy Huff kept 21,000 oil heaters for his 80-acre grove south of Gainesville, and between 1949 and 1983 few winters went by without Huff having to light up the burners at least once. During the harsh freeze of 1962, Huff kept all of his heaters burning night and day. Although every tree dropped both fruit and leaves, those trees near the burners recovered by the next growing season. In recent years, high fuel costs and the citrus belt's southward migration have largely eliminated the use of heaters, except to protect specimen trees or high-value crops.[31]

Growers also employ wind and water to stave off killing freezes, training large fans over the tops of their groves to mix the warm and cold air layers, or spraying water over their trees to form a protective sheet of ice that keeps the surface of the fruit at, but not below, the freezing point. Icing the trees is fraught with risks, however. A stiff wind will negate the advantage of the protective ice, and if the spraying continues for too many hours, the thin sheet becomes a heavy blanket, weighing the tree's limbs past the breaking point, destroying more than just the year's crop.[32]

In 1935, after a freeze destroyed much of the orange crop, Florida and the United States Weather Bureau established the Federal-State Agricultural

Weather Service (also known as the Federal-State Frost Warning Service). The service allied growers with government agencies to minimize the costs of adverse conditions in the natural environment, a technological and institutional response to the environment. For any frost-protection technology to be truly effective, growers needed accurate forecasts of approaching cold fronts. When will the front arrive? How low will temperatures fall, and for how long? Will wind conditions make oil burners worthless, or should a grower stand by through the night to light them? At its peak, the service employed a dozen or so meteorologists, funded by the state through academic affiliation with the University of Florida. In addition, nine field agents collected data weekly during the cold season from as many as four hundred weather stations.[33] The service kept growers informed of its microforecasts by way of a daily teletype service and radio. In the early 1970s, the service modernized and downsized, establishing a twenty-four-hour weather teletype service, while cutting staff and reducing the number of weather stations by half.[34] Statistical inference from old data permitted microforecasting without the expense of actually measuring the temperature at every location.

Other citrus industry alliances, nominally economic in function, have played significant roles in shaping the relationship between their product and nature. Private organizations such as the Florida Citrus Exchange (established in 1909), the Florida Citrus Mutual (established in 1948), and dozens of other trade associations have sought, in the Mutual's words, the "lofty goal" of "bringing supply and demand into sync to maximize profits." Since 1935, with the establishment of the Florida Citrus Commission, a state agency funded by the citrus industry, growers have had enormous power to shape agricultural policy and direct state-sponsored research, through the University of Florida's Citrus Research and Education Center (CREC).[35] It was here, in the early 1940s, that CREC scientists developed the process that would transform the citrus industry.

The single most significant technological change in citrus production in the twentieth century—perhaps even more significant than the development of topworking—was the advent of frozen concentrated orange juice (FCOJ). Concentrate's effect on the citrus industry was similar to the transformation in grain marketing in the Midwest of the mid-nineteenth century. Grain elevators and the new marketing strategies they required transformed corn and wheat from solids, carried from farm to market in discrete sacks, to something "more like liquids: golden streams that flowed like water." Nearly a century later, concentrated orange juice had a similar impact on citrus. As journalist John McPhee observed in 1967, "concentrate has not only changed the landscape and the language; it has, in a sense, turned the orange inside out."[36] Now, instead of marketing boxes of oranges, selected and priced by color, size, and quality, growers sell on the basis of the quantity of fruit sugars in each truckload of citrus brought to the juice plant, as determined by samples analyzed by chemists.[37]

Judging by the status of the canned-juice market in 1940, concentrated orange juice's prospects seemed poor. Most American juice consumers squeezed their own from fresh oranges. Despite steady growth in citrus processing plants since the 1920s, less than one-fifth of Florida's orange crops went into canned citrus fruit and juice in 1940. Canning was a secondary market, essentially a way for growers to dispose of blemished, substandard, or nonstandard sized fruit.[38]

A number of processors experimented with finding palatable concentrates for special markets. Citrus Concentrates, Inc., of Dunedin began concentrating orange juice by a vacuum process used for drying blood plasma. Before the war, Citrus Concentrates sold $1 million of the highly concentrated syrup annually, mostly to hospitals and other institutions. The hot-concentrate process skyrocketed when several Florida processors got Lend-Lease contracts to produce concentrate for British civilians. In 1943, 10 percent of Florida's orange crop went into 5 million gallons of the sweet, semi-liquid jelly, which were shipped to Europe to civilians and soldiers.[39]

The biggest problem with bottled concentrate was its flavor: along with the water, vacuum dehydration removed oils and essences that give fresh orange juice its flavor—McPhee describes the reconstituted product tasting "like a glass of water with two teaspoons of sugar and one aspirin dissolved in it." In 1945, scientists at the Florida Citrus Commission's Citrus Research and Education Center developed a concentration process that recovered (or re-created by approximation, to be more accurate) most of the juice's flavor. They found that when highly concentrated juice was diluted slightly with a mixture of fresh juice, citrus oils, and other flavoring ingredients, the resulting concentrate could be frozen, shipped, and stored. When diluted with three parts water, the mixture produced an acceptable version of fresh juice. The CREC researchers received a patent for the process in 1948 but assigned it to the U.S. Department of Agriculture.[40] In 1945, the new product received its first commercial test when Citrus Concentrates, Inc., sent two refrigerated train carloads of concentrate to People's Drug Stores of Washington, D.C., for use in soda-fountain orange juice.[41]

From 1945 to 1948, postwar economics and turf wars in the new frozen foods industry retarded marketing of concentrated orange juice. After this inauspicious beginning, frozen concentrate sales slowly started growing. By 1948, three big processors, Minute Maid, Snow Crop (Vacuum Foods), and Birds Eye (General Foods) dominated, with a number of small processors successfully competing for what was now a fast-growing sector of the frozen food market. The large processors spent hundreds of thousands of dollars annually promoting concentrate. The entire industry rode on Minute Maid's coattails when legendary crooner Bing Crosby bought 20,000 shares (at 10 cents a share, his investment was only $2,000) and took the title of manager of Bing Crosby Minute Maid Corporation—a marketing subsidiary that among other strategies produced radio shows promoting frozen juice. Production rose from 226,000 gallons in the 1945–46 season to 30 million gallons five years later. The flood of juice drove a boom in overall citrus production, which rose from 42.8 million boxes in 1944–45 to 73.5 million in the 1951–52 season, with concentrated juice consuming over one-fourth of the crop.[42]

To growers in the late 1940s, concentrate seemed to offer a solution to many vexing problems: "The concentrate didn't depend on seasons," a *Business Week* report enthused, "You could store it as long as you liked. By building or reducing inventory at will, you could absorb the fluctuations in crops and thus keep prices on an even keel. It was the solution to everything."[43] Initially, however, unrealistic projections based on skyrocketing demands for the cheap and convenient beverage destabilized prices and production. The high prices producers were willing to pay growers, and the promise of endless new markets drove growers to expand their groves. Florida farmland prices rose 20 percent in twelve months in 1950–51, and by 1954, Florida growers were tending 27.6 million orange trees—78 percent more than in 1945. Between 1954 and 1970, the number of orange trees nearly doubled again.[44]

The resulting overproduction and wild price swings plagued the new industry through the early 1950s, but from its arrival in grocers' freezers, concentrated orange juice created a new market for oranges that accounted for nearly all of the industry's growth. In 1954, approximately half of Florida's 88 million boxes of oranges ended up as FCOJ; in 1998, less than 10 percent of the state's orange crop was consumed fresh, with frozen concentrate and refrigerated single-strength juice consuming 95 percent of the year's 244 million boxes of oranges.[45]

Christian Warren

John McPhee begins his humorous and informative survey of the Florida orange industry in the mid-1960s with his quixotic search for a glass of fresh-squeezed juice in the heart of orange country, "a place where—or so it had once seemed to me—people all but brushed their teeth in fresh orange juice." But reconstituted concentrate was all he was offered, and he was reduced to rustling some oranges from a local grove and squeezing a glass himself. "I had what I wanted," he concluded, "but it had been a long day." Frozen concentrate's share of the orange juice market has dwindled since the 1960s, with the rising popularity of single-strength "not from concentrate" juices (sales of which in 1998–99 were twice that of frozen concentrate). But frozen concentrate—whether in the now old-fashioned six-ounce cans, or reconstituted and sold in refrigerated cartons next to premium "fresh" ("Not From Concentrate") orange juice—dominates the market, with 64 percent of total juice sales.[46]

Frozen concentrate removes citrus yet further from nature. Its ability to erase time, smooth the differences between seasons, and regulate prices makes concentrate a powerful economic factor in the citrus industry's survival. But its removal from nature shows in its taste: consistent regardless of intra- or interseasonal changes, it provides a reliable, if not natural taste, much like other manufactured beverages. Significant numbers of consumers have balked at the artifice and inauthentic flavor, establishing the premium refrigerated juice market. But not even those premium brands can match the taste of that fresh-squeezed juice that made McPhee's long day complete, the same taste that once defined orange juice, squeezed right in the kitchen from fresh oranges, whose spent hulls once filled America's kitchen garbage cans.

Demand for orange juice, regardless of which form consumers choose to buy it, has been the chief factor in the ongoing growth of the citrus belt since the 1950s. Where that growth has occurred, however, is a function of several historical forces. In addition to access to markets and fair weather, competition over land use has shaped the boundaries of Florida's citrus-growing region, especially in the second half of the twentieth century. Florida's citrus region evolved in competition with other land uses. In some places, citrus moved in directly after the lumbermen cleared the pines; in others, citrus production promised a better return on the land than low-intensity uses such as grazing. Tensions often mounted in areas where livestock and citrus regions overlapped: growers erected fences to keep out neighbors' cattle, furtively shot and buried wayward hogs, and sought legislative action to halt the cattlemen's practice of setting fires to clear coarse underbrush and promote fresh growth, fires that frequently burned growers' fences and trees. As citrus began its slow move south after the Civil War, it must have seemed that cattle were the growers' front line. In 1886, Orange County citrus grower Alexander Kelley McClure noted: "the settling up of the country is driving the cattlemen south, down among the Everglades receding before the march of civilization." Recognition of climatic realities by citrus growers would eventually make room for cattle once again in the Orange County region, where Brahman bulls now graze in fields once bristling with citrus trees.[47]

Latitude, of course, is not everything, and many areas that appealed to growers were equally attractive to tourists and new residents. For much of the twentieth century, therefore, population growth and tourism chipped away at the orange's domain, pushing its center farther south and farther from Florida's sunny coasts. Comparing the experience of two neighboring Florida counties, Pinellas and Hillsborough, suggests the shifting dynamics of climate, transportation, and demand for housing and tourist accommodation.

At the beginning of the century, the two counties were one. Bounded on the west by the Gulf coast, Hillsborough County straddled the warm harbor of Tampa Bay and extended inland to the western edge of the Ridge. The area's seasonal swings in temperatures are moderated by sea breezes and the warm waters of Tampa Bay, producing a perfect setting for citriculture. Tampa's harbor of course also provided access to transportation, access greatly enhanced with the introduction, in 1884, of rail lines to the north.[48] As figure 8.3 illustrates, from the time Pinellas County achieved independence from Hillsborough in 1911 until the post–World War II era, the two counties saw similar increases in both citrus production and population.

But the postwar residential building boom gobbled up acres of groves and drove land prices skyward. Citrus production in Pinellas County fell away as more and more growers plowed over their groves and sold out to residential real estate developers. Hillsborough's population growth paralleled that on the west side of Tampa Bay. But most of Hillsborough's population growth occurred on the bay side, while citrus production continued growing and intensifying in Tampa's eastern hinterlands. Further study of local property values, changing tax laws, productivity, and weather history may answer whether this transformation represented creeping suburban sprawl uprooting a thriving citrus economy or an opportunity for profit-maximizing growers to transfer their business to more remote—and slightly less frosty—areas.

The "Disneyfication" of Orlando and its impact on central Florida citrus production presents a very different set of circumstances leading to much the

Christian Warren

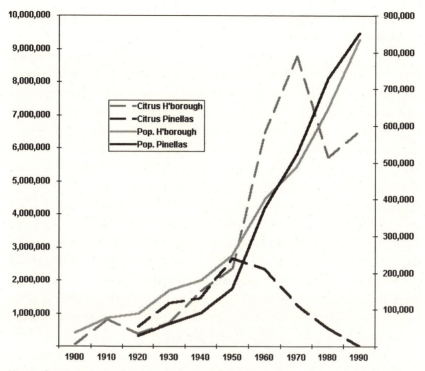

Figure 8.3. Orange production versus population growth.

same result as in Pinellas County: when Mickey came, the citrus growers went away. Here, of course, it was the strategic plans of a giant entertainment enterprise and not the natural attractions of land and water that dictated where the residential and commercial boom would occur.[49] Climate, central location with interstate highway access to both coasts, and cheap land largely determined Disney World's location. The low cost of land in turn made the project's unprecedented scope possible. Walt Disney promised that unlike his first theme park, "Disneyland East" would be built with plenty of breathing room for Disney-owned restaurants and hotels. "It is necessary to control the environment," he asserted. "We learned this at Disneyland."[50]

In October 1964, Disney's land agents secretly purchased their first major central Florida tract—over 8,000 acres of swamp, purchased at a cost of $107 per acre. Much of the 27,400-acre tract Walt Disney World would eventually occupy was undeveloped: swamps, scrub pine forests, and low-intensity cattle land, though some land featured scattered citrus groves. By late 1965, amid growing buzz about who had hired the mysterious land agents and to what end, Disney had secured almost all of its target acreage, at a cost of just

An Overview of the Many Environmental Histories of Florida Citrus

over $5 million, or less than $200 per acre. Once Disney confirmed the company's plans, surrounding land prices skyrocketed.[51]

In 1971, just months before Walt Disney World opened its gates, John Luff, mayor of Windermere, a small town several miles north of the Disney properties, speculated on the coming changes. Luff, who owned Windermere's only store and operated thirty-five citrus groves, estimated that recently approved assessments for water, sewer, and street improvements would drive local taxes up to $500 per lot. He had voted for the improvements, even though, he said, "they would put my groves out of business. But how can you stand in the way of progress?" Luff's interviewer questioned the nature of this progress, predicting, "In ten years, the only orange tree left in Orange County is likely to be in a museum."[52] The drop would not be that drastic, but it was dramatic: Orange County's production of oranges and grapefruit peaked in 1970, with a reported crop of 19.7 million boxes; ten years later, Orange County groves produced less than half that number. The trend continued through 1990, when the county produced just over 1 million boxes—about 5 percent of the 1970 figure. Over the same two decades, the number of acres in groves plummeted from 6,260 to 343, while the county's population nearly doubled.[53]

The inevitable conflict between growers, land developers, and tourist industry promoters should not overshadow the largely symbiotic relationship between the Florida citrus industry and those promoting Florida as a tourist destination, a place to raise a family, start a business, or retire. In the case of early-twentieth-century land developer William J. Howey, this symbiosis was manifested in one person. From 1908 to the early 1930s, Howey found creative ways to market agricultural and residential land, tourism, and citrus products from his base in Lake County. From 1914 to 1920, Howey purchased 60,000 acres of land, which he cleared, planted in citrus, and parceled out to northern investors who contracted for Howey to maintain their land and market the produce. He built a hotel on Little Lake Harris and established the town of Howey-in-the-Hills, which became a popular stop for tourist-investors from both coasts. Howey's seven sales offices—located in major tourist towns from Miami to St. Petersburg—offered land, as well as oranges and Howey's "Lifeguard" brand canned juice.[54] His interest in the life-saving attributes of citrus extended as far as planning the Howey Sanitarium, where he hoped to employ citrus products to treat influenza and chronic illnesses such as diabetes.[55]

Howey's melding of citrus, tourism, and real estate is only one of the more visible examples of a deliberate and fully articulated plan for exploiting the synergies the separate industries offered. As a successful grower, Howey mastered the art and science of citrus cultivation—site selection and preparation, the chemistry of propagation, freeze-protection, harvesting and processing—in short, the alchemy of turning base materials into Florida gold. As a developer in Florida's early twentieth century land booms, he helped create citrus's status as a "natural" feature of the Florida landscape and Floridian culture.

All Floridians live with citrus in their backyards—whether literally or figuratively. Many Florida residents witness up close the seasonal cycles of a productive citrus tree: the scent of blossoms, the sleepy sounds of bees making their rounds, the subtle changes in color and texture as fruit grow and ripen. They walk into their own yard and casually take from their own fruit-laden tree a perfect sun-ripened orange. Many no doubt share Harriet Beecher Stowe's sentiments about that grand tree in her yard: "It gives one a sort of heart thrill of possession to say of such beauty, 'It is mine.'"[56] But their ownership of these "upspringing and abundant" trees also likely brings the sights and smells of the home and garden shop, where they confront row after row of the American chemical industry's newest and most improved products to fertilize and condition their soil or to fend off insects, molds, and bacteria. Like commercial growers, they monitor weather forecasts in winter to be prepared to shield their trees from frosty weather; they grudgingly accede to Department of Agriculture rules for preventing Mediterranean fruit fly; or they wince at the thought of being forced to give up their beloved backyard cornucopia to help eradicate citrus canker.[57]

Whether or not they cultivate backyard citrus trees, Floridians live in a built environment and within a culture shaped in part by intensive citrus production. Over the past two centuries, commercial citrus groves appeared over most of the state: in the north, from coastal towns on the panhandle to the mouth of the St. Johns River; in the south from Miami to the Keys. Most of the old groves disappeared as new ones grew, farther south, farther inland, following changes in transportation, climate, and the movements of human populations, ultimately determining the limits of today's citrus belt. This historical dispersal followed by gradual retreat meant citrus had the potential for a much deeper and broader impact over the development of the politics, culture, and environment of the "Long Frontier" than its current geographic center would indicate. The state's environment and culture were always definitely southern, yet distinctly Floridian. Florida built its reputation on claims of healthy climate, clear water, and a bountiful nature, exemplified by the iconic image of an orange tree replete with fruit. Florida citrus produced a different image for this corner of the South, an image defined less by moonlight and magnolias than by sunshine and orange blossoms.

Notes

1. *St. Petersburg Times,* January 28, 1912.

2. Marjory Stoneman Douglas, *Florida: The Long Frontier* (New York: Harper and Row, 1967); the belated closing of Florida's frontier marks it, in geographer Carolyn Baker Lewis's term, as a "secondary frontier." "Agricultural Evolution on Secondary Frontiers: A Florida Model," in *The Frontier: Comparative Studies,* ed. William W. Savage and Stephen I. Thompson (Norman: University of Oklahoma Press, 1979), 2:205–33.

3. Or roughly 2.6 percent of Florida's land surface; the U.S. Census Bureau, in *Census of Agriculture 1992,* vol. 6, pt. 9, table 31, reported all citrus fruits occupied 887,904 (2.56 percent) of Florida's 34,657,920 acres.

4. Jerry Wood Weeks, "Florida Gold: The Emergence of the Florida Citrus Industry, 1865–1895" (Ph.D. diss., University of North Carolina, 1977) 3; John McPhee, *Oranges* (New York: Noonday Press, 1991). According to McPhee, the Spanish were given mandates to carry citrus to the New World.

5. James J. Miller, *An Environmental History of Northeast Florida* (Gainesville: University Press of Florida, 1998), 104–6. Miller's account is based on Jean Ribault, *The Whole and True Discouerye of Terra Florida* (facsimile reprint of 1563 London edition, Gainesville: University of Florida Press, 1964); T. Frederick Davis, "Early Orange Culture in Florida and the Epocal Cold of 1835," *Florida Historical Quarterly* 15, no. 4 (April 1937): 232–41.

6. Donald Worster, "Transformations of the Earth: Toward an Agroecological Perspective in History," *Journal of American History* 76, no. 4 (March 1990): 1087–106.

7. Karen Ordahl Kupperman, "The Puzzle of the American Climate in the Early Colonial Period," *American Historical Review* 87 (December 1982): 1262–89; Peter H. Wood, *Black Majority: Negroes in Colonial South Carolina from 1670 through the Stono Rebellion* (New York: Knopf, 1974); John A. Attaway, *A History of Florida Citrus Freezes* (Lake Alfred, Fla.: Florida Science Resource, 1997), 5.

8. Jerry Wood Weeks quotes Bernard Romans, British surveyor in the 1760s: "I also regard as a curiosity of the artificial kind the immense orange groves, found in the woods between latitude 28 1/2 and 30 degrees, supposing them originally sprung from the seeds of some oranges formerly dropt, by travelling Spaniards at their camps." Romans, *A Concise Natural History of East and West Florida* (1775; facsimile edition, Gainesville: University of Florida Press, 1962), 278, cited in Weeks, "Florida Gold," 3; Attaway, *A History of Florida Citrus Freezes,* 11.

9. Fish's plantation was 2 miles from St. Augustine, on St. Anastasia Island, which came to be called Fish's Island. Davis, "Early Orange Culture in Florida," 234; Weeks, "Florida Gold," 4; McPhee, *Oranges,* 88.

Christian Warren

10. According to Marjory Stoneman Douglas, Colonel T. H. Dummett purchased the Merritt Island lands between 1820 and 1825. *Florida: The Long Frontier* (New York: Harper and Row, 1967) 225; Weeks, "Florida Gold," 7–8; Davis, "Early Orange Culture in Florida," 235–36.

11. Attaway, *A History of Florida Citrus Freezes*, 14 (quote), 16, 17; on rumors of an iceberg causing the freeze, see Davis, "Early Orange Culture in Florida," 236.

12. Attaway, *A History of Florida Citrus Freezes*, 16; McPhee, *Oranges*, 90–91.

13. Female purple scale insects are parasites that attach themselves to succulent growth on citrus trees and live under a scale of waxy secretions. Florida. Dept. of Agriculture, *Citrus Industry of Florida* (Tallahassee: Department of Agriculture, 1949), 102–4; Richard C. Sawyer, *To Make a Spotless Orange: Biological Control in California* (Ames: Iowa State University Press, 1996), 86.

14. Weeks describes groves in Yalaha and Ocala in 1850, as well as in Orange Mills and East Palatka ("Florida Gold," 10); Attaway describes growth during the 1850s in Alachua, Putnam, and Marion counties, *A History of Florida Citrus Freezes*, 17.

15. F. G. Sampson, "Pioneering in Orange and Lemon Culture in Florida," *Proceedings FSHS* 36 (1923): 194, quoted by Weeks, "Florida Gold," 18–19.

16. Harriet Beecher Stowe, *Palmetto-Leaves* (Gainesville: University of Florida Press, 1968).

17. Ibid., 142; John F. Tenney, *Slavery, Secession and Success: The Memoirs of a Florida Pioneer* (San Antonio: Southern Literary Institute, 1934), 27–28, quoted in Weeks, "Florida Gold," 15.

18. Attaway, *A History of Florida Citrus Freezes*, 18–21.

19. Weeks, "Florida Gold," 79; Michael Sanders, "The Great Freeze of 1894–95 in Pinellas County," *Tampa Bay History* 2 (spring/summer 1980): 5–14; U.S. Census Bureau, *Census of Agriculture, Eleventh Census*, vol. 10, *Statistics of Agriculture*; Florida Dept. of Agriculture, *Citrus Industry of Florida*, 11.

20. Attaway, *A History of Florida Citrus Freezes*, 29–35; Conrad quote from M. S. Arterburn, "A History of Citrus in Mount Dora, Florida to 1900" (master's thesis, Stetson University, 1961), in Attaway, *A History of Florida Citrus Freezes*, 34.

21. An early settler in central Florida recalled one such desertion: one of the nicest homes in Bloomfield "was left fully furnished when the owners went back to where they were from." Nellie King Wright, "Narrative of Bloomfield in the 1890s," unpublished manuscript (1969), 3, quoted in Robert D. Manning, "From Orange to Green 'Gold': The Roots of the Asparagus Fern Industry in Florida," *Florida Historical Quarterly* 62 (April 1984): 464–84; for other examples, see Sanders, "The Great Freeze of 1894–95"; and Lewis, "Agricultural Evolution on Secondary Frontiers," 225.

22. U.S. Census Bureau, *Census of Agriculture, 1890–1910*; eighteen out of twenty-two (81.2 percent) of northern counties that reported some orange production for the 1890 census reported no oranges grown in 1900. Only three of fifteen (20 percent) orange-growing counties south of 29 degrees north reported no production in 1900.

23. In the 1910 census, fifteen out of twenty-two (68.2 percent) northern counties had failed to match 1890's production, while eleven out of fifteen (73.3 percent) southern counties had.

24. McPhee, *Oranges,* 47.

25. Hillsborough County then comprised both today's Hillsborough and Pinellas counties. Between the 1890 and 1910 federal censuses, Hillsborough County's population rose from 14,941 to 78,374 (an increase of 424 percent); while orange production went from 138,515 boxes to 665,461 (an increase of 380 percent). Charlton W. Tebeau, *A History of Florida* (Coral Gables: University of Miami Press, 1971), 287; Mark Derr, *Some Kind of Paradise: A Chronicle of Man and the Land in Florida* (New York: William Morrow, 1989), 45–46.

26. For blow-by-blow accounts of these freezes, see Attaway, *A History of Florida Citrus Freezes,* 275–82.

27. Stowe, *Palmetto-Leaves,* 18.

28. J. W. Cameron and R. K. Soost, "Citrus," in *Evolution of Crop Plants,* ed. N. W. Simmonds (New York: Longman, 1976), 261–65; McPhee, *Oranges,* 63; Stephen Hui, "Sweet Oranges: The Biogeography of *Citrus Sinensis,*" http://stephen.cjb.net.resources/orange.html.

29. Larry Jackson and Frederick S. Davies, *Citrus Growing in Florida,* 4th ed. (Gainesville: University Press of Florida, 1999): 110–23.

30. Recently, historians have studied these themes, though often in settings beyond the Sunshine State. Mark Fiege's study of irrigation in the Snake River Valley employs methodologies and approaches appropriate to an environmental history of irrigation in Florida's citrus industry. *Irrigated Eden: The Making of an Agricultural Landscape in the American West* (Seattle: University of Washington Press, 1999). David McCally's *The Everglades: An Environmental History* includes an excellent introduction to issues of irrigation on the Florida scene (Gainesville: University Press of Florida, 1999). The history of California's citrus industry has received careful scrutiny lately: Richard C. Sawyer, *To Make a Spotless Orange*; Steven Stoll, *The Fruits of Natural Advantage: Making the Industrial Countryside in California* (Berkeley and Los Angeles: University of California Press, 1998).

31. Attaway, *A History of Florida Citrus Freezes,* 276–77; Jackson and Davies, *Citrus Growing in Florida,* 209.

32. Florida Department of Agriculture, *Citrus Industry of Florida,* 118–20; McPhee, *Oranges,* 48–49.

33. Attaway, *A History of Florida Citrus Freezes,* 49–52. During the hurricane season, many of the field agents took assignments forecasting storms.

34. Florida Department of Agriculture, *Citrus Industry of Florida,* 126; Attaway, *A History of Florida Citrus Freezes,* 49–52.

35. James T. Hopkins, *Fifty Years of Citrus: The Florida Citrus Exchange, 1909–1959* (Gainesville: University of Florida Press, 1960); "lofty goal," Florida Citrus Mutual, "History of Florida Citrus Mutual," http://www.fl-citrus-mutual.com/index.cfm?pageid=4.

36. William Cronon, *Nature's Metropolis: Chicago and the Great West* (New York: W. W. Norton, 1991), 113; McPhee, *Oranges,* 127.

37. Florida Cooperative Extension Service, "Frozen Concentrated Orange Juice from Florida Oranges," Fact Sheet FS8, April 1994.

38. A larger share of the grapefruit crop went to market canned.

39. The popular press reported that the small jars that American prisoners-of-war received in their Red Cross packages were highly sought after in the prisoner-guard bartering economy. Back in the states, the market for bottled concentrate did not go beyond institutional and soft-drink markets. J.C. Furnas, "The Big Squeeze," *Saturday Evening Post,* July 1, 1944, 18; "Troubles in Frozen Orange Juice," *Fortune,* March 1952, 102. The syrup originally concentrated 10-to-1, but most was marketed at 7-to-1 (compared with 3-to-1 for frozen concentrate).

40. Although Louis G. MacDowell often is credited with the "invention" of frozen concentrate, several scientists at the CREC, under MacDowell's directorship, worked together on the process. Florida Citrus Mutual, "Florida Citrus: Cultivating an Industry," http://www.fl-citrus-mutual.com/index.cfm?pageID=62; "aspirin," McPhee, *Oranges,* 125.

41. Hopkins, *Fifty Years of Citrus,* 196; "Troubles in Frozen Orange Juice," 102.

42. "Concentrates: Boom Hurts," *Business Week,* February 23, 1952, 77–81; "Troubles in Frozen Orange Juice," 104–5, 166.

43. "Concentrates: Boom Hurts."

44. The data, from federal agricultural censuses, which for 1945 listed 15,502,216 trees of all ages; for 1954 listed 27,618,505 trees; and for 1969 listed 53,641,046 trees.

45. Data from "Concentrates: Boom Hurts," "Citrus Reference Book," www.fred.ifas.ufl.edu/citrus/refbl.html (accessed October 27, 2000); "Troubles in Frozen Orange Juice," 105; Hopkins, *Fifty Years of Citrus,* 242.

46. McPhee, *Oranges,* 17–21; Weeks, "Florida Gold," 34; Nielsen Retail OJ Sales in Grocery Stores, in "Citrus Reference Book," 63.

47. Weeks, "Florida Gold," 49; In 1920, Orange County and its immediate interior neighbors Lake, Seminole, and Sumter counties produced 18 percent of the state's oranges and grapefruit, but only about 2.6 percent of its cattle grazed there; in 1992, the four counties produced only 1.6 percent of the state's oranges and grapefruit, but the cattle population had climbed from 17,000 to over 100,000, accounting for almost 6 percent of the state's cattle. Walt Disney World would have a more profound effect on Orange County, of course.

48. Raymond Arsenault, *St. Petersburg and the Florida Dream, 1888–1950* (Norfolk, Va.: Donning Co., 1988), 49.

49. This description does not disregard the artificial, corporate-manufactured "nature" produced by massive dredging of Tampa Bay's intercoastal waterway, which multiplied the acreage of saleable "useful" waterfront property. Still, as artificial—and destructive—as dredging was, its purpose was to exploit and enhance an existing natural resource. Kissimmee's main attractions were cheap land and its strategic location halfway between existing tourist destinations.

50. "Disneyland East," *Newsweek,* November 29, 1965, 82.

51. Stephen M. Fjellman, *Vinyl Leaves: Walt Disney World and America* (Boulder, Colo.: Westview Press, 1992), 111–13.

52. "Florida Real Estate Boom, *Look,* April 6, 1971, 31.

53. Osceola County, south of Orange County, contained half of the Disney property

but was less intensively developed in the 1960s. Both population and citrus production climbed slowly from 1970 to 1990. Additional study of land competition and citriculture should also include analysis of the impact of the space program on Florida's east coast; for example, see Weeks, "Florida Gold," 227–28, on federal purchase of the original Dummett Groves.

54. Melvin Edward Hughes Jr., "William J. Howey and His Florida Dreams," *Florida Historical Quarterly* 66 (January 1988): 243–64.

55. Ibid., 250.

56. Stowe is quite direct in identifying the economic nature of her admiration, making this statement profoundly ironic, given the chief source of her renown. Stowe, *Palmetto-Leaves*, 17.

57. Florida Department of Agriculture and Consumer Services, "Statewide Citrus Canker Decontamination Plan Launched," Department Press Release, March 29, 2000, http://doacs.state.fl.us/press/2000/03292000_1.html.

Chapter 9

The Public Storm

Hurricanes and the State in Twentieth-Century America

Raymond Arsenault

On August 16, 1888, a powerful hurricane struck the coast of southeastern Florida. The storm's maximum sustained winds may have exceeded 100, or even 125, miles per hour, but no one knows for sure. The storm originated as a tropical depression somewhere in the Atlantic Ocean sometime in late July or early August. The earliest recorded human encounter with the storm occurred on August 14, a few miles off the northern coast of Haiti, but inhabitants of more easterly Caribbean islands may have experienced the storm's high winds and water even earlier. On August 15, the storm battered several of the lower Bahama Islands, inflicting considerable damage and loss of life, but no one in Florida knew about the Bahamians' plight. The Bahamians themselves had only a vague notion of what had just happened, and authorities in Nassau were never able to come up with an exact count of the dead and injured. When the outer winds of the storm began to buffet the coast of Florida on the evening of the 15th, some savvy inhabitants may have suspected that a major hurricane was headed their way. But no one knew for sure. At that point, no one in Florida, or anywhere else for that matter, had any hard evidence about the size, shape, strength, history, or direction of the hurricane. As the fury of the storm became evident on the morning of the 16th, the residents of Dade County, where the eye first made landfall, scrambled for their lives. Understandably, no one had the time, or the inclination, or the expertise, to measure the barometric pressure, wind speed, eye configuration, or any other measurable aspect of the roaring natural monster that was threatening their community. One local man claimed that the tidal surge at the mouth of the Miami River reached 14 feet, but no one ever verified his claim, perhaps because in all of Dade County there was not a single newspaper reporter or meteorologist, amateur or professional.

As the scattered inhabitants of southeastern Florida began to emerge from the rubble, the hurricane swept across the peninsula, sideswiping the village of Fort Myers before continuing west into the Gulf of Mexico. No one tracked the hurricane's exact path across the Gulf, but on August 19 it struck the Louisiana coast somewhere west of New Orleans. In the Louisiana interior, the storm lost strength and fragmented before passing into history unnamed and unknowable. Here, as in Florida, the survivors managed the best they could, burying their dead, rebuilding their homes, and simply carrying on— all without government assistance or media coverage. In the end, the storm left changed lives and vivid memories, but little data and almost no public scrutiny.[1]

A little over a century later, on August 24, 1992, Dade County experienced Hurricane Andrew. The full force of the storm struck the Florida coast at Homestead, at 4:30 in the morning. By that time, few individuals in Homestead or anywhere else regarded Andrew as a stranger. Anyone with access to television, radio, or a morning newspaper already knew something about the character and potential of what some were calling the "storm of the century." A broad array of government officials, both domestic and international, had gathered a wealth of sophisticated data on Andrew, tracking the storm's evolution from its origins as a small tropical depression near the Cape Verde Islands on August 17, to its designation as a tropical storm by the National

Weather Bureau on August 18, to its upgrade to hurricane status on August 23, to its classification as a Category 4 storm on the Saffir/Simpson scale on August 24. Radar-generated images produced by satellite, aviation, and maritime surveillance provided government officials and the public with the exact latitude and longitude of the storm, as well as the changing shape and intensity of the wind and rain. Hourly updates on CNN, the Weather Channel, and other networks allowed the public to monitor every twist and turn in Andrew's journey across the Atlantic, in full color with running commentary from a host of meteorological experts. Moreover, during the last week of August nearly every newspaper in the Western Hemisphere ran a daily, front-page story profiling the storm. Even those who lived thousands of miles from the storm's path had the opportunity to experience the storm vicariously. Indeed, they could hardly avoid doing so.

All of this attention gave Andrew a distinct public personality and a "personal" history defined and documented by a precise set of measurements: peak winds of 175 miles per hour; maximum sustained winds of 145 miles per hour; a maximum recorded gust of 212 miles per hour; a maximum wind radius of 12.5 miles; a minimum barometric pressure of 922 millibars, or 27.23 inches at the time of landfall, the third-lowest ever recorded in North America; a 16.89-foot storm surge at Miami; a death toll of fifty-one; 80,000 homes and 15,000 pleasure boats in the Dade County area badly damaged or destroyed; 1.4 million Dade County homes without electricity; 35 million tons of debris; over $30 billion in damages. The list could go on and on, and often did in the various narratives constructed by government officials and journalists.[2]

The stark contrast between these two accounts—one vague and incomplete and the other precise and comprehensive—is revealing. These two storms—one private and one public, separated by a century of technological innovation, bureaucratic development, and evolving public consciousness—demonstrate that the character and meaning of hurricanes have changed dramatically in the twentieth century. Prior to 1900, the connection between hurricanes and human societies was essentially private; public agencies rarely became involved in individual or communal struggles for survival, and the press paid only fleeting attention to storms large or small. So-called "acts of God" came and went, and no one held out much hope that human vulnerability to such "natural disasters" could be eliminated. Weathering fierce storms was part of life, plain and simple. Only in the twentieth century, after years of governmental activism, did such resignation give way.[3]

As the account of Hurricane Andrew suggests, by the 1990s a sprawling bureaucracy had turned hurricanes into public events of the first order, bringing the expectation and the promise that government agencies would do everything in their power to protect private citizens and private property from the ravages of cyclonic fury. Working in conjunction with state and local authorities, and buttressed by thousands of print and electronic media sources, federal officials drew upon an elaborate network of tracking and warning systems, research facilities, educational publications, evacuation plans, relief efforts, and emergency management teams. All of this promoted a sense of administrative mastery and technological control that stood in sharp contrast to the acknowledged unpredictability and vulnerability of earlier eras. While this sense of mastery and control proved to be somewhat illusory in the case of Andrew's magnitude, few observers questioned the attempt to "manage" the storm. For better or for worse, the shared experience of the "public storm" had become an inescapable part of modern American life.

The evolution of the public storm phenomenon offers historians an interesting case study in institutional development. In recent years, several innovative scholars, including Morton Keller and Theda Skocpol, have deepened our understanding of the transformation and mobilization of governmental institutions in response to changing perceptions of social reality and the function of the state. Even though there has been a great deal of continuity in the nature of the problems addressed during the twentieth century, the scope and scale of governmental activism and regulation have reached levels that would have been unthinkable at the beginning of the century. These shifts in public policy have come in fits and starts, as the pace of change has responded to all manner of contingencies and alternating surges of public expectation and "persistent antistatism," to use Keller's term. When applied to the expanding role of government in the "management" of hurricanes, this new approach to institutional history reveals a complex interplay among bureaucratic structures, technological change, and popular culture.[4] Regrettably, there is little sense of this interplay in the existing literature on hurricanes, most of which offers a narrowly focused, technology-driven view of the subject. Written by ex-bureaucrats or popular science enthusiasts, these tales of wind and water and "Yankee ingenuity" tell us relatively little about the nature of change, the multiple factors influencing public policy, or the larger context of American culture. One notable exception is Ted Steinberg's illuminating and sophisticated recent study, *Acts of God: The Unnatural History of Natural Disaster in America*. Steinberg's interdisciplinary analysis of govern-

Raymond Arsenault

mental and public complicity in "natural" disasters such as floods, earthquakes, tornadoes, and hurricanes complements the present study and should encourage other scholars to explore this neglected area of environmental/political history.

As an expression of the ethos of mastery and management, the saga of the public storm is primarily a story of post–World War II America. But there is an earlier story of less purposeful development that helps to explain why the institutionalization of the public storm took so long to mature. For more than a century, the dominant pattern was one of institutional drift, an inertial legacy that, according to the eminent legal historian J. Willard Hurst, was characteristic of the American experience prior to the second half of the twentieth century.[5] Thus, for a full understanding of the historical evolution and public policy implications of the public storm, we need to pay some attention to the early history of the connections between American meteorology and bureaucracy.

During the colonial and early national eras, official governmental involvement in tracking, predicting, and responding to tropical storms was negligible. Early hurricane research, like the broader study of weather, was a private affair conducted by self-trained meteorologists such as Benjamin Franklin. In the 1740s, Franklin offered the novel hypothesis that dynamic storm systems, not surface winds, determined the movement of tropical storms. Later researchers, including Thomas Jefferson, tried to extend Franklin's insights, but government officials did not offer much assistance until 1814, when the surgeon general ordered daily weather observations at all army posts and hospitals. Three years later, Joseph Meigs, the commissioner of the General Land Office, asked local land-office registrars to keep daily weather records, but military physicians remained the backbone of the national meteorological effort until after the Civil War. The army's data proved useful to scientists such as William Redfield, who published an important series of papers on hurricanes in the 1830s and 1840s. Redfield, one of the first researchers to understand the basic structure of tropical storms, concluded that such storms involved a large mass of cyclonic winds rotating around a center. He was also the first observer to attempt to trace the paths of hurricanes as they moved from the Caribbean region to the American mainland. Unfortunately, since the American government evidenced no interest in Caribbean meteorology, he had to rely on other sources to fill out his tracking charts. One such source was Lt. Col. William Reid of the British Royal Engineers, who began a systematic study of hurricanes in Barbados in 1831.

Reid not only plotted storm tracks but also devised a general "law of storms," which included a list of rules for storm-threatened mariners. In 1847, he initiated what may have been the world's first hurricane warning system, displaying a series of flags that announced the rise and fall of barometric pressure.[6]

By that time, the American meteorological effort had a new look: in 1842, President John Tyler appointed James P. Espy, the author of *Philosophy of Storms,* an influential treatise on thunderstorms, as the federal government's first official meteorologist; and four years later the newly created Smithsonian Institution began to collect weather records while forming a national network of voluntary meteorological observers. In 1849, Joseph Henry, the director of the Smithsonian, announced the creation of a telegraphic warning system that "would solve the problems of American storms." Despite Henry's enthusiasm, none of this had much impact on the ability of ordinary citizens to deal with the annual spate of hurricanes. During the 1850s and 1860s, tropical storms came and went with little or no warning, and few, if any, American citizens expected this state of affairs to change anytime soon.[7]

The first real breakthrough came in 1870 when an unlikely combination of events raised hurricane tracking to a new level of sophistication and promise. In February, a congressional resolution endorsed by President Grant authorized the secretary of war to institute a national weather service. Two months later, the War Department assigned the task to the Army Signal Service, which in November created a new bureau, the Division of Telegrams and Reports for the Benefit of Commerce. Despite its cumbersome title, this division soon presided over a national network of meteorological reporting stations.[8] The second event took place in Havana, Cuba, where Father Benito Viñes, the new director of the Jesuit College of Belén, turned his attention to tropical storm research and the need for a reliable hurricane warning system. The most knowledgeable and imaginative hurricane researcher of his day, Father Viñes was the first forecaster to base his calculations on observations of both the lower and upper atmosphere and the first to analyze the seasonal trajectory of tropical storm activity. Largely in place by 1873, his warning system ultimately "utilized hundreds of volunteer observers, gathered ship reports, issued telegraph warnings to nearby islands, and even developed a 'pony express' between isolated villages to warn residents of approaching hurricanes."[9]

Recognizing the significance of Viñes's work, the Signal Service contracted to receive daily cable reports from weather stations in Havana, Santiago de Cuba, and Kingston, Jamaica. The reports began in early August 1873, allowing the service to issue the nation's first official tropical storm warning on August 23. Other reports and warnings followed, but insufficient funding stymied efforts to expand the reporting system to Puerto Rico, Barbados, and Guadeloupe. Without additional Caribbean reporting stations, the system provided little protection to Americans living on or near the Atlantic or Gulf coasts, a perilous reality that became all too apparent in September 1875, when an unexpected hurricane nearly wiped out the town of Indianola, Texas. This and later disasters added to the public clamor for a more comprehensive reporting system, and by 1880 the Signal Service was receiving daily cables from six Caribbean stations. Even so, the government's commitment to the system remained tenuous; indeed, for several months in 1881 all Caribbean reports were suspended pending the determination of "the legality of spending any part of the appropriations in maintaining a station outside the limits of the United States." In 1882, the reports resumed, and by the end of the decade the newly organized Cuban Meteorological Service was acting as a clearinghouse for hurricane data from several islands, including Antigua and Puerto Rico. But even this expanded warning system inspired little enthusiasm among Gilded Age politicians and bureaucrats. No one in the federal government, it seems, was ready to acknowledge the nation's responsibility to protect its citizens from destructive tropical storms. As late as 1889, Father Viñes's makeshift warning system still received most of its operating funds from private sources, primarily shipping concerns, insurance companies, and merchant associations.[10]

Fortunately, change was in the air—or more literally in the snowdrifts and flood waters of the American heartland. The traditional grumbling about the Signal Service's lack of professionalism and administrative mismanagement turned into a rousing chorus of criticism after the service failed to predict the record-setting blizzards of 1886 and 1887 and the devastating Johnstown, Pennsylvania, flood of 1889. As public dissatisfaction with the Signal Service's weather reporting reached new heights, Congress responded by transferring the government's meteorological duties to civilian control, creating the United States Weather Bureau within the Department of Agriculture. Under the direction of Mark Harrington, a distinguished academic and the founding editor of the *American Meteorological Journal,* the new agency opened its doors in July 1891, just in time for the annual hurricane season. To Harrington's relief, the 1891 hurricane season was relatively uneventful, as was the 1892 season. But his luck ran out the following year, when six hurricanes struck the American mainland. Two of the hurricanes were unusually powerful storms that left death and devastation on a massive scale; together they were responsible for more than four thousand deaths, largely because Americans had little or no warning that the storms were approaching. The 1893 hurricane season was "the second most deadly in the United States since record keeping began," a sobering fact that cast serious doubt on the new agency's capacity to protect the public from nature's fury. The Weather Bureau fared somewhat better in 1894, when its timely warning of a hurricane approaching the southern coast of Rhode Island was credited with saving hundreds of lives among the fishermen of Narragansett Bay. But, in general, the bureau's early efforts to track and forecast tropical storms did not inspire public confidence. By 1896, the bureau had greatly expanded the number of official meteorological reporting stations, including nearly fifty in Florida, but the new system, which had only limited connections to Caribbean reporting stations, brought little relief to coastal residents, who invariably bore the brunt of tropical storm damage. To cite one example, when a fast-moving and powerful hurricane roared across the Gulf of Mexico and struck Cedar Key, Florida, in September 1896, the residents of the tiny Gulf community—and the Weather Bureau—were caught completely off guard.[11]

The Cedar Key storm, which eventually killed 114 people and left a trail of destruction from Florida to Pennsylvania, made a great impression on the American public, including presidential candidate William McKinley. Following America's declaration of war against Spain in 1898, McKinley claimed that he feared hurricanes far more than he feared the Spanish navy. Accordingly, he urged Congress to authorize the creation of a comprehensive hurricane warning system that would protect the Caribbean operations of American military and merchant vessels. The resulting legislation, passed in July 1898, led to the establishment of a Weather Bureau forecasting center at Kingston, Jamaica, and official reporting stations in Cuba, Santo Domingo, Trinidad, Curacao, St. Kitts, and Barbados. Following the end of hostilities, the acquisition of territorial possessions in the Caribbean prompted the bureau to open additional stations in Puerto Rico and Dominica and to transfer the forecasting center to Havana. Convincing host nations or colonies to accept Weather Bureau personnel required diplomatic tact, the promise that American meteorologists would disseminate their findings throughout the Caribbean region, and a plan to train local weather observers who would eventually replace American observers. By 1902, the localization of the staff was virtually complete, as all but one of the Weather Bureau's American-born employees had returned to the United States. Following the onset of Cuban independence in May 1902, the bureau moved the hurricane forecast center from Havana to Washington, where it would remain until 1935. According to Weather Bureau chief Willis Moore, this qualified withdrawal from the Caribbean served the cause of diplomacy and uplifted the morale of bureau employees who were less than enthusiastic about extended tours of duty in the disease-infested tropics. But, as historian Erik Larson recently pointed out, this simple explanation masked a complex story of imperial condescension and bureaucratic cover-up.[12]

Moving the hurricane forecast office from Havana to Washington was actually a calculated effort to avoid a public relations disaster in the wake of the great Galveston, Texas, storm of September 1900. As Larson and other scholars have demonstrated, the Weather Bureau's complicity in the Galveston tragedy—where more than six thousand citizens perished in less than twenty-four hours—is clear: despite repeated observations and bulletins by the College of Belén's tracking stations, no hurricane warning ever reached Galveston, primarily because the Weather Bureau had temporarily banned the cable transmission of Cuban weather reports (ostensibly to prevent "the transmission over Government lines of irresponsible weather information"). To make matters worse, Isaac Cline, the longtime director of the Weather Bureau's Galveston station, had repeatedly assured local residents that the notion that the city could be destroyed by a hurricane was an "absurd delusion." After Cline lost his wife, and nearly lost his daughter, in the storm, Moore tried to deflect criticism of the bureau by portraying Cline as a courageous martyr, "one of the heroic spirits of that awful hour." And sometime later, after Cuban authorities pointed out that they had tried to warn uncooperative American officials about the impending storm, the Weather Bureau chief concocted a diabolical Cuban plot to discredit his agency. As he explained in a plaintive letter to the secretary of agriculture: "I know that there have been many secret influences at work to embarrass the Weather Bureau. . . . It is apparent to me and to every ranking officer . . . in the West Indies that the people do not appreciate our service, that the only thing they want is to kick us and say good-bye." In an age when America was coming to terms with its imperialist urges, Moore's self-serving, anti-Cuban scapegoating found a receptive audience in Washington. Aside from a few War Department leaders who had served in Cuba and who knew enough about the situation to revoke the ban on Cuban weather reports, government officials rallied behind the bureau, which, despite the Galveston fiasco, conducted business as usual until Moore's retirement in 1913.[13]

The inability of Moore and other Weather Bureau officials to work with their Cuban counterparts—unquestionably the most experienced and sophisticated hurricane trackers in the world—had profound consequences, inhibiting scientific advancement and threatening public safety for at least a generation. In 1919, the bureau opened a second hurricane forecast center in San Juan, Puerto Rico, and the proliferation of aviation and radio technology brought some improvement in the bureau's storm warning capabilities by the early 1920s. But the progressive era and its immediate aftermath did not witness any major changes in public expectations or governmental involvement in storm forecasting or management. Tropical storms came and went, usually with little warning, and the government's role was still limited to data collection by the Weather Bureau, the flood-control efforts of the Army Corps of Engineers, and the activities of special military detachments assigned to law enforcement or cleanup duty. Although both the science of meteorology and the scope of the federal government had experienced dramatic advancements since the turn of the century, the fundamental notion that hurricanes were an unpredictable and uncontrollable natural force remained unchallenged.[14]

Interestingly enough, when the challenge did come, its primary catalysts were not science or government, but demography and nature. Beginning in 1926, a series of powerful hurricanes disrupted the Great Florida Boom, causing extensive damage and loss of life in an area that had been all but uninhabited a generation earlier. On the morning of September 20, 1926, a major storm packing peak winds of 138 miles per hour roared into Miami, propelling a 13-foot storm surge into Biscayne Bay. As the eye passed directly over the city, northern transplants who had never experienced a hurricane before emerged from their battered dwellings only to discover a few minutes later that the worst was yet to come. By the end of the day, the death toll was over two hundred, and much of the city was in ruins. The first hurricane to strike the city in twenty years, "the big blow of '26" cost an estimated $1.4 billion in property damage, a staggering figure that exceeded the losses attributed to the great Galveston storm of 1900. It also received more press coverage than any storm since the Galveston hurricane. Much of the coverage was sharply critical of the Weather Bureau, which had a lot of explaining to do in the days and weeks following the storm. Reporters and survivors alike wanted to know why Richard W. Gray, the chief meteorologist at the bureau's

Raymond Arsenault

Miami office, waited until 11:30 p.m. on the nineteenth, less than eight hours before the peak winds struck the city, before issuing an official hurricane warning. Was this the best that the Weather Bureau could do? Some observers feared that it was and argued that federal government should stop wasting tax money on a worthless hurricane warning system. But others took a different tack, suggesting that the time had come for the federal government to assume the responsibility of protecting its citizens from natural disasters. If a mixture of technology and governmental organization could cut a canal through the isthmus of Panama and put military aviators in the air, why couldn't the same combination bring a measure of relief from the ravages of tropical storms?[15]

Such speculation became even more common after the proverbial "flood of the century" inundated the entire Mississippi River region in the spring of 1927. John Barry, the author of *Rising Tide: The Great Mississippi Flood of 1927 and How It Changed America,* has argued that the sheer magnitude of the 1927 flood prompted a revolution in American attitudes toward disaster relief and federal responsibility, and perhaps he is right. But if he had looked eastward to Florida—if he had gazed upon the ruins of the Miami boom—he would have realized that the great Mississippi flood was not the only natural force propelling this revolution. Indeed, Florida provided a second thrust in this direction in 1928, when a devastating hurricane struck the coast near Palm Beach before sweeping across the northern edge of the Everglades. Palm Beach itself escaped the worst ravages of the storm, but the residents of the inland Lake Okeechobee region were not so fortunate. Although the Weather Bureau office in Miami was aware that the storm had already struck Grand Bahama Island, killing more than a thousand Bahamians, the bureau issued its first hurricane warning less than twelve hours before the eye reached the Florida coast. By that time it was too late to get word to the isolated farmers living in the lowlands south and west of the lake. At Belle Glade, where hundreds of migrant workers perished, a low earthen dam quickly gave way to a raging 15-foot storm surge, and other nearby communities suffered a similar fate. The official Florida death count was 1,836, but the actual toll was much higher. Years later, farmers were still "plowing up bones" in the blood-drenched soil of the Okeechobee basin. Although the realization that most of the victims were black migrants tempered the public response to the tragedy, the pressure on the government to do something, anything, about killer storms mounted as the disaster-ridden decade drew to a close.[16]

The first meaningful step toward increased governmental responsibility, the Mississippi Flood Control Act of 1928, had little to do with hurricanes. But a second piece of legislation, the River and Harbors Act of 1930, expanded the notion that the government could use preventive measures to limit the effects of tropical storms. Among other things, the River and Harbors Act authorized the construction of the Hoover Dike, a massive 35- to 45-foot-high concrete ring around Lake Okeechobee. The Army Corps of Engineers completed the first phase of the dike in 1937, the same year Zora Neale Hurston immortalized the victims of the 1928 storm with her searing novel *Their Eyes Were Watching God.* By that time, Franklin Roosevelt's New Deal had undertaken several massive projects designed to tame or harness the forces of nature, including the Tennessee Valley Authority and the Grand Coulee Dam.[17] In this context of rising technological expectations, adopting a more aggressive approach to the hurricane problem seemed logical and fitting. At the same time, in keeping with the New Deal's commitment to governmental innovation, the national hurricane forecast center in Washington underwent a complete reorganization in early 1935. The Washington office was replaced with two regional centers—a primary office in Jacksonville, Florida, and a secondary office in New Orleans. Headquartering the forecasters in population centers that actually experienced tropical storms signaled a renewed dedication among Weather Bureau officials, who promised a new era in hurricane forecasting and protection.[18]

Regrettably, the new era did not come soon enough for the 408 Americans who perished in the Great Labor Day Hurricane of September 1935. One of the most powerful storms in recorded history, the 1935 hurricane carried peak winds approaching 250 miles per hour and a minimum barometric pressure of 26.35 inches, at the time the lowest pressure ever recorded in the Western Hemisphere. The storm struck the Florida Keys just south of Key Largo, where hundreds of World War I Bonus Marchers and Civilian Conservation Corps workers were constructing a highway parallel to the Florida East Coast Railway. The workers had been brought in by the Federal Emergency Relief Agency in 1934 to complete the final 40 miles of the highway link to Key West. Housed in small tents and flimsy shacks, they had virtually no chance to withstand a direct hit from even a minor hurricane. In the end, this vulnerability—and a lack of warning—sealed their fate. Less than twenty-four hours before the hurricane hit the Keys, the Weather Bureau characterized the storm as a minor tropical disturbance with "shifting gales and probably winds of hurricane force." Later, after the bureau discovered that the storm was strengthening, government officials hurriedly dispatched a relief train from Homestead. But the ill-fated train never reached the stranded workers; when a 20-foot storm surge washed over Long and Upper Matecumbe Keys, the train and 41 miles of tracks and trestles were swept into the sea. The tragic drowning of hundreds of workers who had survived the Hoover administration's repression of the Bonus March and the worst ravages of the Great Depression was a bitter irony that shocked and angered many Americans, including Ernest Hemingway, who was then living in Key West. After helping to bury the dead, Hemingway penned a biting essay titled "Who Murdered the Vets?" "Who sent nearly a thousand war veterans, many of them husky, hard-working and simply out of luck, but many of them close to the border of pathological cases, to live in the frame shacks on the Florida Keys, in the hurricane months?" he asked plaintively. Surely, he added, "the clearing of the Anacostia Flats is going to seem an act of kindness compared to the clearing of Upper and Lower Matecumbe."[19]

Weather Bureau officials were relieved that Hemingway did not emphasize their complicity in the workers' deaths. But they also knew that, in the wake of the tragic 1935 storm, hurricane trackers and other government officials would be under increased pressure to protect the public from killer storms. To some, the 1935 Labor Day fiasco provided further proof of nature's uncontrollable power and the futility of governmental attempts to brook that power. But to most Americans, the government's involvement in the episode reinforced the growing expectation that public officials should play an active role in disaster avoidance and relief. Although this expectation would not be fully satisfied or institutionalized until the 1970s, the combination of expanding governmental authority during World War II and a series of unusually active hurricane seasons during the 1940s raised the "public storm" concept to a new level by midcentury.

Recognizing the public's rising expectations, New Deal officials reorganized the Weather Bureau in June 1940, moving it from the Department of Agriculture to the Department of Commerce. Though largely cosmetic, this bureaucratic shuffle raised the profile of government meteorologists, presaging the new responsibilities that would soon descend upon them. The proliferation of military installations in Florida and Texas during the war inevitably linked tropical storm forecasting with national security, prompting the relocation of the forecast office to Miami in 1943. President Roosevelt placed the Miami office under the joint control of the Army Air Corps and the U.S. Navy for the duration of the war, a development that allowed hurricane forecasters to take full advantage of new military-related technologies such as radar and advanced aviation reconnaissance. On July 27, 1943, Army Air Corps Colonel Joseph Duckworth became the first pilot to fly deliberately into the eye of a hurricane. Encountering the storm off the coast of Galveston, he made two flights into the eye—a daring feat that made him an instant folk hero. The romantic era of the "hurricane hunter" had arrived, and by the end of the war, hurricane penetration flights by air corps and navy aircraft had become almost routine, especially in the Pacific, where massive typhoons inflicted heavy damage on American naval vessels in 1944 and 1945.[20]

The war years also witnessed the rise of Grady Norton, a folksy Alabaman who became the first hurricane forecaster to achieve semi-celebrity status. Norton began working for the Weather Bureau in 1915 and became the bureau's chief hurricane forecaster in 1935, but it was in the 1940s that he revolutionized the art and science of storm forecasting. Following the "development of radar and radio direction-finding equipment" that facilitated the observation and measurement of winds throughout the troposphere, Norton "developed a theory that hurricanes moved with the wind flow in the upper troposphere" rather than around a surface high-pressure area. To prove his point, he predicted the path of an October 1944 storm with astonishing accuracy. This feat assured his legendary status among hurricane forecasters, but to most Floridians he was simply the man with the calm, reassuring voice, the oracle who filled the airwaves with dependable warnings and practical advice, first on the radio and later on television. Foreshadowing future generations of weather celebrities, this self-described "wind jammer" from "Fleahop, Alabama," died in folk-hero fashion in October 1954, following a grueling twelve-hour session plotting Hurricane Hazel's path across the Caribbean.[21]

Under Norton's leadership, the hurricane forecast office evolved into a highly visible public agency and an icon of popular culture. An important milestone in this evolution was the decision to provide each hurricane with a name. Attaching anthropomorphic qualities to tropical storms was hardly new. The unpredictable nature of tropical storms, and the uniqueness of each storm, inspired a natural and widespread appreciation for the "personality" and "character" of individual hurricanes. But with the official naming of hurricane "Able" in August 1950, public officials ushered in a new age of meteorological anthropomorphism. In alphabetic fashion, "Able" gave way to "Baker," and so on, as the 1950 storm season worked its way through ten hurricanes, ending with a powerful mid-October storm aptly named "King."

Raymond Arsenault

For three seasons, the Weather Bureau employed traditional military code words as storm names, but in 1953 bureau officials decided to use an alphabetic series of women's names.[22]

The official feminization of hurricanes, following a long tradition of references to "Mother Nature" and other feminized natural entities, quickly caught on with the public and the press. Punctuating hurricane coverage with gendered story lines and language was common practice by the mid-1950s, as reporters described a succession of unruly "women." "The weathermen weren't unaware of the name's meaning," explained a *Miami News* reporter covering Hurricane Donna in 1960, "scientists can be romantics, too. They knew that Donna in the Italian tongue means 'lady.' And like all hurricanes, they spoke of her as 'she.' She was their Donna, their lady." In 1965, the *Miami News* special edition on Hurricane Betsy opened with the phrase "The Lady Was a Tramp!" One reporter referred to Betsy as "one of Nature's angry ballet dancers," the purveyor of a "furious dance" who "unfurls her great skirts and pirouettes before us." In similar fashion, a *Tampa Tribune* story referred to Betsy as a "giddy, oversized maiden." Weather Bureau officials encouraged such rhetoric and frequently cited the unpredictability of hurricanes as a legitimate rationale for feminine designation. "Hurricanes are like the women they're named for," head forecaster Gordon Dunn stated in 1960, "We never outguess them completely."[23]

Such tongue-in-cheek quips were relatively rare for Dunn, a no-nonsense scientist whose professional demeanor complemented the rising sophistication and bureaucratization of hurricane forecasting. After assuming the directorship in 1954, following Grady Norton's death, Dunn guided a major expansion of the Miami forecasting office, which was renamed the National Hurricane Center (NHC) in 1955. A year later, in anticipation of the International Geophysical Year (1957–58), he and other Weather Bureau officials initiated the National Hurricane Research Project (NHRP), an ambitious investigation of the structure of hurricanes. With the age of space capsules and astronauts looming on the horizon, the NHC did not want to be left behind in the high-stakes game of government-sponsored technology. In 1956, the NHC re-equipped its air force hurricane hunters with WB-50s, replacing the outmoded WB-29s that had been used since 1946. Not to be outdone, the U.S. Navy's hurricane hunter squadron was soon using highly sophisticated, four-engine Super Constellations, which propelled hurricane reconnaissance and research into a new era. Utilizing elaborate Doppler radar systems, these flying laboratories quickly became the stuff of legend, inspiring a spate of admiring newspaper and magazine articles, plus several action novels and documentary films. Following the shock of the Soviet Union's 1957 *Sputnik* launch, the hurricane hunters' exploits were welcome news in a nation desperate for signs of American technological achievement.[24]

In April 1961, the cosmonaut Yuri Gagarin's celebrated journey into space, accomplished nearly a month ahead of American astronaut Alan Shepard's space flight, further deflated American confidence. The National Aeronautics and Space Administration (NASA) eventually eclipsed the Soviet space program, but in the meantime Americans were forced to look elsewhere for technological dominance.[25] One potential area of dominance was meteorological research, especially the new science of weather modification. In 1962, the National Hurricane Center launched Project Stormfury, the first extended effort to lessen the frequency and intensity of tropical storms. The idea of physically altering the structure of hurricanes received serious attention as early as the 1940s, when a series of severe hurricane seasons inspired a call for desperate measures, including a proposal to destroy or divert hurricanes with atomic weapons. Following the explosions at Hiroshima and Nagasaki in August 1945, the enterprising county commissioners of Lee County, Florida, offered several thousand acres of land to the army for a proving ground where the effects of atomic energy on hurricanes could be tested.[26]

The army never took Lee County up on its offer, but in 1947 a navy "hurricane hunter" aircraft seeded a hurricane with silver iodide crystals after the storm passed over the Florida peninsula and headed into the open waters of the North Atlantic. Government officials made no claim that the seeding, known as Project Cirrus, had any effect on the storm, but the 1947 hurricane's erratic behavior became a subject of controversy when the NHC resumed seeding experiments in the late 1950s. According to one suspicious Miami journalist, following the 1947 seeding "the hurricane stalled, reformed and then swung back to slash at Savannah, Ga., and the South Carolina coast doing heavy damage."[27] The seeding of Daisy in 1958, Esther in 1961, and Beulah in 1963 produced no measurable impact, but these failures did not calm the fears of conspiracy theorists or deter Project Stormfury scientists from trying again. In September 1965, in the immediate aftermath of Hurricane Betsy, Secretary of Commerce John T. Connor called for a "vigorous national program" to test the feasibility of weather modification. This produced new expectations and additional funding, but little happened until 1969, when the NHC "bombed" Hurricane Debbie with a massive dose of silver iodide crystals. According to project director R. Cecil Gentry, "scientists

Raymond Arsenault

hoped to freeze Debbie to death. Theoretically, water should form around the crystals sowed in the clouds around the hurricane's eye. The water would freeze around the crystals . . . and rob the storm of its heat and energy." Unfortunately for Gentry and Project Stormfury, Hurricane Debbie "barely twitched" under the "massive chemical barrage," leading even Gentry to question the likelihood of major storm modification in the foreseeable future. "Do not look for a breakthrough tomorrow," he warned, a prediction confirmed by the modification project's demise in 1971.[28]

Project Stormfury proved to be a scientific disappointment and a public relations fiasco. But the NHC fared much better in other areas of technological advancement. The completion of the WSR-57 coastal radar warning system in the early 1960s provided the NHC and the American public with nearly continuous surveillance of storm tracks within 150 miles of the east and Gulf coasts. And, by the early 1970s, an extensive network of oceanic buoys gave storm analysts access to direct measurements of oceanic surface conditions. This integrated system of radars and buoys produced an unprecedented mass of data, the utility of which depended on sophisticated computerization. It would be several decades before computer technology harnessed the full potential of the new tracking and warning system. In the meantime, NHC scientists consoled themselves with the wonders of satellite technology.[29]

With the launching of TIROS-1, America's first experimental weather satellite, in April 1960, the science of storm tracking entered a new age. The earliest images from space were crude and difficult to interpret, but NHC scientists soon demonstrated the usefulness of satellite-generated photographs. In the fall of 1961, television images beamed down from TIROS-3 allowed government forecasters to issue an early warning of Hurricane Carla's impending assault on the Texas coast. The warning, which produced the first large-scale hurricane evacuation in American history, reportedly saved hundreds of lives, spurring new interest and investment in weather satellite technology. As the decade progressed, weather satellites became increasingly sophisticated: in 1964, NIMBUS-1 provided the first infrared night photographs from space; in early 1966, ESSA-1 and ESSA-2, equipped with wide-angle television cameras, became the nation's first fully operational weather satellites; and later in the same year, ATS added "spin-scan" capability to the science of satellite photography. In the mid-1970s, geosynchronous satellites gave way to the geostationary models of the GOES (Geostationary Operational Environmental Satellite) series, which produced broad-scale hemispheric photographs at thirty-minute intervals. Full utilization of weather satellites as research tools awaited advances in computer technology. But the problem of unused data did little to offset the conceptual impact of the spectacular images generated by space-based cameras. For the first time, NHC scientists and others could see the full, awe-inspiring outlines of cyclonic power. The shape or body of the storm had become real, transcending and objectifying what earlier had been only an imaginative construct. Photographic and computer-enhanced representations of swirling winds reinforced the anthropomorphic and "personal" nature of tropical storms, giving them life in a new way. This was especially true following the development of McIDAS (Man-computer Interactive Data Access System) software, created at the University of Wisconsin in the mid-1970s, which literally "put the pictures in motion."[30]

All of this took on added cultural significance with the proliferation and maturation of television news. From the mid-1960s on, local and national storm reports featured vivid images of approaching hurricanes, which complemented the steady stream of data provided by the NHC. Videotape technology allowed television editors and reporters to create riveting narratives of storm activity. By splicing satellite photographs, interviews with NHC forecasters, and on-location reporter updates filmed against a backdrop of rising wind and water, television coverage became an integral part of the "public storm" experience. Television, and to a lesser extent print-media graphics, transformed and deepened the vicarious participation of citizens far removed from the storm's path. Hurricanes had become a source of national crisis and concern, a shared experience that engaged and transfixed millions of Americans.[31]

The technological innovations and media advances of the 1960s brought heightened public expectations and increased pressure in Washington. At the same time, a general resurgence of political activism underscored the government's responsibility for "managing" the environment, especially in the context of the Great Society initiatives of the Johnson administration. Accordingly, in July 1965, the National Hurricane Center, along with the rest of the National Weather Bureau, became part of a new agency, the Environmental Sciences Services Administration (ESSA). With this bureaucratic reshuffling, the NHC entered an era of unprecedented expansion and activity. In the fall of 1965, ESSA officials created a twenty-one-person Tropical Analysis Center at the NHC and gave NHC director Gordon Dunn the added responsibility of directing the National Hurricane Warning Service for the entire Atlantic basin. This reorganization concentrated authority in the Miami office and downgraded the responsibilities of the hurricane forecast offices in Boston, New Orleans, Washington, and San Juan, Puerto Rico. By the time Gordon Dunn retired in 1967, the NHC staff had grown to eighty-three, and the public visibility of the Miami office had reached new heights.[32]

Dunn's successor, Robert H. Simpson, expanded the NHC staff to well over one hundred during his six-year tenure (1968–1973), primarily through an increased emphasis on research and development. In 1970, Congress transferred oversight of the NHC to the National Oceanic and Atmospheric Administration (NOAA), a new agency that signified the federal government's growing commitment to meteorological science. Under NOAA's administration, Simpson enhanced the NHC's scientific reputation, creating a Satellite Applications Unit (SAU) and introducing the Saffir-Simpson Scale, a categorization scheme that ranks hurricanes according to wind speed and destructive potential. The introduction of the five-point Saffir-Simpson Scale in 1975 gave the public a convenient means of classifying individual hurricanes and systematized differential levels of expectation and preparedness. Identifying an approaching storm as a potentially catastrophic Category 3 or 4 hurricane gave added force and specificity to the NHC's hurricane watches and warnings, underscored the scientific legitimacy of hurricane forecasting, and focused public attention on the NHC. For some hurricane buffs, it also added to the lore of experience and survival, in the manner of a sports statistic or superlative. As an official government ranking system, the Saffir-Simpson scale had the power to authenticate danger and risk, and to reinforce the profiling of individual storms. Who could resist the gathering drama of an approaching Category 3 or 4 storm, or the tales of damage, loss, and survival that were sure to follow?[33]

The Saffir-Simpson scale was, of course, only one element of a broad set of public policies that encouraged America's growing fascination with hurricanes. During the late 1970s, the federal government's efforts to measure and track tropical storms, aided by the mass media's willingness to disseminate such information, evolved into a comprehensive program of storm "management." In March 1979, President Jimmy Carter issued an executive order creating the Federal Emergency Management Agency (FEMA), the first federal agency empowered to oversee all aspects of disaster prevention and assistance. In the long history of American disaster relief, no governmental authority had ever assumed so much control or responsibility. Prior to the 1930s, state and local authorities shouldered almost all of the burden, although intermittent examples of federal relief began as early as 1803, when an act of Congress provided aid to a fire-ravaged New Hampshire town. During the Great Depression, the Reconstruction Finance Corporation, the Bureau of Public Roads, and the Army Corps of Engineers provided some assistance to stricken communities, but federal efforts remained limited and haphazard until the 1960s, when a series of catastrophic disasters prompted calls for federalization on an unprecedented scale. In 1964, President Lyndon Johnson initiated the practice of designating hard-hit communities as national disaster areas eligible for special federal assistance, and four years later Congress passed the National Flood Insurance Act and created the Office of Emergency Preparedness, an underfunded agency that provided a symbolic focus for federal relief efforts but little more. The devastating effects of Hurricane Camille in 1969 and Hurricane Agnes in 1972 added to the growing public pressure for federal disaster assistance, prompting the Nixon administration to establish the Federal Disaster Assistance Administration (FDAA) as part of the Department of Housing and Urban Development (HUD) in 1973. A year later, the Disaster Relief Act codified the process of national disaster area declarations, replacing an ad hoc system that had been plagued by insufficient follow-through and undue political influence.

Thus, by the mid-1970s federal responsibility for disaster assistance was a given. Washington's contribution involved more than one hundred federal agencies, a testament to the scope, if not the efficiency, of the government's efforts. Unfortunately, these agencies often worked independently or even at cross-purposes, and their activities and policies frequently conflicted with the parallel efforts of state and local authorities. This state of confusion became a major concern of the National Governors Association, which urged President Carter to streamline the federal government's disaster assistance programs. The creation of FEMA went a long way toward solving this problem by merging a number of overlapping federal agencies, including the Federal Insurance Administration, the National Fire Prevention and Control Administration, the National Weather Service Community Preparedness Program, the Federal Disaster Assistance Administration, and the Federal Preparedness Agency of the General Services Administration. FEMA's first director, John Macy, made a concerted effort to coordinate his agency's efforts with those of state and local officials, some of whom were understandably wary of the new mega-agency. He also instituted "an all-hazards approach" to emergency management that emphasized "direction, control and warning systems which are common to the full range of emergencies from small isolated events to the ultimate emergency—war." This flexible approach proved useful during FEMA's first decade, which witnessed a wide range of major disasters, including the toxic chemical contamination of Love Canal, the refugee crisis following the 1980 Mariel boatlift, the nuclear accident at Three Mile Island, and the devastation of Hurricane Hugo.[34]

FEMA's myriad activities—from the formulation of evacuation plans to the dispensing of relief funds—helped to publicize and legitimize the goal of storm management. Working in close cooperation with the NHC and NOAA, FEMA served as a central clearinghouse for information, advice, and regulation. It did so, in part, by encouraging the development of a professional subculture of hurricane experts. In May 1979, the agency cosponsored a national conference on "Hurricanes and Coastal Storms: Awareness, Evacuation, and Mitigation." Held in Orlando, the three-day meeting brought together an unusual mix of academics and public administrators and became a model for the annual conferences that followed. During the 1980s and 1990s, the national hurricane conferences grew in size and influence, signifying the rising academic and professional interest in tropical storms. In 1983, Professor William Gray of Colorado State University issued his first annual hurricane prediction profile, which he derived from measurements of sea temperature, upper-level wind direction, West African rainfall, and a periodic meteorological phenomenon known as "El Niño." Gray's predictions drew considerable publicity, inspiring other meteorological researchers to turn their attention to the mysteries of tropical storms. Indeed, a massive proliferation of hurricane research projects, technical papers, government grants, and local and regional conferences testified to the expansion and professionalization of what some observers were beginning to call "the hurricane business."[35]

Much of this activity was conducted beyond public view, but this became less true in the 1980s as FEMA, along with the NHC, assumed a mediating role between the professional world of hurricane specialists and American popular culture. FEMA and NHC officials presided over an elaborate system of official hurricane "watches" and "warnings" that gave them the power to order the evacuation of millions of citizens. Both before and after storms, the enforcement of public policy and the mobilization of volunteers and resources required communication links that placed government officials in the public eye. Working with the press had become an integral part of storm management. With the approach of the fall hurricane season, many newspapers offered special hurricane preparedness sections that relayed storm emergency procedures, evacuation routes, survival tips, and other words of wisdom from government authorities. Later, when the hurricanes actually materialized, televised storm reports featured regular updates from the NHC. During the 1980s, NHC director Neil Frank became a familiar face to the millions of Americans who listened to his pronouncements on the Cable News Network (CNN), the Weather Channel, and other networks. Frank's successors—Robert Sheets, Jerry Jarrell, and Max Mayfield—continued this tradition, and after his appointment as FEMA director in 1993, James L. Witt joined the list of hurricane media stars. Though something less than folk heroes, these men cultivated a familiarity that accentuated the "public storm" phenomenon.[36]

In doing so, they discovered that turning scientific and organizational expertise into public awareness can be a difficult task. In the public mind, the gospels of prevention and technological sophistication often shaded into expectations of mitigation and decreased risk. Professional hurricane experts knew all too well that storm management could only go so far, but this did not stop some citizens from expecting and demanding near invulnerability to tropical storms. Throughout his long tenure at the NHC, Neil Frank strained to control a revolution of rising public expectations. In 1985, in trying to counter criticism of a new prediction/evacuation system that provided "'odds' on where a storm will strike," Frank freely admitted that "two-thirds to three-fourths of the people who evacuate with 24-hour lead time are going to do so unnecessarily. . . . for every four times we tell you to evacuate, only one will be necessary." And "we're not going to get any better," he explained, "the atmosphere is very complex. . . . We're going to continue to have meteorological surprises." Such admissions did not sit well with some observers. "Despite having at his disposal millions of dollars worth of sophisticated technology, a trained staff, and 20 years experience in South Florida," one Miami reporter complained, "Frank still can't tell people exactly what they want to know: where will the storm hit, when will it hit, and when should we run? Frank can only warn and worry." Another reporter characterized Frank as a "sincere prophet of doom and horror," and still another blanched at his "ominous storm warnings" and sharp criticism of "the federal flood-insurance program, which encourages people to develop in coastal areas where they shouldn't be."[37]

NOAA and FEMA officials often echoed Frank's warnings, but the sheer size of the government's forecasting and emergency apparatus communicated a different message, one of control and technological mastery.[38] Periodic demonstrations of nature's fury, such as the catastrophic destruction of Hurricane Andrew in 1992, reminded Americans of their continued vulnerability.[39] But, as the twentieth century drew to a close, such demonstrations often got lost in the mystique of the "public storm." In conjunction with broad technological change—especially the increasing sophistication and scope of mass media—a century of governmental expansion, from progressivism and the New Deal to the Cold War and the Great Society, had created an institutional context that sustained and deepened this mystique. The same national state that spawned social security, Medicare, and the military-industrial complex redefined hurricanes as threats to national security, producing a social construct that placed powerful restraints on environmental and political consciousness. Far removed from the hurricanes of past centuries—when natural disasters straddled the separate spheres of private risk and governmental indifference—the storms of today occupy a central place in American political and popular culture. From the marble corridors of Washington to the barrier islands of Florida, Texas, and the Carolinas, the "public storm" rages on.

Notes

1. Jay Barnes, *Florida's Hurricane History* (Chapel Hill: University of North Carolina Press, 1998), 73; John M. Williams and Iver W. Duedall, *Florida Hurricanes and Tropical Storms*, rev. ed. (Gainesville: University Press of Florida, 1997), 71, plate 2; National Oceanic and Atmospheric Administration (NOAA), *Tropical Cyclones of the North Atlantic Ocean, 1871–1986*, Historical Climatology Series 6-2 (Asheville: National Climatic Center, 1987).

2. Barnes, *Florida's Hurricane History*, 261–84, 312–14; Williams and Duedall, *Florida Hurricanes and Tropical Storms*, 1–4, 13, 16, 37–42, 82, 102–7, 139; *Miami Herald*, August 10–September 15, 1992; *St. Petersburg Times*, August 18–20, 2002; James B. Elsner and A. Birol Kara, *Hurricanes of the North Atlantic: Climate and Society* (New York: Oxford University Press, 1999), 414–22. See also Walter Gillis Peacock, Betty Hearn Morrow, and Hugh Gladwin, *Hurricane Andrew: Ethnicity, Gender, and the Sociology of Disaster* (London: Routledge, 1997); Eugene F. Provenzo, *Hurricane Andrew, the Public Schools, and the Rebuilding of Community* (Albany: State University of New York Press, 1995); Eugene F. Provenzo and Asterie Baker Provenzo, *In the Eye of Hurricane Andrew* (Gainesville: University Press of Florida, 2002); Roger A. Pielke, *Hurricane Andrew in South Florida: Mesoscale Weather and Societal Responses* (Boulder: National Center for Atmospheric Research, 1995); United States Department of Interior, National Park Service, *Hurricane Andrew: The National Park Service Response in South Florida* (Denver: National Park Service, 1994).

3. See John C. Burnham's appeal for additional research in "A Neglected Field: The

History of Natural Disasters," *Perspectives* (American Historical Association newsletter) (April 1988): 22–24. Although Burnham's suggestions are well-taken, the historical literature on "natural disasters" in the United States is actually extensive. See especially Donald Worster, *Dust Bowl: The Southern Plains in the 1930s* (New York: Oxford University Press, 1979; David McCullough, *The Johnstown Flood* (New York: Simon and Schuster, 1968); Kai T. Erikson, *Everything in Its Path: Destruction of Community in the Buffalo Creek Flood* (New York: Simon and Schuster, 1976); Pete Daniel, *Deep'n As It Come: The 1927 Mississippi River Flood* (New York: Oxford University Press, 1977); John M. Barry, *Rising Tide: The Great Mississippi Flood of 1927 and How It Changed America* (New York: Simon and Schuster, 1997); Steven Biel, *Down with the Old Canoe: A Cultural History of the Titanic Disaster* (New York: Norton, 1996); Mike Davis, *Ecology of Fear: Los Angeles and the Imagination of Disaster* (New York: Henry Holt, 1998); and Ted Steinberg, *Acts of God: The Unnatural History of Natural Disaster in America* (New York: Oxford University Press, 2000). On hurricanes, see Isaac R. Tannehill, *Hurricanes: Their Nature and History* (Princeton: Princeton University Press, 1938); Marjory Stoneman Douglas, *Hurricane* (New York: Rinehart and Company, 1958); David M. Ludlum, *Early American Hurricanes, 1492–1970* (Boston: American Meteorological Society, 1963); Gordon E. Dunn and Banner I. Miller, *Atlantic Hurricanes*, rev. ed. (Baton Rouge: Louisiana State University Press, 1964); Thomas Helm, *Hurricanes: Weather at Its Worst* (New York: Dodd, Mead and Company, 1967); Jerry Rosenfeld, *Eye of the Storm: Inside the World's Deadliest Hurricanes, Tornadoes, and Blizzards* (New York: Plenum, 1999); Erik Larson, *Isaac's Storm: A Man, A Time, and the Deadliest Hurricane in History* (New York: Crown, 1999); Peter Davies, *Inside the Hurricane: Face to Face with Nature's Deadliest Storms* (New York: Henry Holt, 2000); and Elsner and Kara, *Hurricanes of the North Atlantic*. See also Sebastian Junger, *The Perfect Storm: A True Story of Men and the Sea* (New York: Norton, 1997).

4. See Morton Keller's groundbreaking trilogy: *Affairs of State: Public Life in Late Nineteenth Century America* (Cambridge: Harvard University Press, 1977); *Regulating a New Society: Public Policy and Social Change in America, 1900–1933* (Cambridge: Harvard University Press, 1979); and *Regulating a New Economy: Public Policy and Economic Change in America, 1900–1933* (Cambridge: Harvard University Press, 1990). See also Theda Skocpol, *Protecting Soldiers and Mothers: The Political Origins of Social Policy in the United States* (Cambridge: Harvard University Press, 1992). Peter Evans, Dietrich Rueschmeyer, and Theda Skocpol, eds., *Bringing the State Back In* (New York: Cambridge University Press, 1985).

5. J. Willard Hurst, *Law and the Conditions of Freedom in the Nineteenth-Century United States* (Madison: University of Wisconsin Press, 1964).

6. Robert C. Sheets, "The National Hurricane Center—Past, Present, and Future," *Weather and Forecasting* 5 (June 1990): 189–90; Larson, *Isaac's Storm*, 37–53, 121–22; Mark Monmonier, *Air Apparent: How Meteorologists Learned To Map, Predict, and Dramatize Weather* (Chicago: University of Chicago Press, 1999), 18–42; James Rodger Fleming, *Meteorology in America, 1800–1870* (Baltimore: Johns Hopkins University Press, 1990), 23–73; Donald R. Whitnah, *A History of the United States Weather Bureau* (Urbana: University of Illinois Press, 1961), 1–13; Patrick Hughes, *A Century of Weather*

Service: A History of the Birth and Growth of the National Weather Service, 1870–1970
(New York: Gordon and Breach, 1970), 3–16, 189–90; Douglas, *Hurricane*, 217–26;
Gizela Kutzbach, *The Thermal Theory of Cyclones: A History of Meteorological Thought in
the Nineteenth Century* (Boston: American Meteorological Society, 1979); Barnes, *Florida's Hurricane History*, 33; Edgar B. Calvert, "The Hurricane Warning Service and Its
Reorganization," *Monthly Weather Review* 63 (April 1935): 85; William C. Redfield,
"Remarks on the Prevailing Storms of the Atlantic Coast, of the Northeastern States,"
American Journal of Science 20 (1831): 17–51; William C. Redfield, "On Three Several
Hurricanes of the American Seas and Their Relations to the Northers, So Called, of the
Gulf of Mexico, and the Bay of Honduras, with Charts Illustrating the Same," *American Journal of Science*, 2d ser., vol. 2 (1846): 311–34; Lt. Col. William Reid, *An Attempt
To Develop The Law of Storms* (London: John Weale, 1946). See also Ludlum, *Early
American Hurricanes, 1492–1870*; and Dunn and Miller, *Atlantic Hurricanes*, 137–40.

7. Monmonier, *Air Apparent*, 32–54; Fleming, *Meteorology in America, 1800–1870*,
23–81, 142–43; Hughes, *A Century of Weather Service*, 4–5, 16–19; Whitnah, *A History of
the United States Weather Bureau*, 12–15; Douglas, *Hurricane*, 224–30; Marcus Benjamin, "Meteorology," in *The Smithsonian Institution, 1846–1896: The History of Its First
Half Century*, ed. George Brown Goode, 647–78 (Washington D.C.: Smithsonian Institution, 1897); Maxime Bocher, "The Meteorological Labors of Dove, Redfield, and
Espy," *American Meteorological Journal* 5 (1888): 1–13; James P. Espy, *The Philosophy of
Storms* (Boston: Little and Brown, 1841); James P. Espy, *First Report on Meteorology to
the Surgeon General of the United States Army* (Washington, D.C.: 1843).

8. *Congressional Globe*, 41st Cong., 2d sess., vol. 42, pt. 2 (February 9, 1870), 1160;
U.S. Army Signal Service, *Report of the Chief Signal Officer to the Secretary of War for the
Year 1872* (Washington, D.C.: 1872); Whitnah, *A History of the United States Weather
Bureau*, 19–58; Hughes, *A Century of Weather Service: A History of the Birth and Growth
of the National Weather Service, 1870–1970*, 19–23; Sheets, "The National Hurricane
Center," 190; Calvert, "The Hurricane Warning Service and Its Reorganization," 85;
Monmonier, *Air Apparent*, 7–8, 12, 48–53, 158–59.

9. Barnes, *Florida's Hurricane History*, 33, 67; Calvert, "The Hurricane Warning
Service and Its Reorganization," 85; Larson, *Isaac's Storm*, 102–3; Douglas, *Hurricane*,
230–36; Rosenfeld, *Eye of the Storm*, 230–32; Dunn and Miller, *Atlantic Hurricanes*,
140–42; Benito Vines, *Investigation of the Cyclonic Circulation and the Translatory
Movement of West Indian Hurricanes* (Washington, D.C.: U.S. Weather Bureau, 1898);
Benito Vines, *Practical Hints about West Indian Hurricanes* (Washington, D.C.: U. S.
Weather Bureau, 1885). See also Louis A. Perez, *Winds of Change: Hurricanes and the
Transformation of Nineteenth-Century Cuba* (Chapel Hill: University of North Carolina
Press, 2001).

10. Calvert, "The Hurricane Warning Service and Its Reorganization," 85–86;
Barnes, *Florida's Hurricane History*, 67–68; Sheets, "The National Hurricane Center,"
190; Hughes, *A Century of Weather Service*, 23–28, 192–93; Dunn and Miller, *Atlantic
Hurricanes*, 140–42; Douglas, *Hurricane*, 230–46.

11. Whitnah, *A History of the United States Weather Bureau*, 22–100; Hughes, *A
Century of Weather Service*, 26–28, 34, 36–38; Monmonier, *Air Apparent*, 53, 164;

Larson, *Isaac's Storm,* 69–72; Barnes, *Florida's Hurricane History,* 74. On the Johnstown flood, see McCullough, *The Johnstown Flood.*

12. Calvert, "The Hurricane Warning Service and Its Reorganization," 86; Larson, *Isaac's Storm,* 72–74, 102–8; Sheets, "The National Hurricane Center," 194; Gordon E. Dunn, "A Brief History of the United States Hurricane Warning Service," *Muse News* 3 (1971): 140–43; Hughes, *A Century of Weather Service,* 42; Douglas, *Hurricane,* 249–53.

13. Larson, *Isaac's Storm,* 100–142, 230–58, 267–72; Douglas, *Hurricane,* 253–58; Willis Moore to secretary of agriculture, September 21, 1900, box 1475, General Correspondence, Department of Agriculture, National Archives, Washington, D.C. For other accounts of the 1900 Galveston hurricane, see Isaac Cline, "Special Report on the Galveston Hurricane of September 8, 1900," *Monthly Weather Review* (November 16, 1900): 372–74; Joseph L. Cline, *When the Heavens Frowned* (Dallas: Mathias, Van Nort and Company, 1946); Gary Cartwright, "The Big Blow," *Texas Monthly* (August 1990): 76–81; John Coulter, ed., *The Complete Story of the Galveston Horror* (United Publishers of America, 1900); David G. McComb, *Galveston: A History* (Austin: University of Texas Press, 1986); and David Ballingrud, "Without Warning," *St. Petersburg Times,* May 28, 2000. On Moore's controversial career, see Whitnah, *A History of the United States Weather Bureau,* 82–130, 178.

14. Whitnah, *A History of the United States Weather Bureau,* 131–200; Sheets, "The National Hurricane Center," 194; Calvert, "The Hurricane Warning Service and Its Reorganization," 86; Hughes, *A Century of Weather Service,* 44–68; Dunn, "A Brief History of the United States Hurricane Warning Service," 141–43. Voluminous information on the activities and administration of the National Weather Bureau during these years can be found in Records of the Weather Bureau, record group 27, sections 5.1 and 5.2, National Archives, Washington, D.C. On the flood-control activities of the Army Corps of Engineers in the early twentieth century, see Barry, *Rising Tide,* 115, 157–60, 165–68; and John Ferrell, *From Single to Multi-Purpose Planning: The Role of the Army Engineers in River Development Policy, 1824–1930* (Washington, D.C.: U.S. Army Corps of Engineers, 1976).

15. *Miami Herald,* September 16–30, 1926; *Miami News,* September 16–30, 1926; Barnes, *Florida's Hurricane History,* 111–26; Steinberg, *Acts of God,* 51–61; Williams and Duedall, *Florida Hurricanes and Tropical Storms,* 14–15, 75, plate 6; Douglas, *Hurricane,* 258–67; Howard Kleinberg and L. F. Reardon, *The Florida Hurricane and Disaster, 1926* (Miami: Centennial Press, 1992); *The Florida Hurricane Which Devastated Miami, Hollywood, Ft. Lauderdale, . . .* (Chicago: American Autochrome, 1926); Joseph Hugh Reese, *Florida's Great Hurricane* (Miami: L. E. Fesler, 1926); Garnet Varner Walsh, *Hurricane, 1926* (Chicago: Petit Oiseau Press, 1958). See also Clarence Walker Barron, *Lessons from Florida Winds* (1927; reprint, New York: *Wall Street Journal*); and *Lessons of the Storm* (Pittsburgh: Jones and Laughlin Steel Corp., 1926).

16. Barry, *Rising Tide,* 363–426; Lawrence E. Will, *Okeechobee Hurricane and the Hoover Dike,* 2d ed. (St. Petersburg: Great Outdoors, 1967); Barnes, *Florida's Hurricane History,* 127–40; Douglas, *Hurricane,* 267–71; Steinberg, *Acts of God,* 59–63. The most comprehensive study of the 1928 Okeechobee hurricane is Eric L. Gross, "Somebody

got drowned, Lord: Florida and the Great Okeechobee Hurricane Disaster of 1928" (Ph.D. diss., Florida State University, 1995). See also Eliot Kleinberg, *Black Cloud: The Great Florida Hurricane of 1928* (New York: Carroll and Graf, 2003); Robert Mykle, *Killer 'Cane: The Deadly Hurricane of 1928* (New York: Cooper Square Press, 2002); William Fox, "The Night 2,000 Died," *St. Petersburg Times,* September 14, 1986; and Jeff Klinkenberg, "A Storm of Memories," *St. Petersburg Times,* July 12, 1992.

17. Barry, *Rising Tide,* 399–407; Will, *Okeechobee Hurricane and the Hoover Dike,* 179–93; Gross, "Somebody got drowned"; Alfred Jackson Hanna and Kathryn Abbey Hanna, *Lake Okeechobee: Wellspring of the Everglades* (Indianapolis: Bobbs-Merrill, 1948); Julie Hauserman, "Welcome to Dike Okeechobee," *St. Petersburg Times,* May 31, 2000; Zora Neale Hurston, *Their Eyes Were Watching God* (Philadelphia: J. B. Lippincott, 1937); Marc Reisner, *Cadillac Desert: The American West and Its Disappearing Water,* rev. ed. (New York: Penguin, 1993), 135–68; Fredrick J. Dobney, *River Engineers on the Middle Mississippi: A History of the St. Louis District, U. S. Army Corps of Engineers* (Washington, D.C.: GPO, 1978).

18. U. S. Weather Bureau, *Annual Report, 1934–35* (Washington, D.C.: GPO, 1935), 9–10; Sheets, "The National Hurricane Center," 195–96; Calvert, "The Hurricane Center and Its Reorganization," 87–88; Dunn, "A Brief History of the United States Hurricane Warning Service," 141–42; Whitnah, *A History of the United States Weather Bureau,* 135–36; Robert W. Burpee, "Grady Norton: Hurricane Forecaster and Communicator Extraordinaire," *Weather Forecasting* 3 (September 1988): 247–50.

19. W. F. McDonald, "The Hurricane of 31 August to 6 September 1935," *Monthly Weather Review* 63 (September 1935): 269–71; Barnes, *Florida's Hurricane History,* 144–59; Douglas, *Hurricane,* 271–79; Steinberg, *Acts of God,* 63–68; Rodman Bethel, *Flagler's Folly: The Railroad That Went to Sea and Was Blown Away* (Key West: R. Bethel, 1987); Whitnah, *A History of the United States Weather Bureau,* 136; Burpee, "Grady Norton: Hurricane Forecaster and Communicator Extraordinaire," 247–48; Ernest Hemingway, "Who Killed the Vets?" *New Masses,* September 17, 1935, 9–10. See also *Hearings on H.R. 9486 before the House Committee on World War Veterans' Legislation,* 74th Cong., 2d sess., 1936; Gary Dean Best, *FDR and the Bonus Marchers, 1933–35* (Westport, Conn.: Praeger, 1992).

20. Sheets, "The National Hurricane Center," 196, 199–200; Douglas, *Hurricane,* 352–55; Whitnah, *A History of the United States Weather Bureau,* 201–16; Barnes, *Florida's Hurricane History,* 34; Helm, *Hurricanes: Weather at Its Worst,* 51–63; Elsner and Kara, *Hurricanes of the North Atlantic,* 41–42; Rosenfeld, *Eye of the Storm,* 238–39; Dunn and Miller, *Atlantic Hurricanes,* 145, 156; Davies, *Inside the Hurricane,* 79–82.

21. Burpee, "Grady Norton: Hurricane Forecaster and Communicator Extraordinaire," 247–53; Sheets, "The National Hurricane Center," 196; Dunn and Miller, *Atlantic Hurricanes,* 136, 145, 183, 202, 236, 269; Douglas, *Hurricane,* 292–93, 300; Grady Norton, "Hurricane Forecasting (A Soliloquy)," unpublished ms. (1947), National Hurricane Center Library, Miami.

22. "Alice to Wallis," *Time,* June 15, 1953; Barnes, *Florida's Hurricane History,* 35–38; Helm, *Hurricanes: Weather at Its Worst,* 104; Douglas, *Hurricane,* 293; Steinberg, *Acts*

of God, 67–68. The idea of using women's names to identify hurricanes appeared as early as 1941 in George Stewart's novel *Storm* (New York: Random House, 1941).

23. Dunn and Miller, *Atlantic Hurricanes*, 8–9. Barnes, in *Florida's Hurricane History*, notes: "Air force and navy meteorologists who tracked the movements of typhoons across the wide expanses of the Pacific frequently assigned female names to storms. This system became official in 1953, when the Weather Bureau began using female names for storms in the Atlantic. It continued through the late 1970s, until women's groups and several countries lobbied the World Meteorological Organization to change the naming system. In 1979 men's names and names of international origin were added to the lists" (38). *Miami News*, September 16, 1960, September 8, 1965, September 11, 1965; *Tampa Tribune*, September 10, 1965; *Miami Herald*, September 11, 1960. The newspaper accounts cited above, and hundreds of others, can be found in scrapbooks located at the National Hurricane Center Library in Miami. See especially the scrapbook labeled "Newspaper Articles on Hurricane Donna, Hurricane Cleo, and other Hurricanes from *The Miami Herald* and *The Miami News* from 1960 to 1964" (hereafter cited as NHC Scrapbook 1960–1964). See also "Another Sexist Bastion Falls," *New York Times*, May 13, 1978.

24. Sheets, "The National Hurricane Center," 196, 199–201, 204; Douglas, *Hurricane*, 355–58; Davies, *Inside the Hurricane*, 80–82; Helm, *Hurricanes: Weather at Its Worst*, 50–63, 128–29; Rosenfeld, *Eye of the Storm*, 238–41; Isaac Tannehill, *Hurricane Hunters* (New York: Dodd, Mead and Company, 1954; *Miami Herald*, September 3, 1977, August 10, 1978, September 3, 1978; *Miami News*, August 29, 1979, August 4, 1980, August 17, 1983, NHC Scrapbook 1950–1985, National Hurricane Center Library, Miami. See also R. M. Markus, N. F. Halbiesen, and J. F. Fuller, *Air Weather Service, Our Heritage, 1937–1987* (Scott Air Force Base, Ill.: Military Airlift Command, U.S. Air Force, 1987); and the novel by former air force pilot and hurricane hunter William C. Anderson: *Hurricane Hunters* (New York: Crown, 1972). On the International Geophysical Year, see Walter Sullivan, *Assault on the Unknown: The International Geophysical Year* (New York: McGraw-Hill, 1961).

25. For an overview of the "space race" between the United States and the Soviet Union, see James Schefter, *The Race: The Uncensored Story of How America Beat Russia to the Moon* (New York: Doubleday, 1999).

26. *Bradenton Herald*, August 21, 1945; *Tampa Daily Times*, August 9, 1945.

27. *Miami News*, August 19, 1969, August 28, 1969 (quotation); *Ft. Lauderdale News*, September 12, 1965, in NHC Scrapbook 1966–1969; Rosenfeld, *Eye of the Storm*, 136; Elsner and Kara, *Hurricanes of the North Atlantic*, 380; Dunn and Miller, *Atlantic Hurricanes*, 294; Douglas, *Hurricane*, 292; Barnes, *Florida's Hurricane History*, 177–80; Davies, *Inside the Hurricane*, 82–86.

28. *Miami Herald*, August 30, 1964, NHC Scrapbook 1960–1964; *Miami Herald*, September 15, 1965 (Connor quote), NHC Scrapbook 1966–1969; *Miami Herald*, June 20, 1972, August 1–2, 1978; *Ft. Lauderdale News*, September 12, 1965, August 24, 1969 (Gentry quote); *Miami News*, August 18–19, 1969, all in NHC Scrapbook 1950–1985. See also the following NHC Scrapbook 1950–1985 clippings: "Gov't Weather Tampering Is Causing World Floods," *National Tattler*, December 24, 1972; and "Rainmaking

on Protests 'Ridiculous,'" *Hollywood Sun-Tattler,* August 24, 1972, which reported the National Weather Service's denial "that it seeded clouded over Miami Beach to bring down rain on protesters outside the Republican National Convention." On Project Stormfury, see Robert C. Gentry, "Hurricane Modification," in *Weather and Climate,* ed. W. N. Hess (New York: John Wiley and Sons, 1974); Robert Sheets, "Tropical Cyclone Modification: The Project Stormfury Hypothesis," NOAA Technical Report ERL 414-AOML 30 (1981), 1–52; Sheets, "The National Hurricane Center," 200; Dunn and Miller, *Atlantic Hurricanes,* 294–96; Rosenfeld, *Eye of the Storm,* 245–48; Davies, *Inside the Hurricane,* 79–102; Elsner and Kara, *Hurricanes of the North Atlantic,* 380; Hughes, *A Century of Weather Service,* 181, 200; and Barnes, *Florida's Hurricane History,* 229–30. On the emerging science of weather modification, see Senate Committee on Foreign Relations, *Weather Modification,* 93rd Cong., 2d sess., 1974; Frederick Sargent, "A Dangerous Game: Taming the Weather," *Bulletin of the American Meteorological Society* 48 (1967): 452–58; W. R. Derrick Sewell, ed., *Human Dimensions of Weather Modification* (Chicago: University of Chicago Press, 1966); Robert G. Fleagle, ed., *Weather Modification: Science and Public Policy* (Seattle: University of Washington Press, 1969); National Research Council, *Weather and Climate Modification: Problems and Progress* (Washington, D.C.: National Academy of Sciences, 1973); Steinberg, *Acts of God,* 127–47; and the *Journal of Weather Modification* (1969–).

29. Sheets, "The National Hurricane Center," 197–99, 204–5; NOAA, Federal Coordinator for Meteorological Services and Supporting Research, *National Hurricane Operations Plan, 1972* (Washington, D.C.: U.S. Department of Commerce, 1972), FCM 72-2.

30. James F. W. Purdom and W. Paul Menzel, "Evolution of Satellite Observations in the United States and Their Use in Meteorology," in *Historical Essays on Meteorology, 1919–1995,* ed. James Rodger Fleming, 103–17 (Boston: American Meteorological Society, 1996); J. D. Johnson, F. C. Parmenter, and R. Anderson, "Environmental Satellites: Systems, Data Interpretation, and Applications," *NOAA NESS* (October 1976), (NOAA S/T 76-241); Sheets, "The National Hurricane Center," 197–99, 201–4; Dunn and Miller, *Atlantic Hurricanes,* 291–94; Elsner and Kara, *Hurricanes of the North Atlantic,* 42–43; Rosenfeld, *Eye of the Storm,* 236–38; and E. A. Smith, "The McIDAS System," *IEEE Transactions: Geosciences* (GE-13) (1975): 123–28. See also E. C. Barrett and D. W. Martin, *The Use of Satellite Data in Rainfall Monitoring* (New York: Academic Press, 1981). See also *Miami News,* August 26, 1964, NHC Scrapbook 1960–1964; and *Miami Herald,* November 22, 1975, May 26, 1982, July 19, 1982, August 29, 1984, and c. 1974 *Herald* clipping "Machines Speed Weather Data," all in NHC Scrapbook 1950–1985.

31. On the maturation of television news, see Erik Barnouw, *Tube of Plenty: The Evolution of American Television,* 2d rev. ed. (New York: Oxford University Press, 1990); David Schoenbrun, *On and Off the Air: An Informal History of CBS News* (New York: E. P. Dutton, 1989); and the six-part documentary video series *Dawn of the Eye* (Princeton: Films for the Humanities and Social Sciences, 1997), especially pt. 4, "The Powers That Be, 1960–75," and pt. 5, "The Electronic Battalions, 1975–88."

32. Sheets, "The National Hurricane Center," 196–97; National Weather Bureau,

Office of the Federal Coordinator, *Report of the 1966 Interdepartmental Hurricane Warning Conference, Atlantic* (Washington, D.C.: GPO, 1966), 1–49. See also the voluminous clippings in the NHC Scrapbook 1966–1969, especially *Miami News,* September 8, 1965.

33. Sheets, "The National Hurricane Center," 197; Elsner and Kara, *Hurricanes of the North Atlantic,* 21–24, 44, 137–38, 382; Barnes, *Florida's Hurricane History,* 13–14; Rosenfeld, *Eye of the Storm,* 18–19, 239–41, 249. On Simpson's tenure as NHC director, see *Miami News,* August 27–28, 1969; *Miami Herald,* August 27, 1969, NHC Scrapbook 1966–1969; *Miami Herald,* August 22, 1969, May 30, 1974; *U.S. News and World Report,* September 8, 1969, 33, NHC Scrapbook 1950–1985. See also Robert H. Simpson and H. Riehl, *The Hurricane and Its Impact* (Baton Rouge: Louisiana State University Press, 1980).

34. For a history of FEMA and its predecessors, see "History of the Federal Emergency Management Agency," http://fema.gov/about/history.htm.; Peter J. May, *Recovering from Catastrophes: Federal Disaster Relief Policy and Politics* (Westport, Conn.: Greenwood, 1985; and Steinberg, *Acts of God,* 106–14, 173–95. See also *Miami Herald,* September 10, 1965, September 12, 1965, *Ft. Lauderdale News,* September 16, 1965; *Miami News,* June 7, 1966, NHC Scrapbook 1966–1969; Ron Sachs, "Storm Target Areas Urged to Obey Warnings Quickly," NHC Scrapbook clipping, ca. September 1974, *Miami Herald,* May 30, 1982, June 1, 1982; L. Erik Calonius, "Hurricane Experts Say the State of Their Art Can't Avert a Disaster," *Wall Street Journal,* October 14, 1983, all in NHC Scrapbook 1950–1985; Douglas C. Dacy and Howard Kunreuther, *The Economics of Natural Disasters: Implications for Federal Policy* (New York: Free Press, 1969); U.S. General Accounting Office, *Federal Disaster Assistance: What Should the Policy Be?* (Washington, D.C.: GAO, 1980); U.S. General Accounting Office, *Requests for Federal Disaster Assistance Need Better Evaluation: Report to the Congress* (Washington, D.C.: GAO, 1981); Federal Emergency Management Agency, *This Is the Federal Emergency Management Agency* (Washington, D.C.: FEMA, 1982); U.S. General Accounting Office, *Consolidation of Federal Assistance Resources Will Enhance the Federal-State Emergency Management Effort: Summary: Report* (Washington, D.C.: GAO, 1983; House Committee on Government Operations, *Federal Assistance to States and Communities for Hurricane Preparedness Planning: Twentieth Report* (Washington, D.C.: GPO, 1983); Committee on Appropriations, Subcommittee on HUD-Independent Agencies, *Federal Flood Insurance Program: Hearing before a Subcommittee of the Committee on Appropriations, United States Senate,* 97th Cong., 1st sess., Special Hearing, Federal Emergency Management Agency, Nondepartmental Witnesses (Washington, D.C.: GPO, 1981).

35. Earl J. Baker, ed., *Hurricanes and Coastal Storms: Awareness, Evacuation, and Mitigation,* Florida Sea Grant College Report 33 (Gainesville: Florida Sea Grant and Marine Advisory Program, 1980); Lawrence S. Tait, ed., *Hurricanes . . . Different Faces in Different Places (17th: 1995: Atlantic City, N.J.)* (Tallahassee: National Hurricane Conference, 1995). On the evolution of hurricane research in the 1980s and 1990s, see Elsner and Kara, *Hurricanes of the North Atlantic*; Sheets, "The National Hurricane Center," 207–30; and the periodic technical reports published by the NHC and NOAA.

Raymond Arsenault

On William Gray, see Elsner and Kara, *Hurricanes of the North Atlantic,* 334, 344; William M. Gray, "Global View of the Origins of Tropical Disturbances and Storms," *Monthly Weather Review* 96 (1968): 669–700; Gray, "Hurricanes: Their Formation, Structure, and Likely Role in the Tropical Circulation," in *Meteorology over the Tropical Oceans,* ed. D. B. Shaw (London: Royal Meteorological Society, 1979), 155–218; Gray, "Atlantic Seasonal Hurricane Frequency," pt. 1, "El Niño and 30 mb Quasi Biennial Oscillation Influences," and pt. 2, "Forecasting Its Variability," *Monthly Weather Review* 112 (1984): 1649–83; Gray and C. W. Landsea, "African Rainfall as a Precursor of Hurricane-Related Destruction on the U.S. East Coast," *Bulletin of the American Meteorological Society* 73 (1992): 1352–64; Gray et al., *Summary of Atlantic Tropical Cyclone Activity and Verification of Authors' Seasonal Prediction* (Fort Collins: Colorado State University, 1995); *St. Petersburg Times,* August 9, 1998; and Gray's Web site: http://Tropical.atmos.colostate.edu/forecasts/index.html. On El Niño, see Cesar N. Caviedes, *El Niño in History: Storming through the Ages* (Gainesville: University Press of Florida, 2001).

36. Frank served as NHC director from 1973 to 1987, when he was replaced by Robert C. Sheets. See Neil L. Frank, "The Hard Facts about Hurricanes," *NOAA Magazine* 4 (1974): 4–9; and various clippings in the NHC Scrapbook 1950–1985, esp. *Miami News,* May 29, 1982, *Miami Herald,* September 24, 1975, May 29, 1976, June 1, 1980, June 1, 1982, June 6, 1982, July 29, 1982, November 20, 1982, November 25, 1982, September 12, 1984, March 10, 1985, and Neil Frank, interview by K. Demaret, *People* 20 (August 29, 1983): 87–88. On the growing celebrity status of hurricane forecasters, see the series of profiles by Mike Clary in the *Miami Herald,* March 5, 1984, June 6, 1984, July 29, 1984, June 3, 1984; and Al Burt, "The Calm Before," *Miami Herald,* March 10, 1985, all in the NHC Scrapbook 1950–1985. For examples of the special "hurricane sections" issued by many major newspapers, see *Miami Herald,* June 27, 1982, July 28, 1983, NHC Scrapbook 1950–1985; and "Hurricane Guide," *St. Petersburg Times,* May 28, 2000. On Witt's tenure at FEMA, see Steinberg, *Acts of God,* 190–95.

37. *People* 20 (August 29, 1983): 87–88; Burt, "The Calm Before," *Miami Herald,* March 10, 1985, June 1, 1980; all in NHC Scrapbook 1950–1985. In a September 24, 1975, *Miami Herald* story by Sam Jacobs, "She Was Surprise to Most," Frank stated: "I know people find it hard to believe that we can send a rocket to the moon and have it land just a few feet from where we planned it to and then I say that I can only predict a hurricane to within 50 miles, but it's true." A year later, NHC forecaster Gilbert Clark confessed: "We're the first to admit we can't predict what they'll do. They can move so crazily, wobble as much as 50 miles in either direction. It's almost like they're alive." *Miami Herald,* August 9, 1976, NHC Scrapbook 1950–1985.

38. *Miami News,* May 31, 1979, May 29, 1981, *Miami Herald,* May 26, 1982, May 30, 1982, June 1, 1982, July 28, 1983, *Sun Reporter,* May 29, 1982; Calonius, "Hurricane Experts Say the State of Their Art Can't Avert a Disaster," *Wall Street Journal,* October 14, 1983, all in NHC Scrapbook 1950–1985; Erik Larson, "Waiting for Hurricane X," *Time,* September 7, 1998, 62–66.

39. See Pielke, *Hurricane Andrew in South Florida*; Roger A. Pielke, "Reframing the

U. S. Hurricane Problem," *Society and Natural Resources* 10 (1997): 485–99; Provenzo and Provenzo, *In the Eye of Hurricane Andrew; St. Petersburg Times*, August 18–20, 2002; Roger M. Wakimoto and Peter G. Black, "Damage Survey of Hurricane Andrew and Its Relationship to the Eyewall," *Bulletin of the American Meteorological Society* (February 1994): 189–200; Hugh E. Willoughby and Peter G. Black, "Hurricane Andrew in Florida: Dynamics of a Disaster," *Bulletin of the American Meteorological Society* (March 1996): 543–49; and Committee on Governmental Affairs, *Rebuilding FEMA: Preparing for the Next Disaster*, 103rd Cong., 1st sess., May 18, 1993 (Washington, D.C.: GPO, 1994). During the past decade, several important studies have explored recent trends in the politics and culture of "natural" disasters. See especially Andrew Ross, *Strange Weather: Culture, Science, and Technology in the Age of Limits* (London: Verso, 1991); Rutherford H. Platt, *Disasters and Democracy: The Politics of Extreme Natural Events* (Washington, D.C.: Island Press, 1999); Davis, *Ecology of Fear*; and Steinberg, *Acts of God*.

Raymond Arsenault

Part 3

Despoliation

Chapter 10

Alligators and Plume Birds

The Despoliation of Florida's Living Aesthetic

Jack E. Davis

Florida is an imagined place. It has long been so, with outsiders historically acting as the creators of its image. The Spanish, for example, originally suspected that Florida was an island, and an unidentified cartographer named it Bimini. Juan Ponce de León eventually learned otherwise, while the myth of gold and silver and a magical wellspring lured him into a futile search for wealth and eternal youth. What he did find, what he did not have to imagine, was natural beauty, and during the flowering of spring he renamed the peninsula La Florida. Yet this enchanting place seemed simultaneously savage and repulsive. Most of the peninsula was an impassable quagmire, and the indigenous people, namely the Ais and Calusa, resisted Juan Ponce's wanderings and cost him his life. During the next four hundred years, people called Florida a garden and a paradise, as if to invalidate Ponce's fate. One late-nineteenth-century travel writer labeled Florida the "Eden of the South," and, still, Eden was not without contrasts. Other observers were disdainful of Florida's desolate scrub lands, malarial swamps, indeed, the landscape's "dreary monotony." Writing from her winter cottage on the St. Johns River in the 1870s, Harriet Beecher Stowe said that her adopted state was "like a piece of embroidery," with "one side all tag-rag and thrums . . . and the other side showing flowers and arabesques and brilliant coloring."[1]

Whatever Florida was, beautiful or repulsive, nature usually defined it. Its popular identity lay at the intersection between culture—the images that people like Stowe perpetuated—and the natural environment. Nature was Florida's living aesthetic—the indigenous and distinct flora, fauna, and climate that brought life and color to the landscape and gave the state its character apart from human creations. In no other period was the living aesthetic arguably more popular than in the last half of the nineteenth century, when a national public was discovering Florida in newspapers, magazines, travel guides, dime novels, and children's books. Many of those readers joined an expanding class of leisure seekers and traveled to Florida for vacation. Northern physicians prescribed Florida's healthful climate to patients in need of convalescence. An increasing number of visitors stayed to become permanent residents, giving Florida a population of nearly 500,000 at the turn of the century. When much of the state still remained a harsh wilderness, natural beauty was less of an inducement for permanent relocation than were low taxes, cheap land, commercial ventures, and the chance for a new start.

Yet, whatever the reason to go to Florida, the living aesthetic rarely escaped the attention of the settler and the visitor. The nineteenth-century correspondences and journals of soldiers, vacationers, and new residents are replete with commentary about Florida nature. In a series of letters written in 1855 to his wife in New York, the historian George Bancroft referred to Florida as a "land of Fountains," an appellative inspired by the state's many freshwater springs. His contemporary and a travel writer from New York, Daniel F. Tyler expressed a common sentiment when he reported on his stay at Green Cove Springs, Florida: "You realize a moral, as well as a physical benefit, from this communion with the primitive world." Writing home to his son in 1874, L. D. Huston said of Florida, "so far it is a perfect Eden—they tell me that it is about the same all year round, and if it is, then goodbye to the north." A few years later, a California newspaper tempted readers with letters from Samuel C. Upham, who told of bounties around his Manatee River homestead: "The rivers are overflowing with fish, and the forests are overrun with game. . . . The climate is delightful—sort of an earthly Paradise." Minnie Moore-Willson, who moved to Kissimmee from the Midwest in the 1880s with her husband, a real-estate developer, compared "Florida's Scenic Wonders," in particular the Everglades, with California's Yosemite Valley, Montana's Yellowstone, and Arizona's Grand Canyon.[2]

Some of the country's best-known writers brought similar images to a larger audience. In nature, they discovered Florida's sense of place. Constance Woolson set her most successful novel, *East Angles* (1886), in Florida and gave it an Edenic seduction reminiscent of William Bartram's Elysium, albeit one that ultimately eluded the book's protagonist. Henry James reviewed and liked Woolson's novel, and he went to Florida. Whereas Woolson made many trips to Florida, James spent barely six days there on a single occasion. But the sometimes jaded author stayed long enough to become "Byronically foolish about the St. Johns River," as he put it. "That was the charm," he wrote, "the velvet air, the extravagant plants, the palms, the oranges, the cacti . . .—one might also have been in a corner of Naples or of Genoa." Writing for *Scribner's Monthly Magazine* in the 1870s, Edward King was enchanted with the St. Johns tributary, the Ocklawaha River, which with its "sylvan peace and perfect beauty" offered perfect tranquility to the traveler. What lay upstream was even better. Here was Silver Springs, Ponce de León's Fountain of Youth, according to King, "one of the wonders of the world."[3]

One of the most distinctive features of Florida's living aesthetic was its highly visible wildlife. The state was virtually unsurpassed as a life-generating habitat, and with its geographic reach into subtropical latitudes, its environment was flush with plants and animals that set Florida apart from the rest of the country. The most exotic and frequently noted Florida wildlife were alligators and plume birds. Stowe saw them on the St. Johns River, King on the Ocklawaha. They inhabited the entire state, from the panhandle to the Everglades, and in great abundance. "[O]ne of the most distinguished figures of the Florida wilds," Frank M. Chapman of the American Museum of Natural History observed, were the showy wading birds. Alligators were "so thick" in the water, said a contemporary, that "you can walk across on their heads." Together, birds and alligators were beauty and beast, chief renderings of the two sides of Florida's created image.[4]

There was great vogue in these and many other indigenous creatures and plants of Florida. Just as tourists paid money to spend time in Florida, those things that embodied the state's image were merchantable. They were harvested for sale on global and local markets as fashion apparel and souvenirs. The trade in Florida nature was a conspicuous public enterprise, and no more evident than when its products were on display as storefront commodities. In Jacksonville, shops along the famous Bay Street, known as "Curio Row," sold novelties of nature as early as the 1870s. A contemporary travel guide written by the southern lyricist Sidney Lanier said of Bay Street's inventory: "These curiosities are sea-beans, alligator's teeth, plumes of herons and curlew's feathers, crane's wings, mangrove and orange [wood] walking canes, coral branches, coquina figurines, and many others."[5]

The market for such items gave rise to an army of commercial wildlife hunters. They penetrated the Fakahatchee Strand for orchids, combed the beaches of southwest Florida for sea shells, waded through nearby swamps to cut cypress knees, plundered the shores for sea turtles and turtle eggs, ambushed mangrove islands everywhere for plume birds, and followed the nocturnal bellowing of reptiles for alligator hides. The state passed laws to protect wildlife. But market demand hardly abated, and protective legislation often did little more than turn legal hunters into unrepentant poachers. The money made from shooting wildlife remained ever seductive. Custodians of the marketplace—consumers, retailers, wholesalers, and commercial wildlife hunters—turned Florida into arguably the most hostile place in the world for wildlife, especially alligators and plume birds.

In the end, harvesting novelties of nature threatened those things that gave Florida its original splendor. Development and drainage were important catalysts in the transformation of Florida's popular image, but the destruction of wildlife preceded both and forged its own change. Along with agricultural and forest products, hunted wildlife was one of Florida's principal export commodities. Those of greatest demand, while supplies lasted, were parts of alligators and feathers of wading birds. Their commodification continued the story of wildlife destruction played out on the American frontier many times over. In the affairs of humans and nature, the Florida saga must be counted as one of the bloodiest. Equally important, it dislodged the living aesthetic as the centerpiece in Florida's popular image. Out of the violence, moreover, came a notable and generally overlooked event in Florida history: The near-extermination of certain wildlife species—again, not development or drainage—led to the birth of organized conservation in the state. What was happening in Florida was of national concern. The state and its activists were not simply caught up in a broad wave of conservation enthusiasm that swept the country; they helped energize it. Despite their initiatives, the grim future for Florida's wildlife and its original image was clear.

One of the most desirable of Florida's wild creatures, and one of the most easily culled from nature, was the North American alligator. The giant reptile prowled freshwater swamps, streams, and lakes as far north as South Carolina and as far west as Texas, but the identity of one of the country's most exotic states, Florida, was linked to one of the continent's most exotic creatures. The first known illustration of the North American alligator done by a westerner was that of Jacques LeMoyne, who accompanied French soldier-settlers to Florida in the sixteenth century. In his 1591 sketch, one of two alligators dominates the scene, which includes thirteen native hunters. The alligator evokes terror if not also evil. Although it breathes no fire, it is dragonlike and exaggerated in size, eclipsing that of its bare-bodied pursuers. In the background, seven natives with spears and clubs have overcome the second alligator as it struggles on its back, suggesting not only the fate of its counterpart but that nature itself, no matter how treacherous, can be subdued.

When the naturalist William Bartram explored the southern British colonies two centuries later, Florida produced the first extensive reports of alligators. In the colony of East Florida, Bartram found an aquatic wonderland. He had learned long before that tranquility was counterbalanced by chaos and upheaval, but he was not prepared for what he encountered in Florida. His most enduring example of violence in nature is his depiction—in illustration and narrative—of alligators, "terrible" monsters that gathered in "incredible" numbers. His too are oversized, medieval representations of dragons, with "clouds of vapor issuing from their wide nostrils." Bartram's critics believed that his reports of roaring, bloodletting, man-hunting reptiles were too fantastical to be true, and indeed alligators do not blow steam. Nevertheless, according to one of his biographers, his descriptions of alligators were "undeniably the most famous passages in all of his writings."[6]

In later centuries, the prehistoric reptiles continued to represent the darker side of Florida's allure. The fictional story of Alligator Ike in an 1883 issue of *Beadle's New York Dime Library* linked, for example, alligator hunting to the "mire" of the Everglades and to outlawry in Florida's backcountry. A national reading audience encountered many such tales of the gruesome beasts that dwelled in Florida's swamplands, which in themselves invited an image of mysterious and uncivilized places, suitable only for wild and savage things. By the late nineteenth century, alligators had become part of Florida lore, portrayed in magazines, books, and travel guides as "uncouth monsters," as one writer described them. Around this time, authors of children's books discovered Florida as a popular setting for their stories, and human-eating alligators served as a favored "nemesis" for their young heroes. But along with terror, the alligator had the ability to evoke fascination. No matter how abhorrent, it was still an awe-inspiring wonder of nature. As late as the last decades of the twentieth century, the alligator was the wild creature that Florida visitors wanted to see most.[7]

A century earlier, visitors and others wanted to possess one, or some part of one, in one form or another. From pens where he kept thousands of hatchlings behind his St. Petersburg sundry store, Bill Carpenter shipped baby alligators as live curios to customers around the country. Few objects of nature seemed so versatile as a consumer product. Travel writer Julian Ralph came to that conclusion when he walked Jacksonville's Bay Street in the 1890s. Bay Street, he said, "is fit to be called Alligator Avenue, because of the myriad ways in which that animal is offered as a sacrifice to the curiosity and thoughtlessness of the crowds. . . . I saw them stuffed and skinned, turned into bags, or kept in tanks and boxes and cages; their babies made into ornaments or on sale as toys; their claws used as purses, their teeth as jewelry, their eggs as curios." This kind of exploitation was a perfectly acceptable use of alligators. One of the main characters in a 1914 children's novel, *The Moving Picture Girls under the Palms, or, Lost in the Wilds of Florida*, asked: "What would we do for valises and satchels if we had no alligators?"[8]

No one was perhaps more aware of the public's fascination with the alligator than Kirk Munroe. The author of over thirty books for boys and south Florida's first notable writer, Munroe made alligators synonymous with spirited adventure and probably popularized their connection to Florida more than anyone. He was also quite familiar with their extraction from the wild— the supply-side of the alligator market. In an 1892 *Cosmopolitan* story, he told about an expedition with Seminole Indians that was typical of the way alligators were hunted. The pursuit usually occurred at night, when the reptiles were more active. Hunters did not see their prey, Munroe noted; they heard them. "Darkness had hardly well set in before muttered bellowings began to sound from the stream." After a cormorant shot earlier that day was strewn downstream of the hunters' boat, a torch was lit to illuminate the alligators' eyes, showing against the black in pairs "luridly red." When the first alligator advanced on the bait, a Seminole sent a shot "through one of his glowing eyeballs." Using a harpoon to feel for the sinking body, another Seminole speared it and dragged it to shore, where it was later retrieved and skinned with the rest of the catch. Munroe took aim at the sixth and last alligator shot that night. "The report of the rifle was instantly followed by such a flurry of whirling, thrashing and splashing, such showers of spray and bloody foam, such a lashing of the water with furious blows and such commotion generally that it was as if a small cyclone had, without warning, been dropped from the heavens into that quiet spot."[9]

The takings had to be substantial to be worth the evening's labor of Munroe's Seminole companions. The market value of the hide was found only in the skin of the belly and the clawed feet. Before 1916, when alligators were the only wild game that hunters could legally pursue year-round, their hides usually fetched ten cents a foot. Leaving feet and claws attached added another twenty-five cents. When Frank Stranahan, a pioneer Ft. Lauderdale merchant made rich by nature's wealth, paid two dollars for an eight-foot hide in 1901, he was offering top dollar. Used for necklaces, the teeth brought five to eight dollars a pound. Stranahan gave a nickel for each fresh alligator egg and was known to buy them by the thousands from Seminoles. He would then either resell the eggs in bulk to a dealer in Jacksonville or hatch them and sell the babies to tourists. A six-inch live alligator typically sold for twenty-five cents.[10]

Although not operating on the retail side, Indians were as much involved in the alligator trade as whites. Before contact with Europeans, few native cultures regarded wildlife as superfluous, and yet whites did eventually draw Indians into their commercial activity as trading partners and into their employment as hunting guides for sportsmen and naturalists. The environmental consequences of that partnership were significant. Whites and Indians killed turtles, bears, wildcats, birds, alligators, deer, otters, and raccoons. Florida in the last quarter of the nineteenth century resembled the British North American colonies in the seventeenth and eighteenth centuries. Animals were still shot and trapped in the old ways, and consumption was pursued systematically and without thought of conservation. Seminoles were the area's principal hunters before the 1890s, and whites served as traders and middlemen for dealers in Jacksonville, New York, and Havana. Alcohol, which traders had been using since the colonial period, was one of the most effective means of luring Seminoles into the commercial economy. By historian Harry Kersey's account, cash for raccoon and otter pelts, deer and alligator hides, and wading-bird plumes represented 66 percent of the cash income for the Everglades Indians.[11]

Wildlife populations paid heavily for the activity of whites and Indians. Plundering in Florida was like that of the bison on the Great Plains, the timber wolf in the Northeast and Northwest, and the beaver in New England. Beginning in the 1880s, tens of thousands of alligator hides, rolled up and packed in wooden barrels, left Florida annually for leather companies in the Northeast and in Europe. Many were sent to Japan, where they were tanned, made into souvenirs, and exported back to Florida for sale to tourists. A total of 2.5 million alligator hides were harvested from the Florida wilds between 1880 and 1894. The state's ecosystem lost an unrecorded number more alligators in the eggs plundered from nests. Hunting restrictions instituted in 1916 sent the price of hides skyrocketing but hardly initiated a trend against the slaughter. As late as the 1940s, a brokerage in Gainesville received 80,000 hides annually. The reptiles' numbers had become so "pitifully reduced" by then, according to Thomas Barbour, the director of the Comparative Museum of Zoology at Harvard University, that they had turned into "craven beasts, seldom seen by day." Not until 1962 did the state ban the hunting of alligators altogether.[12]

In the days before an animal's ecological contribution was understood, much less considered, wildlife protection required that an animal either serve as sport game or induce sympathy. The alligator met neither essential. Even conservationists showed little more than indifference for the "saurians," as they were sometimes called. One exception among early conservationists was A. W. Dimock, an Everglades adventurer and a repentant alligator hunter. In 1908, he proclaimed that if federal and state governments could provide protection to bison and game birds, they could do the same for alligators. As early as 1880, Daniel F. Tyler called for such a measure—"*the sooner the better.*" Yet the problem in wildlife protection in Florida, even for favored animals, was not so much in the lack of legislation as in the lack of enforcement of legislation.[13]

Lawmakers were generally dedicated sportsmen who showed little desire to change Florida from a hunter's paradise where every season was open season. A common scene orchestrated on steamers ferrying passengers up and down the state's waterways, for example, included men with hunting rifles standing at the gunwales freely taking pot shots at wildlife. The steamer was equivalent to the railroad trains in the western territories from which men fired through open windows at the bison that then still crowded the plains.

Jack E. Davis

Like grazing wildlife, an alligator sunning on a bank or a turtle floating at the water's surface hardly tested the skill of a shooter. On more than one steamer, Harriet Beecher Stowe stood by impotently as a witness to the carefree violence. It outraged her. "Now and then those sons of Nimrod in their zeal put to peril the nerves, if not lives, of passengers," she wrote. "One such actually fired at an alligator across a crowd of ladies . . . and persisted in so firing a second time, after being requested to desist. If the object were merely to show the skill of the marksman, why not practice upon inanimate objects? . . . Certainly this is an inherent savagery difficult to account for. Killing for killing's sake belongs not even to the tiger. The tiger kills for food; man, for amusement."[14]

Stowe tolerated killing for food or the market, however, even the fashion market. The more significant wildlife destruction, immeasurable in its impact, on the Florida frontier was executed for those reasons. A similar kind and level of destruction had come to pass with each successive shift of the American frontier, from the eastern seaboard colonies to the western territories to the Florida subtropics. On each frontier, nature rendered the bounty, and the western cultural desire for profit provided the motive for taking it. But in Florida, the culture-nature dynamic often included an additional motive. Vanity combined with profit to drive the destruction. On frontiers outside Florida, bison hides, deerskins, and beaver pelts, like alligator hides, were less objects of beauty than of practicality. Wearers of the soft and elegant plume feathers of Florida's wading birds, by contrast, were yielding to fashion. Bird feathers of a wide variety were in vogue among middle- and upper-class women, who were transferring a bit of nature's beauty to themselves and thus stimulating a multimillion-dollar market for its demand.

The feathers of Florida's plume birds were the most prized among nature's novelties. For newcomers to the state, snowy egrets, great egrets, little blue herons, great blue herons, roseate spoonbills, ibises, and wood storks were an odd thing to see stepping about on their stick legs with inverted knees in marshes and along pond and bay edges. When not in flight, some birds stood to the height of a grown man's chest. While wood storks preferred the solitude of cypress trees, most others tended toward nesting in integrated avian colonies in mangroves, called rookeries. A wildlife photographer in 1909 said that egrets would light on mangroves in such large numbers that their white lace made an island "look like a huge snow-drift." At least three Florida rookeries were each believed to provide habitat for a million birds.

So plentiful in the sky was avian life that people used to say, the "air is alive."[15]

With its warm temperatures, dry and wet seasons, mangrove islands and forests, and plentiful storehouse of fish, Florida was perfectly suited as a habitat for migrating wading birds. For thousands of years, they had lived unmolested in Florida. Their bloodline dated to the Pleistocene, when their ancestors lived with mammoths, bison, horses, camels, llamas, and sloths, indigenous fauna that failed to survive geologic and climatic changes combined with the crude weapons of early humans. The birds, more flexible and adaptable, did. What they would not be able to endure was the modern hunter's gun. As state Audubon vice president Kirk Munroe put it early in the twentieth century, Florida was the "paradise of plume hunters and the purgatory of all birds."[16]

Sportsmen, taxidermists, and naturalists all partook in the pursuit of plume birds. The job of the naturalist was to observe wild flora and fauna in an undisturbed setting and in a laboratory. Killing was part of the calling. John James Audubon, whose name became synonymous with wildlife protection, shot thousands of birds so he could portray them on canvas. Latter-day naturalists collected specimens for museums of natural history in Europe and the United Sates, including the Smithsonian Institution. One naturalist recalled once approaching a rookery of pelicans and stopping to watch parents feeding their young, marveling at the adult's "wonderful" instinctive ability to "find its own nest among so many thousand." He then killed eighteen specimens in the name of science.[17]

One of the earliest sportsmen and naturalists to hunt in south Florida was Charles B. Cory, a Bostonian heir to a silk and wine fortune who first brought his gun to Florida in the 1870s. Cory, who fancied the title "professor," traveled around the world, sending back reports to magazines and scientific journals with his observations of nature. When in Florida, he indulged his passions for the high society of Palm Beach and the sport of tracking and shooting wild game. These were hardly mutually exclusive passions among other male members of his class, who were not naturalists but sportsmen. Cory was as much the latter as the former. He organized his hunts like safaris. Wearing an English field helmet that complemented his twisted handlebar mustache, he made a habit of having his photograph taken with his most prized quarry, such as a panther or a black bear. In 1895, the professor opened the Florida Museum of Natural History in Palm Beach, where he installed his trophies as the museum's exhibits.[18]

Jack E. Davis

Sportsmen were less interested in killing peaceful wading birds than in big game, which was supposed to give measure to a male hunter's manhood. Although sportsmen were sometimes "callous hearted," as Minnie Moore-Willson put it, and wanton in their destruction, their impact was minimal when measured against the activities of commercial hunters. The naturalist caused even less damage.[19]

Market hunters began plundering rookeries in the early 1880s. Selling feathers had become a lucrative endeavor generated by the millinery industry in New York and Europe, which fixed feathers of all kinds, even whole birds, to women's hats as ornamental trimming. The plumage of egrets and their long-beaked cousins were especially popular. When working as a volunteer for the American Ornithological Union (AOU) in 1886, Frank Chapman over the course of two afternoons counted 160 birds on the hats of women walking about New York City's uptown shopping district. Feathers provided an important source of supply for the $17-million-a-year millinery industry in New York, which alone employed 20,000 workers, most under sweatshop conditions. Plume hunters operated in their own harsh environment, but their work could enrich them. One young white hunter said that "a day's wages of plume-hunting" was equal to a month of "'gator hunting." Seminoles peddled feathers to tourists at hotels for several dollars apiece. Most feathers, though, were sold to millinery agents, who paid twelve to seventeen dollars per ounce, depending on the kind and quality of feather. Hunters got the price of gold—thirty-two dollars an ounce—for the snowy egret's fluffy mating feathers, known as aigrettes. One ounce of feathers required killing four egrets.[20]

Not surprisingly, many locals drew their existence from trade in plume birds. Florida was not the sort of place where the average individual who lived off the land or sea could hope to get rich. Life was in some ways more difficult for Florida pioneers, especially those living in south Florida, where the birds concentrated, than for those who settled on the plains of the Great West. Indian raids had not been a threat since the Seminole wars ended in 1858, but before the days of dredges and drainage canals, there was little range land for livestock. There was plenty of freshwater for staple crops, but comparatively less consistently dry terra firma in which to plant them. Settlers had always shot birds for a source of protein for the family table. They called the egret the Chokoloskee chicken. "The pot-hunter has good reason for killing birds," wrote University of Miami biologist John C. Gifford in 1925. But once millinery agents began paying for feathers, the hunting habits of locals changed dramatically. Said Audubon warden Oscar Baynard, the money earned from pluming was simply a "terrible temptation to many real fine fellows."[21]

The feather trade occurred in a global market. Plumers carried their guns into the wilds of Australia, the Middle and Far East, South America, and southern Europe, and they shipped their feathers across regions, continents, and oceans. With the Everglades as a prime bird habitat, few places in the world could match the size of the avian population and the ensemble of species in Florida. In 1902, commercial sales rooms in London reported an inventory of 48,240 ounces in plumes, equivalent to the destruction of 192,000 egrets and two to three times as many nestlings and eggs, all from the United States and most from Florida. Hunters cleaned out whole rookeries up and down Florida's coasts and in the Everglades. Without exaggeration, Moore-Willson called the Everglades the "chief slaughter grounds for the birds of America." The birds, she wrote, "are taking their last meals."[22]

The region was crowded with plume hunters, who penetrated deeper and deeper into the swamp, leaving virtually no avian life behind. They typically pursued their trade in a callous and highly destructive manner. The New York feather agent J. H. Batty maintained a business relationship with as many as two hundred commercial hunters in Florida, supplying them with breechloading shotguns designed with a twelve-gauge barrel and a less destructive and quieter .22-caliber barrel, used for small birds and close-range shooting. Birds were hunted year-round, but the heaviest takings occurred in late spring when rookeries were considered "ripe." Nuptial feathers remained at their finest then, and hatchlings were fresh out of their eggs. The adult birds were not likely to abandon their nests at the sound of gunfire. They instead rose up in defensive hover to protect their young, only to become easier targets of their predators.[23]

Extermination was not the goal of hunters, but it was very nearly the result. As early as 1887, ornithologist W.E.D. Scott reported that once-bustling rookeries had been turned into eerie ghost islands. As a consequence of the demand for the more expensive "snowy product," conservationists in 1911 could count only ten egret colonies in the Carolinas, Georgia, and Florida. William T. Hornaday, the director of the Bronx Zoo, estimated a 77 percent decline in Florida's bird population between 1881 and 1894. By the turn of the century, roseate spoonbills and snowy egrets had all but disappeared, the great white heron totaled approximately 200, the reddish egret survived with one pair, and the flamingo deserted Florida and never returned on its own after 1907. Victims of target practice and pot shots, the swallow-tailed and Everglades kites fell to endangered levels, where they remained indefinitely. The change was so remarkable that the president of the local Audubon in Tampa was moved to write in a 1916 issue of *Bird-Lore* that he had actually seen an egret recently fly over the city.[24]

Not even sympathetic naturalists considered the consequences of losing so many vital inhabitants of a given ecosystem, of the imbalance that might afflict the local food chain. Instead, they were aroused by the cruelty of the plume trade, and nothing unsettled them more than the image of hundreds of distressed nestlings. Intending to tap into these emotions, William Dutcher, the first president of the National Association of Audubon Societies, cited in a pamphlet the "horror" of an eyewitness to a recently raided heronry.

> What a holocaust! . . . What a monument of human callousness! There were fifty birds ruthlessly destroyed, beside their young (about 200) left to die of starvation! . . . [T]he parentless young ones could be seen staggering in the nests, some of them falling with a splash into the water . . . while others simply stretched themselves out on the nest and so expired. Others, again, were seen trying in vain to attract the attention of passing Egrets, which were flying with food in their bills to feed their own young. . . . How could anyone but a cold-blooded, callous monster destroy in this wholesale manner such beautiful birds—the embodiment of all that is pure, graceful, and good?"[25]

A few hunters themselves had a difficult time stomaching such a sight. One was ruined for his trade after returning to see the remains of a shot-out rookery. "I am done with bird hunting forever!" he wrote. Another, who was able to kill and skin alligators by the dozen without a tincture of misgiving, believed he had not been "doing God's service" after he killed mother egrets and allowed crows to carry off the young. The day after his first kill, the young hunter who preferred the money from plume hunting to alligator hunting grieved for the orphaned nestlings: "I couldn't stand it, hearing those hungry little birds."[26]

The federal and state governments passed laws to protect the birds, but the millinery industry fought the laws, and most hunters ignored them. It is unclear whether the state was trying to protect the lives of birds or the vocation of some of its citizens when it created its first restrictive legislation in 1879, which prohibited aliens from killing plume birds. Whatever the law's intent, the peak years of plume hunting, by alien and citizen alike, were yet to come. The Frenchman Jean Le Chevalier, for example, one of the wealthiest in the plume business, practiced without the slightest interference from the authorities. Although the legislature outlawed the commercial hunting of egrets and other plume birds in 1891, it again provided no enforcement provisions. A year later, one agent delivered 130,000 Florida birds to the millinery industry. Nongame birds everywhere were under siege, and in 1900, Congress passed the Lacey Act to outlaw interstate commerce of any birds killed in violation of state law. A few months later, Florida lawmakers enacted the first law prohibiting the killing of nongame birds. New York, which in 1910 outlawed the interstate importation of bird feathers, was more vigilant about enforcing its laws than was Florida. Enforcement, however, pushed many milliners to relocate to Pennsylvania, and those that remained imported feathers from agents in Europe, who bought from agents in Havana, who bought from smuggling poachers in Florida. At the time, Frank Chapman predicted the extinction of several bird species in Florida.[27]

The story of Florida's vanishing image included citizens who tried to save the birds, and by virtue of their efforts, they introduced wildlife conservation to the state. Beauty, not the beast, awakened these new conservationists. As William Dutcher argued in making a case for saving Florida's birds, they were "the embodiment of all that is pure, graceful, and good." Birds, especially nesting ones, also betrayed innocence, a trait that could not be granted to alligators inhabiting fetid swamps. Beauty and innocence made a potent combination that aroused nationwide concern for the plight of Florida's birds.[28]

The chief antagonist of hunters and millinery interests in the plume wars was the National Association of Audubon Societies. State societies, including Florida, established the National Association in 1905. Mrs. Kingsmill Marrs, Florida Audubon's representative at the organizing meeting, recalled: "I was one of a group of persons who met to consider if they should make a bold plunge into the stormy sea of opposition to Audubon measures and bird protection existing in Florida." Florida birds were not the sole reason for the founding of the National Association, but the plumage issue lent a sense of urgency to the meeting. The National Association quickly began spearheading an aggressive lobbying and publicity campaign. In newspapers and magazines ranging from *Ladies Home Journal* to *Popular Mechanics*, ornithologists and other experts wrote about empty rookeries and empty skies and the bloody connection of these conditions to women's fashion. National Audubon pushed for the creation of bird sanctuaries, and state societies sponsored education campaigns. With the backing of National Audubon and the Florida chapter, President Theodore Roosevelt in 1913 designated Pelican Island on the Florida east coast a federal bird sanctuary, making it the country's first national wildlife refuge. Audubon provided a warden.[29]

The state society with the most at stake in the struggle to save birds was Florida. In early March 1900 in Maitland, six men and nine women organized the Florida Audubon Society. Theirs was the first state society established in the South outside of Tennessee, five years before the formation of the National Association. They elected a board of officers who came from the ranks of the social elite: a clergyman, a college president, a judge, a former army general, and a writer. They made Kirk Munroe, Governor William S. Jennings, and President Roosevelt honorary vice presidents. The Florida group's principal aim was to educate the public about the "wanton destruction of wild birds and their eggs," to discourage the purchase of feathers for ornamentation, and to emphasize the distinction between bird protection and game-bird protection.[30]

Florida Audubon recorded its first lobbying success when the state legislature passed the nongame-bird law in 1901. Although regarded as model legislation for other states to emulate, it carried a modest penalty—a fine of five dollars and confiscation of the feather bounty—and it bore no teeth for enforcement. The law did prohibit the shooting of birds for target practice and made bird study compulsory in public schools, but Florida Audubon initially failed to convince lawmakers to establish a permanent game commission and to expand the nongame-bird list to include shorebirds, ducks, hawks, robins, and many other species. As a whole, according to Audubon activists, Florida's legislators were willing to restrict the activities of "negroes and crackers" but not their own pastime indulgences.[31]

Nor would they appropriate money for game wardens. Audubon had fought hard for them. Publicly employed game wardens were a relatively new concept. Rangers patrolling federal lands were largely a creation of the National Park Service, which came into being in 1916, and Florida employed its first wardens only after it established a permanent Game and Freshwater Fish Commission in 1943. Instead, the American Ornithological Union hired four wildlife wardens in 1902, and National Audubon accepted the responsibility for their supervision and salary, thirty-five dollars a month.[32]

Within a few years of the deployment of the Audubon wardens, two were killed. In 1905, a well-known plume hunter named Walter Smith shot thirty-five-year-old Guy Bradley off the coast of Flamingo, making Bradley the first recognized martyr of Florida conservation. Three years later in Port Charlotte, Florida, the patrol boat of Columbus McLeod was discovered submerged with sand bags. The sixty-year-old warden's shredded hat was found inside with bits of hair, skull, and brain matter clinging to it. His body was never recovered.[33]

Despite national awareness of Bradley's death and the illicit plume trade, the demand for feathers remained steady. An egret fund established in 1906 had failed to generate the finances to establish an adequate warden defense, and wanting to avoid more bloodshed, Audubon officials all but surrendered the Florida battlegrounds to poachers. Frank Chapman, who served as National Audubon treasurer, lamented that Florida's last large rookery, Cuthbert, "will have to go . . . no law or man to protect it." Audubon instead focused on lobbying for strengthened bird-protection laws. At the behest of the national organization, and responding to an estimated 200,000 letters from concerned citizens, Congress added a ban on imported plume fashions to the Federal Tariff Act of 1913. Senator George McLean made a passionate speech in support of the proviso, which was countered by his less sympathetic colleague James Reed. The Missouri senator said: "I really honestly want to know why there should be any sympathy or sentiment about a long-legged, long-beaked, long-necked bird that lives in the swamps. . . . let humanity utilize this bird for the only purpose that evidently the Lord made it for, namely so that we could get aigrettes for the bonnets of our beautiful ladies."[34]

Reed's views were far from extreme, but a few people thought against the mainstream. If not most, many were women. At the height of the bird slaughter, local women's garden clubs in Florida pushed for the creation of bird sanctuaries in their communities, and twenty had been created by the time Roosevelt established Pelican Island. Many of these women were also active in the Florida Federation of Women's Clubs, which maintained committees on conservation and on birds. In 1916, under the leadership of May Mann Jennings, whose husband was a former governor of Florida, the Florida Federation of Women's Clubs successfully lobbied the state legislature for the creation of Florida's first state park, Royal Palm Park in the Everglades. The royal palm was the most stately and elegant of the palm species found in Florida. They were few in number and a favorite of poachers, who removed them to sell as ornamental plantings or cut them to secure their seeds. The federation lobbied for the park to provide a sanctuary for a rare stand of native royal palms and also for diminishing plume birds. The state's commitment to the park, however, was as limited as its enforcement of bird-protection laws. The federation was given the responsibility of maintaining and operating the park without the benefit of state money. Royal Palm remained Florida's only state park for two decades, and the Florida Federation of Women's Clubs earned the distinction of being the only women's organization in the country to operate such an enterprise. Eventually, the federation would offer Royal Palm to the National Park Service. Spurred by that donation, Florida's first congresswoman, Ruth Bryan Owen, a Florida federation member, co-sponsored legislation to create Everglades National Park.[35]

Despite the efforts of Florida's early conservationists, plume hunting continued into the 1940s. The shrinking size of the bird population, combined with a change in hat fashions, the Great Depression, and the establishment of the Florida Game and Fish Commission in 1943, finally brought an end to plume hunting. Protecting Florida's birds, even while ignoring the slaughter of alligators, was a noble effort. But the damage had been done. Development was well on its way by the early twentieth century, and the continued destruction of habitat would prevent the full recovery of wildlife populations.

By the early decades of the twentieth century, a growing number of people recognized that vanishing wildlife was changing Florida's living aesthetic. In a 1908 *Harper's* article, conservationist and writer A. W. Dimock was one of the few to lament "the passing of the Florida alligator," which he said "has always been the picturesque and popular feature of the peninsula." In a rare observation for the time, he made reference to the alligator's ecological value, noting the wildlife that thrived around the water holes alligators dug during the dry season and the rise in the number of water moccasins in response to their predator's decline. But Dimock was primarily concerned with the disappearing spirit and character that alligators gave to the Florida landscape. So was Daniel F. Tyler. Tyler expressed his concern twenty-eight years earlier and based his observation on the St. Johns River area. Hunters inflicted their damage there first before moving down into the wildlife-rich Everglades, where Dimock spent most of his time. Both men believed that hunters were not solely at fault for the animal's demise. They blamed Florida officials for permitting, as Dimock wrote, "the destruction of an attraction and an asset worth millions to the State." The alligator's habitat and "sustenance" remained "secure," he believed. The state's signature reptile could recover, and with it so too could old Florida. The solution was simple. Let the alligator alone, he pleaded, so that its population would rebound and "restore life and attractiveness to the waterways of a great national playground."[36]

Tyler placed the reptile together with its avian complement in their significance to the idea of Florida. "The Florida tourist," he wrote in 1880, "will be disappointed at not seeing more alligators and beautiful birds of plumage." Without its big birds, Florida was like rosebushes without their blooms, and its own bushes had been picked nearly clean. Minnie Moore-Willson found a suitable analogue in literature: "[W]ere we to take from Wordsworth his bird verses, how sadly mutilated would be the writings of our great English poet." Once again, the hunter—the "Hun descendent," Moore-Willson called him —was not solely to blame. The men and women who vacationed in Florida belonged to the social class that favored feathered hats. Dimock summarized, "The tourist has murdered the birds that beckoned him." Twenty years later, people still grieved for Florida. In a 1928 *Miami News* article entitled "Everglades Paradise Wrecked by Blunders," Florida resident Charles Torrey Simpson said that "It was birds that gave color and glory to the whole. . . . They filled the air, they crowded the water. . . . Only a few are now left of uncounted millions; they are mostly a lovely memory."[37]

Simpson belonged to a generation of Florida naturalists whose interests ran deeper than their research. They wrote about Florida's changing landscape and positioned themselves as advocates of its preservation. Few were as observant of and as disturbed by Florida's "tragedy" as John Kunkel Small of the New York Botanical Garden. In his 1929 book *From Eden to Sahara*, he called Florida a "natural history museum." A botanist, he worried that what had already happened to Florida's birds was happening to its vegetation. Change was a process of nature, he observed, slow and orderly with results that were "constructive—and satisfactory." Human-initiated change, by contrast, was comparatively "crude" and "rapid," leading to destruction and chaos. Since the beginning of human history, he wrote with the conviction of a conservationist, "the forces of destruction have gathered until today their action is fast and furious, and the results superlative." This was Florida's future. "Yesterday a botanical paradise! Tomorrow, the desert!"[38]

Small sympathized with his south Florida colleague John C. Gifford, who was greatly concerned for imperiled Florida fauna. A man of science, Gifford believed that nature existed for the benefit of humans, and he trusted in their inventive powers to improve upon it. His own contribution had come with the introduction to south Florida of the melaleuca and other water-absorbing trees, which were imported to help dry up the Everglades. In Gifford's mind, certain human imprints, such as the conversion of wetlands to productive forests and farmlands, were good. Others were not. The devastation of Florida wildlife, for example, was a great human folly. "The whole of South Florida should be one big bird sanctuary," he argued in 1925, while failing to understand how his own "improvements" were destroying bird habitat. "Wild bird life like beautiful plant life gives pleasure to every normal person." Yet too many men, especially white men, "easily revert to a very primitive state" when they "'tote' guns" into the wilderness. There they become "naturally vindictive toward anything that stands in their way." Gifford feared next for the future of Florida's "majestic" trees, believing that they were "destined like the flamingo, the parakeet and ibis and many other choice products of nature to pass on. . . . [T]he Florida of yesterday must no doubt in time fall before the juggernaut of modern progress."[39]

As the four naturalists indicated, birds and alligators were the first to fall before the juggernaut. So much else of Florida nature, its living aesthetic, would go their way. By the end of the century, the list of endangered and threatened species in Florida had become long: 530 plants and animals. Some of those on the list managed to climb back from a critical decline in numbers.

The alligator population was one. After receiving state protection in 1962 and federal protection in 1973, and despite habitat destruction, the alligator regenerated itself remarkably quickly. Scientists and state officials regarded the alligator comeback as a great success story in conservation. But the count of the alligator population was (and is) based on density figures and not absolute numbers. The exact number of the population size before its slaughter is unknown, and given that half of Florida's wetlands have been lost since then, it is safe to say that the population never restored itself fully. Yet it did increasingly clash with Florida's exploding human population. By 1979, the state had downgraded the alligator's endangered status to a species of special concern. State officials and some biologists began applying the label "nuisance" to the alligator, and in 1978 the state instituted a program to control (that is, exterminate) individual wayward alligators. Nine years later, the Florida Game and Freshwater Fish Commission adopted an alligator harvest program, which included the issuance of a limited number of hunting permits. The program was billed as a way to enhance the economic value of a "renewable natural resource" and thus stimulate conservation incentives. An unsuccessful challenger of the harvest program said, "The alligator symbolically and historically is the most important animal in the state of Florida." The alligator as commodity, nevertheless, gained official status. In 2003, licensed hunters bagged 2,576 game alligators and 6,759 "nuisance" alligators.[40]

Wading birds staged their own comeback, although they too failed to reach population sizes of old. Development destroyed an average of 26,030 acres of wetlands annually between the mid-1970s and mid-1980s, and polluted water and diminishing fish stocks added to the birds' struggle to survive in Florida. Equally important, meddling with water levels in the Everglades—the principal habitat area of plume birds—made nesting conditions inconsistent from one year to the next. Birds either failed to produce healthy offspring or they abandoned the region altogether for more suitable places. In the last decades of the twentieth century, for example, degraded conditions in south Florida compelled a sizeable number from North America's largest breeding colony of wood storks in North America to seek sanctuary somewhere else. Although the total number of wood storks in the United States increased during that period, a growing number were moving their breeding grounds northward, reaching as far as South Carolina. The activity of the birds, an indicator species for the ecological health of the Everglades, spoke volumes about local and state environmental policies. Similar readings can be taken from the habits of the roseate spoonbill, which historically nested only in Florida Bay at the end of the Everglades. In 2003, the largest breeding colony of the pink birds was found in Tampa Bay, once a nearly dead body of water that benefited from intensive cleanup efforts of environmentalists and local governments.[41]

Florida's popular identity as a place began with nature. It was enchanting at the same time that it was savage. Plume birds and alligators symbolized these opposing qualities. Ultimately, Florida seduced, but it also changed. It had only recently evolved from frontier conditions, the first attempts at Everglades drainage had failed miserably, and railroads had only begun to penetrate the peninsula by the time hunters had done their damage to the indigenous wildlife. The landscape for the most part was physically unchanged, but the life upon it was less eye-catching. People still came to Florida, and in greater and greater numbers than before, but the scenery and the sounds were different. Florida gravitated more toward the artificial and away from the living aesthetic that had been so central to a sense of place. In the course of a few decades beginning in the late nineteenth century, Florida had grown less diverse, less natural, less original. It looked and felt more like what humans imagined it ought to be.

Jack E. Davis

Notes

1. Elliot James Mackle Jr., "The Eden of the South: Florida's Image in American Travel Literature and Painting, 1865–1900" (Ph.D. diss., Emory University, 1977), 110; Harriet Beecher Stowe, *Palmetto Leaves* (Boston: J. F. Osgood and Co., 1873; reprint, Gainesville: University Press of Florida, 1999), 26; Tommy R. Thompson, "Florida in American Popular Magazines, 1870–1970," *Florida Historical Quarterly* 82 (summer 2003): 1–14.

2. Minnie Moore-Willson, *The Birds of the Everglades and Their Neighbors the Seminole Indians* (Tampa: Tampa Tribune Publishing Company, 1920), electronic version, Florida Heritage Collection (Publication of Archival Library and Museum Materials), http://webluis.fcla.edu (hereafter cited as FHC), 7; L. D. Huston to his son, March 17, 1874, box 7, miscellaneous manuscript collection, P. K. Yonge Library of Florida History, University of Florida, Gainesville (hereafter cited as PKY); Samuel C. Upham, *Notes from Sunland, on the Manatee River, Gulf Coast of South Florida: Its Climate, Soil and Productions: Land of the Orange and Guava, the Pine-apple, Date and Cassava* (Philadelphia: E. Claxton and Company, 1881), electronic version, FHC; Patricia Clark, ed., "'A Tale to Tell from Paradise Itself': George Bancroft's Letters from Florida, March 1855," *Florida Historical Quarterly* 48 (January 1970): 268; Daniel F. Tyler, *Where to Go in Florida* (New York: Hopcraft, 1880), "Author's Apology."

3. Anne E. Rowe, *The Idea of Florida in the American Literary Imagination* (Gainesville: University Press of Florida, 1992), 30–43, 56, 58–65; Mackle, "The Eden of the South," 115.

4. Frank M. Chapman, *Camps and Cruises of an Ornithologist* (New York: D. Appleton and Company, 1908), 123; Mark Derr, *Some Kind of Paradise: A Chronicle of Man and the Land in Florida* (New York: William Morrow and Company, 1989), 260–61, 384.

5. Quoted in Tome Staley, "Florida Alligator Carvings," *Antiques and Art Around Florida* (winter/spring 1998), on-line version: http://aarf.com/fealig98.htm.

6. Thomas P. Slaughter, *The Natures of John and William Bartram* (New York: Vintage Books, 1997), 199–203; William Bartram, "The Alligators of the St. Johns River," in *Alligator Tales*, ed. Kevin M. McCarthy (Sarasota, Fla.: Pineapple Press, 1998), 3–12.

7. Captain Fred Whittaker, "Alligator Ike; or, The Secret of the Everglade," *Beadle's New York Dime Library* 19 (July 18, 1883): 1–11; Kirk Munroe, "Catching Alligators," *Harper's Weekly* (April 12, 1884): 233; Peter A. Soderbergh, "Florida's Image in Juvenile Fiction, 1909–1914," *Florida Historical Quarterly* 51 (October 1972): 160; John Richard Bothwell, "How an Alligator Sold St. Petersburg," in *Alligator Tales*, 161–64.

8. Julian Ralph, *Dixie, or, Southern Scenes and Sketches* (New York: Harper and Brothers, 1896); Alonzo Church, "A Dash through the Everglades," *Tequesta* 9 (1949): 19; John Whipple Potter Jenks, *Hunting in Florida in 1874* (privately published, 1884), 47; Soderbergh, "Florida's Image in Juvenile Literature," 159–60; *Tampa Morning Tribune*, March 20, 1898; Bothwell, "How an Alligator Sold St. Petersburg."

9. Kirk Munroe, "Alligator Hunting with Seminoles," in *Alligator Tales*, 59–67;

Munroe, "Catching Alligators," 233; Hugh L. Willoughby, *A Canoe Journey of Exploration,* 81; Kirk Munroe, Miscellaneous Vita, Kirk Munroe Collection, box 2, Special Collections, Rollins College Library, Winter Park, Florida; Irving Leonard, *The Florida Biography of Kirk Munroe: Narrative and Biographical* (Chuluota, Fla.: Mickler House Publishers, 1975), 1–17, 19–32; Jenks, *Hunting in Florida in 1874,* 47.

10. Lawrence Will, *Cracker History of Okeechobee: "Custard Apple, Moonvine, Catfish and Moonshine"* (Belle Glade, Fla.: Glades Historical Society, 1977) 92–93; Harry A. Kersey Jr., *Pelts, Plumes, and Hides: White Traders among the Seminole Indians, 1870–1930* (Gainesville: University Presses of Florida, 1975), 37, 47–49, 52, 54–55, 77, 130, 132; Andrew H. Brown, "Haunting Heart of the Everglades," *National Geographic* 93 (February 1948): 152; Harry A. Kersey Jr., *The Stranahans of Fort Lauderdale: A Pioneer Family of New River* (Gainesville: University Press of Florida, 2003), 77, 85; Bothwell, "How an Alligator Sold St. Petersburg," 161–64.

11. Will, *Cracker History of Okeechobee,* 91–93; Kersey, *Pelts, Plumes, and Hides,* 36–37, 44–45, 49–53, 117, 130–33; Derr, *Some Kind of Paradise,* 133.

12. Charlton W. Tebeau, *Man in the Everglades: 2000 Years of Human History in the Everglades National Park* (Coral Gables: University of Miami Press, 1986), 44; "In the 'Glades: Prof. C. B. Cory Tells about What He Saw in the Everglades," (reprinted from *The Tropical Sun,* May 23, 1895), *Broward Legacy* 14 (winter/spring): 23; "Shall We Protect the Pelican?" Florida Audubon Society pamphlet (n.d.), Conservation folder, Special Collections, Rollins College; Mary Douthit Conrad, "Homesteading in Florida during the 1890s," *Tequesta* 16 (1957): 9; W.E.D. Scott, "The Present Condition of Some of the Bird Rookeries of the Gulf Coast," second paper, *The Auk: A Quarterly Journal of Ornithology* 4 (July 1887): 217; ibid., third paper, *The Auk: A Quarterly Journal of Ornithology* 4 (October 1887): 276–77; Hanna and Hanna, *Lake Okeechobee,* 341; Kersey, *Pelts, Plumes, and Hides,* 47, 48, 130, 132; Derr, *Some Kind of Paradise,* 141–42; Brown, "Haunting Heart of the Everglades," 152; Thomas Barbour, *That Vanishing Eden: A Naturalist's Florida* (Boston: Little, Brown and Company, 1944), 178, 193; John C. Gifford, *Billy Bowlegs and the Seminole War* (Coconut Grove, Fla.: Triangle Company, 1925), 24.

13. A. W. Dimock, "The Passing of the Florida Alligator," in *Alligator Tales,* 96–106; Will, *Cracker History of Okeechobee,* 92–93; Tyler, *Where to Go in Florida,* 21.

14. William Cronon, *Nature's Metropolis: Chicago and the Great West* (New York: W. W. Norton and Company, 1991), 216–18; Stowe, *Palmetto Leaves,* 260–61; Moore-Willson, *The Birds of the Everglades,* 17.

15. Derr, *Some Kind of Paradise,* 139; Marjory Stoneman Douglas, *The Everglades: River of Grass* (Sarasota, Fla.: Pineapple Press, 1997), 279; "About the Aigrette," *Bird-Lore* 11 (October 1909): 232; Archie Carr, "The Bird and the Behemoth," in *The Wild Heart of Florida,* ed., Jeff Ripple and Susan Cerulean (Gainesville: University Press of Florida, 1999), 40–42; A. C. Bent, "Nesting Habits of the Herodiones in Florida," *The Auk: A Quarterly Journal of Ornithology* 21 (January 1904): 20–29; Lawrence E. Will, *Dredgeman of Cape Sable* (St. Petersburg, Fla.: Great Outdoors Publishing, 1967), 55.

16. Barry Reese, "Plume Wars" (unpublished honors seminar paper in possession of the editors, University of South Florida), 38.

Jack E. Davis

17. Jenks, *Hunting in Florida in 1874*, 53–54.

18. Howard A. Kelly, "The Everglades National Park," *The Journal of the Maryland Academy of Sciences* 2 (January 1931): 39; Charles B. Cory, "Descriptions of Six Supposed New Species of Birds from the Islands of Old Providence and St. Andrews, Caribbean Sea," *The Auk: A Quarterly Journal of Ornithology* 4 (July 1887): 177.

19. Moore-Willson, *The Birds of the Everglades*, 17.

20. "About the Aigrette," 232; *South Florida Courier*, April 17, 1886; Will, *Cracker History of Okeechobee*, 94; Derr, *Some Kind of Paradise*, 136–37; Alfred Jackson Hanna and Kathryn Abbey Hanna, *Lake Okeechobee: Wellspring of the Everglades* (Indianapolis: Bobbs-Merrill Company, 1948), 340–41; Reese, "The Plume Wars."

21. Gifford, *Billy Bowlegs and the Seminole War*, 53; Oscar E. Baynard to A. J. Hanna, September 24, 1947, Plume Hunting folder, Alfred J. Hanna Papers, Special Collections, Rollins College; Marjory Stoneman Douglas, "Wings," *Saturday Evening Post*, March 14, 1931, 79; Lucy Worthington Blackman, *The Florida Audubon Society: 1900– 1935*, n.p., n.d., 30–31.

22. Moore-Willson, *The Birds of the Everglades*, 7, 8; Douglas, "Wings," 78; Lawrence E. Will, *Okeechobee Boats and Skippers* (St. Petersburg, Fla.: Great Outdoors Publishing, 1965), 15–72, 129–42; Kersey, *Pelts, Plumes, and Hides*, 52–63, 75–77, 104–5, 132.

23. Jenks, *Hunting in Florida in 1874*, 53–54; Douglas, *River of Grass*, 279.

24. "Florida Still Asleep," *Bird-Lore* (February 1, 1916); Reese, "The Plume Wars"; Orr, *Saving American Birds*, 237; Will, *Cracker History of Okeechobee*, 93, 95; Stephen Fox, *The American Conservation Movement: John Muir and His Legacy* (Madison: University of Wisconsin Press, 1981), 148–51; Douglas, *River of Grass*, 279; W.E.D. Scott, "The Present Condition of Some of the Bird Rookeries of the Gulf Coast," first paper, *The Auk: A Quarterly Journal of Ornithology* 4 (April 1887): 135–44; T. Gilbert Pearson to Mrs. W. S. Jennings, April 1, 1916, May Mann Jennings Papers (hereafter cited as MMJ), box 9, PKY; Bent, "Nesting Habits of the Herodiones in Florida," 23–29; Derr, *Some Kind of Paradise*, 140; Harold H. Bailey, *The Birds of Florida* (Baltimore: Waverly Press, 1925), 31; Steven Beissinger, "A Faithful, Fickle Hawk," *Natural History* (January 1988), 43–50; Reese, "The Plume Wars."

25. William Dutcher, "The Horrors of the Plume Trade," The National Association of Audubon Societies, special leaflet no. 21 (n.d.), Plume hunting folder, Hanna Papers.

26. Jim Huffstodt, "The Reign of the Plume Hunter," *Florida Wildlife* (March-April 1992): 3; *American Eagle*, September 2, 1926; Loren G. Brown, *Totch: A Life in the Everglades* (Gainesville: University Press of Florida, 1993), 11; "Autobiography of C. G. McKinney" (1928) 8, on the website "Reclaiming the Everglades: South Florida's Natural History, 1884–1934" (Publication of Archival Library and Museum Materials), http://everglades.fiu.edu/reclaim/; "About the Aigrette," 232; Orr, *Saving American Birds*, 30–31.

27. Robin W. Doughty, *Feather Fashions and Bird Preservation: A Study in Nature Protection* (Berkeley and Los Angeles: University of California Press, 1975); Ann Vileisis, *Discovering the Unknown Landscape: A History of America's Wetlands* (Washington, D.C.: Island Press, 1997), 151–56; Oscar E. Baynard to A. J. Hanna, September 24,

1947; Blackman, *The Florida Audubon Society,* 21; Hanna and Hanna, *Lake Okeechobee,* 340–41; Derr, *Some Kind of Paradise,* 136–38; Douglas, "Wings," 78; "Summary of the Bird Laws of Florida and Federal Regulations Applying to Migratory Birds," Florida Audubon Society pamphlet, 1915–1916, and A. Gray to A. J. Hanna, September 11, 1947, Plume hunting folder, Hanna Papers; John H. Baker, "Saving Man's Wildlife Heritage," *National Geographic* 106 (November 1954), 584; Chapman, *Camps and Cruises,* 148.

28. Dutcher, "The Horrors of the Plume Trade."

29. Blackman, *The Florida Audubon Society,* 13, 15, 27; "About the Aigrette," 232–33; Baker, "Saving Man's Wildlife," 584; *Tampa Tribune,* March 14, 2003; "This Is Not a Pretty Story," *Ladies Home Journal,* February 1914, 5; "Most Beautiful Bird Saved from Extinction by Law," *Popular Mechanics,* August 1930, 210; *Tampa Tribune,* March 14, 2003.

30. Blackman, *The Florida Audubon Society,* 1–34; Todd Pearson, *The First One Hundred Years: Being a Description of the Origins, History, and Prospects of the Florida Audubon Society and Its Seventy-Five Years,* n.p., n.d., 1–10.

31. Stuart McIver, "Death of a Bird Warden," *South Florida History Magazine* 29 (fall 2001): 24–25; Emily Perry Dieterich, "Birds of a Feather: The Coconut Grove Audubon Society, 1915–1917," *Tequesta* 45 (1985): 6–7.

32. Ibid.; James T. Huffstodt, *Everglades Lawmen: True Stories of Games Wardens in the Glades* (Sarasota, Fla.: Pineapple Press, 2000), x, 5.

33. "Pioneering Conservation in Florida: How the Egrets Found a Friend," *Florida Game and Fish* 3 (April 1942): 1; Charles M. Brookfield and Oliver Griswold, *They Called It Tropical: True Tales of the Romantic Everglades, Cape Sable, and the Florida Keys* (Miami: Historical Association of Southern Florida, 1985), 68; Reese, "The Plume Wars"; McIver, "The Death of a Bird Warden," 24, 27; Huffstodt, "The Reign of the Plume Hunters," 4; Blackman, *The Florida Audubon Society,* 17, 19, 26–27, 28. For a comprehensive study of the life and murder of Guy Bradley, see Stewart B. McIver, *Death in the Everglades: The Murder of Guy Bradley, America's First Martyr to Environmentalism* (Gainesville: University Press of Florida, 2003).

34. Reese, "The Plume Wars," 41, 48; Fox, *The American Conservation Movement,* 155, 157; Blackman, *The Florida Audubon Society,* 26–27; Orr, *Saving American Birds,* 12.

35. John Kunkel Small, *From Eden to Sahara: Florida's Tragedy* (Lancaster, Penn.: Science Press Printing Company, 1929), 67; Lucy Worthington Blackman, *The Florida Federation of Women's Clubs, 1895–1939* (Jacksonville, Fla.: Southern Historical Publishing Associates, 1939), 21, 33–34; Mrs. W. S. Jennings, "Royal Palm State Park," *Tropic Magazine* 4 (April 1916): 10–16, 26; *Miami Herald,* November 24, 1916; C. B. Reynolds, "Royal Palm State Park," *Mr. Foster's Travel Magazine* 6 (January 1919), n.p.; May Mann Jennings to Mrs. M. L. Stanley, April 30, 1917, MMJ, box 10; telegram, Bryan Jennings to May Mann Jennings, June 2, 1915, MMJ, box 10; Linda D. Vance, *May Mann Jennings: Florida's Genteel Activist* (Gainesville: University Press of Florida, 1985), 54–60, 118–21, 125–26; Sally Vicker, "Ruth Bryan Owen: Florida's First Congresswoman and Lifetime Activist," *Florida Historical Quarterly* 77 (spring 1999), 466–67.

Jack E. Davis

36. A. W. Dimock, "The Passing of the Florida Alligator," in *Alligator Tales*, 96–106; Tyler, *Where to Go in Florida*, 20–21.

37. Ibid.; Moore-Willson, *The Birds of the Everglades*, 7, 17; Elizabeth Ogren Rothra, *Florida's Pioneer Naturalist: The Life of Charles Torrey Simpson* (Gainesville: University Press of Florida, 1995), 182–83.

38. Small, *From Eden to Sahara*, 111, 113.

39. Gifford, *Billy Bowlegs and the Seminole War*, 53, 69; "John Clayton Gifford," on "Reclaiming the Everglades" website.

40. *Public Waters Alligator Harvest Training and Orientation Manual* (Florida Fish and Wildlife Conservation Commission, 2003), 3–4; Allan R. Woodward and Clinton T. Moore, "American Alligators in Florida," U.S. Department of the Interior National Biological Service website, http://biology.usgs.gov/s+t/noframe/d052.htm.

41. Woodward and Moore, "American Alligators in Florida"; Richard Wolkomir and Joyce Wolkomir, "In Search of Sanctuary," *Smithsonian* 31 (February 2001): 72–78; *Tampa Tribune*, May 6, 2003.

Chapter 11

Blasting through Paradise

The Construction and Consequences of the Tamiami Trail

Gary Garrett

In his 1916 book *Winter Journeys in the South,* John Martin Hammond complained about transportation difficulties in Florida. Traveling north or south within the state presented few problems, but when the author found himself in Miami, on the east coast, and wanted to try the tarpon fishing in Ft. Myers, on the west coast, the geographical barriers proved frustrating:

> I could go to Key West and then take a coasting steamer which plied up the west coast, thus going around the toe of Florida and making a two days' trip to get to my hundred-mile-distant destination; I could go to Jacksonville and then down by the Atlantic Coast Line, another two days'

jaunt; or, getting desperate, I could take the new route through the Everglades, going up the drainage canal from Fort Lauderdale to Lake Okeechobee, thence over to the head of the Caloosahatchee river and down, a three days' trip altogether.[1]

Clearly, Hammond believed, Florida's coast-to-coast travel options needed some improvement, and many Florida business and political leaders agreed. Disappointed fishermen meant lost revenue for the tourist trade. Poor transportation hampered all Florida industries and inhibited the long-range growth of the state. One year before Hammond's book was published, powerful Floridians resolved to create the direct route required to make it easier for a Miami tourist to catch a Ft. Myers tarpon.[2]

In the summer of 1915, local bond issues passed in both Miami and Ft. Myers, officially launching a road-building project with the ambitious goal of creating a paved highway running west from Miami to the Gulf of Mexico, then north through Ft. Myers and all the way to Tampa. This highway, almost immediately dubbed the "Tamiami Trail," gained fame long before its completion. The bold route taken, straight through the heart of the southern Everglades and the Big Cypress Swamp, evoked stirring images of engineering heroes battling snakes, alligators, and trackless saw grass in the name of progress. When finally finished in 1928, the Tamiami Trail stretched 273 miles through seven counties and represented for many people the ultimate triumph of modernity over nature. "Festival Will Proclaim Conquest of Everglades" read a typical headline celebrating the opening of the highway, and in this case "conquest" proved to be no exaggeration.[3]

The bifurcation of south Florida by the Tamiami Trail disrupted an ecosystem of more than 4 million acres, inflicting injuries to the land, water, and inhabitants that continue to be felt today and may yet prove fatal. Unlike other ecological disasters such as the Oklahoma Dust Bowl of the 1930s, the environmental devastation caused by this "engineering marvel" did not result from ignorance and miscalculation. This highway stands as the crowning achievement of a decades-long campaign to rid south Florida of the Everglades completely, and the evidence of this can be seen in the origin, construction, and consequences of the Tamiami Trail.[4]

The idea of building a highway across the south Florida wetlands shares roots with the notion of railroads across the Great Plains and through the Rocky Mountains. The geography may have differed, but as historians have written:

Had Frederick Jackson Turner looked southward instead of westward in 1880, he would have discovered a state emotionally and physically tied to the frontier. The vast territory south of Tampa and Orlando was still largely uninhabited, with only a handful of Seminole Indians and plume hunters living in the subtropical region.[5]

That handful of Seminoles, according to ornithologist and sportsman Charles B. Cory, numbered just under 400 in 1896, and the forbidding area they occupied stretched all the way south from Lake Okeechobee to the end of the Florida peninsula. The comparison of this region with the Great West is an apt one, for the same mission of conquest and progress that Turner found in the settlers of Kansas and South Dakota can be seen in the pioneers testing the borders of the Everglades. The western settlers, challenged and threatened by scarcity of water, shoved the Indians aside and plowed the land, determined to find water somehow or to learn to live without it. Equally dauntless, their counterparts invading south Florida faced a very different problem: the summer rains, natural springs, and the water flowing south from Lake Okeechobee combined in such manner as to confine new settlers to the coasts and virtually deny them use of the interior altogether. In the best Turner tradition, they determined to conquer this problem by draining off the water, shoving the Indians aside, and plowing the land.[6]

Plans to drain south Florida's wetlands date back as far as 1845, when the state legislature sought federal assistance for a survey of the Everglades. This request led to the 1848 report by St. Augustine attorney Buckingham Smith that established the feasibility of lowering the water level in Lake Okeechobee and drying out south Florida by deepening rivers and digging canals. In 1850, the United States deeded most of the Everglades to the State of Florida on condition that such plans be followed. "But Indian hostilities delayed active operations for ten years, and the outbreak of the Civil War remanded the enterprise to the study of theorists," explained William Wallace Harney in the March 1884 issue of *Harper's New Monthly Magazine*. Fortunately for progress, Harney noted, the passing of nearly forty years had brought railroads, investment money, and more people to Florida, and the time clearly had arrived to proceed with the great project. His prophetic article devoted eight pages of text and diagrams to the three themes that future drainage advocates would stress: feasibility, benefits, and propriety.[7]

Feasibility meant simply that the Everglades could be drained if the water flowing south from Lake Okeechobee could be diverted, and Harney's article focused on the efforts of Philadelphia millionaire Hamilton Disston to achieve this goal. The first of the great drainage advocates with money to back his dreams, Disston combined state reclamation contracts and land purchases to control half of south Florida in the 1880s. His dredging crews deepened and straightened the Kissimmee and Caloosahatchee Rivers, draining adjacent acres and making both waterways steamboat accessible. His drive to lower the level of Lake Okeechobee began with a string of canals linking the great lake with the renovated Caloosahatchee, but the collapse of his financial empire in 1896 stopped the developer's plans.[8]

Disston's failure set the stage for Napoleon Broward, who converted Everglades drainage from a private enterprise to a public project. A corporation-fighting progressive, Broward based his 1904 campaign for governor almost entirely on an "Empire of the Everglades" platform aimed at staving off railroad claims against state-owned wetlands and finishing the dredging job Disston started. The governor found the wetlands a tougher opponent than the railroads and left office in 1909 with just 15 miles of canal completed. But the agency Broward fostered, the Everglades Drainage District, covered the eastern half of south Florida, and the dredging continued.[9] In 1916, the "Back to Broward" League lobbied for increased drainage by restating Harney's feasibility theory from thirty-two years before:

> The Everglades, while nearly level, slopes gradually from about six feet above sea level in the southern and eastern portions near the coast, to about 20 feet above sea level near Lake Okeechobee. With this elevation it can readily be seen that it is not a difficult engineering feat to build enough control canals to carry off the flood waters from the lake, and enough other canals and laterals to carry off the rainwater that falls upon the Everglades proper.[10]

The benefits expected from this seemingly simple yet frustratingly difficult project centered around agriculture. Underneath the Everglades vegetation and water lay a thick bed of ancient muck, rich and black and untouched by plows, that drainage advocates believed could grow almost anything. Given the region's rainfall and twelve-month growing season, William Wallace Harney believed drainage would "develop an area of fertility unrivalled even by the loamy bottoms of the Mississippi." This belief was handed down like a religion over the decades, and advocates claimed the Everglades could support 50,000 family farms and make Florida the most productive farming state in the nation. Forty-two years after Harney's article in *Harper's, South* magazine predicted that Everglades muck would make south Florida the "market garden of the earth."[11]

These grand drainage and farming plans required nothing less than the utter destruction of the natural flora and fauna of the Everglades, and advocates as early as Harney cloaked the propriety of such action in terms of the "land reclaimed." "Reclamation" implied the rightful taking back of property lost or stolen, as if the alligators and saw grass had conspired with nature itself to deprive the new Floridians of their land. A 1916 prodrainage cartoon featured two baby cranes asking from their nest in the Everglades, "Mother! When do we have to move out?" "Not during the present administration," replied their politically astute parent, and with nature thus cast as the enemy of progress, drainage advocates owed and made apologies to no one. Nature had rendered the Everglades "worthless, covered with water, inaccessible," and only reclamation could make things right.[12]

Politicians and newspapers linked "drainage" with "reclamation" in the same way they would come to link the Tamiami Trail with "conquest." Edwin Asa Dix and John Nowry MacGonigle unwittingly foreshadowed both the difference and the similarity between these concepts in their 1905 article for *Century Magazine* that lyrically described the mysteries and wonders of a region "still marked on the latest maps, 'Unexplored.'" After stating their belief that the "taming and reclaiming of the Everglades" would be accomplished eventually, they warned readers that it nonetheless remained "an enormous task," for "the fortress will be taken by siege, not by assault." They were wrong.[13]

In April 1915, an informal meeting in Tallahassee between Francis W. Perry and James F. Jaudon launched the assault that Dix and MacGonigle failed to anticipate. Perry, the president of the Ft. Myers Chamber of Commerce, and Jaudon, the Miami tax assessor, agreed to return to their respective cities and garner support for building a highway through the Everglades. Their efforts proved spectacular. The Central Florida Highway Association, in its inaugural meeting in Orlando on June 10, officially adopted the Tamiami Trail as a project to be supported, and two members of that association, L. P. Dickie and D. C. Gillett, secretary and president respectively of the Tampa Board of Trade, claimed credit for naming the road, originally coined simply "Tamiam." In July, the *Fort Myers Press* announced the raising of $65,000 in Dade County and $150,000 in Broward County for work on the Tamiami Trail. The following month, Lee County sold bonds to build the road from Ft. Myers south to Marco, and Dade County fielded a full survey crew to mark

Gary Garrett

the route from Miami to the Lee County line. Perry and Jaudon's dream road had progressed from a two-man idea to an officially planned Miami-to-Tampa highway with a catchy name and initial funding in less than four months.[14]

This rapid progress did not come without controversy. Even as Miami began its survey work and Lee County sold bonds for the stretch of road to Marco, business and civic leaders from Immokalee, in the center of Lee County, and LaBelle, to the north, argued for the routing of the highway through their towns. Advocates of the Dixie Highway, long planned and finally under construction from Chicago to Miami, jealously guarded against state funding for the Tamiami Trail. But no controversy focused on the viability of the project. The "can do" spirit still reigned in south Florida, and seemingly no one doubted modern civilization's ability to harness the Everglades successfully. Two weeks after the Ft. Myers–Marco road bond sale, the Lee County Commission announced plans to celebrate the opening of the Tamiami Trail "during the latter part of January, 1917." Then, the commissioners maintained, "we should be ready to run an automobile excursion from Tampa to Miami over the trail."[15]

The commissioners erred in their estimate by more than eleven years, and it is difficult to ascribe their excess optimism to mere naïvety. In 1915, Ft. Myers boasted no paved road to anywhere. Throughout the 1890s, the town could be reached only by ship, and while the railroad from Tampa finally arrived in 1904, and the first automobile arrived in 1908, Ft. Myers remained in 1915 arguably the most isolated "little city" in the United States. No road at all ran west from Miami or north from the Marco-Naples area. No road bridge spanned the Caloosahatchee River north of Ft. Myers, and even if one existed, no road ran north from the other side of the river. Fully six years of Tamiami Trail construction, including a new bridge over Charlotte Harbor, would be required before a car could travel from Tampa to Punta Gorda, and there still would be no road from there to the Caloosahatchee and still no bridge across the river to Ft. Myers.[16]

Given their city's remoteness, the necessity of building from scratch almost every mile of highway and bridge from Miami to Tampa, and the ignorance of everyone regarding how to make a road through the Everglades, the Lee County Commission's confidence that the Tamiami Trail could be built in eighteen months seems groundless. Possibly the need to float a $125,000 bond to pay for the Marco–Dade County portion of the highway shortly after raising $177,500 for the Ft. Myers–Marco portion encouraged the commissioners to be optimistic. Potential financial benefits may have encouraged them as well. J. H. Tatum, of the Miami Chamber of Commerce, advised the Lee County Board of Commissioners on August 2, 1915, that property values would skyrocket with completion of the project. Dade County had experienced this with the building of roads south of Miami, Tatum stated, and Everglades land "has been selling for $250 an acre that was bringing $5 an acre before the roads."[17]

In fairness to the Lee County officials, Miami's projections for completion proved wrong also, and the economic temptations clearly played well on both coasts. The new highway promised far more than transportation between distant, growing cities. As the Tamiami Trail Commission reported, from the beginning officials considered the highway an extension of the ongoing drainage efforts:

> The idea actuating the Dade County Commissioners was that the drainage of the Everglades would be promoted by the construction of the proposed road, because it was the plan to dig a canal and use the rock excavated from the canal for road bed. The canal would constitute a waterway of value in draining the adjacent lands, and the drainage thus effected would enhance their value to the State.[18]

Given the previous difficulties experienced with Everglades drainage canals, officials might have expected road building that depended upon canal digging to be problematic. Miami, with its larger tax base and a far smaller stretch of road to build, pressed ahead with construction through Dade County. Ft. Myers, with its 1910 census of 2,463 and vast tracts of unimproved land and accordingly lower property values, could not compete. With 110 miles of highway to construct, more than three times that of Dade County, and with more than half of its portion of the Trail directly through the Everglades and Big Cypress Swamp, Lee County ran out of money in 1919 and thereafter concerned itself primarily with the road north and efforts to get a bridge built across the Caloosahatchee.[19]

Work on the highway south of Ft. Myers halted for four years. In 1923, Lee County finally completed the long-awaited Caloosahatchee bridge, but the Tamiami Trail still ran east from Naples for about 30 miles and simply ended in the swamp. The road from Miami was stalled at the Dade County line. "In the early 1920s," wrote Marjory Stoneman Douglas decades later, "we used to fish at the end of Dade County's 40 miles where the roadway seemed to have been stopped forever." The famous author of *The Everglades: River of Grass* demonstrated a vaguely troubled ambivalence toward the Trail during this period, writing sadly of the violated wilderness and proudly of the highway's promise. In her 1923 poem "Everglades," she tried to have it both ways:

They shall remain inviolable and themselves.
They shall give themselves tremendously and still be virgin.
They shall lend themselves to the crooked scheming of schemers
And remain untouched.[20]

The Everglades had been penetrated from east and west, but the heart of its interior remained intact. That did not, however, mean the invaders were quitting, and the ever-resourceful James F. Jaudon led the renewed assault. As president of the Chevelier Corporation, Jaudon offered to complete the Tamiami Trail by extending the Dade County section of the highway west through Monroe County to meet the section of finished road in Lee County. Running parallel to but 7 miles south of the original plan, the new route would take the Trail through Chevelier-owned real estate, with Jaudon's company paying the cost in anticipation of rising land values. Dade and Lee Counties agreed, and in 1921 Chevelier began construction, but the work proceeded far too slowly. Overtaken by events, the company would lose its chance to complete the highway. The great push to finish the Tamiami Trail would come from the west coast, and 1923 would be remembered as the turning point in the struggle. The fate of the wetlands waited in Ft. Myers, where the "Trailblazers" were bound for glory, and Barron G. Collier would make history.[21]

On April 4, 1923, twenty-three men in eight Model T Fords and one 3,000-pound vehicle called an Elcar left Ft. Myers to generate publicity for the Tamiami Trail and prove the trip to Miami could be made in automobiles. They called themselves the "Trailblazers" and expected the entire trip to take three days. The only anticipated difficulty, the 40-mile stretch of the proposed Tamiami Trail route through the Everglades, turned the adventure into a tortuous nightmare lasting over three weeks. Lost and without provisions, the Trailblazers lived on venison and wild turkey and depended entirely upon their Seminole guides to lead them to Miami. Their plight generated immense publicity, with the national press reporting the news or lack of news from them daily, and served to underscore the true "last frontier" conditions of the Everglades. While the Trailblazers accomplished nothing instrumental in the travel across the Tamiami Trail, they did make themselves forever a part of its history. The trip became legendary, and its importance and difficulty grew larger over time in the public mind until many believed, as the *St. Petersburg Times* reported in 1972, that it was the Trailblazers' "determined efforts that proved the 'Glades tameable and forged the way for the completion of the Tamiami Trail."[22]

Barron G. Collier's contribution to the Trail would be more difficult to exaggerate and a most interesting study for those intrigued by the role of whim in history. A high school dropout from Memphis born in 1873, Collier made himself a millionaire in the advertising business and bought Useppa Island, near Ft. Myers, as a vacation property in 1911. He began serious investing in Florida ten years later with the purchase of an unprofitable citrus grove at Deep Lake Hammock in southern Lee County. The property included a rickety railroad built for shipping fruit that ran 14 miles south through the Big Cypress Swamp to Allen's River and the tiny town of Everglade at the edge of the Ten Thousand Islands. Without explanation, Collier selected Everglade as his base of operations and began dredging landfill to raise more of the soggy town above sea level. While his work crews deepened Allen's River and enlarged Everglade, the developer continued his land acquisition and soon owned over 1.3 million acres, virtually all undeveloped Lee County property.[23]

In May 1923, the State of Florida accepted an offer from Barron G. Collier that it could not refuse easily. The millionaire wanted the southern 1,300,480 acres of Lee County lopped off and renamed Collier County. In exchange, Collier agreed to guarantee financing for the completion of the Tamiami Trail. Objecting to the loss of over half their county's land, Ft. Myers interests fought the idea furiously, but the highway Collier proposed to complete had gone without Lee County funds for construction since 1919, and the Chevelier Corporation's work in Monroe County showed little promise. Stunned by Collier's intention to return to the original Trail route, Jaudon's company rallied Monroe, Dade, and Lee county politicians, editorial writers, and landowners against the rich New Yorker, but they were no match for a man who could count J. P. Morgan and William Randolph Hearst as friends and advisors.[24]

"I intend to build the Tamiami Trail through Collier County just as fast as it is possible to do it," Collier told the *Ft. Myers Press* in his first interview after the legislature awarded him his own county. He did not "blame the people of Ft. Myers and the rest of Lee County for the attitude they have taken," but he had some "big developing" to do. "I felt that I could do it much better with a friendly county administration," he told the reporter. As the owner of four-fifths of the new county, Collier had reason to expect its administrators to be "friendly."[25]

True to his word, the millionaire put his Everglade construction crew and dredge to work on the highway immediately. But the new county, not its owner, paid for the work. Collier prudently used his money as collateral so the new "friendly county administration" could float a $350,000 loan for the Tamiami Trail. Everglade, renamed Everglades as Florida's newest county seat, became the center of Trail construction activity. Dredgemaster Otto Neal, hired to purchase and deliver Collier's first dredge to Everglades, helped dig a canal 4 miles north to intersect the Trail route at Carnestown. This crucial first step allowed equipment and supplies to be barged to the construction site and provided a way for workers to come and go. Under the direction of engineer Charles G. Washbon, Collier's small workforce dredged west from Carnestown and reached the abandoned Lee County portion of the Trail in December 1923.[26]

Construction slowed immediately when the dredgers reversed course and began digging their way east toward Miami. Solid rock was discovered beneath the saw grass and muck from Carnestown to the Dade County line, and progress on the Trail slowed nearly to a standstill. "The problem," explained the *Fort Myers Tropical News*, "was to break through this rock, dig it out to form a drainage canal, and use the material for the road." Collier's workers used explosives to loosen the rock, but according to Neal, "It was difficult to determine the amount of dynamite necessary for each 'shot' and ofttimes we were compelled to reblow the holes." The purchase of Collier's first Bay City "walking dredge" improved efficiency considerably, but through 1924 the size and speed of the Tamiami Trail construction crew struggling east from Carnestown looked a lot like Chevelier Corporation's disappointing performance heading west from Dade County. Conquering the Everglades would require more workers, more dredges, more dynamite, and a new leader.[27]

In 1925, Barron G. Collier hired engineer D. Graham Copeland to finish building the Tamiami Trail. A fourteen-year U.S. Navy veteran and director of construction projects throughout the world, Copeland turned Everglades into Collier's company town, with whistles announcing the times to wake up, eat lunch, and quit work. It seems unlikely that Collier could have found a better man to lead an assault against the formidable terrain. "His decisions were instantaneous," dredgemaster Neal recalled in 1928, "not 'goin' off half cocked' as the saying is, but the man just knew what had to be done."[28] Copeland's no-nonsense style is displayed in his 1930 report to the Everglades Drainage

District, in which he cited the chain of title to the Everglades before arguing for their continued drainage:

> The chain of title to the Everglades is briefly:
> Aborigines by right of settlement.
> The Crown of Spain by right of conquest.
> The Crown of England by right of conquest.
> The Crown of Spain by right of cession.
> The United States by right of purchase.[29]

With the new man in charge, the construction of the Trail proceeded slowly but relentlessly. Exploding 2,584,000 sticks of dynamite, described by Copeland as "one carload a month" and by Charles G. Washbon as "thirty to forty boxes daily," Collier's workers blasted their way toward Miami. The highly regimented operation began with clearing crews of fifteen to twenty-five men who slashed vegetation and laid rails for the drilling crews that followed. The drillers used Ingersoll-Rand compressors and drills with 16-foot bits mounted on railway cars. These machines bored 12-foot holes, three across, every 6 feet along the entire canal route. Blasting crews following the drillers cleaned out the holes with Fairbanks Morse jetting pumps and stuffed from ten to forty sticks of dynamite in each hole. Dredging crews following the blasters operated three Bay City dredges that worked in shifts. The dredges scooped up the loosened rock in one-yard dippers and piled it on the Trail route, creating a canal and a road simultaneously. Still more workers followed, using one 5-ton and two 10-ton Holt tractors to grade the newly dredged rock.[30]

Seventy-five-man work crews lived in trailers dragged behind dredges and received between twenty and sixty dollars per month for braving heat, bugs, water, and whatever crawling creatures they might encounter. Otto Neal believed the "clearing and blasting crews received the brunt of the manual labor." Often in water up to their waists, the clearing workers "were sometimes away from town for two months at a time because of the difficulty in getting back," and their supplies were carried to them by oxen or on their own shoulders. Two six-ox teams "with drivers and helpers" accompanied the drilling and blasting crews to haul the gasoline and dynamite, and according to Washbon, the average ox lasted two weeks. The Trail construction work was grim and dangerous for oxen and men alike, but "an average progress of two hundred and fifty feet per day was maintained under these difficulties."[31]

While the firm hand and organizational genius of D. Graham Copeland can be seen in the drive to build the Tamiami Trail east from Carnestown, the influence of Florida State Road Department (SRD) specifications and money is unmistakable as well. The department officially recognized and began surveying the Trail in 1924 and assumed financial responsibility for it the following year. The quadrupling and quintupling of Barron G. Collier's workers and machines that began in 1925 coincided with SRD contracts awarded to Collier's engineering and construction firm. Collier and Copeland finished building the famous highway, but SRD paid for it. Collier's legendary role in the construction of the Tamiami Trail is secure, but cost figures through 1927 tell a little-known story:

Dade County	$585,000
Monroe County	$210,000
Chevelier Corporation	$333,000
Collier County	$1,100,000
Lee County	$1,084,000
State Road Department	$3,570,965[32]

Collier's support from SRD extended to his insistence on sticking to the original Trail route all the way through Collier County. Ignoring the work already completed by the Chevelier Corporation, D. Graham Copeland's construction crews built 20 miles of parallel highway just 7 miles north of the Monroe County road. In a 1926 Miami Chamber of Commerce "open forum" meeting, citizens voiced their frustration over SRD's intention to spend many months and hundreds of thousands of dollars building 27 more miles of Trail in Collier County instead of turning the highway south and building 7 miles to connect with a road that already ran to Dade County. Their failure to change SRD hearts and minds produced one of the unintentional consequences of the Tamiami Trail. Purchased by SRD and dubbed the South Loop, the Monroe County stretch of highway eventually became Loop Road, a scenic nature route through part of the Big Cypress National Preserve.[33]

The intentional consequences of the Tamiami Trail include the nearly successful drainage of the Everglades. The highway's role in the grand scheme to dry out south Florida is manifest, but the extent of the damage it caused is unclear. Before Disston's drainage work began in the 1880s, the complex hydrology of the Everglades and the Big Cypress Swamp centered around sheet water slowly flowing south across nearly flat plains extending from Lake Okeechobee to Florida Bay. Periodic overflows from the great lake combined with abundant rainfall, spring water, and a subtropical climate to create vast and diverse wetlands alive with a flora and fauna mix unique in the world. Water drained slowly, almost imperceptibly, over a gradient averaging less than three inches per mile, providing perfect protection for centuries of vegetation forming the thick layers of peat that became known as Everglades muck. Lack of hydrological studies from this era and the disruptive effects of other drainage projects completed before and during construction of the Trail make determining the direct impact of the road and its canal difficult to measure. But when seen as an integral part of the long, concerted effort to reclaim the Everglades, the highway was an ecological disaster.[34]

The completion of the Tamiami Trail in April 1928 cut the Everglades and the Big Cypress Swamp in half with a 30-foot-wide highway-dam and a drainage canal running the width of the entire state. The fifth major drainage construction in three decades of reclamation work, the Trail and the four major canals completed before 1920 by the Everglades Drainage District reduced water levels throughout south Florida. The transformation of the vast region proceeded slowly, but warning signs of devastation appeared quickly. In 1915, U.S. Agricultural Department surveyors documented numerous vegetation changes associated with water loss in the Everglades interior. In 1917, civil engineer John King, who worked for James F. Jaudon, noted decreasing bird populations attributed to the loss of feeding grounds. Exposed to the open air, the famous Everglades muck began disappearing as well. Between subsidence, oxidation, and fires, the average peat thickness along the eastern Tamiami Canal decreased nearly 2 feet from 1918 to 1940, and along the Miami Canal the drop was 3 feet. Writing in 1932, naturalist Charles Torrey Simpson lamented plant and animal losses associated with Everglades drainage and declared, "I feel that no more complete botch has been made of any project within the lifetime of any of my readers."[35]

In addition to lowering Everglades water levels, the Tamiami Trail opened the south Florida interior to agriculture, logging, tourists, and moonshiners. The *Miami Herald* predicted "thousands of tourists" making the "grand tour" between the Florida coasts, but "the greater value of the Trail will be its power to develop this section of the state agriculturally and industrially." The collapse of the stock market in 1929 and the advent of the Great Depression delayed many of the tourists and much of the development, but the highway's impact on the region remained immense. The combined population of Collier's two largest towns, Everglades and Naples, tripled in the decade between 1925 and 1935, rising from 314 to 1,090. Ft. Myers increased from 6,674 to 10,312 in the same period. The Tamiami Trail became a common feature in

Florida guide books, with descriptions of vanishing wildlife and roadside Seminole camps where "each winter thousands of tourists visit these thatched encampments, and each one leaves some silver behind."[36]

Encouraged by the guide books and a popular song, "Tamiami Trail," that celebrated the Everglades as a "land of romance" where "every peach on the beach" was "strummin' a ukulele," tourists traveled the Trail for fun and adventure, often contributing to the destruction of plant and animal life. Charles Torrey Simpson described a magnificent hammock along the highway in Collier County where 500 royal palms had been reduced to less than 50 after being cut down or "dug up and sold to be planted in householders' yards." He recalled pre-Trail days with schools of fish in the Gulf of Mexico "packed like sardines in a box reaching way up and down the coast" and complained bitterly about "the average fishing tourist" who wanted to "get an immense catch and have it strung up" for a picture "to be bragged about ad nauseam." The Federal Writers' Project's tour description of the Trail promised a "canal side of the road . . . alive with birds, reptiles and fishes," and a highway that became a death scene "in the early morning after night traffic" left the "mangled corpses of snakes" and the "bodies of raccoons and other small animals crushed when blinded by headlights."[37]

The New Deal writers also promised Indians along the Trail, and the influence of the highway and its tourists and their "silver" on the culture of the Seminoles proved devastating. After escaping to the Everglades to avoid banishment to Oklahoma in the aftermath of the wars of the 1850s, the Seminoles managed to limit their contact with white culture for decades. The Tamiami Trail ended their isolation forever. In 1928, with the opening of the highway, the *Miami Herald* reported that while some Indians were moving farther back into the Everglades, "some of the bolder Seminole women are selling souvenirs along the trail."[38] Almost overnight Indian hunters and fishermen became tourist guides and sideshow attractions, and women began giving birth to mixed-race children. Agent Roy Nash of the Bureau of Indian Affairs noted in his 1932 survey:

Two Seminole women last winter set up camp beside the Tamiami Trail and discreetly offered their services as prostitutes. There is nothing startling in this change of attitude. Men of a dominant economic group have always been able to possess the women of a decidedly inferior economic group. And now that Florida has five hundred primitive hunters surrounded by a civilization possessing wealth, luxury, and bootleg liquor, an increase of sexual intimacy between white men and Seminole women is as inevitable as the sequence of day and night.[39]

Alcohol abuse became an enormous problem among the Seminoles, especially when moonshiners took advantage of the Trail to hide their stills deep in the Everglades. The highway also brought missionaries, hunters, bird-watchers, and tourist-trap operators, presenting the Indians with a confusing array of white people seeking their services, souls, and other possessions. In his gratitude for their services as guides and hunters during the construction of the Tamiami Trail, Barron G. Collier, always proud of his good relations with the Indians, granted every Seminole unrestricted passage on his bus line for life. The price of those tickets may have been too high.[40]

Five months after the Trail opened, the deadly hurricane of 1928 caused an overflow from Lake Okeechobee that flooded thousands of Everglades acres, overwhelmed the new muck farms, and drowned hundreds of workers. Charged with making Everglades agriculture safe, the United States Army Corps of Engineers began construction of the Herbert Hoover Dike in 1930. This levee eventually encircled Lake Okeechobee and marked the beginning of a new phase of water management for the Everglades watershed. Over the last half of the twentieth century, the Corps of Engineers constructed a hydrological nightmare in south Florida, fragmenting the Everglades with a maze of canals and levees that increased in total length from 440 miles in 1929 to around 1,500 miles in 2002. Controlling this maze, the South Florida Water Management District (SFWMD) worked diligently to reduce the role of nature in the Sunshine State.[41]

Established by the state legislature in 1972 and operating under Corps of Engineers permits, SFWMD roughly doubled the size of the old Everglades Drainage District. Using computers, flood gates, and pumping stations, the agency developed procedures for "dictating the quantity, quality, distribution, and timing of water release" throughout the Everglades, and by the 1990s over half the wetlands and an estimated 90 percent of the birds had vanished. The sugar industry boomed, and the runoff from its fertilizers damaged the Everglades more each year. Mercury found its way into the water, and the Florida Game and Fresh Water Fish Commission reported: "We will not be able to eat the fish in the Everglades in our lifetime." Governor Broward's "Empire of the Everglades" seemed well within sight and the conquest of nature nearly complete, thanks in no small part to the Tamiami Trail.[42]

"The Everglades were dying," wrote Marjory Stoneman Douglas in 1947,

Gary Garrett

opening the final pages of *The Everglades: River of Grass.* Aptly titled "The Eleventh Hour," the last chapter described the environmental conditions and the long campaign that led to the establishment of Everglades National Park. Five decades later, when the wetlands were so near death that ecologist John C. Ogden described them as "Everglades in name only," the public outcry reached national, bipartisan proportions. In December 2000, the political result, a $7.8 billion, fifty-year engineering and reconstruction program called the Comprehensive Everglades Restoration Plan (CERP), authorized the Corps of Engineers to reverse a half century's work. Included among CERP's sixty-eight major engineering projects was the raising of 30 miles of the Tamiami Trail. After seventy-five years of blocking the flow of Everglades water, the highway lost its environmental acceptability. Corps engineers planned to build a series of bridges to reduce the Trail's presence, but many environmentalists and Everglades National Park officials simply wanted the road to go away.[43]

Back in 1916, during the height of the initial Trail optimism, a Ft. Myers special committee laid plans for a new annual celebration intended to rival the Mardi Gras of New Orleans and be known as "The Conquest of Florida." Such dreams had come to nothing by 1923, but the intervention of a New York millionaire breathed new life into the delayed assault, and the "Opening of the Tamiami Trail" motorcade so naïvely planned in Ft. Myers in 1915 finally traveled from Tampa to Miami nearly thirteen years later. The date of the grand event, April 26, 1928, occasioned special edition newspapers throughout Florida, with parades, receptions, and parties from Tampa to Miami. The next year saw no mention of the highway's first anniversary in either the *Collier County News* or the *Fort Myers Press*. The fifth, tenth, and twentieth anniversaries brought the same result.[44]

Historian William Cronon has argued that the railroads of the Midwest came to seem a part of nature to the very people who built them. The same might be said of the Tamiami Trail. Once built, its makers could take the highway for granted as something naturally there to be used. The Trail had been special only as a symbol, and the conquest seemed finished. But the difficulties encountered by Collier's blasting crews foreshadowed the wetlands' natural resiliency. Survivors of centuries of hurricanes, droughts, and fires, the Everglades and Big Cypress Swamp proved more adept at a war of attrition than the Tamiami Trail. Eventually replaced by the faster, more convenient Alligator Alley interstate 30 miles to the north, the Trail never developed the teeming business and industrial traffic envisioned by its backers.

Gradually surrounded by ever-expanding public lands, the Trail shrank in significance as the "Save Our Everglades" movement grew. Seven decades after Barron G. Collier and the Florida State Road Department arrogantly bypassed Chevelier's highway in Monroe County and inadvertently created the Loop Road, the Trail itself seemed on its way to becoming a scenic nature route.[45]

Notes

1. John Martin Hammond, *Winter Journeys in the South* (Philadelphia: J. B. Lippincott, 1916), 87.

2. Ibid., 88; Joseph Reese, *History of the Tamiami Trail and a Brief Review of the Road Construction Movement in Florida* (Miami: Tamiami Trail Commissioners of Dade County, Florida, 1928), 4–7.

3. "The Tamiami Trail," *Collier County News*, April 26, 1928; "Festival Will Proclaim Conquest of Everglades," *Fort Myers Tropical News*, April 25, 1928; "Marco Road Bonds Sold," *Fort Myers Press*, August 3, 1915; Reese, *History of the Tamiami Trail*, 13–16.

4. "Engineering Marvel," *Collier County News*, April 26, 1928; Mark Derr, *Some Kind of Paradise: A Chronicle of Man and the Land in Florida* (New York: William Morrow, 1989), 164; Donald Worster, *Dust Bowl: The Southern Plains in the 1930s* (New York: Oxford University Press, 1979), 5; Alan Mairson, "The Everglades: Dying for Help," *National Geographic* (April 199): 6.

5. Gary R. Mormino and George E. Pozzetta, *The Immigrant World of Ybor City: Italians and Their Neighbors in Tampa* (Chicago: University of Illinois Press, 1987), 46.

6. Charles B. Cory, *Hunting and Fishing in Florida, Including a Key to the Water Birds Known to Occur in the State* (Boston: Estes and Lauriat, 1896), 7; Frederick Jackson Turner, *The Frontier in American History* (Huntington, N.Y.: Krieger Publishing, 1976), 212. Regarding frontier attitude: "If the thing was one proper to be done, then the most immediate, rough and ready, effective way was the best way."

7. Nelson Manfred Blake, *Land into Water/Water into Land: A History of Water Management in Florida* (Gainesville: University Presses of Florida, 1980) 33–37; William Wallace Harney, "The Drainage of the Everglades," *Harper's New Monthly Magazine*, March 1884, 598–605.

8. Blake, *Land into Water*, 73–82; Charlton W. Tebeau, *A History of Florida* (Coral Gables: University of Miami Press, 1971), 278–82.

9. Blake, *Land into Water*, 94–105; Tebeau, *History of Florida*, 327–34, 346–50. For Broward, see also Samuel Proctor, *Napoleon Bonaparte Broward: Florida's Fighting Democrat* (Gainesville: University of Florida Press, 1950).

10. *"Back to Broward" League* (Ft. Lauderdale: The League, 1916), 1.

11. Harney, 604; *"Back to Broward" League*, 1; Henry Fitzgerald, "A Five Million-Acre Garden," *South*, September 1926, 1.

12. Harney, 605; *"Back to Broward" League*, 1, 6, 17.

Gary Garrett

13. Edwin Asa Dix and John Nowry MacGonigle, "The Everglades of Florida: A Region of Mystery," *Century Magazine*, February 1905, 514.

14. Reese, *History of the Tamiami Trail*, 6–9; "Captain Jaudon Originator of Idea for Tamiami Trail," *Fort Myers Tropical News*, April 25, 1928, Florida Highways section; "Believe Road Will Prove Of Great Value," *Fort Myers Press*, July 20, 1915; "Marco Road Bonds Sold," *Fort Myers Press*, August 3, 1915; "Dade County Has Started Work On Survey," *Fort Myers Press*, August 6, 1915.

15. "Sentiment Favors the LaBelle Route," *Fort Myers Press*, August 3, 1915: 1; Karl H. Grismer, *The Story of Ft. Myers: The History of the Land of the Caloosahatchee and Southwest Florida* (St. Petersburg, Fla.: St. Petersburg Printing Company, 1949), 214–15; "Opening of Trail Planned," *Fort Myers Press*, August 21, 1915.

16. Grismer, *Story of Ft. Myers*, 164, 186, 213.

17. Ibid., 213; "Tamiami Trail Delegate Here," *Fort Myers Press*, August 2, 1915.

18. Reese, *History of Tamiami Trail*, 13, 17.

19. Grismer, *Story of Ft. Myers*, 193; Charlton W. Tebeau, *Florida's Last Frontier: The Story of Collier County* (Coral Gables: University of Miami Press, 1957), 224; Reese, *History of Tamiami Trail*, 17.

20. Tebeau, *Florida's Last Frontier*, 222; Grismer, *Story of Ft. Myers*, 193; Marjory Stoneman Douglas, *Florida: The Long Frontier* (New York: Harper and Row, 1967) 267; For Douglas's ambivalence, see her poems "Everglades" (1921) and "The Tamiami Trail" (1923) and the quoted poem "Everglades" (1923) in *The Wide Brim: Early Poems and Ponderings of Marjory Stoneman Douglas*, ed. Jack E. Davis (Gainesville: University Press of Florida, 2002), 44, 65–67.

21. Reese, *History of the Tamiami Trail*, 17; Derr, *Some Kind of Paradise*, 166–67; Tebeau, *Florida's Last Frontier*, 225.

22. "Blazing the Tamiami Trail," *American Eagle*, April 11, 1946: 1; "Tamiami Trailblazers Recall It Took 22 Days To Miami," *St. Petersburg Times*, April 18, 1972; Tebeau, *Florida's Last Frontier*, 225–28.

23. Tebeau, *Florida's Last Frontier*, 119–26; "Barron Collier: Super Salesman Poured Millions into Florida," *Florida Trend*, January 1972, 40–50; Anthony Weitzel, "The Collier Story," *Naples Daily News*, September 1, 1994.

24. "Lee County Citizens Lose Out in Fight Trisecting County," *Fort Myers Press*, May 4, 1923; "The Lost Cause," *Fort Myers Press*, May 4, 1923: 2; Reese, *History of the Tamiami Trail*, 17–20.

25. "Barron Collier Tells the Fort Myers Press, in First Interview after His County Is Created, of Development Plans," *Fort Myers Press*, May 7, 1923.

26. Otto Neal, "Early Stages of Trail Building Reviewed," Tamiami Trail History Notes, 1927–1928, Marjory Stoneman Douglas Papers (Richter Library, University of Miami, Coral Gables, Florida), http://everglades.fiu.edu/reclaim. The canal to Carnestown eventually extended all the way to Immokalee and provided fill for the parallel road constructed. Called the Barron River Canal (Allen's River was renamed in honor of Collier), this was the first major drainage project in the Big Cypress Swamp. See the introduction and Benjamin F. McPherson, "The Big Cypress Swamp" in *Environments of South Florida Present and Past*, ed. Patrick J. Gleason (Coral Gables: Miami Geologi-

cal Society, 1984), 2:x, 69–70; "C. G. Washbon Gives Striking Picture of Magnitude of Work," *Tamiami Trail History Notes, 1927–1928*, on "Reclaiming the Everglades" website, http://everglades.fiu.edu/reclaim.

27. "Former Navy Officer Chief Engineer for Collier Works," *Fort Myers Tropical News,* April 25, 1928; "C. G. Washbon," 7. The Bay City Walking Dredge was designed to straddle a 20-foot-wide canal and "walk" by means of mechanical "shoes" as digging advanced. Ideal for rugged terrain, the dredge could travel one mile per day. For specifications, see "Bay City Walking Dredge No. 489: A National Historic Mechanical Engineering Landmark," *American Society of Mechanical Engineers* (February 19, 1994).

28. Tebeau, *Florida's Last Frontier,* 87; "Barron Collier Tells," *Fort Myers Press,* May 7, 1923: 1; "Collier Story," *Naples Daily News,* September 1, 1994; "Former Navy Officer Chief Engineer for Collier Works," *Fort Myers Tropical News,* April 25, 1928; "Early Stages of Trail Building Reviewed by Neal, Dredgemaster," *Collier County News,* April 26, 1928.

29. D. Graham Copeland, *Policy: A Report to the Board of Commissioners of the Everglades Drainage District* (Ft. Myers: Ft. Myers Press, 1930), 3.

30. D. Graham Copeland, "Importance of Three M's on Trail Stressed," *Tamiami Trail History Notes, 1927–1928*, on "Reclaiming the Everglades" website, http://everglades.fiu.edu/reclaim; Neal, "Early Stages of Trail Building"; "C. G. Washbon," 6.

31. "Collier County Road Built of Solid Rock," *Fort Myers Tropical News,* April 25, 1928; "Collier," *Naples Daily News,* September 1, 1994; Neal, "Early Stages of Trail Building," 3; "C. G. Washbon," 6.

32. Reese, *History of the Tamiami Trail,* 24; "C. G. Washbon," 5.

33. Reese, *History of the Tamiami Trail,* 17–19; "Open Forum Meeting of Chamber of Commerce at Central High School, Miami Fla. on night of 26 April 1926 for discussing the Tamiami Trail," *Tamiami Trail History Notes, 1927–1928*, on "Reclaiming the Everglades" website, http://everglades.fiu.edu/reclaim; Ted Levin, *Liquid Land: A Journey through the Florida Everglades* (Athens: University of Georgia Press, 2003), 100, 102.

34. Garald Parker, "Hydrology of the Pre-Drainage System of the Everglades in Southern Florida," in *Environments of South Florida,* 28–37. For an overview of the Everglades ecosystem, see Thomas E. Lodge, *The Everglades Handbook: Understanding the Ecosystem* (Delray Beach, Fla.: St. Lucie Press, 1994).

35. Derr, *Some Kind of Paradise,* 164. The four canals running from Lake Okeechobee to the Atlantic were the Miami (1913), North New River (1912), Hillsboro (1915), and West Palm Beach (1920). The Everglades Drainage District encompassed the eastern half of south Florida, from Okeechobee south to the Tamiami Trail. For canals and water-loss sources quotes, see Fred Sklar et al., "The Effects of Altered Hydrology on the Ecology of the Everglades," in *The Everlgades, Florida Bay, and Coral Reefs of the Florida Keys: An Ecosystem Sourcebook,* ed. James W. Porter and Karen G. Porter (Boca Raton, Fla.: CRC Press, 2002), 39–49; Charles Torrey Simpson, *Florida Wild Life: Observations on the Flora and Fauna of the State and the Influence of Climate and Environment on Their Development* (New York: Macmillan, 1932), 189.

36. "The Trail Is Finished," *Miami Herald*, April 26, 1928; Nathan Mayo, commissioner of agriculture, *The Sixth Census of the State of Florida 1935* (Tallahassee: Department of Agriculture, 1935), 85, 91; John E. Jennings Jr., *Our American Tropics* (New York: Thomas Crowell Company, 1938), 61.

37. Cliff Friend and Joseph H. Santly, *Tamiami Trail* (New York: Jerome H. Remick and Co.: 1936); Charles Torrey Simpson, *Florida Wild Life*, 187, 184, 193; Federal Writers' Project, *Florida: A Guide to the Southernmost State* (New York: Oxford University Press, 1939), 407.

38. Derr, *Some Kind of Paradise*, 164; "Highway Sends Seminoles Away," *Miami Herald*, April 26, 1928.

39. Roy Nash, *Survey of the Seminole Indians of Florida* (Washington, D.C.: U.S. Department of Interior, 1932), 24.

40. Nash, *Survey of the Seminole Indians*, 46. See also Patsy West, *The Enduring Seminoles: From Alligator Wrestling to Ecotourism* (Gainesville: University of Florida Press, 1998).

41. Alan D. Steinman et al., "The Past, Present, and Future Hydrology and Ecology of Lake Okeechobee and Its Watersheds," *The Everglades, Florida Bay, and Coral Reefs of the Florida Keys*, 19–37; Blake, *Land into Water*, 230, 255–70.

42. Mairson, "The Everglades," 17; Jeff Klinkenberg, "A Culture Endangered," *St. Petersburg Times*, December 13, 1992; Levin, *Liquid Land*, 3–11.

43. Marjory Stoneman Douglas, *The Everglades: River of Grass* (New York: Rinehart and Company, 1947), 349–85; Levin, *Liquid Land*, 233–34; Public Law 106-541, 106th Cong. (December 11, 2000), *Water Resources Development Act of 2000*.

44. "The Conquest of Florida Is Name Chosen," *Fort Myers Press*, November 16, 1916; "Fort Myers All Set for Opening Program Today," *Fort Myers Tropical News*, April 26, 1928.

45. William Cronon, *Nature's Metropolis: Chicago and the Great West* (New York: W. W. Norton, 1991), 72–73; Levin, *Liquid Land*, 112, 216; United States Geological Survey, "Alligator Alley," http://sofia.usgs.gov/virtual_tour/alalley; The Everglades Foundation, "Save Our Everglades," http://www.saveoureverglades.org. For a summary of expanding public lands in southwest Florida, see Jeff Ripple, *Southwest Florida's Wetland Wilderness: Big Cypress Swamp and the Ten Thousand Islands* (Gainesville: University Press of Florida, 1996), 45–57.

Chapter 12

Lake Apopka

From Natural Wonder to Unnatural Disaster

Nano Riley

Lake Apopka was once one of Florida's most beautiful bodies of water and its second-largest lake. In a state surrounded by water, and known for its many wonderful lakes and rivers, Lake Apopka was also famous for its abundance of fish, and in the early twentieth century, people said the water was so clear that fishermen could sit in a boat and target the bass they wanted to catch. The marshy wetlands along its vegetation-lined shores were home to a huge population of alligators and provided feeding areas for birds and a breeding area for the lake's fish.[1]

But after fifty years of human manipulation in the name of improvement,

Lake Apopka is no longer an angler's paradise and a natural wonder—it is now considered the most polluted lake in Florida and is better known for its series of environmental tragedies, such as the deaths of waterbirds and alligators, and massive fish kills. The cleanup efforts have also been dotted with mistakes and failures, but biologists, state and federal agencies, and environmental groups have not given up. The latest plans amend previous shortcomings, and there is hope that new measures will restore Lake Apopka to its former glory.

As part of a complex, living ecosystem of marshes and rivers extending both north and south from the center of the state, Lake Apopka lies in the northeast corner of Orange County, just north of Orlando, and stretches into the southeast part of Lake County, where its watershed forms the headwaters of the Ocklawaha River. The Ocklawaha River basin itself spans 568 square miles of lakes and wetlands in Lake County, where Lake Apopka is the largest of the lakes in the Harris Chain, a string of lovely lakes traversing central Florida's lake country that also includes Lake Beauclair, Lake Dora, Lake Eustis, Lake Griffin, Lake Harris, Little Lake Harris, Lake Carlton, and Lake Yale. These watery marshlands form the Ocklawaha River, which in turn joins the St. Johns River, one of Florida's largest and most navigable rivers, that flows north and into the Atlantic Ocean near Jacksonville.[2]

Florida's native people lodged on the shores of Lake Apopka as early as 7500 BC, where they hunted and fished the lake's teeming waters. When the Spaniards arrived in Florida in the sixteenth century, the Acuera band of the Timucua confederation supposedly dwelled in the Apopka area, but by 1730 these natives had disappeared, victims of war and the European diseases. In the nineteenth century, there was a Seminole village on Lake Apopka, or Ahapopka, as the Indians pronounced it, which existed until the outbreak of the Second Seminole War in the mid-1830s. It was not until after the Armed Occupation Act of 1842, at the end of that war, that the first white pioneers arrived to settle on the shores of the great lake to farm the 160 acres they received to colonize the primeval area.[3]

Toward the end of the nineteenth century, people were improving navigation in the area by connecting the natural waterways with the easily navigated St. Johns River, and the Ocklawaha. Lake Apopka remained free from human intervention until the late 1800s, when the Apopka-Beauclaire Canal was built at the north end of the lake, connecting it to Lake Beauclaire in an effort to increase the navigable waters for travel. Things began to change during the land boom of the 1920s, when the lakeshore town of Winter

Garden began dumping raw sewage and wastewater from its citrus process-ing plants directly into its waters. However, by far the lake's most serious damage came about in the early 1940s, when World War II was in full swing and fear of a nationwide food shortage gripped the country. In 1941, the Army Corps of Engineers constructed a levee along the north shore to drain 20,000 acres of shallow marsh for farming. Large areas along the lake's edge were drained, allowing farmers to use the rich muck from the lake's bottom as farmland. In 1947, after a hurricane struck the area, the first of the recorded algae blooms occurred, foreshadowing further degradation.[4]

Jim Connors oversaw much of the early restoration in the 1990s as former project manager for the St. Johns River Water Management District (SJRWMD), one of five regional water districts in Florida. The district is re-sponsible for managing all the groundwater and surface water within its nineteen-county area of northeast and east central Florida.

"Before the muck farms began, Lake Apopka was the second-largest lake in Florida," said Connors. "Now it is the most polluted lake in Florida. Dur-ing the 1940s, when muck farming began, and the farmers built levees and drainage canals, the lake went from 51,000 acres to 31,000 acres, so now it's the fourth-largest lake in Florida."

"The farms used gravity runoff," Connor explained. "Farms were actually below the level of the lake, so the farmers flooded the fields to kill nematodes, then pumped the water back in. This eventually led to a buildup of sediment five feet thick on the bottom of lake."[5]

Lake Apopka's pollution is rooted in these efforts to control nature for the benefit of humanity. In Florida, a state where farmers can grow crops year-round, draining the marshy land at the lake's edge to increase productivity seemed like a good idea. The warm climate allowed farmers to produce three crops per year in the exposed, fertile muck. However, as farmers began drain-ing water from these muck farms along the shore back into what was left of Lake Apopka, the lake's nutrient load increased, and the massive influx of nutrients spawned the algae blooms that became continuous. The water of-ten turned pea-green, causing fish kills, and the thick growth of sediment formed on the lake's bottom blocked sunlight from nourishing the natural vegetation that provided habitat for native fish. In addition to the algae growth, the 1950s saw the lake overgrown with water hyacinths, a non-native invasive water plant introduced for its lovely lavender-blue bloom. The hya-cinths, which thrive on polluted water, choked many of Florida's waterways.

In the 1950s, the only way authorities handled aquatic weeds was to spray a powerful herbicide.[6]

Unfortunately, no one at the time suspected the impact this drainage and constant farming would have on the lake and its inhabitants over the next fifty years. The area was named the "Zellwood Drainage District," and 19,000 acres of the muck land was deeded to farm interests. Farmers established their own rules and the right to irrigate their fields with Lake Apopka's waters. For nearly fifty years, farms discharged phosphorus and pesticides into the lake, and the degradation of the water quality in Lake Apopka and the adjoining Harris Chain of Lakes continued.[7]

Now Lake Apopka stands as lifeless testimony to what can happen to a pristine body of water when humans tamper with nature. After the years of fish kills caused by the algae blooms, the deaths of hundreds of alligators in the mid-1980s, and most recently, the deaths of an estimated one thousand waterfowl during a failed restoration effort that reflooded the lake's shores in the winter of 1998 and 1999, Florida is now reevaluating its measures to restore the once-beautiful lake and striving to find new answers in an attempt to correct previous problems.

In recent years, environmentalists around the globe have followed the sad story of Lake Apopka, a textbook case of a beautiful, living lake ruined in the name of improvement. The toll has been heavy, not only on birds, fish, and alligators that live and feed at the lake but also on the people who worked the farms. The story is also an example of how costly the effects of pollution can be to change, and how this can affect human lives. It is a dicey problem, and emotionally charged for people on both sides of the issue.

Lake Apopka first received worldwide attention in 1992, when local breeders, who raise alligators for hides, were unable to obtain viable alligator eggs from the lake, which normally supported a large and healthy population of alligators. Biologists noticed there were fewer alligators than in recent years, and the eggs the breeders collected did not hatch. Unable to explain the problem, they began an investigation to discover what was wrong. Their findings uncovered an unexpected problem: Many of the male alligators had increased levels of estrogen that caused undeveloped, infantile penises, while others were not properly gender-defined.[8]

The scientists and biologists were stumped. When the reports became public, there was a stampede to the lake's shores. Scientists and the media flew in from as far away as China to view Lake Apopka and to cover the curious story. There were no ready explanations for the problem, but evidence pointed to Tower Chemical's terrible spill of the toxic chemical dicofol in 1980 that killed 90 percent of the lake's alligator population. Nevertheless, alligators had rebounded since the spill, and the lake was now considered clean. Baffled biologists had no explanation for the gator's strange deformity. Eventually, Louis Guillette, a specialist on reptile reproduction from the University of Florida, hit on a possible cause. The synthetic chemicals acted as hormones, influencing the reproductive organs of the reptiles. Guillette also discovered that many red-eared terrapins in Lake Apopka were neither male nor female. Since the lake connects to the entire Harris Chain, abnormalities turned up in the adjoining lakes. Something had to be done. It was time for cleanup.[9]

Early efforts to correct the pollution problem began in 1971, when the dam and lock to the Apopka-Beauclaire Canal was opened to lower the lake level and consolidate the floating bits of sediment. But after the lake dropped 2 feet from its former depth, thousands of fish died, along with twenty-one alligators and an unknown number of turtles. Unfortunately, the lowering of the lake caused a concentration of bacteria in the remaining water. It was another well-meaning cure gone wrong. By 1979, the Environmental Protection Agency planned another draw-down of the lake, to take place gradually over a nine-month period, but farther downstream, residents on the Harris Chain of Lakes worried about being flooded with polluted water, while lakefront residents worried about more wildlife deaths, and citrus grove owners worried about the loss of frost protection for their crops. And the expense was estimated at about $20 million, nearly twice the cost of the draw-down done in 1971.[10]

Throughout the 1980s, various groups formed to develop a viable plan to save Lake Apopka, one that would not create further damage. In 1987, the Florida Surface Water Improvement and Management (SWIM) Act directed the St. Johns Water Management District to restore Lake Apopka. The SWIM program funded many of the projects completed by the Lake Apopka Restoration Council, a group created by the Florida legislature in 1985 to find an economic and environmentally sound way to restore Lake Apopka. In 1991, a new group of activists formed the Friends of Lake Apopka (FOLA) and dedicated itself to the care of the lake after the decision of the St. Johns Management District's governing board to grant the Zellwood Muck Farms a permanent permit that would have allowed it to continue dumping polluted water into Lake Apopka. After the discovery of the sterile alligators, FOLA decided to lobby for drastic measures. Representatives Everett Kelly and Bill Sublette, with Florida senator Buddy Dye, introduced the bill that became the Lake Apopka Restoration Act of 1996.[11]

"Cleanup attempts failed because there was no holistic approach," said Jim Connor. The state finally decided the only thing to do was to buy out the muck farms that lined the north bank of the lake. Most of the growers—hard-working men who staked their claims just after World War II—had farmed the fertile soil since the 1940s. Now they owned small empires, operated by their sons and grandsons. Naturally, they did not want to sell.

"The Zellwood Drainage and Water Control District included about twelve farms working together to cut the cost of pumping and levees," said Connor. "The growers were feisty and fought giving up their farms.

"A. Duda, a large international agricultural company, acted alone," Connor explained. "They dealt with the pollution problem by building a large retention pond system to reduce the phosphorus in the water prior to pumping it back into the lake." But the Zellwood collective became difficult.

"They balked when we established standards," he said. "Duda realized it would be cheaper to rectify their drainage system rather than sue. Farms were given a consent order that gave them time to put an interceptor system in to reduce the pollution."

Finally, growers agreed to the buy-out offered by the state because they found it was too expensive to comply with the new regulations. It was cheaper for the growers to sell to the state and let the St. Johns River Water Management District do the restoration, said Connor. By 2000, nearly 90 percent of the muck farms belonged to the State of Florida, and the cost of the buy-out exceeded $100 million.[12]

Ending the application of pesticides and fertilizers was necessary to clean up Lake Apopka and avert the associated impacts to the adjoining Harris Chain of Lakes. Then in 1998, with the majority of farmlands out of production and an end to the use of pesticides and fertilizers, restoration could begin.

The flooding of the lakeshore began in the late summer of that year, and it was a sight to see. Standing on the massive dikes surrounding the shallow lake, the former vegetable rows were still visible in many places as the water slowly crept across the lake. Bits of dead cornstalks poked out of the water, ghostly remnants of the famous Zellwood sweet corn, to serve as perches for the aquatic birds. Farther out on the lake, hundreds of waterbirds feasted on the lake's fare. Pelicans swooped from above as wood storks and herons stood on long legs and trolled the bottom for a tidbit. Nearby an alligator sunned itself on the side of a drainage ditch. With all of the humans gone, and the farm machinery silent, the wildlife returned. Everything seemed to be regenerating, and there was hope for Lake Apopka.

Then in November 1998, several months after the reflooding of the muck farms, an estimated 676 birds—mostly white pelicans, wood storks, and great blue herons—died on the shores of Lake Apopka. The U.S. Fish and Wildlife Service ordered a study of the bird deaths. In March 1999, necropsies on the dead birds revealed high levels of toxaphenes, dieldrin, and even DDT, long banned for use on crops in the United States. Officials did not lay the blame on residues from the former farmlands but said the deaths could be due to a "hot spot," an area of concentrated toxicity left from a chemical spill. Bird lovers feared the deaths exceeded 800, because many more birds that visited the lake flew away, possibly dying someplace else. In all, about 1,000 birds of twenty-two different species were found dead statewide. White pelicans and other fish-eating birds such as herons, and even a few eagles, died in the highest numbers, and there were also significant numbers of fish found dead on the reflooded muck. Even so, officials were reluctant to restrict fishing in the lake.[13]

Though the number of deaths shocked the bird lovers of the Lake Apopka area, some scientists did not find them new. Gian Basili, an avian expert with the Florida Audubon Society, said that birds feeding in flooded farm fields on Lake Apopka might have been dying for years, but at levels too low to attract attention. After the lake was reflooded, more than 41,000 birds—including 4,370 white pelicans—were recorded feeding at one time, and the total number of birds feeding on fish and other organisms at the site during the winter of 1998 was far higher, Basili said. He cited organochlorine pesticides, such as DDT, that were once widely used by the Zellwood farmers, long-lasting nerve toxins that accumulated in the tissues of small fish, so the large birds that ate many of the fish were poisoned at high rates.[14]

But Lake Apopka's influence is far-reaching, affecting far more than wildlife. Some people involved with Lake Apopka's restoration efforts find there is too little attention paid to the human element in this environmental drama. When the state bought the farms, many farmworkers found themselves out of a job. As often happens, government's decision to clean up pollution did not figure in the cost of the farmworkers' lost jobs.

Jeannie Economos was the Lake Apopka project coordinator for the Farmworker Association of Florida during the period of the state and federally funded muck farm buyout, and the association's office in Apopka is head-quarters for the retraining project for farmworkers who have lost their jobs. Economos estimated that about 2,500 workers lost jobs when the farms shut down, and with the extended families of these farmworkers, many thousands more were affected.

"The original buyout was expanded, and the state spent more than $100 million for the farmland, while legislation allotted a mere $200,000 for job retraining of the displaced farmworkers," she said. "Most of the farmworkers have worked on farms all of their lives and have no other skills."

The Lake Apopka packinghouse owned by A. Duda closed down. The mul-timillion-dollar international company, the largest of the muck farms bought out by the state in 1998, was supposed to keep its packinghouse open for two years, but Economos noted that the company closed it in 1999.

"It employed 160 to 170 people who came back to Apopka to work, but they now have no work," said Economos. "They offered these people work in other farm areas of the state, such as Lake Placid, but they don't want to go there because there is no housing. They'd have to rent their own places and that's too expensive for most of these farmworkers. They don't have first and last month's rent, and security deposits. They had trailers here, but now they have no work so they have to get their things out of the trailers and they have no place to go. The majority are people of color, all are low-income, and a large percentage of them are immigrants. Approximately 40 percent are women."[15]

Margie Lee Pitter, now in her sixties, labored as a field worker in the farms around Lake Apopka throughout the 1960s and 1970s, when pesticides were sprayed from crop duster planes as workers stooped in the fields picking veg-etables. After thirty-five years as a farmworker in the area, she worked her last day in a carrot packinghouse on July 31, 1998. That was the day farming along Lake Apopka's polluted banks officially ended, and the muck farming that was a way of life in Apopka ended with it. Since the farming stopped and the packinghouse closed, Pitter has worked several different jobs, but she felt comfortable with none of them. The quiet, dignified woman came to learn computer skills at the Farm Worker Ministry office in Apopka, something she hopes will provide a satisfactory income so she will not have to go on public assistance. In her soft voice, Pitter shared her story.

"I never had no kids. I had four miscarriages, but never had any kids. Just a few years ago, a nurse with the health service came and talked to us about safety and health, and she asked if I had any kids. When I told her I had four miscarriages, she said that might be because of the pesticides in the fields. I never had any idea about that.

"When I started working in the 1960s, the boss just told us to go over to the side of the field when the plane came over with the spray so we wouldn't get sprayed on, but we all felt the mist in our faces 'cause it blew around. Sometimes we all had headaches, blurry vision and felt sick, but nobody told us it might be the chemicals."[16]

Pitter wore skirts over her jeans when she worked in the fields because there were no portable bathrooms provided for the field workers in those days, and she recalled she used to come home covered with black dust, like a coal miner, from the dry muck that blew around in the fields. She and thousands of others never knew the consequences of the pesticides sprayed overhead by the crop dusters. Most of those exposed to the toxins ignored the telltale signs of chemical poisoning. Back in those days, before the law required farmers to tell workers what pesticides they were using, hazards involved many different chemicals, including DDT and others that are now completely banned in the United States. Few people realized the damage pesticides could do, even though most had been developed for chemical warfare during World War II. Pesticides can cause skin irritation from handling without gloves, and lung damage from the fumes if no mask is used. There is an increased incidence of reproductive organ cancer among farmworker women at a much younger age than the average population, as well as a higher incidence of birth defects among their children, yet in Pitter's day, people knew little of the long-term effects.[17]

In addition to the lack of money provided for retraining these displaced workers, little has been done to assess their health. Not only were they exposed to toxic chemicals in the fields, their health may have been affected by tainted wells close to the restoration area. The Farm Workers Association held a meeting in the nearby town of Apopka after the bird deaths in the winter of 1998 and 1999 to address concerns of members of the community, specifically farmworkers, with respect to the news linking pesticide and bird deaths at the lake.

"We don't know who could be affected because health effects are so wide and so varied that unless you do a survey in depth, people say things are not related," said Economos. "We're hoping to get funding for a survey and use that data to do a large health study that would document some health problems. Lake Apopka is a very significant chapter in the study of endocrine-altering abilities of synthetic chemicals. We need the Department of Health to take a serious look at this, but they say the levels of chemicals are not significant enough to affect anyone."

Since the lake is the site of two Superfund sites, residents were concerned about a small rural community near Zellwood that depends on well water. "The EPA says local wells are not contaminated," said Economos, but she said she was unsure about how thorough the tests were.[18]

In June 2001, the Southeast Region of the U.S. Fish and Wildlife Service released the study of the bird deaths at Lake Apopka that occurred two years earlier as the lake was reflooded to restore the natural littoral zone where the farmland had been. The findings confirmed what many had expected. Necropsies on several wood storks, American white pelicans, and one bald eagle found dead on the lake in the spring of 1999 revealed elevated brain levels of DDT, dieldrin, and oxychlordane, all potent organophosphates used by growers on the muck farms. However, the report states, "None of these residues reached the level to be lethal." Toxaphene was also present in the birds' brains, but again the report states, "a reference could not be found for a lethal threshold of toxaphene in the brain."

The reports verified elevated levels of organochlorines, including DDT, dieldrin, toxaphene, and heptachlor, among others, in minnows, catfish, tilapia, and gar collected from the lake for testing. All in all, it was a toxic cocktail awaiting the migratory birds that visit Lake Apopka in the winter and dine on its fish.[19]

Tom MacKenzie, spokesman for the Southeast Region of the U.S. Fish and Wildlife Service, said that whenever birds are killed it is a federal crime. "We look into it to see who's responsible. So we looked at the St. Johns River Water Management District to see if they were culpable."[20]

After a thorough study of the restoration efforts, in October 2003 Thomas Sansonetti, assistant attorney general for the Justice Department's Environment and Natural Resources Division, and Paul Perez, U.S. attorney for the Middle District of Florida, issued a Memorandum of Understanding (MOU) with the St. Johns River Water Management District that ended a criminal investigation and natural resource damages claims. The MOU resolved criminal charges against the St. Johns River Water Management District under the Migratory Bird Treaty Act (MBTA), the Endangered Species Act (ESA), and the Bald and Golden Eagle Protection Act, plus certain civil claims for natural resource damages under the Comprehensive Environmental Response, Compensation and Liability Act.

Because the St. Johns River Water Management District sold thirty-year conservation easements on much of this property to the Natural Resource Conservation Service of the U.S. Department of Agriculture, it was allegedly liable for its conduct from the fall of 1998 through the spring of 1999, when over 1,000 migratory birds, including endangered wood storks, eagles, and other protected birds died in and near the northern shore of the lake. According to the agreement, the United States agreed not to file criminal charges against St. Johns River Water Management District for wildlife violations, so long as it does not materially breach the terms of the memorandum, which holds the district to strict environmental rules in any restoration effort. The MOU has no effect on whether or not restoration in any form may continue; however, any restoration that is done must be in compliance with existing laws regarding migratory, threatened, or endangered birds.

The MOU now requires the SJRWMD to do the following: (1) bring all of its properties into compliance with the ESA and other wildlife statutes; (2) reimburse the wildlife rehabilitators that worked on affected birds the approximately $90,000 collectively that they expended in this effort to save the poisoned birds, including Uncle Donald's Farm, Audubon Society Birds of Prey Center, and the Suncoast Seabird Sanctuary; (3) run a conference to educate other water districts regarding the wildlife laws; (4) acknowledge the causes of the birds' death and its role therein; (5) provide training to its employees; (6) conduct a five-year program to monitor pesticide levels in Lake Apopka; (7) monitor wood stork populations on its properties for five years; (8) and develop an active management plan for threatened or endangered species on at least 200 acres of its properties.[21]

Part of the suit stemmed from the fact that in early November 1997, before the reflooding of the farms, biologists completed a risk assessment for the first large parcel purchased by the state. It found, among other things, that the pesticide levels of DDT and toxaphene on the property presented an increased risk for predatory birds eating fish from any restored wetlands on the site. Other organochlorine pesticides were detected at relatively higher levels on the second group of properties purchased. At the time, the comparative study of these two sites looked only at levels of DDT and toxaphene, omitting complete assessments of other pesticides such as dieldrin. Nevertheless, even with this information, in the late summer and fall of 1998 during peak migration, the district continued with the shallow flooding of these two large sections of the properties, leading to the deaths of over 1,000 migratory birds on or near the properties. According to a statement from the U.S. Fish and Wildlife Service, Southeast Region, "certain organochlorine compounds, including dieldrin, toxaphene and DDT and its metabolites found on the flooded farmland were primary causative factors in, or the cause of, the bird deaths."

Currently, Lake Apopka's cleanup is ongoing, but the lessons learned offer information that will prove invaluable in other wetland restoration areas, in both national and international efforts to restore ecosystems damaged by past agricultural practices. Much of the information concerns bioaccumulation, the process where chemicals accumulate in the tissues of organisms in a concentrated form greater than that found in the water and soils. When the pelicans, herons, and other aquatic birds ate the fish, they also ingested the concentrated pesticides. Since the birds are higher on the food chain, the amount of chemicals they consumed in the fish proved lethal.

The district also cleaned up a five-acre toxaphene "hot spot" that scientists believe figured prominently in the bird deaths, and they have also developed an early-warning system for reflooded lands in order to spot potential problems that can arise from pesticide residues. But most of the previously reflooded land remains dry, becoming an upland shrub community covered with prairie vegetation. However, beginning in June 2002, 700 acres—part of the Duda tract on the lake's north shore with the lowest levels of pesticide residues—are being converted to wetlands in a pilot project. The district has monitored this program intensively. To date there have been no bird deaths.

Another requirement for SJRWMD is mitigation for the polluted wetlands on Lake Apopka's shores that cannot be restored. Efforts are now underway to restore the Matanzas Marsh, a tract of approximately 8,465 acres in St. Johns County, as a mitigation area for the endangered wood storks. The project protects and monitors wood stork populations at the rookery located in the marshland. The total purchase price was approximately $40 million, and the district contributed $10 million of this price, while the Florida Department of Environmental Protection will pay the remainder.

No herbicides or pesticides can be used on the Matanzas Marsh property within the drainage area of the colony, except as necessary to control an outbreak or invasion of non-native plants or animals. That could only happen in an area where the wood stork colony would not be affected, provided that USFWS agrees to the pesticide use. Other conditions of the Matanzas Marsh mitigation prohibit "additional roadways or improvements on existing roadways, towers, power lines, canals and drainage features," and any new building construction. And at Lake Apopka, the MOU states that SJRWMD must coordinate with county health officials and set up a five-year plan for monitoring pesticide levels in the lake's fish.[22]

The Lake Apopka restoration will probably continue for years, because it took years for the degradation to occur. But the unsettling story of the near-total destruction of this once-glorious lake is a bellwether for other areas of natural significance where restoration is planned. Around the country, as people begin to comprehend the importance of natural ecosystems, the story of Lake Apopka serves as a guide for ecologists, who can learn from some of the mistakes and avoid such problems in future restoration projects.

"It's a noble goal to recover damaged lands," said Tom MacKenzie, "but it's hard to undo fifty years of abuse."

Notes

1. Friends of Lake Apopka website, "History of Lake Apopka," http://www.fola.org/who/lakehist.htm.

2. Ibid.; Nelson M. Blake, *Land into Water/Water into Land: A History of Water Management in Florida* (Gainesville: University Presses of Florida, 1980), 120–29.

3. Apopka Historical Society website, http://www.apopkamuseum.org/history.htm. The source of the name "Apopka" is believed to be of Creek origin from *aha*, meaning potato, and *papka*, for eating place, hence "potato-eating place."

4. St. Johns River Water Management District website, "Project Overview: Lake Apopka Restoration Project," http://sjr.state.fl.us/programs/acq_restoration/s_water/lapopka/project.html.

5. Jim Connor, former Lake Apopka restoration project manager, St. Johns Water Management District, interview by author, April 15, 2000.

6. "History of Lake Apopka"; Blake, *Land into Water*, 120–29; "Project Overview."

7. "History of Lake Apopka."

8. Theo Colburn, Dianne Dumanoski, and John Peterson Myers, *Our Stolen Future: Are We Threatening Our Fertility, Intelligence, and Survival?* (New York: Plume Books, 1997).

9. Ibid.

10. "Project Overview."

11. "History of Lake Apopka."

12. Connor interview.

13. St. Johns River Water Management District website, "Questions and Answers: The Lake Apopka Agreement," http://sjr.state.fl.us/programs/acq_restoration/s_water/lapopka/Q-A.html.

14. Jerry Jackson, "Bird Deaths May Not Be New, Expert Says High Death Tolls May Have Just Made Lake Apopka's Problem More Visible," *Orlando Sentinel*, March 12, 1999.

Nano Riley

15. Jeanne Economos, former coordinator for the Lake Apopka project for the Farmworker Association of Florida, interviews by author, June 21, 1999, January 12, 2004.

16. Margie Lee Pitter, displaced Lake Apopka farmworker, interview by author, June 21, 1999.

17. "Farmworker Women's Health Project," *Network News* (National Women's Health Network) 17 (November 1992): 6.

18. Economos interview.

19. U.S. Fish and Wildlife Service, "Lake Apopka Bird Deaths Investigation, Summary Findings Update," July 26, 2001, http://southeast.fws.gov/law/News/LakeApopka/apopka_index.html.

20. Tom MacKenzie, spokesman for the Southeast Region of the U.S. Fish and Wildlife Service, interview by author, January 12, 2004.

21. U.S. Department of Justice, "Memorandum of Understanding Resolves Criminal Investigation and Natural Resource Damage Claims against St. Johns River Water Management District," October 8, 2003, www.usdoj.gov.

22. "Questions and Answers: The Lake Apopka Agreement."

Part 4

Conservation and Environmentalism

Chapter 13

"Conservation Is Now a Dead Word"

Marjory Stoneman Douglas and the Transformation of American Environmentalism

Jack E. Davis

The mood of the assembly was as hostile as the evening was hot. Marjory Stoneman Douglas, the last speaker of the night, was accustomed to both. Crowded in the high-school auditorium were several hundred landowners from an east Everglades community that owed its existence to levees and drainage canals. To those in attendance, Douglas was the "anti-Christ," a sentimental environmentalist who was willing to trade their livelihoods and their homes to save birds and alligators and snakes. "Go back to Russia, granny," someone shouted when her time came to speak. Against an eruption of boos and jeers, the ninety-one-year-old Douglas moved confidently down the center aisle to have her say before county commissioners. Her task that night was to convince the commission to limit construction on 155,000 acres of privately held land "of critical environmental concern." Some people in the audience were appropriately defensive, for Douglas, the sanctified "Grandmother of the Everglades," was known for capturing the ear of policymakers and, indeed, the hearts of the American people. After pulling the microphone down to her 5-foot frame, she waited for a break in the escalating noise. "You damn butterfly chaser," came a voice from above the din. Finally, she said, "Look. I'm an old lady. I've been here since eight o'clock. It's now eleven. I've got all night, and I'm used to the heat." In the end, the commissioners voted the way of the environmentalists.[1]

The elderly woman who made it her civic duty to save the Everglades from the continuing enterprise of drainage, development, and bureaucratic control was no simple butterfly chaser. Former Assistant Secretary of Interior Nathaniel Reed described Douglas as "that tiny, slim, perfectly dressed, [but] utterly ferocious grande dame who can make a redneck shake in his boots." Douglas had established herself as an expert on Florida history and the environment in 1947 when she published *The Everglades: River of Grass,* a pathbreaking book that later became the green bible of Florida environmentalists. Even Douglas's antagonists respected her knowledge and foresight. Through many years of lobbying, writing, educating, and cajoling, she helped raise the plight of the Everglades to the top of the national agenda, resulting in important state and federal legislation that signified changing environmental policy. Countless honors and awards acknowledged her work as a writer and environmentalist. The one that capped her public career was the Presidential Medal of Freedom, the government's highest civilian honor, which she received at age 103. When she died in 1998 at age 108, she had been one of the most celebrated environmental leaders in the last decades of the twentieth century. President Clinton, who once described Douglas as Mother Nature herself, said she had been "both an inspiration and mentor for a generation."[2]

Spanning much of the twentieth century, the long sweep of Douglas's public life provides an ideal case study for American environmentalism and its rise as a movement out of the traditions of progressive conservation. By studying Douglas, one encounters the linkages between the modern environmental movement and early conservation impulses.[3] Her life in a burgeoning Miami at the beginning of the twentieth century reveals the diverse nature of early conservation, including the influence of organized women and their

Jack E. Davis

myriad progressive reforms. Miami's juxtaposition to the Everglades—still an uncharted wilderness but one that was believed to offer great economic potential—forced civic-minded women to take stock of both urban and extra-urban environments. Douglas combines the inquiry of progressive-era attitudes toward the two environments into a single individual, one who reconciled a utilitarian outlook with wilderness preservation. Her shift away from a progressive-conservation understanding of the human relationship with the nonhuman world is particularly revealing of the role that ecology played in shaping modern environmental sensibilities. Her extraordinary resurrection in the last decades of her life as a public activist, and one more assertive than before, dramatizes the larger transformation in American environmentalism. Many of the characteristics that scholars identify with the contemporary movement, one can find in Douglas's later life: the deployment of grassroots activism; the lessons of ecological science; the rise of environmental justice; the admixture of anthropocentrism and biophilia; and the socialized sensibilities of womanhood.

From the moment that she moved to Miami in 1915, at age twenty-five, her life became forever enmeshed with the city and its wetland environs. Raised in Taunton, Massachusetts, and educated at Wellesley College, she saw south Florida as a refuge from the fallout of a bad marriage and the pain of her mother's recent death. As she later testified, the "white light" of the subtropical sun, the "snappy golden and peacock weather," and the palpable civic energy of a young Miami quickly buoyed her spirits. Her father, Frank Stoneman, whom she had not seen in fifteen years, had moved to Florida in the 1890s and started the city's first morning daily newspaper, which became the *Miami Herald*. When he brought her onto the newspaper, she embarked on a writing career that lasted more than eighty years, including twenty devoted to short stories and over fifty to books. Four years older than Miami, she found her new city poised for its own expanded horizons. The south Florida city was an urban island of approximately 11,000 residents in a frontier wilderness. Fanning out across the state, the Everglades made a natural boundary for the city's westward growth in the days before successful drainage. Pine forests with a dense palmetto understory lay to the north, and to the south wetlands ran to the sea. The city's hinterland was as wild as any nineteenth-century territory in the American West. Extended to Miami in 1896, the Florida East Coast Railroad opened the south Florida territory to unforeseen levels of growth and exploitation.[4]

Although on a much smaller scale, Miami's relationship to its hinterland was similar to that of Chicago in the nineteenth century, as William Cronon has described that region. At the same time that Miami's growth benefited from agribusiness outside the city center, the railroad delivered an urban culture to rural south Florida. Commercial agriculture—sugarcane, citrus, and truck farming—developed out from the urban realm in lockstep with the city's growth. One Miami land company, for example, sold 10,000 farms in 10-acre tracts in a six-year period before World War I. Eventually, small independent husbandmen would sell out to well-financed commercial farmers and growers, many with northern corporate parentage. Land companies, corporate farmers, and politicians alike believed that once the rich peaty Everglades soil was liberated from the "bondage of inundation," as one observer put it, the region would offer unlimited possibilities for agricultural expansion and profit.[5]

The growth of agribusiness was dependent on an affordable and reliable means by which to ship its products, but if not for the city the railroad would likely have been longer in coming. Its owner, petroleum-tycoon-turned-land-speculator Henry Flagler, was in part lured by the profits of shipping products of the soil. But he wanted to transport people—vacationers and conventioneers—to and from Miami as much as anything else. Real estate salespeople, who helped energize the local economy in the early decades, contributed to Flagler's profits by carving out thousands of home lots on the eastern fringes of the Everglades and selling them to seasonal residents and permanently relocated northerners. Boosters found in south Florida a different kind of wealth of nature than that exploited in the Great West. They were selling a favorable climate, beautiful waterfront views, interminable sunshine, and a subtropical landscape of exotic birds, trees, and reptiles. Miami, indeed, was emerging as a metropolis of nature. Boosters surely realized this in their own way and on their own terms, but they lacked a sophisticated understanding of the essential connection of Miami's assets to the environment outside the city's limits. The breezes blowing off the Gulf Stream in the Atlantic assured pleasant temperatures year-round; the rains that cooled summer afternoons and watered the crops drifted in from offshore and from over the Everglades; the stick-legged birds that trimmed the city landscape and the sky above emanated from habitats elsewhere; and the mangroves that lowered waterfront property values spawned sea life that fed people and provided some with a livelihood or sport. The perilousness of the boosters' ignorance was demonstrated most acutely in their attempts to drain the Everglades, first in the 1880s and then throughout much of the twentieth century. In pursuing that end, they were destroying the nucleus of the south Florida environment and endangering that which had been responsible for their city's very existence.[6]

The group that initiated the first attempts to save at least part of the Everglades was the Florida Federation of Women's Clubs (FFWC). As many scholars have noted, years before women could vote, their civic and charitable organizations assumed an important role in progressive reform of the late nineteenth and early twentieth centuries. Soon after moving to Miami, Douglas took note of the average woman's club as a "self-produced university . . . a small, respectable pot, boiling away unnoticed, a stirring of minds, a spirit of inquiry, a new awareness of ideas." Many women's organizations, particularly the more influential white, middle-to-upper-class groups, integrated social concerns—child welfare, school reform, and pure-food regulations—with conservation agendas. The national General Federation of Women's Clubs (GFWC) maintained a conservation department, and among its lobbying accomplishments were state and national laws to protect forests, waters, and wildlife. Gifford Pinchot, whose mother chaired the conservation committee of the Daughters of American Revolution, observed in 1910 that "few people realize what women have already done for conservation." Women, as did men, may have associated the concept of conservation principally with rural spaces, but progressive reformers devoted much of their attention to the urban environment, which bore the consequences of rapid growth and industrialization. It was not uncommon, for example, for a women's poetry club to take up the issue of city beautification, and it was women generally who organized for improved sanitary conditions and smoke- and noise-abatement ordinances.[7]

Founded in 1895, the FFWC addressed a broad range of issues at the state level. It adopted a legislative agenda that focused on compulsory school attendance, Seminole Indian welfare, public health, and improved roads. Some of the organization's most successful efforts came out of its conservation committee, which devoted many years toward the establishment of Florida's first forest reserves. The FFWC's most notable accomplishment was another first, the creation of Florida's earliest state park. In 1916, the same year that Congress authorized the National Park Service, Florida legislators voted to set aside state land to match that donated by Mary Flagler, FFWC member and widow of Henry Flagler, to establish Royal Palm State Park. The legislature left the FFWC with the responsibility of developing and operating the park with its own funds. The organization then set out to accomplish two principal

Marjory Stoneman Douglas and American Environmentalism

goals: to preserve a rare natural stand of royal palms and to provide protective habitat for wading birds of the Everglades.[8]

Protecting plume birds was a major concern in the country when in 1905 women of the FFWC first floated the idea for an Everglades park. It was the year that plume hunters shot and killed Guy Bradley, a game warden whom the National Association of Audubon Societies had hired to protect the rookeries in Monroe County. Throughout the South, white and Indian poachers slaughtered wading birds, prized for their valuable plumage, by the tens of thousands. Bird feathers, and even whole birds, were all the rage in women's hats, and for decades poaching in Florida's wild country fed a veritable market of destruction for profit and vanity. The FFWC's first petition to Congress, in 1896, supported an initially unsuccessful bill to outlaw trade in ornamental bird feathers. In Florida, a number of FFWC members were officers in the state Audubon Society, which eight women and six men founded in 1900. A year later, Florida lawmakers for the second time strengthened bird-protection legislation originally enacted in 1877. Despite passage of state and federal laws, the efforts of the Audubon Society, and the establishment of Royal Palm Park, the slaughter of plume birds continued until the 1940s. According to some estimates, poaching and habitat encroachment eventually reduced the Everglades bird population by 90 percent.[9]

After moving to Miami, Douglas quickly gravitated to women's clubs for initiation into their world of civic activism. Having gone to work as a staff reporter and the society-page editor for the *Miami Herald,* she was recruited to coordinate publicity for the work of the FFWC and the Florida Equal Suffrage Association. She also traveled to the state capitol in Tallahassee in 1916 with a seasoned group of club women to lobby for woman's suffrage. In Miami, she and her fellow club women questioned the values and wealth of a city that ignored its social responsibilities to the poverty-stricken while it fixated on growth. The local powers that be had managed to segregate blacks and the poor from the rest of the citizenry, and the lack of health codes allowed city leaders to deny the most basic services to some neighborhoods for half a century. In 1922, Douglas organized a fund that provided milk to needy babies. She was writing a daily column for the *Herald* at the time and used commentary and even poetry to agitate for improved conditions in child welfare, public education, and sanitation. She simultaneously blasted corrupt politics and government, convict leasing, and the trade tariff, which she said amounted to a heartless burden on European cities struggling to rebuild from the rubble of war.[10]

Jack E. Davis

Douglas's social concerns were shaped by family history, a liberal education, and personal experience. Although she rejected any religious affiliation and died a self-proclaimed agnostic, she credited her humanitarian values to her Quaker roots on her father's side of the family. She appreciated the Society of Friends' support of woman's suffrage, and she admired her own Quaker grandparents' principled stand against slavery. In her autobiography, she described the Quaker Levi Coffin, the reputed president of the Underground Railroad, as the ancestor who influenced her most as a "free thinker and activist." She also attributed her expanding social consciousness to her professors at Wellesley College. One, Emily Greene Balch, a Quaker pacifist and future Nobel Peace Prize recipient, introduced her students to slum conditions in Boston. When Douglas later served as a Red Cross correspondent touring Europe after World War I, she once again encountered human misery. She subsequently discovered similar conditions in Miami's urban environment.[11]

Douglas's direct involvement with women's clubs tapered off when she left the Red Cross and returned to the *Miami Herald* in 1920. While she shared her club sisters' interests in social reform and conservation, her views on sexuality were comparatively more extreme. Supporting the Nineteenth Amendment had been consistent with the position of women's organizations generally, but when the National Women's Party first proposed the Equal Rights Amendment in 1923, Douglas's open endorsement distinguished her from the many club women who preferred to stand upon a pedestal. The whole issue of separate spheres for the sexes made her skeptical. "It's a little bit late in the day for men to object that women are getting outside their proper sphere," she wrote in 1922. It is no coincidence that many of Douglas's short stories feature fiercely independent and determined women who have unburdened themselves from a man's possession. Douglas wanted women to have the freedom to chose their own path in life, whether motherhood, a career, or both lay at the end. After her failed marriage, which she valued as a learning experience, she was unwilling to submit to the financial support of a man, and she chose for herself the life of a single, professional woman.[12]

As a journalist with enough latitude to focus on ideals that were important to her, she engaged in a sort of professional activism. Similar to her club women counterparts, the expansive list of social reforms to which she gave press included conservation. Just as there were social benefits to reap from woman's suffrage, honest government, well-nourished children, and an educated citizenry, there was enriched life to come from a healthy and unspoiled environment. In the city, social issues were more often than not tied to environmental problems. In a 1923 column, she wrote: "Child welfare ought really to cover all sorts of topics, such as better water and sanitation and good roads, and clean streets and public parks and playgrounds." Miami's runaway growth and land-boom years of the 1920s, which seemed to marginalize quality-of-life concerns, irritated her. In response, she used her pen to lobby for zoning ordinances, public parks, tree planting, and landscaped boulevards. Her concept of what made a beautiful and livable city was suggestive of the City Beautiful movement and the principles of the period's leading urban reformers, such as Jane Addams, Mira Lloyd Dock, and Alice Hamilton; and landscape architects, such as Frederick Law Olmsted, John Nolen, and Beatrix Farrand. No Florida city had yet embraced the planning movement that landscape artists tended to endorse, but Douglas hoped that Miami would. Ultimately, she was disappointed. "I could argue that land should be set aside for parks, while land was cheap, I could talk about this new thing, zoning, and the newer and hazier thing, city planning, little realizing myself, as the tide of automobiles thickened in the narrow streets, that no planning of that day could have foreseen what the automobile would do to the entire country."[13]

Although it is unclear from existing records, Douglas was likely aware of the work of Olmsted and Nolen if not also the less-well-known Farrand, whose pioneering work opened the profession to women. Douglas had a curious mind, and she read voraciously and widely. It was from the academic journal *Social Forces* that she obtained a deeper understanding of regionalism, the idea that constructive relationships between cultures and their natural surroundings should be maximized to dramatize regional distinctiveness and the diverse whole of American culture. An officer in the Miami Women's Club introduced Douglas to regionalism, and after studying it further she promoted it in her column. The subtropical world of south Florida was the primary source of its distinctiveness, she wrote on numerous occasions. From the unique and natural, the right kind of architects, developers, engineers, and landscape designers—those who approached their professions as art—could transform Miami into one of the great cities of the world. It was a simple matter of south Florida's transplanted northern population living with its new environment rather than imposing on it ways of another region. "All we need, really, is a change from a near frigid to a tropical attitude of mind."[14]

Jack E. Davis

Douglas claimed to be pragmatic in her views of humans and their relationship with the natural world. The needless destruction of plant and animal life simply carried no social value. Any landscape was an open portfolio of natural beauty and civilization's most accessible and important aesthetic resource, an underutilized model for human creative talent. Taking a Quaker-stewardship view of nature, Douglas loved creatures of the wild, from the low-slung sand crab to the stilted seabird. Yet at the same time that she made a "plea for wider justice" for all living things and rejected the idea of lower and higher life-forms, she was not above reducing species to categories of good and bad.[15]

Her early values toward both the urban and extra-urban environments define her, like her club women counterparts, as a progressive conservationist. Although she celebrated the abundance, beauty, and opportunity of Florida, she recognized that her frontier region lacked the immensity of the American West and that the sustenance of civilization required exploitation, indeed leaving a cultural imprint on nature. She lacked the romantic and religious associations that might have aligned her with the less-pronounced preservationist strain of the early conservation movement. In telling moments of self-reflection, for example, she regretted that her mind was given too much to scientific and analytical reasoning, more rational than emotional, for her own creative needs as a fiction writer. It makes sense then that progressive conservation appealed to her pragmatic inclinations. When she looked at the city streets below her newspaper office, she envisioned scientifically managed growth that allowed for green space and improved the quality of life for all residents. When she turned west toward the country, she accepted rational exploitation—the sustainable use of resources—that benefited the largest constituency possible.[16]

Thinking within the prevailing intellectual contexts of progressivism and regionalism, Douglas believed that the economic promise of her city was tied to the distinctiveness of the hinterland. Most unique of all in the south Florida country were the Everglades. She did not so much oppose the utility of development as she did the reckless spending on drainage projects and the indifference to the wholesale destruction of the Everglades. "The wealth of south Florida, but even more important, the meaning and significance of south Florida," she wrote in 1923, "lies in the black muck of the Everglades and the inevitable development of this country to be the great tropic agricultural center of the world." Consistent with her regionalist vision, she wanted to see not the advance of traditional agriculture but the cultivation of "lavish" tropical growths of the kind that her friend David Fairchild, a local entomologist turned botanist, was introducing to the area. In her column, garden club speeches, and even in *River of Grass,* she sang Fairchild's praises for importing plants that enhanced the tropical appearance of south Florida, a place that was, in truth, subtropical. In later years, exotic plants would be identified as a metastasizing floral cancer consuming the Everglades ecosystem.[17]

At the same time that she supported agriculture, an industry that would ultimately become her chief nemesis, she lauded a great engineering feat that unified the vastness of the region into a more accessible space. After engineers in the 1920s began dynamiting and dredging their way across the Everglades in their endeavor to complete the Tamiami Trail, Douglas dedicated two odes to the progress symbolized in the U.S. highway that would connect Miami to Tampa. She justified its construction with the proclamation that the Everglades "sever" the civilizations of Florida's east and west coasts, which more properly should become "one, hence, forever." As in the case of agricultural development, she would later change her position on the "greatness" of the highway that formed a veritable dam against the flow of the river of grass.[18]

Although Douglas had not taken part in the creation of Royal Palm State Park, she always supported a protected space in the Everglades. At one point, she wrote but never published a story, "Women and Birds," that alludes to the prodigious female struggle behind the park's founding and development. When the FFWC in 1929 offered Royal Palm in support of a proposal to create an Everglades national park, Douglas was invited to join the Tropic Everglades National Park Association, which was charged with turning the proposal into a reality. Various women of the FFWC and Florida congresswoman Ruth Bryan Owen, who cosponsored the bill to establish Everglades National Park, fed the stream of women around the country who helped to shape the national park system both as advocates and naturalists. Why Douglas was chosen to serve on the association over others who had been actively involved with Royal Palm Park is unclear.[19] Her introduction to the Everglades had come only nine years earlier, five years after she moved to Miami, and other than fishing on Sunday afternoons in a drainage canal, her exposure to the Everglades had been limited to views from a distance. Her first real immersion occurred when a congressional delegation, state officials, a few select conservationists, and members of the park association spent two days boating and hiking through the Everglades (stumbling upon plume hunters at one point) and sailing overhead in a dirigible.[20]

Jack E. Davis

The 1930 excursion inspired her first important publication written in defense of the nonhuman world. Appearing in a 1931 issue of *Saturday Evening Post*, "Wings" expressed alarm over the illegal trade in bird feathers that lingered after a change in hat fashion slowed their demand. Two of her most popular short stories followed the trip as well. The 1905 killing of Guy Bradley provided the plot for "Plumes" (1930), the story of a convict turned bird protector who fears that his own lifeless body will end up in the tangle of mangroves. In "A Flight of Ibis" (1935), the protagonist is a sympathetic photographer who uses camera flash and film to save a colony of birds from would-be poachers. The two stories offered Douglas's most powerful evocation of the human abuse of nature to that date. She set most of her stories in south Florida because she believed the regional environment lent them an original quality. But even as she brought attention to the indigenous beauty that so enthralled her, nature remained a backdrop to a human story. In a similar vein, independent women frequent her stories, and yet a gendered sensibility never distinguishes her depictions of nature. Her style lent itself only slightly to that of "literary domestics," who illuminated maternal behavior and domestic life among plants and animals. She was influenced more so by conventional nature writers like William Henry Hudson, the Argentine-born author of *Green Mansions* to the writing of whose biography she later devoted twenty years.[21]

Two decades of writing short stories for magazines followed Douglas's departure from the newspaper in 1923 and served as a prelude to her most important literary achievement: *The Everglades: River of Grass*. She was in the midst of writing a novel—one about a south Florida homesteading couple who persevere against the "beauty and terror" of both nature and humanity—when she was approached by her friend Hervey Allen, editor of Rinehart Books' Rivers of America series. She had planned for the novel to serve as her transition into book writing. But a proposal from Allen to contribute to his series intervened, and she instead produced *River of Grass*. Enthusiastic reviews greeted its fall 1947 release, and it soon made the New York *Herald Tribune*'s "What America Is Reading" list. In the same newspaper, Marjorie Kinnan Rawlings recommended Douglas's book "to all readers concerned with . . . the great relations of man to nature." Harnett T. Kane wrote of Douglas in a review for the *Atlanta Journal*, "few Americans have ever written so sensitively, so skillfully, so magnificently of any part of their land." *River of Grass* changed not only her literary career; the process of creating the book transformed her life in unforeseen ways, and its publication lifted her to the crest of a wave that carried the country into a new era of environmental awareness.[22]

Douglas spent several years researching and writing *River of Grass,* consulting with experts in both the physical and social sciences. She relied heavily on the advice of Garald Parker of the U.S. Geological Survey, who described himself as a "geologist-biologist-hydrologist." At the time that he met Douglas, Parker was engaged in pioneering research into groundwater flow in south Florida; the limestone rock basin on which the Everglades floated; "soil-water-plant relationships"; and the ecological impact of development, agriculture, and drainage. His Everglades research would yield more than forty scientific papers and reports, some of which served as Douglas's introduction to ecology. She began to understand the Everglades as one large hydrological system that extended to Lake Okeechobee and beyond to the "lakes and marshes" of central Florida. Parker's work, Douglas wrote his wife years later, was "really the basis for a great deal of my knowledge of the area." It also influenced the structure of the natural history section of her book, which contains subtitles such as "The Grass," "The Water," "The Rock," and "Life on the Rock."[23]

When Douglas met Parker, ecology was still an inchoate field of study, its insights just beginning to take hold in the scientific community. Although Aldo Leopold's 1949 *A Sand County Almanac* is credited with shifting the gaze of the conservation community to ecological concepts, *River of Grass* appeared nearly two years earlier. The two books prompted readers to look at nature through new lenses, with Leopold advocating a revised land ethic and Douglas offering a redefinition of the Everglades. Douglas's plea for a more ecologically informed relationship is less explicit than Leopold's. She in fact devoted more space in her book to the human history of the Everglades than to natural history. Yet the regionalist philosophy that had long before shaped her own land ethic remained influential. Throughout her narrative, she encouraged readers to see the reciprocal exchanges between culture and nature as the basis for the integrity of place. In the case of the south Florida region, Douglas argued, using the language of ecology, "the old subtle balance . . . had been destroyed." Some students of her magnum opus have equated Douglas's open contempt for human "greed," "inertia," and "foolishness" as a tone that anticipated by fifteen years Rachel Carson's memorable statement in *Silent Spring* that the "'control of nature' is a phrase conceived in arrogance" and in the belief that "nature exists for the convenience of man." Although highly praised for its literary achievements, *River of Grass*'s greatest contribution is an ecological one. In prose that appealed to a general audience, Douglas portrayed the Everglades as the lifeblood of an entire regional ecosystem. She was in fact the first person to conceptualize the Everglades as a living river, rather than a fetid swamp, one that flowed from Lake Okeechobee to Florida Bay, around hummock islands and through cypress groves and saw grass. "That was," her friend and fellow writer Helen Muir declared, "her genius."[24]

The idea of a river of grass caught on. Douglas had the good fortune to have her book released a few weeks before President Truman dedicated Everglades National Park on December 6, 1947. Congress passed legislation in 1934 to create the park, but a lack of appropriations delayed its actual establishment for thirteen years. By the time of the dedication ceremony, Douglas's metaphor gave a new visual reference and meaning to the Everglades environment. Florida's senior senator, Claude Pepper, spoke of the "river of grass" in his speech at the ceremony, and newspapers soon adopted it to affirm the park's distinctiveness. Swamps had historically been devalued as wastelands in the Western mind, but rivers had always been attached with commercial or romantic importance. The river of grass was recognized for yet another reason. If Everglades National Park was unique in kind, it was equally so in origins. Not only was it the first national park to honor a wetland; it was the first established to preserve a "treasury of biological wealth," whereas with its predecessors, Congress sought to safeguard extraordinary geological features and a part of the national trust.[25]

One might reasonably conclude that the existence of the Everglades signaled a shifting in environmental thought evident in *A Sand County Almanac*. Yet developments unfolding at the time of the park dedication eventually showed that while one government agency was receptive to new ideas, another remained wedded to the traditional policy of nature control. After a massive September hurricane forced the waters of Lake Okeechobee over its rim and surrounding levees, causing untold damage in agriculture and personal property, nearly every county in Florida drafted resolutions demanding adequate flood control. Letters from voters concurring with this demand poured into the offices of Florida's U.S. senators. Pointing out that more than 2,000 people had died in Everglades floods since 1900, the *Miami Herald* proclaimed that the "Everglades remain untamed." Soon after the 1947 hurricane, the Army Corps of Engineers announced a comprehensive plan for flood control and water conservation. Even the author of *River of Grass* endorsed the need to triumph over rebellious nature. Her conversion from a progressive conservationist to an ecologically enlightened environmentalist was not yet complete. In later years, Douglas described corps engineers as men with lingering childhood fetishes for playing with mud, but in 1948 she put her faith in their project. An unpublished article of hers hailed it as "second in all our history only to the majestic scope of the Panama Canal."[26]

Ten years later, after settling into a productive career of book writing, Douglas published an exhaustively researched history of hurricanes, a phenomenon of nature that humans had failed to control and, as she made clear, one that shaped the course of human history. *Hurricane* (1958) was the third of ten fiction and nonfiction books that succeeded *River of Grass*. Her life during that period remained busy. In the late 1940s, she served as an officer and president of a "slum" clearance committee, which forced a change in local sanitation codes. In 1950, she became a charter member of the first American Civil Liberties Union chapter organized in the South, serving a short stint as its director. She assumed the editorship of the University of Miami Press for a brief period and then tried her hand at running her own press, which she called Hurricane House. When she was seventy-six, the Wellesley College Alumnae association awarded her a fellowship to begin research on the W. H. Hudson biography. By the late 1960s, she had reached a point in life in which she still felt the desire, but not the pressure, to publish.[27]

Just as she was slowing her gait, however, public awareness of environmental problems was escalating. Ecological disasters as well as industrial air and water pollution, by no means new problems, were exacerbated by modern technologies and a status-oriented consumer society that within two generations would nearly double in population and grow increasingly materialistic. In counteraction to its own consumption-growth tendencies, that same society spawned new national and grassroots organizations, typically white and middle class, that invested their energy in improving standards of public health. Activists still sought an aesthetically pleasing environment, but now they framed it as a manifestation of healthy living. One goal could not logically be separated from the other; nor could the urban from the extra-urban, or social justice from environmental abuse. Leopold and Carson tried to convey the ideas of the human-nature nexus and the seamless web of life. Even so, the older, well-established conservation organizations, such as the Sierra Club, National Audubon Society, and National Wildlife Federation, were slow to range out beyond wilderness preservation until a broadening constituency of invigorated citizens forced their hand. The measurable impact of local citizens' groups—by virtue of their size, insufficient finances, virtually all-volunteer staffs, and ephemeral nature—was limited. Successful outcomes were generally, though not always, left to national groups, which were turning professional, growing exponentially, and acquiring new sources of funding. The grassroots organization that Douglas founded would prove to be exceptional by turning a local issue into one of national importance.[28]

A four-year drought in the Everglades, continued ecological insults, and bureaucratic bungling beckoned Douglas's complete conversion to modern environmentalist strategies and goals. Long dry spells were part of Everglades history, and for centuries the indigenous flora and fauna had survived natural extremes. But in the 1960s, as nature writer and scholar Wallace Stegner observed firsthand, in words reminiscent of *River of Grass,* "inertia, conflict of interests, competing land uses, natural disasters, and human mismanagement have combined to place an incomparable million-acre preserve in danger of imminent extinction." Post–World War II population expansion pressured the Everglades on every flank. "You were just hurled along by the force and impetus of this population [growth]," said Douglas of its haste as it approached 6 million by century's end. The Army Corps of Engineers kept the population dry with its flood-control project, which resulted in the construction of some 720 miles of levees, 1,000 miles of canals, and 200 water-control devices. The latest phase of the project converted the meandering Kissimmee River, the main watershed artery to Lake Okeechobee, into a formless drainage canal. The labyrinthine system gave state bureaucrats at the South Florida Water Management District control over crucial aspects of Everglades ecology. By decade's end, the project rivaled the Tennessee Valley Authority in size, spiraled to $1 billion in costs, and continued without a planned completion. One of the corps' creations was the 1,000-square-mile Everglades Agricultural Area (EAA), which was almost twice the original size of the national park. After the drought hit, the water management district diverted water to the EAA that would otherwise feed the Everglades and the national park, while the corps simultaneously pumped billions of gallons of Lake Okeechobee water to the ocean. Outside of rain, the park received no hydration for four years, and yet the EAA never went without. Plans for oil exploration added to the region's problems. After the Park Service and environmentalists won an allotment of water for the park, they also managed to keep petroleum companies at bay. Environmentalists then turned their attention to an aggressively lobbied proposal to locate a jetport in the middle of the Everglades.[29]

A loose coalition with no organizational base, Everglades environmentalists also turned to Douglas in 1969. They believed that her credibility as the popular author of *River of Grass* and as a longtime resident of south Florida would provide a "formidable force" in their battle against the jetport. They also hoped that she would attract support from influential citizens' groups, such as women's clubs. To help, Douglas created Friends of the Everglades (FOE), organizing chapters in the counties surrounding the Everglades and running the operations with secretaries from her home office full-time. FOE quickly launched a public-education campaign against the jetport. Concurrently, future Earth Day founder Senator Gaylord Nelson leaked a Department of the Interior report predicting that the jetport would literally kill the Everglades, and former Interior Secretary Stewart Udall, hired as a consultant by the Dade County Port Authority, recommended its relocation. The Nixon administration responded by withdrawing funding for the project. The defeat of the jetport was FOE's first victory in its larger mission to undo the damage of the corps and agribusiness.[30]

Douglas brought grassroots organizational experience, personal historical knowledge, and the moral authority of a pioneer Floridian to the new age of activism. Within a few years, FOE posted nearly 3,000 members from thirty-eight states and provided an anchor for a number of environmental coalitions. The accumulated problems of fifty years and an enlarged capacity to subdue nature had taken their toll on the Everglades. All combined to render old progressive philosophies obsolete if not also responsible for the current state of things. "Conservation is now a dead word," Douglas declared in 1982. "You can't conserve what you haven't got. That's why we [FOE] are for restoration." Douglas was expressing a central concept in a new age of environmentalism that included Superfund cleanups, forest restoration, resource recovery, and predator reintroduction. Convincing the public and policymakers to "repair" the Everglades, as FOE expressed the concept, required not just educating them in the fundamentals of ecology but backing such a plan with predictive scientific data.[31]

Douglas teamed up with arguably the best-equipped scientist in Florida to translate those data into policy change. A professor of applied ecology at the University of Miami, Arthur Marshall had been a fellow protagonist with Douglas in the jetport struggle. Twenty-nine years her junior, he belonged to a generation of politically minded Florida scientists who found role models in Leopold and Carson and who in the 1970s were instrumental in using the authority of their research and knowledge to prevent a number of ecological blunders. Their own spiritual forbears in Florida history were naturalists, including Charles Torrey Simpson, John Kunkel Small, and Thomas Barbour, who in the early twentieth century were predicting environmental doom in works with titles such as *From Eden to Sahara, That Vanishing Eden,* and "In Memoriam." An inspiration herself, Douglas gave the last chapter in *River of Grass* the foreboding title "The Eleventh Hour." A generation later, Marshall earned the sobriquet "prophet" for creating predictive models that accurately determined the fate of ecosystems. In 1983, he gave the Everglades twenty years to survive.[32]

While his naturalist predecessors lamented the eventual loss of a wilderness conceptually detached from the city, Marshall saw the urban and extraurban environments as a connected system. The mushrooming city landscape had obviously imposed stresses on the Everglades, but the altered hinterland in turn affected urban life. Marshall spoke in terms of a large-scale ecosystem of water, wildlife, and weather. Tying everything together was his "rain machine" thesis, which attributed south Florida's extraordinary droughts and microclimatic changes to decreased evaporation resulting from wetlands drainage and urban sprawl. Just as she had depended on Garald Parker three decades earlier, Douglas looked to Marshall to teach her about the most current findings in ecology. Having argued in 1947 that the city was dependent upon the "store of water in the permeable rock" of the Everglades, she latched onto his "rain machine" thesis, and FOE published a pamphlet entitled "Who Knows the Rain—The Nature and Origin of Rainfall in South Florida." She also preached the gospel of ecological doom in countless press interviews; before regulatory boards and the state legislature; and in talks to citizens' groups, university audiences, and women's clubs. If current policy persists, went her refrain, the Everglades will dry up and south Florida will transform from a humid to an arid region.[33]

Douglas found a seemingly strange bedfellow in another person, Johnny Jones, head of the Florida Wildlife Federation. A master plumber by vocation, Jones possessed an artisan's understanding of the corps' colossal Everglades system. By avocation, he was an avid hunter whose hobby displeased Douglas. For more than a century, women had been trying to save animals from various enemies, including hunters. Douglas had been an early participant in that tradition and helped usher it into the contemporary movement by adding the alligator, Everglades deer, and Florida panther to her perpetual concern for wading birds. Heir to a parallel tradition, Jones presided over a state chapter of one of the older conservation groups, linked to an early faction of American conservation when sportsmen organized for game preserves and incidentally wilderness protection; at the same time, he personified the diverse interests in contemporary environmentalism. Like Douglas, Jones understood the ecological significance of wildlife habitat, but he also believed, for example, in hunting deer to reduce their population in distressed environments for the benefit of the animals and their habitat. Douglas, by contrast, distrusted wildlife management just as she did water management, arguing that harvesting deer reduced the principal food source for the endangered panther and tampered with natural ecological balances. Deep down, she knew that little remained natural about ecological balances in the Everglades since they were a controlled environment, and she respected Jones as an expert lobbyist. He and his organization came with a successful track record, which included sponsorship of the state's endangered species act and an environmentally sensitive lands-purchase law.[34]

Jones formed a third in a triumvirate with Douglas and Marshall. They first joined forces after Marshall created Water!—a coalition organization of fifteen citizens' groups. With Marshall providing the scientific research and knowledge, Jones conducting behind-the-scenes lobbying, and Douglas chairing the organization and generating publicity and disseminating educational information, the three worked to implement the so-called Marshall plan, an eighteen-point blueprint for the repair of the Everglades. Their first major triumph came in 1976 when lawmakers passed a bill, written mostly by Jones, mandating the development of measures to restore the oxbow flow of the Kissimmee River. In 1983, Governor Bob Graham unveiled the ambitious $100 million "Save Our Everglades" program to "reestablish the natural ecological functions of the Everglades." Soon afterward, he and Douglas shoveled Kissimmee River dirt in a ceremony kicking off the initial phase of dechannelization.[35]

Not everyone celebrated the moment. Wealthy and politically powerful sugar planters, known collectively as Big Sugar, put up a solid wall of resistance to cleaning up Lake Okeechobee and restoring the natural flow of the Everglades. Sugar plantations consumed nearly 500,000 acres in the EAA, forming an artificial and polluted barrier between Lake Okeechobee and the Everglades. The water conservation end of the corps' flood-control project gave priority to agricultural interests, and for years Big Sugar and cattle ranchers dominated the board of the water management district. In 1979, FOE and the Florida Wildlife Federation sued the water management district and the Florida Sugar Cane League to stop the backpumping of fertilizer- and pesticide-laden water into the nearly eutrophic Lake Okeechobee, the same water that flowed into the Everglades. The suit was just one battle in a pro-tracted war in which Douglas made herself into a "public relations night-mare" for Big Sugar, a war to which Douglas would never see a victorious end. Eighteen months before her death, for example, Big Sugar spent $35 million to defeat a constitutional amendment mandating a one-cent-per-pound sugar tax to fund the cleanup of the Everglades system.[36]

If Big Sugar was willing to exploit nature in the blind pursuit of profit, Douglas recognized that it was equally indiscriminate with farm labor. Al-though environmental concerns dominated her public agenda after forming FOE, she never lost sight of the kind of social issues that had shaped her conservation views decades earlier. Big Sugar was notorious for exposing its underpaid labor, mostly West Indian immigrants, to harsh and dangerous working and living conditions. Douglas had done research in the West Indies for a 1952 *Saturday Review* article, and she saw firsthand the abject conditions of the working people in many countries. She blamed those conditions in part on U.S. government import protections that eliminated foreign competi-tion while generating a pool of cheap offshore labor. Just as trade tariffs hurt European economies after World War I, import measures—tightened after Fidel Castro took control of sugar-rich Cuba—crippled the economically im-portant sugar industry in Caribbean countries. In search of work, West Indi-ans came to cut cane in south Florida. In 1947, Douglas prefigured the latter-day concepts of environmental justice when in *River of Grass* she related the white aggression against Everglades Indians of the nineteenth century with the destruction of nature and the twentieth-century subjugation of migrant farmworkers, mostly black, with the commercial reclamation of Everglades wetlands. The experience of cane workers was an all too familiar link to the earlier history. Douglas lent her name and support to Florida Rural Legal Services, an organization that was dedicated to protecting the welfare of mi-grant farm laborers, particularly sugarcane workers in the inland town of Belle Glade. In a 1985 letter to Governor Bob Graham, urging him to estab-lish a committee to survey the conditions of migrant workers, Douglas wrote, "I feel greatly at fault in not having made a loud public protest about Belle Glade before this."[37]

Douglas did, as she always had, make a loud roar on the issue of women's rights. Not long after she organized Friends of the Everglades, the former suffragist also emerged as an outspoken champion of the Equal Rights Amendment, testifying before the state legislature for its adoption fifty-nine years after her first visit to Tallahassee on behalf of suffrage. Then as later, environmental conditions and social welfare were for her two parts of the same agenda. In a 1974 speech to the American Association of University Women, in which she endorsed the ERA, Douglas could have easily been speaking fifty years earlier when she told her audience to think of the health of the environment—its air and water quality—as they would think of the cleanliness of their home. "The problem of the environment is the extension of good housekeeping of the thinking woman." Consistent with modern feminist thought and the message of many national women's liberation organizations, the idea of Earth as home reflected a belief in an enlightened sex rather than an endorsement of the domesticated-woman stereotype. Douglas did not go as far as radical ecofeminists and equate the treatment of nature with the male treatment of women. But she believed that as a historically dominated group, women possessed a commonsense understanding of qualities of life, whether it be human or nonhuman life, and the interconnectedness of those qualities. She was surrounded by women who sustained the unbroken thread to earlier generations that cared about the environment and sensed the human-nature nexus. Reminiscent of the earlier days, the conservation department of the Coral Gables Woman's Club was a co-litigant in the 1979 suit brought against Big Sugar. At any given time, most of the officers of the FOE were female, and when Douglas stepped down at age 100 as president, her successor was a woman.[38]

As for the rights of nature, Douglas never saw the advantage of crusading for that reason alone. She was biophilic but not biocentric. "My opponents accuse me of caring more about birds and fish than people, but they can't prove that," she declared. She simply believed in balance. "If we can save water for people, we can save it for the birds and fish, too." She understood the health of the environment and all its creatures as a barometer for the physical—as well as the moral—well-being of humanity. Like other middle-class Americans who provided the mass support for the contemporary environmental movement, Douglas was a creature of suburban living, one who had always refrained from communing closely with the wild. She hardly ever visited the Everglades. "To be a friend of the Everglades is not necessarily to spend time wandering around out there," she wrote in her autobiography, when she was ninety-six. "It's too buggy, too wet, too generally inhospitable." Yet like Marshall, she recognized that urban life was inextricably linked to the extra-urban, that Miami's existence was dependent on its rural hinterland. As go the Everglades, protected or destroyed, so go the sustaining elements of human life.[39]

Jack E. Davis

Douglas's own life was extraordinary. When she died in 1998, she left a legacy that others proceeded to build upon. But she never accepted the illusion of victory. "No one is satisfied with their life's work," she was quoted saying the week of her 104th birthday. "There is always the need to carry on. The most important thing is to prepare competent people to follow you." The future of the Everglades indeed remained uncertain even after President Clinton signed the highly touted $7.8 billion Comprehensive Everglades Restoration Act in December 2000. The Kissimmee River had not yet been fully reconverted; an $88 million restoration project that Congress approved in 1989 for the eastern section of Everglades National Park remained unfinished; and while one state agency spent millions of dollars to remove phosphorous berm from Lake Okeechobee, the water management district continued backpumping agricultural runoff into it. Although Interior Secretary Bruce Babbitt claimed that the signing of the 2000 Restoration Act opened an "entirely new chapter in conservation history," *Audubon* magazine speculated that the project had "no better chance of being launched than any of the previous attempts to save the Everglades." Douglas was no longer alive, but her organization issued a resolution criticizing the project in part because it was, as Babbitt called it, conservation. It ensured the continued existence of the EAA, gave too much discretion to the corps and the water management district, and, in essence, left humans in control of nature.[40]

Douglas's place in the history of American environmentalism is less ambiguous than the future of the Everglades. She lived and illuminated the flux of history in the course of a century. Evident in her own life experiences is the vitality of the female dimension in environmental history. She was a product of women's early realm of organized activism, which included wilderness protection and a healthy urban environment. She was not so much a prophet as a messenger, who delivered the prevailing ideas of conservation to her newspaper readers and sounded in her short stories the warning of wildlife destruction. She navigated the changing currents in twentieth-century environmentalism and exhorted others to do the same, first with *River of Grass* and then as a grassroots leader with national visibility. She synthesized into activism the lessons of the emergent field of ecological science, all the while demonstrating her own conversion. If conservation and wildlife protection—the dominant ideas in early environmentalism—once informed her consciousness, ecology eventually became her context. Nature and humans were no longer distinct but rather part of one expansive, interconnected system. The urban environment, that of human species, was ecologically bound with the extra-urban environment, that of non-human species.

When Douglas died, the environmental consciousness of Americans was coming around to this way of thinking, and Douglas, whose life was a bridge across two eras, had helped force this turn. Specifically, her early life provided the personal building blocks that gave form to her values, beliefs, and activities of her senior years, and along the way she discarded that which was no longer useful, kept that which remained pertinent, and adopted that which fit new purposes. In a parallel truth, early-twentieth-century conservation impulses, in all their varied dimensions, were a necessary thrust for the American transition to contemporary environmentalism.

Notes

1. "'It's Never Too Late for Anything,'" undated *Miami News* clipping in folder 11, box 39, Marjory Stoneman Douglas Papers, Archives and Special Collections Department, Otto G. Richter Library, University of Miami, Coral Gables (hereafter cited as MSD); "The Elocutioner," undated *Miami Herald* clipping in MSD, folder 12, box 39; interview with Joe Podgor, August 10, 2000. A similar rendition of this event is found in perhaps the most insightful popular article on Douglas and the Everglades, by Steve Yates, "Marjory Stoneman Douglas and the Glades Crusade," *Audubon* 85 (March 1983): 112–27.

2. *USA Today,* May 17, 1998; *Miami Herald,* May 14–15, 1998; *New York Times,* May 15, 1998; Stephen W. Byers, "Don't Mess with Her Wetlands," *New York Times Magazine,* January 3, 1999, 46; Valerie Gladstone, "Marjory Stoneman Douglas," *Ms,* January/February 1989, 68–70.

3. Early environmental historians such as Samuel P. Hays and Roderick Nash tended to emphasize discontinuities between the early conservation movement and the modern environmental movement. But more recently, scholars have leaned toward the position of Robert Gottlieb, who has argued that the two eras are more closely related than historians originally observed. See Samuel P. Hays, "From Conservation to Environment: Environmental Politics in the United States since World War II," *Environmental Review* 6 (fall 1982), 14–29; Roderick Nash, *American Environmentalism: Readings in Conservation History,* 3rd ed. (New York: McGraw-Hill, 1990), 187–89; Robert Gottlieb, *Forcing the Spring: The Transformation of the American Environmental Movement* (Washington, D.C.: Island Press, 1993).

4. Raymond A. Mohl, "Miami: The Ethnic Cauldron," in *Sunbelt Cities: Politics and Growth since World War II,* ed. Richard M. Bernard and Bradley R. Rice (Austin: University of Texas Press, 1983), 59; Edward N. Akin, *Flagler: Rockefeller Partner and Florida Baron* (Gainesville: University Press of Florida, 1992); Marjory Stoneman Douglas, "When You and I Were Young, Miami," *Tropic Magazine* (*Miami Herald*), November 5, 1967, 16–22, 36; Jack E. Davis, ed., *The Wide Brim: Early Poems and Ponderings of*

Marjory Stoneman Douglas (Gainesville: University Press of Florida, 2001), 57. The best narrative of Douglas's life is her 1987 autobiography, written with John Rothchild, *Marjory Stoneman Douglas: Voice of the River* (Sarasota, Fla.: Pineapple Press, 1987).

5. J. E. Dovell, "The Everglades—Florida's Frontier," pt. 1, *Economic Leaflets* 6 (April 1947): 1; William Cronon, *Nature's Metropolis: Chicago and the Great West* (New York: W. W. Norton, 1993), 5–19, 23–259, and generally; J. E. Dovell, "The Everglades—Florida's Frontier," pt. 1, *Economic Leaflets* 6 (April 1947); Christopher F. Meindl, "Past Perceptions of the Great American Wetland: Florida's Everglades during the Early Twentieth Century," *Environmental History* 5 (July 2000): 381, 385–90. Records of many of the early land companies can be found on the "Reclaiming the Everglades" website, produced by the Publication of Archival Library and Museum Materials, State University System of Florida, http://susdl.fcla.edu.

6. Dovell, "The Everglades—Florida's Frontier," pt. 1; D. LeBaron Perrine, "The Remaking of Florida," *Tropic Magazine*, February 1926, 185–199; *Miami Herald*, May 25, 1930; Mark S. Foster, *Castles in the Sand: The Life and Times of Carl Graham Fisher* (Gainesville: University Press of Florida, 2000), 136–71; Akin, *Flagler*, 112–13; Helen Muir, *Miami U.S.A.* (Gainesville: University Press of Florida, 2000), 47–53, 95–103; Douglas, "When You and I Were Young, Miami."

7. Douglas, "When You and I Were Young, Miami," 19–20. On women's clubs and women and progressive reform, see Carolyn Merchant, "Women of the Progressive Conservation Movement, 1900–1916," *Environmental Review* 8 (spring 1984): 57–86; Dorothy Schneider and Carl J. Schneider, *American Women in the Progressive Era, 1900–1920* (New York: Anchor Books, 1993); Karen J. Blair, *The Clubwoman as Feminist: True Womanhood Redefined, 1868–1914* (New York: Holmes and Meier Publishers, 1980), 83, 103–6; Cameron Binkley, "'No Better Heritage Than Living Trees'— Women's Clubs and Early Conservation in Humboldt County," *Western Historical Quarterly* 33 (summer 2002): 179–203; Glenda Riley, *Women and Nature: Saving the 'Wild' West* (Lincoln: University of Nebraska Press, 1999), 97–113. Historians once overstated pollution concerns as distinctive to the contemporary environmental movement, in part as a result of overlooking the early activities of women. In recent years, scholars have offered a corrective to that oversight. See, for example, David Stradling, *Smokestacks and Progress: Environmentalists, Engineers, and Air Quality in America, 1881–1951* (Baltimore: Johns Hopkins University Press, 1999), 52–55, 59, 93; Suellen M. Hoy, "'Municipal Housekeeping': The Role of Women in Improving Urban Sanitation Practices, 1880–1917," in *Pollution and Reform in American Cities, 1870–1930*, ed. Martin V. Melosi (Austin: University of Texas Press, 1980), 173–98; Maureen A. Flanagan, "The City Profitable, The City Livable: Environmental Policy, Gender, and Power in Chicago in the 1910s," *Journal of Urban History* 22 (January 1996): 163–90; Harold L. Platt, "Jane Addams and the Ward Boss Revisited: Class, Politics, and Public Health in Chicago, 1890–1930," *Environmental History* 5 (April 2000): 194–222.

8. Lucy Worthington Blackman, *The Florida Federation of Women's Clubs, 1895–1939* (Jacksonville, Fla.: Southern Historical Publishing Associates, 1939), 21, 33–34; Mrs. W. S. Jennings, "Royal Palm State Park," *Tropic Magazine*, April 1916, 10–16, 26; Mi-

ami Herald, November 24, 1916; C. B. Reynolds, "Royal Palm State Park," *Mr. Foster's Travel Magazine* 6 (January 1919), n.p.; May Mann Jennings to Mrs. M. L. Stanley, April 30, 1917, May Mann Jennings Papers (hereafter cited as MMJ), box 10, Special Collections, George Smathers Libraries, University of Florida, Gainesville (hereafter cited as GSL); telegram, Bryan Jennings to May Mann Jennings, June 2, 1915, MMJ, box 10; Linda D. Vance, *May Mann Jennings: Florida's Genteel Activist* (Gainesville: University Presses of Florida, 1985), 54–60, 118–21, 125–26.

9. Lucy Worthington Blackman, *The Florida Audubon Society, 1900–1935* (n.p., n.d.), 6–8, 20, 45; Robin W. Doughty, *Feather Fashions and Bird Preservation: A Study in Nature Protection* (Berkeley and Los Angeles: University of California Press, 1975); Mark Derr, *Some Kind of Paradise: A Chronicle of Man and the Land in Florida* (New York: William Morrow and Company, 1989), 137–40; Marjory Stoneman Douglas, "Wings," *Saturday Evening Post,* March 14, 1931, 10–11, 74, 77–78; Oliver H. Orr Jr., *Saving American Birds: T. Gilbert Pearson and the Founding of the Audubon Movement* (Gainesville: University Press of Florida, 1992), 30–31, 47–51, 124–25, 154–55, 237; Harry A. Kersey, *Pelts, Plumes, and Hides: White Traders among the Seminole Indians, 1870–1930* (Gainesville: University Presses of Florida, 1975), 36–37, 65, 76–77, 81, 117, 131–33.

10. James C. Clark, "Florida's Limits on Women," *Florida Magazine (Orlando Sentinel),* May 20, 1990, 25; *Orlando Sentinel Star,* November 9 1975; *Miami Herald,* December 30, 1922, February 18, 1974, August 25, 1976, November 11, 1985; letter to May Mann Jennings, December 2, 1917, MMJ, Correspondence file, Sept.-Dec. 1917, Jan.-Feb. 1918, box 12; Letter to May Mann Jennings, December 2, 1917, MMJ, Correspondence file, Sept.-Dec. 1917, Jan.-Feb. 1918, box 12; Douglas, "When You and I Were Young, Miami"; Marjory Stoneman Douglas to Dorothy Vaile, July 18, 1985, MSD, folder 78, box 44.

11. Douglas, *Voice of the River,* 37, 76; Marjory Stoneman Douglas card, Personnel Files, Hazel Braugh Record Center and Archives, American Red Cross, Falls Church, Virginia; Marjory Stoneman Douglas, "Years I Have Seen: A Prologue," MSD, Florida, Prologue folder, box 2; Marjory Stoneman Douglas, "Cities Face Their Slums," *Ladies Home Journal,* October 1950, 23, 224–25; Mercedes M. Randall, *Improper Bostonian: Emily Greene Balch* (New York: Twayne Publishers, 1964); Cathy Shaw, "The Friend of the Everglades," *Wellesley Magazine* (summer 1983): 15.

12. Merchant, "Women of the Progressive Conservation Movement," 80; Vera Norwood, *Made from This Earth: American Women and Nature* (Chapel Hill: University of North Carolina Press, 1993), 29–30; Hoy, "'Municipal Housekeeping,'" 194; *Miami Herald,* December 2, 1922, December 27, 1922, March 10, 1923; J. M. Willson to J. E. Mosely, October 18, 1928, "Reclaiming the Everglades"; Marjory Stoneman Douglas, "Alumnae Achievement Award," 31. Three good examples of such stories are "Women and Birds" (unpublished story); "Pineland," *Saturday Evening Post,* August 15, 1925; and "Wind before Morning," *Saturday Evening Post,* June 8, 1935.

13. *Miami Herald,* January 29, 1923, March 8, 1923, May 11, 1923; "The Remarkable Marjory Stoneman Douglas," *Miamian,* September 1970, 62; Douglas, untitled manuscript, 29; Stanley K. Schultz, *Constructing Urban Culture: American Cities and City*

Planning, 1800–1920 (Philadelphia, 1989); Diana Balmori, Diane Kostial McGuire, and Eleanor M. McPeck, *Beatrix Farrand's American Landscapes: Her Gardens and Campuses* (Sagaponack, N.Y.: Sagapress, 1985); Norwood, *Made from the Earth,* 110–11, 114–17; Douglas, "When You and I Were Young, Miami." On the City Beautiful movement, generally, see William H. Wilson, *The City Beautiful Movement* (Baltimore: Johns Hopkins University Press, 1989). On Addams, Dock, Hamilton, and other women urban reformers, see, Platt, "Jane Addams and the Ward Boss Revisited"; Christopher C. Sellers, *Hazards of the Job: From Industrial Disease to Environmental Health Science* (Chapel Hill: University of North Carolina Press, 1997), 69–106; Wilson, *The City Beautiful Movement,* 44, 57–58, 126–46.

14. Douglas, untitled manuscript, 31–32; Marjory Stoneman Douglas, *The Everglades: River of Grass* (Marietta, Ga.: Mockingbird Books, 1992), 134–35; Marjory Stoneman Douglas, *Florida: The Long Frontier* (New York: Harper and Row, 1967), 262; Lydia Allen DeVilbiss to Marjory Stoneman Douglas, December 7, 1947, MSD, folder 42, box 42; *Miami Herald,* October 30, 1922, November 11, 1922. On the subject of regionalism, see Merrill Jensen, ed., *Regionalism in America* (Madison: University of Wisconsin Press, 1965); Daniel Joseph Singal, *The War Within: From Victorian to Modernist Thought in the South, 1919–1945* (Chapel Hill: University of North Carolina Press, 1982), 148–52.

15. Marjory Stoneman Douglas, "The Everglades Remembered," *Florida Naturalist* (December 1983), 8–9, 15; *Miami Herald,* January 3, 1921; Mary Schmich, "Our Lady of the 'Glades," *Chicago Tribune* clipping, MSD, folder 11, box 39; Gottlieb, *Forcing the Spring,* 212–18.

16. On the subject of progressive conservation, see Hays, *Conservation and the Gospel of Efficiency.*

17. *Miami Herald,* October 12, 1922, March 20, 1923, March 30, 1923, April 12, 1923; Douglas, *River of Grass,* 129–31, 176, 260; *Exotic Invaders of the Everglades,* MSD, report, folder 72, box 28. Douglas remained a lifelong supporter of Fairchild's work, and in 1937, she published a pamphlet supporting the public purchase and preservation of Fairchild's gardens. See Marjory Stoneman Douglas, *An Argument for a Botanical Garden in South Florida to be Called the Fairchild Tropical Garden* (Coral Gables, Fla.: Craftsmen of Kells Press, 1937).

18. *Miami Herald,* April 16, 1923, April 18, 1923; Thomas E. Will, "Conservation in Earnest," Thomas E. Will Papers, box 33, Special Collections, GSL; Charlton W. Tebeau, *Man in the Everglades: 2000 Years of Human History in the Everglades National Park* (Miami: University of Miami Press, 1968), 21–22.

19. Extant documents are unclear about how many people and who served on the Tropic Everglades National Park Association.

20. Ernest F. Coe, "The Proposed Tropic Everglades National Park Location in the Cape Sable Region of South Florida," October 25, 1928, "Reclaiming the Everglades"; Tebeau, *Man in the Everglades,* 166–81; Vance, *May Mann Jennings,* 80–86, 88, 90–93, 112, 114–15, 117–18, 130–31; Sally Vicker, "Ruth Bryan Owen: Florida's First Congresswoman and Lifetime Activist," *Florida Historical Quarterly* 77 (spring 1999): 466–67; Douglas, *Florida,* 282; Marjory Stoneman Douglas, "The Forgotten Man Who Saved

the Everglades," *Audubon* 73 (September 1971), 79–96; Franklin D. Roosevelt, Executive Order No. 6883, October 22, 1934, Florida State Library, Tallahassee. On women and national parks, see Polly Welts Kaufman, *National Parks and the Woman's Voice: A History* (Albuquerque: University of New Mexico Press, 1996); and Riley, *Women and Nature*, 17, 75, 83, 101, 109–10, 126, 128, 145–47, 163, 157.

21. Douglas, "Wings"; Marjory Stoneman Douglas, "Plumes," *Saturday Evening Post*, June 14, 1930, 8–9, 112, 114, 117–18, 121; Marjory Stoneman Douglas, "A Flight of Ibis," *Saturday Evening Post*, December 21, 1935, 12–13, 69–70, 72; Mildred Campbell to Literary Editor, July 30, 1930, MSD, folder 46, box 30; Kevin M. McCarthy, "How Marjory Stoneman Douglas Crusaded for Southern Florida in Her Short Works," special issue, *Journal of Florida Literature* 8 (1997), 15–21. On women nature writers, see Norwood, *Made from the Earth*, 25–53, 172–208; Rachel Stein, *Shifting the Ground: American Women Writers' Revision of Nature, Gender, and Race* (Charlottesville: University Press of Virginia, 1997), 4–5, 14–15, 24, 26–31, 34–52, 117–22; Judith Boice, *Mother Earth: Through the Eyes of Women Photographers and Writers* (San Francisco: Sierra Club Books, 1992); Thomas S. Edwards and Elizabeth A. De Wolfe, eds., *Such News of the Land: U.S. Women Nature Writers* (Hanover, N.H.: University Press of New England, 2001).

22. Marjory Stoneman Douglas, *Road to the Sun* (New York: Rinehart, 1952); Melissa Walker, "Marjory Stoneman Douglas," in *American Nature Writers*, ed. John Elder (New York: Charles Scribner's Sons, 1996), 240; Douglas, *River of Grass*; Agreement, Farrar and Rinehart and Marjory Stoneman Douglas, November 23, 1943, MSD, folder 110, box 47; Harnett T. Kane, review of *The Everglades: River of Grass*, MSD, folder 48, box 42; *New York Herald Tribune*, December 7, 1947; Marjory Stoneman Douglas to Marjorie Kinnan Rawlings, December 8, 1947, Marjorie Kinnan Rawlings Papers, Special Collections, GSL, Douglas, Marjory—ALS to MKR, 1947, December 8 folder.

23. Abbreviated Resume, Garald G. Parker Sr., Garald G. Parker Collection (hereafter cited as GGP), Special Collections, University of South Florida Library, University of South Florida, Tampa; Garald G. Parker, "Truth about the Everglades," unpublished paper (n.d.), MSD, folder 27, box 25; Marjory Stoneman Douglas to Mrs. Parker, MSD, folder 21, box 40; Douglas, *River of Grass*, 8–17.

24. Matt Schudel, "Marjory's Place," *Orlando Sentinel Sunshine*, May 2, 1999; Douglas, *River of Grass*, 291, 292, 298–99; Michael P. Branch, "Writing the Swamp: Marjory Stoneman Douglas and *The Everglades: River of Grass*," in *Such News of the Land*, 128, 132–33; Helen Muir, interview by the author, March 11, 1999; Rachel Carson, *Silent Spring* (New York: Houghton Mifflin Company, 1987), 297; Nash, *Wilderness and the American Mind*, 182–99.

25. *Zephyrhills News*, June 27, 1947; dedication ceremony for Everglades National Park, Everglades, Florida, December 6, 1947, program and addresses, MMJ, box 22; "Glistening River," undated newspaper clipping, series 201, folder 1, box 35, Claude Pepper Papers, Claude Pepper Library, Florida State University Library, Tallahassee; "A Great Day for Florida," undated newspaper clipping, Claude Pepper Library, series 201, folder 1, box 35. On the history of the American image of wetlands, see Ann Vileisis, *Discovering the Unknown Landscape: A History of America's Wetlands* (Washing-

ton, D.C.: Island Press, 1997); on the Everglades specifically, see Meindl, "Past Perceptions of the Great American Wetland," 378–95.

26. *Miami Herald*, September 18–27, 1947, November 2, 1947; Marjory Stoneman Douglas, "The Everglades Face the Future," *Trailways Magazine* 9 (fall 1944), 9–10, 26, 28; Marjory Stoneman Douglas, "What Are They Doing to the Everglades?" unpublished manuscript, Marjory Stoneman Douglas, Reclaiming the Everglades; "Estimate of Agricultural Losses in Broward County from Storms of September 21 and October 5, 1948 and Resulting High Waters," Spessard Holland Papers, Special Collections, GSL, Flood Control Permanent folder, box 287 (see same folder for letters and resolutions supporting flood control); Department of the Army Corps of Engineers, Public Notice, December 31, 1947, and A. G. Mathews, chief engineer, Florida State Board of Conservation, report, March 10, 1949, Claude Pepper Papers, series 201, folder 1, box 34 (see series 201, folder 11, box 33 in Claude Pepper Papers for letters and resolutions supporting flood control). Even the National Audubon Society supported the flood-control plan: John H. Banks to Spessard Holland, July 12, 1948, Spessard Holland Papers, Flood Control Hearing folder, box 287.

27. Burt (*Reader's Digest*) to Marjory Stoneman Douglas, July 2, 1953, Marjory Stoneman Douglas Papers, box 2, Elizabeth Virrick Collection, Historical Museum of South Florida, Miami, Florida (hereafter cited as EVC); Marjory Stoneman Douglas, "Slum Clearance, Community Style," unpublished article manuscript, n.d., EVC, box 2; Marjory Stoneman Douglas and Elizabeth Virrick, "People against Slums," book prospectus, n.d., EVC, box 2; List, Organizations List—Dade County Individuals Belonging to Various Groups folder, box 12, Florida Legislative Investigation Committee Collection, Florida State Archives, Tallahassee; Greater Miami Chapter, American Civil Liberties Union "Dear Friend" circular, signed by Arnold M. Greenfield, n.d., Publications—ACLU folder, box 17, Florida Legislative Investigation Committee Collection; application for charter, American Civil Liberties Union of Greater Miami, Dade County, Florida, July 22, 1955, American Civil Liberties Union of Greater Miami, 1955–1959, American Civil Liberties Union of Florida Records, Special Collections, GSL, folder 1, box 1; "The Winner of the Horton-Hallowell Fellowship," *Wellesley Alumnae Magazine* (January 1967), 32, 38. For a history of the black experience in Miami, see Marvin Dunn, *Black Miami in the Twentieth Century* (Gainesville: University Press of Florida, 1997).

28. For general studies of the modern environmental movement, see Philip Shabecoff, *A Fierce Green Fire: The American Environmental Movement* (New York: Hill and Wang, 1993), 111–28; Kirkpatrick Sale, *The Green Revolution: The American Environmental Movement, 1962–1992* (New York: Hill and Wang, 1993), 11–45; Gottlieb, *Forcing the Spring*, 75–114, 117–77; Stephen Fox, *The American Conservation Movement: John Muir and His Legacy* (Madison: University of Wisconsin Press, 1981), 250–53, 262–329; and on Florida, see Scott Hamilton Dewey, "'Is This What We Came to Florida For?': Florida Women and the Fight against Air Pollution in the 1960s," *Florida Historical Quarterly* 77 (spring 1999): 503–31.

29. Peggy Poor, "Can Man Come to Terms with Nature in Florida Everglades?" *Florida Magazine* (*Orlando Sentinel*), April 19, 1970; *Orlando Evening Star*, April 14,

1971; Marquis Childs, "The Everglades in an Era of Reprieve: A New Awareness May Help to Preserve One of America's Treasures, Which Has Had Bleak Times," *Smithsonian* 1 (June 1970): 5–13; Peter Farb, "Disaster Threatens the Everglades," *Audubon* 67 (September-October 1965): 302–7; Wallace Stegner, "Last Chance for the Everglades," *Saturday Review*, May 6, 1967, 22–23, 72–73; Central and South Florida Flood Control District news release, July 12, 1974, GGP; Jackson Price to Claude Pepper, June 3, 1966, Claude Pepper Papers, series 301, folder 2, box 767; and District Corps of Engineers, Jacksonville, Florida, news release, April 14, 1966, Claude Pepper Papers, series 301, folder 4, box 613.

30. "Conservation—Jets v. Everglades," *Time*, August 22 1969, 42–43; newspapers clippings, David O. True Collection, Special Collections, University of South Florida Library, Tampa, Everglades folder, box 25; Charles R. Jeter to Marjory Stoneman Douglas, August 26, 1982, Arthur R. Marshall Papers, Special Collections, GSL, Everglades Jetport folder, box 2.

31. *Sarasota Herald-Tribune*, November 28, 1982; Joe Podgor interview; Franklin Adams, interview by the author, August 8, 2000.

32. Thomas T. Ankersen, "Law, Science and Little Old Ladies: The Many Hands That Made a Movement," *Forum* (summer 1995): 31–33; Marjory Stoneman Douglas to Arthur Marshall, February 5, 1971, Arthur R. Marshall Papers, folder 28, box 1. For the works of early Florida naturalists, see John Kunkel Small, *From Eden to Sahara: Florida's Tragedy* (Lancaster, Penn.: Science Press Printing Company, 1929); Charles Torrey Simpson, *In Lower Florida Wilds* (New York: G. P. Putnam's Sons, 1920); Charles Torrey Simpson, *Out of Doors in Florida: The Adventures of a Naturalist Together with Essays on the Wild Life and Geology of the State* (Miami: E. B. Douglas Company, 1923); and Thomas Barbour, *That Vanishing Eden: A Naturalist's Florida* (Boston: Little, Brown, 1944). In *Our Vanishing Wild Life: Its Extermination and Preservation* (New York: New York Zoological Society, 1913), New York Zoological Society president William T. Hornaday also sounded the alarm about Florida's vanishing wilderness.

33. *Tallahassee Democrat*, May 19, 1981; *Sarasota Herald-Tribune*, November 28, 1982; Allan Dodds Frank, "Without Water, Everything Stops," *Forbes*, December 2, 1984, 63–64, 68, 72; Yates, "Marjory Stoneman Douglas and the Glades Crusade," 118; Ankersen, "Law, Science and Little Old Ladies," 31–33; Douglas, *River of Grass*, 296–97.

34. John C. Jones and Marianna Jones, interview by the author, August 11, 2000; *Tallahassee Democrat*, May 19, 1981; *Miami Herald*, August 15, 1982; "Birds Have Personality," undated newspaper clipping, MSD, folder 11, box 39; John C. Jones to Nathaniel P. Reed, July 21, 1982, MSD, folder 27, box 25; Marjory Stoneman Douglas to Lawton Chiles, February 26, 1986, MSD, folder 51, box 26; John C. Jones to Marjory Stoneman Douglas, February 20, 1982, MSD, folder 51, box 26; John C. Jones to Marjory Stoneman Douglas, June 2, 1982, MSD, folder 51, box 26; Marjory Stoneman Douglas to John C. Jones, February 8, 1982, MSD, folder 51, box 26.

35. Jones and Jones interview; "The Kissimmee River . . . A Trip into the Past," June 1976 news clipping provided by John C. and Marianna Jones, West Palm Beach, Florida; Water! conference program, February 22, 1976, MSD, folder 8, box 23; Water! Member organizations list, MSD, folder 8, box 23; "Unlikely Allies Team Up," undated

newspaper clipping, MSD, folder 6, box 24; "Restoration of the Kissimmee River," resolution, n.d., MSD, folder 8, box 23; Arthur R. Marshall to Members of the Coalition to Repair the Everglades, memo, n.d., MSD, folder 89, box 45; press release, "Graham Announces Save Our Everglades Program," August 9, 1983, Governor Robert Graham Papers, correspondence folder, box 44, Florida State Archives.

36. *Florida Wildlife Federation, et al. v. State of Florida Department of Environmental Regulation, et al.,* DOAH case no. 79-256, MSD, folder 89, box 45; "Forever Glades," *Audubon,* special issue, "The Everglades Rises Again," 103 (July–August 2001): 61; *St. Petersburg Times,* December 21, 1987, June 5, 1989, May 15, 1998; *Orlando Sentinel,* September 18, 1990, January 22, 1990, January 11, 1991; David McCally, *The Everglades: An Environmental History* (Gainesville: University Press of Florida, 1999), 172–73; Alec Wilkinson, *Big Sugar: Seasons in the Cane Fields of Florida* (New York: Alfred A. Knopf, 1989); Derr, *Some Kind of Paradise,* 95–96, 172–73.

37. Marjory Stoneman Douglas to Robert Graham, October 17, 1985; Rob Williams to Marjory Stoneman Douglas, January 24, 1986; Robert A. Williams, memorandum, January 24, 1986, all in MSD, Social Concerns folder, box 12; Bob Graham to Marjory Stoneman Douglas, July 16, 1982, MSD, folder 47, box 26; *Orlando Sentinel,* January 1, 1984, September 18, 1990; McCally, *Everglades,* 154–57; Cindy Hahamovitch, *Fruits of Their Labor: Atlantic Coast Farmworkers and the Making of Migrant Poverty, 1870–1945* (Chapel Hill: University of North Carolina Press, 1997), 113–37; Branch, "Writing the Swamp," 131; Franklin Adams, and Joe Podgor interviews. Douglas devoted ten chapters of *River of Grass* to the history of Glades Indians; for the experience of migrant farmworkers, see 275–80.

38. *Miami Herald,* December 2, 1922, December, 27, 1922, March 10, 1923, February 18, 1974, August 25, 1976; Orlando *Sentinel Star,* November 9, 1975; *Sarasota Herald-Tribune,* November 28, 1982; *Orlando Sentinel Star,* November 9, 1975; *Orlando Sentinel,* April 8, 1990; Jim Clark, "Florida Waffled on Passing Equal Rights Amendment," *Orlando Sentinel, Florida Magazine,* March 30, 1997. On modern feminism and environmentalism, see, for example, Carolyn Merchant, *Earthcare: Women and the Environment* (New York: Routledge, 1995), 88–89, 145–49.

39. *Tallahassee Democrat,* May 19, 1981; Holly M. Hays, "Marjory Stoneman Douglas: Conservationist of the Century," *Florida Living,* August 1992, 54; *St. Petersburg Times,* June 5, 1989; *Orlando Sentinel,* May 26, 1986; *Miami Herald,* May 21, 1983; Schmich, "Our Lady of the 'Glades"; Douglas, *Voice of the River,* 233.

40. *St. Petersburg Times,* October 20, 2000, February 2, 2001; *Birmingham News,* August 10, 2001; "Anatomy of a Deal," in "The Everglades Rises Again," special issue, *Audubon* 103 (July–August 2001): 50–51; "Biodiversity Legal Foundation—Friends of the Everglades-Florida Biodiversity Project, resolution, October 2, 2000, http://www.everglades.org; *Glade Runner* (winter 2001–2): 4, 6–7.

There is no shortage of land to cause the panic to dredge
bays and bayous. What is needed is good city planning.
It is not good business to not plan and spoil
our most important assets.

St. Petersburg Times, 1957

The whole Bay has been raped.

State Representative Dorothy Sample, 1984

Chapter 14

A *"Monstrous Desecration"*

Dredge and Fill in Boca Ciega Bay

Bruce Stephenson

Shortly before his death, Governor LeRoy Collins called the indiscriminate dredging and filling of Boca Ciega Bay a "monstrous desecration."[1] Despite Collins's legal and administrative challenges, one of Florida's most productive and beautiful estuaries was laid to waste. It was not just the loss of the coastal lagoon off St. Petersburg that haunted Collins but also the knowledge that similar environmental catastrophes marked Florida's run to prosperity. Moreover, Boca Ciega's demise was a product of neither ignorance nor an apathetic public; Florida's first ecologists and grassroots activists combined to fight and articulate the costs of dredging and filling the estuary. Rather,

Boca Ciega fell victim "to that gleam," as one St. Petersburg resident put it, that "just never died in the 'Progress Boys' eyes."[2]

The filling and degradation of Boca Ciega Bay provoked a heated political controversy that lasted from the early 1950s to 1970. Elected officials, courts, and agencies, from the local to the federal level were entangled in a confusing mix of legalities and politics as they tried to reach a solution agreeable to both developers and conservation groups. The effort to protect Boca Ciega also forced municipal officials to reevaluate their planning process. It was obvious that the giant dredges rearranging the landscape were diminishing the bay's aesthetic appeal, but, in 1956, state biologists revealed that dredging and filling was also destroying the marine ecosystem. Their study, which introduced ecology into the decision-making process, ensured that city building in St. Petersburg—and the rest of Florida—would never be the same.

By the mid-1950s, grassroots opponents to projects that threatened America's scenic natural areas had become increasingly vocal. Although these movements were spontaneous and often occurred without a central organization or a coordinated plan of action, they expressed a strong common desire. Whether they were fighting dams in the Southwest, clear-cutting in the Northwest, or dredging projects in Florida, conservationists battled for a new set of public priorities. Previously Americans had viewed the natural world as a commodity to exploit as efficiently as possible. Now they wanted protection for the scenic lands and waters that played such an integral role in their quality of life. When its leaders, reasoning from the nascent science of ecology, challenged traditional notions of property rights and progress, the budding environmental movement introduced a radical concept into the mainstream of American thought.[3]

Ecology was deemed the "subversive science" once activists started using its theories to challenge the idea of progress. The ecological hypothesis—that natural communities evolve toward an efficient point of equilibrium—goes against the capitalist ethos of endless growth and ever-increasing consumption. By bringing ecology into the debate over the preservation of natural resources, conservationists moved beyond questions of aesthetics. By 1970, ecologists were contending that maintaining the health of the ecosystem was crucial to sustaining human life. A society predicated on growth and consumption, environmentalists contended, could be as destructive as it was creative.[4] Boca Ciega Bay presented an important and early test case for a nation wrestling with the issue of environmental protection.

Boca Ciega Bay: Subtropical Sublime

"Here stands the work of godly hands, the flowering peninsula of Pinellas, with her cluster of green islands and keys. Like gorgeous strings of emerald and jade, sweeping over the master plan of divine dreams."[5] The beauty that William Straub, editor of the *St. Petersburg Times,* described in 1929 was the product of a recent geologic transformation. The "strings of emerald and jade" running parallel, in a north-south formation, to the Pinellas subpeninsula were once sandbars that gradually formed over three to four thousand years into barrier islands. Sediment deposited by the waves accumulated around any obstacle, usually vegetation, to form dunes. The Gulf of Mexico's winds and waves fostered the sand dunes' continued growth, and, once the dunes had reached a height somewhere between 3 and 6 feet, they provided a stable foundation for the fragile barrier islands.

Besides anchoring the beaches, the dune system sheltered the islands' landward side, where colonies of palm and pine habitat flourished. The barrier islands' seaward coasts featured white sand beaches, while the bayside shores held a mixture of mangroves and marine grasses. Red mangroves played an especially important role in the estuarine ecosystem. Their prop roots trapped loose materials and leaf litter, creating habitats for marine life and buffering the island from storm tides. The mangrove was a vital link in the food chain. When mangroves dropped their nutrient-rich leaves, the leaves nourished detritus consumers like shrimp, a primary food source for larger fish. The trees' prop roots also hosted scores of marine creatures—tunicates, sponges, barnacles, oysters, mussels, and other mollusks—that played an integral role in the estuary lying between the mainland and the barrier islands.

Boca Ciega Bay is the largest coastal lagoon separating the Pinellas offshore isles from the mainland. It averages 2 miles in width and runs 16 miles along the southern edge of the subpeninsula. When Straub penned his paean to Pinellas, the bay was between 2 and 6 feet deep with dense mangrove swamps fringing most of its 90-mile shoreline. The mangroves' extensive root system restricted the seaward movement of upland sediments, helping to keep the brackish bay water clean and clear. The bay's vast underwater meadows of turtle grass prevented erosion of the lagoon floor while serving as both a nursery and feeding ground for the abundant marine life. Its waters teemed with fish—including tarpon, bonita, trout, and mullet—and shellfish, such as stone crabs, clams, oysters, scallops, and shrimp. Rookeries,

Bruce Stephenson

although depleted from the ravages of plume hunters in the early 1900s, still housed large wading birds such as snowy egrets, roseate spoonbills, and blue herons on the edge of Boca Ciega's abundant waters.[6]

The barrier islands cushioned Boca Ciega from the tropical storms and hurricanes that swept through region. The dunes and mangroves acted like shock absorbers and bore the brunt of the storms. Yet despite a dune system's amazing resilience, a barrier island could wash away in minutes when hurricane floodwaters or a storm surge made its eventual seaward return. Such a backwash occurs when hurricane winds change direction and combine with gravitational forces to force the storm surge over—and sometimes through—any obstacle in its way.[7]

In 1848, the most powerful recorded hurricane to hit the west coast of Florida literally blew the water out of Tampa Bay, exposing large sand flats, during the backwash stage. The entire barrier island chain from Pinellas south to Sanibel flooded when the Gulf of Mexico's waters rose 14.3 feet above normal. The storm surge reshaped Pinellas's barrier island chain. It carved out two new inlets, washed away some keys, and built up others with sands dredged from both land and seas. Although the mainland escaped such punishment, two-thirds of the Pinellas peninsula experienced heavy flooding. Fortunately, in 1848 Pinellas's barrier islands were uninhabited, and only a few hardy settlers inhabited the peninsula's higher elevations.[8]

A Vision of Eden: Florida's First City Plan

The initial effort to protect Boca Ciega Bay occurred in 1922, when John Nolen, the nation's premier city planner, found St. Petersburg and the surrounding Pinellas peninsula an ideal place to build a model "resort city." The city's 1920 population of 14,237 had almost doubled when St. Petersburg's Planning Board hired the Boston planner to design Florida's first comprehensive city plan. Given the Planning Board's concerns over the city's haphazard expansion, Nolen presented a plan and accompanying land-use controls to preserve the "natural advantages that belong to the St. Petersburg region." He designed an interconnected system of parks and preserves to access nature and, at the same time, protect the region's most sensitive and vital natural resources (for example, wetlands and barrier islands). Gulf-front parks would enhance tourism, while neighborhoods were clustered within green borders and placed within walking distance (one-half mile) of shopping centers and schools.[9]

A "Monstrous Desecration": Dredge and Fill in Boca Ciega Bay

Nolen's supporters faced the unenviable task of trying to sell a system of land-use controls to a populace reveling in the allure of quick riches and speculation. "The city planning referendum was as abusive as any ever held in St. Petersburg, and that is saying a great deal," the *St. Petersburg Times* reported.[10] On August 28, 1923, the pecuniary magic of the Great Florida Land Boom consumed voters, and they sent Florida's first city planning initiative crashing to an ignominious defeat. The proplanning forces gained a mere 13 percent of the vote, and the citizens of St. Petersburg hurtled into the future without plan or any sense of limitation.

Five years later, St. Petersburg was saddled with the nation's highest per-capita public debt. During the boom years (1922–26), elected officials instituted a unique system of "entrepreneurial socialism." The city underwrote the construction of a road system and other improvements to enhance speculation rather than meet market demand. By 1930, St. Petersburg's 40,000 residents were paying off an infrastructure to support a city of 250,000. To regain a measure of fiscal security, the city council adopted a scaled-down version of Nolen's work. The new plan provided a general guide to development, including provisions to protect Boca Ciega Bay.[11] Nolen recommended that the city institute a "bulkhead line" that limited fills to areas contiguous with the existing coast line. A failure to do so would create an "unhappy situation on the shoreline," he wrote, "through the excessive and illogical building out into the water."[12]

City leaders failed to heed Nolen's advice. By the early 1950s, the postwar building boom had exhausted the city's supply of waterfront property. To meet demand for this prime commodity in a burgeoning city (St. Petersburg's population tripled to 181,200 between 1940 and 1960), developers initiated extensive dredging and filling operations in Boca Ciega Bay. These projects rearranged the landscape to such a degree, one citizen declared, that if local officials kept "explaining away the dangers of dredge and fill, St. Petersburg will become an inland city." In 1957, after surveying the countless fills in Boca Ciega Bay, Governor LeRoy Collins commented, "Pretty soon we are going to have to drill to find water there."[13]

Boca Ciega Bay and the Ecology of Progress

By the mid-1950s, Boca Ciega Bay was hardly a pristine body of water. During the Depression, the U.S. Army Corps of Engineers had tied the coastal lagoon into the Intercoastal Waterway by dredging a 15-foot-deep channel. The corps deposited the bay bottom in large piles that formed "spoil islands." Several hundred acres of bountiful marine habitat were covered with dredged mud and sand, and the grasses that had held the sandy bottom material could not grow in the deep channels, which led to increased levels of turbidity. The flow of partially treated sewage and storm water runoff generated by new development in St. Petersburg also lowered the bay's water quality.

Despite these problems, Boca Ciega Bay remained one of the nation's most prolific marine systems. Mangroves dotted its shores, and vast expanses of turtle grass covered the southern half of the bay. The largest concentration of turtle grass, and one of Tampa Bay's most fertile fisheries, lay off Cats Blank Point in southwest St. Petersburg. In 1953, in excess of 4 million pounds of fish were taken in Pinellas County—more than any other county in Florida. Forty percent of this haul came from Boca Ciega Bay. Hundreds of tourists and residents enjoyed shell fishing along the mudflats, while a viable shrimping industry boosted the local economy.[14]

In 1953, Albert Furen, a local developer who owned 6 acres of shoreline property at Cat's Blank Point, purchased the rights to fill 504 acres of bay bottom adjoining his holdings from the Trustees for the Internal Improvement Fund (TIIF). The TIIF, a commission chaired by the governor and comprising the state's independently elected cabinet members, was established in 1855 after the federal government had previously deeded to Florida all unowned land "wet and unfit for cultivation." From its inception, the TIIF was a primary revenue-generating source for the state, and it rarely restricted the sale of Florida's land and water.[15]

In response to the indiscriminate dredging and filling of Florida's bays during the postwar building boom, in the early 1950s, conservation groups from coastal communities called on the state to restrict these projects fouling some of Florida's most beautiful and productive waters. In St. Petersburg, the Alliance for the Conservation of Natural Resources (ACNR) had risen to combat development in Boca Ciega Bay. The group inundated local officials with letters of protest, jammed public meetings, and claimed up to 20,000 members.[16] During the 1953 gubernatorial contest, LeRoy Collins promised to resolve this dredge-and-fill issue for obvious political reasons. Yet, this constituted more than an opportunistic campaign pledge. Collins believed that protecting the state's bays was integral to maintaining the magnetic lure Florida held over the nation.

After his election, Collins stepped into the national spotlight when he attempted to break racial segregation's hold on Florida, but he did not forget his promise to the conservationists.[17] He imposed a two-year moratorium on the TIIF's sale of submerged lands, giving the state time to develop a program for regulating coastal building. He established the State Land Use and Control Committee (SLUCC) to explore ways to regulate dredge-and-fill operations in Florida waters.[18] Furen's fill soon became a focal point for the Collins administration. As Ney Landrum, one of the governor's aides, claimed, "Things were entirely out of control in Pinellas and something had to be done."[19]

In Pinellas, where "dredges were as routine as seagulls," elected officials openly abetted dredging operations.[20] The county commission had never opposed a single fill proposal, and it seemed probable that the St. Petersburg City Council would extend city utilities to Furen's project. The Collins administration feared this massive fill would devastate Boca Ciega Bay and set an alarming precedent because it was "not related in a bona fide manner" to Furen's six-acre shoreline holding. If St. Petersburg's city council supported Furen, the governor warned council members and the Pinellas County Commission, the state would intervene.[21]

In December 1956, the St. Petersburg City Council voted four to three to negotiate with Furen about providing city services; the following March, the county commission gave its initial approval on the Furen fill. Collins backed up his threat by sending a condemnation act to the legislature. If it passed, Furen's submerged lands would return to the state. When the large Pinellas delegation threatened to block his draft act, Collins had the state attorney general, Richard Ervin, retain Tampa attorney Thomas Shackleford on behalf of the governor and the Florida State Board of Conservation. In April, Ervin warned the county commission that if they sanctioned the fill and refused to reopen the case with the state, Shackleford would file suit in circuit court.[22]

The Collins administration's effort to regulate dredge-and-fill operations received strong support from Nelson Poynter, publisher of the *St. Petersburg Times*. In increasingly Republican Pinellas County, Poynter gave Collins's Democratic administration outspoken support, especially on this issue. Poynter's generous 1953 campaign contribution to Collins undoubtedly helped influenced the new governor's decision to set a moratorium on the sale of submerged land. Yet, at the same time, Poynter and Collins were of a kindred spirit. They both felt Pinellas's "sparkling waters" represented gifts of nature that required protection from developers like Furen.[23] "Furen and his partisans equate progress with quick profit," a *Times* editorial read. "Op-

ponents think progress has a much wider and infinitely deeper meaning—
Growth can be benign or cancerous."[24]

Since the early 1900s when William Straub penned his first editorials, the
St. Petersburg Times had advocated the conservation of natural resources. In
the mid-1950s, the *Times* became the standard bearer for Florida's nascent
ecology movement after Nelson Poynter struck up a friendship with the naturalist Rachel Carson. Carson, whose classic *Silent Spring* (1962) awakened the
nation to the dangers of chemical pesticides, was immersed in research at the
St. Petersburg Marine Research Lab when Poynter made her acquaintance in
the early 1950s. Her studies of marine life produced a best seller in 1951, *The
Sea Around Us* (1951), followed by *The Edge of the Sea* (1955), a work designed
to "take the seashore out of the category of scenery and make it come alive."[25]
Carson's eloquent and evolving ecological prose caught the newspaperman's
attention. As their friendship deepened, Poynter learned that the unabated
dredging and filling could extinguish the complex web of marine life that
Carson had so carefully chronicled.[26]

After consultations with Carson, Poynter's campaign against dredge and
fill intensified. In 1955, the *Times* devoted a series to describing how filling
portions of Boca Ciega Bay would upset the sustaining balance of the entire
estuarine system. Before the TIIF's moratorium on dredge and fill ended,
Poynter advised the state to analyze the potential ecological costs of such
projects in Boca Ciega Bay. He also urged the city council and the county
commission to incorporate the results of such a study into a plan for regulating coastal development.

In 1956, a *St. Petersburg Times* editorial found the destruction of Boca
Ciega Bay especially "distressing for citizens interested in good planning
and preserving natural resources," revealing the city's "ill-conceived planning philosophy."[27] In 1940, the city had hired Bartholomew and Associates
to craft a new city plan. Casting off Nolen's work as the "optimistic opinions of
an ideal city," the firm opted for a plan based on a "thorough analysis of the
facts." The plan started from the premise that a more "efficient physical infrastructure" would improve the city's economic health and, in turn, make it a
more appealing draw for tourists.[28] The Bartholomew planners, however,
paid scant attention to the natural environment and, the *Times* claimed, omit-
ted "human motivation" from their formulaic approach. "People flocked to
the Pinellas area for its beautiful waters"; yet the Bartholomew plan contained no guidelines to preserve these natural resources. Local politicians

ignored Poynter's plea for environmental planning, but the plight of Boca Ciega Bay drew attention from outside the region.[29]

Ecology and Planning

In 1955, the U.S. Fish and Wildlife Service (USFWS) reported that Boca Ciega's "priceless assets" of marine life and habitat were in peril. Given the "serious threat of impending dredging projects and the need for a *comprehensive plan* [emphasis added] to insure preservation of these resources," the USFWS urged, "a prompt and intensive study of this problem is warranted." The agency recommended that the Florida State Board of Conservation undertake the study, because regulating fill projects fell under the state's jurisdiction.[30]

The board immediately commissioned Robert Hutton, a former professor of marine biology at the University of Miami, to study the effects of dredging and filling on Boca Ciega Bay. He oversaw the project while Ken Woodburn, the first ecologist employed by the state, performed most of the fieldwork. Five years earlier, the state had established a marine laboratory in St. Petersburg, and the research team had already analyzed portions of the bay. Between September 25, 1955, and January 1, 1956, Woodburn and Hutton studied fifteen sites located throughout the bay. They recorded hydrologic changes, analyzed bottom samples, and accumulated a mass of data from examining mangroves, sea grasses, algae, plankton, bacteria, echinoderms, fish, mollusks, and shrimp. Hutton also used the work of Robert Ingle, who had studied the effects of dredging in other southern states, for comparative analysis.

In late 1956, Hutton completed his report, *The Ecology of Boca Ciega Bay, with Special Reference to Dredging and Filling Operations*. This study was the first ecological analysis that the state had sponsored to assess the impact of development on an important natural resource. Hutton concluded that Boca Ciega Bay would suffer irreparable damage if the Furen project proceeded. Continuing to dredge and fill would heavily curtail commercial fishing because vast expanses of turtle grass, the bay's "keystone species,"[31] would be sacrificed for waterfront homes. Ecologists determine the health of natural systems by analyzing keystone species, which perform vital functions in the system and affect many other organisms. Turtle grass was essential to Boca Ciega Bay; without it, the estuary's interrelated web of land and marine life would collapse.

Besides providing a nursery for marine life, the root structure of the turtle grass kept the sandy soils lining the bay bottom from dispersing. Allowing additional dredging projects to eliminate turtle grass would cover the bay bottom with silt while choking out a good portion of the remaining stands. Turtle grass was the catalyst for the organic decomposition of waste, and it could not survive in the deeper, dredged portions of the bay. Without this vital species, the ecosystem's ability to recycle waste would be impaired and the bay's water quality would drop exponentially. Where dredging had already occurred, Hutton found that sulfate-producing bacteria from a combination of human waste and storm-water runoff had created a rank, black ooze that covered the bottom of the bay. Unless dredge-and-fill operations ceased, the bacteria that infested this anaerobic mud would spread throughout the bay and intensify the growing public health risk. While dredge-and-fill projects were an inexpensive method for developers to create waterfront real estate, the public had to bear the cost of, as Woodburn put it, "permanent pollution." The destructive potential of the Furen project "should be weighed," Hutton concluded, against expected benefits of the project before dredging is permitted to proceed.[32]

In March 1957, Hutton's findings played an important role in the framing of the "Bulkhead Law," the SLUCC's proposal to regulate dredge-and-fill operations. The idea was hardly new (the Nolen firm had presented a similar proposal), but the time had now come to deal with the nearly intractable problem. Every deed to waterfront real estate in Florida carried a riparian provision that allowed landowners to extend existing lot lines into the water as far as the bulkhead, which was usually set at the edge of navigable channels. Property owners could fill the area between the coast and the bulkhead line with material excavated from the adjacent bay bottoms.[33] The Bulkhead Law would preserve waterfront property owners' access to existing channels, but all fill projects would have to meet minimum standards of health, safety, and welfare. The SLUCC defined welfare as the "conservation of wildlife, prevention of erosion, and damage of natural beauty." Its definition of health included the "prevention of pollution." The Bulkhead Law also granted all cities and counties the authority to regulate fills through zoning. In addition to the Bulkhead Law, Collins requested legislation to regain the bottomlands Furen held either by buying them or by exercising the right of eminent domain.[34]

In 1957, Collins made a special address before the opening session of the state legislature, alerting Floridians to the pillaging of the state's most magnificent bays. Local officials had not only abused the public trust; they "actually encouraged the misuse of Florida's natural resources." Since county and municipal governments appeared unwilling to protect Florida's waters, Collins announced that the state would regulate waterfront development.[35]

While the governor's conservation agenda was taking shape, Lee Ratner, a multimillionaire developer from Chicago, bought out Furen. Ratner claimed that his project would fill a gap in St. Petersburg's housing market by creating an exclusive setting for northern businessmen. "It has been proven that buyers of this type tend to bring their business enterprises to Florida," he claimed. Ratner's attorney, Leonard Bursten, a young lawyer who had started his career as an investigator for Senator Joseph McCarthy, promised that his client would negotiate with all governmental agencies to improve the design of the project.[36]

Lee Ratner had millions of dollars but a less than sterling reputation. Earlier in the decade, his advertisements in northern papers convinced buyers to purchase thousands of acres of unseen land near Fort Myers. Many of these novice investors found that their "fabulous, improved lots" were watery plots in an impassable cypress swamp. Ratner's fraudulent scheme forced the state legislature to call a special session to regulate land sales.[37]

Ratner personified the slick postwar developer.[38] In addition to his brash demeanor and questionable business tactics, he employed an entourage of lawyers and consultants to run through Florida's weak but growing list of regulations. Well-placed political contributions and questionable ethics completed an operational scheme seen throughout the Sunshine State. During the 1950s, elected officials seldom worried if developers misled them. For the "good ol' boy crowd," these entrepreneurs were simply trying to advance commerce and prosperity. It was just a matter of time before local officials began, Florida historian John Rothchild writes, "codifying the promotional slogans into the county zoning."[39]

On April 11, 1957, the Pinellas County Commission approved the Ratner Fill, as it had become known. At the end of the meeting, Shackleford handed commissioners a petition for a rehearing and warned them that he would pursue the issue in court. Bursten claimed that the effort to block the project was "just because the people in Tallahassee disliked his client." He described the TIIF as a "bunch of bleeding hearts" and doubted the honesty of Hutton and Woodburn. Following in the steps of his former employer Joe McCarthy, Bursten derided Hutton as a government lackey who had "deliberately set out to wreck my client's plans." The aggressive young lawyer made a parting shot at Floyd Brown, the representative of the Alliance for the Conservation of Natural Resources (ACNR): "Instead of 20,000 members he is supposed to represent, the number had dwindled to a death march of a handful."

Mrs. Robert Davis, an ACNR officer and president of the St. Petersburg Garden Club, immediately challenged Bursten. "If you want us to bring 1,000 members up here to protest this fill, we'll do it." Since the city council had voted to work with Furen in December, the ACNR had sent more than two thousand letters of protest. Floyd Brown also informed Shackleford that the ACNR would join the state board of conservation as a plaintiff if the state went to court against Ratner.[40]

Davis, Brown (a high school science teacher), and Mary Bigelow had formed the ACNR in 1954. Bigelow devoted the most time to the organization. She had visited St. Petersburg in the early 1940s and had become enchanted with the region's natural beauty. In 1951, she moved to St. Petersburg. Three years later, she awoke one morning to the dull roar of a dredge. Incensed that her waterfront vista was being transformed into a subdivision, she organized the ACNR by gathering members from eight civic organizations. Between 1954 and 1958, she traveled to Tallahassee numerous times to testify before the TIIF as the ACNR's representative.[41]

On April 23, 1957, Bigelow was in Tallahassee when Ratner's lawyers and William Windom, St. Petersburg's city manager, appeared before Governor Collins and the rest of the TIIF board. Windom explained that Ratner would modify his project in exchange for the deeds to an additional section of the bay. When Windom admitted, despite Bursten's vehement objection (when Windom made his statement Bursten leaped up to and almost over the bar separating the audience from the TIIF) that Ratner intended to fill more than the area granted under the existing deed, Collins shook his head in disbelief. When the governor spoke, he chastised Windom for representing Ratner and endorsing a project "contrary to the interests of the city." He also informed Windom that the state would continue its effort to stop Ratner's project: "We have not counted ourselves out of the picture, even if you have." Windom apologized for having given the impression that the city wanted Collins to change his stance.

Gerald Gould, the lawyer in charge of marketing the project, appeared next before the TIIF board. Gould complained that the state government had placed private citizens in jeopardy because agencies were "constantly changing their positions." The previous administration had already deeded the lands his client held, and Gould argued that the state's efforts to regulate development were inconsistent with his client's legal standing. He also stated that he had a letter binding Florida's chief executive to "our legal position and moral position." Collins bristled as he told Gould, "I don't know who had told you what, but I do think I have a pretty good knowledge of what has been said at this table, which is the official place that governs our conduct." The governor countered that the previous administration's decision represented a "considerable stretching of state policy." Then he asked Gould to produce his letter. The counselor haltingly admitted, "I'm not sure just where that letter is." The governor warned him to be more careful in what he said, and Gould managed to stammer, "I'll try to get that letter." Collins suspended the discussion when Gould claimed that the governor had made certain promises to Ratner. Collins had never spoken with Ratner, he informed Gould, and the state would do whatever it could to stop his client's project. After the governor's declaration, Gould backed away from the stand, slumped down next to Bursten, and began murmuring into his briefcase.[42]

Collins's stand ushered in a new era. A multimillion-dollar project funded by northern capital was no longer an unquestioned good in Florida. While turning productive estuaries into subdivisions added to the local tax rolls, destroying Florida's natural resources compromised the public welfare. Collins represented a growing constituency that had come to see that the benefits of protecting an important natural system outweighed the profits from private development.

In June, despite opposition from the entire Pinellas delegation, the state legislature passed an amended version of the Bulkhead Law. The bill's chief supporters came from coastal communities that feared their bays would suffer the same fate as Boca Ciega Bay unless the state took action. When Representative Thomas Carey of St. Petersburg tried to exempt Pinellas from the regulations, a Fort Myers representative noted that in "Pinellas you are filling everything around there except the Sunshine Parkway" (the bridge between Bradenton and St. Petersburg). Carey countered that although the fish faced relocation, "We are putting people where we are filling." Later Carey tried to shuttle the bill into committee, in hope that it would die a slow death. This motion lost after a representative from Bradenton, William Grimes, made the comment that if "we study this bill all summer isn't it possible Manatee County bays might end up as bad as Pinellas County bays?" Carey also failed to get a special exemption for the Ratner Fill, setting the stage for an important test of the state's new legislation.[43]

While the Bulkhead Law represented an important step in the effort to regulate coastal development, it did little to alter existing building practices.

The bill encouraged cities and counties to establish bulkhead lines, but it did not give any specific guidelines. In addition, the state legislature failed to provide funding for the technical assistance needed to design bulkhead lines properly. While the act gave the TIIF the right to withdraw lands from sale if the "conservation of natural resources were imperiled," there was no definition of what constituted peril. This flaw became only too apparent at the rehearing.[44]

In December 1957, the county commission reopened proceedings on the Ratner proposal with expert testimony from Ratner's consultants.[45] James B. Lackey, a marine biology professor from the University of Florida, testified that his employer's project would "encourage fish and marine life." Deep channels on each side of the project would flush water into the most polluted section of the bay (north of the project), which would improve water circulation, disperse bacterial pollutants, and even regenerate the dying scallop population. John Dequine, a fish biologist for the Southern Fish Culture Company, backed up Lackey's testimony and added that fishing opportunities would actually improve. The dredging operation would create deeper pools where fish would congregate, and the angle of the fabricated underwater slopes would also help to attract fish. "The heights of sophistry were reached," according to Ken Woodburn, "when one consultant testified that sea grass beds were of little consequence to fish populations in Boca Ciega because fish came and went with the tides."[46] Perhaps even more outrageous, but at least truthful, was the testimony of J. Hardin Peterson, a former U.S. representative and Furen's attorney. He claimed his client's work would greatly benefit St. Petersburg by buffering the city during a hurricane. "I would suggest," commented John Orr, the lawyer representing the ACNR, "this human buffer they are going to put out there certainly won't be in the real estate ads."[47]

Robert Hutton, author of *The Ecology of Boca Ciega Bay*, testified for the state. But before he could refute Ratner's consultants, he endured hours of interrogation by Bursten. Bursten first tried to discredit *The Ecology of Boca Ciega Bay* by challenging Hutton's scientific credibility. After questioning the scientist three separate times over his "compensation from the state," the lawyer tried to prove that Hutton was incapable of understanding the Ratner project. Hutton finally received a respite when the state's attorney gained the floor. When asked what effect Ratner's project would have on the bay, Hutton reiterated his premise that the destruction of turtle grass beds would devastate the bay's marine system. Besides filling 500 acres of prime fishing grounds, the dredging operations would deepen the shallow water surrounding the huge fill to a depth of between 7 and 25 feet. Turtle grass thrived in depths of 2 to 4 feet, and Hutton had never found it in water deeper than 6 ½ feet. He pointed out that eliminating an estimated thousand acres of turtle grass would increase the siltation problem, lower the water quality, and accelerate the spread of anaerobic muck across the bottom of the bay. He also doubted that trading boat channels for grass flats would enhance fishing. "In my opinion," he concluded, "the elimination of Cats Blank Point would materially and adversely harm marine life."

The "Rape" of Boca Ciega Bay

The Pinellas County Commission ignored Hutton's testimony and voted unanimously for Ratner to proceed. This was hardly surprising, especially after the county administrator, Dewey Morris, warned the ACNR to drop its opposition because the Ratner Fill would come "hell or high water."[48] The antifill forces received more bad news when the ACNR and Shackleford challenged the commission's decision in the local circuit court and lost. Judge S. H. Harris ruled that the TIIF's original sale to Furen was consistent with sound governing policy "and that public policy [was] irreversible."[49]

The Collins administration contested the ruling, appealing jointly with the ACNR and the TIIF. In addition, the ACNR, the TIIF, and John Brantley, a St. Petersburg council member, challenged Ratner's title in a separate case. The coalition gained a minor victory when Attorney General Ervin ruled that the TIIF could not grant title to submerged land off Cats Blank Point because St. Petersburg, not the state, held the rights to this domain.

On January 8, 1959, with court challenges still pending, Ratner's lawyers tried to force Collins's hand. A year had passed since the county commission had issued Ratner's dredging permit, and if the operation did not begin within the year, the permit would lapse. Bursten informed Ervin that unless the Collins administration agreed to a compromise his client would begin dredging. Collins responded to Bursten's threat by having the circuit court issue a restraining order against Ratner's project. He also informed Bursten that his administration would "resist to the fullest extent we can under the law and under legal obligations we have in the premises."[50]

A month later the state court of appeals affirmed the lower court's ruling on the Ratner project. The ACNR and Ervin immediately petitioned the state supreme court. The petitioners claimed that the TIIF had exceeded its pow-

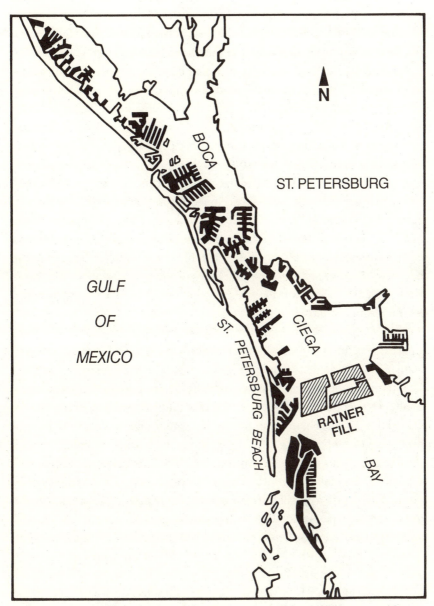

Figure 14.1. By 1970, 25 percent of Boca Ciega Bay had been filled. At roughly 500 acres, the Ratner Fill was the largest of the fills in the bay.

ers by selling lands outside its jurisdiction. The Florida Supreme Court denied this motion and ruled that it would not hear complaints against the actions of a state agency. With no legal means of redress, the Collins administration had little choice but to cut a deal. Ratner agreed to a slight modification of the project, decreasing its size from 515 to 445 acres. He also donated land to Florida Presbyterian (now Eckerd) College and dedicated a right-of-way for the Bayway, a toll road that would link the south beach communities to St. Petersburg.[51]

In 1961, Ratner's firm completed its dredging operation. The location and size of this fill not only intensified the bay's decline; it also ensured that Boca Ciega could never be restored to its past health. By 1964, this once-shallow coastal lagoon, with its vast meadows of turtle grass, had been transformed into a channelized cesspool. Fills occupied 12.5 percent of the bay's 20,000 acres, while dredging operations had altered another 5,000 acres to build the fills. The "suburbanization" of the bay left the water discolored, stagnant, and laden with pollutants. As a layer of anaerobic muck replaced the sand of the bay bottom, commercial fishing interests saw their catches plummet. By the late 1960s, Boca Ciega was Florida's most polluted bay, and fishing fleets had left for cleaner waters.[52]

After Collins left office, the next significant legislation to protect Boca Ciega Bay came in 1966, when the wealthy investor and environmentalist Nathaniel Reed joined Claude Kirk's administration. In a surprise victory, Kirk returned the governor's office to the Republican Party for the first time in almost a century. One of Kirk's first appointments went to Reed, who accepted the post of "environmental advisor" and immediately set out to limit dredge-and-fill operations. During the 1967 legislative session, Kirk and Reed teamed with Representative Tom Randell of Fort Myers to secure passage of the Randell Act, which required developers seeking dredge-and-fill permits to furnish a detailed environmental study meeting strict state guidelines. Reed also persuaded Kirk to oppose any applications that significantly altered coastal habitats. Before the Randell Act passed, Florida approved an average of 2,000 fill projects a year. By 1970, that number had shrunk to 200.[53]

In 1969, Florida's bays received additional protection when Kirk signed the Aquatic Preserve Bill into law. Representative Dorothy Sample, a Republican attorney from St. Petersburg, spurred a bipartisan effort that prohibited dredging in designated preserves. She also convinced her colleagues to make Boca Ciega Bay Florida's first aquatic preserve.[54]

Bruce Stephenson

During the late 1960s, new federal statutes also helped end dredge-and-fill operations in Boca Ciega Bay. In 1968, Congress passed the National Estuary Protection Act, which encouraged local municipalities to protect the biological integrity of estuaries through planning. In addition, it called for federal agencies to consider the ecological impacts fostered by development projects in coastal areas. In 1970, the federal courts first interpreted the National Estuary Protection Act in *Zabel v. Tabb,* a case involving a dredge-and-fill project in Boca Ciega Bay that followed on the heels of the Ratner controversy.[55]

Zabel v. Tabb: An Environmental Precedent

In 1958, Alfred Zabel requested a permit from the Pinellas County Commission to fill twelve acres of Boca Ciega Bay. Although it was tiny compared with the Ratner Fill, Zabel's proposal to expand his trailer park into the bay attracted fierce opposition from local homeowners. The case went to the Florida Supreme Court twice before the TIIF was forced to grant a permit in 1965. As a last—and usually pro forma—step, the project required approval from the Army Corps of Engineers.

But when the project came in for review, the corps' Jacksonville office was inundated with protests. Colonel R. A. Tabb planned to postpone his decision until after the corps had held a public meeting in St. Petersburg. In November 1966, more than a hundred citizens showed up to speak against the project. Only one person agreed with Zabel's attorney, Thomas Harris, who declared, "It's our land, we can do with it what we want." After the meeting, Tabb's staff consulted with other governmental agencies about the environmental impact of Zabel's project. The biologists at the Marine Research Laboratory in St. Petersburg provided the most information. Robert Ingle, a marine biologist who had worked with Hutton in the 1950s, was the director of the laboratory. In a meeting with the corps' scientists, he restated most of Hutton's testimony from the previous decade. He also told them that the dredging and filling of Boca Ciega Bay had cost the fishing industry $1.4 million a year.[56]

In March 1967, Tabb denied Zabel's request for a permit. This was the first time the corps had ever denied a project because of its potential to damage the environment. Harris immediately filed suit against the U.S. Army Corps of Engineers and Tabb in federal court. The Tampa circuit court ruled against the corps because the proposed project did not impede navigation. The court took the view that protecting the environment was an ancillary issue. In

1968, however, with the passage of the National Estuary Protection Act, the corps' responsibilities increased. The corps had to amend its permit and include an examination of the effects of proposed work on "fish and wildlife, conservation, pollution, aesthetics, ecology and the general public interest."[57] After revising its procedure for obtaining permits, the army appealed the circuit court's ruling in *Zabel v. Tabb*. In 1970, the case went before the federal appellate court in New Orleans. It drew national attention; both developers and environmentalists waited to see if courts would uphold the National Estuary Protection Act.

In a precedent-setting decision, the court ruled that the project's destructive potential provided sufficient reason for refusing the dredging permit. The court found that, though projects like Zabel's had routinely received clearance a decade earlier, science had now clearly revealed the disastrous effects of dredge-and-fill projects on marine ecosystems. It was imperative that the government change its policies. Americans had become "aware of civilization's potential destruction," Judge John R. Brown stated, "from breathing its own polluted air and drinking its own infected water and the immeasurable loss from a silent-spring disturbance of nature's economy." Zabel appealed the decision, but the Supreme Court refused to hear the case, and a new standard was set for Boca Ciega Bay and the nation.[58]

In 1970, the federal courts also sent Leonard Bursten, Ratner's attorney, to prison. Bursten had left Florida in the early 1960s to represent a group of high-rolling developers in Beverly Hills, where his intimidating tactics caught the attention of a task force investigating fraudulent real estate dealings. The Los Angles police later implicated Bursten in a scheme that involved bribing city officials, but before this case reached the courts Bursten was sentenced to prison for tax fraud. While serving as Ratner's counselor in 1957, Bursten had earned over $160,000, none of which he reported as earned income.[59]

Boca Ciega Bay's degraded condition stabilized in the 1970s. By the end of the decade, the city's sewage plant had stopped discharging partially treated sewage into the bay. Efforts to preserve and replace such vital species as mangroves and turtle grass even brought about minor improvements, but the bay remained an environmental hazard.[60] The U.S. Department of Commerce has featured Boca Ciega Bay in a film, *Estuarine Heritage,* that it distributed to coastal communities revealing unregulated development's disastrous consequences. Polluted urban bays are hardly uncommon, but no other bay in the nation suffered such extensive damage in such a short period. Between 1940 and 1970, more than 80 percent of all Boca Ciega's marine grasses were lost, and 70 percent of the bay's nursery areas were destroyed. In 1940, Wilson Hubbard, captain of a charter boat, could fish in the bay from his 14-foot skiff, using only a hook and a line, and consistently pull in over 100 pounds of speckled trout a day. "You could look right through to the bottom," he recalled, "and see the fish swimming around." In the late 1980s, Hubbard still ran charter-fishing boats, but never in Boca Ciega Bay. Another commercial fisherman, who had brought in giant hauls before the Ratner Fill, lamented that there was nothing in the bay. "It's just so thick and heavy looking I wouldn't hardly swim in it, let alone fish it." In 1986, the county's chief health official discouraged swimming in the bay. "Why swim in it," he asked, "if you don't have to?" Shell fishing remains banned in most of the bay, and attempts to replant turtle grass have generally failed because of the poor flushing and heavy siltation.[61]

Perhaps the most salient reminder of Boca Ciega's demise comes from Governor Collins. Shortly before his death in 1991, Florida's senior statesman despaired that his administration did not do enough to protect the state's natural resources. Although he introduced many reforms through his office, the rape of Boca Ciega Bay still haunted him—so much so that, on flights to Tampa Bay, he always faced away from the coastal lagoon off St. Petersburg. What happened there was a "monstrous desecration" that he could never bring himself to view.

Unfortunately, the lessons learned in Boca Ciega Bay have been lost on Florida's present leaders. Governor Jeb Bush supports running an expressway through the Wekiva River Basin, the linchpin to central Florida's water supply and key habitat for the Florida black bear. Building a highway in this area is a risky endeavor because the region's water supply is already under tremendous pressure, and, if unchecked, new development will speed the depletion of groundwater resources. The governor appointed a task force to study the highway alignment and accompanying land-use issues in fall 2002. In the 2003 legislature, opposition arose to the task force's recommendation that the state acquire lands and impose controls to protect the Wekiva Basin springhead and aquifer recharge potential. The governor failed to support, much less champion, this initiative, and it suffered a quick death. He ignored appeals to designate the Wekiva as an area of "Critical State Concern" and appointed another task force, the Wekiva River Basin Coordination Committee (WRBCC) to study this issue. Following the original task force's lead, the WRBCC has proposed a similar series of recommendations to prevent suburban development from filling the Wekiva Basin springshed.[62] The question remains, however, will Jeb Bush fight the "monstrous desecration" of a unique Florida ecosystem?

If Governor Bush fails to build on LeRoy Collins's legacy and the bipartisan environmentalism that came to define state politics, Floridians will bear more than financial and ecological costs—they will suffer an extinction of experience. The vision of paradise that runs through Florida history emanates from a unique subtropical landscape. The memorable places and settings that define the Wekiva Basin tied generations together in a special bond, and losing them abrogates a common history. Hurtling into a future ignorant of nature's bounds and built to the lines of marketing slogans and optimum traffic flows will lock our children into an increasingly commercialized, engineered landscape, which hosts the highest pedestrian death rates in the nation.[63] Bereft of the wonderment that greeted previous Floridians' encounters with nature, it is hard to fathom how their humanity will not suffer. Destroying natural places that sustain life and enlighten our senses not only eliminates vital resources humans can never replicate, it represents acts of nihilism that extinguish a set of human experiences that are as old as our species.

Notes

1. LeRoy Collins, telephone interview by author, July 11, 1990.

2. *St. Petersburg Times*, April 3, 1957.

3. Samuel P. Hays, *Beauty, Health and Permanence: Environmental Politics in the United States, 1955–1985* (New York: Cambridge University Press, 1987), 1–39.

4. Donald Worster, *Nature's Economy: A History of Ecological Ideas* (New York: Oxford University Press, 1985), 205–20.

5. William Straub, *History of Pinellas County* (St. Augustine: Record Company, 1930), 11.

6. Pinellas County Planning Department (hereafter cited as PCPD), *The Conservation of Natural Resources Element of the Pinellas County Comprehensive Plan* (Clearwater, Fla., 1980), 45, 108–9; Roy R. Lewis and Ernest D. Estevez, *The Ecology of Tampa Bay, Florida: An Estuarine Profile* (Slidell, La.: U.S. Fish and Wildlife Service, Department of the Interior, 1988), 65–79; Robert F. Hutton, *The Ecology of Boca Ciega Bay with Special Reference to Dredging and Filling Operations* (St. Petersburg: Florida State Board of Conservation Marine Laboratory, 1956), 12–18, 47–63.

7. Robert H. Simpson and Herbert Riehl, *The Hurricane and Its Impact* (Baton Rouge: Louisiana State University, 1981), 221, 244–46, PCPD, Conservation of Nature Resources Element, 110.

Bruce Stephenson

8. Karl H. Grismer, *The Story of St. Petersburg* (St. Petersburg,: P. K. Smith and Company, 1948), 19.

9. John Nolen, *St. Petersburg Today, St. Petersburg Tomorrow* (St. Petersburg, 1923), John Nolen Papers (hereafter cited as NP), Division of Manuscripts and Special Collections, Cornell University, Ithaca, N.Y.

10. *St. Petersburg Times,* April 4, 1929.

11. R. Bruce Stephenson, *Visions of Eden: Environmentalism, Urban Planning and City Building in St. Petersburg, Florida, 1990–1995* (Columbus: Ohio State University Press, 1997), 70–102.

12. John Nolen, *A Report on City Planning Proposals for St. Petersburg, Florida* (St. Petersburg, 1926).

13. *St. Petersburg Times,* April 13, 1958; LeRoy Collins Papers, Special Collections, University of South Florida, Tampa.

14. Hutton, *The Ecology of Boca Ciega Bay,* 4.

15. Nelson Blake, *Land into Water/Water into Land: A History of Water Management in Florida* (Gainesville: University Presses of Florida, 1980), 38–59.

16. The problem of filling is first documented in *Florida Water Resources Study Commission Report on Water Problems* (Tallahassee: Florida Board of Conservation, 1956).

17. Tom Wagy, *Governor LeRoy Collins of Florida: Spokesman for the New South* (Tuscaloosa: University of Alabama Press, 1985), 74–83, 120–43.

18. Sheldon Plager and Frank Maloney, *Controlling Waterfront Development* (Gainesville: University of Florida, Public Administration Clearing Service, 1968), 30–31.

19. Ney Landrum, telephone interview by author, August 7, 1990.

20. John Rothchild, *Up for Grabs: A Trip through Time and Space in the Sunshine State* (New York: Viking, 1985), 33.

21. *St. Petersburg Times,* March 13, 1957.

22. Ibid., February 13, 1957. The Pinellas County Commission also served as the Pinellas Water and Navigation Control Authority by a special act of the state legislature, passed in 1955.

23. Robert N. Pierce, *A Sacred Trust: Nelson Poynter and the St. Petersburg Times* (Gainesville: University Press of Florida, 1993), 261.

24. *St. Petersburg Times,* February 22, 1956.

25. Carson quoted in *The Wilderness Reader,* ed. Frank Bergon (New York: Signet Books, 1980), 290.

26. Ibid.; Pierce, *A Sacred Trust,* 260–61.

27. *St. Petersburg Times,* February 22, 1956.

28. Harland Bartholomew and Associates, St. Petersburg Comprehensive Plan (St. Louis, 1941), Government Publications, Washington University, St. Louis, Missouri.

29. *St. Petersburg Times,* February 22, 1956.

30. Hutton, *The Ecology of Boca Ciega Bay,* 7–9.

31. According to E. O. Wilson, "The loss of a keystone species is like a drill accidentally striking a power line. It causes lights to go out all over." Wilson quoted in G. Tyler

Miller, *Living in the Environment* (Belmont, Calif.: Wadsworth Publishing Company, 1994), 101.

32. Kenneth Woodburn, interview by author, August 6, 1990; Hutton, *The Ecology of Boca Ciega Bay*, 81.

33. Rothchild, *Up for Grabs*, 32.

34. Plager and Maloney, *Controlling Waterfront Development*, 13.

35. *St. Petersburg Times*, April 3, 1957.

36. Ibid., March 6, 1957.

37. Ibid.; Rothchild, *Up for Grabs*, 83–103.

38. Rothchild, *Up for Grabs*, 84–86; Jonathan Raban, "The Gaudy Green Eden," in *Florida Leadership Forum, Progress or Decline, Issues of Growth Management: A Reader* (Tallahassee: Florida Endowment for the Humanities, 1986), 181–86.

39. Rothchild, *Up for Grabs*, 96.

40. *St. Petersburg Times*, April 12, 1957.

41. Ibid., October 13, 1958.

42. Ibid., April 14, 1957.

43. Ibid., May 17, 1957, and June 5, 1957.

44. Plager and Maloney, *Controlling Waterfront Development*, 26–39.

45. All quoted material is from Pinellas County Commission, Excerpts from Furen-Ratner Fill Hearings (Clearwater, Fla.: December 6, 7, 10, 11, 17, 18, 1957), Pinellas County Court House, Clearwater, Florida.

46. Woodburn interview, August 6, 1990.

47. *St. Petersburg Times*, January 7, 1958.

48. Ibid., September 28, 1958.

49. Ibid., January 17, 1958.

50. Ibid., January 9, 1959.

51. Ibid., February 27, 1959, July 10, 1959, and August 19, 1959.

52. Roy R. Lewis, "Impacts of Dredging in the Tampa Bay Estuary, 1876–1976," in *Conference of the Coastal Society: Time Stressed Environments,* ed. E. L. Pruitt (Arlington, Va.: n.p., 1977), 47–51; J. L. Taylor and C. H. Saloman, "Some Effects of Hydraulic Dredging and Coastal Development in Boca Ciega Bay," *U.S. Fish and Wildlife Service Bulletin* 67 (February 1968): 213–41.

53. Blake, *Land into Water/Water into Land,* 197; Luther J. Carter, *The Florida Experience: Land and Water Policy in a Growth State* (Baltimore: Johns Hopkins University Press, 1974), 53–54.

54. PCPD, The History of Pinellas County (Clearwater, Fla., 1986), 44; *St. Petersburg Independent,* May 23, 1969.

55. Joseph Siry, *Marshes on the Ocean Shore* (College Station: Texas A & M University Press, 1984), 178–82.

56. Taylor and Saloman, "Hydraulic Dredging and Coastal Development"; *St. Petersburg Times,* May 5, 1966, and November 30, 1966.

57. Rutherford H. Platt, *Land Use Control: Geography, Law, and Public Policy* (Englewood Cliffs, N.J.: Prentice Hall, 1991), 330.

58. *Zabel v. Tabb,* 430 F2d 199 (1970).

Bruce Stephenson

59. *St. Petersburg Times*, March 28, 1970.

60. Tampa Bay Regional Planning Council, *The Future of Tampa Bay* (St. Petersburg, 1985), 151–56.

61. *St. Petersburg Times*, February 12, 1985; *St. Petersburg Independent*, April 15, 1986; Lewis and Estevez, *The Ecology of Tampa Bay, Florida*, 89–127.

62. The *Orlando Sentinel* has run a series or articles and editorials on the proposed expressway through the Wekiva Protection Area and Basin. The most comprehensive articles are found in the January 3, 2003, and August 24, 2003, editions. Also see "Florida's Water Crisis," a series that ran in the *Sentinel* between March 3, 2002, and November 17, 2002. Governor Bush is entertaining the expensive proposition of pumping water from north Florida south to meet anticipated demand. *New York Times*, September 27, 2003.

63. Orlando, Tampa Bay, and West Palm Beach are the nation's three most dangerous metropolitan areas for pedestrians and bicyclists. For children, these cities are especially dangerous. While children make up 5 percent of fatalities in vehicle accidents, they account for 11 percent of pedestrian deaths. Surface Transportation Policy Project, "Mean Streets 2002" (Washington, D.C., 2003), www.transact.org/report.

Chapter 15

"We Must Free Ourselves . . .
from the Tattered Fetters of the Booster Mentality"

Big Cypress Swamp and the Politics
of Environmental Protection in 1970s Florida

Gordon E. Harvey

Between the 1950s and 1970s, investors, primarily from the North, bought
thousands of acres in and around Big Cypress Swamp, which lies mostly in
Collier County in southwest Florida, for up to $2,500 an acre on the install-
ment plan—twenty dollars down and twenty dollars a month. Leonard Rosen's
Gulf American Land Corporation sold most of this land with plans to carve
dozens of subdivisions out of the wetlands and swamplands of south Florida.
After building Cape Coral out of a mangrove swamp on the Gulf coast, Rosen

set his eyes on Big Cypress, purchased the equivalent of the size of Manhattan out of the swamp, and dreamed of a city of 400,000 satisfied customers. To prepare the swampland for construction, Rosen constructed a multitude of canals, almost 183 miles in all, and built more than 800 miles of access roads in what he now called Golden Gate Estates. The land sold for almost $2,500 an acre. But few landowners ever occupied their land. By 1997, Rosen's dream of 400,000 residents barely amounted to fifty houses. In the early 1970s, the vacant land attracted drug smugglers and Cuban exiles, who used it for their various, and at times nefarious, purposes. Golden Gate Estates was a symbol of all that could go wrong environmentally for a swamp that was the lifeblood of south Florida's water resources and the Everglades itself. It was also emblematic of the carelessness that most often followed the crusade for industrial and residential development in the nation, especially in the South. By the end of the 1960s, there developed a movement to correct what University of Florida ecologist Howard T. Odum called the "culture of development."[1]

In July 971, newly inaugurated Florida governor Reubin Askew addressed a Dade County conference on Florida's air and water resources. Askew indicted humans for mishandling their natural surroundings and lamented recent environmental hazards and disasters in Florida such as a deadly bacteria strain in Lake Apopka caused by high levels of nutrients from local farms, municipal sewage, citrus groves, citrus processing plants, and water hyacinth debris. The damage was hastened by C-38, a 52-mile canal built in the 1960s by transforming the meandering 90-mile Kissimmee River into a flood-control waterway. The canal channeled fertilizer runoff from surrounding farmland directly into the lake. Before the end of summer, Askew predicted, Lake Apopka's surface would be "white with shad turned belly up." It was to Askew the latest in a long line of examples of man "befouling his environment." "Unlike the animals," Askew explained, humans are "guilty of years of thoughtlessness and neglect. But also unlike the animals, we have the ability to protect and restore—as well as the ability to spoil and destroy."[2] For a governor of a southern state in need of industrial and commercial investment and with a history of environmental indifference, Askew chose strong language to announce that he had committed his administration to aggressive environmental correction and protection. On a matter of direct concern to his audience, he declared that "the day of the septic tank—which still serves more than a half million Dade County residents—must pass. It has no place in an urban area."[3]

Not the first Floridian to express grave concern for the state's environment, Askew was most certainly the most powerful when he uttered his remarks. The state's unique environment and favorable climate set it apart from other states. Traveling along portions of the St. Johns River in 1773, William Bartram wondered at Florida's untouched beauty, finding himself in "a blessed unviolated spot of earth."[4] Bartram was not alone in his affinity for Florida's splendor. He was joined by Ralph Waldo Emerson, Harriet Beecher Stowe, and Stephen Crane. Henry James praised the state's "velvet air" and "royal palms." And Ernest Hemingway described Florida as "the last wild country." Florida's own Marjory Stoneman Douglas celebrated the state's environment, especially the Everglades, and declared, in a book considered by Hodding Carter as comparable with Bartram's *Travels*, that there was only one Everglades.[5]

By 1970, Florida offered little of the wild frontier and immaculate beauty praised by literary notables. For many of the same reasons that the state was fêted in literature, it had become an attractive place to live and visit. In the two hundred years since Bartram's visit, Florida's population had grown from roughly 100,000 Native Americans to almost 10 million residents. Most of the state's population explosion took place after World War II. Between 1940 and 1970, Florida's population grew from 1.8 million to 7 million, and by 1980 to 11 million. Tourism added another 32 million to the number of people who put demands on the state's resources. Six years later, the number of tourists, who are generally more casual about consuming energy and creating waste, increased by 54 percent.[6] With an increase of 564 percent between 1930 and 1980, Florida's population growth outpaced that of every other state.[7]

Such growth hastened the state's environmental decline. Residing by the millions in coastal cities and along freshwater bodies in south and central Florida, the population was centered in those areas least equipped to tolerate such numbers. As Florida writer Mark Derr notes, Florida had become a "victim of its allure."[8] In his landmark history of Florida, Charlton Tebeau lamented in 1971 the condition of the state's natural resources. It was, he concluded, the result of the pioneer view of nature and the land as "something to be used without limit for their profit and pleasure." Tebeau reported that extraction still ruled over preservation.[9]

In September 1969, "Conservation 70s, Inc.," an environmentally focused citizens' group, conducted weekend workshops for legislators and state agencies to build awareness of the state's fragile environmental condition. Established in July 1969 in Orlando, "C-70s," as it was popularly known, warned state leaders of future "ecotastrophes," which could only be measured by years and decades rather than hours and days. The group asserted that barring aggressive protection, the Everglades would dry out within eighty years. It tried to counter the state's long history of environmental indifference, which often included actions detrimental to the environment. For example, a 1958 Florida Water Resource Conference concluded that the state had too much water and recommended channeling the Kissimmee River to drain parts of central Florida, which resulted in the construction of C-38. Canals constructed in Brevard, Palm Beach, Broward, and Dade counties drained wetlands to make way for agricultural and residential expansion. Cut at sea level, the canals allowed seawater to intrude into the freshwater supply.[10]

In the year of Askew's election, a group of federal ecologists recommended aggressive action to preserve the Everglades and the water sources that gave it life. The group explained that the Everglades system was larger than the national park proper, that the system actually began in the upper Kissimmee River basin of central Florida and drained to the south via marshland into Lake Okeechobee. The lake and Big Cypress Swamp to the northwest drained into the Everglades, giving it most of its water. Since the 1880s, humans had upset the delicate balance of the Everglades system by introducing swamp drainage, flood control, canal building, and residential and commercial development, all of which had the effect of carving the system into pieces, thereby weakening and threatening its vitality. Few had realized the complex interdependency of the state's natural assets. In the 1970s, the Everglades housed dozens of endangered species, provided bountiful data for ecologists studying the role of water in nature, and, according to one amateur anthropologist, provided a home for Bigfoot. The water system was a major "recharge" area for the Biscayne Aquifer, which served as the primary water supply for the heavily populated Gold Coast of Florida. Without urgent action, the group warned, south Florida's water supply would be inadequate to meet the needs of the growing population as early as 1976.[11]

Such conclusions were echoed by Arthur R. Marshall, a University of Miami ecologist best known for his expertise on the Everglades, whom Askew commissioned to undertake a detailed assessment of south Florida's water supply. Marshall sadly reported that the Everglades had approached the end of its resiliency, giving it twenty more years of life. He pointed out that draining of the surrounding areas for residential and commercial development had reduced the park's ability to hold water. "Should we continue on our past course of environmental insensitivity or indifference," warned Marshall, "we shall see a snow-balling degeneration of major resources of the Everglades commence in this decade—within the term of this administration." Marshall could find no other instance where "species extirpation has resulted from maltreatment of a national park." Flood control and drainage efforts had resulted in numerous fires and unnatural dry periods that had plagued the park for most of the twentieth century. The Hoover Dike, a Depression-era flood-control and land-reclamation project that followed deadly hurricanes in 1926 and 1928, contributed to the Everglades' decline. The dike dried out the Everglades for half the year, longer than its natural winter drought period, resulting in a series of fires. In every decade following 1926, the Everglades suffered at least two major burns. What had occurred, wrote Marshall, was "evapo-transpiration." As the land area decreased, the park's ability to hold water also declined, which reduced the amount of rain-causing evaporation, resulting in less rainfall in south Florida and a reduction of the water table. In short, human intervention had reduced the amount of rainfall in the region.[12] Marshall's report ended with an ominous thought: "the United States was the first nation in the history of the world to establish a system of national parks. Must we be the first nation and state to destroy one?"[13]

The poster child for Florida's environmental problems in the 1970s was Big Cypress Swamp and its watershed. Considered by many as the last truly wild place in Florida, Big Cypress rested northwest of the Everglades and 60 miles from Miami and covered large portions of Collier, Hendry, Palm Beach, Broward, Dade, and Monroe counties. Home to Seminole and Miccosukee Indians, Big Cypress housed a number of endangered species and plants while supplying the Everglades with more than half its water supply; if the Everglades had a "heart," it was the 2,450-square-mile Big Cypress. The swamp was originally included within the boundary of Everglades National Park in the 1930s. It was later removed after an oil strike in the Pineland region near Sunniland fostered a land boom and a move by oil companies and others to remove Big Cypress from federal protection. The popularity of cypress wood for decks, bleachers, coffins, barrels, and P.T. boats during World War II made a target of the swamp's grand virgin-growth trees. Between 1943 and 1957, cypress was extensively logged from the area. By 1946, the state, responding to landowner pressure, had negotiated the reduction of Everglades National Park boundaries by almost one-third, leaving Big Cypress Swamp and other endangered ecological sites in Florida without federal or state protection.[14]

Removal of Big Cypress from federal protection corresponded with an increase in the migration of south Floridians away from Miami. "Cuban refugees, Civil Rights legislation demanding integrated schools and housing, and a perception that government was reaching too deep within their lives," Derr writes, precipitated a white-flight response to change.[15] Other residents came to the area because of the Miami-Dade County jetport, planned for construction within Big Cypress. The swamp received scant attention from few people other than environmentalists until the 1969 jetport controversy made it a topic of national concern. Proposed and planned by the Miami-Dade Port Authority, the jetport was designed to occupy 39 square miles (an area larger than the City of Miami proper) north of the Everglades and within the territory of Big Cypress. With its large runways and immense size, the jetport could handle up to 200,000 flights a year and would have been larger than the airports of New York, Los Angeles, and Washington, D.C., combined. Outrage at the potential for environmental destruction, and intervention by the Nixon administration, resulted in the jetport's relocation away from the swamp. Following Nixon's intervention, the U.S. Department of the Interior promised future action to protect the swamp. Property owners who had relocated to the area in anticipation of jetport-related growth pledged future action to protect not Big Cypress but rather their property interests and values.[16]

In September 1971, Askew assembled 150 science, government, agriculture, and conservation experts for a Governor's Conference on Water Management in south Florida. In the plenary session, Askew reprised his call for a "peace between the people and their place . . . between the natural environment and the man-made settlement." For centuries, said Askew, humans had been "awfully busy" undoing the work of nature. Lamenting the rise of sewage levels in Biscayne Bay, the decline of fish and game levels at Lake Okeechobee, and the general disregard for water preservation all over the state, Askew quoted *Silent Spring* author and catalyst of the modern environmental movement Rachel Carson in his call to arms: "If the Bill of Rights contains no guarantee that a citizen shall be secure against lethal poisons distributed either by private individuals or public officials, it is . . . only because our forefathers . . . could conceive of no such problem." The time had come, declared Askew, to stop "viewing our environment through prisms of profit, politics, geography or local pride." Someone else may have directly caused such problems, said Askew, but "somehow, we all know, we're to blame."[17]

Askew charged the conferees with determining how best to address such questions as the necessity for a south Florida regional water authority. Who would control such an agency—federal, state, or local officials, or all three? How should the state protect and preserve its environment and threatened water supply? Growth, Askew explained, was desirable and necessary for the state's economic well-being, but at what cost? How could the state effectively balance its economic and environmental needs, which, after all, were not necessarily mutually exclusive? As an example of the wholesale deterioration of Florida's water supply, Askew presented the case of Biscayne Bay. In 1920, the bay had abundant freshwater springs, but by 1971, one had to travel 12 miles inland to find freshwater. Failure to forestall further declines meant "disastrous" results to the state economy and environment. Askew's economic argument—lost revenues from declines in tourism and investment and increased expenditures for restoration—had a stronger impact than moral platitudes. For Florida, tourism was the lifeblood of its economy. With millions of visitors each year coming to its beaches and parks, especially Everglades National Park, the state was set to lose millions of dollars of revenue if its natural attractions fell into decline.[18]

The *Miami Herald* declared that Askew's water conference "may be one of the most important conferences held in Florida." Warning that is was too early to undertake "victory dances in the dangerous contest between those who would save and those who would destroy the environment," the *St. Petersburg Times* nonetheless saw signs of a "new ballgame." Without action to protect Florida's environment, the *Times* warned, Florida might become the world's only desert with 60 inches of rainfall annually. The *Tampa Tribune* described the conferees as "heretics" to the established order, but "prophets" to the environmentally concerned. The newspaper predicted that the conference "has probably set in motion a statewide political power struggle."[19]

The conferees published a seven-page list of recommendations. They included putting an end to indiscriminate draining of wetlands, preserving muck lands by re-flooding and re-vegetating with saw grass, and protecting Lake Okeechobee and Big Cypress Swamp and its watershed as vital sources of freshwater for the state. For Big Cypress, the conference urged preservation by land acquisition and strict land-use controls. To administer such activities, the group suggested the creation of an interagency committee to consider short-term water problems, and the formation by the state of long-term water- and land-use plans. The group also urged that the state treat water problems as regional issues, not local or state problems, since bodies of water rarely observed human-made boundaries. Long relying on a more reactionary "firefighter" approach to environmental threats, environmentalists now had a blueprint for a more proactive course.[20]

Using the recommendations as a policy blueprint, Askew lobbied Florida's congressional delegation to introduce federal legislation for Big Cypress acquisition. Askew's push to protect Big Cypress came at a time when national presidential politics intensified as Democratic hopefuls postured to become the person to challenge incumbent Richard Nixon. As environmentalism grew as a major issue in the 1970s, those seeking to unseat Nixon attempted to seize upon such concerns as a means of gaining an issue over the president.[21]

Askew's appeals did not go unheeded. As 1971 ended, presidential posturing among Democrats had begun in earnest. A collection of U.S. senators and presidential candidates—Maine's Edmund Muskie, Minnesota's Hubert Humphrey, South Dakota's George McGovern, and Washington's Henry "Scoop" Jackson—had all but declared their candidacies and displayed an interest in environmental legislation. Jackson chaired the Senate's Committee on Interior and Insular Affairs, conducted hearings on the Everglades in 1969, and had displayed an appreciation for protecting the national park. In August 1971, Florida senator Lawton Chiles—with Jackson and Florida's other U.S. senator, Ed Gurney—sponsored a bill for the federal purchase of all land within or connected to Big Cypress. As Jackson, Gurney, and Chiles ushered their bill through the Senate, Askew lobbied Interior Secretary Rogers Morton, urging that he, too, pursue aggressive protection of Big Cypress through acquisition. Acquisition, explained Askew, was "the only sure method to protect the heart of this natural ecosystem and at the same time treat the landowners fairly." Florida had help within the Interior Department. Deputy Interior Secretary Nathaniel Reed, former environmental adviser to Claude Kirk and past chair of the Florida Department of Air and Water Pollution Control, pressed Morton to give "maximum personal attention" to Big Cypress while citing the administration's "excellent record" in protecting the area with its intervention in the jetport controversy. Morton agreed that acquisition was a better option than regulating the area with a heavy federal hand.[22]

Nixon's interest in Big Cypress was primarily political. Nothing close to an environmentalist, Nixon nevertheless appreciated the political value of environmental issues. To that end, Nixon created the Council on Environmental Quality, which served as a clearinghouse for environmental policy during the Nixon years. Among other things, that council recommended to Nixon the creation of the Environmental Protection Agency (EPA) in 1970. Undersecretary of the Interior John Whitaker once succinctly condensed Nixon's interest in the environment: "what better, higher, priority than re-election."[23] It came as no surprise when Nixon announced in November 1971 that he planned to submit to Congress a bill authorizing and expenditure of $156 million to buy 547,000 acres of Big Cypress to protect it "from private development that would destroy it."[24]

In November 1971 and again in April 1972, Jackson's committee held hearings in Dade County and Washington, D.C., on Big Cypress and water conditions in south Florida. It listened to testimony from various ecologists, environmentalists, and Askew himself. Askew's testimony offered little that he had not already stated publicly, and he repeated his warnings of dire consequences if the swamp went unprotected. Demand for land in and around the swamp continued to grow with 1{1/4}-acre plots near the Tamiami Trail selling for $2,500. Local officials in Collier County had tried to slow the land boom by placing a moratorium on zoning changes, but they had few other means at their disposal. Acquisition remained the only effective way to protect the swamp and the interests of property owners. To that end, Florida was prepared to commit $40 million as a good-faith effort. But, Askew concluded, "Florida alone cannot save or acquire the heart of Big Cypress Watershed." The $40 million was the largest amount the state had ever committed to a single acquisition and was not far off the total amount the state had spent in its history for park and recreational land acquisition.[25]

In January 1972, in a shallow media exercise to exhibit their concern for the swamp, Interior Secretary Rogers Morton and National Park Service Director George Hartzog accompanied Nixon's daughter, Julie Eisenhower, on a tour of the swamp at Robert's Lake Strand near Monroe Station. Outfitted in waders and flanked by Eisenhower's secret service detail and members of the national media, the group ventured more than a hundred yards into the swamp. After Morton retrieved empty beer cans from the water, the three took an airboat ride into the heart of the swamp, where he repeated the administration's commitment to preservation through acquisition.[26]

As Congress mulled over legislation that would protect the swamp, the Florida legislature met in February 1972. In opening remarks that spanned sixty pages and lasted for an hour, Askew posited a catalog of legislative proposals: an eighteen-month moratorium on executions; establishment of a blue-ribbon commission to study the death penalty "quietly, calmly and compassionately"; consumer protection legislation; an end to the elected cabinet; and broad new powers in the area of environmental protection. For the environment, Askew requested a merger of the state's several environmental agencies to be replaced by a "superagency," which would consolidate the power and responsibility of the Department of Natural Resources, the Pollution Control Department, the Game and Freshwater Fish Commission, and the trustees of the State's Internal Improvement Fund. "It is not melodramatic to say," Askew said, "that Florida, like California, is in great danger of becoming a 'paradise lost.' It is not offbeat and alarmist to say that continued failure to control growth and development in this state will lead to economic as well as environmental disaster." Askew's sweeping environmental proposals included a Land and Water Management Bill, which would allow the state to designate for protection and preservation certain "areas of critical state concern." He also requested a bond issue of up to $240 million to purchase endangered lands, of which $40 million would go toward purchasing Big Cypress. Askew also proposed that the Department of Natural Resources, of which the governor and his cabinet were the executive board, be given the power to regulate oil and gas drilling, including requiring oil and gas companies to obtain permission from the state to launch new drilling or exploration activities on public lands. It was an ambitious series of proposals, and Askew appealed to the legislature to join him in preserving the state for "the people and for all the other living things which make Florida a place worth living."[27]

Askew's consolidation proposals sought to remove power from up to six cabinet members and set him at odds with many in state government who believed that he was less concerned with streamlining state government than he was in increasing his power. Askew granted that he pushed such reforms "knowing full well that they expose me to the charge of power-grabbing." But to suggest as much, Askew argued, was an "affront to the legislature" and "an unjustified lack of confidence in the people. I sincerely hope that Florida's great needs will not be eclipsed by that kind of phrase-making." It was imperative to look beyond politics: "The importance of action in these areas to the future of Florida transcends any of the politics of the moment." Cabinet members and officials with the state's Natural Resources and Agriculture departments attacked the proposals. They were among those who still smarted from a series of constitutional reforms in 1968 and 1969 that resulted in

Florida's elected cabinet losing budget-making authority to the legislature. Under the current system, the governor and the trustees of the state Internal Improvements Fund, by majority vote, made decisions on land sales and purchases. Askew wanted to abolish the trustees and move that power to a new Lands Commission comprised of himself and the cabinet, with the governor holding a veto. Furthermore, Askew's planned superagency, the Environmental Affairs Department, would be led by gubernatorial appointees and would comprise three new boards: the State Lands Commission, the Game and Freshwater Fish Commission, and the Environmental Quality Commission. The *St. Petersburg Times* saw "political dynamite" in Askew's plans. Others, like State Senator Mallory Horne, complained that Askew had posited "the biggest single assault on the power of the cabinet in the sixteen years I've been in the legislature." Supporters, led by Representative Jim Reeves, a Democrat from Askew's hometown of Pensacola, predicted quick approval in the state house.[28]

Askew had asked for another round of landmark reforms from an already tired legislature, battered and bruised from a December 1971 special session that resulted in the enactment of a corporate income tax amendment to the state constitution. Now, three months later, Askew sought another Herculean effort to pass more contentious and potentially divisive legislation. To that end, he spent no small amount of time stroking the collective legislative ego: "This is probably the last hurrah for what I believe is the greatest legislature in the history of our state. Let's make it one which will never be forgotten by students of responsive and responsible government."[29]

The movement to acquire Big Cypress met opposition from landowners and those who believed that the government was trying to abolish their property rights. Collier County had one of the larger of such groups. James G. Pace, president of the Landowners Conservation and Protective Association, called for the government to abandon hopes of acquisition. He argued that the imminent danger to Big Cypress and Everglades was overstated. Rather, Pace urged the government to spend a much smaller amount of money ($25 million) to develop water-conservation areas on publicly owned land. Pace attacked the state for what he considered Marxism run amok. He had bristled at comments made by State Attorney General Robert Shevin, who had, according to Pace, said that in some instances the rights of individual property owners were subservient to the rights of the state and citizenry as a whole, especially when it came to water resources. To Pace, Shevin's comments smacked of communism: "I have never read Karl Marx, but this is the principle of the governments of Russia, China, Cuba, Chile and other countries with ideologies different from ours."[30]

Another group, the East Collier Landowners Improvement Committee, echoed Pace's sentiments. The organization's Research Director, Ellis Chism, asserted that taking Big Cypress from the landowners would amount to a felony: "what greater crime can there be against people than to take this land where they planned and dreamed to live the balance of their lives in this choice climate and location in our nation?" Chism asserted that purchasing the land was inherently unfair because the government would never pay market value for such valuable plots of land. Frontage land near Alligator Alley had recently sold for $10,000 for 1{1/4} acres. Land at Ochopee near the Tamiami Trail had sold for almost $20,000 per acre, while an oil firm had paid the Walt Disney Company $300,000 for an acre near Walt Disney World. And what of the American promise of liberty, asked Chism. Cuban émigrés lived in the area: "These Cubans have been made to believe that democracy will protect their God-given rights." He warned that the nation would not sit idly by while the state committed a "criminal act against God's creatures while you prefer our land be preserved for snakes and alligators." To Chism, his crusade reflected the great revolutionary Spirit of '76: "We are fighting to re-establish the great nation of our forefather's [sic] dreams and hopes so we can protect our children from persons like you." Not willing to let their arguments about patriotism, democracy, and freedom speak for themselves, the group also relied on misinformation. One of the more damaging rumors was that the government planned to ban hunting in any federally or state-protected wildlife area and prohibit all-terrain vehicles, such as swamp buggies. In fact, the Big Cypress legislation before Congress expressly protected, but heavily regulated, hunting rights. And swamp vehicles were allowed, but only on preexisting trails.[31] Assistant Interior Secretary Nathaniel Reed warned Floridians and conservation groups not to believe the "bag of lies" emanating from opposition groups.[32]

Askew's attempt to create an environmental superagency failed in the state Senate after passing the House. A noble effort to consolidate the immense size and far-flung powers of various state departments and agencies, the bill ran headlong into the intricacies of state government and bureaucracy. Signs of failure appeared shortly after the bill arrived in the legislature. The state attorney general issued an opinion that held that one agency under target for consolidation, the Florida Game and Freshwater Fish Commission, was a "law unto itself," in that it was the only environmental-related state agency specifically written into the new state constitution and could not be abolished by the legislature short of a constitutional amendment. Director O. Earle Frye was hurt by Askew's proposal, explaining that his agency had always "tried to fit into the family of state agencies" by submitting regular budgets and annual reports even when not required.[33]

If Askew suffered a political setback with consolidation, it was overshadowed by the passage of the most sweeping environmental legislation in Florida history. With widespread support in the legislature, five major environmental bills became law following the 1972 legislative session.[34] The 1972 Water Management Act gave the state authority to label endangered land as "Areas of Critical State Concern," and to subject such areas to strict usage regulations. Development in such areas required approval of the State Land Planning Commission. Acknowledging that environmental problems rarely observed human-made borders, the legislation allowed critical areas to be addressed in their entirety with little interference from county lines or bureaucratic tangles between counties. The Department of Natural Resources gained regulatory authority over oil and gas drilling in Florida. The state was also divided into five water management districts, each overseen by a commissioner appointed by the governor, with broad power to regulate water usage. They were also charged with developing a state water-use plan. The Land Conservation Act authorized a $240 million bond issue to fund the purchase of endangered and recreational lands and required the Department of Natural Resources to prepare a comprehensive plan for the preservation of endangered lands. Yet another act banned coastline drilling near aquatic preserves or within freshwater areas. In all, the 1972 environmental legislation set Florida apart from its fellow southern states while drawing high praise from Loring Lovelle, president of C-70s. Lovelle declared that Florida was now "head and shoulders above any other state, as well as the federal government in land and water management."[35]

Florida was not alone in placing environmental spending measures on the ballot. Each of the forty state legislatures that met in regular session in 1972 considered some form of land-use or water legislation. In the South, Kentucky and Virginia joined Florida in ushering environmental protection legislation through their respective state houses. Especially daunting for Florida was gaining voter approval for spending increases and bond issues in a time of taxpayer revolt.[36]

Florida state law required voter approval for all state bond issues. To cultivate popular support for the referendum, Askew allied with state legislators

Bob Graham and Jack Shreve, both of whom had been named "outstanding legislators" of the 1972 session by C-70s for their commitment to the environment and their role in ushering the landmark environmental legislation. Graham chaired "Lands For You, Inc.," an organization formed by concerned citizens in favor of environmental protection. The bond issue also received endorsements from groups such as the League of Women Voters, Sierra Club, Jaycees, C-70s, Florida Home Builders Association, and Florida Association of Realtors. Harris Mullen, publisher of *Florida Trend* and chair of Florida's influential public interest organization, Council of 100, aggressively campaigned for the bond referendum by arguing that the state had a moral and legal responsibility to protect its environment; and that voters had to realize that the economy and the environment were "indivisible."[37]

In November 1972, Florida voters joined those from California, Washington, and New York in approving major bond issues. Three-quarters of all bond issues placed before voters in 1972 met approval, a stunning reversal from the previous year, when American voters only approved one out of five bond issues before them. Bond issues were so successful nationwide that the *New York Times* declared the taxpayer revolt of the late 1960s and early 1970s all but dead. Florida's $240 million proposal ranked among the largest bond issues of the year but still paled in comparison with New York's $1.15 billion proposal for pollution control and land preservation, and California's $516 million issue. Florida's success can be credited, in part, to the support of popular public officials, such as Graham and Askew, and the increasing awareness of the state's symbiotic relationship with its environment.[38]

In the wake of the successful bond referendum and 1972's landmark environmental legislation, the Nixon administration announced its intent to pursue congressional appropriations to purchase 547,000 acres of Big Cypress Swamp "to protect it from private development that would surely destroy it." This announcement came just days following an announcement by Scoop Jackson of hearings to be held in Miami on a bill authored by Jackson, Chiles, and Gurney and co-sponsored by former presidential candidates Edmund Muskie and Hubert Humphrey. As to the inevitable question of whose idea came first, Nixon's interior secretary Rogers Morton asserted that Nixon first had the urge to save Big Cypress, to which Chiles responded that he had taken the idea to Morton in early 1972 and received a cool response to the idea of outright purchase. Morton had then suggested stricter regulation over acquisition. Jabbing the administration, Chiles concluded that: "I'm delighted that the administration has come around to our concept of buying this watershed area. It is the only real route to preserving and protecting the area and at the same time being fair to landowners."[39]

There was little difference between the several Big Cypress bills before Congress. Land acreage ranged from 547,000 acres to 585,000 acres, while the amount of the purchase ranged from Nixon's proposed $156 million to Florida Representative Claude Pepper's $200 million. The Nixon bill departed from the others in allowing for the presence of oil wells and oil exploration within the swamp, but only with state approval. Askew endorsed the Nixon bill as the vehicle to purchase the swamp. The state had committed $40 million toward the swamp's purchase as a show of good faith that Florida would carry its burden in environmental protection; the sum had been large enough to spur the Nixon White House to action.[40]

In its 1973 session, the Florida legislature enhanced and expanded the environmental protection laws it enacted in 1972. The *St. Petersburg Times* had dubbed 1972 the "year of the environment" in Florida but gave 1973 equal importance because the legislature now had to fund the environmental laws it had created. Among the more important results of the 1973 legislature was the formal naming of Big Cypress as an "Area of Critical State Concern," which required the Askew administration to determine boundaries of protection; as well as a commitment that the $40 million from the recently passed environmentally endangered lands bond issue be used toward land acquisition in Big Cypress Swamp. Following up on the 1972 creation of water-management districts, the 1973 legislature formally established district boundaries and enacted the Florida Electric Power Plant Siting Act, which gave the Department of Pollution Control centralized regulatory authority over locations of new power plants. Finally, a fifteen-member commission was formed to study the energy needs of Florida to be included as part of the state's comprehensive plan.[41]

In speeches before the Florida Audubon Society and Manatee County Chamber of Commerce, Askew repeated his call for responsible growth. For too long, state leaders had sacrificed the state's environmental future on the altar of boosterism. In the inevitable conflict between growth and preservation, growth had won for too long—and with disastrous results. Askew called for a new age of controlled growth in which a state could seek both expansion and environmental protection:

> Everyday another parking lot or another shopping center or another lofty high rise removes a little bit of the green and open spaces that have

made our state the back yard of America. We cannot build a wall around Florida. But we can build a wall around indifference. We can build a wall around greed. We must free ourselves—and free Florida—from the tattered fetters of the booster mentality. We must continue to grow. But we must continue to seek to control that growth. The Spanish explorers searched in vain for eternal youth in the pristine wilderness of Florida. They never realized that the secret was there—all around them—all the time. They never knew, as we know now, that we can be forever young, and forever productive, if we only cherish our natural environment.[42]

The state now had to protect, preserve, and restore the state's natural resources. To that end, Askew called for an inventory of the state's environment, an "environmental databank," to allow for proper protection and management and the establishment of a Natural Resources Institute to provide guidance in such areas.[43]

In 1974, Congress voted to establish Big Cypress National Preserve, the first in the national park system. The Chiles-Jackson bill to purchase the swamp was introduced to the Senate in August 1971, and the Nixon administration's version of the bill was introduced in February 1972. Shortly thereafter, the House of Representatives took up consideration of the bill. The Senate version of the Big Cypress bill, the one sponsored by Chiles, picked up no less than sixteen co-sponsors over the next few months, including such luminaries as Edward M. Kennedy, Hubert Humphrey, Thomas Eagleton, Mike Mansfield, Howard Cannon, and Edmund Muskie. Bounced from one Congress to another, the Big Cypress protection bill did not come up for a final vote until 1974. Endorsed by party leaders on both sides of the aisle, the final measure authorized spending $116.9 million for acquisition of Big Cypress (while mandating that the state spend the $40 million designated under Florida's Big Cypress Preserve Act toward the same purpose) to purchase over a six-year period 570,000 acres. It was the largest appropriation for a single federal park or recreation area, and 522,000 acres was the largest acquisition of private land in the history of the National Park Service.[44]

There were 22,000 landowners affected by the bill. Many of these were absentee owners who had yet to make a single improvement. But a "significant number" were Florida residents who used their land to erect hunting shacks for recreation. The bill allowed owners of improved property, which included hunting shacks, to retain rights to their property for up to twenty-five years or, if they chose, to sell their property for fair-market value, less

whatever rights they retained.[45] If the owner of the property exercised ownership of the improved property in a manner contrary to the purposes of the act,
then the state could undertake procedures to terminate ownership. To preserve the swamp's natural values," the National Park Service was to manage
and maintain the area. The Seminole and Miccosukee Indians were allowed
to continue their traditional activities within the swamp. The Big Cypress
National Preserve legislation did not abolish the right of oil companies to
explore for oil within the swamp, but it did place such activities under the
regulatory eye of the Florida Department of Natural Resources, headed by the
governor and his cabinet. Big Cypress was regularly explored for oil, with
approval from the Askew administration, although Askew had unsuccess-
fully sought for a way to ban such activity.[46]

To the *New York Times,* the legislation was an "invaluable contribution" to
saving the Everglades. The *Times* credited Nixon for overruling his budget
officials to push the legislation, but it also made clear that Askew and other
Florida leaders were the impetus behind the bill. Had Askew not persuaded
the state to put up $40 million in good-faith money, the *Times* judged, the
bill's passage would have been "improbable" and a "national treasure" would
remain unprotected.[47]

Askew found that not all residents of the area supported the bill; some, in
fact, sensed a communist plot to deprive them of their property rights and
stated that they would "rather give my land to the communists." However, the
more serious protests came from the East Collier Landowners Improvement
Committee, Inc. Announcing that it was "united for justice and freedom,"
the committee used mass-distribution of flyers and well-placed newspaper
advertisements. The twelve-year-old group—with 440 members and claiming to speak for 35,000 landowners in the Big Cypress area—disagreed with
ecologists that Big Cypress was the main water source for the Everglades. In
fact, it asserted, Big Cypress was not technically a swamp since most of the
land was above water. It also took exception at a U.S. Interior Department
decision that owners of less than 40 acres could not negotiate sale price nor
retain mineral rights—a major bone of contention since rumors and speculation had pointed toward massive oil deposits in the area. To no avail, the
group accused the government of racial inequality in swamp acquisition,
since an estimated 4,000 black families were among landowners, albeit
mostly absentee, in the Big Cypress area.[48]

Fearing a loss of tax revenue, Collier County officials appealed to the
government to either remove portions of the swamp that resided within the

county from protection or provide compensation. Askew explained to the Collier Board of Commissioners that in fact its loss was actually a gain. With so much protected land within its borders, the county would be relieved of the need to construct roads, sewers, and bridges in those undeveloped areas. Therefore, lost property taxes were not lost after all, since they would not be required for infrastructure that no longer needed building. Plus, the state and federal government was investing $156 million in the area by acquiring the preserve in the first place, and the federal government was taking responsibility for managing the preserve.[49]

The land and water legislation passed by the Florida legislature in 1972 and 1973 established a foundation for Florida's environmental policy for the rest of the century and into the next. Succeeding Askew, Bob Graham built upon those efforts to reclaim endangered land for the state's future with his "Save Our Everglades" initiative. By 1978, more than 327,871 acres of Big Cypress had been purchased. A few years later, the state forced Gulf America Corporation to deed more than 10,000 acres of wetlands to the state, pay $1 million to the state for monitoring and correction of future pollution problems, build fewer housing units than planned, and conduct a $19 million environmental correction to reverse flood-control projects that had damaged the wetlands of the area around Cape Coral Estates. By 1979, Florida found itself in an ongoing dispute with Alabama and Georgia over modification of the Apalachicola River for industrial use. Those who used the upper portions of the river and its tributaries in Alabama and Georgia claimed that Florida was acting "selfishly" in not allowing dredging or canal construction to allow for increased barge traffic. Less than a year later, Florida succeeded in having Apalachicola Bay named a national sanctuary. The trend was clear—the state had decided to become a proactive guardian of its natural resources.[50]

In 1992, Florida ranked highest among southern states in a "Green Index," which weighed each state's concern for and protection of the environment—its "Green Areas." After eighteenth-ranked Florida and twenty-third ranked North Carolina, no southern state ranked higher than thirty-second, and a list of the usual suspects filled out positions forty-five through fifty: Tennessee, Texas, Mississippi, Arkansas, Louisiana, and Alabama. Florida's high ranking can be traced back to the environmental legislative sessions of 1972. In the 1970s, many Floridians realized that perhaps one of the fundamental principles of the environment and ecology—that everything is related to everything else—also applied to the economy, politics, and industrial development. They realized that the death of south Florida's main water supplier and popular tourist attraction would also distress the state's economy. Perhaps Florida's sixteen-year "age of moderation" ruled over by Reubin Askew and later Bob Graham allowed for the environmental reforms of the early 1970s to become part of the political and economic landscape, not easily dismantled in later years by less moderate legislators and governors.[51]

In his seminal work on southern industrialization and economic development, James Cobb argues that the obsession with industrial growth in the post–Civil War South served as a double-edged sword. Southern states went to great lengths—including tax breaks, free or cheap land, a general business-friendly climate, and an active indifference to the environment—to attract industrial firms. The federal outgrowth of the environmental movement caused more than a few southern congressmen to rail against the government and cry that new environmental regulations were little more than a Yankee or communist conspiracy to keep Dixie down. But the region was in danger of losing that which had set it apart and attracted residents and tourists.[52]

As Cobb writes, environmental protection offered no competition to the job production for an impoverished region. But environmental protection was necessary for the region to preserve the very thing that had attracted millions of visitors and new residents from industrial cities in the North. The irony was apparent: to attract industry, the South could not be overly concerned with the environment, but to attract residents and tourists, the region could not simply let its natural attractions fall into a state of decline. This is especially so with Florida, which attracts more tourists each year than many states' populations combined. No longer indifferent to the woes of its natural resources, Florida and the federal government acted to protect Big Cypress. Reflecting the mood of a growing southern middle class that was sensitive to the symbiosis that existed between the human-made world and the natural environment, Florida preserved important parcels of what Hemingway described as the "last wild country."[53]

Notes

1. For a study of land sales in Florida, see John Rothchild, *Up for Grabs: A Trip through Time and Space in the Sunshine State* (New York: Viking, 1985); *USA Today*, December 5, 1997. An excellent study of how politics in Tampa responded to the city's tremendous growth during the twentieth century is Robert Kerstein, *Politics and Growth in Twentieth-Century Tampa* (Gainesville: University Press of Florida,

2001), esp. 183–84, 187, 260–76; Howard T. Odum, Elizabeth C. Odum, and Mark T. Brown, *Environment and Society in Florida* (Boca Raton: Lewis Publishers, 1998), 5.

2. Nearly 200,000 of the 775,000 agricultural acres surrounding the lake were occupied by sugarcane. Nutrients from these and other farms, such as dairy farms, had contributed to killing the lake because of too many nutrients. Mark Derr, *Some Kind of Paradise: A Chronicle of Man and the Land in Florida* (Gainesville: University Press of Florida, 1998), 357–58; Reubin Askew remarks before Air and Water Conference, July 2, 1971, in the Reubin O'D. Askew Papers, S65, box 2, Florida State Archives, Tallahassee; *Orlando Sentinel,* July 3, 1971.

3. Reubin Askew remarks before Air and Water Conference.

4. Bartram quote cited in Anne Rowe, *The Idea of Florida in the American Literary Imagination* (Baton Rouge: Louisiana State University Press, 1986), 3–5.

5. James and Hemingway quoted in Rowe, *The Idea of Florida in the American Literary Imagination,* 3–5; Allen Morris and Joan Perry Morris, *The Florida Almanac, 1997–98* (Tallahassee: Peninsular Press, 1998), 446. Douglas's treatment of the Everglades has become a classic in its exploration of the park and its import to Florida. See Marjory Stoneman Douglas, *The Everglades: River of Grass* (New York: Rinehart, 1947).

6. Derr, *Some Kind of Paradise,* 313–14; 337–38.

7. For excellent studies of the role of tourism in the shaping of southern history, see Richard D. Starnes, ed., *Southern Journeys: Tourism, History, and Culture in the Modern South* (Tuscaloosa: University of Alabama Press, 2003); and Daniel S. Pierce, *The Great Smokies: From Natural Habitat to National Park* (Knoxville: University of Tennessee Press, 2000). Since 1970, the state has grown by 6 million people every twenty years, or by 300,000 a year, or by 6,000 a week. Derr, *Some Kind of Paradise,* 339.

8. Since 1930, Florida has been primarily an urban state, with almost 75 percent of the population residing on 6 percent of the land. Derr, *Some Kind of Paradise,* 13, 313–14.

9. Charlton W. Tebeau, *A History of Florida* (Coral Gables: University of Miami Press, 1971), 345; Marjory Stoneman Douglas, *Florida: The Long Frontier* (New York: Harper and Row, 1967), 273–75. John Egerton explores the nature of the southern land relative to the South's assimilation/disappearance into a greater American nation (or vice versa) circa 1974. John Egerton, *The Americanization of Dixie: The Southernization of America* (New York: Harper's Magazine Press, 1974), 48–74.

10. Since salt water is heavier than freshwater, the salt water would creep into the freshwater supply if not "forced" back by freshwater flowing out to sea. Cutting canals at sea level allowed for saltwater migration into the freshwater supply. Fred Ward, "The Imperiled Everglades," *National Geographic* 141 (January 1972): 1–27; proceedings of Conservation 70's Conference, September 13–14, 1969; Askew Papers, S949, box 7.

11. One of the first things Askew did was to appoint people to the South Florida Flood Control District governing board who were more interested in conservation than in drainage and flood control. A. Durand Jones, "Big Cypress Swamp and the Everglades: No Solutions Yet," *Living Wilderness* (winter 1973–74): 28–36; *St. Petersburg Times,* n.d., ca. August 1970, in Askew Papers S949, box 5; *Miami Herald,* October 11,

1976; Report of the Special Study Team of the Florida Everglades, August 1970, in Askew Papers, S949, box 5.

12. Fires occurred in 1926, 1928, 1931, 1932, 1935, 1937, 1943, 1945–47, 1950–52, 1962, 1965, 1971, 1973; Derr, *Some Kind of Paradise*, 324–27; Arthur R. Marshall statement to governor's cabinet, "A Review of Water Resource Projects and Problems in Central and South Florida," April 13, 1971, Tallahassee, Florida, Askew Papers, S949, box 3.

13. Arthur R. Marshall statement to governor's cabinet, "A Review of Water Resource Projects and Problems in Central and South Florida," April 13, 1971, Tallahassee, Florida, Askew Papers, S949, box 3.

14. Derr, *Some Kind of Paradise*, 329, 330, 331, 356; O. E. Frye Jr., "Big Cypress Swamp," *Florida Wildlife* (June 1972): 17–22; *New York Times*, June 22, 1975.

15. Derr, *Some Kind of Paradise*, 356.

16. J. Brooks Flippen, *Nixon and the Environment* (Albuquerque: University of New Mexico Press, 2000), 31–33, 39–56; *New York Times*, June 22, 1975; Tebeau, *A History of Florida*, 356–57, 359–60; Frye, "Big Cypress Swamp"; Derr, *Some Kind of Paradise*, 356–57; Frye, "Big Cypress Swamp"; *New York Times*, June 22, 1975.

17. Askew remarks at opening session of Governor's Conference on Water Management in South Florida, Miami Beach, September 22, 1971; marked draft copy of Askew remarks; both in Askew Papers, S65, box 2; Askew press release and agenda for Governor's Conference on Water Management in South Florida, Miami Beach, September 22, 1971; Askew Papers S949, box 6.

18. Ibid.; Askew speech before Keep Florida Beautiful luncheon, Tallahassee, July 14, 1971, Askew Papers S65, box 2; *Tallahassee Democrat*, July 14, 1971; Askew press release, October 22, 1971; Askew press release, November 5, 1971, Askew Papers, S949, box 16.

19. *St. Petersburg Times*, September 23, 1971; *Miami Herald*, September 23, 24, 1971; *Tampa Tribune*, September 23, 24, 1971.

20. Jones, "Big Cypress Swamp and the Everglades"; Reubin Askew, "Conclusions and Recommendations of the Recent Governor's Conference on Water Management in South Florida," *Florida Conservation News* (November 1971): 2; copy located in Askew Papers, S949, box 16.

21. Askew letters to Florida congressional delegation, all dated July 23, 1971, Askew Papers, S949, box 3; *St. Petersburg Times*, August 30, 1971; *Florida Times-Union*, August 12, 1971.

22. O. E. Frye Jr., "Big Cypress Swamp," *Florida Wildlife*, June 1972, 17–21. The Chiles bill was styled S2465, "A bill to establish the Everglades–Big Cypress Recreation Area in the State of Florida, and for other purposes," 92nd Cong., 1st sess., *Congressional Record* 117 (August 6, 1971): 30219; Askew to Rogers Morton, July 20, 1971; and Nathaniel Reed to Morton, February 5, 1971, both in Askew Papers, S949, box 3; Flippen, *Nixon and the Environment*, 153.

23. Flippen, *Nixon and the Environment*, 153; Frye, "Big Cypress Swamp"; "Oral History Interview with William D. Ruckelshaus, January 1993" (Washington, D.C.:

U.S. Environmental Protection Agency, Office of Administration, Management and Organization Division).

24. *New York Times,* November 24, 1971; *Miami Herald,* November 24, 1971; *St Petersburg Times,* November 25, 1971.

25. The state had reached an agreement with the General Acceptance Corporation to purchase more than 17,000 acres of the Fakahatchee Strand and 9,500 acres of wetlands adjacent to the strand. Senator Henry "Scoop" Jackson to Askew, November 24, 1971; Askew Papers S949, box 3; testimony by Reubin Askew and special assistant Jay Landers before the U.S. Senate Subcommittee on Parks and Recreation of the Committee on Interior and Insular Affairs, 92nd Cong., 2d sess., 1971, on S2465 and S3139, both in Askew Papers, S949, box 3.

26. *Miami Herald,* January 4–6, 1972; *New York Times,* January 5, 1972, January 6, 1972.

27. The environmental agency consolidation that Askew requested would have drastically cut the number of administration employees from 310 to a figure considerably less than that. *St. Petersburg Times,* February 2, 1972, February 4, 1972; *Panama City News Herald,* February 1, 1972, February 2, 1972, February 6, 1972; "Address of Reubin O'D. Askew Governor of Florida before the Florida Legislature, Tallahassee, Florida, 1 February 1972," Askew Papers, S126, box 20; "Major Environmental Laws since the 1971 Governor's Conference on Water Management," internal memo, no date, ca. August 1973, Askew Papers, S78, box 5.

28. The 1968 Constitutional Reforms also established a natural resources provision in the state's constitution, which stated that "it shall be the policy of the state to conserve and protect its natural resources and scenic beauty." See *Constitution of the State of Florida,* article II, section 7; See also John C. Tucker, "Constitutional Codification of an Environmental Ethic," *Florida Law Review* 52 (April 2000): 299–327; For a primer on cabinet restructuring under Florida's several constitutions, see Deborah K. Kearney, "The Florida Cabinet in the Age of Aquarius, *Florida Law Review* 52 (April 2000): 425–56; see also Rebecca Mae Salokar, "Constitutional Politics in Florida: Pregnant Sows or Deliberative Revision," paper presented at the American Political Science Association (APSA), August 30, 2001, in possession of author.

29. *Panama City News-Herald,* February 2, 1972; *St. Petersburg Times,* February 2, 1972.

30. *Tampa Times,* April 21, 1972; James G. Pace to "Fellow Property Owners," no date, ca. May 1971; in Askew Papers, S949, box 3.

31. Nathaniel Reed to John Jones (of the Florida Wildlife Federation), March 22, 1972, in Askew Papers, S949, box 3; William Merrihue (Collier County Conservancy) to Askew, October 4, 1973, Askew Papers, S953, box 2.

32. *Naples Daily News,* December 9, 1971; Ellis Chism to President Richard Nixon and Members of Congress, no date, ca. April 1972; in Askew Papers, S949, box 3; Nathaniel Reed to John Jones, March 22, 1972, in Askew Papers, S949, box 3.

33. *Pensacola Journal,* September 15, 1972; *Florida Times Union,* September 15, 1972; *Panama City News Herald,* February 10, 1972; Michael V. Gannon, *Florida: A Short History* (Gainesville: University Press of Florida, 1993), 138–39. The superagency bill

passed the state house easily but failed in the Florida Senate's Natural Resources Committee in the face of stiff cabinet opposition. Askew's related proposal to replace the elected education commissioner with an appointed commissioner also failed. It was a major blow to Askew's political ego and his plans to streamline the cabinet and agencies of state government. *Pensacola Journal*, September 15, 1972; *Florida Times Union*, September 15, 1972; *Panama City News Herald*, February 10, 1972; Gordon Harvey, *A Question of Justice: New South Governors and Education* (Tuscaloosa: University of Alabama Press, 2002), 85; Greg Johnson memo to Askew, July 5, 1972, Askew Papers, S126, box 6.

34. The success of the 1972 legislative session for Askew cannot be overestimated. A survey of legislative support for Askew's proposals revealed that he enjoyed higher support (47 percent out of a possible 100) from Republicans than he did from a group of thirty Democrats his advisers named "non-supportive Democrats," who gave Askew only 32 percent. The remaining fifty Democrats gave Askew 81 percent support. His lowest support came from Lee and Collier counties, where large portions of Big Cypress lay. The Alachua, Marion, and Dade county delegations gave Askew support from 88 percent to 93 percent. Internal memo from Greg Johnson to Askew, July 29, 1972, Askew Papers, S942, box 3.

35. "Major Florida Environmental Laws since the 1971 Governor's Conference on Water Management," internal memo, n.d., ca. May 1973, Askew Papers, S78, box 5; *Land Planning News* 1 (September 1972), copy in Askew Papers, S949, box 5; Conservation-70's press release, April 10, 1972, Askew Papers, S949, box 5.

36. Authority for appropriating bond revenue rested in the hands of the governor and cabinet to act as the executive board of the Department of Natural Resources. Massachusetts alone saw the introduction of 322 environmentally focused bills. *Miami Herald*, November 3, 1972. Those states, along with Florida, that adopted or debated means of responding to new federal legislation or to respond to environmental needs included Arizona, California, Colorado, Hawaii, Idaho, Indiana, Kentucky, Massachusetts, New Mexico, Ohio, Oklahoma, and Virginia. Most other states dealt with water usage issues. *New York Times*, April 1, 1972, July 2, 1972, October 21, 1972, November 9, 1972; "Florida Land and Water Management Act of 1972," *Florida Statutes*, 373.013; "Florida Water Resources Act of 1972," *Florida Statutes*, 380.012.

37. Conservation 70's press release, April 10, 1972, Askew Papers S949, box 5; remarks of Harris Mullen to the Environmental Standards Committee, Tallahassee, Florida, September 12–13, 1972, in Askew Papers, S949, box 5; *Miami Herald*, November 3, 1972; Arnold Greenfield to Askew, November 14, 1972, Askew Papers, S942, box 2.

38. *New York Times*, October 21, 1972, November 9, 1972; *Miami Herald*, November 3, 1972.

39. *New York Times*, November 24, 1972.

40. Askew Press Conference Transcript, n.d., ca. November 1972; Askew Papers, S949, box 3; "Comparison of Congressional Proposals for the Big Cypress Swamp," internal memo, n.d., ca. April 1973, Askew Papers, S953, box 2.

41. Bills to make beaches and coastal areas eligible to be named Areas of Critical

State Concern and to expand wetlands protection authority of the state did not survive committee consideration. Guy Spicola (chair of Senate Committee on Environmental Protection) memo to committee members, June 7, 1973, Askew Papers, S78, box 5; "Major Florida Environmental Laws since the 1971 Governor's Conference on Water Management," internal memo, n.d., ca. spring 1973, Askew Papers, S78, box 5; *St. Petersburg Times*, March 25, 1973; "Proposed Area of Critical State Concern: Big Cypress Watershed," Report No. CA-73, Florida Department of Administration, Division of State Planning, 1973, Askew Papers, S949, box 3.

42. *St. Petersburg Times*, April 12, 1974; Associated Press article on Askew Speech before Florida Audubon Society, n.d., ca. April 10, 1974, Askew Papers, S78, box 5; Askew speech before Bradenton, Florida, Chamber of Commerce, July 11, 1974, Askew Papers, S78, box 5.

43. Askew's proposal for an environmental databank and resource institute did not pass through the legislature. HB 3633 was defeated in 1974. Askew speech before Bradenton, Florida, Chamber of Commerce, July 11, 1974, Askew Papers, S78, box 5. Legislative Information Division, Florida State Legislature, *History of Legislation, 1974 Regular Session, Florida Legislature* (Tallahassee: Legislative Information Division, 1974).

44. In the weeks following passage of the Big Cypress legislation, some owners of unimproved land hastily built shacks in order to maintain their rights to the land. Jones, "Big Cypress Swamp."

45. Ibid.

46. Unimproved property, which comprised the vast majority of the land in the preserve, was exempt from the Uniform Relocation Assistance and Real Property Acquisition Act of 1970, which waived the need for an appraisal and the property owners' right to accompany appraisers of land units of forty acres or less. The legislation also mandated that if the state constructed Interstate 75 through the area commonly known as the "Tamiami Trail," it would be restricted to a limited-access roadway "designed and constructed in a manner which will enhance the values of the preserve and cause the least possible adverse environmental impact." "Establishment of Big Cypress National Preserve in the State of Florida," *Congressional Record* 120 (September 9, 1974): 30468–474. President Nixon signed the bill into law (PL 93-440) on October 11, 1974, See *Congressional Record* (October 17, 1974): 36017; *New York Times*, June 22, 1975; *Tallahassee Democrat*, March 13, 1975.

47. *New York Times*, October 12, 1973.

48. Ibid.; *Naples Daily News*, November 13, 1973; Anti-Askew Flyer distributed by East Collier Landowners Improvement Committee, n.d., ca. April 1974, Askew Papers, S949, box 15; *Ft. Myers News-Press*, April 14, 1974; *Miami Herald*, February 11, 1974; *St. Petersburg Times*, March 22, 1973; *Tallahassee Democrat*, March 13, 1975.

49. Resolution of the Collier County Board of Commissioners Requesting Property Tax Compensation, July 22, 1975, Askew Papers, S953, box 2; Stephen G. Mitchell (chair, Collier County Board of Commissioners) to Askew, July 31, 1975; Askew to Mitchell, August 13, 1975; both in Askew Papers, S953, box 2; *Tallahassee Democrat*, March 13, 1975; *Miami Herald*, October 10, 1976; Jane Love memo to Askew, June 4,

1975; Ken Woodburn to Jim Anthrop, June 9, 1975; both in Askew Papers, S942, box 6; Minutes of Florida Water Management Advisory Board, April 14, 1976, Askew Papers, S495, box 1.

50. *Miami Herald*, July 1, 1976, October 10, 1976, November 7, 1976, December 20, 1976; March 6, 1977, August 14, 1977; October 25, 1978; July 29, 1979, September 28, 1979; February 15, 1980.

51. The "green index" is cited in Gavin Wright's afterword, *The Second Wave: Southern Industrialization from the 1940s to the 1970s*, ed. Philip Scranton (Athens: University of Georgia Press, 2001), 286–300; see also Bob Hall and Mary Lee Kerr, *1991–92 Green Index* (Washington, D.C.: Island Press, 1991).

52. James C. Cobb, *Industrialization and Southern Society, 1877–1984* (Lexington: University Press of Kentucky, 1984), 2, 134–35.

53. Ibid. For more on the growth of a new environmentally conscious middle class, see Samuel Hays, *Beauty, Health, and Permanence: Environmental Politics in the United States* (New York: Cambridge University Press, 1987); Hemingway quote in Rowe, *The Idea of Florida in the American Literary Imagination*, 5.

Gordon E. Harvey

Chapter 16

"The Big Ditch"

The Rise and Fall of the Cross-Florida Barge Canal

Lee Irby

By March 1972, Marjorie Carr had grown restive. For ten years, she and a group of environmentalists had engaged various governmental entities in a long campaign of attrition to decide the fate of the Cross-Florida Barge Canal. A year before, both a federal judge and President Richard Nixon had ordered a halt to the construction of the proposed 107-mile human-made waterway across central Florida. Marjorie Carr seemingly had won her long fight, yet to the victor had gone no spoils. "It is springtime in Florida and another growing season has started," she wired Nixon. "When will restoration begin in the Ocklawaha River Valley?" This question dogged Carr for the next fifteen years. Even as she struggled against the ravages of lung cancer in 1997, when she was eighty-one, she wondered: "Will I see it run free or not? I don't know." Carr wanted nothing more than to see the pristine Ocklawaha River running its natural course beneath cypress trees and stands of saw palmetto. The Rodman Dam had blocked the river's flow since the fall of 1968, flooding thousands of acres, creating a huge pool of water over what had been pristine hardwood forest.[1]

The history of the Cross-Florida Barge Canal represents in microcosm a larger collision of forces that have battled to shape the modern Florida landscape. In the canal's history reside four hundred years of turmoil, triumph, and tenacity, exhibited by both those who sought the canal's creation and those who organized to oppose it. The arguments in favor of the canal reflect a decidedly "commodified" worldview, one in which human beings lord over nature, an entity that exists primarily as fodder for an ever-expanding marketplace. The fruits of nature belonged to those who were sufficiently "civilized" to turn them into commodities. Such an attitude toward nature prevailed in the United States unchallenged until the mid-twentieth century, when "environmentalism" arose to contest the wanton disfigurement of the natural world. Although its antecedents stretch back to the mid- to late nineteenth century, environmentalism did not become a political force to be reckoned with until the 1960s, at about the same time that work on the canal began in earnest. Thus, at the Cross-Florida Barge Canal intersect two diametrically opposed views of nature and of the human place within the natural world.[2]

Dreams Dashed

Florida's unique geography fueled the dream of a cross-state canal almost from the first days that Europeans landed upon the peninsula. A long finger of land jutting into the Caribbean, Florida's shape demanded that mariners wanting to sail from the Gulf coast to the Atlantic (or vice versa) ply the dangerous waters of the Florida Straits, where near present-day Key West lurk coral reefs capable of wrecking any size vessel. Additionally, in time of war, a canal capable of spiriting small boats across Florida would bestow an advantage upon the forces that utilized it. The first European conquistadors embraced these two desires: improvement of shipping and defense. Pedro Menéndez de Avilés became *adelantado* (a self-funded invader in the name of the king) of Florida in 1565, undertaking the arduous task of settling the inhospitable peninsula in the belief that it would eventually enrich him. In requesting the position of *adelantado* from Philip II, Menéndez mentioned both the trading possibilities and the defensive posture of Florida, perhaps knowing that Philip himself was interested in finding a navigable path across the peninsula. Jean Ribault had vaguely indicated in 1563 that a waterway across Florida existed that would allow the journey to be made in twenty days. During the sacking of the French at Fort Caroline, Menéndez learned from a captured soldier that the St. Johns River had "two mouths," one on the Atlantic and another on the Gulf. After dispatching the French, Menéndez began a search to confirm this claim. First, he started up the St. Johns from the Atlantic and got as far as Lake George before being turned away by defending Indians. Next he tried the opposite approach, by looking for the alleged mouth of the St. Johns along the Gulf coast. Although Indians had described a way of sailing up the St. Johns to a large lake, and then from the lake down another river to the Gulf, Menéndez did not understand that this journey entailed portage between certain lakes and rivers. Thus, his efforts to locate a waterway across Florida failed, although his argument in favor of a cross-state waterway would remain essentially unchanged for four hundred years.[3]

The British added another dimension to the desire to find passage across north central Florida. Whereas Menéndez had looked for a natural body of water that would facilitate trade and aid in defense, Governor James Grant of East Florida in 1765 first proposed the construction of a "river-canal" of 150 miles, along with a road, across the peninsula. Grant estimated that such a project would cost 500 guineas, to be raised in Florida, Charles Town, and Georgia, and that fifty slaves could finish the work in a year. Thus, from its earliest days, the cross-state canal has seen low-cost estimates and time of completion schedules that bordered on the unreal. Grant's proposal for a built canal remains telling when considering that cartographers of that era continued to depict Florida as a place where rivers flowed freely from the Atlantic to the Gulf. Perhaps Grant knew better, having had seen the area. Yet his plan also indicated a burgeoning faith in engineering, in a rationalist approach to the natural world, that mankind could reform it to suit the needs of a market-driven economy. Menéndez struggled against the topography as it existed, whereas Grant assumed that such topography existed at the behest of those who owned the land. But Grant's plans came to nothing, and in 1783 Florida again became a Spanish possession.[4]

During the early nineteenth century, the United States experienced the beginning of the transportation revolution that would come to mark the century's relentless drive toward market expansion. Canals played an integral role in the transformation of the American economy, and as Florida entered the nation as a territory in 1821, canal building was rampant. The case for one across Florida relied on reasoning first promulgated by Pedro Menéndez some two centuries earlier: improvement of shipping and defense. By the 1820s, the maritime industry possessed full knowledge of the dangers of the reef at Key West. So many ships had wrecked upon it that an entire salvage industry had emerged on the island. Additionally, ships passing through the Florida Straits came perilously close to Cuba, and canal proponents deftly used the promise of national security to bolster their claims. In 1824, the Florida legislative council issued a memorial to Congress in which the template for the pro-canal argument clearly stood out: "Such a canal, by opening passage from the Gulf of Mexico to the Atlantic would in an eminent degree, develop the agricultural resources of Florida, enhance the value of public lands, promote the intercourse and enlarge the commerce of the Atlantic and western states and in time of war give celerity and energy to the operations of the general government." Eventually, powerful figures like Daniel Webster and John Calhoun urged action for a cross-state canal, and in 1826 Congress passed a bill authorizing the first survey of a possible canal route across Florida.[5]

The results of this survey proved to be disappointing to the canal boosters. Engineers spent nearly three years in Florida, examining all areas below the St. Marys River to the north and a line between Tampa Bay and Cape Canaveral to the south. The engineers sought to locate the best route for a canal, yet they concluded that "a ship canal destined to connect, through the peninsula, the Atlantic with the Gulf of Mexico, is not practicable." The impediment to building a ship canal would remain unchanged into the late twentieth century: "the ridge of the peninsula of Florida . . . does not offer, at any place, either natural reservoirs or heads of streams adequate to the supply of a canal having very large dimensions."[6] In other words, by 1829 engineers understood that building a ship canal across Florida entailed finding enough water to fill the big ditch. During the next fifty years, Congress authorized five more surveys, and none of them unequivocally recommended building a canal. Even private companies that endeavored to build the canal met with failure, despite the generous terms granted by the state legislature. By 1900, plans for a cross-state canal appeared to be dead.[7]

While Florida congressional leaders continued to keep the canal flame alive, Theodore Roosevelt gave the canal an implicit boost, causing enough momentum that in the early twentieth century Congress again ordered re-

Lee Irby

evaluations of the plans for a cross-state canal. In 1907, Roosevelt claimed that railroads did not have the carrying capacity to keep up with the pace of American business and urged the creation of inland waterways linking the Eastern Seaboard to the Gulf of Mexico. To adherents of the New South philosophy, such talk fit neatly into their vision of an economically ascendant region, a South divorced from its seemingly backward ways. In many regards, Florida embraced the New South creed with particular gusto, evidenced by the grandiose railroad and hotel building of Henry Flagler and Henry Plant in the late 1800s. A cross-state canal would bestow upon the Sunshine State the imprimatur of progress that canal proponents eagerly sought, while at the same time offering competition to the railroads.[8]

In 1911, a special board of engineers, at the request of Congress, again looked into the canal, and found that a canal only 12 feet deep "would have no great value" as a shipping route and was "not worthy of prosecution." Undeterred by this setback, canal backers in the Florida legislature pushed through a bill creating a Canal Commission in 1921, the same year that the United States Senate, spurred by Floridian Duncan Fletcher, called for a reevaluation of the 1911 report. The task fell to Colonel Gilbert A. Youngberg, U.S. district engineer for Florida, who issued his reevaluation in 1923. Carefully weighing the changes in technology that came in a great torrent in the early twentieth century, Youngberg nonetheless found that a cross-state barge canal would benefit only local shipping and would offer no great advantage to national defense (the canal would be too small). He recommended that Congress not fund a survey of what would be an unjustifiable project.[9]

Here it appeared that the canal had again died, or at least had received such a mortal wound that reviving it would seem almost impossible. No study, no survey, had argued for building a big ditch across Florida—and the Army Corps of Engineers had always seemed willing to build anything. But the canal's death began to resemble something out of a George Romero film: the corpse—ministered to by the same necromantic Florida lawmakers determined to bring it back—only appeared to be lifeless. They needed an *ex machina* intervention, however. While the Great Depression brought the nation to its knees in the 1930s, it offered canal boosters a welcome tonic, allowing their dream to once again stir.[10]

Keeping Men Busy

Although Congress authorized small sums to conduct surveys of possible canal routes across northern Florida and southern Georgia in 1927 and 1930, not until the implosion of the American economy in the early 1930s did the possibility of actually building a canal approach reality. Events began to gather a momentum that had been missing from earlier efforts to promote the canal. Until 1931, no engineer had solved the puzzle of justifying the expenditure of the hundreds of millions of dollars on the canal, despite the repeated surveys authorized by Congress. But times indeed were changing in the 1930s. In 1931, the City of Jacksonville hired the firm of Hills and Youngberg for $15,000 to make an economic study of the project—the same Gilbert A. Youngberg who eight years earlier had recommended that Congress not spend another dime on surveys for the project. But Youngberg had since retired from government, and now his calculations produced a different result. Based on 1929 data alone, he argued, a *ship* canal would have saved $15,927,500 in shipping costs, whereas in a 1923 report, he had concluded a *barge* canal to be of little value, since its size would accommodate neither large commercial nor large military vessels. It is important to keep in mind the differences between the two: a barge canal would be 12 feet deep, whereas a ship canal must go down 35 feet. The impetus in the 1930s centered on a ship canal, the type dismissed in the 1829 survey as "impracticable." A ship canal might pay off in the long run, but no one knew whether one could be built in Florida, with its aquifer percolating beneath the limestone.[11]

Besides Youngberg's optimistic report, canal proponents geared themselves up for a political fight and began assembling munitions. Supporters from Texas, Louisiana, Mississippi, Alabama, and Florida gathered in New Orleans in March 1932 and formed the National Gulf-Atlantic Ship Canal Association, selecting as its president General Charles P. Summerall, who claimed: "It is estimated that more tonnage will pass through the canal than through any other ship canal in the world." This organization proved to be an effective body, coordinating efforts that had thus far been diffuse. Within two weeks of its formation, the Canal Association picked up key endorsements from Senator Huey P. Long of Louisiana and influential columnist Arthur Brisbane. The same arguments that Pedro Menéndez advanced in 1565 still held sway: a canal would improve shipping and boost national defense. "It is a disgrace to this country, proof of sluggishness, that the canal from the Atlantic to the Gulf has been so long delayed," wrote Brisbane.[12]

But without the Depression, perhaps even these efforts would have languished in the dustbin of futility. The Depression threatened industrial capitalism as nothing else in the country ever had. Even diehard opponents of federal intervention into the "private sector" gave ground, albeit not much. Locked in a tough battle for reelection, with the Bonus Army encamped right outside his doorstep, President Herbert Hoover in July 1932 signed into law the creation of the Reconstruction Finance Corporation (RFC), which would provide loans to private companies engaged in "self-liquidating" projects for "public use." The Canal Association quickly applied for a loan, citing the usual benefits that a cross-state canal would provide, except that it added one new dimension: the canal would "provide as much or more man-hours of labor than any other similar public or private work now proposed" and would constitute "unemployment relief." The Canal Association asked for $160 million, later amended to $118 million, without specifying the canal's route. That one change alone—the promise of unemployment relief—carried more weight than the dozens of charts showing by how much shipping costs would be reduced. Unemployed men posed a threat to the existence of the capitalist system; they must be kept busy, lest they begin experimenting with ideologies inimical to the "American way of life."[13]

Canal supporters seemed to understand that approval of massive public works projects like the canal would stave off potential anarchy: "Times on Cap Hill are indeed trying at this particular time," wrote Congressman Lex Green of Starke. "It is one of the most critical moments in the history of the Republic." But Green also added that the new president, Franklin Delano Roosevelt, was showing interest in the canal project.[14] In case the new president did not understand the link between joblessness and civic disorder, the Florida legislature in May 1933 passed a joint resolution calling on FDR to approve the canal project, and at the top of the list of benefits was that the canal "will give employment to a vast amount of human labor, thus greatly relieving the distress due to the unemployment crisis." Almost as an afterthought, the resolution mentioned the commercial and military assets. In June, Congress passed the National Industrial Recovery Act, authorizing the president to spend $3.3 billion on construction projects. The canal's fate then became the property of the Public Works Administration, headed by Harold Ickes, and for the next year, the canal entered a holding pattern.[15]

During this caesura, however, engineers decided on the definitive route that any cross-state canal should take. This decision alone would have great impact on the future of environmentalism in Florida, because in December 1933, a special board of engineers reported to the president that the best route, out of twenty-eight considered, was the one designated 13-B. This route would stretch from the mouth of the St. Johns, down the Ocklawaha, skirt just past Ocala, and meet up with the Withlacoochee River, before emptying at Yankeetown into the Gulf. Never had this issue seen such unanimity of opinion, and once settled, the issue of "where to build it" died out. Hence, to build the canal meant to disturb the Ocklawaha River, one of the earliest of Florida's tourist attractions. So well-known was the pristine beauty of the Ocklawaha that visiting national dignitaries took steamboat rides down it, including the famous excursion of Ulysses S. Grant in January 1880. That engineers slated it for sacrifice fifty years later indicated the level to which certain Americans remained alienated from the natural world in the early twentieth century. A culture of consumerism stood poised to undo with alacrity what natural forces had spent millennia creating.[16]

Although engineers had decided where to build it, other fundamental questions remained unanswered, including the decision on the type of canal and, more important, whether to build a canal at all. The special board in December 1933 recommended building a lock-type ship canal, because a sea-level canal would "seriously disturb the natural ground-water table, with the probable results of not only damaging the source of water supply, but also entailing inestimable damages to agriculture over a wide area contiguous to the canal." Further, this board found no economic justification for building a ship or barge canal at that time. This conclusion caused ten senators from the Gulf states to write FDR, urging him to appoint a board of review, which he did. In June 1934, the board of review issued its report, agreeing with the earlier board that 13-B was the best route but dismissing concerns that the sea-level canal would damage Florida's water resources and denying that the project was economically unjustifiable. The board of review also determined that a sea-level canal had many advantages over the lock-type; namely, it would cost less and be easier to build and maintain. For the past 110 years, engineers had dismissed a sea-level canal across Florida, but the nation's economic collapse had changed the political landscape in ways that canal backers, including FDR, were quick to understand.[17]

Yet even as FDR seemed ready in 1935 to fund the canal, opposition to it had already arisen. Railroad interests in Florida had much to lose from any canal that might traverse the state, and thus they joined forces to condemn the project, blasting it for its enormous cost. More significantly, railroad lobbyists had discerned that engineers disagreed about possible damage to the Floridan Aquifer from which much of the state derives its drinking water. The American Association of Railroads even published a colorful pamphlet entitled *Not Worth Its Salt,* which detailed the danger of saltwater incursion into the aquifer and other groundwater once canal construction cut into the Ocala limestone near the Summit Ridge, the highest point the canal would have to reach. Once the salt water polluted the aquifer, "there is no power on earth which can ever turn it back again," the pamphlet warned. Loss of freshwater alarmed the citrus industry, and its displeasure found voice in the *Florida Grower,* which echoed the complaints of the railroads. "Florida may suffer immeasurable and everlasting damage to its water supply," wrote its editor, Marvin Walker, in June 1935, as FDR deliberated the canal's fate. Even the head of the Public Works Administration, Harold Ickes, admittedly no fan of the canal, in a statement perhaps intended to sway FDR, cited the "serious adverse effects . . . upon the important underground water supplies." The effort was to no avail, as four days later, on August 30, 1935, the president authorized the spending of $5 million to begin construction. On September 19, FDR ceremonially touched off the first dynamite blast for the cross-state ship canal by pressing a button from his Hyde Park home.[18]

But opposition to the canal, especially the threat to the water supply, contained the template for future environmental policy. In February 1936, a group called the Central and South Florida Water Conservation Committee urged "that the canal construction should be delayed sufficiently to permit a *comprehensive geological and engineering investigation* of the water situation, to make sure that the surface and underground water supplies . . . will not be adversely affected" (emphasis added). This group in effect desired that an environmental impact statement be done for the project, and that qualified experts determine what exactly would happen to the natural world once huge cranes began digging the big ditch. Such an attitude predated the law enacting such impact statements by almost forty years and thus constitutes an important statement by a group of individuals who believed that concern for the environment belonged in public policy.[19]

Roosevelt's own attitude toward potential contamination of Florida's aquifer illustrates the casual regard many people held for the natural world. Ickes continued to bring to FDR's attention the concerns about saltwater incursion, including at one poignant December 1935 meeting where Ickes again spoke to the president about possible "impregnation of salt water into the underground water courses." Roosevelt offered another hypothesis, one devoid of geological and engineering investigation. Since many Caribbean islands are surrounded by salt water, FDR mused to Ickes, and can still draw freshwater from wells, then "the canal would not have the effect that some geologists predict that it would have." Ickes quickly pointed out that he didn't "pretend to know," since he was "no geologist." No such caution deterred FDR. That Roosevelt felt confident to base such an important decision upon mere personal speculation indicates how farseeing was the Central and South Florida Water Conservation Committee's call for a more rigorous approach.[20]

But the FDR-approved $5 million expenditure, a fraction of the estimated $146,000,000 cost, would be the last money spent on cross-Florida canal construction for nearly thirty years. In December 1935, FDR ceded control of large-scale WPA funding to Congress, meaning that big-ticket items would now have to be officially appropriated. At the same time, opposition to the canal remained strong in Florida, and in Congress, Senator Arthur Vandenberg of Michigan began assailing the administration for its overly generous dispensation of public funds, the cross-Florida canal being foremost among his complaints. The canal's stewards on Capitol Hill could not coax enough support to fund the project, and work on the canal came to a stop in June 1936. The area around the construction site had become something of a boomtown, as thousands of workers trailed into Marion County. When the money ran out, four enormous bridge piers stood in stark relief against the flat landscape, and the empty buildings became a WPA school. Given that out West, the Army Corps of Engineers and the Bureau of Reclamation fought each other to spend millions on dams of marginal economic benefit, creating the dam-building frenzy of the 1930s that characterized what Marc Reisner called the "Go-Go Years," it seems incredible that the cross-Florida canal would become the embodiment of New Deal excess. Yet unlike the dams, the canal competed directly with a major industry, the railroads, whose attacks on the canal laid the groundwork for all subsequent attacks. Somehow environmental damage had entered the equation, far ahead of the national consciousness-raising of the 1960s.[21]

Even as the cross-Florida canal died yet again, a victim of anti–New Deal sentiment, events would soon conspire to revive it yet again. This time the savior was Adolph Hitler. Even as the canal begged for money, the world lurched toward war. The timing could not have been better, as even canal supporters in Congress seemed to be losing their ardor. "Neither of our senators have done a lick of work since you left here," vented H. H. Buckman, Canal Association secretary, in March 1941. But Pearl Harbor and Germany's U-boats changed the dynamic considerably. Now "the defensive value of the canal," according to Walter F. Coachman Jr., a booster from Jacksonville, would aid the cause. "Recent sinking of ships off the Atlantic Seaboard . . .

beyond. The Florida Audubon Society, the Nature Conservancy, the Florida Federation of Garden Clubs, and the Izaak Walton League joined in the fight begun by Anthony and Carr. Senator William Proxmire denounced the canal from the Senate floor, and the *New York Times* urged a cautious approach.[32]

Essentially, canal opponents followed two concurrent policies. Since Congress had to approve funds for the canal every budget cycle, one goal became working on Congress not to authorize another appropriation. "It isn't too late to save the Ocklawaha," Carr explained in 1965. "The canal lives from appropriation to appropriation." Thus, the House Subcommittee on Public Works received letters from canal opponents, a campaign that canal boosters derided as financed by the railroads. Yet defunding appeared to be a long shot, even as Congress appropriated smaller sums for construction than the Army Corps of Engineers had requested. The leaders of the "Save the Ocklawaha" movement therefore sought a less risky solution: diverting the path of the canal so that it would miss the river altogether. Finally granted a public hearing on the canal in Tallahassee on January 25, 1966, canal opponents ascertained that rerouting the canal away from the Ocklawaha would cost approximately $10 million, about half the cost of a B-52 bomber, as Anthony pointed out. Yet the alternative route plan went nowhere, and the Ocklawaha's destruction seemed inevitable.[33]

Indeed, the heavy machinery began laying waste to pristine forests along the Withlacoochee and the Ocklawaha. Canal opponents responded by forming the Florida Defenders of the Environment (FDE) in May 1969, with the stated purpose of "serv[ing] as a coordinating body for the collection and dissemination of information pertaining to [the] environment."[34] One leading member was John H. Couse, a former resident along the Ocklawaha River whose property was condemned by the Army Corps of Engineers, then smashed by the crusher-crawlers to make room for the Rodman Pool. "Most people in Florida don't know what is happening with the barge canal," he said in 1970. "If they were informed, given the truth, they would not sit back while special interests play Russian roulette with their homes, their future." The FDE believed that the truth about possible environmental degradation would motivate people politically. While public relations had played a significant role in a Sierra Club campaign to stop a dam at Marble Canyon in 1967, FDE opted for an approach that relied upon the collection of scientific data that would catalogue the damage done to entire ecosystem, from groundwater to nesting birds.[35]

The FDE published its findings in March 1970. *Environmental Impact of the Cross-Florida Barge Canal* centered on the concept of comparison; that is, to understand environmental damage done by a project, one must "compare conditions as they existed, or still exist, before the construction . . . with those that can be predicted if plans . . . were to be carried out." The factors included in such a comparison must include both physical and biological systems: geology, hydrology, climate, and soils, along with measuring how plants, animals, and humans "interact" with such systems. The FDE concluded that the canal would cause fracture zones in the limestone that would allow leakage of pollutants into the aquifer. It would destroy the habitat of a "full spectrum of plant and animal life native to north central Florida," while creating a "debris-choked reservoir, heavily invaded by exotic water weeds," part of a canal system already "antiquated . . . [and] too shallow for the newer trans-Gulf barges." These findings became part of a lawsuit filed by the Environmental Defense Fund on behalf of the FDE in September 1970, which sought an injunction to halt construction on the canal and a drawdown of 5 feet of the Rodman Pool to stop further drowning of the forest.[36]

The FDE's effort to link politics with ecology proved to be successful in ways perhaps the group's founders could not have predicted. They fought to save the Ocklawaha River, figuring that a fight to scrap the entire project would be futile. Yet in the end, the exact opposite happened: the entire canal project came to a grinding halt, but the Ocklawaha River remained blocked, and the Rodman Dam continued to prevent the migration of mullet and other fish. When President Richard Nixon stopped construction of the canal by executive order in January 1971, he justified his action because of "potentially serious environmental damages," especially to the "Ocklawaha River— a uniquely beautiful, semi-tropical stream, one of a very few of its kind in the United States, which would be destroyed by the construction of the canal."[37] Thus, the findings put forth in the FDE's 1970 impact statement provided political cover for elected officials to take the steps necessary to kill the project. In December 1976, the Florida cabinet asked Congress to deauthorize the project, a sentiment echoed in May 1977 by President Jimmy Carter. U.S. Representative Buddy McKay expressed the trajectory many Floridians followed in regard to the canal: "We all are part of the same history— my grandfather favored the canal, my father favored it, I favored it myself until I became aware of how the cutting of the summit reach would threaten . . . a very fragile water system. You know, back [then], we looked at water very differently. . . . You got rid of water." Buddy McKay, like Lawton Chiles and many others, had undergone a raising of consciousness, wherein they came to question the relationship established between humanity and nature as represented by the canal. McKay's change in attitude reflected a larger trend in Florida, which by 1974 was the only state in the country where "overpopulation" was the first major concern.[38]

Canal backers never again got Congress to authorize money for construction, and in 1990, the Water Resources Act explicitly deauthorized the canal. But killing the project did not mean that the Ocklawaha River ecosystem would be restored. Restoration involved one task: removal of the Rodman Dam so that the river could run wild again. Like defenders of the Hetch-Hetchy Valley dam project near Yosemite National Park, barge canal proponents who for decades had boasted of the defensive and commercial benefits of the project now unearthed one more advantage that had escaped attention: the canal, with its dam and reservoir, had created an ecosystem worth protecting. It is of critical importance to grasp how this position evolved, in that such views constitute a profound shift in prodevelopment ideology. New South and Sunbelt boosters spoke of "growth" as an exaltation, the one true goal of any government. Yet many Floridians turned against growth during the 1970s, even as their state kept growing. Floridians opposed growth, while simultaneously thinking that "environmentalists" had gone too far, had become too extreme. Therefore, developers could claim that within "growth" resided "new opportunities" not just for people but for organisms and ecosystems. The debate over restoring the Ocklawaha River contains a clear example of such inversion of ecological ethos.[39]

From the early 1960s, even canal backers understood that the big ditch would alter the landscape. But such changes did not mean that wildlife habitat would be degraded. In fact, the canal might actually enhance fish and wildlife resources. In 1965, the Florida Game and Fresh Water Fish Commission issued a policy statement that in effect supported canal construction, claiming that "our findings indicate that there will be certain adverse effects on fish and wildlife resources but that these are overshadowed by increased fishing and wildlife hunting opportunities associated with construction of Rodman and Eureka reservoirs." This theme of "increased opportunity" became the rallying cry of canal backers, even after the Game and Fish Commission reversed its position in 1969 and withdrew support of the canal. Charles Bennett stood in the House of Representatives in May 1971 and extolled the virtues of the Rodman Dam and Pool. Foremost among the benefits were the "new recreation sites" being constructed, construction that Bennett admitted would "have an effect upon the plants and animals of the small area of the Ocklawaha River which has already been altered by widening." But such "effect" would also "provide habitat for a wide variety of desirable sport and commercial species." Bennett's language reflected the ascendancy of the environmental movement, with its concern for "habitat" and "species," even while arguing against a return to the natural state of the river.[40]

The Army Corps of Engineers further complicated the dialogue emerging in the mid-1970s. Although Nixon had ordered a halt to construction, a federal court in 1973 ruled that Nixon's executive order was unconstitutional but held in place an injunction pending completion of a restudy of "environmental and economic factors."[41] The Army Corps of Engineers undertook this task and spent three years gathering evidence and writing a multivolume magnum opus, issued in February 1977. The corps examined all alternatives, from a total completion of the project to total restoration of the rivers. Yet the corps arbitrarily equated total completion with total restoration, as if those two choices contained the same level of extremism. The corps decided that the alternative that best exampled a maximization of "environmental quality" would "preserve the existing setting with the lake [Rodman Pool] at 18 feet." The corps concluded that "Lake Ocklawaha's [Rodman Pool] potential as an experimental laboratory, potentially involving the scientific and pedagogic communities, state and federal agencies, and the public, is a resource which should not be *destroyed* hastily" (emphasis added). The corps anointed the dam and reservoir as valuable assets which if dismantled would constitute some rash act of ecoterrorism, although Richard Nixon himself had urged for the river's restoration.[42]

Although the corps attempted to portray the Rodman Pool as some veritable learning community, what value it had was mostly as a bass-fishing site. A canal that was to speed shipping, aid in defense, create jobs, and stave off Fidel Castro became by the early 1980s a sacred fishing hole. Even if the FDE could not get authorization to have the river restored, the group wanted the reservoir drawn down, or emptied, so that trees might not drown. Partial restoration would be preferable to none at all. But emptying the reservoir would interfere with national bass fishing tournaments held at the pool since 1973. Dam backers claimed that over 400,000 people visited the pool every year, and that it was becoming a national attraction. A cottage industry sprang up in Palatka: skilled fishing guides could charge $200 a day on the weekends, an economic benefit not accounted for in any study of the canal.[43]

But beyond the bass fishing, supporters pointed to the "ecosystem" that the Rodman Dam and Pool have created. Such an assertion marks the culmination of a long process in which both canal supporters and the Army Corps of Engineers discounted restoration of the river as belonging to environmental extremism, much like civil rights activists in the 1960s were branded as extreme for advocating the rule of federal law. In such a process, the center invariably shifts far to the right politically. Hence, in 1985, longtime canal booster George Linville boasted of the abundance of game at the Rodman Pool: "[T]he eagles are roosting there and the alligators that are there, the osprey that are; all those wildlife people, wildlife animals and insects and bugs and all these other things that people claim to be interested in, are in place currently today, feeding, roosting, nesting, and in fact reproducing in that waterway."[44]

Linville argued against deauthorizing the canal, yet his essential points lived on after Congress voted to kill the project in 1990. Canal backers turned the tables: tearing down the Rodman Dam would entail destroying an ecosystem. "As you are aware, the issue of the Rodman Reservoir ecosystem is very important to my constituency," wrote State Senator George Kirkpatrick to the Florida Department of Environmental Protection (DEP) in 1995. More ardently than any other public figure, Kirkpatrick resisted restoration of the Ocklawaha River, labeling such efforts as the intent "to destroy the Rodman Ecosystem." His assertion merely reflected the same attitude toward natural habitat displayed by the Army Corps of Engineers in 1977, and expressed succinctly by Putnam County commissioner Bonnie Allender in 1985: "Our environment was meant by God to be used by man for man's benefit. Man should use his intelligence to improve his surroundings by proper utilization and conservation."[45]

In the name of saving the Rodman Reservoir, George Kirkpatrick and his bass-fishing allies beat back every attempt to fund the restoration of the Ocklawaha. In 1993, he managed votes enough for an eighteen-month study of restoration, at the cost of $900,000, although lawmakers might not have known what they were voting on. The study, issued in 1995, came to an unambiguous conclusion: "Historically, the Governor and Cabinet clearly and consistently have supported restoration of the Ocklawaha River. These reports indicate the current policy should remain unchanged." Kirkpatrick called the restoration project a boondoggle and claimed it would cost over $100 million (the DEP had estimated $30 million). When the DEP began filing for the required permits for restoration, Kirkpatrick charged that the agency was taking improper action and kept restoration funds out of the budget while inserting operating funds to keep the reservoir open. In 1998, the Florida Senate voted to change the name of the Rodman Dam to the George Kirkpatrick Dam. Although Kirkpatrick died in February 2003, other powerful north Florida legislators have taken up the cause of preserving the reservoir, despite the professions of Governor Jeb Bush, who has spoken out in favor of the Ocklawaha's restoration by 2006.[46]

"A river is a work of art by nature," Marjorie Carr once said. More than anyone else, she came to embody the fight to save the Ocklawaha, and with its salvation, cleanse Florida of a misguided defacement of a national treasure. That she died without seeing the river run wild in no way diminishes her legacy. Yet the dam that blocks the flow of the Ocklawaha River symbolizes a larger obstruction. On one side of it stand those who work to amend and heal past wounds inflicted on a fragile environment; on the opposite side are amassed those, smaller in number but equally determined, who profit from an unnatural landscape and fear any change to it, although such changes might actually improve the economic well-being of those who live nearest the river. Arguments akin to those about the Ocklawaha can be heard in a dozen other places in Florida, from Key West to Pensacola. Florida is a house divided against itself, and the stasis that has resulted from the intractable nature of such division will not lead to meaningful policy changes that could save the remaining wild slivers of the Sunshine State.

Notes

1. Carr to Nixon, March 9, 1972, Marjorie Carr Papers, Florida Defenders of the Environment, Gainesville, Florida, Doc. 733; *Gainesville Sun,* June 13, 1997.

2. For a brilliant discussion of "commodification" and nature, see William Cronon, *Changes in the Land: Indians, Colonists, and the Ecology of New England* (New York: Hill and Wang, 1983), 159–70. For a history of the American environmental movement, see Philip Shabecoff, *A Fierce Green Fire: The American Environmental Movement* (New York: Hill and Wang, 1993).

3. Charles E. Bennett, "Early History of the Cross-Florida Barge Canal," *Florida Historical Quarterly* 45 (October 1966), 132–33; Henry Barber, "The History of the Florida Cross-State Canal" (Ph.D. diss., University of Georgia, 1969), 1–7; Eugene Lyon, "Settlement and Survival," *The New History of Florida,* ed. Michael Gannon (Gainesville: University Press of Florida, 1996), 40–46.

4. Barber, "History," 10–12.

5. Quoted in Bennett, "Early History," 136; Barber, "History," 13–32.

6. *Message from the President of the United States in Relation to the Survey of a Route*

for a Canal between the Gulf of Mexico and the Atlantic Ocean, 20th Cong., 2d sess., 1829, S. Doc. 102, 51.

7. Bennett, "Early History," 141–42; Barber, "History," 78. Of the canal companies chartered by the state legislature, Barber writes: "None of these companies turned a spade of dirt." The Gulf Coast and Florida Peninsula Canal Company would have gotten 10 miles of public land on either side of any canal it could have built.

8. Barber, "History," 96. For an examination of identity within the New South, see Paul M. Gaston, *The New South Creed* (Baton Rouge: Louisiana State University Press, 1970).

9. Barber, "History," 106–16; Bennett, "Early History," 143–44.

10. Nelson Manfred Blake, *Land into Water/Water into Land: A History of Water Management in Florida* (Gainesville: University Presses of Florida, 1980), 151.

11. *Documentary History of the Florida Canal: Ten-Year Period January 1927 to June 1936*, 74th Cong., 2d sess., 1936, Doc. No. 275, 8–25; Barber, "History," 125–28; Blake, *Land into Water/Water into Land*, 154.

12. *Documentary History*, 27–28.

13. Ibid., 33; Blake, *Land into Water/Water into Land*, 152; Barber, "History," 132–33. For a treatment of the troubles workers encountered during the early 1930s, see Lizbeth Cohen, *Making a New Deal: Industrial Workers in Chicago, 1919–1939* (Cambridge: Cambridge University Press, 1990).

14. Green to Bert Dosh, March 22, 1933, Bert Dosh Papers, box 2, Special Collections, P. K. Yonge Library of Florida History, University of Florida, Gainesville.

15. *Documentary History*, 82; Barber, "History," 135–37; Blake, *Land into Water/Water into Land*, 154; J. Richard Sewell, "Cross-Florida Barge Canal, 1927–1968," *Florida Historical Quarterly* 46 (April 1968), 369–70.

16. Barber, "History," 139.

17. Ibid., 140–47; *Documentary History*, 104–10; Blake, *Land into Water/Water into Land*, 156.

18. *Not Worth Its Salt: The Proposed Ship Canal . . . A Salt Water Project . . . Will Contaminate the Fresh Water That Makes Florida the Winter Garden of the East* (New York: American Association of Railroads, [1935?]), 5. Pamphlet located at P. K. Yonge Library of Florida History. See also Barber, "History," 155–164; *Documentary History*, 74; Blake, *Land into Water/Water into Land*, 157. By late 1935, much of the early New Deal momentum had waned, and Roosevelt's critics, namely Huey Long and Father Coughlin, were berating him. Perhaps FDR approved the $5 million to silence Long in particular, a southerner who would draw considerable support in north Florida. See Alan Brinkley, *Voices of Protest: Huey Long, Father Coughlin, and the Great Depression* (New York: Knopf, 1982), 3–7.

19. Frank Kay Anderson, *A Brief Against the Present Construction of the Proposed Florida Cross-State Ship Canal* (Sanford: Central and South Florida Water Conservation Committee, 1936), 12.

20. *The Secret Diary of Harold L. Ickes: The First Thousand Days, 1933–1936* (New York: Simon and Schuster, 1954), 488–89.

21. Blake, *Land into Water/Water into Land*, 161–63; Barber, "History," 171–99;

Documentary History, 184–201; Shabecoff, *Fire*, 91–110; Marc Reisner, *Cadillac Desert: The American West and Its Disappearing Water* (New York: Penguin Books, 1986), 145–68. A Gallup poll of 1939 found that half the nation had not heard of the cross-Florida canal, and of those that had, about 75 percent opposed it. See Benjamin F. Rogers, "The Florida Ship Canal Project," *Florida Historical Quarterly* 36 (July 1957), 21.

22. Buckman to Bert Dosh, March 14, 1941, and January 24, 1942, in Dosh Papers, box 2; House Committee on Rivers and Harbors, *Enlargement and Extension of the Gulf Intercoastal Waterway, Including the Construction of a Barge Channel and Pipe Line Across Northern Florida*, 77th Cong., 2d sess., May 18–22, 1942; Blake, *Land into Water/Water into Land*, 164–65.

23. Buckman to Perry, January 25, 1951, in Dosh Papers, box 2. For an analysis of the cultural aspects of the Cold War, see Stephen J. Whitfield, *The Culture of the Cold War* (Baltimore: Johns Hopkins University Press, 1991).

24. Blake, *Land into Water/Water into Land*, 199; Bennett to Dosh, July 9, 1958, Dosh Papers, box 3; Sewell, "Canal," 377–78.

25. Collins to House Appropriations Committee, May 1, 1958, Dosh Papers, box 2.

26. Dosh to Spessard Holland, June 19, 1959, Dosh Papers, box 2; Ellender to Spessard Holland, June 25, 1959, Dosh Papers, box 2.

27. Ship Canal Authority, "Because We Shall Need It, It Must Be Ready Now!" July 1960, Dosh Papers, box 2.

28. Clipping, undated, Dosh Papers, box 2. Nixon, however, carried Florida in the election of 1960. Population data taken from State of Florida, Development Commission, *Population of Florida* (Tallahassee, 1959), 1–2. Dosh to John Bailey, December 28, 1963, Dosh Papers, box 2.

29. Blake, *Land into Water/Water into Land*, 202–3; Sewell, "Canal," 383–84.

30. *Florida Times-Union*, February 7, 1965; Blake, *Land into Water/Water into Land*, 205.

31. Howard T. Odum et al., *Environment and Society in Florida* (Boca Raton, Fla.: Lewis Publishers, 1998), 408.

32. Citizens for the Conservation of Florida's Natural and Economic Resources, *A Brief Summary of the Destruction of Natural Resources That Will Result from the Construction of the Cross-Florida Barge Canal* (Gainesville: n.p., n.d). Found in Melissa Shepard Carver, "Florida Defenders of the Environment: A Case Study of a Volunteer Organization's Media Utilization" (master's thesis, University of Florida, 1973), 101–3; Blake, *Land into Water/Water into Land*, 204–5.

33. *St. Petersburg Times*, May 10, 1965; Carver, "Case Study," 30–33; Blake, *Land into Water/Water into Land*, 204–5; Barber, "History," 277–78. Between 1964 and 1969, Congress appropriated $46,862,000 for the canal, leaving the Army Corps of Engineers short by about $26 million.

34. Florida Defenders of the Environment, "Articles of Incorporation," May 31, 1969, in Carver, "Case Study," 111.

35. *Palm Beach Post*, June 22, 1970. For a treatment of the Marble Dam controversy, see Reisner, *Cadillac Desert*, 253–89.

36. Florida Defenders of the Environment, *Environmental Impact of the Cross-*

Florida Barge Canal with special emphasis on the Ocklawaha Regional Ecosystem (Gainesville: n.p., 1970), 1–3, 7; *Tampa Tribune,* December 16, 1970.

37. Press release, Office of the White House press secretary, January 19, 1971, in Carr Papers, file 977A.

38. *Barge Canal Hearings,* 47; Patrick H. Caddell to FDE, July 17, 1974, in Arthur Marshall Papers, P. K. Yonge Library of Florida History, box 5.

39. Ibid.

40. *Florida Times-Union,* February 4, 1965; *Congressional Record,* 91st Cong., 2d sess., E4504, found in Carr Papers, Bennett file.

41. *Canal Authority of Florida v. Callaway,* 489 F.2d 567; Army Corps of Engineers, *Cross-Florida Barge Canal Restudy Report: Summary* (Jacksonville, 1976), 1–2.

42. Army Corps of Engineers, *Cross Florida Barge Canal Restudy Report: Final Summary* (Jacksonville, 1977), 40–41.

43. *St. Petersburg Times,* September 24, 1995.

44. *Canal Hearings,* 132.

45. Kirkpatrick to Virginia Wetherell, September 5, 1995, in Carr Papers, Kirkpatrick file; *Canal Hearings,* 52.

46. Virginia Wetherell to Lawton Chiles, January 17, 1995, Carr Papers, Kirkpatrick file; *St. Petersburg Times,* December 23, 1994, January 29, 1995, May 11, 1995, and March 15, 1998; *Gainesville Sun,* April 16, 1998; *Sarasota Herald-Tribune,* July 15, 2003.

Contributors

Raymond Arsenault is the John Hope Franklin Professor of Southern History at the University of South Florida, St. Petersburg. His published works include "The End of the Long Hot Summer: The Air Conditioner and Southern Culture" (1984) and *St. Petersburg and the Florida Dream, 1888–1950* (UPF, 1996).

Frederick R. Davis is an assistant professor of history at Florida State University. He is the author of *A Naturalist's Life: Archie Carr, Sea Turtles, and Conservation* (forthcoming).

Jack E. Davis is an associate professor of history at the University of Florida. He is the author or editor of several books, including *Marjory Stoneman Douglas: A Life with the Everglades* (forthcoming).

Gary Garrett is an assistant professor of history at Chowan College. He is currently writing a book on the environmental history of the Houston ship channel.

Thomas Hallock is a visiting scholar in the Florida Studies Program at the University of South Florida, St. Petersburg. He is the author of *From the Fallen Tree: Frontier Narratives, Environmental Politics, and the Roots of a National Pastoral, 1749–1826*, and editor of *The Traveler: Newsletter of the Bartram Trail Conference*.

Gordon Harvey is an assistant professor of history at the University of Louisiana, Monroe. He is the author of *A Question of Justice: New South Governors and Education, 1968–1976* (2002).

Lee Irby is an assistant professor of history at Eckerd College, St. Petersburg. He has published many articles and essays on Florida history, including "Taking Out the Trailer Trash: The Battle over Mobile Homes in St. Petersburg, 1920–1970," which won the *Florida Historical Quarterly*'s Arthur Thompson prize in 2001. His novel *7,000 Clams* was published by Doubleday in 2005.

David McCally is the author of *The Everglades: An Environmental History* (UPF, 1999).

Christopher Meindl is an assistant professor of interdisciplinary social science at the University of South Florida, St. Petersburg, and the author of several journal articles on Florida geography and ecology. His research focuses on Florida and human-environment interaction, especially in wetlands.

Dave Nelson is a doctoral student at Florida State University, and an archivist with the Florida State Archives. He is currently writing a book entitled *Relief and Recreation: The Civilian Conservation Corps and the Florida Park Service, 1935–1943*.

Gordon Patterson is a professor of history at Florida Institute of Technology. He is the author of *The Mosquito Wars: The History of Mosquito Control in Florida* (UPF, 2004).

Charlotte Porter is a curator at the Museum of Natural History, University of Florida. She is the author of a forthcoming book on William Bartram's travels in Florida, and she is co-editing a collection of essays sponsored by the Bartram Trail Commission.

has given the canal an up-trend in Washington." Canal backers deftly managed to include their project in an omnibus rivers and harbors bill—a *barge* canal, the type dismissed for its military use nineteen years before. But the nation was at war, and as Representative Joseph Mansfield of Texas noted, "while the people of the East are enduring great sacrifices, the people of the Southwest are suffering great financial loss" as oil could not be safely moved from the region. Thus, along with the canal, Congress approved a pipeline across Florida. This measure passed the Senate by one vote, indicating the opposition to the project that lingered from the mid-1930s. But the law lacked an appropriation for building the canal; it simply authorized the canal's existence. Other higher priority projects stood ahead of it, and when the war ended, so too did many of the rationalizations proffered for building it in the first place.[22]

If They Build It

The Cold War pitted two nations against each other between which existed innumerable similarities. Both nations used the context of the Cold War to erect bulging bureaucracies dedicated to proclaiming themselves to be the world's greatest country. The so-called arms race conformed to larger cultural patterns in which national defense became for both the United States and the Soviet Union an avenue to demonstrate the efficacy of their respective political systems. As the Cold War heated up in the 1950s, canal backers understood the semiotics involved. They had an authorized canal but no money for it. "No project of this kind has a ghost of a chance of getting started," wrote Buckman to newspaper magnate and canal champion John Perry, "unless *it is certified by the President* as being necessary in national defense. . . . [T]his is no job for a boy." The canal needed to signify America's might, needed to make a glorious contribution to the cause. In 1935, the canal would avert a potential revolt of the masses; two decades later, backers pinned all their hopes upon Pedro Menéndez's reasoning of 1565: defense.[23]

In 1951, President Harry Truman asked the Department of Defense to review the canal project, but its findings proved to be no help. The Joint Chiefs of Staff found that "the military aspects of the proposed project are so limited that they should not be used as the primary basis for decision on this matter." For a project that had received its share of death sentences, this one would appear to be irrevocable. But the canal did not die. Instead, the Army Corps of Engineers designated it for economic restudy in 1954, and Congress funded this task in 1958. In 1942, the corps had adduced the benefit-to-cost ratio to be 0.19 to 1, far short of the minimum 1-to-1 ratio needed for approval. In 1958, the ratio had risen to 1.05 to 1, meaning that for every dollar spent, the canal would return a nickel. Canal proponents found reason for hope. "The cross Florida barge canal is closer to enactment than ever before and your steadfast support is a large factor in this," wrote Congressman Charles Bennett to *Ocala Star-Banner* editor Bert Dosh. "*It will be built.*"[24]

Yet, even armed with an improved benefit-to-cost ratio, canal supporters still had trouble getting money out of Congress. Governor Leroy Collins wrote the House Appropriations Committee in support of the project, declaring that the canal would have "tremendous strategic importance in our nation's defense planning."[25] Even though Senator Spessard Holland promised to help obtain funding, in 1959 canal backers could not wrestle $160,000 for planning, "a sum . . . so small that is almost negligible in any appropriations bill," complained Bert Dosh. Senator Allen Ellender, who chaired the Appropriations Committee, explained why he would not spend a dime on the canal: the benefit-to-cost ratio "is a very slim margin [1.05 to 1.0]. It is my considered judgment that there are other more urgently needed projects in Florida."[26]

As 1960 dawned, again it appeared that the big ditch had met its maker. But just as Hitler had helped authorize the canal in 1942, so too did another world figure assist canal boosters in their efforts. By 1960, Americans understood that Fidel Castro's rise to power in Cuba would entail true revolution; America's exploitation of the island's resources and people came to an end, and Castro himself embraced the financial aid of the Soviet Union. The Cold War now lurked 90 miles from American soil. Canal backers jumped into the fray. "The unmistakable trend of recent developments in the Western Hemisphere with respect to the increasing communistic influence poses a present and continuing threat to our lines of communication," wrote the Ship Canal Authority in 1960. Not just Cuba posed a threat: the Canal Authority cited "Chinese laborers" being brought to "less developed" islands in the Bahamas as evidence of the red menace, more proof that "Because We Shall Need It, It Must Be Ready Now!"[27]

But Florida's incredible population growth proved to be an even bigger ally of the canal than the bearded visage of Fidel Castro. By the 1960 presidential election, Florida had become the twelfth-largest state, having nearly doubled in population since 1950. To win votes in the Sunshine State, John F. Kennedy campaigned as a staunch canal advocate. To canal-backing congressman Charles Bennett: "If I am elected President I will be glad to cooperate with you in making this project a reality. I regard it not only as important to Florida but to the economy of our entire country, which must fully utilize all of our natural resources if we are to achieve necessary economic expansion." Thus, screamed Kennedy advertisements in Ocala, "A Vote for Kennedy is a Vote for the Cross-Florida Canal!" Yet, even after his election, supporters wondered whether Kennedy used the canal as a "possible pawn," especially as he positioned for reelection in 1964. But Kennedy lived up to his word and pushed for actual construction funds, which the House of Representatives approved on November 19, 1963, less than a week before his assassination. Lyndon Johnson, perhaps the most astute politician of his generation, needed little prodding to fathom the relationship between important votes in north Florida and the canal, although canal supporters explained the dynamic anyway. "Since approval by Congress of the $1 million appropriation," Dosh wrote in December 1963, "there has been a decided change in the political situation in Florida. The Goldwater boom . . . is definitely on the wane." Dutifully, LBJ presided over the second ceremonial dynamite blasting in February 1964 to inaugurate the canal's rebirth.[28]

So construction on the canal began again, twenty-eight years after the Public Works Administration workers had stopped. It would be a barge canal, previously dismissed as too narrow to help either shipping or defense. But as Florida's population continued to increase, thereby increasing its importance in presidential politics, so too did the Army Corps of Engineers continue to calculate better benefit-to-cost ratios, reaching a high of 1.7 to 1.0 by 1969. The canal backers fancied themselves as kingmakers, at the center of a power nexus that seemed to be firmly entrenched. Florida stood poised as a Sunbelt potentate, symbolized by the canal and all the light industry it would spawn. Yet even as canal supporters celebrated their apparent victory in their struggle to "utilize" Florida's "natural resources," a challenge to this Sunbelt ideology emerged. The Sunbelt promised growth in ways the New South never could, but in Florida some began to wonder if growth might not be ruinous, especially to the environment. As the cranes once again ate into the Florida landscape, a group of citizens plotted to save a river from destruction. It would become a battle for the Sunbelt's soul.[29]

Rape of the Lock

Then the heavy machinery came. "The cross-Florida barge canal south of here is beginning to take shape as a giant dragline snaps and chews its way through sandy timber and pastureland of Putnam County," reported the *Florida Times-Union* in 1965, in describing the desolation that would come to the Ocklawaha River. Besides the massive dragline, its bucket capable of lift-ing an automobile-sized chunk of earth, there also appeared the "crusher-crawler," which resembled a tank. It knocked over trees and then crushed them in order to carve out space for the Rodman Pool, a reservoir for the St. Johns Lock. By 1965, a group of citizens had come together to stop the ma-chines, specifically to stop the destruction of the Ocklawaha River. Other citi-zens fought if not for the canal's completion, then for the retention of a built environment that they believed constituted an ecosystem worthy of protec-tion in its own right. Their arguments back and forth, once initiated in the 1960s, basically remained unchanged into the twenty-first century. Huge forces collided, forces that have come to define the complex relationship be-tween politics and the environment not just in Florida but also in the United States.[30]

At its core, this battle centered on the definition of "ecosystem." One text-book defines "ecosystem" as "a community of organisms in interaction with the environment." Notice that the definition does not include the word "natu-ral," meaning that an ecosystem, broadly conceived, can be one produced by humans that replaces an ecosystem evolved through natural selection. Thus, when the cranes and crushers began destroying the riverine forests of the Withlacoochee and the Ocklawaha, and dams and locks disturbed the water flows of those rivers, one ecosystem in effect replaced another. The question emerged: which ecosystem would remain in place, the natural one or the built one? Which organisms would interact with what environment?[31]

Even before official funding for the canal came in 1964, concerned citi-zens had rallied to stop the destruction of the Ocklawaha River. In November 1962, David Anthony and Marjorie Carr of the Gainesville Audubon Society, along with Marjorie Bielling, pushed the Florida Game and Fresh Water Fish Commission to hold a public hearing on the proposed canal, especially focus-ing on its environmental impact. From their grassroots effort emerged a larger organization, the Citizens for the Conservation of Florida's Natural and Economic Resources, which sent out thousands of brochures warning of the massive flooding that the Rodman Dam would cause along 45 miles of the Ocklawaha. "This flooding," the brochure read, "will destroy the river-type fish habitat and productive hydric hammock game habitat and *replace them* with equal acreage of shallow lake-type habitat and low quality water-fowl areas" (emphasis added). Their efforts found allies all over Florida and

Contributors

Raymond Arsenault is the John Hope Franklin Professor of Southern History at the University of South Florida, St. Petersburg. His published works include "The End of the Long Hot Summer: The Air Conditioner and Southern Culture" (1984) and *St. Petersburg and the Florida Dream, 1888–1950* (UPF, 1996).

Frederick R. Davis is an assistant professor of history at Florida State University. He is the author of *A Naturalist's Life: Archie Carr, Sea Turtles, and Conservation* (forthcoming).

Jack E. Davis is an associate professor of history at the University of Florida. He is the author or editor of several books, including *Marjory Stoneman Douglas: A Life with the Everglades* (forthcoming).

Gary Garrett is an assistant professor of history at Chowan College. He is currently writing a book on the environmental history of the Houston ship channel.

Thomas Hallock is a visiting scholar in the Florida Studies Program at the University of South Florida, St. Petersburg. He is the author of *From the Fallen Tree: Frontier Narratives, Environmental Politics, and the Roots of a National Pastoral, 1749–1826,* and editor of *The Traveler: Newsletter of the Bartram Trail Conference.*

Gordon Harvey is an assistant professor of history at the University of Louisiana, Monroe. He is the author of *A Question of Justice: New South Governors and Education, 1968–1976* (2002).

Lee Irby is an assistant professor of history at Eckerd College, St. Petersburg. He has published many articles and essays on Florida history, including "Taking Out the Trailer Trash: The Battle over Mobile Homes in St. Petersburg, 1920–1970," which won the *Florida Historical Quarterly*'s Arthur Thompson prize in 2001. His novel *7,000 Clams* was published by Doubleday in 2005.

David McCally is the author of *The Everglades: An Environmental History* (UPF, 1999).

Christopher Meindl is an assistant professor of interdisciplinary social science at the University of South Florida, St. Petersburg, and the author of several journal articles on Florida geography and ecology. His research focuses on Florida and human-environment interaction, especially in wetlands.

Dave Nelson is a doctoral student at Florida State University, and an archivist with the Florida State Archives. He is currently writing a book entitled *Relief and Recreation: The Civilian Conservation Corps and the Florida Park Service, 1935–1943.*

Gordon Patterson is a professor of history at Florida Institute of Technology. He is the author of *The Mosquito Wars: The History of Mosquito Control in Florida* (UPF, 2004).

Charlotte Porter is a curator at the Museum of Natural History, University of Florida. She is the author of a forthcoming book on William Bartram's travels in Florida, and she is co-editing a collection of essays sponsored by the Bartram Trail Commission.

Nano Riley is a native Floridian and freelance writer who lives in St. Petersburg, Florida. Her book *Florida's Farmworkers in the Twenty-first Century*, published by the University Press of Florida (2003), won the Carolyn Washbon Award from the Florida Historical Society.

Bruce Stephenson is a professor of environmental studies at Rollins College. He is the author of *Visions of Eden: Environmentalism, Urban Planning, and City Building in St. Petersburg, Florida, 1900–1995* (1997).

Christopher Warren is academy historian at the New York Academy of Medicine. His book *Brush with Death: A Social History of Lead Poisoning* (2000) won the Arthur Viseltear Award from the American Public Health Association.

Index

A. Duda, 285, 287

Acts of God: The Unnatural History of Natural Disaster in America, 204–5

Acuera, 281

Addams, Jane, 304

Ais, 236

Alabama, 131, 367, 380

Alachua County, 48, 79, 182

Alachua Sink, 53

Alaska, 127

Algal blooms, 282

Allen, Hervey, 307

Allender, Bonnie, 393

Allen's River, 268

Alliance for the Conservation of Natural Resources (ACNR), 331, 336–40

Alligator Alley, 275, 361

Alligator Ike, 239

Alligators, 237–41, 253–54, 264, 281, 283–84, 286, 297, 313

Altvater, A. C., 103

Amelia Island, 97

America: A Prophecy, 64

American Association of Railroads, 382

American Association of University Women, 316

American Civil Liberties Union, 310

American Cyanamid Company, 167

American Federation of Labor (AFL), 93

American Meteorological Journal, 207

American Museum of Natural History, 237

American Ornithological Union (AOU), 245, 249

American Ornithology, 59

American Red Cross, 303

American Revolution, 48, 51, 58

Amos Quito, 172
Anacostia Flats, 213
Anthony, David, 388–89
Apalachicola Bay, 367
Apalachicola National Forest, 100–101, 104, 106
Apalachicola River, 97, 117, 367
Apopka, 287
Apopka-Beauclaire Canal, 281
Aquatic Preserve Bill, 342
Aquifers, 152–54, 353, 380, 382–83
Arcadia, 10
Arctic, 187
"Area of Critical State Concern," 345, 362, 364
Arizona, 237
Arkansas, 367
Armed Occupation Act, 281
Askew, Reuben, 16, 351–68
Atala, 61–62
Atlanta Journal, 307
Atlantic Coast, 121, 179–81, 207
Atlantic Coastal Ridge, 148, 153, 156
Atlantic Coast Line Railroad, 260
Atlantic Ocean, 149, 201, 203, 216, 219, 300, 376–78, 380, 384
ATS satellite, 217
Audubon (magazine), 87, 317
Audubon, John James, 63, 244
Audubon Society Birds of Prey Center, 290
Australia, 246
Australian pine, 85

B-52 bomber, 389
Babbitt, Bruce, 317
Bahamas, 82, 201–2, 386
Baker, Harry Lee, 94, 101
Balch, Emily Greene, 303
Bald and Golden Eagle Protection Act, 289
Bancroft, George, 236
Barbados, 179–80, 205, 207, 208
Barnacles, 328
Barbour, Thomas 3, 74–75, 77–78, 81, 87, 242, 313
Barry, John, 211
Bartholomew and Associates, 333

Barton, Benjamin Smith, 58
Bartram, John, 33, 87
Bartram, William, 7, 33, 47–66, 87, 237–38, 352
Basili, Gian, 286
Batty, J. H., 246
Bay City dredge, 269–70
Baynard, Oscar, 246
Beadle's New York Dime Library, 239
Belle Glade, 211, 315
Bennett, Charles, 386–87, 391–92
Bermuda, 82
Berner, Lewis, 81
Beverly Hills, Calif., 344
Bielling, Marjorie, 388
Big Cypress National Preserve, 271, 365–66
Big Cypress Preserve Act, 365
Big Cypress Swamp, 16, 17, 117, 261, 266, 268, 271–72, 275, 350–74
Big Cypress Watershed, 358
Bigelow, Margaret Porter, 77
Bigelow, Mary, 337
Big Sugar, 314–16
Bimini, 235
Bing Crosby Minute Maid Corporation, 190
Bioaccumulation, 289
Birds Eye (General Foods), 190
Biscayne Aquifer, 152–54, 353
Biscayne Bay, 210, 355–56
Blake, Nelson Manfred, 4, 132
Blake, William, 64
Blue Ridge Parkway, 98
Board of Consulting Engineers, 148
Boca Ciega Bay, 326–49
Bolles, Richard J., 144–46
Bonita, 328
Bonus Army, 381
Bonus Marchers, 94, 212
Born of the Sun, 88
Boston, 219, 244, 303, 329
Botanic Garden, The, 64
Boy Scouts, 171
Bradenton, 338
Bradley, Guy, 250, 302, 307
Brahman bulls, 192

Brantley, John, 340
Brazilian pepper, 85
Brevard County, 353
Brewster, 167–68, 172
Brisbane, Arthur, 380
British, 179–80, 180, 189, 241, 205, 377
British Royal Engineers, 205
Brodie, L. R., 104
Bronx Zoo, 246
Broward, Napoleon, 124, 144, 146–48, 263, 274
Broward County, 5, 264, 353–54
Brown, Floyd, 336–37
Brown, John R., 344
Brown, Lesley, 171–72
Buck, William J., 167–68
Buckman, H. H., 384–85
Bulkhead Law, 335, 338
Bursten, Leonard, 336–39, 344
Burton-Swartz Cypress Company, 163, 166–67
Bush, George H. W., 130
Bush, Jeb, 345–46, 394
Business Week, 190
Byrd, Hiram, 161

C-38 canal (Kissimmee River), 351, 353
Cabell, James Branch, 3
Cabeza de Vaca, Alvar Nuñez, 28
Cabinet of Natural History, 62
Calhoun, John C., 378
California, 131, 237, 363, 391
Caloosahatchee canal, 149, 151
Caloosahatchee River, 261, 263, 265–66
Calusa, 236
Cambridge, Mass., 77
Camp Johnson, 162–65
Canal Authority, 386
Canal Commission, 379
Cannon, Howard, 365
Cape Canaveral, 120, 378
Cape Coral, 350
Cape Coral Estates, 367
Cape Sable, 85
Cape Verde Islands, 202
Carey, Thomas, 338

Caribbean, 80–83, 201, 205, 207–8, 214, 315, 376, 383
Caribbean Conservation Corporation, 83
Carnegie Museum, 74–75
Carnestown, 269–71
Carolinas, 223
Carpenter, Bill, 240
Carr, Archie, 8, 19, 72–89
Carr, Marjorie Harris, 17, 375, 388–89, 394
Carson, Rachel, 16, 308, 310, 312, 333, 355
Carter, Jimmy, 219, 220, 390
Castro, Fidel, 315, 386, 392
Catesby, Mark, 32
Catfish, 289
Catholicism, 161
Catlin, George, 62
Cats Blank Point, 331, 340
Catts, Sidney J., 161–62, 164
Cedar Key, 84, 117, 121; storm, 208
Central and Southern Florida Project Comprehensive Review Study, 142–43, 147, 154–57
Central and South Florida Water Conservation Committee, 383–84
Central Florida Highway Association, 264
Century Magazine, 264
Chapman, Frank, 3, 237, 245, 250
Charles Town (later Charleston, S.C.), 180, 377
Charlotte Harbor, 265
Check List of North American Amphibians and Reptiles, 78
Cherokees, 51, 64
Chevelier Corporation, 267, 269, 271, 276
Chicago, Ill., 265, 336
Chicago Drainage Canal, 149
Chicago River, 149
Chicago Sanitary District, 149
Chile, 361
Chiles, Lawton, 357, 363–65, 390
China, 180, 186, 283, 361
Chinese laborers, 386
Chipola River, 97
Chism, Ellis, 361
Choctawahatchee National Forest, 104

Christian Union, 182

Citizens for the Conservation of Florida's Natural and Economic Resources, 388

Citrus, 11, 12, 177–200, 237, 282, 284, 300

Citrus Concentrates, Inc, 189

City Beautiful movement, 304

Civilian Conservation Corps (CCC), 8–9, 92–106, 212

Civil rights, 249, 302, 315, 355, 393

Civil War, 87, 181, 192, 205, 262, 368

Clams, *328*

Classification of Wetlands and Deepwater Habitats of the United States, 127

Clean Water Act, 128

Cline, Isaac, 209

Clinton, Bill, 298, 317

CNN (Cable News Network), 203, 222

Coachman, Walter F., Jr., 384

Cobb, James, 368

Coffin, Levi, 303

"Cold Sunday," 181

Cold War, 223, 385–86

Coleridge, Samuel Taylor, 61

Collier, Barron G., 267–71, 274–76

Collier, Sam, 153

Collier County, 268, 271–73, 350, 354, 358, 360, 366

Collier County Board of Commissioners, 367

Collier County News, 275

Collins, LeRoy, 16, 326, 331–32, 335–38, 342, 345–46, 386

Collins Administration, 332, 340–41

Colorado, 124, 144

Colorado State University, 127, 221

"Columbian Exchange," 179

Comparative Museum of Zoology (Harvard University), 242

Comprehensive Everglades Restoration Project, 10–11, 275, 317

Comprehensive Report on Central and Southern Florida for Flood Control and Other Purposes, 144, 152–53

Concise Natural History of East and West Florida, A, 37

Connor, John T., 216

Connors, Jim, 282, 285

Conrad, Lottie, 183

Conservation, 82–89, 92–106, 298, 301, 303, 305, 310, 312–13, 317–18, 327–32

Conservation 70s, Inc. (C-70s), 352, 362–63

Contribution to the Herpetology of Florida, 78

Copeland, D. Graham, 269–71

Coral Gables Women's Club, 316

Cornell University, 74–75

Cory, Charles B., 244, 262

Cosmopolitan, 240

Costa Rica, 72, 80–81, 84

Council of 100, 363

Council on Environmental Quality, 358

Couse, John H., 389

Cowkeeper (Creek/Seminole Chief), 52–54, 57, 59

Cox, W. H., 161–62, 164

Cracker culture, 88

Crane, Stephen, 1, 352

Creeks (Indians), 48, 50–53, 55, 57, 60, 65–66

Cronon, William, 275

Crosby, Bing, 190

Cross-Florida Barge Canal, 87, 375–97

Cuba, 206–9, 355, 361, 378, 386

Cuban émigrés and refugees, 361, 355

Cuban Meteorological Service, 207

Curacao, 208

Cuthbert rookery, 250

Cutler, Phoebe, 98

Cypress, 309

Dade County, 98, 202–3, 264–66, 268–69, 271, 312, 351, 353–54, 358

Dade County Port Authority, 312

Dahl, Thomas, 130–32

Darwin, Erasmus, 64

Daughters of the American Revolution, 301

Davidson College, 73

Davis, Robert, Mrs., 337

Daytona Beach, 121, 160, 172–73

Daytona Conference, 172–73

DDT, 165, 286, 288–91

De Brahm, John Gerar William, 34

De Castellanos, Juan, 30

De Chateaubriand, François-René, 61
Declaration of Independence, 49, 65
Deep Lake Hammock, 268
Deer, 313
De la Bazares, Guido, 34
DeLand, 183
De Paiva, Juan, 38
De Pysière, Giles, 25–26
Dequine, John, 339
Derr, Mark, 352, 355
Desalination, 18
De Segura, Andrés, 27–28
De Velasco, Juan Lopez 33
Dickie, L. P., 264
Dickinson, John 28
Dicofol, 284
Dimock, A. W., 242, 251–52
Disaster Relief Act, 220
Disney, Walt, 63, 193
Disneyland, 193
Disston, Hamilton, 123, 263, 271
Distinguished Service Medal, 160
Dix, Edwin Asa, 264
Dixie Highway, 265
Dock, Mira Lloyd, 304
Dominica, 208
Doppler radar, 215
Dosh, Bert, 386
Douglas, Marjory Stoneman, 3, 16, 124, 178, 266, 274, 297–25, 352
Dovell, Junius E., 3
Dredging, 306, 326–49
Dry Tortugas, 82
Duckworth, Joseph, 214
Dummett, Douglas, 180–81
Dunedin, 189
Dunes, 328–29
Dunn, Gordon, 215, 218–19
Dust Bowl, 261
Dutcher, William, 247, 248
Dye, Buddy, 285

Eagles, 286, 289–90
Eagleton, Thomas, 365
Earth Day, 312

East Angles, 237
East Collier Landowners Improvement Committee, Inc., 361, 366
East Florida 48–54, 56–58, 62, 64–65, 239, 377
Eckerd College, 342
Ecology of Boca Ciega Bay, with Special Reference to Dredging and Filling Operations, The, 334
Economos, Jeannie, 286–88
Ecosystem Restoration, 154
Ecosystems of Florida, 102
Eden, 8, 13, 186
Edge of the Sea, The, 333
Egrets, 246
Eisenhower, Julie, 358
Elcar, 267
Ellender, Allen, 386
Ellicott, Andrew 34
"El Nino," 221
Emergency Civilian Works, 94
Emergency Wetlands Resources Act, 127
Emerson, Ralph Waldo, 352
Endangered Species Act (ESA), 289–90
English. See British
Environmental Defense Fund, 390
Environmental Impact of the Cross-Florida Barge Canal, 390
Environmental Protection Agency (EPA), 284, 358
Environmental Quality Commission, 360
Environmental Sciences Services Administration (ESSA), 218
Environment and Natural Resources Division (U.S. Department of Justice), 289
Equal Rights Amendment, 303, 315–16
Ervin, Richard, 332, 340
Escuela Agricola Panamerica, 81
Espy, James P., 206
ESSA 1 and 2 satellites, 217
Estuarine Heritage, 344
Europe, 123, 180, 189, 241–42, 244–46, 248, 302–3, 315, 376
Europe: A Prophecy, 64
Europeans, 376, 241
Evelyn, John, 51

Everglades, 10, 11, 14, 16, 82, 85, 95, 114, 117, 118–19, 122, 124–26, 141–59, 192, 211, 237, 238, 242, 247, 250–53, 261–75, 297–318, 351–57, 360; Agricultural Area (EAA), 311, 314, 316; Drainage District, 150, 153, 263, 269, 270, 272, 274; Engineering Board of Review, 144, 149–51; National Park, 152, 251, 275, 306, 309, 317, 353–54, 356
Everglades, The (Time-Life Books), 84–85, 87
Everglades Land Sales Company, 147
Everglades: River of Grass, The, 3, 266, 274, 298, 306–17
Ewel, Katherine, 115

Fairchild, David, 3, 306
Fairchild Tropical Gardens, 97
Fakahatchee Strand, 238
Far East, 246
Farm Bill (1985), 130
Farm Worker Ministry (Apopka), 287
Farmworkers, 286–88, 315
Farmworkers Association of Florida, 286–88
Farrand, Beatrix, 304
Fechner, Robert, 93–94, 96
Federal Disaster Assistance Administration (FDAA), 220
Federal Emergency Management Agency (FEMA), 219–22
Federal Emergency Relief Agency (FERA), 212
Federal Geographic Data Committee, 129
Federal Insurance Administration, 220
Federal Preparedness Agency of the General Services Administration, 220
Federal-State Agricultural Weather Service, 187–88
Federal-State Frost Warning Service, 187–88
Federal Tariff Act (1913), 250
Federal Writers' Project, 273
Federation of Garden Clubs, 389
Fellsmere, 124, 126
Fernandez de Oviedo y Valdez, Gonzalo, 32
Fernandina, 98
Fish, Jesse, 180
Fish kills, 281, 282–84
Flagler, Henry, 183, 300, 379

Flagler, Mary, 301
Flamingo, 250
Fleahop, Ala., 214
Fletcher, Duncan U., 146, 379
"Flight of Ibis, A," 307
Floriana Park subdivision, 178
Florida Anti-Mosquito Association (FAMA), 160, 173
Florida Association of Realtors, 363
Florida Audubon Society, 3, 248–49, 286, 364, 389
Florida Bay, 271, 254, 309
Florida Buggist, 161
Florida Bureau of Venereal Disease, 168
Florida Caverns State Park, 97, 106
Florida Child Welfare Bureau, 168
Florida Citrus Commission, 188; Research and Education Center, 189
Florida Citrus Exchange, 188
Florida Citrus Mutual, 188
Florida Defenders of the Environment (FDE), 17, 389–90, 392
Florida Department of Agriculture, 125, 359
Florida Department of Air and Water Pollution, 357
Florida Department of Environmental Protection (DEP), 130, 393
Florida Department of Environmental Regulation, 130
Florida Department of Health, 288–89. *See* also Florida State Board of Health
Florida Department of Natural Resources, 359, 362, 366
Florida Department of Pollution Control, 359
Florida East Coast Railroad, 141, 212, 299
Florida Electric Power Plant Siting Act, 364
Florida Entomological Society, 161
Florida Environmental Affairs Department, 360
Florida Equal Suffrage Association, 302
Florida Federation of Women's Clubs (FFWC), 95, 250–51, 301–2, 306
Florida Forest Service, 96, 102, 105
Florida Game and Freshwater Fish Commission, 249, 251, 274, 353, 359–62, 388, 391

Florida Grower, 383

Florida Health Notes, 161–62

Florida Home Builders Association, 363

Florida Keys, 86, 195, 212–13

Florida legislature, 130, 144, 149, 153, 168, 172, 284, 301, 335; state senate, 167, 284–85, 301, 335, 386

Florida Militia, 180

Florida Museum of Natural History in Palm Beach, 244

Floridan Aquifer, 154, 382

Florida Natural Areas Inventory, 118

Florida Naturalist, 74

Florida Panther, 313–14

Florida Park Service, 96–97, 99

Florida Presbyterian College. *See* Eckerd College

Florida Rural Legal Services, 315

Florida's Last Frontier, 3

Florida State Archives, 99

Florida State Board of Conservation, 332, 334

Florida State Board of Health, 161–62, 164–65, 167–68, 171–72. *See also* Florida Department of Health

Florida State Bureau of Engineering, 162, 164

Florida State College for Women (FSCW), 76

Florida State Land Planning Commission, 362

Florida State Lands Commission, 360

Florida State Land Use and Control Committee (SLUCC), 332, 335

Florida State Livestock Sanitary Board, 100

Florida State Road Department, 271, 276

Florida State University (FSU), 76

Florida Straits, 376

Florida Supreme Court, 340–41, 343

Florida Surface Water Improvement and Management (SWIM), 284

Florida: The Long Frontier, 3

Florida Times-Union (Jacksonville), 388

Florida Trend, 363

Florida Water Resource Conference, 353

Florida Wildlife Federation, 313, 314

"Flower Hunter" (Puc Puggy), 52, 54–57, 65

Forbes, Juan, 35

Forest Fires in Florida, 95

Forest Fire Prevention Week, 103

Fort Caroline, 26, 36, 377

Fort Clinch, 97, 98, 101

Fort Lauderdale, 124, 144–45, 241, 261

Fort Myers, 202, 260–61, 264–69, 272, 275, 336, 338, 342

Fort Myers Press, 264, 268, 275

Fort Myers Tropical News, 269

Fort Worth, Tex., 73

Foster, J. G., 165

Fothergill, John, 48–50, 58

Fountain of Youth, 29–30, 237

Frank, Neil, 222

Franklin, Benjamin, 49, 205

Frayer, W. E., 127–31

Fredine, C. Gordon, 128–32

Freezes: of 1835, 181, 183; of 1894–95, 183; of 1962, 187

French, 179, 239, 377

Friends of the Everglades (FOE), 312–16

Friends of Lake Apopka (FOLA), 284–85

From Eden to Sahara, 87, 252, 313

Frostproof, 183

Frye, O. Earle, 362

Furen, Albert, 331–38, 340

Gagarin, Yuri, 216

Gaige, Helen, 74

Gainesville, 79, 83, 84, 86, 172, 182, 187, 242, 388

Gainesville Audubon Society, 388

Galveston, Tex., 209–10, 214

Gar, 289

Garcilaso de la Vega, el Inca, 31

General Federation of Women's Clubs (GFWC), 301

General Land Office, 205

Genoa, Italy, 237

"Gentleman of the South, A," 35

Gentry, R. Cecil, 216–17

Georgia, 180–81, 246, 367, 377, 380

Geostationary Operational Environmental Satellite (GOES), 217

Germany, 384

Gifford, John C., 252–53
Gilded Age, 181
Gillett, D. C., 264
Gold Coast, 353
Golden Gate Estates, 351
Goldhead Branch State Park, 97, 100–102,
     104–5
Goldwater, Barry, 387
Gorgas, Dr. William, 162
Gould, Gerald, 337–38
Governor's Conference on Water Manage-
     ment, 355
Graham, Bob, 153, 314–15, 363, 367–68
Graham, Ernest, 153
Grand Bahama Island, 211
Grand Canyon, 237
Grand Coulee Dam, 212
Grant, James, 377
Grant, Ulysses S., 206, 382
Gray, Richard W., 210–11
Gray, William, 221
Great Alachua Savanna 48, 52, 54, 60–61, 65
Great Depression, 94, 150, 213, 220, 272, 251,
     330, 379
Great Florida Boom, 210
Great Labor Day Hurricane, 212
Great Plains, 242, 261
Greater Antilles, 82
"Green Areas," 367
Green Cove Springs, 95, 236
Greene, Ralph, 164, 166, 168
"Green Index," 367
Green, Lex, 381
Green Mansions, 307
Green Swamp, 117
Greynolds Park, 97–98
Grimes, William, 338
Guadeloupe, 207
Guillette, Louis, 284
Gulf America Corporation, 367
Gulf American Land Corporation, 350
Gulf coast, 207, 217, 180–81, 192
"Gulf-Island Cotton Mouths, The," 76
Gulf of Mexico, 117, 121, 164, 202, 208, 261,
     273, 328, 376–80, 382

Gulf Stream, 82, 180, 300
Gurney, Ed, 357, 363

Hakluyt, Richard, 35
Halcrow, Sir William and·Partners (engineer-
     ing firm), 81
Halifax River, 180
Hall, A. W., 170–71
Hamilton, Alice, 304
Hammond, John Martin, 260–61
Hampson, Paul, 128
Handbook of Turtles, 80–81
Hanna, Alfred Jackson, 3
Harney, William Wallace, 262–64
Harrington, Mark, 207
Harris, J. R., 170
Harris, S. H., 340
Harris, Thomas, 343
Harris Chain of Lakes, 281, 284–85
Harrub, C. N., 163
Harper's, 251
Harper's New Monthly Magazine, 262–63
Hartzog, George, 358
Harvard University, 74–75, 77, 242
Havana, 206, 208–9, 241, 248
Hawaii, 127
Hawthorne Formation, 154
Hazen, Allen, 147
Hearst, William Randolph, 268
Heath, Buck, 106
Hefner, John, 127–32
Hemingway, Ernest, 213, 352, 368
Hendry County, 354
Henry, Joseph, 206
Hererra y Tordesilla, Antonio, 32
Herons, 285–86
Hetch-Hetchy Valley, 391
High Jungles and Low, 82
Highlands County, 181
Highlands Hammock State Park, 92, 97, 100,
     103, 105–6
Hills and Youngberg law firm, 380
Hillsborough County, 183, 192
Hillsborough River, 97, 99, 180
Hillsborough River State Park, 97, 99

Hiroshima, 216
History of Florida, A, 3
Hitler, Adolph, 384, 386
Holland, Spessard, 386
Holt tractors, 270
Homestead, 202, 213
Honduras, 72, 80–82
Hoover, Herbert, 150, 381
Hoover Dike, 212, 274, 354
Hornaday, William T., 246
Horne, Mallory, 360
House Subcommittee on Public Works (U.S.), 389
Howard, Leland Osian, 160–61
Howey, William J., 194–95
Howey-in-the-Hills, 194
Howey Sanitarium, 194
Hoyt, Roy, 101
Hubbard, Wilson, 345
Hudson, William Henry, 307, 309
Huff, Buddy, 187
Hugh Taylor Birch State Park, 106
Humble Petition, 34–35
Humphrey, Hubert, 357, 363, 365
Hurricane, 310
Hurricane House, 310
Hurricane hunters, 214–16
Hurricanes, 201–32, 309–10, 329; Able, 214;
    Agnes, 220; Andrew, 12, 202–4, 223; Baker,
    214; Betsy, 215–16; Beulah, 216; Carla, 217;
    Camille, 220; Daisy, 216; Debbie, 216–17;
    Donna, 215; Esther, 216; Hugo, 221; King,
    214
Hurst, J. Willard, 205
Hurston, Zora Neale, 212
Huston, L. D., 236
Hutchins, Thomas 34
Hutton, Robert, 334–36, 339–40, 343

Ickes, Harold, 96, 381, 383
Immokalee, 265
Indians. *See* Native Americans
Indian Removal Act of 1828, 62
Indian River, 180–81
Indian River Lagoon, 120

Indiana, 131
Indianola, Tex., 207
Ingersoll-Rand, 270
Inferno, 64
Ingle, Robert, 334, 343
"In Memoriam," 313
Internal Improvement Fund, 148, 359–60
International Geophysical Year, 215
Intracoastal Waterway, 330
Iowa, 131
Ishom, Randolph, 149
Izaak Walton League, 389

Jackson, Henry "Scoop," 357–58, 363, 365
Jacksonville, 5, 36, 103, 162–63, 169–70, 181,
    212, 238, 240–41, 260, 343, 380, 384
Jamaica, 207–8
James, Henry, 1, 237, 352
Japan, 242
Jarrell, Jerry, 222
Jaudon, James F., 264–65, 267, 272
Jaycees, 363
Jefferson, Thomas, 205
Jennings, May Mann, 95–96, 102, 250
Jennings, S. Bryan, 96
Jennings, William S., 95, 249
Jesuit College of Belén, 206, 209
Jonah's Pond, 86
John Burroughs Medal, 83
Johnson, Lyndon B., 220, 387
Johnson administration, 218
Johnstown flood, 207
Joint Chiefs of Staff, 385
Jones, Johnny, 313–14

Kane, Harnett T., 307
Kansas, 262
Kautz, Randy, 128
Keller, Morton, 204
Kelly, Everett, 285
Kennedy, Edward M., 365
Kennedy, John F., 386–87
Kentucky, 362
Kersey, Harry, 241
Key Largo, 85, 212

Keystone City, 183
Key West, 212, 260, 376, 378, 394
Khan, Kubla, 61, 63
King, Edward, 237
King, John, 272
Kingsessing, Pa., 56–58
Kingston, Jamaica, 207–8
Kirk, Claude, 19, 342, 357
Kirkpatrick, George, 393
Kirkpatrick Dam, 394
Kissimmee, 237
Kissimmee River, 263, 311, 314, 351, 353
Kushlan, James, 118–19

LaBelle, 265
Lacey Act, 248
Lackey, James B., 339
Ladies Home Journal, 248
Lake Alice, 85–86
Lake Apopka, 15, 280–93, 351
Lake Apopka Restoration Act of 1996, 285
Lake Apopka Restoration Council, 284
Lake Beauclair, 281
Lake Carlton, 281
Lake City, 103
Lake County, 181, 194, 281
Lake Dora, 281
Lake Eustis, 281
Lake George, 54, 377
Lake Griffin, 281
Lake Harris, 281
Lake Mattamuckeet, 146
Lake Michigan, 149
Lake Myakka, 99–100
Lake Ocklawaha. *See* Rodman Pool
Lake Okeechobee, 17, 118, 124, 144, 146, 148–
    52, 154–55, 211–12, 260, 262–63, 271, 274,
    308–9, 311, 314, 316, 353, 355–56
Lake Placid, 287
Lake, Sheeler, 104
Lake Yale, 281
Land and Water Management Bill, 359
Land Boom (Florida), 281, 330
Land Conservation Act, 362
Land into Water, 132

Landowners Conservation and Protective
    Association, 360
Landrum, Ney, 332
Lands for You, Inc., 363
Lane, Franklin, 98
Lanier, Sidney, 1, 63, 238
Laudonnière, René, 36–37
Lawson, A. D., 97
Lawson, Erik, 209
League of Women Voters, 363
Le Challeux, Nicolas, 36
Le Chevalier, Jean, 247
Lecouris, George, 101, 104
Lee County, 216, 264–69, 271
Lee County Commission, 265–66
Lehtinen, Dexter, 154
Leighton, Marshall O., 149
LeMoyne, Jacques, 37, 239
Leopold, Aldo, 308, 310, 312
Lignumvitae Key, 86
Linville, George, 393
Little Lake Harris, 194, 281
Lodge, Thomas, 60
Loftin, U. C., 161
Long, Huey P., 380
Long and Upper Matecumbe Keys, 213
Long Warrior (Creek leader), 55
Loop Road, 276
Lopez de Mendoza Grajales, Francisco, 32
López de Velasco, Juan, 33–34
Los Angeles, Calif., 344
Louisiana, 202, 367, 380
Love Canal, 221
Lovelle, Loring, 362
Loves of the Plants, 64
Lower Creeks (Indians), 48, 50, 52, 53, 57, 60;
    snake taboo, 55
Luff, John, 194
Lykes, John, 163

MacGonigle, John Nowry, 264
MacKenzie, Tom, 289, 292
Madeira Bay, 85
Maine, 357
Malaria Control Work, 163

Manatee County, 338, 364

Manatee County Chamber of Commerce, 364

Manatee River, 237

Mandarin, 182

Mangroves, 120–21, 125, 132, 300, 307, 328–29, 331, 334

Manhattan, 351

Man in the Everglades, 3

Mansfield, Joseph, 385

Mansfield, Mike, 365

Marble Canyon, 389

Marchand, Lewis J., 78

Marco Island, 85, 264–65

Mardi Gras, 275

Marianna, 78, 103

Mariel boatlift, 221

Marion County, 182, 384

Marrs, Kingsmill, Mrs., 248

Marshall, Arthur, 312–14, 316, 353–54

Marshes, 118–20, 124–25, 132–33, 156, 291, 328

Martyr, Peter (Pietro Martire d'Anghiera), 29

Marx, Karl, 360

Marxism, 360

Massachusetts Institute of Technology (MIT), 162

Matanzas Marsh, 291

Matecumbe (Upper and Lower), 213

Mather, Stephen, 98

Matheson Hammock, 97

Mattamuckeet Lake reclamation project, 146

Mayfield, Max, 222

McCarthy, Joseph, 336

McClure, Alexander Kelley, 192

McEntee, James, 94

McGovern, George, 357

McIDAS (Man-computer Interactive Data Access System), 218

McKay, Buddy, 390–91

McKinley, William, 208

McLean, George, 250

McLeod, Columbus, 250

McPhee, John, 189, 191

Mead, Daniel W., 147

Mead, Metcalf, and Hazen Report, 143, 148

Mediterranean fruit fly, 195

Meigs, Joseph, 205

Melbourne, 124

Melish, John, 34

Memorandum of Understanding (MOU), 289–92

Memphis, Tenn., 268

Menéndez de Avilés, Pedro, 36, 376–78, 380, 385

Mercury, 274

Merritt Island, 180–81

Metcalf, Leonard, 147

Meuse-Argonne offensive, 160

Mexico, 80

Miami, 14, 124, 148, 150, 152, 171–72, 194–95, 203, 210–11, 213, 215–16, 219, 222, 260–61, 264–67, 269, 275, 298–306, 316, 354–55, 363; city commission, 168–69

Miami Canal, 148, 272

Miami Chamber of Commerce, 266, 271

Miami-Dade County, 121

Miami-Dade County jetport, 312, 355

Miami-Dade Port Authority, 355

Miami Daily Metropolis, 169; "Bulletins on the Mosquito Campaign," 169

Miami Herald, 252, 272–73, 302, 303, 309, 356

Miami Mosquito Campaign, 169–70, 172

Miami News, 215

Miami River, 148, 202

Miami Rocklands, 152–53

Miami Women's Club, 304

Miccosukee, 354, 366

Michigan, 384

Middle East, 246

Midgley Realty, 177–78

Midwest, 188, 237

Migratory Bird Treaty Act (MBTA), 289

Milanich, Jerald T., 38

Minnesota, 357

Minute Maid, 190

Mississippi, 367, 380

Mississippi Flood Control Act of 1928, 212

Mississippi River, 50, 211, 263

Missouri, 250

Mobile, Ala., 73

Model T Fords, 267
Monroe County, 267–68, 271, 276, 302, 354
Monroe Station, 358
Montague, Clay, 119–20
Montana, 124, 131, 237
Monticello, 172
Moore, Willis, 209–10
Moore's Prairie, 88
Moore-Willson, Minnie, 237, 245–46, 252
Morgan, J. P., 268
Morocco, 179
Morris, Dewey, 340
Morse, Fairbanks, 270
Morse, Jedediah, 34
Morton, Roger, 357–58, 363
Mosquitoes, 160–76
Mosquitoes and Mosquito Control, 169
Mount Royal, 56
Moving Picture Girls under the Palms, or, Lost in the Wilds of Florida, The, 240
Moznette, George, 169–70
Muck farming, 282, 284–87
Muir, Helen, 309
Muir, John, 95
Mullen, Harris, 363
Munroe, Kirk, 240–41, 244, 249
Muskie, Edmund, 357, 363, 365
Myakka Rattler, 100
Myakka River State Park, 97, 99–100, 102, 105
Myers, Ronald, 102

Nagasaki, Japan, 216
Naples, Fla., 265–66, 272
Naples, Italy, 237
Narragansett Bay, R.I., 208
Nash, Roy, 273
Nassau, Bahamas, 202
National Aeronautic and Space Administration (NASA), 216
National Association of Audubon Societies, 247, 248–50, 302
National Audubon Society, 310
National Estuary Protection Act, 343–44
National Flood Insurance Act, 220
National Geographic, 63

National Governors Association, 220
National Gulf-Atlantic Ship Canal Association, 380, 384
National Hurricane Center (NHC), 215–19, 221
National Hurricane Research Project, 215
National Hurricane Warning Service, 218
National Industrial Recovery Act, 381
National Oceanic and Atmospheric Administration (NOAA), 219, 221
National Park Service, 93–94, 96–99, 249, 251, 301, 311, 358, 365
National Weather Bureau, 203, 218
National Wetlands Inventory, 126–27, 129–30
National Wildlife Federation, 310
National Women's Party, 303
Native Americans, 98, 101, 241–42, 273, 302, 314, 352; Acuera, 281; Ais, 236; Calusa, 236; Creeks, also Lower Creeks, 48, 50–53, 55, 57, 60, 65–66; Miccosukee, 354, 366; Seminole, 240, 245, 281, 301, 354, 366; Timucua, 281; writing of, 27
Naturalist at Large, 77
Naturalist in Florida, A, 85, 87
Natural Resource Conservation Service, 290
Natural Resources Institute, 365
Nature Conservancy, 389
Naufragios, 28
Neal, Otto, 269–70
Nelson, Gaylord, 312
Netting, M. Graham, 74–75
New Deal, 92–93, 106, 212–13, 223, 273, 384
New Hampshire, 131, 220
New Jersey, 162
New Mexico, 124
New Orleans, La., 50, 202, 212, 219, 275, 380
New Orleans *Times-Democrat*, 155–56
New River, 144
New Smyrna, 172
New York, 59, 93, 180, 236, 241, 245–46, 248, 252, 307, 363, 366, 389
New York Botanical Garden, 252
New York *Herald Tribune*, 307
New York State's Fish and Game Commission, 93

New York Times, 363, 366, 389

Niagara Falls, 59

NIMBUS-1, 217

Nineteenth Amendment, 303

Nixon, Richard, 355–58, 363–64, 375, 390, 392

Nixon administration, 220, 355, 363–65

Nobel Peace Prize, 303

Nolen, John, 304, 329–30, 333

North America, 180, 203

North Carolina, 146, 246, 367

Northeast, 242

Northwest, 242

Norton, Grady, 214–15

Not Worth Its Salt, 382

Nova Scotia, 180

Nyasaland (Malawi), 72, 81

Ocala, 103, 117, 382, 386–87

Ocala limestone, 383

Ocala National Forest, 104

Ocala Star-Banner, 386

Ochopee, 361

Ocklawaha River, 17, 86, 117, 181, 237, 281, 376, 381–82, 388–94; valley, 375, 389–91

Ocmulgee River, 49

O'Connell, Stephen C., 86

Odum, Howard T., 351

Ogden, John C., 275

O. Henry Prize, 83

Okeechobee County courthouse, 153

Okefenokee Swamp, 117

Oklahoma, 261, 273

Oleta River, 98

Olmsted, Frederick Law, 98, 304

Orange County, 192, 194, 281

Orlando, 123, 192, 221, 262, 264, 281, 353

Orr, John, 339

Osceola National Forest, 104

O'Sullivan, Maurice, 35

Owen, Ruth Bryan, 251, 306

Pace, James G., 360–61

Pacific Ocean, 214

Palatka, 34, 182, 392

Palm Beach, 211, 244

Palm Beach County, 353–54

Palmetto Club, 160

Palmetto Leaves, 63

Panama, 149, 162, 211, 310

Panama Canal, 310

Panama Canal Commission, 149

Panama Zone, 162

Panic of 1893, 123

Parker, Garald, 308

Patterson, Gordon, 120

Payne's Prairie, 48, 83–84, 86

Peake, Charles, 82

Peale, Charles Wilson, 59, 62

Pearl Harbor, 105, 384

Pelican Island, 249–50

Pennsylvania, 207–8, 248

Pensacola, 103, 360, 394

People's Drug Stores, 189

Pepper, Claude, 309, 364

Perez, Paul, 289

Perkins, Edmund T., 149

Perkins, Frances, 93

Perry, 164–68, 172

Perry, Francis W., 264–65

Perry, John, 385

Perry Project, 165–66, 172

Pesticides, 160–76, 283–92, 314

Peterson, J. Hardin, 339

Philadelphia, Pa., 123, 263

Phillip II, 376

Philosophy of Storms, 206

Phosphate mining, 167

Pinchot, Gifford, 95, 301

Pineland, 354

Pinellas County, 192–93, 331–32, 338; Commission, 336, 339–40, 343

Pinellas peninsula, 183, 328, 329–32

Pitter, Margie Lee, 287–88

Plant, Henry, 379

Pleistocene, 244

"Plumes," 307

Polk County, 167

Ponce de León, Juan, 26, 37, 62, 235–37

Popenoe, Wilson, 81

Popular Mechanics, 248

Port Charlotte, 250
Porter, Joseph, 161–64, 173
Poynter, Nelson, 332–34
Presidential Medal of Freedom, 298
Principal Navigations, 35
Proceedings of the Florida Academy of Sciences
    (journal), 76
Progressivism, 298–305, 312
Prohibition, 161
Project Cirrus, 216
Project Stormfury, 216–17
Proxmire, William, 389
Public Works Administration (PWA), 381, 383,
    387
"Puc Puggy" (the Flower Hunter), 52, 54, 59
Puerto Rico, 207–8, 210, 219
Punta Gorda, 265
Purgatorio, 64
Putnam County, 388, 393

Quito, Amos, 160

Railroads, 123, 141, 182–83, 185, 192, 260, 300,
    379
Ralph, Julian, 240
Randell, Tom, 342
Randell Act, 342
Randolph, John, 121
Randolph Commission, 151
Randolph Report, 143, 149–51
Ratner, Lee, 336–40, 344
Ratner Fill, 338, 340–41, 343, 345
Rawlings, Marjorie Kinnan, 307
Reconstruction Finance Corporation, 220, 381
Red-eared terrapin, 284
Redfield, William, 205
Reed, James, 250
Reed, Nathaniel, 19, 298, 342, 357, 361
Reeves, Jim, 360
Reid, William, 205–6
Reisner, Marc, 384
Relacion, 28
Republican Party, 342
Rhode Island, 208
Ribault, Jean, 35–36, 179, 377

Ridge, The, 181–82, 186, 192
*Rising Tide: The Great Mississippi Flood of 1927
    and How It Changed America,* 211
River and Harbors Act of 1930, 212
River of May. *See* St. Johns River
Rivers of America Series, 307
Roberts, William, 33
Robert's Lake Strand, 358
Rocky Mountains, 261
Rodman Dam, 376, 388, 390–94
Rodman Ecosystem, 393
Rodman Pool (Lake Ocklawaha), 388–93
Rodman Reservoir, 393
Rolle, Denys, 34–35
Rollins College, 3, 73
Romans, Bernard, 33, 37–38
Romero, George, 379
Rookeries, 245, 250, 328–29
Roosevelt, Franklin Delano, 93–94, 212–13,
    382–84
Roosevelt, Theodore, 98, 249, 378
Rosalynde: Eupheus Golden Legacie, 60
Roseate Spoonbill, 254
Rosen, Leonard, 350
Rothchild, John, 336
Royal Canadian Mounted Police, 160
Royal Palm State Park, 96–97, 250–51, 301–2,
    306
Royal Society of London, 49
Rural American Sports, 62
Russia, 297, 361

Saffir-Simpson Scale, 219
St. Anastasia Island, 180
St. Augustine, 27, 32, 34–35, 49, 120, 143, 179–
    81, 262
St. Cloud, 123
St. Johns, a Paradise of Diversities, The, 3
St. Johns County, 291
St. Johns Lock, 388
St. Johns River, 3, 5, 8, 33–36, 49, 52, 54–55,
    63, 179–82, 195, 236–37, 251, 281, 352, 377,
    381
St. Johns River Water Management District
    (SJRWMD), 282, 284–85, 289–92

St. Kitts, 208

St. Lucie control canal, 150–51

St. Lucie River, 149

St. Marys River, 54, 378

St. Petersburg, 38, 177, 194, 240, 326–27, 329–43, 345, 356, 360, 364; City Council, 332, 340; Planning Board, 329

St. Petersburg Garden Club, 336

St. Petersburg Marine Research Lab, 333, 343

St. Petersburg Times, 326, 332–34, 356, 360, 364

Salt Springs, 61

Sample, Dorothy, 326, 342

Sampson, F. G., 182

Sand County Almanac, A, 308–9

Sanibel Island, 329

San Juan, P.R., 210, 219

Sansonetti, Thomas, 289

Santiago de Cuba, 207

Santo Domingo, Dominican Republic, 208

Sarasota, 97, 103

Saturday Evening Post, 307

Saturday Review, 315

Savannah, Ga., 73, 216

"Save Our Everglades," 314, 367

"Save the Ocklawaha," 389

Saw grass, 264, 269, 309

Scales, J. H., 167

Science Sub-Group, 154–55

Scoggin, Lewis, 104

Scott, W.E.D, 246

Scribner's Monthly Magazine, 237

Sea Around Us, The, 333

Sebring, 97

Second Seminole War, 281

Seminoles, 48, 52–53, 240–41, 245, 262, 267, 273–74, 281, 301, 354, 366

Shackleford, Thomas, 332, 336–37, 340

Shaw, Samuel P., 128, 132

Sheets, Robert, 222

Shepard, Alan, 216

Shevin, Robert, 360

Sholtz, Dave, 96, 103

Shreve, Jack, 363

Sierra Club, 310, 363, 389

Silent Spring, 308, 333, 355

Silver iodide crystals, 216

Silver Springs, 5, 237

Simons, George, 162, 163–73

Simpson, Charles Torrey, 3, 252, 272–73, 313

Simpson, Robert H., 219

Skocpol, Theda, 204

Small, John Kunkel, 3, 9, 87, 252, 313

Smith, Buckingham, 122, 143, 262

Smith, Walter, 250

Smith Report, 143

Smithsonian Institution, 39, 206, 244; Tropical Research Institute, 75

Smoky Mountain National Park, 98

Snow Crop (Vacuum Foods), 190

Social Forces, 304

Society of Friends, 303

Soil Science Society of Florida, 152

South, 182, 196

South America, 246

South Carolina, 131, 179, 216, 239, 246, 254

South Dakota, 262, 357

Southeast Asia, 186

Southern Fish Culture Company, 339

South Florida Water Management District (SFWMD), 18, 274, 311, 317

South magazine, 263

Soviet Union, 216, 385, 386

Spain, 50, 59, 180, 208

Spanish, 1, 179–80, 186, 235, 281, 365, 376–78

Sparke, John, 35

Sputnik, 216

State Board of Forestry, 94

Steamboats, 242, 382

Stegner, Wallace, 311

Steinberg, Ted, 4, 204

Stejneger, Leonhard, 74, 77–79

Stokes Landing, 55

Stone crabs, 328

Stoneman, Frank, 124, 299

Stork, William, 32

Stoutamire, Ralph, 125

Stowe, Calvin, 182

Stowe, Harriet Beecher, 1, 63, 182, 186, 195, 236, 243, 352

Stranahan, Frank, 241
Straub, William, 328, 333
Sublette, Bill, 285
Summerall, Charles P., 380
Summit Ridge, 383
Suncoast Seabird Sanctuary, 290
Sunniland, 354
Sunshine Parkway, 338
Super Constellations, 215
Superfund, 312
Suwannee River, 87–88, 117
Suwannee River State Park, 106
Swamp Land Acts, 122–23
Swamps, 121–23, 125, 132–33, 164, 236, 239,
    253, 280, 291, 297–318, 350–74. *See also*
    Wetlands
Swartz, E. G., 167
Swingle, W. T., 186

Tabb, R. A., 343
Taft, William Howard, 149
Tallahassee, 103, 161, 170, 172, 183, 302, 315,
    336–37, 389
Tamiami Canal, 272
Tamiami Trail, 14, 156, 260–79, 306, 358, 361;
    Commission, 266
Tampa, 14, 18, 170–72, 183, 261, 262, 265, 275,
    306; City Commission, 171–72
Tampa Bay, 120, 177, 181, 183, 192, 254, 329,
    331, 345, 378
Tampa Board of Trade, 264
Tampa Tribune, 215, 356
Tangerine Avenue (St. Petersburg), 178
Tarpon, 260–61, 328
Tatum, J. H., 266
Taunton, Mass., 299
Taylor, Edward H., 74
Taylor County, 164–66
Taylor County Herald, 165
Tebeau, Charlton, 3, 352
Tennessee, 249, 367
Tennessee Valley Authority, 212, 311
Tenney, John, 182
Ten Thousand Islands, 85, 268
Tent Town Topics, 101

Texas, 207, 209, 213, 217, 223, 239, 367, 380,
    385
That Vanishing Eden, 75, 87
Their Eyes Were Watching God, 212
Thompson, Charles, 49
Three Mile Island, 221
Tilapia, 289
Time-Life American Wilderness Series, 84–85
Timucua, 179, 281
TIROS-1 and 3 (satellites), 217
Titusville, 172
Tomoka State Park, 106
Torreya State Park, 97, 99
Torreya tree, 97
Tortuguero, Costa Rica, 84
Tower Chemical, 284
"Trailblazers," 267–68
Travels, 47–54, 57, 60–66, 88, 352
Trinidad, 208
Tropical Analysis Center, 218
Tropic Everglades National Park Association,
    306
Truman, Harry, 309, 385
Trustees for the Internal Improvement Fund
    (TIIF), 331, 333, 336–37, 339–40, 343
Tsu, Lao, 157
Turck, Raymond, 160–61, 168, 172–73
Turkeys, 267
Turner, Frederick Jackson, 178, 262
Tuttle, Julia, 185
Tyler, Daniel F., 236, 251–52
Tyler, John, 206
Typhoons, 214

U-Boats, 384
Udall, Stewart, 312
Ulendo, 81, 83, 86
Umatilla, 73
Uncle Donald's Farm, 290
Uncle Tom's Cabin, 63
Underground Railroad, 303
U.S. Army, 162–63
U.S. Army Air Corps, 213–14
U.S. Army Corps of Engineers, 86, 114, 129,
    142, 148, 151–53, 210, 212, 220, 274–75,

282, 309–11, 316, 330, 343–44, 379, 384–87, 389, 392–93

U.S. Army Signal Service, 206–7; Division of Telegrams and Reports for the Benefit of Commerce, 206

U.S. Bureau of Indian Affairs, 273

U.S. Bureau of Public Roads, 220

U.S. Bureau of Reclamation, 384

U.S. Committee on Interior and Insular Affairs, 357

U.S. Congress, 122, 132, 142, 146, 151, 207, 219, 220, 248, 250, 285, 301–2, 309, 384–89, 365; Moss Committee, 146–47

U.S. Department of Agriculture, 124–25, 130, 169, 189, 195, 207, 213, 272, 290; Bureau of Irrigation and Drainage Investigations, 145–46

U.S. Department of Commerce, 213, 344

U.S. Department of Defense, 380

U.S. Department of Housing and Urban Development, 220

U.S. Department of the Interior, 298, 312, 355, 357–58, 366; Fish and Wildlife Service (USFWS), 76, 126–127, 286, 289–91, 334; Office of Biological Services, 126

U.S. Forestry Service, 93–95, 101–2

U.S. Geological Survey, 308

U.S. Government Military Reservation, 162–63

U.S. House of Representatives. See U.S. Congress

U.S. Navy, 213, 215

U.S. Office of Emergency Preparedness, 220

U.S. Public Health Service, 162, 165–66

U.S. Senate. See U.S. Congress

U.S. Treasury, 143

U.S. Weather Bureau, 183, 187, 207–15

U.S. Weather Service, 148

University of Florida, 73–75, 77, 81, 85–87, 132, 161, 339, 351; Citrus Research and Education Center, 188; College of Agriculture, 105

University of Kansas, 74

University of Miami, 312, 334, 353

University of Miami Press, 310

University of Michigan, 74

University of Pennsylvania, 57–58

University of Wisconsin, 218

Upham, Samuel C., 237

Useppa Island, 268

Valencia, Spain, 179

Vandenberg, Arthur, 384

Vanishing Eden, The, 313

Venereal disease, 168

Vero Beach, 124

Villa, Pancho, 160–61

Viñes, Father Benito, 206–7

Vinten, C. R., 102

Virginia, 121, 362

Vogel, Cathleen C., 143

Wacahoota jubilee, 88

Walker, Marvin, 383

Walt Disney Company, 361

Walt Disney World, 193–94, 361

War Department, 206, 209

War of 1812, 87

Warren S. Henderson Wetlands Protection Act, 130

Washbon, Charles G., 269–70

Washington, 209, 212, 218–20, 357, 363

Washington, D.C., 189, 358, 385

Water! (organization), 314

Water Conservation Areas, 152

Waterfowl, 281, 285–86, 289, 302

Water hyacinths, 282

Water Management Act (1972), 362

Water Resources Act (1990), 391

WB-29 (aircraft), 215

WB-50 (aircraft), 215

Weather Channel, 203, 222

Webster, Daniel, 378

Weedon Island, 38–39

Weisman, Brent, 39

Wekiva River, 345–46

Wekiva River Basin Coordination Committee (WRBCC), 345–46

Wellesley College, 299, 303

Wellesley College Alumnae Association, 309

West, 262

Western Hemisphere, 203, 212

West Florida, 50, 54, 59

West Indies, 315

West Palm Beach, 124, 172

Wetlands, 118–19, 121–33, 143, 148, 151, 254, 280, 291, 297–318. *See also* Swamps

Whitaker, John, 358

"Who Knows the Rain—The Nature and Origin of Rainfall in South Florida," 313

Whole and True Discovery of Terra Florida, 35–36

"Who Murdered the Vets?" 213

Wiegert, Richard, 119–20

Will, Thomas Elmer, 124

Williams, Major Archie, 156

Wilson, Alexander, 58–59

Wilson, E. O., 86

Wilson, Woodrow, 98, 162

Windermere, 194

Windom, William, 337

"Wings," 307

Windward Road, The, 81–83

Winter Garden, 281–82

Winter Journeys in the South, 260

Withlacoochee River, 382, 388–89

Witt, James L., 222

"Women and Birds," 306

Woodburn, Ken, 334–36, 339

Wood storks, 254, 285, 289–90

Woolson, Constance, 237

Wordsworth, William, 61, 252

Works Progress Administration (WPA), 384

World War I, 160, 162–64, 212, 300, 302–3, 315

World War II, 152, 205, 213, 214, 192, 282, 285, 288, 311, 352, 354

Worster, Donald, 2, 179

Wright, Albert Hazen, 74–75, 79

Wright, James O., 125, 143, 146–47

Wright Report, 143

WSR-57 (coastal radar warning system), 217

Wyoming, 98, 124, 237

Xanadu, 61

Yankeetown, 382

Yellowstone, Wyo., 98, 237

Yosemite National Park, 391

Yosemite Valley, 237

Youngberg, Gilbert A., 379–80

Zabel, Alfred, 343–44

Zabel v. Tabb, 343–44

Zellwood Drainage and Water Control District, 283, 285

Zellwood Muck Farms, 284–87

The Florida History and Culture Series
Edited by Raymond Arsenault and Gary R. Mormino

Al Burt's Florida: Snow birds, Sand Castles, and Self-Rising Crackers, by Al Burt (1997)

Black Miami in the Twentieth Century, by Marvin Dunn (1997)

Gladesmen: Gator Hunters, Moonshiners, and Skiffers, by Glen Simmons and Laura Ogden (1998)

"Come to My Sunland": Letters of Julia Daniels Moseley from the Florida Frontier, 1882–1886, by Julia Winifred Moseley and Betty Powers Crislip (1998)

The Enduring Seminoles: From Alligator Wrestling to Ecotourism, by Patsy West (1998)

Government in the Sunshine State: Florida since Statehood, by David R. Colburn and Lance deHaven-Smith (1999)

The Everglades: An Environmental History, by David McCally (1999), first paperback edition, 2001

Beechers, Stowes, and Yankee Strangers: The Transformation of Florida, by John T. Foster Jr., and Sarah Whitmer Foster (1999)

The Tropic of Cracker, by Al Burt (1999)

Balancing Evils Judiciously: The Proslavery Writings of Zephaniah Kingsley, edited and annotated by Daniel W. Stowell (1999)

Hitler's Soldiers in the Sunshine State: German POWs in Florida, by Robert D. Billinger Jr. (2000)

Cassadaga: The South's Oldest Spiritualist Community, edited by John J. Guthrie, Phillip Charles Lucas, and Gary Monroe (2000)

Claude Pepper and Ed Ball: Politics, Purpose, and Power, by Tracy E. Danese (2000)

Pensacola during the Civil War: A Thorn in the Side of the Confederacy, by George F. Pearce (2000)

Castles in the Sand: The Life and Times of Carl Graham Fisher, by Mark S. Foster (2000)

Miami, U.S.A., by Helen Muir (2000)

Politics and Growth in Twentieth-Century Tampa, by Robert Kerstein (2001)

The Invisible Empire: The Ku Klux Klan in Florida, by Michael Newton (2001)

The Wide Brim: Early Poems and Ponderings of Marjory Stoneman Douglas, edited by Jack E. Davis (2002)

The Architecture of Leisure: The Florida Resort Hotels of Henry Flagler and Henry Plant, by Susan R. Braden (2002)

Florida's Space Coast: The Impact of NASA on the Sunshine State, by William Barnaby Faherty, S.J. (2002)

In the Eye of Hurricane Andrew, by Eugene F. Provenzo Jr. and Asterie Baker Provenzo (2002)

Florida's Farmworkers in the Twenty-first Century, text by Nano Riley and photographs by Davida Johns (2003)

Making Waves: Female Activists in Twentieth-Century Florida, edited by Jack E. Davis and Kari Frederickson (2003)

Orange Journalism: Voices from Florida Newspapers, by Julian M. Pleasants (2003)

The Stranahans of Ft. Lauderdale: A Pioneer Family of New River, by Harry A. Kersey Jr. (2003)

Death in the Everglades: The Murder of Guy Bradley, America's First Martyr to Environmentalism, by Stuart B. McIver (2003)

Jacksonville: The Consolidation Story, from Civil Rights to the Jaguars, by James B. Crooks (2004)

Seasons of Real Florida, by Jeff Klinkenberg (2004)

The Seminole Wars: The Nation's Longest Indian Conflict, by John and Mary Lou Missall (2004)

The Mosquito Wars: A History of Mosquito Control in Florida, by Gordon Patterson (2004)

Land of Sunshine, State of Dreams: A Social History of Florida, by Gary Mormino (2005)

Paradise Lost? The Environmental History of Florida, edited by Jack E. Davis and Raymond Arsenault (2005)